TELECOMMUNICATIONS ACT HANDBOOK

A Complete Reference for Business

Leon T. Knauer • Ronald K. Machtley • Thomas M. Lynch
Wilkinson, Barker, Knauer & Quinn

Government Institutes, Inc.
Rockville, Maryland

Library of Congress Cataloging-in-Publication Data

Telecommunications Act handbook : a complete reference for
business / edited by Leon T. Knauer, Ronald K. Machtley,
Thomas M. Lynch.
     p.   cm.
Includes bibliographical references and index.
ISBN 0-86587-545-6
    1. Telecommunication--Law and legislation--United States.
    2. United States. Telecommunications Act of 1996.
I. Knauer, Leon T., 1932- . II. Machtley, Ronald K., 1948- . III. Lynch,
Thomas M., 1968- .
KF2766.T44   1996
343.7309'94--dc20
[347.303994]   96-24661
                                 CIP

Printed in the United States of America

For Traude Knauer, Kati Machtley
and Jennifer M. Lynch, Esq.

Summary Table of Contents

Table of Contents

Figures

Foreword

For more than three years, my House colleagues and I worked to enact comprehensive telecommunications reform legislation into law. In my view, passage of the Telecommunications Act of 1996 will be ranked as one of the 104th Congress' most significant accomplishments.

Now, like millions of other Americans, I eagerly look forward to the telecommunications revolution that that legislation surely will create, both here at home as well as abroad. But because telecommunications reform is still a work in progress, and because technology continues to evolve, the full impact of the Telecommunications Act of 1996 will not be felt for some time.

"The Telecommunications Act Handbook" is a valuable resource for anyone working in the telecommunications industry. But it's an equally valuable resource for individuals just interested in learning more about the Telecommunications Act of 1996 — and the changes it will bring about in the telecommunications industry.

This publication is not simply a dry recitation of the provisions of the new telecommunications law. Instead, it puts the new law in context — helping telecommunications professionals and laymen alike understand why it's important, and how it will affect their lives. It also summarizes the history and development of each sector of the telecommunications industry, and then clearly explains how the Telecommunications Act of 1996 will change each industry sector. In particular, the chapter discussing the Act's legislative history is an especially valuable resource for those wanting a better understanding of how and why Congress dealt with — or didn't deal with — certain telecommunications issues.

I expect "The Telecommunications Act Handbook" to be a helpful source of information for many years to come, and I commend my friend and former colleague — "the gentleman from Rhode Island, Ron Machtley" — for his efforts to make the Handbook a reality.

CONGRESSMAN JACK FIELDS
CHAIRMAN, SUBCOMMITTEE ON TELECOMMUNICATIONS AND FINANCE
U.S. HOUSE OF REPRESENTATIVES

Preface

The law firm of Wilkinson, Barker, Knauer & Quinn has been closely associated with regulatory and legislative developments in the telecommunications field for over thirty years. Based on these years of experience, we have undertaken this analysis of the Telecommunications Act of 1996 from an historical and practical perspective so that the challenges, risks and benefits confronting this new telecommunications age will become apparent to the reader.

This book is not a highly technical, heavily cited legal treatise. Rather, our objective is to provide business executives and non-legal scholars with an understanding of the new framework that will govern telecommunications activities for years to come.

Major credit for supervising the compilation of this text is extended to those of my partners who direct the various areas of the telecommunications practice of the firm. Each of these partners has been associated with Wilkinson, Barker, Knauer & Quinn for many years. All are acknowledged leaders in the communications bar and have been responsible for whatever success our firm has achieved in the communications area. Those are L. Andrew Tollin and Kathryn A. Zachem in the common carrier field (including mobile), Kenneth E. Satten for broadcast and Paul S. Quinn, one of the founders of our firm, on legislative matters.

Appreciation is also extended to Ronald K. Machtley and Thomas M. Lynch, who coordinated the overall firm effort, to those other members of our firm who authored the various chapters, and to Michael D. Sullivan who was constantly available to contribute his acknowledged expertise on the regulations and procedures of the Federal Communications Commission. Concurrently with the publication of this book, Mr. Machtley will become the President of Bryant College in Smithfield, Rhode Island. Although he will be missed, his contribution herein will endure.

Our gratitude is also extended to Dr. Klaus W. Grewlich, Director General of the Confederation of European Paper Industries, Brussels, Belgium, and former Director General for International Business Development, Deutsche Telekom, Bonn, Germany, the only non-member of our firm who compiled the final chapter on global communications. Needless to say, the views expressed in this book are those of the authors and do not necessarily represent the views of the firm or its clients.

A special compliment is due to those gentlemen who have been pioneers in the regulatory arena and whom I have the privilege to call friends — Commissioner James Quello of the FCC, and Dr. Christian Schwarz-Schilling, former Minister of Telecommunications in Germany. Their efforts to effect real reform in telecommunications has truly been a public service to their respective countries.

Lastly, I recall with enthusiasm the issues which have confronted the telecommunications industry over the last thirty years. Whether stemming from legislative initiatives, regulatory rulings, or appellate decisions related to the Communications Act of 1934, or to the basic industry restructuring such as the breakup of AT&T, the industry has always been presented with exciting and unique challenges. It is clear that these challenges will accelerate as the implementation of the Telecommunications Act of 1996 progresses.

LEON T. KNAUER

Chapter 1

Legislative History of the Telecommunications Act of 1996

By William H. Boger, Esq.

On February 8, 1996, President Clinton signed into law the "Telecommunications Act of 1996" (P.L. 104-104), thereby putting in place the most significant changes in U.S. telecommunications law in over 60 years. Although the groundwork leading up to enactment of this legislation took years of work by several Congresses, the following legislative history concentrates on actions taken from 1994-1996 by the second session of the 103d Congress, and the 104th Congress.

103D CONGRESS

The 103d Congress began with high hopes for telecommunications reform. President Clinton had just defeated incumbent George Bush for the Presidency in the 1992 elections, and jurisdiction over telecommunications legislation was in the hands of the powerful Democratic Chairmen of the Senate and House Commerce Committees, Ernest Hollings (D-SC) and John Dingell (D-MI). They were pressured by various sectors of the telecommunications market, particularly by the enormous Regional Holding Companies (RHCs), to move forward on telecommunications reform legislation that would deregulate and open up long-distance and local exchange markets to competition.

After extensive hearings throughout 1993 and early 1994, on June 28, 1994, the House passed two telecommunications bills by overwhelming bipartisan votes of 423-5 and 423-4 respectively. The "Antitrust

Communications Reform Act" (H.R. 3626) removed the remaining line-of-business restrictions from the Bell Operating Companies (BOCs) and allowed their entry into the long-distance and equipment manufacturing markets. The BOCs strongly supported the bill's market entry test provisions, which allowed them to enter long distance when there was "no substantial possibility" that they could use their local facilities to impede competition. The "Communications Competition and Information Infrastructure Reform Act" (H.R. 3636) allowed local telephone companies to provide cable television service, and cable companies to provide telephone service. It also opened the local loop to competition by requiring all common carriers to allow other telecommunications and information services to access their switches and equipment and to make their networks completely interconnectable at a technically and economically reasonable point.

On August 11, 1994, the Senate Commerce Committee cleared the "Communications Act of 1994" (S. 1822) by a strong bipartisan 18-2 vote. S. 1822 combined elements of both House bills, but contained a stricter market entry provision for the BOCs, including additional unbundling requirements, which proponents said were designed to increase the chances of rapid growth of competition in local exchange services. This was opposed by the BOCs and most Senate Republicans, including Minority Leader Robert Dole (R-KS), who threatened a filibuster. Due to this opposition, on September 23, 1994, Chairman Hollings released a public statement declaring S. 1822 dead for the rest of the 103d Congress. This turned out to be an accurate prediction.

104TH CONGRESS

The 1994 elections brought dramatic changes as Republicans took control of Congress by obtaining majorities in the Senate, and, for the first time in 40 years, the House of Representatives. The new Chairman of the Senate Commerce Committee, Senator Larry Pressler (R-SD) immediately promised to move forward quickly on telecommunications reform legislation. On January 31, 1995, Senate Commerce Committee Republicans released the first draft of a bill that was later to become S. 652, the "Telecommunications Competition Deregulation Act of 1995." The Republicans modified the Hollings bill from the 103d Congress (S. 1822) by eliminating cable price controls and limits on broadcast ownership, allowing greater foreign investment in U.S. companies, prohibiting states from regulating telephone company profits and easing the restrictions imposed on entry by the BOCs into long-distance service. In addition, the draft bill contained a "competitive checklist" of requirements that the BOCs had to meet prior to entry into long distance.

S. 652 was introduced by Chairman Pressler on March 30, 1995, after the Senate Commerce Committee held hearings on January 9, March 2 and March 21. On March 23 the bill was marked up and reported 17-2 by the Commerce Committee (S. Rept. 104-23). Several amendments were adopted, including an amendment sponsored by Senators Exon (D-NE) and Gorton (R-WA) that extended prohibitions against obscene and indecent telephone calls to electronic communications, such as e-mail.

In the House, the new Republican Chairman of the Commerce Committee, Tom Bliley (R-VA) promised similar action. On May 3, Bliley introduced the "Communications Act of 1995" (H.R. 1555). Hearings were held on May 10 and the House Commerce Committee's Tele-communications and Finance Subcommittee reported H.R. 1555 by voice vote on May 17, 1995. The Subcommittee considered, but deferred for full committee consideration, three divisive amendments dealing with cable television price controls, broadcast ownership limits and foreign investment in U.S. broadcast and telephone companies. The first, sponsored by Congressmen Edward Markey (D-MA) and Dan Schaefer (R-CO), was an attempt to win over opponents in Congress and at the White House by requiring more imminent competition before removing the price controls on cable television. The second, sponsored by Congressman Cliff Stearns (R-FL), was an amendment that would ease ownership limits on radio and television stations. It received much criticism from Members concerned about the potential concentration of media power. The third, sponsored by Congressman Michael Oxley (R-OH), was an amendment allowing unlimited foreign investment in U.S. telecommunications companies.

On May 25, 1995, the full House Commerce Committee reported H.R. 1555 38-5 (H. Rept. 104-2040). With respect to the three divisive amendments deferred by the Subcommittee, the Committee adopted them with the following modifications: (1) they ended cable price control on "expanded basic" programs and cable equipment; (2) they removed all ownership limits on radio stations and raised the ownership limit for television, letting a single network or chain reach up to 50 percent of U.S. households; and (3) they allowed the FCC to block foreign investment in U.S. telecommunications companies for national security or other public-interest reasons, unless the investor's country allowed the U.S. companies to make unlimited investments.

Additionally, the Committee adopted several other major amendments including: (1) new obligations on local phone companies to share their networks with competitors, except in some rural areas; (2) requiring BOCs to use a separate subsidiary for electronic publishing; (3) requiring local telephone companies to use a separate subsidiary for video programming; (4) requiring long-distance companies to continue charging no more for long-distance calls in rural areas than they do for comparable urban calls; and (5) restricting the ability of companies to charge fees for services provided via toll-free calls.

On June 7, Senate floor action began on S. 652. After days of debate and numerous amendments, the Senate passed S. 652 81-18 on June

15. The bill included a major amendment that would require each BOC to share its network with at least one competitor before seeking permission from the FCC to offer long-distance service or to manufacture telecommunications equipment. Additionally, the FCC would have to consult with the Department of Justice before deciding whether the BOC's expansion into long distance was in the public's best interest. The bill would also ease much of the price regulation on small cable systems and larger systems' "expanded basic" program tiers before they faced competing cable providers.

While the Senate bill was similar in its framework to the bill reported by the House Commerce Committee, certain details varied. For example, both bills would require the BOCs to face competition in their local markets before offering long-distance service, but the House bill set a higher threshold for competition that would require local telephone companies to share their networks with would-be competitors within eighteen months, as compared to the Senate bill's lesser requirement of 160 days. The House bill also did not contain a provision giving the Justice Department a role in advising the Federal Communications Commission (FCC) before it granted a BOC application to provide long-distance service.

During this time, discussions continued on the House side — fueled by the unhappiness of the BOCs with the entry provisions. And in an unusual and almost unprecedented action, the House Republican leaders announced several amendments to the Committee-passed bill on July 13. The provision that required a BOC wishing to enter the long-distance market must face at least one competitor offering services over its own equipment that are "comparable in price, features and scope" to the BOC's services, was modified by dropping the comparability requirement and allowing the BOC to qualify even if its competitors relied in part on the BOC's facilities to deliver their services (resale). Two other changes also aided the BOCs. The first gave the FCC only six months, not eighteen, to promulgate regulations to implement the checklist, and the second provided that each BOC would be required to use a separate subsidiary for long distance for only the first eighteen months after enactment of the bill, not the three years previously required.

On August 4, the House passed H.R. 1555 as amended by the House Republican Leadership by a 305-117 vote. Then, in a procedural maneuver designed to facilitate a Conference with the Senate, on October 12 the House took up S. 652, struck the Senate provisions, and passed it by voice vote with the text of H.R. 1555 as passed by the House on August 4.

A House-Senate Conference convened on October 25 and continued throughout November and into December. On December 6, House Conferees voted 17-16 largely along party lines to support new provisions prohibiting the dissemination of "indecent" material to minors on computer networks and online services. This created a new role for the federal government by authorizing the FCC to regulate the largely unstructured and unregulated Internet.

During the Conference, the Democrats and the Clinton Administration were successful in using the threat of a Senate filibuster to obtain major concessions from the Republicans. For instance, the long-distance entry provisions were modified to impose some of the most stringent elements of the House and Senate bills on the BOCs, and price controls for major cable operators were retained until April 1999, or until local companies offered comparable service, instead of being eliminated immediately. Further, existing barriers to ownership of multiple media outlets in the same market were largely left in place and states were permitted to continue regulating telephone company profits. Also, the significant requirement that the Justice Department must approve the BOCs' entry into long distance, found in the Senate bill, was reduced to only a "consultative" role. Finally, the Senate provision allowing greater ownership of U.S. companies by foreigners was dropped when Hollings was unable to reach agreement with House Republicans.

On December 12, the Conferees announced agreement on several important provisions including: (1) deregulation of all cable prices by a "date certain," *i.e.,* March 31, 1999; (2) elimination of the current ban on telephone companies' offering television programming; and (3) giving television broadcasters the first opportunity to purchase spectrum if the FCC decides to offer it for the creation of a new generation of digital television broadcasts, known as high definition television (HDTV).

Progress continued, and, on December 20, Vice President Al Gore announced that a deal had been reached. This proved to be premature, however, and the Conference stalled. One major issue holding up an agreement was the indecency standard sponsored by the House Republicans, and another dealt with auctioning digital television spectrum, which was raised at the last minute by Majority Leader Bob Dole (R-KS). Dole argued that giving this spectrum away to broadcasters instead of holding auctions to sell it amounted to "corporate welfare." However, he was mollified by statements of Chairman Pressler that hearings would be held on spectrum allocation in April, and by FCC Chairman Hundt that the FCC would not issue new licenses to broadcasters for digital use until Congress acted. With these assurances, Dole relented.

The House adopted the Conference Report on February 1, 1996, 414-16, and the Senate followed suit on the same day 91-5. Despite the overwhelming bipartisan approval of the Conference Report, some Republicans complained that they had given too much away to the Democrats. Democrat John Dingell added fuel to this by stating during the February 1 House floor debate on the Conference Report that the final product was very close to the legislation passed in 1994. In some respects this was true, but the new law contained many provisions, such as those eliminating cable price controls and relaxation of broadcast ownership

7

rules, that would not have been included in a Democrat-sponsored bill. In addition, almost all new regulations on the BOCs expire within three to five years, existing and new FCC regulations are to be reviewed biannually and eliminated if unnecessary, and the FCC is given broad "forbearance" authority not to enforce most of the new Act, the surviving provisions of the Communications Act, and their own implementing regulations.

On February 8, 1996, President Clinton signed the bill (P.L. 104-104) into law. In his signing statement the President said, "[t]oday, with the stroke of a pen, our laws will catch up with our future. We will help to create an open marketplace where competition and innovation can move as quick as light."

Chapter 2

Telephony

By Thomas M. Lynch, Esq.

The history of telecommunications in the United States is the story of remarkable technology and the evolution of competition. In the last hundred years or so, the American people have been both observers and captives as telecommunications precipitously influenced their lives. As bystanders in the struggle between the principles of capitalism and the essence of democracy, consumers have witnessed the undaunted efforts of state and federal governments as they tried simultaneously to contain and encourage the burgeoning telecom monopolies. The Telecommunications Act of 1996 is an attempt to finally permit the effective self-regulation of an industry that began in 1844 with Samuel Morse's prophetic words, "What hath God wrought!"

The Telecom Act represents a shift from acceptance of natural monopolies to fulfillment of the current political trend toward laissez-faire reliance on market forces. Ironically, it also marks the return to principles of competition that flourished at the dawn of telephony. And though the Telecommunications Act of 1996 may testify to the ability of elected representatives to deliver something for every segment of the industry, it has also paved the way for pivotal changes in the life of the average American — much like the telephone did in 1876.

This chapter presents a brief history of telephony in the United States and then examines how the Telecommunications Act of 1996 changes the current landscape of regulation and operation in the landline aspects of the telecommunications industry. The principal provisions of Title I of the Act are explained, with reference to their historical context.

9

FROM BELL TO BREAKUP — A HISTORY OF TELEPHONY

Local Exchange and Interexchange Services

In the summer of 1875, not long after the Civil War, Alexander Graham Bell, following years of telephony research, discovered certain principles of electromagnetics which he would only later come to fully understand. He found that by converting the differences in acoustic pressure found in speech to analogous differences in electrical signal amplitudes, such electrical signals could be transported through a copper wire to loudspeakers, which then converted the electrical signals back to sound waves. Following that discovery, he invented the basic elements of a telephone: the electromagnetic microphone and the speaker, and on March 10, 1876, Bell spoke the first words into a working telephone to his assistant in an adjacent room, "Mr. Watson, come here, I want you."

Signaling devices were invented next by Bell and Watson, the culmination of which was the telephone ringer, and soon Bell began to install telephones commercially on a modest basis. Initially, two lines were established for each telephone, one for speaking and the other for listening, so the user did not have to move the same device continuously between mouth and ear.

The first telephones were directly connected to each other by wires, and therefore could only be used to reach individuals at either end point. In 1878, with the proliferation of telephones and telephone wires, the need for the telephone "exchange" became evident. The first exchanges were simple switchboards that permitted each telephone to reach any other telephone connected to the same switchboard. Switching was initially done manually by swift but rowdy boys and later by polite female operators, generally working in banks of switches for the Bell Telephone Company (incorporated in 1877). Ultimately, automatic switching systems were developed which interpreted a series of pulses to raise and then rotate a shaft to make the appropriate connection. Dialing devices were invented in 1898 to generate the pulses, and the first fully automated switching system was available in Omaha just 75 years ago.

These "local exchanges" worked reasonably well for their communities, but the linking of exchanges to provide "interexchange" service between distant cities was not practical because signals tended to deteriorate over great distances. "Loading coils" developed by a penniless Serbian immigrant in 1899 permitted long-distance transmissions to a limited extent. But the real breakthrough came in 1906 when Lee DeForest developed the "audion," a vacuum tube electronic amplifier that could be used to amplify electric signals. Used as "repeaters" at appropriate intervals on a telephone wire, audions could ensure that a telephone signal would be transmitted across any distance with little degradation of quality. AT&T, initially a subsidiary of the Bell Telephone Company formed in 1885 to provide long distance, purchased the audion patent from DeForest in 1913 and interexchange service became a critical component of telephony shortly thereafter.

Monopoly and Initial Regulation

Prior to the invention of the audion, local exchanges were built and operated by the Bell Telephone Company or its successor AT&T, and also by many independent phone companies. There were at least two local exchange competitors in nearly half of all cities with phone service by 1902. Competition had already forced the Bell Telephone Company to reorganize into its subsidiary, AT&T, and by 1907, the independent phone companies owned as many local exchanges as AT&T. The latter's average rates had been cut in half through vigorous competition. The technological advantage, however, belonged to AT&T, and open competition was soon to be abruptly ended.

AT&T's Long Lines division had been providing interexchange service with loading coils prior to the acquisition of the audion patent. With the audion technology, AT&T significantly improved and expanded its long-distance offering. AT&T's decided advantage in interexchange service and its 1881 acquisition of Western Electric, the largest telecommunications equipment manufacturer in the world, were the seeds of its growing monopoly. By interconnecting only AT&T's local exchanges to its superior long-distance lines, refusing to sell equipment to independents, and restricting interconnection even to those independents that did not compete with it, AT&T began a process of driving the independents to sell their local exchanges to AT&T or go out of business.

Thirty-four years after Bell's discovery, and just after AT&T had purchased its most likely competitor, the once formidable Western Union, Congress became nervous with the growing monopolies of the day and so passed the Mann-Elkins Act of 1910 to regulate, among other industries, telecommunications. The Mann-Elkins Act established the Interstate Commerce Commission and permitted it to regulate telecommunications providers as common carriers. The ICC did not rise to the challenge, however, and in 1912 the U.S. Department of Justice threatened the AT&T monolith with an antitrust suit. In July of 1913, a vice president of AT&T, Nathan Kingsbury, responded by letter to the Department of Justice proposing a settlement. In the Kingsbury Commitment, as it has become known, AT&T agreed to stop buying competitors and to connect the remaining independents to its long-distance lines. It also agreed to sell Western Union. The Justice Department approved the deal and achieved a significant victory. But the times they were a-changing.

The Kingsbury Commitment had restricted AT&T's ability to acquire local exchange operators, and in an interpretation of the Attorney

General, it even required AT&T's local exchanges in some circumstances to interconnect with *all* long-distance carriers — something the Kingsbury Commitment had conveniently forgotten to mention. But with World War I looming just around the corner, public policy shifted from the preservation of competition to the establishment of a ubiquitous and efficient telephone network. The Postmaster General took over operation of the telephone system from 1918 to August of 1919 and explicitly encouraged the consolidation of competing systems into one national system. After the War, in 1921, Congress overrode the Kingsbury Commitment with the Willis-Graham Act, and permitted the ICC to exempt AT&T from antitrust laws when acquiring other telephone companies. The country was apparently becoming comfortable with monopolies.

In 1929, the Great Depression emptied the pocketbooks of Americans. Distrust mounted between the average citizen and the large corporation, and in response the Communications Act of 1934 was enacted to regulate the communications industry through a new body, the Federal Communications Commission. Although the Communications Act was principally enacted to regulate radio broadcasting, it was also designed to take over from the ICC the regulation of telephony as a common carrier activity. The Act's boldly stated purpose was, "to make available, so far as possible, to all the people of the United States a rapid, efficient, Nationwide and worldwide wire and radio communication service with adequate facilities at reasonable charges." Thus, "universal service" and reasonable telephone rates became the touchstones of telecommunications law, essentially conceding to AT&T its monopoly status — so long as it was a benign monopoly.

And indeed AT&T was quite a monopoly. When the Communications Act became law, AT&T was providing nearly all interexchange service in the United States, and most of the local exchange service. Eighteen Bell Operating Companies (BOCs) handled local calls, and they were all joined together by AT&T's Long Lines division. Virtually all telephone equipment was manufactured and owned by AT&T's subsidiary, Western Electric; subscribers leased the equipment from AT&T, which jealously restricted all attachments to such equipment. See Figure 1 for a diagram of AT&T.

Conceding for a time that monopoly ownership of the BOCs and the long-distance division were needed for the operation of an efficient utility, Congress began to investigate in 1935 whether AT&T's ownership of Western Electric was really necessary. In spite of price regulation, complaints were raised that AT&T, through Western Electric, had been inflating the costs paid by the BOCs for telephone switching and other equipment, the result being an increase in the cost of, and regulated prices for, telephone service. The FCC was ordered to study the issue, and four years later it produced a report that verified the inflation of AT&T's rate base. But war loomed again.

World War II distracted the Congress and afforded AT&T an opportunity to prove its American loyalties. Close cooperation with the Department of Defense, including Western Electric's management of the Atomic Energy Commission's Sandia Laboratories, gained for AT&T a powerful supporter. When the Department of Justice resumed its attack on Western Electric in 1949, asking the court to separate Western Electric from AT&T, the Defense Department rose in support of its ally. The result was the 1956 Consent Decree, which permitted AT&T to keep Western Electric, and merely required Western Electric to license its equipment patents to competing manufacturers. The Decree also limited the BOCs to providing common carrier communications services, something they were already

14

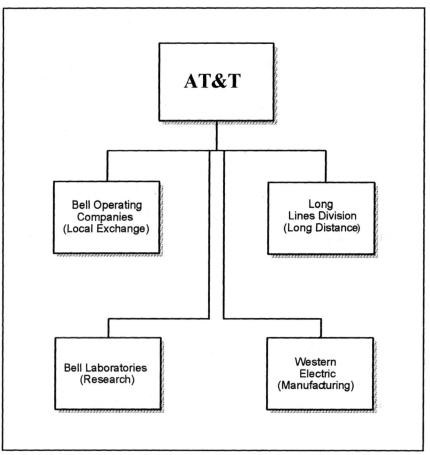

Figure 1 - *Diagram of AT&T before the breakup.*

doing almost exclusively. In short, the 1956 Consent Decree was a slap on the wrist.

Left intact, AT&T became surprisingly efficient and its Bell System more productive. In 1956, over 70 percent of America's households had a telephone, compared to only thirteen in the United Kingdom and less than ten in France and Germany. Over the years that followed, telephone service became even more universal, rates declined and long-distance service spread out across the nation — connecting everyone's telephone to everyone else's. Bell Laboratories was hard at work on new inventions, and coaxial cable, microwave radio transmission, laser technology, and most importantly, the transistor were introduced.

AT&T's technological innovations were, ironically, the catalyst of its demise. With new technologies, customer premises equipment became cheaper and soon large corporations could afford to purchase private exchanges for internal communication. In addition, corporations increasingly demanded private links between their distant offices; and where there is demand, supply will surely follow. In 1959, the FCC opened up the microwave spectrum for private use, as well as common carrier transmissions.

In 1963, Microwave Communications, Inc. (MCI), a small upstart company with a dream, applied for a license to offer common carrier microwave service between St. Louis and Chicago. Microwave had become an excellent substitute for landline long-distance services and MCI planned to lease microwave capacity to businesses that needed private-line long-distance connections between their branches in the two cities. Approval of the application was not automatic, however, because the FCC's mandate essentially protected the monopoly status of AT&T, allowing competitors only if to do so would be in the "public interest." The Commission had previously reasoned that the public interest did not permit competitors because to allow them in most cases would permit "cream-skimming." That is, AT&T was required to maintain an entire nationwide network, and built into its rates was a cross-subsidy which charged urban and business users more for telephone service so rural customers, for example, would not have to pay the enormous costs required to extend a phone line to them. Permitting competitors to undercut the rates for urban and business routes would be unfair since AT&T bore upon itself a broad public mandate of universal service.

MCI countered AT&T's inevitable cream-skimming argument with the proposition that they would only provide "interplant and interoffice" communications for private networks, and thus would not be competing with AT&T's long-distance services offered to the public. By a vote of four to three, the FCC approved MCI's application in 1969. Immediately thereafter, MCI and others flooded the Commission with requests for approval of microwave links in different markets. Inundated with applications, the FCC ultimately created a new class of carrier, the "Specialized Common Carrier." And shortly thereafter, in 1971, the Commission began a proceeding to permit the Specialized Common Carriers to interconnect with the BOCs' local exchanges to allow users of MCI's private network to reach any telephone outside the network.

The FCC decided in favor of interconnection generally, but MCI had to wrest full rights to interconnection from AT&T through years of court proceedings. Nonetheless, in 1972, MCI began operations. By 1974, its microwave network served 40 cities all over America. MCI now had its foot in the door. After several years of litigation with an infuriated AT&T, MCI began to offer "Execunet" services that permitted subscribers to call any telephone number using MCI's network by first dialing an MCI access code. Thus direct competition for standard long distance had begun.

Sensing competition may be possible in long distance, and spurred on by MCI, the Department of Justice filed its third antitrust suit against AT&T in November of 1974. The suit alleged monopolization of both long-distance service and the manufacture of telecommunications equipment. The case languished for four years until the district judge in charge became terminally ill and the matter was reassigned to Judge Harold H. Greene on his first day on the federal bench.

The Breakup of the Bell System

The trial in the third antitrust action against AT&T began in 1981. Four months later, in denying a motion to dismiss filed by AT&T, Judge Greene found the government's evidence showed that AT&T was attempting to restrict interconnection to its local exchanges. Greene's opinion also included a number of other findings that were less than favorable to AT&T, although he did dismiss the claims of cross-subsidy and predatory pricing with respect to telecommunications equipment. It didn't take AT&T long to realize where the trial was heading, and it quickly renewed negotiations with the Department of Justice.

In 1982, after several failed negotiations, AT&T and the Justice Department finally reached an agreement that would change the industry dramatically: the multi-billion dollar Bell Operating Companies were to be split off from AT&T and required to provide access to all interexchange providers, the 1956 business restrictions on AT&T were to be dissolved, although AT&T was temporarily prevented from entering the electronic publishing business, and the BOCs were to be subjected to new line-of-business restrictions. Judge Greene approved the agreement but made certain modifications to ensure judicial oversight. Greene's order ratifying the deal, and modifying the "Final Judgment" of the 1956 Decree, was aptly named the "Modification of Final Judgment" (commonly called the "MFJ"). The MFJ gave AT&T six months to draft a plan of reorganization to be approved by the Department of Justice and the court.

AT&T now had a unique opportunity to design the structure of its future rival. Under AT&T's plan, the BOCs were not to be held by a single, large holding company, although this structure would have been acceptable under the MFJ. Instead, the BOCs were to be divided up among seven Regional Holding Companies (RHCs). But each RHC, and each of the BOCs it controlled, provided telephone service throughout a wide territory

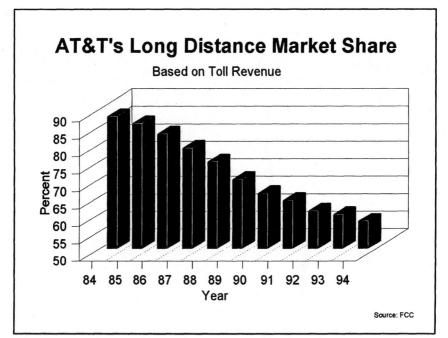

Figure 2 - *Decline of AT&T's market share since the breakup.*

where AT&T provided (and planned to continue providing) long-distance service. As a result, the MFJ limited the amount of territory in which the BOCs could provide telephone service. To simulate the local exchanges of old which served specific communities, to restrict the operating areas of the BOCs' local exchanges, and to preserve AT&T's business of providing long-distance service within each BOC's territory, the MFJ established new, fairly small BOC service areas called "Local Access and Transport Areas" (LATAs). See Figure 3 for a map of the LATAs. BOCs were forbidden under the MFJ from providing interexchange service between LATAs — interexchange was reserved for AT&T and its ostensible competitors.

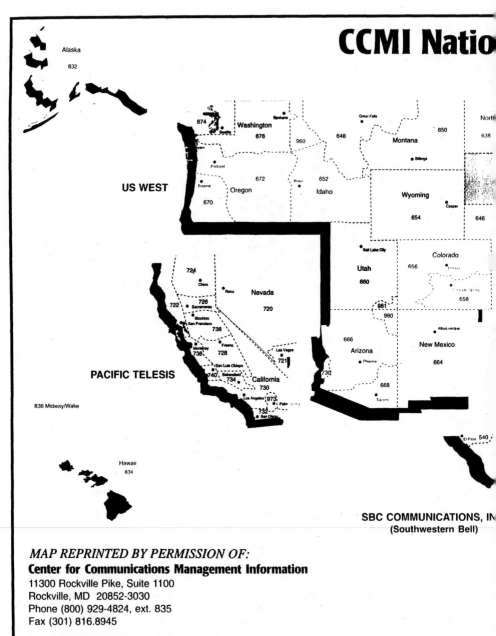

CCMI Natio

Alaska
832

US WEST

Washington
674
Seattle
876
Spokane
960
648

Montana
Great Falls
650
Nor
638
Billings

Portland

Oregon
Eugene
672
672
Boise
652
Idaho
670

Wyoming
654
Casper
646

Salt Lake City
Utah
660
Colorado
656
658

PACIFIC TELESIS

California

724
Chico
726
722
Sacramento
Reno
Nevada
720
981
980

Stockton
San Francisco
738
736
Monterey
728
Fresno
San Luis Obispo
740
734
Bakersfield
730
732
Los Angeles
973
Palm
San Diego
Las Vegas
721
730
666
Arizona
Phoenix
668
Tucson
New Mexico
Albuquerque
664

836 Midway/Wake

El Paso 540

Hawaii
834

SBC COMMUNICATIONS, IN
(Southwestern Bell)

MAP REPRINTED BY PERMISSION OF:
Center for Communications Management Information
11300 Rockville Pike, Suite 1100
Rockville, MD 20852-3030
Phone (800) 929-4824, ext. 835
Fax (301) 816.8945

I LATA Map

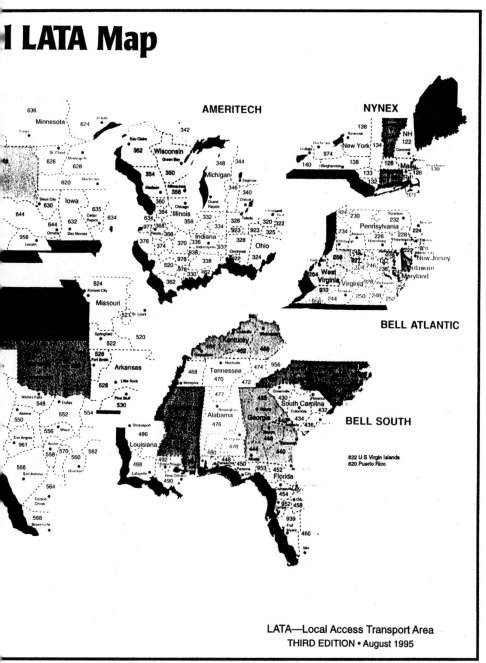

LATA—Local Access Transport Area
THIRD EDITION • August 1995

Figure 3 *- Local Access and Transport Areas established by the MFJ.*

21

The BOCs were prohibited from doing a number of other things, too. They couldn't provide information services (broadly defined to cover any information transmitted via telecommunications). They couldn't manufacture telecommunications equipment (Western Electric stayed with AT&T). And they couldn't provide any product or service except local exchange service and access for their subscribers to long-distance providers. In short, the MFJ once again ratified the premise that local exchange was a natural monopoly and could be tolerated as such if regulated. The BOCs were the designated monopolies, controlled by the Regional Holding Companies, and the still-massive AT&T was to be set loose (without most of its line-of-business restrictions) into the competitive marketplace.

AT&T's plan was approved in 1983, and effective January 1, 1984, the BOCs became legally separated from AT&T — delivered into the hands of the newly-formed Regional Holding Companies. AT&T was forced to compete in the interexchange marketplace, though there was hardly competition at first. See Figure 2. And Judge Greene became a one-man regulator as he issued hundreds of orders enforcing, interpreting and applying the MFJ over the next twelve years. In 1991, the ban on BOC provision of information services was lifted, but the paradigm established by the MFJ was virtually untouched: the BOCs remained in monopoly local exchange service, while everything else was competitive (and the BOCs were largely excluded).

Meanwhile, technology continued to outpace that paradigm. The millions of miles of coaxial cable and microwave circuits used for telephony, private line and network television transmissions were increasingly used to carry high-speed computer data as well. Through fiber-optic technology it became cheaper to carry ever larger amounts of telecommunications traffic. And wireless telephony had taken hold; cellular telephones introduced in the early 1980s served over 25 million subscribers, and a new group of wireless services rolled out in 1995, called personal communications services, appeared capable of supplanting the wireline local exchange service to some extent. The market was bursting with opportunity, the BOCs sought to enter the long-distance business, and the local exchange came under pressure for competitive entry. Out of this technological cataclysm came the Telecommunications Act of 1996.

THE TELECOMMUNICATIONS ACT OF 1996 — A NEW PARADIGM?

The Telecommunications Act of 1996 is based on the premise that no sector of the telecommunications marketplace should be immune from competition. This proposition is a dramatic reversal of the theory that local exchange is a natural monopoly and should be regulated as such. But a paradigm in which local exchange and long distance are open to competition is nothing new. Until AT&T dominated the telephony marketplace by forbidding competitors access to its long-distance lines, competition in local exchange was thriving. As noted above, in 1902 almost half of all cities were served by at least two local exchange providers.

Despite this retroactive application of the seemingly obvious principles of competition, the Telecom Act does contain a new schematic for telephony: the Telecom Act generally requires interconnection of all telecommunications carriers. In 1902, no telephone company was required to interconnect with any other. Subscribers to a local exchange could only communicate with other subscribers of the same exchange. But now, taking a page from the access requirements applicable to long distance, the Telecom Act finally mandates interconnection that will, for example, permit Pac Bell subscribers to call and be called by subscribers of new upstart local exchange companies. Moreover, the former monopoly local exchange providers have new resale obligations and must unbundle their network elements to permit competitors to create new services with which to better compete.

The new Act also sets up important incentives for the entrenched BOCs to comply with these mandates: they are allowed to compete in the interexchange market only after satisfying a "competitive checklist" of items designed to stimulate local exchange competition. See Figure 4. Despite this significant initial regulation, the goal of the Act is the development of a telecommunications marketplace regulated principally, if not entirely, by competition. The following explains how the United States Congress has attempted to inject competition into virtually every segment of the telephony marketplace.

Local Exchange — Not Just for BOCs Anymore

How does one take an industry that has been a monopoly for nearly a century and suddenly open it up to competition? Entrenched companies will almost certainly benefit from economies of scale, existing plant, consumer loyalty, market presence and many other advantages that can be more evenly shared in a developing industry subject to competition. Congress' answer in the Telecom Act is to mandate and restrict certain commercial behavior. Needless to say, the Bell Operating Companies are most heavily effected by the new legislation.

Unlocking the BOCs

The Telecommunications Act of 1996 places rather specific obligations on the Bell Operating Companies and other local exchange carriers existing at the time the Act was passed. Referring to the BOCs and the other incumbents collectively as "incumbent local exchange carriers," the Act mandates strict interconnection, resale and unbundling obligations in an effort to allow would-be competitors to construct and configure competing local networks in the quickest and cheapest manner possible. Each of these obligations is discussed below.

Interconnection. As we have seen, the Bell Operating Companies have been subject to certain interconnection requirements since at least 1984. All long-distance carriers may access the BOCs' local exchanges, and wireless service providers may also interconnect to permit their subscribers to reach landline telephones. The Telecom Act, however, broadens the interconnection requirement substantially. The Telecom Act requires that *all* providers of telecommunications services have a duty to interconnect with all other such telecommunications carriers. "Telecommunications service" is defined broadly in the Telecom Act to mean the offering of services to transmit a user's information between points specified by him. This language is obviously meant to apply in contexts other than local exchange. As discussed in Chapter 5, the FCC is currently considering whether the interconnection provisions of the Telecom Act apply to commercial mobile service providers. But while the courts and the FCC determine precisely the impact of the Telecom Act's interconnection language, including whether it applies to interexchange carriers and wireless providers, the incumbent LECs must contend with a more severe, and specific, obligation.

The Bell Operating Companies, and the other incumbent local exchange carriers, excluding certain rural telephone companies, must permit any telecommunications carrier wishing to provide local exchange services to interconnect with their local exchange network at any technically feasible point. The FCC has tentatively concluded that the definition of "technically feasible point" will at least cover those points where the incumbents have previously permitted interconnection. Furthermore, such interconnection must be at least equal in quality to that provided by the incumbent LEC to itself or any other carrier, and must be on just and reasonable rates and terms. The incumbents have an affirmative obligation to negotiate with would-be competitors and, as described below, if the incumbents prove to be intransigent, the competitors have a statutory recourse to state-conducted arbitration.

In practical terms, the Act's interconnection mandate would appear to mean that if, for example, the owners of an apartment building wish to provide local exchange services to their tenants, they may interconnect their switching equipment to the incumbent local exchange carrier's network at the nearest "technically feasible" node, and in so doing will have lopped off a portion of such carrier's customer base.

The FCC issued a notice of proposed rulemaking in April of 1996 to seek public comment on future interconnection guidelines. Although the notice contained more questions than concrete suggestions, it highlights the overwhelming complexity of the rules which the Commission must fashion by August 8, 1996. As if the August deadline were not enough to encourage the FCC to move quickly, squabbles among would-be competitors and the Bell Operating Companies have already begun. In the spirit of the early years, MCI recently sued a BOC over the terms of interconnection to a local exchange network and several BOCs have suspended negotiations with potential competitors to consider the implications of the Telecom Act. Furthermore, MCI has taken to lobbying both the FCC and state regulators, requesting that all interconnection agreements reached with the BOCs be made public.

The Act's interconnection requirements, extensive as they are for an incumbent, may be supplemented by state regulation. In addition to the rules that will be established by the FCC to govern interconnection, the state in which an incumbent LEC provides service may also regulate interconnection and other requirements. In addition, if the incumbents and their potential competitors are unable to reach a voluntary agreement as to rates, the state is given the power to determine the "just and reasonable rate" for interconnection, the calculation of which must be based on the incumbent LEC's cost of providing such interconnection. The Telecom Act, drafted by a Republican-controlled Congress, provides broad latitude to the states to prescribe and enforce such regulations so long as they do not prevent the Act's implementation.

The state commissions have already been fairly active with respect to interconnection — some 25 states had taken some legislative or regulatory action prior to enactment of the Telecom Act. Following enactment, the states have continued their interest in regulating interconnection. In March, after Ameritech and Time Warner Communications were unable to reach agreement on interconnection terms, the Ohio Public Utilities Commission ordered Ameritech to file tariffs allowing Time Warner and others to interconnect, and specified terms by which Ameritech will be compensated. Similarly, the Washington Utilities and Transportation Commission rejected interconnection tariffs filed by a BOC in January and outlined specific terms that must be included. Many other public utility commissions already have stringent interconnection requirements in place. The interplay between the FCC's regulations and the state's requirements with respect to interconnection will probably be among the most hotly contested issues arising from the Telecom Act.

In addition to the general interconnection requirements outlined above, all incumbent LECs are required to permit their competitors to locate equipment necessary for interconnection on the incumbent's premises. The FCC tried to require the BOCs to provide space in their central offices for competitors' equipment several years ago. However, the Court of Appeals for the D.C. Circuit vacated the FCC's orders on the grounds that to require such physical collocation amounted to a taking of the BOCs' property, which was not authorized by the Communications Act of 1934. The Telecom Act now specifically provides such authorization.

Resale. The cost of purchasing, installing and maintaining a network of sufficient size to compete with an incumbent local exchange carrier is substantial. AT&T, for example, has estimated that it would have to invest billions of dollars to construct new facilities in local markets in order to be able to reach twenty percent of the 117 million access lines served by the BOCs. In addition, those competitors that are able to muster enough resources to construct a large network may be limited as to the types of services they are able to offer. To address such obstacles, the Telecom Act requires incumbent LECs to offer for resale, at wholesale rates, all telecommunications services they provide to consumers. With this requirement, competitors seeking a market presence will be able, for example, to construct local exchange networks covering half a city, and rely on resale to cover the other half. Other competitors may be able to construct local exchange transport networks, but to provide a full panoply of services could resell an incumbent's 411 and operator services, for example.

Resale seems to be the means by which most competitors will enter the market on a large scale, even those with facilities-based networks such as cable companies. Many metropolitan areas are covered with a patchwork of disparate cable franchises because such franchises are awarded separately by counties and municipalities. Thus, cable companies typically have physical facilities in only part of a geographic area. Cable companies can augment the telephone services they are able to offer over their own facilities with resale of the LEC's service in order to establish a competitive presence throughout a broader area. Therefore, the implementation of resale requirements will be one of the more important duties of state and federal regulators — particularly the state regulators.

Under the Telecom Act, states are charged with the responsibility of setting the "wholesale" rates for the resale of telecommunications services. Although the FCC is considering establishing specific guidelines by which the rates are calculated, under the Act, the state commission must determine the wholesale rates "on the basis of retail rates charged to subscribers for the telecommunications service requested, excluding the portion thereof attributable to any marketing, billing, collection, and other costs." Thus, the wholesale rate is really a discounted retail rate — starting with the cost to consumers rather than the cost to the incumbent LEC. This formula, explicitly required by the Telecom Act, may lead to the "cream-skimming" bemoaned by AT&T just before the breakup. Specifically, those portions of an incumbent's network that are priced below cost in an effort to provide universal service to distant and expensive locations, for example, will be ripe for resale — a competitor will surely find it cheaper to purchase deep-discounted carriage, priced far below its cost, than to build a network to cover the same territory.

Few states have addressed the resale pricing issue, and among those that have, a significant disparity exists ranging from a three percent discount off retail rates for residential services in Illinois to 25 percent discounts in Tennessee. The disparity is indicative of a larger problem: if the discount is too high, facilities-based competitors such as cable companies, MFS Communications and Teleport may be discouraged from making further capital investments in favor of relying on resale, and if the discount is too low, competitors may be unable to cover large territories with their competitive offerings.

The BOCs have a strong incentive to comply with these resale obligations. After all, as discussed below, the BOCs will be permitted to enter the lucrative long-distance market if they have a facilities-based local exchange competitor in their back yard. Although pure resale would not qualify as facilities-based, a competitor would likely combine resale and facilities to provide competitive service. The sooner the BOCs' competitors have entered the local exchange business, the sooner the BOCs will have the opportunity make billions more dollars in long distance.

As an example of a cooperative attitude that the BOCs may adopt with respect to resale, the California Public Utilities Commission recently set the rates, effective March 31, 1996, that Pacific Bell and GTE can charge resellers for the purchase of local lines. Finding that Pac Bell's residential rates were already priced below cost, the California PUC nonetheless concluded that "some discount off those retail rates was still needed to spur resale competition." But Pac Bell didn't complain, instead they sent "Welcome to California" baskets of oranges, wine and other goodies to some 60 resellers approved by the PUC in the same proceeding. A spokesman stated that Pac Bell expected a similar basket when they enter the long-distance business.

Unbundled Access to Network Elements. As described above, the early switching systems were run by banks of polite operators, physically connecting one caller to another with the switchboard. Switching systems rapidly developed from that point to the rather complex, computer-operated systems we use today. The modern local exchange network consists of a physical transmission infrastructure and a logical infrastructure. Placing a call today involves advance signaling, diagnostic and testing procedures, switching, and transport, among other processes. Many of the elements of a phone system contain built-in redundancy to ensure quality and accuracy. A new local exchange competitor may find it difficult to build an entire local exchange network on the scale of the competing BOC's, with all of the switching and other processes that have evolved since 1876. Consequently, the Telecom Act requires incumbent LECs to "unbundle" their networks at technically feasible points to make individual components, or "network elements," available to would-be competitors on a modular basis. The unbundling must be complete — a competitor must be able to combine the modules to provide the underlying telecommunications service if desired. In addition, as with interconnection, the incumbent LECs must permit competitors to physically collocate equipment on the incumbent's premises which is necessary to take advantage of the unbundling.

To some extent, the BOCs have already undertaken unbundling efforts. In the 1980s, as a condition to permitting the BOCs to provide enhanced services such as voice mail, the FCC required the BOCs to unbundle the basic elements of their networks that were necessary to provide the enhanced services, and make such basic service elements available to competitors. In this way, competitors could provide, for example, voice mail or on-line computer services without having to duplicate substantial portions of the BOC's expensive network. This "Open Network Architecture" (ONA) requirement, however, was limited to enhanced services. The Telecom Act goes much further by requiring the incumbent LECs to unbundle the elements of their network necessary to provide local exchange telecommunications service.

Throughout the ongoing ONA proceedings, the FCC has maintained that unbundling the networks of the BOCs is a long and complex process. The FCC did not contemplate that the type of unbundling required by the Telecom Act would be possible in the near future. But with rewards like entry into long distance, the BOCs have an incentive to unbundle the local exchange as quickly as possible. The BOCs had already been considering replacing components of their networks to provide greater flexibility for themselves in switch control and the provision of new features. And such new components were already under ONA-type scrutiny in the FCC's *Intelligent Networks* proceeding. With the potential to enter the interexchange business, it would be logical for the BOCs to accelerate their plans to upgrade their local exchange networks.

The FCC is charged with the responsibility to determine by August 8, 1996, which network elements should be unbundled. This is a vast and complex undertaking. In making this assessment, the FCC must consider, at a minimum, whether access to confidential and proprietary elements is necessary, and whether failure to provide access to such elements would impair the ability of the carrier seeking access to provide the services it seeks to offer.

However, the states will play a significant role as well. As with interconnection, a state commission may impose standards and requirements more stringent that those adopted by the FCC — so long as such requirements do not prevent implementation of the Telecom Act. Some states have shown their hand already. The California Public Utilities Commission, for example, released in 1993 an extensive list of unbundling requirements of the type envisioned by the Telecom Act. The list includes transport, switching, call processing, and call management capabilities, resources used to support the operations, management, service initiation, maintenance, repair or marketing of such capabilities, electronic service order entry and status systems, diagnostic, monitoring, testing and network reconfiguration systems, and traffic data collection systems. Under the California PUC's plan, each of these network elements would be unbundled and available for a competitor to purchase rather than duplicate. This list may serve as a model for other state regulators eager for competition.

In addition to supplementing the FCC's list of what must be unbundled, the states are also given the authority to set the "just and reasonable" rates the incumbent LECs may charge for the unbundled elements. Unlike the resale rates, however, the Telecom Act provides a formula for calculating such network element rates that is based on the cost (determined without reference to a rate-of-return) of providing the unbundled element. The rates established by the states *may* include a reasonable profit.

Practical Considerations

As discussed above, the Telecommunications Act of 1996 places significant and specific obligations on the incumbent local exchange carriers. These obligations are intended to prevent the incumbent LECs from discriminating against their would-be competitors and are also designed to force the incumbents to share the benefits and economies of scale they have realized over the past 100 years without competition.

The Telecom Act also places other obligations on *all* local exchange carriers, including new local exchange companies. Under a paradigm in which all telecommunications carriers are interconnected, including local exchange carriers, certain practical issues must be addressed. In addition to the general obligation to interconnect, discussed above, other requirements imposed on all local exchange carriers (with a few exceptions) are number portability, dialing parity, pole access and reciprocal compensation arrangements.

Number Portability. The telephone number is the principal means by which the majority of people are contacted today. Consequently, most individuals and businesses are reluctant to change their phone numbers once established. As new competitors enter the local exchange market, they will undoubtedly find it difficult to attract the customers of the BOCs (and vice versa) if to do so means the customers will have to change their phone numbers. The Telecom Act addresses this dilemma by requiring all local exchange carriers to allow customers to keep their telephone numbers if they change to a different local exchange carrier — known as "number portability" — to the extent technically feasible.

Presently, number portability is only technically feasible with respect to some services. For example, the toll-free 800 numbers offered by long-distance carriers are fully portable, both with respect to the location of the subscriber and the carrier providing the number. Initially, the interexchange carriers permitted 800 subscribers to retain their telephone number when changing the location at which the call is terminated. When local exchange carriers implemented an 800 number database access system in 1993, 800 subscribers were also able to keep their number while changing the long-distance carrier that provided the 800 number. Number portability of service providers at the local exchange level is not yet available, however, and indeed was not necessary under the old paradigm where the local exchange was considered a natural monopoly.

The present method of assigning and processing telephone numbers is part of the portability problem. A telephone number issued today identifies the particular switch operated by a particular service provider in the first three of its seven digits. With such a numbering system, local exchange telephone numbers are inherently unportable. The Commission began a proceeding in 1995 to study the number portability issue and an order is expected in May of 1996. In the meantime, AT&T's "location routing number" (LRN) system and others are emerging as potential solutions to the portability problem. Under the LRN system, a unique 10-digit location routing number is assigned to each end office of each local exchange carrier. The LRN is transparent to the subscriber, so when he changes carriers his phone number remains the same but the LRN changes to reflect the new carrier's end office. LRN will undergo testing in Illinois beginning the second quarter of 1997. Similar portability solutions, such as Local Area Number Portability (LANP) and Carrier Portability Code (CPC), are being tested in Washington State and New York, respectively.

Although there are presently some technological and equipment-related barriers to full number portability, as with resale and interconnection, the BOCs have a powerful incentive to provide solutions as quickly as possible. In order to enter the long-distance business, the Telecom Act requires the BOCs to provide number portability on the local exchange level, or until the FCC (or a state PUC) requires full number portability, the BOCs must provide interim number portability by using "work-arounds," such as "remote call forwarding, direct inward dialing trunks, or other comparable arrangements." These temporary solutions may be costly to the BOCs, but entry into the long-distance marketplace may be worth the price.

Somewhat related to number portability is numbering administration — the assignment of telephone numbers. Currently, numbering administration is handled by Bellcore (which is owned by the BOCs) and the local exchange carriers. Congress was concerned that leaving the assignment of numbers in the hands of the incumbent LECs could result in new competitors receiving unfavorable treatment, such as having to use a new area code or being assigned a prefix such as "666," which some customers may perceive as unlucky. To avoid this situation, the Telecom Act requires the Commission to create or designate an impartial entity to administer telecommunications numbers and to make such numbers available on an equitable basis. The Commission had already designated the North American Numbering Council in 1995 to fulfill this role.

Dialing Parity. As noted above, when MCI first began to offer its "Execunet" long-distance services, its subscribers had to dial a five-digit "access code" in order to bypass AT&T's long-distance services and affirmatively select MCI's. The inconvenience was sufficient to deter many potential subscribers from switching to MCI. The same inconvenience does not exist today with respect to most long-distance providers — subscribers merely dial 1 + the telephone number and the routing of the call over the appropriate long-distance provider is transparent. But some resellers of long-distance service and providers of intraLATA toll service still require their subscribers to dial an access code.

Because resale is likely to be a significant means of entry for new local exchange competitors, the Telecom Act sought to eliminate the inconvenience of access codes by requiring all local exchange carriers to provide dialing parity to competitors that wish to use their networks. Thus, if a landlord wishes to resell phone service to his tenants as part of the rent, such tenants will not be required to dial an additional five digits before calling the local pizza delivery service. In addition, all LECs must permit their competitors "to have nondiscriminatory access to telephone numbers, operator services, directory assistance, and directory listing, with no unreasonable dialing delays."

There is one significant exception to the dialing parity obligation, however. Presently, the BOCs are allowed to charge an additional fee for calls originating and terminating within a LATA but between distant points. Such "short-haul" long-distance fees may be assessed by Bell Atlantic, for example, on a call between Washington, D.C. and a distant suburb in Virginia. Resellers are permitted to offer the same intraLATA toll services, but subscribers wishing to use the reseller's service must first dial additional digits to select that carrier. As discussed above, the Telecom Act generally eliminates such access codes in favor of dialing parity. However, the Act exempts a BOC from providing dialing parity with respect to intraLATA toll calls (unless a state had already required it by December 19, 1995) until such BOC has been authorized to provide interLATA service in-region (discussed below) or February 3, 1999, whichever is earlier. Consequently, a new competitor that chooses to resell a BOC's intraLATA short-haul service must require its subscribers to dial the access code. Many would-be competitors have complained that this loophole frustrates their attempt to provide local exchange service in competition with the BOCs.

The FCC has until August 8, 1996, in which to establish regulations implementing the dialing parity requirements. As with all provisions described in this section, the states may require more stringent compliance so long as to do so would not prevent implementation of the Telecom Act.

Pole Access. The incumbent LECs have enjoyed years in which to obtain permits from local authorities to dig up streets and plant telephone poles. They have benefitted from the rights of eminent domain exercised by state and local governments on their behalf. And they have acquired easements over significant amounts of property in the United States for the purpose of maintaining their telephone networks. Because a new facilities-based competitor will need access to these same rights of way in order to provide local exchange service to a former incumbent LEC customer, the Telecom Act requires all LECs to "afford access to poles, ducts, conduits, and rights-of-way ... to competing providers of telecommunications services on rates, terms and conditions consistent with Section 224."

That section of the Communications Act was originally enacted to give cable television companies access to utility poles and ducts. As amended by the Telecom Act, it permits the FCC to regulate pole attachments and access to rights-of-way, but expressly reserves regulatory authority to the states where they are actively engaged in such regulation. Note, however, that through amendments to Section 224 by the Telecom Act, the regulation of pole attachment conditions and rates does not extend to circumstances where an incumbent LEC wishes to take advantage of a new local exchange carrier's rights-of-way. Thus, while new local exchange competitors must afford access to their pole and ducts, even to the incumbent LECs, the new carriers will not necessarily be subject to federal regulation of the amounts they can charge or the conditions they may impose. The states, however, have the authority to impose such regulations.

Reciprocal Compensation Arrangements. When all telecommunications carriers interconnect their networks, the traffic generated by any individual user may be carried over many different carriers' networks. Thus, it is necessary to establish how the carriers will be compensated amongst themselves for transporting and terminating traffic. The Telecom Act provides that all local exchange carriers must "establish reciprocal compensation arrangements for the transport and termination of telecommunications." A clearinghouse may ultimately develop to facilitate reciprocal compensation, although the Act does not currently contemplate one.

The Telecom Act further provides that with respect to incumbent LECs, the terms and conditions for reciprocal compensation will not be considered reasonable unless the costs of carriage are based on "a reasonable approximation of the additional costs of terminating such calls." Depending on how it is interpreted, the Telecom Act may favor the new competitors if it requires the incumbent LECs to price their carriage on a relatively small marginal cost basis instead of a distributed basis that would capture the significant costs they incurred in building their large networks.

Although the FCC is given authority to establish regulations implementing this requirement, the states may also adopt regulations that don't interfere with the implementation of the Telecom Act. The new legislation prevents this process from becoming overly regulatory, however, by forbidding the use of rate regulation proceedings to "establish with particularity the additional costs of transporting or terminating calls."

Making It Work

The Duty to Negotiate and a Mechanism for Entry. None of the requirements described above will have their intended effect unless the incumbent LECs and their would-be competitors negotiate in good faith. As described in the history above, prior to the breakup, MCI litigated with AT&T for years before finally winning full rights to interconnect to its local exchanges. The Telecom Act seeks to speed up this process by requiring all incumbent LECs to negotiate in good faith the particular terms and conditions of agreements designed to fulfill the requirements described above, namely: interconnection, resale, unbundled access, number portability, dialing parity, pole access and reciprocal compensation arrangements. The requesting telecommunications carrier must also negotiate in good faith.

To ensure the implementation of this duty to negotiate, the Telecom Act provides a set of procedures to cover voluntary negotiations and involuntary negotiations. If an incumbent LEC receives a request for interconnection, resale or network elements, as described above, it may negotiate and enter into a binding agreement (with the state commission's help as mediator on sticky points if necessary) with respect to the particular request. A voluntarily negotiated agreement is exempt from many of the interconnection and other requirements described above and the implementing federal and state regulations. The presumption is that a freely negotiated agreement will contain all provisions necessary to satisfy the new competitor.

If open issues remain unresolved after 135 days, either party may request the state public utilities commission to arbitrate the open issues. The state commission's resolution of these issues must comply with the Telecom Act and the regulations drafted pursuant to it. If the state commission is called upon to establish rates through arbitration, it must follow the Telecom Act's specific standards for pricing interconnection and the transport and termination of traffic, as discussed above.

Once all issues are resolved either voluntarily or by arbitration, the agreement must be submitted to the state commission for approval. The state commission may only reject negotiated provisions of an agreement if it finds that such agreement discriminates against a telecommunications carrier not a party to the agreement, or the implementation of the agreement is not "consistent with the public interest, convenience, and necessity." This latter standard is extremely open-ended and has been used in the past by the FCC for, among other things, preventing competition in local exchange. Resort to this means of rejecting a voluntary agreement will surely be contentious.

Filing a Statement of General Terms and Conditions. The Telecom Act offers each BOC a chance to file with the state commission a statement of the terms and conditions that such BOC generally offers in that state to comply with the requirements of the Telecom Act with respect to interconnection, resale, unbundling, number portability, dialing parity, pole access, and reciprocal compensation, as well as the associated regulations promulgated by the FCC and the state commission. This establishes a tariff-like alternative for standard interconnection arrangements, obviating the need for the BOC to negotiate separate agreements concerning the same matters with every telecommunications carrier. The state commission may only reject the statement if its terms for interconnection, resale, *etc.*, and the pricing terms within the statement, fail to comply with the Telecom Act and the relevant state and federal regulations. Filing such a statement will not relieve a BOC of its duty to negotiate in good faith with would-be competitors.

Going Forward

Opening the $98 billion local exchange market to real competition will take time. The extent to which it may be realized will depend on the efforts of inventors, entrepreneurs and the FCC and state regulators. Nonetheless, the reforms set forth in the Telecom Act establish an environment that will foster competition. Many of the specific regulations and governing principles will be established by the FCC and the various states over the next few months, including with respect to such crucial issues as terms for interconnection, resale rates, and the technical feasibility of number portability and unbundling. See Appendix 4 for the FCC's timetable to implement the requirements of the Telecom Act.

Competitors, both large and small, are ready to exploit the reforms presented by the Telecom Act. AT&T has filed to offer local exchange service in all fifty states and estimates it will have one-third of the local exchange market in the United States within five to ten years. In addition, alternative access providers have begun to negotiate with the Bell Operating Companies to exercise rights granted to them under the Telecom Act. Appendix 3 shows, state by state, the status of competition in local exchange.

Universal Service

In 1908, Theodore Vail, the president of AT&T, announced a new slogan for his company: "One Policy, One System, Universal Service." The American people were beginning to consider telephone service a necessity and AT&T had begun to make its case to the public that, through one company, such universal service would materialize more quickly than through competition. As the history above points out, the Postmaster General in 1918 agreed and when that office took over administration of AT&T's networks during World War I, consolidation of competitors into AT&T was a priority.

Which Services Must Be Universal?

Even though regulation of telephony today is based on open competition, universal service is still a priority. But while most people agree that basic telephone service should be made available to everyone, a considerable difference of opinion exists as to whether other services should be universally available at a standard low price. Through its "Lifeline Assistance" project, the FCC currently administers a universal service program pursuant to which interexchange carriers contribute $750 million each year to support the provision of telephone service to rural areas and low-income individuals. But that fund only supports plain old telephone service.

The Telecom Act requires the creation of a federal-state joint board to determine which services should be made available universally, how the cost of such services should be supported and other such issues. The FCC established that Joint Board on March 8, 1996. The Joint Board has until November 8 to complete its review of the FCC's regulations and make specific suggestions to the FCC regarding compliance with the Telecom Act. The ultimate decisions rest with the Commission.

The Telecom Act contains criteria for assessing which services will be included in universal service — the definition of which will evolve pursuant to the Act. The criteria require the Commission and the Joint Board to consider the extent to which a particular telecommunications service (1) is essential to education, public health or public safety, (2) has been subscribed to by a substantial majority of residential customers, (3) is being deployed in public telecommunications networks, and (4) is consistent with the public interest, convenience and necessity. Only time will tell what services will meet these criteria.

To provide further guidance, the Telecom Act contains specific principles that will assist the Joint Board in making critical decisions about the types and extent of universal service to be offered. The principles set forth by the Act are: quality services at affordable rates, access to advanced telecommunications and information services in all regions of the nation, access at comparable rates by rural and high-cost areas to the same types of services available in urban areas, equitable contribution by all telecommunications carriers, specific federal and state support mechanisms, and access to advanced telecommunications services by schools, health care providers and libraries. The Telecom Act provides elsewhere that interexchange carriers may not charge higher rates for subscribers in rural and high-cost areas than the rates charged to subscribers in urban areas.

The Telecom Act also provides that an interexchange carrier's rates must be the same in all states.

The Commission has moved quickly on universal service and in a notice of proposed rulemaking issued on March 8, 1996, the Commission proposed the following services should be included among the core services comprising universal service: (1) voice grade access to the public switched network, with the ability to place and receive calls, (2) touch-tone, (3) single party service (one subscriber per local loop), (4) access to emergency services (911), and (5) access to operator services. The Commission proposed providing these core services to rural, insular and high-cost areas. The Commission also proposed providing such services to low-income consumers based on a suggestion to that effect in the legislative history of the Telecom Act, although the Act does not explicitly provide for such "universal access." The Act does, however, give the FCC broad latitude to fashion universal service guidelines and also explicitly authorizes the FCC to continue its Lifeline Assistance project. The Act further requires telecommunications carriers to ensure their services are accessible by customers with disabilities to the extent such access is readily achievable. These provisions have the flavor of "universal access."

Who Should Contribute? Who Should Receive?

The Telecom Act provides that "every telecommunications carrier that provides interstate telecommunications services shall contribute, on an equitable and nondiscriminatory basis, to the specific, predictable and sufficient mechanisms established by the Commission to preserve and advance universal service." The Commission may exempt carriers from this requirement if their contribution would be minimal. Some debate has arisen whether all types of telecommunications carriers will be required to contribute. The issue is particularly sensitive with respect to wireless service providers. In addition, there is some question as to whether public data networks and online systems, whether or not interconnected to the public switched network, may also be required to contribute.

In addition to the federal program, states may also adopt universal service plans, with more extensive definitions of universal service, and all telecommunications carriers that provide intrastate telecommunications services must contribute to such state's universal service program. With these requirements, initially the interexchange service providers will fund the federal universal service program, as they do now, and the incumbent LECs will fund the local programs. But with the entry of the BOCs into long distance, and interexchange carriers into local exchange, this distribution may change.

On the receiving end, amounts collected for the federal universal service program will be paid to "eligible telecommunications carriers." Under the Telecom Act, an eligible telecommunications carrier is one designated by a state commission that will, throughout a service area specified by the state commission, offer the federal universal services through its own facilities (with partial resale if necessary) and advertise the availability of such services. If no carrier is willing to serve an area, the state commission may press one into service.

At least initially, the BOCs will provide most of the universal services through their local exchanges. But as they enter the interexchange business, and begin to contribute to the federal universal service program (while still providing most of the universal services), the BOCs may be placed at a competitive disadvantage. In short, they may end up paying for, and providing, most of the universal service in the United States — a situation that AT&T claimed justified its monopoly position before the breakup.

Infrastructure and Qualifying Carriers

The universal service provisions of the Telecom Act contain a requirement to help small carriers that wish to provide services included within the definition of universal service. The Act provides that incumbent LECs must make available to any "qualifying carrier" "such public switched network infrastructure, technology, information and telecommunications facilities and functions" as may be requested by such qualifying carrier to serve their particular service area. A qualifying carrier is defined as one that has been designated as an eligible telecommunications carrier and that also "lacks economies of scale or scope."

This provision essentially encourages new local exchange companies to deploy networks in unserved areas and requires the incumbent LECs to share their switches and technology to help the new carrier get started. The Act provides exceptions, however, by affirmatively stating that the incumbent LECs do not have to provide such infrastructure if it is "economically unreasonable," and also that they don't have to provide infrastructure to a carrier that will use it to compete directly with them. Considering the incumbents will now be subject to real competition, it is unlikely they will welcome the opportunity to share their infrastructure and technology with potential competitors.

Long Distance: "Baby" Bells No Longer?

As discussed in the history above, when AT&T was broken up in 1984, the Bell Operating Companies were spun off to provide local exchange service but were prohibited from providing interexchange service between the newly defined LATAs. AT&T was unleashed virtually without restrictions to act as the nation's dominant long-distance carrier. Held back by the chains of the MFJ, the BOCs have yearned to provide long-distance service in competition with AT&T, MCI, Sprint and others. The Telecom Act has finally set them free to do so — almost.

Out of Region InterLATA Services

The MFJ prohibited the Bell Operating Companies from providing interLATA services both within the states where they operated local exchanges and outside those regions. Thus, NYNEX, even though it had local exchange facilities only in certain sections of the Northeast, was prohibited from providing long-distance services even in California. The BOCs were essentially restricted to providing local exchange service as natural monopolies, with apparently no right to do anything else. The holes in that model began to show in 1987 when Judge Greene permitted the BOCs to provide services other than local exchange. Even limited exceptions for interexchange in wireless were permitted in 1995. But the general restrictions remained on interexchange service, wherever provided (including, for a time, foreign countries).

The Telecom Act opens the doors to BOC interexchange entry at least part of the way. The Act immediately permits the BOCs to provide interLATA services originating outside their regions. This means that a BOC can immediately start marketing long-distance services that compete with AT&T, MCI and Sprint to subscribers that live in states other than where that BOC operates local exchange facilities. The Act does not require that such long-distance calls handled by the BOCs must also terminate out of region. In other words, the BOCs are not restricted to carrying calls that only originate and terminate outside their regions — being forced to hand off those calls headed in region to another long-distance carrier. The BOCs may carry long-distance calls into their regions, across LATA boundaries, for termination.

Furthermore, the Telecom Act does not require that the BOCs provide such long-distance service through a separate subsidiary. To prevent cross-subsidization and abuse of market power, the FCC and Judge Greene have at times required the BOCs to create separate subsidiaries to provide certain services. Similarly, the Telecom Act requires a separate subsidiary for some of the BOCs' new ventures, but out-of-region interexchange is not one of those requiring separation. Nevertheless, the FCC has tentatively proposed that unless the BOCs use a separate subsidiary for out-of-region interexchange service, they will be regulated as dominant carriers — which entails significant tariffing requirements and other regulatory red tape. The FCC has received complaints from both BOCs and long-distance carriers about this proposed rule. The BOCs complain that the structural separation requirements violate the Telecom Act, and the long-distance providers complain that the BOCs should not be classified as non-dominant whether separated from their long-distance operations or not. With such disagreement over a relatively minor regulation compared to say, interconnection, the complexity of addressing the requirements of the Telecom Act are becoming painfully obvious.

All of the BOCs are either offering or have announced plans to offer long-distance services out of their regions. Bell Atlantic adopted the most ambitious schedule and announced that it plans to offer long-distance service in five states by the end of the second quarter of 1996. And once again, as MCI did to initiate long distance competition in 1969, the BOCs appear in many cases to be targeting the low-cost, high traffic routes first.

Incidental InterLATA Services

The Telecom Act also permits the Bell Operating Companies to immediately provide certain "incidental interLATA services" originating in any state, including in-region, without a separate subsidiary. This provision permits a BOC to carry interLATA traffic that may be required in connection with another service the BOC offers. These "incidental" services include audio and video programming services (including interactive services), alarm monitoring services (though other restrictions apply), information retrieval services, and most importantly, wireless services such as cellular, paging and personal communications services. The significance of the wireless revolution and of permitting the BOCs to provide interLATA services to their wireless customers is discussed more fully in Chapter 5.

In-Region InterLATA Services

Although the Bell Operating Companies have been freed to provide out-of-region and incidental interexchange services immediately upon passage of the Telecom Act, they may not provide interexchange services originating within their regions until certain conditions are satisfied. Specifically, the Telecom Act establishes a "checklist" that ensures that real competition exists or may develop without hindrance before the BOCs may provide long-distance service in-region.

Before a BOC may provide in-region interLATA service in any particular state, it must first prove to the FCC that it currently faces local exchange competition in that state from a facilities-based competitor that is receiving or is offered each element of a competitive checklist set forth in the Telecom Act. See Figure 4. The competitor must provide local exchange service predominantly over its own telephone exchange facilities — pure resellers won't qualify. Alternatively, if after December 8, 1996, no would-be competitor has requested access during the previous three months, the FCC may grant a BOC permission to enter the interexchange business

---

Competitive Checklist

1. Interconnection at technically feasible points.

2. Nondiscriminatory access to network elements.

3. Nondiscriminatory access to the poles, ducts, conduits and rights-of-way.

4. Local loop transmission from the central office to the customer's premises, unbundled from local switching or other services.

5. Local transport from the trunk side of a wireline local exchange carrier switch unbundled from switching or other services.

6. Local switching unbundled from transport, local loop transmission or other services.

7. Nondiscriminatory access to (i) 911, (ii) directory assistance and (iii) operator call completion services.

8. White pages directory listings for customers of the other carrier's telephone exchange service.

9. Nondiscriminatory access to telephone numbers.

10. Nondiscriminatory access to databases and associated signalling necessary for call routing and completion.

11. Number portability.

12. Dialing parity.

13. Reciprocal compensation arrangements.

14. Resale.

Figure 4 - The Telecom Act's "competitive checklist."

if the BOC has filed with the state commission an approved statement of general terms of access and interconnection that complies with the competitive checklist. For purposes of determining whether the BOC has received a request for interconnection, would-be competitors that do not negotiate in good faith or that breach an agreement for interconnection will not be considered.

The fourteen-point competitive checklist set forth in the Telecom Act contains all the provisions described above that the BOCs must provide to potential local exchange competitors, and elaborates certain unbundling and access requirements. The checklist includes interconnection, resale, unbundled access to network elements, pole access, nondiscriminatory access to telephone numbers, number portability, dialing parity, white pages listings and reciprocal compensation arrangements. Unbundling of specific elements is required, including local loop transmission from the central office to the customer's premises, local transport from the trunk side of a wireline switch, and local switching. In addition, the BOC must provide nondiscriminatory access to emergency services (911), directory assistance, operator call completion, and access to databases and associated signaling necessary for call routing. The FCC may not add to the competitive checklist.

The decision to permit a BOC to enter the long-distance business in-region ultimately rests with the FCC, but the Commission is required to consult with the Attorney General. The Attorney General must provide the FCC with an evaluation of the BOC's application using whatever standard it deems appropriate. The FCC must give "substantial weight" to the Attorney General's evaluation, but is not bound to follow it. The FCC must also consult with the appropriate state commission to ensure the BOC has a facilities-based competitor or has filed a conforming statement of general terms that satisfy the requirements of the checklist as described above. All this must take place within 90 days after the BOC files its application to provide in-region long-distance services. This short statutory deadline will likely complicate the FCC's difficult task of considering a wide variety of interests in determining whether a BOC may enter the long-distance business. Subsequent orders may be necessary to clarify or modify approvals issued within the 90-day period.

Once approved, a BOC may provide in-region interexchange services for the first three years only through a separate subsidiary. The FCC may extend this period of separation by rule or order. The subsidiary must be completely separate from the BOC, with different books, directors, officers, employees, and credit arrangements. All transactions with the BOC must be on an arm's length basis and accounted for in accordance with standards set by the Commission. Every two years a joint federal-state audit must be conducted to ensure compliance with the separation requirements.

To dilute any potential advantages a Bell Operating Company may have by virtue of its market presence, the Telecom Act forbids a BOC from jointly marketing its local exchange and long-distance services as a package unless the BOC permits certain small long-distance companies to bundle the BOC's local exchange service with their long-distance offerings; to offer a single package to subscribers that includes, perhaps transparently from a billing perspective, the BOC's local exchange service. Restrictions apply to the largest interexchange carriers' ability to do so, however. Because the BOCs are restrained from jointly marketing local and long-distance services until they are actually permitted to provide in-region interexchange service, a long-distance carrier that serves more than five percent of the nation's presubscribed access lines — namely, AT&T, MCI and Sprint — may not jointly market its long-distance service and resold local exchange service obtained from the BOC until the BOC is authorized to provide in-region interexchange service, or three years has passed, whichever is earlier. Congress thus attempted to protect the BOCs from AT&T, and vice versa, until each had enough time to become fairly established in the other's market.

Going Forward

Entry into the $70 billion long-distance business for the BOCs may be worth the obligations, restrictions and waiting periods imposed on them. Although some companies have begun providing alternative local exchange services through coaxial cable and fiber-based networks, the BOCs may enter the in-region long-distance business far sooner than they face extensive competition at home. Ameritech, which has already been subject to strict interconnection and resale obligations from state regulators, stated that it expects to offer in-region interexchange service by December of 1996. BellSouth has asserted that it already meets the checklist requirements in Florida and Georgia and expects to start marketing in-region interexchange service to its customers over the next 18 months. And the dual mergers of Bell Atlantic and NYNEX, and Pacific Telesis and SBC Communications, both announced in April 1996, positions these combined companies, smaller in size only to AT&T among telecommunications players, to become serious contenders in the long-distance business.

Just opening the doors to out-of-region long distance is a great benefit to the BOCs that may lead to a demonstrable shrinking of the market shares of AT&T, MCI and Sprint. NYNEX has plans to commence marketing long-distance service immediately to customers out-of-region that have a "northeast affinity," such as retirees in Florida with families in New York, and out-of-town college students. Other BOCs have similar plans.

Regardless of when the BOCs enter the long-distance business, and no matter how soon serious competition exists on the local level, the Telecom Act provides a workable framework that will permit new and existing companies to compete for consumer subscription and loyalty. And with competition as the intended regulator, we should not be surprised to find new services, new competitors, and even new innovation in the delivery of telephone service. Although it may not be wholly obvious yet, over the next decade the average American will be demonstrably affected by the Telecommunications Act of 1996 — almost certainly for the better.

Chapter 3

Broadcast

By Camille Hansen, Esq.

Over time, technology has consistently increased and improved the methods by which Americans receive news, entertainment and other information. Among the most significant technologies, Gutenberg's printing press and the discovery of radio waves are unparalleled in their impact on the aspirations and interaction of people. Audio and video transmissions have become essential to most Americans, and the number of channels of information into the home has increased. But even as "wired" delivery systems become more common, radio and television broadcast remain the least expensive and most preferred media in the nation.

Broadcast communication has long been regulated by the federal government, and the Telecommunications Act of 1996 continues the tradition. Although the provisions of the Act make relatively minor changes in the overall regulation of television and radio (with the exceptions of radio ownership and the V-Chip), Congress seized upon the opportunity to address new forms of broadcasting in the Act, such as high definition television (HDTV) and direct broadcast satellite (DBS). This chapter provides a brief history of broadcast in America and then discusses how Titles II and V of the Telecom Act modify the time-honored model of broadcast regulation.

A BROADCAST PRIMER

As French philosopher Simone Weil once noted, "The future is made up of the same stuff as the present." This is fundamentally true in broadcasting, where the past, the present and the future may all be traced to "the same stuff," namely, radio waves. The initial discovery of radio waves in 1881 by Heinrich Hertz hardly contemplated the vast commercialization of the medium in years to come. Even Guglielmo Marconi, credited with sending the first trans-Atlantic "wireless" message in 1901, only envisioned the maritime potential of such transmissions. Indeed, David Sarnoff's vision of a "Radio Music Box" was disregarded when he first pursued the idea as an employee of the Marconi Wireless Telegraph Company in 1915. It took decades and many early experimenters to develop "broadcasting" as it is known today.

The Advent of Radio

Marconi's wireless telegraph was used initially to transmit and receive signals from ships at sea. The medium was unregulated and many amateurs also dabbled with radio transmission on land. The cacaphony resulting from overlapping signals began to reduce the safety advantages of carrying a wireless telegraph aboard a ship, and events involving failed radio communication, such as the 1912 Titanic disaster, prompted the U.S. government to regulate radio broadcasting. In the Radio Act of 1912, Congress expanded the control of the government over broadcasting by instituting licensing requirements, call letters and waveband assignments according to class of service (*i.e.,* government, ship, coastal and amateur).

What began as a public curiosity quickly became a public passion by the 1920s. No longer just for hobbyists and amateurs, radio assumed cultural and commercial significance for people of all ages and interests, as it developed into an indispensable source of news, information, entertainment, and education. In 1921, "broadcasting" earned its own service classification. By 1922, nearly 400,000 receiving sets were in use in the United States, and that number increased to over a million during 1923.

For those looking to make a profit in the growing radio industry, the initial focus was placed on the production and sale of radio equipment rather than the broadcasts themselves, which generated no income and were viewed as largely philanthropic in nature. Companies invested in and operated stations as a means of promoting public goodwill though program offerings. As gradual experimentation with advertising on the radio proved successful in the early 1920s, the profitable aspect of broadcasting came to light.

With the growing popularity of the airwaves came growing competition for their use. Because the Act of 1912 did not grant discretionary power to the Secretary of Commerce to establish regulations to specify frequencies, limit power output, or restrict hours of operation, it was determined in 1926 that licensees essentially had the freedom to use any frequency and any power level they desired. The courts kept the airwaves open in accordance with the law, holding in one case that interference with other frequency assignments was not grounds for denial of a license application, and in another that operation on a frequency other than the one assigned was not subject to penalty. Without authorized supervision governing the airwaves, too many stations began vying for and broadcasting on the same frequencies. As the airwaves began to encroach chaotically upon one another causing major signal interference, the laws of physics demanded recognition.

In response, Congress endeavored to create a new, more workable regulatory scheme. The Radio Act of 1927 created a five-member, bipartisan Federal Radio Commission, which was to regulate and facilitate equal broadcast service in all areas across the country. The Commission was empowered to "classify radio stations, assign frequencies, decide upon power and hours of operation for any station, regulate equipment used, and make rules with respect to chain or network broadcasting."

By 1929, more than 10 million radios were in use across the nation, with most listeners tuning in for four to six hours a day. In 1932, the number of radio sets had increased to 18 million, and by 1936, an estimated 45 million radios were used in the United States. The rise in radio's popularity and pervasiveness in these years was even more significant in light of the great economic crisis faced by the nation at this time — even the Great Depression did not halt its growth.

In 1933, under the direction of President Franklin D. Roosevelt, a committee was formed to study the regulation of electronic communications in the United States and suggest a means of bringing broadcasting and telephony under the same statutory jurisdiction. The following year, President Roosevelt took the recommendations of the committee to Congress, proposing that a single independent agency be formed to oversee all services relying on "wires, cables, or radio as a medium of transmission." The result was the formation of the seven-member Federal Communications Commission through the enactment of the Communications Act of 1934.

The Rise of Television

It was about this time that television made its debut on the broadcast stage. Although the Communications Act was written to regulate radio and was never specifically amended to include television, it has always been read to be equally applicable to television. Employing the same electronic technologies which had facilitated radio broadcasts, experimental television stations were tested in the late 1920s and began battling with radio stations for frequency use. The conflict became significant enough by 1937 that the FCC allocated frequencies for experimental stations.

From that point, the development of television moved quickly. Television sets were sold for private ownership in 1938. The FCC authorized certain channels for television broadcast use in 1940 and established standards for black-and-white broadcasts in 1941. By 1945, there were six commercial stations in operation and 10,000 television receivers in use in the United States. Twenty more station licenses were issued by the summer of 1946. In 1950, standards for color television sets were promulgated by the Commission.

In spite of the advances, many were skeptical about the future of television, feeling the cost — both to consumers for the purchase of receivers and to stations for the production and airing of programming — would be too prohibitive. Television did experience a loss during the initial years. In 1948 alone, the industry reported an overall loss of $15 million. Eventually, however, as networks were formed that provided programming to affiliated stations and receiver sets became more affordable for consumers, television found its financial footing and made its way into American homes.

Ownership Limitations

Owning broadcast stations became an enticing venture, both because of their lucrative nature and the power to impact the minds of the public. To thwart monopolization of broadcast properties and promote competition in the industry, early legislation adopted ownership rules for both national and local markets.

Control over national ownership was maintained by limiting the power and pervasiveness of the networks, which were defined by the FCC in 1941 as "the simultaneous broadcasting of an identical program by two or more connected stations." Network broadcasting really began after 1926 when NBC (National Broadcasting Company) and then CBS (Columbia

Broadcasting System) acquired numerous affiliate stations and began chain broadcasting. Such broadcasting offered significant advantages, as it enabled all parts of the nation to receive higher quality programming than a local station could afford to produce on its own, and also attracted advertisers wishing to target national audiences. Network affiliations were economically rewarding for affiliate stations, for both the national advertising revenues they received as well as the cash paid by the networks for carrying network programming.

To limit the influence of networks over local stations and avoid too much concentration of power in the industry, anticompetitive regulations to govern the national radio networks were established in the 1940s. Restrictions were placed on network-affiliate agreements, networks were limited to acquiring only a certain number of stations in any given market, and common ownership of more than one network by a single entity was prohibited. These standards governing the national radio networks were made applicable to television networks in 1946.

To prevent concentration of power and control in local markets, the FCC also established "duopoly" rules in 1943 to govern local broadcast station ownership — limiting licensees to one same-service station within a given market or area. "Service contours," defined as the area covered by radio wave emissions, were created in 1964 to govern local duopoly ownership, and in 1970, the "one-to-a-market" rule was implemented to prohibit owners of AM, FM or television stations from acquiring additional stations in the same market. That rule was modified a year later to permit common ownership of AM and FM stations and radio and UHF television stations (on a case-by-case basis) in any particular market.

As the number of stations in each market increased, creating numerous information and alternative programming sources, the Commission acknowledged that its fears about monopolization and abuse of control were unrealized. It was thus prompted to ease up on ownership restrictions as regulators recognized that the possible economic and administrative benefits of joint ownership could help stations operate more efficiently. The national limits have gradually increased over the years — going from the "rule of sevens" (allowing ownership of seven AM, seven FM and seven TV stations by a common entity) in the early 1950s, to the "12-12-12" rule in 1985, and reaching a limit of twenty AM and twenty FM stations by September 1994. Similarly, steps toward further deregulation in the local broadcast markets led to a modification of radio duopoly and one-to-a-market rules in 1989. Duopoly rules were changed to allow common ownership of stations with greater overlap into defined service contours, and one-to-a-market rules were relaxed to permit multiple ownership in the top 25 markets, or where a "failed" broadcast station was involved in other markets.

THE TELECOMMUNICATIONS ACT OF 1996

The Telecommunications Act of 1996 dramatically reorganizes the regulation of telephony and cable, as discussed in Chapters 2 and 4 respectively, but with respect to broadcast, the Act merely supplements existing regulations. The Telecom Act contains relaxations of the broadcast ownership limitations, and widens the scope of broadcast regulation to encompass new technologies such as high definition television and direct broadcast satellite. In addition, the Act contains new requirements aimed at regulating the content of video programming. Each of these isolated provisions of the Telecom Act is discussed below.

Relaxed Ownership Restrictions

As discussed above, to prevent concentration of media power in a few dominant individuals or corporations, traditional broadcast regulation has limited the number of radio and television stations that a single entity may own on a national level, and also on a local level. Over the years, the limits have been increased as additional stations have broadened the diversity of viewpoints and the threat of media concentration has been reduced.

National Limits

The new legislation eliminates the national ownership cap on radio and television stations entirely, leaving no limit on the number of television or radio stations one company can own nationally. Note, however, that televison broadcasters are still limited with respect to the percentage of American homes they may reach. Under the Telecom Act, no single television broadcaster may reach more than 35 percent of the national audience — up from the previous coverage limit of 25 percent.

Local Limits

In the local radio markets, the new legislation will have the effect of allowing greater concentration of ownership. The size of the market will continue to determine the number of stations single entities may own in order to prevent too much concentration of power. Loosening of regulations has resulted in a new eight-station ownership limit for broadcasters in markets with 45 or more commercial radio stations, a seven-station limit in markets with 30-44 stations, a six-station limit in markets with 15-29 stations, and a five-station limit in markets with 14 or fewer stations, so long as no single owner owns more than half the stations in the market. This is an increase from previous limitations of four stations in large markets and three in small markets. There are additional guidelines within these parameters with which broadcasters must comply. For example, in a market with a six-station limit, no more than four of the stations owned by a single broadcaster may be AM or FM. FCC service contour rules will still apply, as AM and FM station markets will continue to be defined by "principal community contours" or signal strength, and will be evaluated on a case-by-case basis.

The Telecom Act also gives the FCC discretion to decide the future of the television duopoly rule which currently limits local television ownership to one station per market by a single entity. Specifically, the Commission has been directed to examine the possibility of loosening regulations to allow UHF/UHF combinations and VHF/UHF combinations, as well as VHF/VHF combinations in compelling circumstances. The Act requires that existing one-to-a-market waiver policies be extended to the top 50 markets.

Cross-Ownership Restrictions

The Broadcast-Newspaper Cross Ownership rule, adopted in 1975, is still in effect, prohibiting ownership of both a newspaper and a broadcast license within the same community. However, deregulation in this area may also be possible in the future. The Act permits common ownership of broadcast networks and cable systems and allows cross-ownership of cable and wireless cable services, so long as the cable operator remains subject to effective competition.

Renewals

The new legislation results in longer license terms for broadcasters. Originally, all broadcast licenses were subject to renewal every three years. Since 1981, license terms have been seven years for radio licenses and five years for television licenses. The public trustee scheme of the

Communications Act of 1934 required that renewals be granted upon a showing that the licensee had served the public interest during the license term.

The new legislation extends all broadcast license and license renewal terms to eight years and streamlines the renewal process. Shorter renewal periods are permitted when found to be in the public interest. Incumbent broadcasters are given a presumptive right to renewal upon a finding by the Commission that the station has served the public interest, convenience and necessity, and committed no serious rule violations or other violations indicative of a "pattern of abuse." Significantly, the legislation eliminates the FCC's traditional comparative renewal procedures, making it difficult for challengers to compete for licenses, unless the FCC first denies the renewal application on noncompliance or other grounds. Thus, broadcasters are given the right to apply for renewal without having to deal with competing applications. This eliminates a potentially expensive and time-consuming trial-type hearing concerning a station's renewal.

Benefits of the Expanded Limits for Broadcasters

The expansion of these national and local limits translates into potential for more ownership consolidation and greater operating efficiencies for broadcasters, who can save money through economies of scale. The deregulation is seen as a benefit to competition in the radio industry, as common ownership of more stations can help licensees realize greater operating efficiencies from combined sales, programming, administrative, promotion and production activities. Ownership of more stations can also help broadcasters to extend their programming to target multiple groups of niche listeners and advertiser demographics, although critics and consumer groups worry that consolidation of ownership will create undue concentration of control and limit editorial diversity. The expansion of both the local and national limits is already having a significant impact on the radio industry. Consolidation, both on the national and local levels, is proceeding at a fast pace and is changing the face of radio ownership.

Addressing New Technologies

High Definition Television

Fueled by the public popularity of television, many innovations have been employed to build upon and perfect the television prototype. High-definition television, more generally referred to as advanced television (ATV), has been touted as the most revolutionary development in video technology since the introduction of color television in the 1950s. Use of digital technology promises to heighten the quality of television-viewing, offering wide-screen pictures, improved color rendition, significantly sharper images and greater detail, and compact disc quality sound. As the amount of spectrum a digital television channel requires is roughly half of what a single analog channel presently uses, conversion from current television systems would result in greatly expanded transmission capabilities for broadcast stations. Additionally, digital TV receivers would enable eventual incorporation of computer and other technologies to facilitate easy access to other services offered along the information superhighway.

The new legislation authorizes allocation of a relatively large portion of spectrum in a highly desirable frequency range for provision of high definition television. The primary source of controversy in this area stems from the provision in the legislation allowing spectrum to be provided at no charge to broadcasters to facilitate the transition to high definition television. Other industry players are concerned that the spectrum may be too valuable for HDTV use, and support a general auction of the spectrum, based on the belief that market forces should govern the use of the spectrum so that potentially more valuable services could be offered on the channels.

Estimates of the value of the spectrum designated for HDTV use range from $10 billion to $100 billion. Those favoring auction of the spectrum primarily include other spectrum users, such as wireless telecommunications providers, that have already had to participate in auctions to secure use of the spectrum. Auctions are currently being conducted for several wireless services, including interactive video and data services (IVDS), specialized mobile radio (SMR) licenses, and multipoint distribution services (MDS), also called "wireless cable." Citing the 1993 mandate by Congress that all spectrum allocated for new services must be auctioned off by the FCC, opponents say that broadcasters should not be exempt from the auction plan. On the other side of the battle are television licensees, who oppose auctions on fairness and economic grounds. They claim that other licensees (*e.g.,* radio and cellular telephone) continue to have free use of the spectrum, making it unfair to require television licensees to pay. Moreover, previous government actions and statements have suggested that the spectrum would be made available to them at no cost, prompting the industry to already invest an estimated $500 million into the development of HDTV. Finally, an auction seems especially unfair given the FCC's plan to reclaim the currently licensed spectrum from television licensees once the transition to HDTV is complete and to hold auctions for that spectrum at that time. Since many currently existing broadcast stations purchased their spectrum licenses from other broadcasters at a premium, an auction for HDTV spectrum would mean these broadcasters would be paying twice for the same portion of spectrum.

From an economic standpoint, many broadcasters claim their financial resources are too limited to cover the cost of licenses in addition to the substantial expenditures required for conversion to HDTV. The National Association of Broadcasters (NAB) has estimated a cost of $8 to $10 million per station for the necessary equipment upgrades, new transmission towers, and engineering and legal costs, saying any additional cost would be prohibitive to small and rural stations. The FCC estimates that a conversion can be installed for as little as $500,000. Nonetheless, broadcasters claim that if they have to pay for licenses in an auction, they will be unable to offer free over-the-air television service and still compete with cable and satellite; they argue that the cost of procuring a license would ultimately necessitate taxing viewers, in the form of subscription fees, to help defray the expense. Moreover, broadcasters believe that auctioning the spectrum could kill the ability of the industry to transition to HDTV.

The resolution of the conflict concerning auctioning HDTV spectrum will likely be resolved by Congress. To date, a number of legislative efforts to auction the spectrum have been unsuccessful. However, until licenses are issued, the dispute is likely to resurface any time Congress is considering budget proposals.

Spectrum Flexibility Rules

Whether the licenses are given without charge for use by broadcasters or auctioned to the highest bidder, the estimated expense for conversion to HDTV and the uncertain level of consumer interest in HDTV programming has raised questions about the practicality of requiring broadcast stations to be limited in the use of their allotted spectrum to HDTV alone. "Spectrum flexibility" has thus been proposed in the Telecom Act to enable broadcasters to use the spectrum in whatever way they choose — requiring one "advanced" television channel to be provided free to the public and subject to public interest obligations (*e.g.*, lowest unit charge, equal time, and children's programming requirements), but allowing the remainder of the transmission ability to be used for other "ancillary and supplementary services" (*i.e.*, non-program services) as desired. Digital technology would enable broadcasters to not only provide one channel of HDTV on six megahertz of spectrum, but also additional channels of standard analog television, or high quality radio signals, cellular telephone services, interactive data services, or any combination of the above.

The spectrum flexibility proposal means that subscription-based services like paging and data services would likely be permissible on these channels, so long as they cause no interference to the provision of HDTV services. The Telecom Act instructs the Commission to "establish a program to assess and collect from the [HDTV] licensee" a fee, if a subscription fee is charged to viewers for any of the offered services over the spectrum. This provision aims at discouraging unjust enrichment from the public spectrum resource. Fee amounts assessed on licensees would be determined by considering the portion of spectrum used for subscription services and the amount of time these services are provided over the airwaves.

Direct Broadcast Satellite

Direct broadcast satellite systems involve a system of high-power communications satellites that transmit television signals to earth stations, commonly known as satellite dishes. More specifically, the service retransmits signals from earth to high-powered geostationary satellites for direct reception by home terminals. DBS service was initially authorized by the Commission in June 1982, and was foreseen at that time as an alternative information provider that would offer competition to cable television in the future. Much like the beginning of cable, DBS service began as Television Receive-Only (TVRO) which transmitted cable and broadcasting programming to homes that were in rural areas not wired for standard cable. Governed by the same "interim rules" adopted in the early 1980s, 500 megahertz of spectrum is currently allocated for DBS use.

The Commission regulates DBS service on a case-by-case basis, depending on the type of service the direct broadcaster chooses to provide: if programming channels itself, the operator is subject to broadcast regulation; if providing a common carrier service, those are the rules under which the service will be regulated. After a decade of fairly stagnant activity in the direct broadcast satellite business, three companies launched satellites and began offering DBS service in the early 1990s.

One contributing factor to the recent rise in DBS activity is the development and use of easily installed, relatively small dishes, generally eighteen inches to three feet in diameter, replacing the large and expensive dishes once required to receive satellite transmissions. Because of the smaller size and reduced cost, DBS services are expected to start commanding a stronger competitive force for the broadcast and cable industries in the near future, as they are utilized by pay television services. Increased satellite power and relaxed FCC regulation have also contributed to DBS development, as well as digital compression which allows greater channel carriage abilities. DBS providers in 1995 were reporting tremendous growth, already serving more than two million homes in the U.S. and creating predictions for future declining growth margins in the cable industry.

DBS systems offer several advantages over other services. Regulations governing DBS are fairly relaxed compared to land-based services. DBS can be more cost-effective and thereby more profitable than cable, as the cost of DBS systems is largely entry-based and up-front in nature — primarily incurred in the placement of satellites in orbit which then disseminate signals to individual home terminals. Once the satellites are launched, there are no significant additional costs to the DBS operator, who can then recoup the fixed cost of entry through access to a large potential subscriber base across the entire country. Moreover, if the service proves to be unprofitable for the operator, the satellite costs can still be recovered by employing the satellite for use in other commercial ventures.

A primary goal of the Telecom Act is to facilitate development of the telecommunications infrastructure in the private sector in order to provide a "wide array of integrated services," based on the premise that innovation and technology development is best fostered by competition, rather than regulation.

The Act gives the FCC the authority to regulate direct-to-home services, such as DBS, and specifically instructs the Commission to promulgate rules that would serve to eliminate restrictions inhibiting a viewer's ability to receive such over-the-air services. In response thereto, the Commission has recently acted to strengthen a 1986 rule dealing with unreasonable local regulation to facilitate easy public access to satellite signals. New rules preempt most local and state government restrictions on the installation of small satellite dishes for both home and commercial use. Specifically, the FCC has adopted "bright line tests" to determine whether relevant local regulations are unreasonable: for receiver dishes one meter or less in diameter, ordinances preventing installation are deemed presumptively unreasonable, as are those for receiver dishes between one- and two-meters in commercial areas. While local governments may tax equipment sales, taxation of DBS services is prohibited.

Regulating Television Obscenity and Violence

The development of HDTV and DBS services manifest the dominant role of television and satellite programming in American homes. In response to public interest and demand, technology has developed to offer better equipment, more channels, and a greater variety of programming to meet the interests of people of all ages at any given time of day. While technology has increased the quantity of programming options available to viewers, it has no control over the quality of the abundant programming traveling the public's airwaves. With the help of technology, however, parents and industry leaders may be aided in their efforts to control or screen program content.

Increased televised violence and sexual content have prompted discussions of a television content ratings code similar in effect to the movie industry ratings code. Motivated by pressure from Congress and the White House, the television industry is looking to establish a television content code as a means of offering parents greater control over childrens' viewing. The code can help parents determine what types of things their children should or should not see. The Telecom Act gives the TV industry a year to comply with the new rating requirements. If the industry is unable to comply or proposes a system that is unacceptable by Commission standards, the FCC is authorized to form its own committee to develop an industry-wide television content code. The four major commercial networks are expected to endorse a ratings system and set an industry standard. The legislation suggests that programs are to be given ratings so that parents have control to tune out programs characterized as "objectionable" for children by the ratings board.

The movie ratings system, the adoption of which has been proposed as a means of rating television programs, is seen by some to be too general for television standards: G (general audiences), PG (parental guidance suggested), PG-13 (some material may be inappropriate for children under 13), R (restricted; under 17 requires accompanying parent or adult guardian), and NC-17 (no children 17 and under admitted). Some in the industry fear that most current shows would likely not qualify as G or PG and support a more content-specific standard, such as one that breaks down and identifies the objectionable material (*e.g.*, nudity, graphic violence, adult situations, adult subject matter, or sexual innuendo).

There are many who question the wisdom and the effectiveness of requiring television program ratings. The vast quantity and wide variety of television programs that would be subject to ratings have made the proposed system a difficult one with which to comply. The subjective nature of the decisions that would be required of any commission or group charged with the task of determining which programs are "objectionable" has also been raised as a potential problem.

Moreover, the ratings system may pose new economic challenges to stations. While actual use of the ratings system to rate shows may be left as discretionary with the stations or networks, the type of rating — or the lack thereof — given to a certain program may affect advertiser preferences, and may influence the size of the viewing audience. If, as a general consensus, advertisers do not want their products associated with certain program ratings, this may reflect itself in the content of future television programs. As an advertiser-supported business, commercial television may be even more driven to produce the types of programs dictated by the marketplace.

In addition to the ratings system proposed to help parents guide the viewing of their children, the new law proposes a controversial technological means of blocking transmission of objectionable programming. Under the Telecom Act, manufacturers of television sets have two years to install a "V-Chip," or violence chip in all TVs larger than thirteen inches, to detect violence-signals and block them if the consumer so desires. Use of the chip would be solely voluntary, left to the discretion of parents.

If the V-Chip required by the new legislation survives its opposition, it will make use of whatever comprehensive program rating system for television is adopted, assigning each television program a rating based on its content. The chip could be used to program a television to block all programs with a particular designated rating and show only programs with a rating code that would be appropriate for family viewing. Some have suggested that it will be more of a "C-Chip," or choice chip, that could be used to block any "objectionable" programming, rather than just violence.

There are some drawbacks and limitations posed by the V-Chip. For example, families will have to buy new sets in order to get the benefit of the V-Chip technology. The cost of the chip is not expected to add more than a dollar to the retail cost of each television set.

Moverover, the proposed chip faces stiff legal opposition from networks and cable television entities on First Amendment grounds. Proponents contend there are no censorship or First Amendment issues involved, as the V-Chip is merely a tool offering parents control and information about television programming so they can assume greater responsibility for proactively interceding to shape their childrens' viewing habits. Opponents to the V-Chip say the system would not be voluntary because parents would not be the ones determining which programs are objectionable, but rather would be relying and acting on ratings assessed by others, namely the government. In essence, a "viewing standard" would be imposed by an imperfect and subjective ratings system. Regardlessoftheir alleged weaknesses, the success of the legislation's proposed tools regarding content review hinges ultimately on parental involvement.

The V-Chip is one of the most controversial elements of the Telecom Act and is likely to remain controversial in the future.

Chapter 4

Cable Television

By Robert D. Primosch, Esq.

> When you have got an elephant by the hind legs and he is
> trying to run away, it's best to let him run.
>
> — *Abraham Lincoln*

For the past dozen years or so, federal regulation of cable television has often resembled a prolonged struggle with Lincoln's elephant. After deregulating the industry in 1984, Congress discovered that cable television had become a much bigger animal than it had bargained for: what was once a loose collection of operators serving primarily rural areas had evolved into a hugely successful but highly consolidated industry that is now the sole source of multichannel video service for millions of Americans. Thus in 1992 Congress restrained the industry's hind legs through comprehensive regulation of its rates, customer service and programming. Now, less than four years later, Congress appears to have heeded Lincoln's advice and has deregulated the industry again, in the hope that competition from telephone companies and others will achieve what regulation did not.

This chapter examines how the Telecommunications Act of 1996 resolves the issues of greatest relevance to cable subscribers: (1) who may provide cable television service; (2) the types of services that may be offered through a cable television system; and (3) the cost of those services. Although many of the Act's specific provisions are discussed herein, the significance of the Act lies in the larger picture, in how it implements Congress' desire to create competition in new markets and provide consumers with an unprecedented variety of video, voice and data services from any number of sources. This will have a profound effect not only on how consumers live but on how they spend their entertainment dollars in the 21st century. In other words, where cable television is concerned, the millennium appears to have arrived.

THE PENDULUM SWINGS: A BRIEF HISTORY OF CABLE REGULATION

Ironically, the debate over how to regulate cable television arises to some extent from the very characteristics that make the medium so popular. Due to the scarcity of electromagnetic spectrum, a conventional off-air television station transmits programming on one channel within a specific area to avoid interference to other stations. By contrast, a cable television system transmits multiple channels of programming through a single wire to as many homes as permitted by state or local government authorities, without the same spectrum constraints. Indeed, it is generally agreed that advances in digital technology will enable cable systems to eventually carry hundreds of channels of programming. Arguably, then, cable gives its audience the best of both worlds, albeit for a monthly fee: it enables subscribers to continue watching popular network and independent television programming (often with improved picture quality) *and* have access to a full menu of programming from once obscure nonbroadcast sources that have now become staples of television viewing (*e.g.,* CNN, ESPN, MTV). Not surprisingly, the American public appears to like the formula. In 1994, cable subscribership in the United States grew to nearly 60 million, representing 65.2 percent of all homes passed by cable.

A cable television system, however, relies heavily on physical plant to deliver its programming to subscribers, and thus requires significant capital investment. In 1994 alone, the cable industry invested $3.8 billion in construction of new plant and equipment. Most of these capital costs are "sunk" costs, meaning that the operator's cable system probably cannot be put to another equally profitable use if video distribution becomes unprofitable. Hence, most areas of the United States have been served by only one cable system, either because the system negotiated an exclusive franchise or because a second provider could not "overbuild" and market its services profitably against an entrenched cable system. Over time, the cable industry took on the characteristics of a natural monopoly, which in turn fueled the drive for federal legislation.

Still, it is sometimes easy to forget that the prominence of cable television in American life is a fairly recent development. The earliest cable systems, built during the 1950s, served rural areas which due to mountainous terrain and other factors could not receive television signals over the air. During that time, cable systems acted almost entirely as passive retransmitters of television broadcast programming. Cable networks such as CNN and ESPN did not exist, and cable systems usually did not originate much, if any, of their own programming. Regulation of cable television was primarily a local matter, with cities and other local government bodies awarding franchises to cable operators who wished to construct and operate their systems along public rights-of-way. Since the Federal Communications Commission (FCC) had not yet claimed any jurisdiction over cable television, the industry remained free of comprehensive federal regulation.

During the 1960s, however, cable television systems expanded into more populated areas where local television stations enjoyed substantial viewership. These stations subsequently complained that cable systems were beginning to "siphon" their audiences by importing the signals of stations from other markets. Hence, in the name of protecting the economic viability of local broadcast television, the FCC adopted what are now known as "must-carry" rules, requiring cable systems to carry local stations. The FCC also adopted "non-duplication" rules, restricting cable systems from importing distant stations that duplicated local programming.

At about the same time, there were signs that the accelerating economic and technological development of cable television was beginning to outpace the ability of the cities to regulate the industry with limited resources. Accordingly, in 1972 the FCC adopted an extensive federal regulatory plan for cable television which, among other things, required a cable operator to obtain a "certificate of compliance" from the FCC, verifying the operator's qualifications and the feasibility of its proposed cable system. The 1972 rules also established construction deadlines, minimum channel capacity requirements, and limitations on the "franchise fees" an operator would be required to pay to a city in return for a franchise. Finally, initiating a debate which persists to this day, the FCC determined that local franchising authorities should be allowed to regulate cable rates for "basic service," defined in layman's terms as the bottom-level "tier" of service taken by all cable subscribers.

Many of the 1972 rules proved to be short-lived. Cable television soon outgrew its status as a niche-oriented, rural based service, and many major urban areas were now being wired for cable. Furthermore, in 1975, Time Inc. began delivering HBO via satellite to cable systems around the country, and many other national programming services followed suit. As a result, cable systems could now move beyond mere retransmission of local television stations and deliver more channels of movies, sports, news and specialized programming to subscribers. In addition, some cable systems were developing "two-way" capabilities, and thus had the potential to provide a wide range of communications and data transmission services to government agencies, educational institutions and private business.

The FCC thus concluded that its 1972 rules had become outdated, and that the cable industry's potential could not be fully realized under extensive federal regulation. Between 1976 and 1978, the FCC eliminated all federal standards for basic service rate regulation, thus leaving all rate regulation matters to the cities. It also eliminated various franchising requirements (including minimum construction schedules), and converted its certification requirement into a simple registration obligation, which did not require the FCC to review a cable operator's qualifications in depth. The FCC's must-carry rules survived, though a federal appeals court would rule them unconstitutional in 1984.

Against this backdrop, Congress passed the Cable Communications Policy Act of 1984, the first piece of comprehensive federal legislation directed specifically at the cable industry. In so doing, Congress did not intend to reverse the deregulatory course already taken by the FCC. Rather, Congress passed the bill largely in response to problems that had arisen within the local franchising process. In the heat of competing for franchises, some cable operators had oversold their capabilities and delivered less than they had promised. By the same token, cities had come to demand expensive, state-of-the-art systems without any serious economic justification, producing a bidding frenzy after which the winning cable operator could not build out its proposed facilities within any reasonable length of time. Moreover, as cable operators expanded their service offerings, franchising authorities began adopting new rules to address such issues as rate regulation, franchise fees, and customer service requirements. These rules varied from community to community, producing a patchwork regulatory scheme that highlighted the need for a national cable policy.

Thus, in the 1984 Act Congress attempted to bring some order to the franchising process. The Act established broad guidelines for what a city may include in a cable franchise; placed specific limits on franchise fees; and set forth procedures and standards for renewal and modification of franchises. The 1984 Act also gave cable operators a federal right of access to public rights-of-way and to easements designated for similar uses by utility companies. Finally, the 1984 Act permitted franchising authorities to require that certain cable channels be set aside for public, educational and governmental (PEG) use, and required that cable operators lease a percentage of their channels to independent commercial programmers.

The portion of the 1984 Act which eventually triggered the most debate, however, was its provision effectively deregulating rates for basic cable service after December 30, 1986. The basis for deregulation was Congress's belief that the availability of other sources of programming within a given market would keep cable rates reasonable. But the 1984 Act also included provisions which (1) enabled franchising authorities to continue issuing exclusive franchises, and (2) prohibited telephone companies from owning and operating cable systems within their own service areas. Moreover, the economics of overbuilding an entrenched cable operator remained prohibitive. As a result, the competition envisioned by Congress never materialized, leaving basic service rates unchecked in many parts of the country.

In some respects, federal deregulation of cable television in the 1984 Act achieved its desired ends. Between 1985 and 1992, cable penetration had increased from 37 percent to approximately 61 percent of television households in the United States. Monthly revenue per subscriber nearly doubled, and annual cable advertising revenues increased five-fold, from less than $600 million to $3 billion. The cable industry also invested substantially in capital improvements and programming. Prior to the 1984 Act, cable systems typically offered 24 channels or less; by 1992, 30 to 53 channels had become the norm. According to statistics provided by the National Cable Television Association, basic cable networks spent $1.5 billion for programming in 1991, nearly four times the amount spent in 1984.

Ultimately, Congress determined that these benefits did not compensate for the fact that cable operators had increased their rates, in some instances much more than the rate of inflation. Service quality also had become an issue: Congress collected written evidence and heard testimony from state regulators citing a substantial number of subscriber complaints about poor service. Some of the larger cable operators had acquired significant ownership interests in a number of cable networks, raising concerns over whether those networks would be made available on fair and equitable terms to cable's competitors. Whether or not deserved, cable's image on Capitol Hill had become that of an industry with little or no market incentive to limit rate increases, offer consistently high customer service or compete fairly with new multichannel delivery systems.

Empowered by consumer demand for change (and with the political winds blowing in the required direction), Congress enacted the Cable Consumer Protection and Competition Act of 1992, which imposed federal regulation on virtually all facets of cable television service. Most significantly, the 1992 Act :

- allowed local franchising authorities to regulate basic cable rates until an alternative service provider became available and subscribed to by a minimum percentage of homes in the franchise area;

- allowed a single subscriber or franchising authority to obtain FCC review of a cable system's rates for "cable programming services" (*i.e.*, those services carried above the basic tier, excluding "pay cable" services such as HBO);

- prohibited cable operators from owning wireless cable or satellite master antenna television (SMATV) systems within their own franchise areas;

- prohibited municipalities from issuing exclusive franchises, but retained the ban on telephone companies owning cable systems within their service areas;

- required the FCC to adopt comprehensive customer service standards for cable systems;

- except in limited circumstances, required cable networks to sell their product to cable's competitors;

- required the FCC to impose restrictions on the number of subscribers that may be reached nationwide by a single cable operator, and on the number of programming services owned by a cable operator which may be carried on the operator's cable system;

- reinstated a broader version of the FCC's must-carry rules, requiring cable systems to carry a wider range of local commercial and educational television stations (these rules are currently under challenge again, this time before the United States Supreme Court); and

- generally prohibited a cable operator from selling a cable system within three years of acquisition.

Between 1992 and 1996, a number of developments motivated Congress to once again consider deregulating the cable industry. First, some of the competition envisioned by Congress in 1984 had finally taken shape. A company called DirecTv, in tandem with United States Satellite Broadcasting, Inc., launched a high-power, direct broadcast satellite (DBS) service, delivering multiple channels of programming to an eighteen-inch dish installed at the subscriber's home. Similarly, a company called PRIMESTAR launched a medium power DBS service utilizing 36-inch home dishes. As of the date of this writing, DirecTv and PRIMESTAR combined were approaching 2,000,000 subscribers and counting.

In addition, certain Regional Holding Companies have made substantial investments in, or outright acquisitions of, companies providing "wireless cable" service. A wireless cable system differs from the conventional wired cable system largely in how it delivers programming to the subscriber. Whereas a conventional wired system utilizes coaxial cable and/or fiber optic lines strung along utility poles or underground conduits, a wireless cable system utilizes microwave frequencies allocated by the FCC, which are received at the subscriber's home with a special antenna. Since a wireless cable system does not use hardwire and thus does not use public rights-of-way, it does not require a local franchise and is not otherwise subject to regulation as a "cable system." Though frequency limitations currently restrict wireless cable systems to 32 or 33 channels, digital technology will enable wireless cable to offer a mix of services comparable in quantity and quality to that of conventional cable systems. It is estimated that wireless cable will reach approximately 3,000,000 subscribers by the year 2000.

Furthermore, a number of lower courts have ruled that the 1984 Act's ban prohibiting a telephone company from owning a cable system in its own service area is unconstitutional. In this context, it became necessary for Congress to evaluate whether continued federal enforcement of the ban is appropriate.

Finally, the FCC's experience with rate regulation after the 1992 Act had been tortuous. Though the FCC labored mightily to construct a rate regulation formula that satisfied consumers and cable operators alike, the drain on the agency's resources was substantial, and some have argued that certain cable operators were actually able to *increase* their rates by virtue of loopholes in the FCC's regulatory scheme. The fact that a single subscriber could commence a rate inquiry was particularly burdensome: in one case, a total of 100 franchises serving over 500,000 subscribers were subject to rate regulation by virtue of a single complaint. This has led the FCC to settle a large volume of outstanding rate complaints by entering into "social contracts" with cable system operators, under which complaints are dismissed in exchange for the operator's commitment to upgrade facilities, issue refunds and limit rate increases in the future. The evolving nature of the cable industry as a whole also has required the FCC to continually fine-tune its rules. As a result, the FCC has reconsidered all or a portion of its rate regulation scheme thirteen times, and further rulemakings on the subject continue to this day.

Thus, Congress deregulated the cable industry again, this time in the Telecommunications Act of 1996. As discussed below, the Telecom Act modifies or eliminates portions of the 1984 and 1992 Acts to facilitate more competition to incumbent cable systems, provides greater opportunity for deregulation of basic service rates, and eliminates rate regulation of cable programming services for smaller cable systems immediately and for all cable systems after three years. The Telecom Act also includes provisions which should facilitate easier entry by cable operators into telephony and other non-video services. To be sure, many of the regulatory provisions in the 1992 Act remain in place, and cable operators still need local franchises to operate their systems. But the Telecom Act will nonetheless transform the cable industry as we now know it: though Congress has not yet allowed the elephant to run entirely free, it has at least resolved to let him walk around a bit.

PRO-COMPETITIVE PROVISIONS OF THE TELECOM ACT

The Telephone Companies Arrive

For some time it has been widely assumed that telephone companies, and particularly the Regional Holding Companies (RHCs), offer the greatest prospect for creating real competition with incumbent cable operators. Recent statistics reflect that the four largest cable system operators (TCI, Time Warner, Continental Cablevision and Comcast) served more than half the cable subscribers in the United States. See Figure 5. Hence, telephone companies have been viewed as the only entities with sufficient size and resources to compete successfully in cable's backyard. Indeed, in the wake of the recent court decisions declaring the telephone-cable cross-ownership ban unconstitutional, at least one RHC (Ameritech) has been implementing an aggressive plan to seek cable franchises and overbuild existing cable operators within its own service area.

Historically, the difficulty with allowing telephone companies into the cable business has been the fact that cable systems often must use a telephone company's poles and conduit space to construct their own facilities. Further, there have been concerns that telephone companies would use revenues collected from telephone rate payers to impermissibly cross-subsidize their investments in cable television. Thus in 1970, when the cable industry was still in its infancy and in greater need of protection, the FCC adopted rules (subsequently amended in 1981 and included in the 1984 Cable Act) which prohibited telephone companies from owning and operating cable television systems within their own service areas. At most, a telephone company could (1) own and operate a cable system outside of its own service area, where it did not have control over poles and conduits, or (2) lease channel capacity to an unaffiliated cable operator, but without

Top Five Multiple System Cable Operators

System Operator	Number of Subscribers	Homes Passed	Miles of Plant	Estimated % of Market
Telecommunications, Inc.	12,000,000	19,000,000	260,000	21.70
Time Warner	7,500,000	12,295,000	125,000	13.60
Comcast	5,582,000	est. 7,000,000	64,000	6.00
Cox Communications	3,196,184	5,013,158	50,255	10.00
Continental Cablevision	3,009,001	5,311,428	54,054	5.40
TOTALS	31,287,185	est. 48,609,586	553,309	56.70%

Figure 5 - Top five multiple system cable operators.

having any interest in or control of the programming carried on those channels.

Twenty-five years later, with the cable industry now more the elephant than the mouse, Congress has concluded that telephone company entry into the cable business would promote competition, stimulate investment in new technologies and maximize consumer choice of services. Accordingly, in the Telecom Act Congress repealed the telephone company/cable television cross-ownership ban, thereby allowing telephone companies to construct and operate franchised cable television systems in their own service areas. In so doing, however, Congress determined that competition was unlikely to flourish if telephone companies were simply allowed to buy out existing cable operators and thereby substitute themselves as the only cable operators in their own markets. Congress thus adopted provisions that generally prohibit a telephone company from acquiring a ten percent or greater interest in or managing an existing cable system within the telephone company's service area. (Conversely, the Act prohibits a cable operator from acquiring a ten percent or greater ownership interest or a management interest in a local exchange carrier within its own franchise area.)

The Telecom Act also generally prohibits a telephone company and a cable operator with overlapping service areas from entering into joint ventures for the purpose of providing video programming to subscribers. Under certain circumstances, a telephone company may acquire a controlling interest in or provide financing to a cable system in its own region if the system is not located in one of the top 25 markets and is not the largest system in the market.

The restrictions described above also do not apply to telephone company acquisitions of cable systems in rural areas (fewer than 35,000 persons) if the cable system does not serve more than ten percent of the telephone company's subscribers, nor do they apply to acquisitions of certain smaller systems in markets outside the top 100. There is also an exception for smaller telephone companies, *i.e.*, those with less than $100,000,000 in annual operating revenue. The rule will not apply to these companies if the cable system being acquired serves no more than 20,000 subscribers, and if no more than 12,000 of those subscribers live in an urbanized area. In any case, the FCC may waive the Telecom Act's telephone/cable buyout restrictions in situations of economic distress or where otherwise necessary to serve the public interest, provided that the franchising authority has consented to the waiver.

Interestingly, though the Telecom Act generally prohibits telephone companies and cable systems in the same service area from entering into joint ventures for the purpose of providing video programming, it does not prohibit telephone company/cable operator joint ventures for the purpose of *constructing* cable or other types of systems which deliver that programming to the subscriber. Moreover, the Telecom Act directs the FCC to adopt rules allowing telephone companies to use a local cable system's drop cables into the subscriber's home, with the cable system's consent and on reasonable terms and conditions.

A Different Animal: Open Video Systems

The Telecom Act includes a twist that, if taken advantage of by telephone companies, may change the nature of how companies that create video programming reach cable subscribers. Normally, a cable television operator has the final say over which programming services are carried on its cable system, except for must-carry, PEG and leased access channels. Under the Act, however, a telephone company may effectively exempt itself from local franchising requirements and most cable rate regulation by sacrificing some of this control over its channels. The concept behind this new type of facility, called an "open video system" (OVS), is that a telephone company should be subject to fewer regulatory burdens if it is willing to make the majority of its channel capacity available to unaffiliated programmers on a nondiscriminatory basis.

Though the FCC has yet to adopt final rules for open video systems, the Telecom Act provides some general guidelines for what open video systems are supposed to look like. Where demand for channels exceeds supply, an operator of an open video system may control no more than one-third of its channels; the rest must be made available on a nondiscriminatory basis to unaffiliated programmers on reasonable terms and conditions. An OVS operator will not be required to carry duplicate channels of the same programming, provided that subscribers are provided ready and immediate access to that programming. The charges which unaffiliated programmers must pay for OVS channels will be determined by the FCC.

The principal advantage of operating an OVS rather than a conventional cable system is that an OVS does not require a local franchise, nor is it subject to most of the rate regulation provisions of the Telecom Act. However, it should also be noted that while OVS operators will not be required to pay franchise fees, the Act allows municipalities to charge an OVS fees that are the functional equivalent of the franchise fees currently paid by cable operators.

Until the FCC adopts its final OVS rules, it is difficult to know whether telephone companies will view an OVS as an attractive alternative to the traditional cable model. Over the past few years, the FCC has experimented with a similar concept called "video dial-tone" (VDT), which to date has not created significant competition to cable. Boiled to its essence, a video dial-tone system differs from an OVS system in that a VDT system is regulated as a common carrier whereas an OVS system is not. Video dial-tone raised a number of complex issues, including how telephone companies should allocate costs between video and telephony services, and whether the portion of a VDT system programmed by the telephone company should be regulated as a cable system and thus should be required to obtain a franchise. The resulting regulatory delays dampened the telephone industry's interest in video dial-tone systems, to the point where there is currently only one authorized VDT system operating in the United States. Of course, in the Telecom Act Congress has declared that OVS systems do not need franchises, and has otherwise established relatively clear guidelines for how OVS systems are to be regulated. Nonetheless, many of the issues raised by video dial-tone also apply to OVS (*e.g.,* cross-subsidization and discrimination against unaffiliated programmers). The efficiency with which the FCC resolves these issues, therefore, may well determine whether the OVS concept will emerge as a *bona fide* alternative to cable service.

Wireless Cable and SMATV

As noted above, wireless cable systems do not require franchises and are not subject to rate regulation. Despite these advantages, regulatory delays in licensing wireless cable facilities has delayed construction of many wireless cable systems. In an attempt to ensure that wireless cable would develop as a competitive service separate and apart from wired cable, Congress adopted a provision in the 1992 Act prohibiting a cable operator from holding licenses for wireless cable channels within its own franchise area.

Since 1992, the wireless cable industry, spurred in part by telephone company investment, has emerged to the point where wired cable systems may face significant competition from wireless cable systems, perhaps within the next five years. Moreover, wired cable systems already compete with DBS providers and will continue to do so in the future. Congress therefore perceived that the 1992 Act's ban on cable operator ownership of wireless cable facilities would not be necessary in a fully competitive environment. Accordingly, in the Telecom Act Congress repealed the cable/wireless cable cross-ownership ban in situations where a cable operator is subject to "effective competition." (Congress' precise definition of "effective competition" is discussed later in this chapter.)

The Telecom Act similarly allows a cable operator to construct or acquire satellite master antenna television systems in its franchise area where there is effective competition. SMATV systems provide the functional equivalent of cable television service to apartment buildings, utilizing a satellite dish on the roof of the building to receive and deliver programming through wiring strung through the building's conduits or posted on the building's interior walls. In some instances, SMATV operators are able to serve multiple buildings by connecting them via hardwire cable. The Telecom Act clarifies that these hardwire connections will not require the SMATV operator to obtain a franchise unless they cross public rights-of-way. Hence, it will be possible for a SMATV operator to expand its service by interconnecting commonly or separately-owned buildings located entirely on private property, without having to obtain a franchise.

Satellite Services

Although DBS and other direct-to-home (DTH) satellite services do not require franchises, Congress recognized that state and local authorities could still restrict market entry by applying taxation and zoning laws to satellite providers in a discriminatory manner. Hence, the Act exempts DTH providers from having to collect and remit local taxes and fees on DTH satellite services. The exemption applies only to the programming provided by a DTH service; it does not apply to the sale of satellite reception equipment. The exemption also does not apply to real estate taxes that are otherwise applicable when the DTH provider owns or leases property. Note, however, that the states remain free to tax the sale of DTH service, and they may rebate some or all of those monies to local jurisdictions if they so desire.

The Telecom Act also directs the FCC to adopt rules prohibiting state or local governments from imposing zoning requirements that prevent a subscriber from installing an antenna for the purpose of receiving DBS service. Currently the FCC is proposing to adopt rules that would prohibit zoning requirements directed at one- and two-meter dishes, which would encompass DBS and most other commercially available DTH services.

Other Issues

The Telecom Act repeals the ban on a cable operator owning a television station within its own service area, though the FCC must formally eliminate its cable/broadcast ownership rule for the repeal to take effect. And the Act repeals the three-year "anti-trafficking" rule in the 1992 Act, meaning that a cable operator may sell a cable system at any time to a willing buyer, subject to any required consent of the local franchising authority.

REGULATION OF VIDEO AND NON-VIDEO SERVICES PROVIDED BY CABLE SYSTEMS

Content Restrictions on Video Programming

With one exception, the Telecom Act does not change how video services have been regulated under the 1984 and 1992 Acts. The PEG and leased access provisions of the 1984 Act remain in place, as do the must-carry provisions of the 1992 Act. If upheld in court, however, the exception may have a tumultuous effect on the content of programming carried by cable operators.

The subject of obscenity and indecency in cable programming has become a high profile issue in Washington, as part of the larger debate on what controls are necessary to keep objectionable material in the media away from children. In a series of provisions designed to minimize the availability of harmful material to minors through cable television, telecommunications or computers, the Telecom Act:

- increases the maximum fine for transmitting obscene material over cable television from $10,000 to $100,000;

- requires cable television operators to fully scramble or otherwise block upon subscriber request, at no charge, the audio and video portions of any programming not specifically purchased by a subscriber;

- permits cable operators to refuse to transmit any portion of a PEG or leased access program that contains obscenity, indecency or nudity; and

- requires that cable operators fully scramble or block the video and audio portions of channels featuring sexually explicit programming, so that subscribers who do not purchase the channels cannot receive them.

The ramifications of the latter provision are already being felt among programmers, particularly those who specialize in adult-oriented material. The Playboy Channel, for example, has contended in court that the costs of scrambling Playboy's audio and video feed is so substantial that cable operators may simply drop the service. To date, the courts have stayed the effect of the rule pending further litigation over whether the rule violates the First Amendment.

Availability of Cable Home Equipment

A cable subscriber's home equipment normally consists of four separate items: (1) the home wiring which connects the cable company's wire to the subscriber's television set; (2) the set-top converter box which processes the cable signal for transmission through the subscriber's television set; (3) a remote control unit allowing the subscriber to select the channels he or she wishes to watch; and (4) additional outlets for connections to multiple television sets within the home. As cable systems become more sophisticated and begin to offer a wider variety of programming services, the standard cable home equipment will also include "navigation devices" and other interactive apparatus that will enable the subscriber to more easily view and make selections from a cable operator's entire menu of programming.

In the past, many cable subscribers have relied entirely upon their local cable operator as their sole supplier of cable home equipment. Out of concerns that cable operators were not charging competitive prices for equipment, in the 1992 Act Congress required cable operators to reduce their equipment charges to actual cost. Now, consistent with its overriding idea that competition rather than regulation is the most effective method of keeping cable rates in line, Congress has adopted provisions in the Telecom Act to ensure that consumers are able to purchase cable home equipment from a variety of sources rather than just the cable operator alone.

The Telecom Act requires the FCC to adopt regulations designed to assure the availability of converter boxes, navigation devices and similar interactive equipment from a full range of manufacturers, vendors and retailers. The purpose of these regulations is to help ensure that consumers are not forced to purchase or lease such equipment from their local cable operator. Note, however, that a cable operator may continue to offer such equipment to subscribers, provided that the cable operator's equipment charges are separately stated on the subscriber's bill and are not subsidized by charges for video programming or other services offered over the cable system. The Telecom Act also permits the FCC to waive its regulations where necessary to introduce new cable services or technology, and requires the FCC to eliminate its regulations completely when it determines that the market for cable services and cable home equipment is competitive.

Finally, in recognition of the fact that patchwork local regulation is inappropriate given the current technological environment, the Act prohibits states or local franchising authorities from regulating a cable system's use of any type of subscriber equipment or transmission technology. The Act also directs the FCC to adopt only minimal standards for ensuring technical compatibility between converter boxes, television sets and video cassette recorders. Congress believes that the marketplace should be the primary engine for developing such standards, and that the FCC's compatibility rules must not affect unrelated markets, such as computers and home automation devices.

Non-Video Services

As discussed elsewhere in this book, much of the impetus for the Telecom Act arose not only from a perceived need to promote competition in cable television, but from an equally strong need to promote competition among providers of telephony and other non-video services (*e.g.*, high-speed data, Internet access). Indeed, prior to passage of the Act, a number of larger cable operators had already taken initiatives toward providing local loop services over their cable plant.

The Act's regulatory scheme is designed to minimize regulation of non-video services by local cable franchising authorities. The Act provides that a cable operator is not required to obtain a franchise for telecommunications services it offers over its cable plant. Furthermore, a franchising authority may require a cable operator to pay franchise fees on its revenues from "cable services." But it cannot require a cable operator to pay franchise fees on revenues from its telecommunications services. A franchising authority may, however, charge a cable operator fair and reasonable fees for using public rights-of-way when providing telecommunications services. Also, the Act expands the definition of "cable service" (and therefore the potential revenues subject to franchise fees) to include interactive services (*e.g.*, game channels) and information services made available to the subscriber by the cable operator.

Also, just as cable operators need access to telephone poles and conduits to provide traditional cable television service, they also need access to those same poles and conduits to provide local telephone service. Prior to the Telecom Act, federal law required that, where the states do not regulate the matter, the FCC must ensure that the rates, terms and conditions for use of utility poles and conduits are reasonable. A rate is "just and reasonable" if it assures the utility a recovery of (1) not less than the cost of the additional attachment, and (2) not more than an amount equal to the percentage of the total usable space occupied by the cable operator, multiplied by the sum of the operating expenses and capital costs of the pole (or conduit). It is important to remember that prior to the Telecom Act the law did not give cable companies a right of mandatory access to utility poles or conduits. It was designed only to ensure that cable operators do not pay unreasonable rates for such access.

The Telecom Act refines the law in a manner which should be beneficial to cable operators who wish to provide telecommunications services. First, the Act specifies that rates, terms and conditions for use of a utility's poles or conduits must be just and reasonable regardless of whether the cable operator is providing cable or non-cable services. Second, the Act requires a utility to provide a cable television system with nondiscriminatory access to its poles and/or conduits, except where the cable system's attachment cannot be made due to insufficient capacity or due to technical or safety reasons. Third, the Act provides cable operators and utilities an opportunity to negotiate acceptable pole attachment rates before seeking a ruling at the FCC. Fourth, the Act requires the FCC to adopt regulations specifying that a utility must apportion the cost of providing usable space among all attaching entities according to the amount of space they occupy.

Moreover, utilities must provide prior written notification to attaching entities of any plans to modify or alter its poles or conduits, and may not charge the attaching entities for such modifications if they are solely for the utility's benefit. Finally, to ensure that a utility's control over poles and conduits does not give it an unfair pricing advantage for its own telecommunications services, the Act requires utilities to include in their costs the attachment charges that would ordinarily be applicable to its occupation of the pole/conduit.

Finally, the Telecom Act enhances the ability of cable operators to interconnect with the facilities of local exchange carriers. The Act orders local exchange carriers to unbundle their services and make them available to their competitors. Where a prospective competitor files a request for unbundled local exchange services, the local exchange carrier has nine months to respond with "reasonable prices" for the requested services. These types of services could include local loops, emergency (911), operator services, Signalling System 7 access and billing. Furthermore, telephone companies must now let competitors resell local loop service at a profit. For a more detailed discussion of interconnection and resale issues, see Chapter 2.

SCRIPTING THE FINALE: THE END OF CABLE RATE REGULATION

After over three years of extensive cable regulation at the federal and local level, several factors prompted Congress to consider deregulating cable rates in the Telecom Act. First, as discussed above, Congress' good intentions had been buried under an avalanche of FCC paperwork, and the prospects for real competition had become strong enough to support a market-based solution for regulating cable rates. Second, the "clustering" of cable systems in larger markets was transforming cable television from a community-based to a regionally-based service, suggesting that the FCC's existing rate rules were insufficient to allow cable operators to deploy new technologies on a wider scale. For instance, the FCC's regulations required cable operators to calculate separately the lease charges for analog and digital converter boxes. Unless cable operators are allowed to average their costs of new technology, they are forced to recover the costs of digital converters solely through revenues from higher priced services. Congress observed that this in turn encourages operators to provide digital boxes in upscale areas only, where they are more likely to recover their costs.

Accordingly, Congress has now devised a new rate regulation scheme that redefines "effective competition" in a manner that provides greater opportunity for deregulation of basic tier rates; provides immediate rate regulation relief for smaller systems; completely deregulates rates for cable programming services on all cable systems after three years; and allows cable operators to aggregate their equipment costs on a regional level and average those costs among their subscribers.

Effective Competition

As noted above, the 1992 Act's extensive regulation of cable rates was the offspring of a perceived lack of competition to cable: at the time the 1992 Act was passed, cable's competitors served fewer than five percent of American households. Furthermore, although the 1984 Act allowed local franchising authorities to regulate basic service rates where the cable system was not subject to "effective competition," the FCC's definition of that term was thought to have aggravated the problem. Initially, the FCC determined that effective competition existed where the entire cable community could receive three or more unduplicated broadcast signals. Congress found that under this "three signal" standard, cable systems in approximately 96 percent of all communities were not rate regulated.

In 1991, the FCC constructed a new definition of effective competition. A cable system would be exempt from rate regulation if (1) six unduplicated over-the-air broadcast signals were available in the entire cable community, or (2) an independently owned, competing multichannel delivery service was available to 50 percent of the homes and subscribed to by at least ten percent of the homes passed by the incumbent cable system. This revision was only a mild improvement: 59 percent of the cable systems serving 80 percent of the nation's cable subscribers remained exempt from rate regulation under the "six signal" test, and virtually all of them remained deregulated under the "competing provider" test.

In the 1992 Act, Congress sought to devise an ironclad test for effective competition that would subject most cable systems to rate regulation until a substantial competitor emerged in the market. Eschewing the FCC's prior tests based on availability of television broadcast signals, the 1992 Act defined effective competition to exist where:

- fewer than 30 percent of the households in the franchise area subscribe to the cable service of a cable system;

- the franchise area is served by at least two unaffiliated multichannel video programming distributors offering comparable video programming to at least 50 percent of the households in the franchise area, and at least fifteen percent of the households in the franchise area subscribe to the smaller of the two systems; and

- a multichannel video provider operated by the franchising authority offers video programming to at least 50 percent of the households in the franchise area.

Congress thus accomplished an almost complete about-face from the 1984 Act: because most cable systems enjoyed better than 30 percent penetration and were not subject to an overbuild, the lion's share of the cable industry could now be rate regulated by local franchising authorities (in the case of the basic service tier) or by the FCC (in the case of cable programming services).

In the Telecom Act, Congress has added an additional test for effective competition that will free cable systems from rate regulation upon market entry by telephone companies. Effective competition will be deemed to exist where a local exchange carrier (or any multichannel distributor using the local exchange carrier's facilities) offers video programming to subscribers in the cable system's franchise area by any means, except via direct-to-home satellite services. The local exchange carrier's video programming service must consist of at least twelve channels of programming, and must be available to subscribers for a standard connection fee.

For the cable industry, the principal advantage of this new test is that local exchange carriers may now create effective competition through non-cable technologies (*e.g.* wireless cable) rather than solely through a franchised cable overbuild. Moreover, the new test does not include any subscribership requirements: effective competition is deemed to exist as soon as the local exchange carrier offers its service, regardless of how many subscribers actually purchase it.

Moreover, under the Telecom Act, once a cable system is subject to effective competition, it is no longer obligated to offer uniform rates throughout its service area, and may therefore offer different rates to different sets of subscribers in order to compete with a telephone company or other entity that is providing multichannel video service.

Small System Relief

One of the most hotly debated issues after the 1992 Act was how Congress' rate regulation scheme should apply to small systems. In the Telecom Act, Congress has deregulated the rates charged by "small cable operators" as follows: where a small cable operator serves 50,000 or fewer subscribers in its franchise area, its cable programming service rates are deregulated immediately (its basic tier rates are also deregulated immediately if the operator offered only a single tier of service as of December 31, 1994). A "small cable operator" is defined in the Act as any operator that serves in the aggregate fewer than one percent of all cable subscribers nationwide (*i.e.*, fewer than 617,000 subscribers), and is not affiliated with any entity whose annual gross revenues exceed $250,000,000. An entity is deemed to be "affiliated" with a small cable operator if it has a twenty percent or greater voting equity or non-voting interest in the operator, or if it otherwise holds control of the operator. The purpose of the "twenty percent rule" is to minimize the opportunity for larger operators to obtain small system treatment even where they hold only minority ownership positions in small system operators.

Sunset of Upper Tier Rate Regulation

With many cable operators moving popular cable programming services off the basic service tier (meaning that the cable subscriber must pay a separate, additional fee for channels such as CNN, ESPN and MTV), the extent to which the FCC may regulate the rates for cable programming services is of considerable importance to consumers. Because the FCC's complaint process had become nearly unworkable, Congress considered different options for easing the FCC's administrative burden while ensuring that cable programming service rates remained reasonable until competition arrived.

In the Telecom Act, Congress has attempted to resolve the issue by eliminating all rate regulation of cable programming services for all cable systems beginning March 31, 1999. Congress also raised the bar for parties who wish to bring a cable programming services rate complaint before the FCC. A single subscriber no longer has the power to commence a complaint proceeding; only the local franchising authority may do so, and even then only if it has received complaints from subscribers within 90 days of a cable programming service rate increase.

Aggregation of Equipment Costs

Under the 1992 Act, rates for cable equipment and installations must be based on actual costs. Pursuant to current FCC rules, cable operators establish an Equipment Basket, to which they assign recoverable costs of providing and servicing customer equipment. The cable operator's ability to aggregate equipment costs by category is somewhat limited: the FCC's rules require separate charges for each "significantly different" type of remote control unit, converter box or other customer equipment. Further, although the FCC's rules do under certain circumstances allow cable operators to aggregate equipment costs at the franchise, system, regional and/or company level, some franchising authorities have rejected aggregated region and company-wide costing proposals submitted by cable operators, perhaps due to certain ambiguities in the FCC's rate regulation scheme for cable equipment.

The Telecom Act makes clear that the FCC must allow cable operators to aggregate, on a franchise, system, regional, or company level, their equipment costs into broad categories (such as "converter boxes"). Such aggregation will not be permitted with respect to equipment received by subscribers who receive only a rate regulated basic service tier. The FCC has tentatively concluded that under this provision, equipment must be categorized by its primary purpose rather than its functionality. For example, the fact that remote control units may have different features will not prevent aggregation of those costs into a single category, since all units serve the same purpose (*i.e.,* allowing remote selection of programming by the subscriber). However, the FCC has tentatively determined that the costs associated with additional outlets should not be aggregated with the costs for initial installations. Finally, the FCC is proposing to allow cable operators to aggregate their installation costs on a "service area" basis, due to the fact that local labor costs may vary widely from system to system.

Miscellaneous Provisions

The Telecom Act allows a cable operator to provide notice of rate changes to subscribers using any reasonable written means at its discretion. Moreover, a cable operator is not required to provide prior notice of any rate change that is the result of a regulatory fee, franchise fee, or any other fee, tax assessment, or charge of any kind imposed by any governmental authority. Finally, when reviewing a cable operator's rates, in limited situations a local franchising authority or the FCC must consider that operator's prior years' losses when determining whether the operator's rates are reasonable.

CONCLUSION

Now that Congress has opened the cages, will the animals run? The answer is yes, though no one is quite sure where they will go. For instance, there is no broad consensus among the Regional Holding Companies about how telephone companies should enter the video business, nor is there any broad consensus regarding exactly when we will see widescale deployment of local telephony over cable plant. In addition, Congress cannot change the fact that these businesses cost money, and thus its desire for full-fledged competition has outpaced the ability of many companies (even the larger ones) to provide it. The sea change envisioned by Congress therefore may not come to fruition for some time. In the Telecom Act, however, the United States has at least the beginnings of a proper blueprint for facilitating genuine consumer choice of cable and telephone service providers.

Chapter 5

Wireless Mobile Communications

By Robert G. Kirk, Esq.

In the last twenty years, there has been tremendous growth in the wireless mobile services industry. The industry has grown from relatively few subscribers in the 1970s to more than 50 million subscribers in 1994. It is likely that more than twenty billion dollars will be spent in the United States just to *acquire* licenses to provide the newest form of wireless mobile services — personal communications services (PCS) — with much more investment needed to build networks and actually provide PCS service.

Not only have wireless services experienced tremendous growth, they also have experienced a convergence. The many wireless mobile services were once viewed as separate and distinct. Specialized mobile radio (SMR) service was different from cellular service, cellular service was different from paging service, *etc.* In the last five years, however, wireless mobile services have become increasingly interchangeable. For example, enhanced SMR services were developed as a potential substitute for cellular service. Given this convergence, Congress reexamined the regulatory treatment of wireless mobile services under the Communications Act in 1993 and determined that all similar wireless mobile services must be subject to similar regulation. Further, Congress authorized the FCC to deregulate (*e.g.,* detariff) wireless services in order to allow market forces to work properly. The 1993 amendment was a watershed for wireless mobile communications. It reshaped the regulatory environment and substantially leveled the competitive playing field from a regulatory standpoint.

Unlike the comprehensive revision of the law governing wireless mobile communications services in 1993, the Telecommunications Act of

1996 does not extensively revamp the wireless rules. The new legislation does, however, affect certain aspects of wireless mobile regulations, as explained in this chapter.

NEW APPLICATIONS FOR AN OLD MEDIUM — A BRIEF HISTORY OF WIRELESS IN AMERICA

Over a century ago, Henrich Hertz developed a way to produce and monitor electromagnetic waves, and constructed a primitive radio transmitter. Although he demonstrated the theoretical feasibility of radio communication, the first practical use of this technology did not occur until 1897, when Guglielmo Marconi established a wireless communications link between a land-based station and a moving tugboat.

Radio development accelerated rapidly during World War I and by the 1930s radio technology was utilized by various police departments to dispatch instructions to radio-equipped patrol cars. After World War II, spurred in large part by the development of new wireless technologies, such as two-way "walkie-talkies," the Federal Communications Commission (FCC) permanently allocated frequencies for wireless mobile applications.

Paging services were implemented in the 1940s and have grown tremendously into the most popular wireless service today. Two-way paging applications are becoming increasingly available, but paging service generally is a one-way service.

Two-way wireless services were also developed during the post-war years. The FCC provided for both private dispatch services, such as the two-way radio used by taxicabs and police forces, and common carrier services, which allow subscribers to make telephone calls from a car phone or a portable handset. In the 1970s, specialized mobile radio (SMR) service blurred this private/common carrier distinction by allowing wireless communications companies to provide dispatch service to customers on a

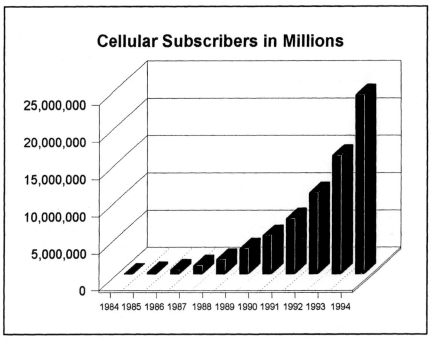

Cellular Subscribers in Millions

Figure 6 - Growth of cellular service in the United States.

commercial basis without common carrier regulation. SMR was generally tailored to serve specific user groups and was not accessible by the general public.

The common carrier mobile phone services available in the mid-1970s were very limited. Cellular telephony expanded wireless phone availability dramatically. Although the seeds of cellular technology were sown in 1947, spectrum was not allocated for cellular use until the late 1970s, when microprocessor technology finally made cellular service possible on a large scale. Two licenses were awarded in each cellular market, with each carrier receiving half of the available cellular spectrum. One license in each market was set aside for use by a local exchange telephone company and the other license was available to another competing entity. These licensees were given the exclusive right to provide service within their assigned markets for a five-year period. Commercial cellular service was first offered in the early 1980s. Cellular systems initially used relatively high-power transmitters to serve large geographic areas from a small number of sites. The coverage "cells" were subdivided over time into a larger number of lower power cells, thereby increasing system capacity.

In 1990, the FCC began a broad inquiry into the development of personal communications services, a family of mobile wireless communications capable of being integrated with a variety of competing networks. It is expected that many of these systems will use a large number of very short-range, low power transmitters known as "microcells" to provide service to large subscriber populations.

REGULATION OF WIRELESS MOBILE RADIO SERVICES BEFORE THE TELECOMMUNICATIONS ACT OF 1996

Initially, paging, cellular, and similar services were subject to both radio (Title III) and common carrier (Title II) regulations under the Communications Act. Title III was applied because radio spectrum was used, and Title II applied to all services that were sold to the general public. Private services and the hybrid SMR service were not subject to Title II, however, because they were not offered "for hire" to the public at large. The Commission drafted separate regulations to govern each service. Thus, one set of FCC regulations existed for SMR, another for paging, and yet another for cellular. Each service became a regulatory island.

The Commission traditionally grouped all wireless mobile services into two regulatory categories: public mobile services and private land mobile services. Originally, public mobile radio services were defined as those radio services which were offered commercially to the general public.

By the 1970s, most such services were interconnected with the wireline telephone network. Private services were defined as services available only to special user groups, such as taxi drivers, public safety officials, or pipeline repair crews. Private mobile services generally were not interconnected, except in limited circumstances. Public mobile services were subject to common carrier regulation under Title II of the Act, radio regulation under Title III, state regulation if the service was intrastate in nature, and alien ownership restrictions. Private land mobile services, on the other hand, were only subject to radio regulation.

Over the years, the distinction between common carrier and private services became clouded as previously distinct services became more and more similar. Paging services, for example, were divided into private and common carrier services even though it was difficult for the public to distinguish between the two types of services. Similarly, the eligible user groups for private services were enlarged to include all businesses, and limits on interconnection were eased. As a result, SMR services and wireless common carrier services were virtually identical in many instances. Increasingly, the FCC focused on the way in which interconnection was achieved to distinguish among functionally similar services. Thus, competing wireless operators were subject to very different regulations.

In 1982, Congress enacted Section 332 of the Communications Act in an attempt to clarify the distinction between private and common carrier services. However, the statute merely codified the functional distinction between private and common carrier status based on interconnection. Private carriers could not interconnect to the public switched network and common carriers, which were now forbidden from providing "dispatch service," were permitted to interconnect to the public switched network. Following enactment of Section 332, however, the Commission modified its interconnection rules for private land mobile systems to allow private carriers such as SMRs to provide interconnected service as long as the operator did not profit from the interconnected portion of the service. In 1991, however, the Commission authorized wide-area or enhanced SMR service which was comparable to cellular in many respects. Thus, functionally equivalent services (*i.e.*, cellular and SMR) became subject to disparate regulation. For example, cellular service was subject to state regulation and states were preempted from regulating enhanced SMR service. It became possible to gain competitive advantages by leveraging regulatory disparities, rather than by creating marketing and service innovations.

Congress responded to the dissimilar regulatory treatment of similar services in 1993 when it amended Section 332 of the Communications Act to require regulatory parity for similar services. To accomplish parity, Section 332 was amended to classify most mobile offerings as "commercial mobile radio services" (CMRS) and to regulate providers of such services as common carriers. Under the revised Section 332, a wireless mobile service is classified as CMRS if it is offered for profit and makes interconnected service available (directly or indirectly) to a substantial portion of the public. Additionally, services which are the "functional equivalent" of CMRS also are deemed CMRS. Thus, the only services that qualify for private carrier regulation under this expansive definition are, practically speaking, either truely private, internal systems, or services that are not interconnected. Accordingly, regulatory disparities between similar services appear to have been eliminated.

In amending Section 332, Congress also encouraged the Commission to limit CMRS regulation because Congress viewed all CMRS to be highly competitive. Congress specifically authorized the FCC to forbear from applying certain common carrier requirements to CMRS providers. Pursuant to this authority, the FCC decided that CMRS providers would no longer be required to comply with some of the common carrier regulations such as those contained in Sections 203 (rate schedules),

204 (FCC authority to determine lawfulness of rates), 205 (FCC authority to impose reasonable rates), 211 (contract filing requirements), and 214 (market entry) of the Communications Act.

The 1993 Act also required all common carriers, such as the Bell Operating Companies (BOCs), to permit CMRS licensees to connect to their networks in a reasonable manner. Additionally, the 1993 Act established a federal regulatory framework to govern the offering of all CMRS. Thus, states were prohibited from imposing rate or entry regulation on CMRS providers. The Act, however, gave the states the right to petition the FCC to reclaim rate regulation authority in the event wireless becomes a substitute for traditional local telephone service.

IMPACT OF THE TELECOMMUNICATIONS ACT OF 1996 ON WIRELESS MOBILE COMMUNICATIONS

Since the Communications Act of 1934 was drafted long before wireless mobile communications were available to the public, it could not have contemplated the present growth and diversity of wireless mobile services nor the associated regulatory issues. For example, wireless mobile services have evolved and grown so rapidly that they may compete with traditional wireline telephone services in the near future. Such a development raises numerous regulatory issues such as interconnection and universal service obligations, as well as state and federal jurisdictional questions.

In passing the Telecom Act, Congress decided it was time to overhaul the Communications Act to provide for a procompetitive, deregulatory national policy framework. As discussed elsewhere, the Telecom Act removes barriers to entry into different aspects of communications, and mandates regulatory reform and forbearance. It also seeks to minimize regulation by allowing competitive market forces, rather than government regulation, to dictate the growth and development of the telecommunications industry. As the drafters of the Act recognized, "We can no longer keep trying to fit everything into the old regulatory boxes - unless we want to incur unacceptable economic costs, competitiveness losses, and deny American consumers access to the latest products and services."

Although the Telecom Act deals primarily with local exchange, long-distance, broadcast, and cable television services, it also affects wireless mobile communications. What follows is an analysis of those provisions of the Telecom Act that may affect the provision of wireless mobile services.

Wireless Local Loop

Traditionally, American consumers obtained residential phone service from a local exchange carrier. The local exchange carrier provided service to the public via a system of wires which physically connected individual homes to the local exchange carrier's nearest switch. Each line from a customer's home to the switch is called a "local loop." In most areas, there is only one company that provides local loops. Thus, residential telephone service may be obtained only from a single local exchange carrier.

Until recently, any entity wishing to offer local residential phone service to customers was required to install its own local loops or resell the service of the existing local exchange carrier (where state law permitted such resale). Of these options, only a duplicative local loop would allow true facilities-based competition because a reseller obtains service at the lowest price offered by a competitor. Establishing a second physical local exchange network covering a broad area, however, would be extremely time consuming and potentially cost prohibitive.

The proliferation and wide spread popularity of wireless mobile communications has raised the possibility that a wireless "local loop" could be established rapidly and inexpensively as a way of providing a competitive alternative to the service of the local exchange carrier. For example, to provide local residential phone service to a new residential neighborhood consisting of seventy homes, wired local loops would require that a wire be connected to each home. No such connections are necessary for a wireless local loop which could offer consumers untethered communications simply by placing a small number of wireless transmitters in the vicinity of the neighborhood. Thus, a wireless local loop provider would have instant access to all consumers located within the area covered by its radio signal. In fact, the rural radio service and the basic exchange telephone radio service (BETRS) already exist as a wireless substitute for traditional wired local loop service in rural areas where it would be too costly to connect homes to the local exchange carrier's network by wire.

Because traditional local exchange service providers have tremendous penetration among the public, serving well over ninety percent of the U.S. population, wireless mobile providers are anxious to get a portion of the local exchange business. The Telecom Act contemplates their entry. As discussed in the next section, the Telecom Act provides that all telecommunications carriers (including wireless) must interconnect their networks. Thus, a wireless local loop subscriber will be able to reach wired telephone users served by a competing carrier. Although the Telecom Act does not subject wireless mobile service providers to local exchange regulation at this time, it gives the FCC authority to extend local exchange regulations to CMRS providers once they become substitutable for traditional local exchange service to a substantial portion of the public.

Interconnection

Prior to the Telecom Act, mobile wireless providers' interconnection rights were contained in Sections 201 and 332(c) of the Communications Act, which provide that a common carrier must establish physical connections with a CMRS provider upon reasonable request.

The Commission has already required local exchange companies to permit wireless providers to interconnect to the local exchange network on terms no less favorable than those offered to the local exchange company's affiliates. The Commission has also required wireless providers and the local exchange companies to negotiate interconnection arrangements in good faith. Further, the FCC has held that cellular carriers are entitled to "mutual compensation," which requires cellular carriers and local exchange carriers to compensate each other for terminating calls originating on each others' networks. The FCC has not actively regulated such interconnection arrangements, however, because most interconnected traffic is local and the interconnection rates have been regulated at the local level.

Shortly before enactment of the Telecom Act, the FCC had begun a proceeding to reevaluate its policies governing interconnection between CMRS providers and local exchange carriers. Subsequently, the FCC invited comment on how the interconnection provision of the Telecom Act affects this type of interconnection. Specifically, the Telecom Act adds to the Communications Act two new sections (Sections 251 and 252) which set forth general interconnection requirements. Section 251 requires all "telecommunications carriers" to interconnect with other tele-communications carriers and imposes interconnection obligations on local exchange carriers. A "telecommunications carrier" is broadly defined in the Act as any provider of telecommunications services, other than an aggregator. Section 252 provides a detailed process for the negotiation, arbitration, and approval of interconnection agreements between local exchange carriers and other telecommunications carriers, and both Section 251 and 252 address the compensation for interconnection, transport, and termination of traffic. Although these sections are largely intended to spur the development of competitive local exchange markets, as discussed in Chapter 2, wireless mobile service providers may fall within the broad definition of a telecommunications service provider. Thus, the FCC will shortly be deciding whether and to what extent interconnection between CMRS providers and local exchange carriers is governed by the new interconnection policies in the Telecom Act.

This is a hotly contested issue. Many wireless carriers argue that this type of interconnection is governed exclusively by Section 332 and not the new provisions of the Telecom Act. These companies support an FCC proposal, made before passage of the Telecom Act, to apply a "bill-and-keep" concept to interconnection between CMRS providers and local exchange carriers. Under bill-and-keep, neither interconnecting party receives compensation from the other. The local exchange companies, on the other hand, oppose the bill-and-keep requirement as inconsistent with the Telecom Act. According to the LECs, the Telecom Act requires parties to negotiate interconnection arrangements, a requirement that would be mooted if bill-and-keep were mandated. They generally argue that CMRS providers should be treated the same as other telecommunications carriers for interconnection purposes and, thus, should be subject to the provisions of Sections 251 and 252.

Accordingly, it is presently unclear exactly how the Telecom Act will affect the interconnection rights and obligations of wireless service providers. The full impact of the Telecom Act on interconnection between CMRS providers and local exchange carries will not be known until the FCC has completed its pending proceeding on this issue, as well as the conclusion of its other rulemaking governing implementation of Sections

251 and 252. Given the highly contentious nature of the interconnection issue, any FCC decisions are sure to be appealed.

Universal Service

As discussed in Chapter 2, the Telecom Act mandates an exhaustive reevaluation of universal service requirements. As part of this evaluation, the Commission and a federal-state joint board must determine who must contribute to the universal service fund and what services will be eligible for universal service support subsidies from this fund. Although wireless service providers have been exempt from universal service obligations to date, the Telecom Act may allow the FCC to require wireless service providers to participate in some universal service programs. Under the Act, all telecommunications carriers that provide interstate services must contribute to the universal service fund, unless their contributions would be minimal under whatever compensation formula is ultimately adopted. Accordingly, wireless services providers that provide interstate services may be required to contribute to the universal service fund.

The news is not all bad for wireless service providers. The Telecom Act may also make it possible for some wireless providers to obtain subsidies from the universal service fund. Pursuant to the Act, universal service subsidies will be paid to eligible telecommunications carriers. These carriers are defined as common carriers that offer services that (1) are essential to education, public health, or public safety, (2) have been subscribed to by a substantial majority of residential subscribers, (3) are of the type being deployed by other carriers in public telecommunications networks, and (4) serve the public interest. As wireless services proliferate, some wireless providers may be able to satisfy the criteria for becoming eligible to receive universal service subsidies.

Incidental InterLATA Services

Pursuant to the MFJ, described in Chapter 2, AT&T was divested of its Bell Operating Companies. The BOCs were authorized to provide local exchange telephone service only within defined geographic areas known as "Local Access and Transport Areas" (LATAs) and were prohibited from carrying telephone service across LATA boundaries. See Figure 3 for a map of the LATAs.

This geographic structure is important from a wireless mobile perspective because the BOCs were permitted to obtain mobile wireless licenses under the MFJ. Wireless mobile service areas, however, did not correspond to LATAs. Accordingly, the BOCs were prohibited from providing wireless mobile services that crossed LATA boundaries, unless they obtained waivers from the Court that administered the MFJ.

Because paging services were being offered by companies largely on a regional or national basis and cellular licenses were awarded for geographic areas which, in many instances, crossed LATA boundaries, the Bell Companies began seeking waivers of the decree to enable their cellular and paging affiliates to provide interLATA services. In many instances, it took years for the Court to act on the waiver requests. Thus, Bell Companies were placed at a disadvantage *vis-a-vis* their competitors that could provide interLATA wireless mobile services without delay.

The Telecommunications Act of 1996 allows the Bell Companies to provide common carrier mobile radio service and other wireless services without restriction. Thus, the Bell Companies can provide CMRS services, either in-region or out-of-region, without regard to statutory separation requirements imposed on the Bell Companies provision of other interLATA services.

117

Equal Access

Not only can the BOCs provide interexchange service to their wireless customers, now they can do so without giving subscribers the option of selecting their long-distance carrier (except through access codes). Until adoption of the Telecom Act, the Bell Companies alone were required to afford their wireless customers a choice of interexchange carriers. In 1992, MCI filed a petition with the FCC requesting that all cellular licensees be subject to the same equal access obligations imposed on the BOCs. Two years later, the Commission proposed to subject all cellular licensees to equal access obligations. The Commission also sought comment on which other CMRS services (*i.e.*, paging, SMR) should be subject to equal access requirements. The Telecom Act mooted this proceeding by eliminating equal access requirements for all CMRS providers. The Commission retains authority, however, to require CMRS providers to allow subscribers to access alternative long-distance providers by dialing a special access code.

Tower Siting

The Telecom Act expands the options of wireless providers in locating transmitter sites. First, local exchange companies are required to afford access by wireless and other telecommunications providers to the poles, ducts, conduits, and rights-of-way on terms and conditions similar to those contained in the pole attachment rules in Section 224 of the Communications Act (as amended by Section 703 of the Telecom Act).

The Telecom Act also discusses the ability of local authorities to regulate the siting of radio facilities. Wireless providers have previously experienced difficulties in obtaining local approval for radio sites. In response, mobile service providers lobbied both the Congress and the FCC to preempt localities from preventing them from building cell sites. Due in large part to the lobbying efforts of wireless providers and localities, Congress addressed this issue in the Telecom Act.

Specifically, Congress stated that it was preserving local authority over siting but indicated that states and localities could not unreasonably discriminate among providers of similar wireless services, nor could they effectively preclude the provision of wireless services by refusing to approve sites needed for deployment of these services. The Telecom Act also requires states and localities to act on siting requests within a reasonable time and stipulates that a denial of such requests must be made in writing and supported by substantial evidence. Further, the Telecom Act precludes states and localities from considering radiation in deciding whether or not to grant a siting request. Any person aggrieved by states or localities acting inconsistently with the Telecom Act is entitled to expedited judicial review of his case.

Finally, the Telecom Act requires the federal government to make public lands and rights-of-way available for the placement of telecommunications facilities. The Telecom Act encourages federal departments and agencies to grant requests to construct radio facilities on public grounds, provided placement of the facilities is not inconsistent with the department's or agency's mission or the use of the public lands. In other words, the Army Corps of Engineers does not have to make environmentally sensitive lands available for the placement of radio facilities.

Joint Marketing

Under the FCC's rules, a Bell Operating Company must provide cellular service through a separate subsidiary and cannot market or sell its traditional wireline local exchange service and cellular service jointly. The

Telecom Act eliminates this restriction. Thus, although a BOC's cellular affiliate must still be operated by a separate subsidiary, it may jointly market its wireline local exchange service and its separated affiliate's cellular.

AT&T/McCaw Consent Decree

In 1994, McCaw merged with AT&T, giving AT&T a tremendous share of the cellular marketplace. In order to obtain consent from the Justice Department for the merger, AT&T entered into a consent decree which required AT&T to: (1) hold McCaw's wireless properties in separate affiliates; (2) provide equal access to new cellular subscribers; (3) not disclose non-public information it receives as a manufacturer from wireless providers to its wireless affiliates. Despite the Justice Department's concern over the anticompetitive effects of the merger absent these conditions, Congress vacated the consent decree on a going forward basis in the Telecom Act.

Miscellaneous

The Communications Act requires that the Commission place applications for broadcast and common carrier authority on public notice, and that such applications cannot be granted unless they serve the public interest and thirty days have passed since they were placed on public notice. A number of other services were subject to these same requirements. The Telecom Act, however, eliminated the public notice requirement with regard to private fixed point-to-point microwave systems. Thus, the Commission may grant applications for such authority without regard to the public notice requirements. The Telecom Act also allows the Commission to waive the construction permit requirement for non-broadcast facilities.

Finally, the Telecom Act empowers the Commission to permit the operation of aviation radio service stations and domestic maritime radio service ship stations. Thus, unless required to carry a radio and obtain a license, boaters and pilots may be freed of the requirement to obtain a license for their on-board radios. This provision is especially ironic given that interference from ship-to-shore radios was a major impetus behind radio regulation in the first place.

CONCLUSION

Clearly, the wireless industry has been the most explosive and exciting in the telecommunications marketplace for the past decade. Small cellular systems serving separate areas have grown into large ventures providing a wide assortment of regional services. Satellite development over the next few years will create the ability to communicate worldwide — with the added benefit of international mobility. While spectrum is limited, sufficient spectrum has been allocated in the U.S. to permit five or more entities to compete throughout the nation, thereby assuring a wide variety of services at lower prices.

Chapter 6

Regulatory Reform

By John J. Smith, Esq.

The reform envisioned by the 104th Congress in drafting the Telecommunications Act of 1996 was premised on the notion that competition is a more effective regulator of marketplace conduct among incumbent competitors and new market participants, and that the open marketplace, with only the barest intervention by the goverment, will better meet the needs of the consumer. To test this premise, the Act reduces the prominence of traditional communications regulation, requiring the Federal Communications Commission to reexamine its regulations and either eliminate or at least forbear from applying them if market forces are working properly. In addition, the Telecom Act redefines the role of the states in shaping the interplay of competitors. This chapter highlights specific reforms embodied in Titles II and IV of the Telecom Act, and provides an overview of general principles of competition which Congress sought to substitute for the previous regulatory regime.

FLEXIBILITY AT THE FEDERAL COMMUNICATIONS COMMISSION

One seemingly obvious way to reduce regulation is to permit the regulator to make reasoned judgments, based upon experience, as to the efficacy of its rules, and to forbear from applying its rules when the circumstances indicate they are unnecessary. However, before the Telecommunications Act of 1996 became law, the FCC had little discretion to do so. Despite the FCC's best attempts to reduce red tape, several judicial decisions had made clear that the FCC had no authority to forbear from regulating, regardless of whether such regulation was helpful or needed.

The Telecom Act finally empowers the Commission to refrain from imposing or continuing to impose any statutory provision or Commission regulation on telecommunications carriers or services. Moreover, the new legislation goes a few steps beyond simply granting to the Commission the power to reduce or eliminate regulation. Congress has mandated that deregulation affirmatively occur when circumstances in the marketplace obviate the need for further oversight and direction.

To this end, the FCC is charged with an independent duty to forbear from regulating if in its judgment regulations or laws are unnecessary to prevent undue discriminatory practices, such as a carrier favoring certain of its customers, or disadvantaging those of its competitors which rely on some of the carrier's services. Before forbearing, however, the Commission must determine that neither "consumers" (not defined in the Act, but presumably including those users of any service, or customers of any carrier, which may be affected) nor the public interest generally would be harmed by the Commission's proposed action or inaction. The Telecom Act expressly provides that the Commission may find that promoting competition through forbearance is in the public interest. Although making such a determination may lead to extensive notice and comment proceedings, at least the regulations are now open for discussion and the truth about the effectiveness and necessity of any given regulation may be realized in the process.

Despite the open invitation to withhold the application of regulations, Congress was careful to ensure that the Commission could not waive the new obligations imposed on incumbent local exchange carriers in the Telecom Act — particularly the BOCs — until they demonstrate compliance. Those obligations, described more fully in Chapter 2, include interconnection, unbundled access to network elements, resale and the duty to negotiate with potential competitors. The Act also ensures that the FCC cannot forbear from enforcing the competitive checklist for BOC entry into interexchange service.

In addition to the general obligation to make independent decisions about whether to forbear from applying a particular regulation, the Telecom Act imposes on the Commission a corresponding duty to respond, in an affirmative and reasoned manner, to petitions filed by carriers seeking the discontinuance or reduction of particular regulations. The Commission has up to one year to make its response and a failure to act (or to justify a limited 90-day extension) automatically results in approval of the petition.

FCC Initiative to Eliminate Interexchange Service Tariffs

In its first exercise of this newly granted forbearance authority, the Commission has proposed "mandatory detariffing" of services offered by all nondominant interexchange carriers. Over a decade ago, the Commission adopted a similar detariffing policy as part of its "Competitive Carrier" proceeding, only to lose in the final round of a series of protracted court battles because Congress had not specifically authorized the FCC to forbear from tariff regulation.

Congress has now given the FCC that authority, although it is still to be decided whether the forbearance authority in the Telecom Act allows the FCC to *mandate* detariffing. Many interexchange carriers argue that the FCC may only adopt a *permissive* detariffing policy, which would still permit carriers to file tariffs, at their option.

As all domestic long-distance carriers, including AT&T, are now classified as nondominant with respect to their domestic service offerings, the mandatory detariffing proposal would sweep away an enormous accumulation of paper filings at the Commission. The FCC's Common Carrier Bureau Chief has estimated that carriers currently file approximately

10,000 tariff revisions each year, amounting to about four million pieces of paper.

It is especially noteworthy that the Commission's initiative would altogether foreclose affected carriers from filing tariffs, in contrast to allowing them the option to file or not to file. Parties have argued that giving the carriers the option of filing would allow them to "game" the tariff procedures, to engage in "price signaling" through publication of their prices, terms and conditions for competitive services. Proponents of mandatory detariffing point to a number of benefits to the consumer (particularly very large users) of telecom services. For example, customers with sufficient bargaining leverage would be in a position to negotiate preferable carrier liability provisions, replacing the constricted credits now offered uniformly by the carriers to compensate for service outages or degradation. Carriers could no longer "trump the contract" with their major customers by filing superseding tariffs affecting the benefit of the bargain struck between supplier and user. Today, carriers legally may unilaterally change the terms of a contract by filing tariff revisions. While rarely invoked (for reasons of keeping good customer relationships), this right injects unnecessary artificial uncertainty into what should be customary private commercial dealings.

BIENNIAL OMNIBUS REVIEW OF REGULATIONS

Acting under a sweeping mandate, every even numbered year after 1997 the Commission must on its own review every outstanding regulation issued under the revised Communications Act which affects the "operations" or "activities" of any telecommunications carrier. The goal will be to determine, in light of meaningful economic competition among industry players, whether further oversight over those operations and activities is necessary to safeguard or promote public interest considerations. As the Telecom Act provides no guidance to the Commission on how to conduct this extensive examination, the FCC can be expected to rely heavily on input from both telecommunications carriers and consumers of their services in reviewing the need for its regulations.

DEVOLUTION OF REGULATORY POWER TO THE STATES

The Telecom Act strikes a new balance between the federal and state governments in regulating telecommunications, and the impact of the rebalancing affects most of the players in telecommunications — the BOCs, other telecommunications carriers, the user community, state commissions and the FCC.

Federal and state relations in telecommunications regulation have often been uneasy. The FCC and the state agencies jealously guard their respective jurisdictional prerogatives and missions. The paradigm of the Communications Act of 1934, unchanged by the Telecom Act, is one of parallel regulatory authority. The federal law, being "federal" in design, recognizes the near equivalency of potentially divergent federal and state regulatory regimes.

Over the previous two decades, the federal courts have wrestled with numerous conflicts arising out of overlapping statutory authority and clashes of regulatory goals and policies. The FCC, in pursuit of national policy to deregulate or liberalize regulation of non-dominant common carriers, introduced several initiatives to preclude or reduce the scope of conflicting PUC regulation. State PUCs have vigorously countered these assertions of federal preemption at each step, challenging the authority of the FCC unilaterally to undermine powers reserved to the states to implement state-wide public policy for telecommunications. The judicial conflict appears to have culminated, through recent Supreme Court decisions, in the direction of greater deference to the states.

Congress has now stepped forward, somewhat tentatively and ambivalently, into this contested territory — the jurisdictional commons where both the Federal Communications Commission and the state public utility commissions graze their flocks. The Telecom Act redefines and extends many of the duties which the state public utility commissions have historically performed under their respective state authorizing statutes. Yet, Congress, mindful that in deregulating at the federal level it may open unintended opportunities for the states to expand their own powers, seeks to close the door to regulatory opportunism, while leaving it just a bit ajar.

The Telecom Act sets out the metes and bounds of a large field of cooperation between the federal and state agencies of government concerned with telecommunications. Conceptually, Congress seems to have struck a balance as follows. The states will have wide discretion to implement federal policy, but with plenty of assistance and oversight from the FCC. Thus the FCC must first erect guideposts to assist state regulators in steering their way through new and unfamiliar territory. Next the states will become actively involved in the details of arrangements among competing local exchange service providers, reviewing their contracts, mediating and arbitrating disputes, and passing upon the general terms and conditions offered by the BOCs and other incumbent LECs to their local exchange competitors.

The following sections outline the principal new authority which the Telecom Act grants to the states, in large part complementary to those duties which the FCC has up to now undertaken with respect to interstate telecommunications matters. For a discussion of the obligations of local exchange carriers to which the state's new powers pertain, see Chapter 2.

Access and Interconnection Arrangements

Under FCC guidelines, the state PUCs must mediate or arbitrate, and ultimately review, contract negotiations and disputes between incumbent local exchange carriers and new competitors over the detailed market-opening arrangements mandated by the Telecom Act. As discussed in Chapter 5, it is an open question whether the new Telecom Act's interconnection provisions apply to commercial mobile services, but they clearly apply to new local exchange competitors. Matters the states must address include requests for interconnection and collocation, unbundling of LEC service elements, resale, pole attachments, and reciprocal compensation, as well as the rates and offering terms for each such arrangement. Inevitably, the PUCs will be drawn into the middle of fierce disputes over pricing, such as the methodology for setting wholesale rates for services to be resold, interconnection and other matters already being contested by incumbent local exchange carriers and their would-be competitors.

BOC In-Region Service Authorizations

As part of the process by which BOCs without facilities-based competitors may ultimately enter in the long-distance business, the state commissions must review and advise the FCC within fixed time frames on statements of general terms and conditions filed by the BOCs for interconnection, resale, unbundling, number portability, dialing parity, *etc.* The PUCs must assess whether such proposals comply with the open network interconnection and access requirements listed above and the additional obligations found in the "competitive checklist" described in Chapter 2. The final word, however, will come from the FCC, subject to inevitable appeals to the courts.

129

Universal Service

Under the Telecom Act, the states have the obligation to ensure that universal service (a term which may evolve under the aegis of a federal-state joint board) is made available at reasonable and affordable rates. Moreover, the state commissions must determine discount rates for certain preferred users of intrastate services — such as educational institutions and libraries. Finally the states will have to designate those entities which are eligible to receive universal service funding and those entities which will contribute to support such funding.

Discretion for Parallel Regulation

Finally, and none too clearly, the Telecom Act accords the states a broad measure of discretion in carrying out their own regulatory mandates — those imposed under the Telecom Act as well as those arising under state law. Thus the state commissions may impose access and interconnection requirements in addition to those set forth in the Telecom Act, so long as they are not inconsistent with the Act — a very wide area in which to roam. The states may define additional public interest duties or standards — relating for example to public safety, welfare, universal and rural services, consumer protection and service quality — provided that such requirements do not favor one competitor or class of competitor over another.

Elsewhere in the Telecom Act Congress seeks to qualify these generous grants of authority and discretion to the states. In just a few, footnote-like, provisions, Congress interjects federal policy deep into the most local of local jurisdiction prerogatives — the right to determine the timing and terms of entry of new participants in the local exchange marketplace. Congress accomplishes this through a handful of techniques: (1) it prohibits the states from maintaining or erecting barriers to would-be players in the local telecommunications marketplace; (2) it expressly directs the FCC to set aside any such impediment; (3) it bars the PUCs from rushing in to fill the void created by FCC deregulation; (4) it precludes enforcement of new PUC regulations or state laws inconsistent with the Telecom Act; and (5) it carves out a place for the FCC to pass upon PUC implementation of state mandates under the new Act.

While to the layman these may seem minor afterthoughts, they are fraught with the potential, perhaps only dimly anticipated, for protracted legal battles over the optimal allocation of regulatory powers between these two levels of government. For example, disagreements will certainly arise where a PUC or state legislature, reasonably interpreting the Telecom Act to accord it the discretion to implement unique state-wide policy, continues in effect or subsequently adopts and enforces regulations or laws which may be similar to provisions which the FCC, as a result of its biennial reexamination, has previously decided to eliminate, or which the FCC believes are impediments to free competitive entry. In most cases it will not be easy to determine that the state regulation or law in question is fatally similar to the regulation eliminated by the FCC. Alternatively, a state may simply declare that its laws or regulations promote federal pro-competition goals, albeit in a manner more fitting to its unique policy concerns. States may also legitimately avoid impairment of publicly beneficial services by incumbent carriers by adapting regulatory regimes at variance with that of the FCC.

Far from putting to rest the jurisdictional animosities of the past, these ambivalent provisions only compound problems inherent to dual jurisdiction regulation. These simple phrases and clauses will conjure as many litigation demons as they exorcise.

REGULATORY HOUSEKEEPING

Perhaps in an effort to spur the FCC to begin its spring-cleaning of outdated regulations, the Telecom Act contains a variety of quick fixes to several existing regulations and eliminates others. These regulatory housekeeping measures are described below.

Tariffs

Among the housekeeping provisions of the Telecom Act are a number of clauses designed to make the filing and modification of tariffs more streamlined. For example, dispute resolutions or investigations by the Commission about charges or other terms in any tariff newly filed or revised after February 8, 1997, must be brought to a conclusion within five months, not twelve to fifteen months as previously provided.

Moreover, approximating the streamlined tariff filing procedures enjoyed by interexchange carriers, the Telecom Act allows local exchange carriers to specify earlier effective dates in their proposed tariff filings: fifteen days for rate increases and seven days for decreases. Long-distance providers may now propose one-day tariff effective dates, except as to international services. The Commission may waive or further modify these local exchange carrier tariffing provisions.

Congress has also authorized the Commission to exempt common carriers from certain other reporting and application requirements: carriers may request relief from advance approval before constructing facilities, and from filing cost allocation manuals and accounting reports more frequently than annually. The Telecom Act further provides for an inflation indexation of the Commission's small carrier rule exemptions whereby it excuses carriers having less than certain annual operating revenues (generally less than $100,000,000) from many record keeping and reporting requirements.

132

The Commission is itself relieved of the task of setting depreciation rates for telco assets, and given flexibility to hire outside auditors to assist in examinations of carrier records.

Privatization of Certain Commission Functions — New Mandates and FCC Initiatives

Among a number of miscellaneous modifications relating to FCC duties for licensing, inspection, and certification requirements, the new legislation allows the Commission to delegate to private organizations many of its responsibilities for testing and certification of communication devices and home electronic products. These functions may now be carried out by responsible private organizations under FCC-promulgated standards and organizational qualifications (*e.g.,* electromagnetic interference standards, independent private testing laboratories).

The Commission over the past few years has taken a number of actions to expedite the equipment authorization process, and now proposes to replace existing certification requirements for personal computers and peripherals with a rule permitting manufacturers to "self-declare" their compliance with FCC technical standards. As the Telecom Act does not expressly proscribe either the form of privatization (*e.g.,* "private laboratories") or the types of products covered, one may expect that manufacturers of many sorts of equipment — microwave ovens, home video appliances, communications receivers, *etc.* — will press for wider expansion of authority to conduct testing internally and to self-certify.

The Commission on its own initiative has conducted a pilot project allowing private sector entities to respond to interference complaints regarding home electronic equipment. It concluded that private intervention in consumer electronics interference matters actually speeds resolution. Such delegations will allow the Commission to focus its limited resources on resolving complaints of interference to public safety, land mobile, common carrier and broadcast radio services.

Other provisions allow the Commission to waive licensing of domestic ship and aircraft radio operators, and personal radio service operators.

Effect on Consent Decrees and Antitrust Laws

The Telecom supersedes three major antitrust decrees: the "Modified Final Judgment," which separated and reorganized AT&T's long-distance, manufacturing and local exchange businesses, the GTE Consent Decree which permitted, among other things, GTE's acquisition of Sprint (which it later sold), and the AT&T-McCaw Consent Decree. All three have been completely supplanted by the new statutory and regulatory schemes affecting the joint provision of interexchange, wireless and local exchange services, and equipment manufacturing.

The new legislation makes few overt changes to existing antitrust laws. Other than a few conforming amendments to other antitrust statutes, the Telecom Act eliminates only one unnecessary provision of the Communications Act, which permitted to FCC to review mergers between "telephone companies," and exempted such mergers from further antitrust challenges.

BOC Manufacturing

An elaborate, and, one might argue, obtuse set of rules governing BOC involvement in manufacturing replaces the MFJ's restrictions on the BOCs manufacture of telecommunications equipment. Under the MFJ, a Regional Holding Company and its affiliates were limited to preliminary pre-manufacturing activities such as specifying generic requirements, which it would then hand off to independent manufacturers for detailed design and fabrication. The new legislation permits each BOC to engage in research and to enter into royalty arrangements with others.

The BOCs may now manufacture telecommunications network and customer premises equipment, but only subject to certain preconditions. These include, (1) prior FCC authorization to provide in-region interLATA service (discussed in Chapter 2), (2) use of a separate subsidiary for manufacturing activities, (3) availability of BOC-manufactured hardware and integrated software to other dependent local exchange carriers on non-preferential terms and conditions, and (4) a general duty to share technical and planning information and not to discriminate in procurements, standards setting, equipment certification, or the sale of telecommunications hardware and software. Other affiliated companies of the BOCs, it would seem, are unaffected by these restrictions and may engage in the full range of manufacturing activities defined in the legislation.

No joint manufacturing activities may be conducted with unaffiliated BOCs, or with Bellcore. Bellcore is subject to special constraints so long as it continues to be affiliated with more than one BOC. A detailed program governing the standards-setting and equipment certification of entities like Bellcore is established to encourage wide participation of interested parties in standards and product certification matters.

Chapter 7

Telecommunications in Germany — A Different Paradigm

By Richard J. Leitermann, Esq.

In the telecommunications industry, the United States has consistently taken the lead role. From Alexander Graham Bell's discovery of electromagnetics, to the breakup of AT&T, to the Telecommunications Act of 1996, the U.S. has set the standard by which other countries abide. Nonetheless, the timing of the world's reaction to American innovation has been less than prompt. Following Bell's invention of the telephone, Europe did not experience real telephony penetration until well into the twentieth century. AT&T, formerly the near-equivalent of the government-owned and operated Postal, Telephone and Telegraph (PTT) entities in Europe, was liberalized between 1982 and 1984, but the PTTs in Europe are just now undergoing a similar process. The Telecommunications Act of 1996 was just recently passed, but Europe will not begin to move on similar reforms until at least 1998.

Although the world's response time to American ingenuity has been slow, countries throughout the world are now undertaking needed liberalization of their telecommunications laws and privatizing government-owned communications entities. The Telecom Act will clearly provide a model for deregulation — and no doubt the rules and regulations adopted by the Federal Communications Commission (FCC) will also serve to provide insight and structure to governments eager for competition.

Among the world's developed nations, Germany is in the upper tier. Although Deutsche Telekom is just now being privatized, the German experience with telecommunications liberalization is similar to that of many countries embarking on telecom reform. This chapter provides the history of Germany's telecommunications industry and regulation and also provides the reader with an insight into the struggles and successes of countries trying to inject competition into their telecom industry in an effort to jump-start their economies.

DEUTSCHE BUNDESPOST: GERMANY'S PTT

Deutsche Bundespost, Germany's Postal Telephone and Telegraph monolith, was a huge enterprise that not only included telecommunications, but also the postal system and a national financial system. Its revenues were greater than any German manufacturing company. The Telecommunications Facilities Law of 1928 expressly conveyed to Deutsche Bundespost the exclusive right to construct and operate *all* telecommunications facilities in Germany. Over time, as technologies developed, Deutsche Bundespost not only provided the same types of services which were provided by AT&T prior to its separation from the Bell Operating Companies in 1984, it also became the principal provider of a number of other services, such as paging, satellite, radio and television.

In 1985, Dr. Christian Schwarz-Schilling, then Minister of Telecommunications and the principal regulator of Deutsche Bundespost, established a commission headed by Professor Eberhard Witte of Munich University, to make recommendations for the reform of the telecommunications industry in Germany. After much debate, the Witte Commission recommended that the telecommunications, postal and banking services be separated and that the Minister of Telecommunications continue to regulate the telecom industry. It was also recommended that a newly created telecommunications entity, Deutsche Bundespost Telekom, be the monopoly provider for basic network and voice telephony services. In addition, the Witte Commission recommended that the equipment market be fully opened to competition and non-voice communications, including data and text, likewise be fully liberalized. The Witte Commission endorsed flexibility in the interconnection of leased lines with Deutsche Bundespost Telekom's switched service, and suggested that tariffs be brought more in line with costs, and that satellite-delivered data be opened to transmission by competitors of Deutsche Bundespost Telekom. The recommendations of the Commission were generally accepted by Minister Schwarz-Schilling and thereafter by the German government.

With acceptance of these recommendations, the transition of the telecommunications sector in Germany began in 1989 and has continued on a progressive basis since. Private entities have capitalized on the competitive opportunities and are presently offering value-added services. In addition, two competing cellular networks currently serve in excess of three million customers, and a personal communications service provider began operations about a year ago. In addition, usage sensitive leased-line tariffs have been implemented, type approval procedures have been liberalized and limited resale of Deutsche Bundespost Telekom's facilities and services has been authorized. While much liberalization has taken place over the past seven years, much more is planned over the next few years to meet deadlines established by the European Commission.

Prior to proceeding, it is important to mention a unique challenge which confronted the German government — the reunification of Germany in 1989. Although the German Democratic Republic had one of the most advanced telephone systems in Eastern Europe, its infrastructure was outdated and, for the most part, inadequate. For example, in Dresden, only one home out of nine had telephone service and the waiting list for telephone service in eastern Germany was in excess of one million people by 1990.

Indeed, the merger of the telephone system in the former German Democratic Republic was not an easy one. The West German government was asked to contribute substantial funds to underwrite the general cost, and there was difficulty in integrating the various private networks established throughout East Germany. Deutsche Bundespost Telekom has already invested about $22 billion in East Germany.

POSTAL REFORM I

Most agree that Postal Reform I, which followed adoption of the Witte Commission's recommendations, has been a success. As stated, the structural aspects of this reform resulted in the creation of three separate entities from the former Deutsche Bundespost: Deutsche Bundespost Telekom (telecommunications), Deutsche Bundespost Postbank (banking) and Deutsche Bundespost Postdienst (postal services). In addition, the Federal Ministry of Post and Telecommunications was given authority to govern these three entities.

While the monopoly of Deutsche Bundespost Telekom did not extend to data and value-added services, and while licenses have been granted for cellular and other mobile services, the market share of private telecommunications enterprises in the German telecommunications sector is still below ten percent. See Figure 7. However, private investment and opportunities are continually expanding and further progressive actions have been taken.

For example, in 1990 the Minister of Posts and Tele-communications issued an order to spur liberalization which provided that licenses would be granted on an extraordinary basis in the event (1) Deutsche Bundespost Telekom did not fulfill its obligation to provide the necessary infrastructure to competitors in terms of type, quality and price of certain requested services, or (2) if a new technology is introduced and its introduction into the marketplace will not negatively affect the obligations of Deutsche Bundespost Telekom to provide essential

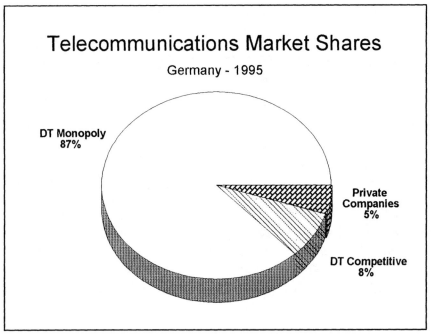

Figure 7 - Competitive and monopoly shares of German market.

(universal) services. Further, at the prodding of the European Commission, the Ministry in 1993 adjusted its regulations for the existing public voice telephony monopoly. More specifically, the Ministry allowed private entities to undertake voice switching for corporate networks and established rules for individual approval for closed user groups. These reforms are almost identical to those demanded by MCI in the United States back in 1963, the granting of which ultimately led to the breakup of AT&T. See Chapter 2 for the relevant history.

In 1993, the Minister also expanded the approval for on-premises facilities, thereby enabling the provision of private wireline telecommunication networks within specified areas.

Most importantly, however, the Minister of Posts and Telecommunications imposed a number of regulatory restrictions on Deutsche Bundespost Telekom because of its monopoly position. These included price regulations for monopoly service, the requirement that Deutsche Bundespost Telekom provide a predefined set of services at prices approved by the Minister and the requirement that Deutsche Bundespost Telekom, in its internal accounting, use such approved prices when providing monopoly services.

Deutsche Bundespost Telekom was further required to provide certain mandatory services such as directory services and public telephones. Moreover, it was mandated that the monopoly provide all ancillary services used for the provision of its own services to competitors on a non-discriminatory basis. In addition, costumer information could not be used by Deutsche Bundespost Telekom without sharing such information with its competitors under identical terms and conditions. Finally, unbundling and interconnection provisions were deemed to apply to Deutsche Bundespost Telekom thereby assuring that the competitors of Deutsche Telekom can select from a menu of services at reasonable rates.

POSTAL REFORM II

The second postal reform became effective on January 1, 1995, the date on which Deutsche Telekom AG was incorporated to succeed the government-owned Deutsche Bundespost Telekom. The main thrust of Postal Reform II is the privatization of Deutsche Telekom — with the first public offering planned for the second half of 1996. It is hoped that by 1999, 50 percent of the stock will be sold to private investors; the German government will not take part in this stock offering. However, even after the stock issuance, the German government will be the major stockholder of Deutsche Telekom. Further privatization through stock sales is planned after 1999.

Another aspect of Postal Reform II is that on December 31, 1997, the German telecommunications market will be completely opened to competition as required by the European Commission. However, simultaneously with Postal Reform II, the government enacted further legislation which addressed the basic regulations for the provision of mandatory services to the German government by Deutsche Telekom. But an amendment to the German Constitution opens the door for complete liberalization of the German telecommunications marketplace by allowing the federal government to rely on private companies to fulfill basic telecommunications service obligations.

Finally, in 1995, the Ministry further clarified the licensing procedures for corporate networks, closed user groups and private networks and, the same year, legislation was enacted which allows private mobile communications network operators to apply for licenses to operate all types of transmission lines if they offer public services. Once these entities are licensed, they will be able to provide network services to other mobile communications operators, thus allowing the sharing of network infrastructure in direct competition to Deutsche Telekom.

WIRELESS, SATELLITE, BROADCAST AND CABLE

Since 1989, the Ministry has made extensive use of its right to license telecommunications services. Over 890 telecommunications service providers have been licensed in Germany, of which over 80 operate under licenses for mobile communications services.

Mobile Communications

Until 1989, Deutsche Bundespost Telekom operated two analog mobile communications (cellular) systems: B-Net and C-Net. Following a European Union regulation on the introduction of the GSM standard in the 900 MHz frequency band, the Ministry in 1989 issued licenses for GSM networks to Deutsche Bundespost Telekom (D1 network) and to a private competitor (Mannesmann Mobilfunk GmbH — D2 network). AirTouch, a U.S. company that once was a part of Pacific Telesis, is a partner of Mannesmann.

Shortly after the start of construction of its network, Mannesmann raised complaints about high fees charged by Deutsche Bundespost Telekom for leased lines necessary to connect base stations to mobile switching centers. The Ministry responded quickly in an attempt to reduce the leased lines fees to an internationally competitive level. However, Deutsche Bundespost Telekom did not decrease its prices to the requested level. In consequence, the Ministry allowed Mannesmann to build its own microwave links between base stations and the mobile switching centers. Notwithstanding this ruling, Mannesmann was required to lease most of its backbone network from Deutsche Bundespost Telekom at high rates.

Once GSM services began operating, Mannesmann, based on its marketing and superior operating abilities, attracted customers at a much faster rate than Deutsche Bundespost Telekom. Currently both systems share about 3.2 million subscribers. Deutsche Bundespost Telekom's market share is presently somewhat below 50 percent (less than 1.5 million subscribers) and Mannesmann enjoys a majority of the subscribers.

In 1993, a license for a DCS 1800 network (E1) was issued by the Minister of Posts and Telecommunications. This network competes with the three national cellular providers and currently serves about 300,000 subscribers in Germany. BellSouth is a partner in this venture. A tender for

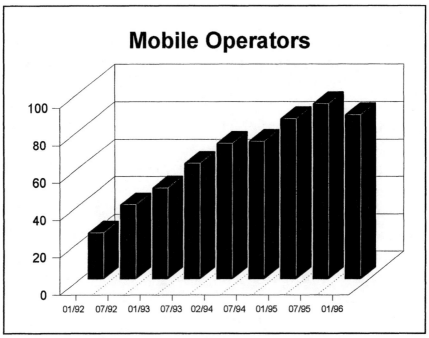

Figure 8 - Mobile operators in Germany.

a second DCS 1800 is planned for the second half of 1996. It is expected that the total number of mobile communications subscribers in Germany by the end of 1999 will be as high as 10.5 million, tripling the current penetration rate from 3.1 percent to over 10 percent.

The Ministry of Posts and Telecommunications also issued licenses to 31 operators to provide regional Trunked Private Mobile Radio (TPMR) networks in Germany. Deutsche Bundespost Telekom has a license to provide national TPMR services. In addition to Deutsche Telekom, two paging network operators have received licenses. The Ministry had also agreed to a resolution by the European Council on the coordinated introduction of a pan-European land based public radio system (ERMES); however, the licensing procedure was delayed because of interference problems with the transmission of television signals in Deutsche Bundespost Telekom's broadband distribution network. To prevent further delay, the Ministry commenced a hearing on licensing procedures in January 1996.

Satellite

In 1990, specific rules were established to license satellite networks and numerous licenses for satellite services have been granted since then. In order to support the delivery of telephony services to the former German Democratic Republic now reunified with Germany, the Ministry of Posts and Telecommunications granted limited licenses for public voice service from and to Eastern Germany. Currently 46 satellite operators are registered in Germany.

Broadcasting and Cable Television

Germany's Constitution allocates the responsibility for broadcasting to the Länder, or state governments. The major reasons for this allocation are based on Germany's history and Constitution which both demonstrate an attempt to limit centralized federal influence on broadcasting media. Furthermore, radio frequencies for broadcasting purposes are considered a limited resource that should be regionally allocated to ensure local programming. Thus, until the 1980s Germany only had two national and one regional broadcasting program. With evolving technologies such as satellite and cable, more spectrum became available and private broadcast

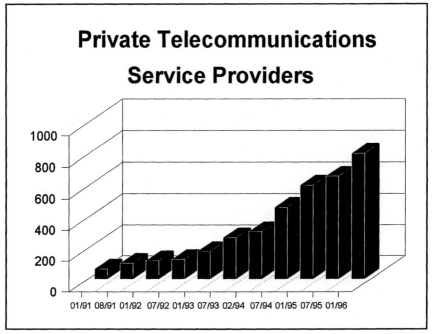

Figure 9 - *Private telecommunications service providers in Germany.*

authorizations were granted. Still, broadcasting licenses may only be granted by the Länder governments.

In general, all broadcasting facilities are included in the network monopoly, and in consequence, all facilities have to be operated by Deutsche Telekom. However, the Länder influence the content of what is broadcast.

The regulations for cable have already been somewhat liberalized. Cable networks with fewer than 25 subscribers that do not use public roadways are generally approved by order of the Minister of Posts and Telecommunications. Cable networks with more than 25 subscribers that do not use public roadways need a specific approval that will be granted for fifteen years, provided that the system does not cause electromagnetic interference. Licenses for cable networks that use public roadways will only be granted if Deutsche Telekom does not intend to provide services in the same area.

Numerous licenses for regional cable networks have been granted. The cable network operators, however, can only redistribute television programs if their cable systems have limited frequency capacity. The new order on the granting of licenses issued in 1995 made clear that cable network operators can use the networks for purposes other than distribution of broadcast signals and, if they qualify for the respective approval, can integrate their cable networks in private telecommunications networks interconnected to the public switched telephone network.

ALTERNATIVE ACCESS PROVIDERS

For the past year, two companies — Metropolitan Fiber Systems and City of London Telecommunications (COLT) — have received authorizations and rights-of-way to provide facilities-based alternative access to business users in Frankfurt for data and closed user group voice services. In consequence, Deutsche Telekom's business tariffs in Frankfurt dropped dramatically. COLT plans to expand its services to other cities in Germany. The three large electric utlity companies (RWE, Veba and Virg) and other smaller companies currently offer private corporate network services on their microwave networks. Deutsche Telekom has responded to this new competition by slashing the rates it charges its corporate customers by up to 35 percent. This practice has been vigorously attacked by the utility companies as an effort to kill competition.

FOREIGN OWNERSHIP RESTRICTIONS

The German telecommunications market has no statutory foreign ownership restrictions. Thus, licenses under the current law (and under the current draft of the new telecommunications law described below) are also granted to foreign entities. As mentioned, one of the cellular operators and the personal communications service licensee have foreign shareholders in excess of 25 percent of their share capital. A large number of the other mobile communications licensees (including satellite) have foreign shareholders or are wholly-owned subsidiaries of foreign companies.

The lack of foreign ownership restrictions and Germany's liberalizations efforts described above caused the European Commission, the U.S. Department of Justice and the Federal Communications Commission to recently approve a venture among Sprint, France Télécom and Deutsche Telekom to establish a global telecommunications service.

GERMANY'S NEW TELECOMMUNICATIONS LAW

In 1995, the Ministry of Telecommunications presented a draft of a new telecommunications law to provide liberalization of a type comparable to the Telecommunications Act of 1996 in the United States. Basically, this new legislation will fully liberalize and open to competition the current network and voice services monopolies, both interexchange and local exchange. There will be no restrictions on the number of licensees who may compete with Deutsche Telekom nor will there be any restrictions on service areas. The only limitation in this expansive legislation is spectrum availability. Those applying to provide alternative network services (such as personal communications services) need only establish their capability, their expertise and their reliability for the operation of telecommunications services. This legislation, if enacted as drafted, will require that Deutsche Telekom provide non-discriminatory access to services and facilities for the cost of efficient provision of those services. In addition, a regulatory authority, similar to the Federal Communications Commission, will be established to regulate and supervise the telecommunications activities of licensees in Germany. This new agency will have authority to impose universal service obligations for telecommunications services on market-dominant operators if market demands are not met and a tender for such services by the regulatory authority is unsuccessful.

Further, in an effort to avoid litigation and administrative delays such as those which have occurred in the United States based on pole attachments and rights-of-way, legislation has been enacted which mandates that the provision of telecommunications services on public streets and rights-of-way shall be free of charge. There has been much objection to this proposal. For example, municipal authorities have argued that there should be a fee comparable to the fees paid by utility companies for the use of public streets. How this issue will be resolved is still uncertain.

Regardless, it is anticipated that the new telecommunications law will be passed by Parliament in the second half of 1996. Immediately upon enactment of this law, all aspects of the German telecommunications marketplace will be fully competitive except for the voice service monopoly (local exchange and interexchange). However, effective January 1, 1998, opportunities will be granted to entities seeking to compete for the voice service business.

CONCLUSION

While the German reform program is not quite as ambitious as the Telecommunications Act of 1996 in the U.S., and while the current state of regulation governing services such as broadcast television, cable and wireless may not be as liberalized as the parallel U.S. markets, Germany is nonetheless undergoing a transition that will open up competitive opportunities in telephony for both German and foreign businesses. Providing these opportunities is critical to the development of effective and innovative telephony networks in Germany. Such networks are, in turn, vital to the development of Germany's economy.

Chapter 8

Global Communications — The Need for a Framework of Ordering Principles

By Dr. Klaus W. Grewlich

As the world becomes more interdependent and interconnected, largely through new communications technologies and services, national and particularly international communications policy rise in importance. At the national and regional level, considerable progress has been achieved toward the admirable goals of privatization, effective competition, and at least partial liberalization of regulatory regimes. The United States' Telecommunications Act of 1996 is a good example of achieving such progress without sacrificing the important social goals of universal telephone service and national security. Germany, after privatizing Deutsche Telekom last year, is likewise preparing to enact its new Telecommunications Law which will lead to full liberalization of alternative infrastructures. Policymakers in many other countries are also preparing their communications agenda for the new era, as are such organizations as the European Union.

These national and regional efforts are important but by no means sufficient to realize the tremendous potential of modern communications. Global policy and legal framework conditions, *i.e.* international ordering principles, are needed to enhance the opportunities of global communications for economic growth, development, employment and cultural exchange, and for keeping potential conflicts under control.

This chapter discusses the current state of technology and competition in the global communications marketplace and proposes a framework of ordering principles by which nations and companies may maximize the potential of telecommunications.

PACE AND GEOGRAPHIC SCOPE OF NEW TECHNOLOGIES

The communications industry is on the threshold of enormous changes. The monopolistic telecommunications structures which date back to around the turn of the century are disappearing, and the monopolists themselves are converging with data processing, publishing, film and television to form massive multimedia conglomerates, the economic and cultural significance of which can at present only be roughly identified. In the current pioneering phase, companies from separate business sectors are trying to enter into this mega-market in accordance with their specific interests and strategies - some through predatory competition and some through strategically-placed cooperation.

Both competition and strategic cooperation are receiving an important stimulus from public policy discussion which has grown up around the catchwords "information society," "multimedia," "data highways" and "global supernetworks." This discussion is now being conducted at the highest political levels, but it is difficult to escape the conclusion that technological innovation and business innovation have outpaced the regulatory and socio-political evolution — at least in theory. Consumer and media expectations for the future "information superhighway" have even outpaced the tremendous surges in technology.

After several failed attempts to realize the future in communications immediately, as evidenced by certain interactive video trials and languishing mergers, some reasons surfaced why it is not so easy to translate the potential benefits into a credible business case. Some of these reasons are regulatory in nature, but there may also have been some sobering messages coming from equipment providers and technical experts that the needed technology has not yet been developed at the right prices. It is true that transmission has doubled in cost/performance roughly every two years and that processing and storage technologies have doubled their cost/performance roughly every three years; but display technology, for instance, has advanced at a slower pace, intelligence in networks is only at its beginning, and increased user control over service functions is still in the research and development stage.

Business awareness of these trends and opportunities is still lower in Europe compared to the U.S. — largely because of the availability of new technologies and because of consumer exposure and demand. For example, in the U.S., more than 60 percent of households are tapped by cable TV systems which are also capable of carrying text and data services. In Europe, only 25 percent are similarly equipped and this figure masks great differences between countries. The penetration in Belgium is 92 percent, and in Greece it is only two percent, at most. As another example, in the U.S. there are 34 personal computers (PCs) per hundred citizens. The European figure overall is ten PCs per hundred, though in the United Kingdom the 22 PCs per hundred is closer to the U.S. level of penetration.

Thus, although the promise of telecommunications is enormous, and large players in the industry are preparing to compete or cooperate, additional advances in technology are required to fully realize the media hype. Furthermore, to foster an environment in which these global networks and strategies may thrive throughout the world, these new technologies must be introduced at reasonable costs to those countries which are lagging.

COMPETITION AND COOPERATION IN COMMUNICATIONS

Competition is toughening in the various sectors of the communications industry. Data processing, equipment manufacturing, software production and the media have all been opened up to the "invisible hand" of competition as an innovation agent over the past century. Today, the telecommunications companies, whose core business has been the nationwide provision of identical services at affordable and universal tariffs to all subscribers, must now in an increasingly liberalized environment face new rivals on home territory and abroad.

There are at least seven different types of players in the various business segments of the communications industry: (1) telecommunications companies (either "niche enterprises" offering a specialized range of services, regional operators or "global players"); (2) manufacturers of information and communications sytems; (3) mobile communications companies; (4) television, cable and satellite program distribution companies; (5) radio and television broadcasters; (6) publishers and film producers; and (7) railway and energy companies which are emerging as innovative users of communications networks.

These players will not just be present as individual competitors. Alliances have begun to be formed, and will continue, initially in response to diverse customer requirements, and thereafter in response to business and technological pressures. However, competition in certain areas and cooperation in others will not be ruled out. For example, international satellite ventures include entities which directly compete with each other in providing cellular, cable or other services. The aphorism of the future is "compete *and* cooperate."

Competition and Cooperation Between Enterprises

Experience shows indeed that companies that fiercely compete with each other in one area, may cooperate in another. Some of the pioneers of this dynamic approach explain the basic idea as "having situational alliances and no enemies." This could well be a new form of diplomacy. Alliances may be horizontal (*e.g.*, between two or three communications companies) or vertical (*e.g.*, telecommunications companies with publishers or film producers). Examples of such alliances are, for instance, Deutsche Telekom and AT&T having formed, together with the Netherlands PTT Telecom, a joint venture in the Ukraine — while all three compete at the same time to provide large multinational corporations with seamless interoffice services. Another example is the joint venture known as "Atlas" between Deutsche Telekom and France Telecom (which is now part of a wider scheme with Sprint under the name "Global One"). See Figures 10, 11 and 12 for charts depicting the three largest global alliances. Yet, Deutsche Telekom and France Telecom continue to compete, most recently in the privatization process for the telephone system of the Czech Republic.

The recent wave of mergers and alliances has created an interesting challenge for antitrust authorities, which must weigh the consequence of these ventures on competition in deciding whether or not to allow them to go through. In fact, given the rapid pace of change in the telecommunications industry, the authorization process itself is perceived to have become an important factor for competition. This has been seen where certain competitors have tried to expedite their own global alliances while trying to slow down the clearance process for rival alliances.

On the other hand, telecommunications companies have to work together, not only in order to be globally present but also to optimize access to networks. Interconnectivity and interoperability, open network provisions, standardization and guarantee of quality are not "God given" but the result of voluntaristic cooperative attitudes.

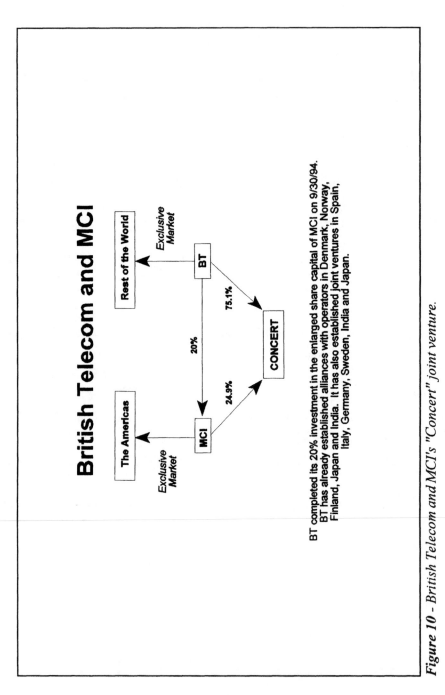

Figure 10 - British Telecom and MCI's "Concert" joint venture.

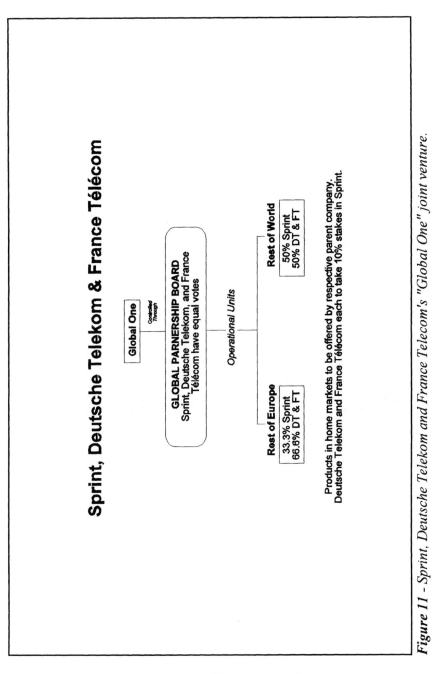

Figure 11 - Sprint, Deutsche Telekom and France Telecom's "Global One" joint venture.

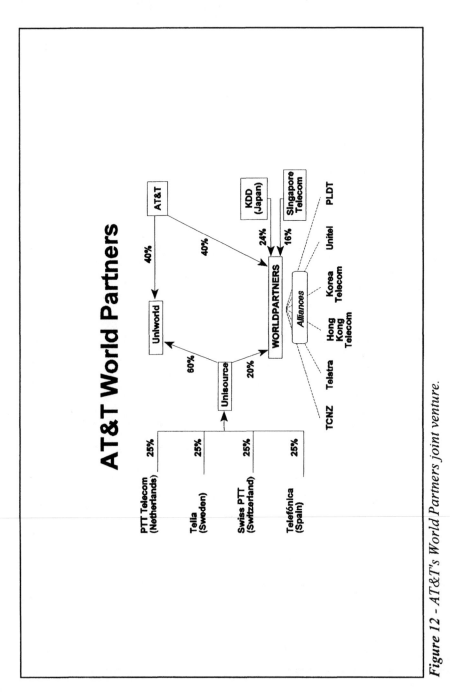

Figure 12 - AT&T's World Partners joint venture.

Competition and Cooperation Between Countries and Regions

The convergence of the telecommunications, computing and entertainment industries has created a technological revolution, which has not gone unnoticed by politicians. Indeed, the information revolution opens new vistas of opportunity which — if promoted in the right way — may do for national economies what Kennedy's "man on the moon" program did for the aerospace industry in the 1960s. Each country wants, of course, to reap the benefits of the global information infrastructure, multimedia and global communications.

Thus, in an effort to attract investment and create new jobs in high tech industries, governments are perceived to be implementing a judicious mix of some "seed money," market liberalization, deregulation and regulation, competition policy, direct investment and proactive trade policy (sometimes called "advocacy"). Some observers, however, criticize that this pragmatic approach to policy has led to a regrettable loss of "fundamental ordering principles."

We are confronted with various national initiatives and responses to new economic challenges. One of the political visions of the Clinton Administration in the U.S. is the creation of a "National Information Infrastructure." Vice President Al Gore has carried the idea of information superhighways one step further in calling for a "Global Information Infrastructure." By making it possible for Americans to access a wide range of multimedia applications, including easy-to-use computer links to libraries, databases, museums and electronic mailboxes, and for education and health applications, the "GII" initiative seeks, like similar schemes in Europe, to create a new culture of communication for consumers, with direct benefits for industry.

The American and the European consumer electronics industry view multimedia as an opportunity to regain ground which was lost to the Japanese microelectronics industry during the 1980s. But Japan has not been an idle bystander. The Japanese Ministry of Post and Telecommunications released a report in May 1994 entitled "Reforms toward the Intellectually Creative Society of the 21st Century." This informative study calls for the creation of a high tech cable network by the year 2010, and predicts the addition of 2.5 million new jobs in the telecommunications industry. The Japanese communications giant NTT seems determined to build most of this Japanese Superhighway while at the same time — as regulation allows — preparing for partnerships and alliances for providing seamless services to global customers.

Europe, too, has recognized the benefits of cultivating an "information society." The European Union's White Paper of December 1993 and the so-called "Bangemann Report" both support the creation of trans-European telecommunications networks. As in the United States, the EU believes that it is primarily the private sector's responsibility to make the necessary investments. The government's role is to provide the right policy framework in which innovation is rewarded.

The Bangemann Report had reached the following conclusions:

- financing the prerequisites for an information society is a task for the private sector;

- the private sector will be supported by liberalization and deregulation measures (that means, among other things, removing monopolies, which would then also involve generally relieving telecommunications companies of certain regulatory burdens which are not necessary in a competitive environment);

• the interconnectivity and interoperability of networks must be guaranteed (like the GSM mobile telephone, other terminals should be useable everywhere in Europe and be able to communicate with one another - complete standardization);

• charges should not be higher than in other highly industrialized regions in the world (in order to rule out any competitive disadvantages for the European economy);

• protection of industrial property, data protection and information security must be guaranteed;

• pioneer projects should be encouraged to develop telecommunications-based teaching programs, university and research networks, methods to meet the specific telecommunications needs of medium-sized and small companies, road transport management systems, improved air traffic control, networks for the health sector, *etc.;* and

• pro-active trade policy, *i.e.* guaranteeing all players equal access to the market.

In framing its regulatory policies, the European Union will very likely base its policies on the research work done in the Organization for Economic Cooperation and Development (OECD), which establishes that "tardiness in undertaking regulatory change can have important negative effects on the economy and society at large, can slow the diffusion of new technologies and services, reduce potential economic efficiency gains, and retards new employment and growth opportunities." Many participants in the first G7-conference on the Information Society held in Brussels in

February 1995 echoed the sentiments for engendering competition and encouraging cooperation among countries and regions.

ELEMENTS OF A FRAMEWORK OF ORDERING PRINCIPLES

The world economy now needs answers to some central political questions. First, will the industrialized countries intensify their cooperation to assure that an open, free-market system of world trade, finance, and information is maintained and can be expanded to include rapidly changing industries like communications, thus creating new employment and new wealth? Second, will all countries have the opportunity to become integrated into this liberal, global economic structure?

Described below are some elements of a proposal on policies and ordering principles which would enhance global communications within the free-market system of world trade and keep potential conflicts under control.

Globalization of Basic Communications Needs

The concept of "globalization" - like any plan to devise a single, universally applicable set of competition policies - might prove too simplistic an approach. There are a number of fairly distinct regions or zones in today's world. First, there are the geographic zones characterized by democracy and well-developed market economies - essentially the member countries of the OECD. Second, there are other geographic areas which display rapid economic growth, but may also have less of a competitive marketplace tradition, and, in some cases, may be experiencing political and social turmoil. These "other zones" range from "OECD-plus-counties" to rapidly developing economies such as those in South-East Asia, to nations including those in much of Africa which continue to face a number of serious economic and social challenges. Reconciling these disparate "zones" throughout the world must be addressed and resolved.

Growth in Emerging Economies

The OECD may represent 75 percent of today's telcoms market, but growth will be centered elsewhere, a powerful incentive for ensuring market access. The pro-competitive policies and free-enterprise assumptions which are relevant to the OECD countries or perhaps the strongly growing "OECD-plus-countries" may prove less acceptable or relevant today in other countries. Certainly, policymakers and politicians must continue to ensure the "OECD-plus-countries" embrace - and continue to embrace - free-market and competition philosophies. But greater effort may be needed if these philosophies are to be embraced and implemented by some developing countries. The desire for market access may accelerate this process.

Universal Access

All too many residents of developing countries lack access to even the most basic telephone services today. Our emphasis globally thus must be on encouraging competition and expanding basic networks, not solely deploying computer-communications systems. A wider objective is to avoid divisions between sections of society with access to information and those without, both within a nation and worldwide.

Positive Adjustment Policies

While the essence of wealth-creation in free market economies is competition between commercial enterprises, attention must be paid to the judicious mixtures of industrial, technology, labor and trade policies in an effort to "optimize" a particular government's national policies or visions. Just as competition between enterprises needs a framework, such as antitrust, to make sure that there are no restrictions on competition, "competition between governments" (for jobs and investment) also needs "ordering principles." Otherwise, unnecessary conflicts may arise. These "ordering principles" should comprise notable multilateral trade policy agreements, arrangements on antitrust and notification laws and procedures and direct investment policies.

As to competing technology policies, past attempts have been made to coordinate "structural policies" between countries. As early as 1983, the OECD promoted what it called "positive adjustment policies" to manage the structural transformation of economies. This allowed, under certain conditions, for a strategy of promoting future-oriented critical technologies as "locomotives of economic growth." Eventually, however, as competition develops, promotion of these industries would have to regress, and finally be completely eliminated.

Utilizing the WTO

The World Trade Organization (WTO) provides opportunities to further develop a framework for this economic transition. It is worth noting that when the General Agreement on Trade in Services (GATS) was negotiated, no one really understood the potential of multimedia and of the communications industry for the growth of the global economy.

The problem for increasingly securing free trade in communication services is that in many cases each of these convergent industries - telecommunications, audiovisual, computers etc. - is regulated in a different way and by different people. Another disadvantage for the political objective of a free-market development towards the global information society is that "the Telecommunications Annex" of the GATS does not really encompass multimedia applications. It is thus essential that multimedia services be brought within the GATS, so that liberal trade practices can be established.

The complexity of such an approach is shown by the difficult experience of the WTO negotiating group on basic telecommunications. There seems to be an irresistible penchant on the part of governments to regulate, as telecommunications and information come to be seen as a more and more economically strategic sector. In view of this, some powerful participants in these negotiations feel they have to maintain a higher level of regulation over international communication services than domestic services to preserve "leverage" when dealing with supposedly less pro-market administrations abroad. Others advocate for avoiding the "reciprocity trap," not in terms of "unilateral disarmament," but in terms of accepting leadership that entails taking risks. On balance, it is essential that international communication services should be offered as a full-fledged multilateral package in the spirit of the WTO and the Bretton Woods System.

Basic Rules: Interconnectivity - Privacy - Encryption

Worldwide, governments are increasing their efforts to regulate on-line services, often applying national principles to a global medium. Copyright, libel and pornography are leading targets for regulatory and law enforcement agencies attempting to deal with the "extra-territoriality" of on-line communications. Here it becomes blatant how hopeless it is to regulate territorially a transnational medium. Like in the field of encryption only a concerted cooperative transnational approach can do justice at the same time to the needs of law enforcement, international networks/free enterprise and individual privacy.

The real objective of regulation and deregulation should be the creation of a "level playing field." Once this field is created, regulation should be phased out as much as possible. But even at that stage of deregulation, some basic rules on interconnectivity, interoperability, and standards will be needed. The same applies to privacy, data protection, and information security. Effective protection of intellectual property rights will also be necessary. Thus, governments face a formidable challenge: phasing out regulations as soon as possible to create a level playing field, optimizing competition policies, and making an extremely important communications network function smoothly in a globalizing world. The Telecom Act is an important first step toward realization of these goals.

Direct Investment

Restrictions on direct investment are typically rationalized as essential to safeguard certain core national assets, critical to effective law enforcement and national defense. In the case of broadcast, cable and other electronic mass media, ownership limitations, particularly foreign ownership restrictions, exist in virtually every country in the world. These latter limitations are most often explained as crucial to maintaining national cultural identity and ensuring an informed electorate.

Governments will need to pay much more attention to ensuring a sound and attractive private investment environment. Licensing provides a more transparent tool with less negative side effects than foreign investment restrictions for securing national security and law enforcement.

As explained above, technological advances will continue to pose serious challenges to the ability of relevant agencies to monitor electronic communications. Governments must cooperate where necessary to ensure that global operators' actions are consistent with attaining an open, pro-competitive environment for a Global Information Society.

Competition Policy

As suggested above, the emergence of global alliances in the telecommunications industry has brought existing nationally-oriented antitrust policies to their limits. The problem with competing national policies is that they cannot be isolated in a global economy. National antitrust rules have unavoidable external effects and can distort trade and investment flows.

For instance, there are many who view Japan as a case in point, where a system of close industrial integration goes beyond what would typically be allowed in other OECD countries. The U.S. has recognized the source of the problem in the "structural impediments" debate. But instead of fighting for an internationally accepted and enforced antitrust policy which would further open the Japanese market to competition, the United States has chosen to use trade policy as its chief weapon. Trade policy may bring some short-term bilateral gains, but in this case an international competition policy would be more effective at solving long-term structural problems, while avoiding unnecessary trade wars.

Deciding on the content of an international antitrust or competition policy is a difficult issue. Cooperation in procedures is good but cannot replace an international antitrust policy in terms of certain basically harmonized ordering principles. The WTO would be an excellent forum for developing such a framework for international antitrust rules.

CONCLUSION

We need to be aware that it is no longer possible for one person, organization, country, or region to derive lasting benefits from communications in today's world without the cooperation of others. The international law of the past, intended to define areas of sovereignty of different states, was simply a law of international coexistence. It is increasingly being replaced by a more highly developed law of international (possibly transnational) cooperation.

This more-enlightened law asks countries to cooperate at the bilateral, regional, and global levels in an ever-increasing number of fields. Where this is not possible, it states that, when anyone adopts new measures, the interests of third parties should be taken into account and the negative consequences be minimized. This spirit, which is the very basis of the OECD, GATT/WTO, and other successful international organizations — is vital for more than just trade and environmental policies. It may contribute to matching global technological progress on political, cultural, and even moral levels.

Appendix 1

The Telecommunications Act of 1996

SEC. 1. SHORT TITLE; REFERENCES.

(a)   Short Title.--This Act may be cited as the "Telecommunications Act of 1996".

(b)   References.--Except as otherwise expressly provided, whenever in this Act an amendment or repeal is expressed in terms of an amendment to, or repeal of, a section or other provision, the reference shall be considered to be made to a section or other provision of the Communications Act of 1934 (47 U.S.C. 151 et seq.).

SEC. 2.   TABLE OF CONTENTS.

The table of contents for this Act is as follows:

"Section 714. Telecommunications Development Fund."

Sec. 708. National Education Technology Funding Corporation.

Sec. 709. Report on the use of advanced telecommunications services for medical purposes.

Sec. 710. Authorization of appropriations.

SEC. 3. DEFINITIONS.

(a) Additional Definitions.--Section 3 (47 U.S.C. 153) is amended--

(1) in subsection (r)

(A) by inserting "(A)" after "means"; and

(B) by inserting before the period at the end the following: ", or (B) comparable service provided through a system of switches, transmission equipment, or other facilities (or combination thereof) by which a subscriber can originate and terminate a telecommunications service"; and

(2) by adding at the end thereof the following:

"(33) Affiliate.--The term 'affiliate' means a person that (directly or indirectly) owns or controls, is owned or controlled by, or is under common ownership or control with, another person. For purposes of this paragraph, the term 'own' means to own an equity interest (or the equivalent thereof) of more than 10 percent.

"(34) AT&T consent decree.--The term 'AT&T Consent Decree' means the order entered August 24, 1982, in the antitrust action styled United States v. Western Electric, Civil Action No. 82-0192, in the United States District Court for the District of Columbia, and includes any judgment or order with respect to such action entered on or after August 24, 1982.

"(35) Bell operating company.--The term 'Bell operating company'--

"(A) means any of the following companies: Bell Telephone Company of Nevada, Illinois Bell Telephone Company, Indiana Bell Telephone Company, Incorporated, Michigan Bell Telephone Company, New England Telephone and Telegraph Company, New Jersey Bell Telephone Company, New York Telephone Company, U S West Communications Company, South Central Bell Telephone Company, Southern Bell Telephone and Telegraph Company, Southwestern Bell Telephone Company, The Bell Telephone Company of Pennsylvania, The Chesapeake and Potomac Telephone Company, The Chesapeake and Potomac Telephone Company of Maryland, The Chesapeake and Potomac Telephone Company of Virginia, The Chesapeake and Potomac Telephone Company of West Virginia, The Diamond State Telephone Company, The Ohio Bell Telephone Company, The Pacific Telephone and Telegraph Company, or Wisconsin Telephone Company; and

"(B) includes any successor or assign of any such company that provides wireline telephone exchange service; but

"(C) does not include an affiliate of any such company, other than an affiliate described in subparagraph (A) or (B).

"(36) Cable service.--The term 'cable service' has the meaning given such term in section 602.

"(37) Cable system.--The term 'cable system' has the meaning given such term in section 602.

"(38) Customer premises equipment.--The term 'customer premises equipment' means equipment employed on the premises of a person (other than a carrier) to originate, route, or terminate telecommunications.

"(39) Dialing parity.--The term 'dialing parity' means that a person that is not an affiliate of a local exchange carrier is able to provide telecommunications services in such a manner that customers have the ability to route automatically, without the use of any access code, their telecommunications to the telecommunications services provider of the customer's designation from among 2 or more telecommunications services providers (including such local exchange carrier).

"(40) Exchange access.--The term 'exchange access' means the offering of access to telephone exchange services or facilities for the purpose of the origination or termination of telephone toll services.

"(41) Information service.--The term 'information service' means the offering of a capability for generating, acquiring, storing, transforming, processing, retrieving, utilizing, or making available information via telecommunications, and includes electronic publishing, but does not include any use of any such capability for the management, control, or operation of a telecommunications system or the management of a telecommunications service.

"(42) Interlata service.--The term 'interLATA service' means telecommunications between a point located in a local access and transport area and a point located outside such area.

"(43) Local access and transport area.--The term 'local access and transport area' or 'LATA' means a contiguous geographic area--

"(A) established before the date of enactment of the Telecommunications Act of 1996 by a Bell operating company such that no exchange area includes points within more than 1 metropolitan statistical area, consolidated metropolitan statistical area, or State, except as expressly permitted under the AT&T Consent Decree; or

"(B) established or modified by a Bell operating company after such date of enactment and approved by the Commission.

"(44) Local exchange carrier.--The term 'local exchange carrier' means any person that is engaged in the provision of telephone exchange service or exchange access. Such term does not include a person insofar as such person is engaged in the provision of a commercial mobile service under section 332(c), except to the extent that the Commission finds that such service should be included in the definition of such term.

"(45) Network element.--The term 'network element' means a facility or equipment used in the provision of a telecommunications service. Such term also includes features, functions, and capabilities that are provided by means of such facility or equipment, including subscriber numbers, databases, signaling systems, and information sufficient for billing and collection or used in the transmission, routing, or other provision of a telecommunications service.

"(46) Number portability.--The term 'number portability' means the ability of users of telecommunications services to retain, at the same location, existing telecommunications numbers without impairment of quality, reliability, or convenience when switching from one telecommunications carrier to another.

"(47) Rural telephone company.--The term 'rural telephone company' means a local exchange carrier operating entity to the extent that such entity--

"(A) provides common carrier service to any local exchange carrier study area that does not include either--

"(i) any incorporated place of 10,000 inhabitants or more, or any part thereof, based on the most recently available population statistics of the Bureau of the Census; or

"(ii) any territory, incorporated or unincorporated, included in an urbanized area, as defined by the Bureau of the Census as of August 10, 1993;

"(B) provides telephone exchange service, including exchange access, to fewer than 50,000 access lines;

"(C) provides telephone exchange service to any local exchange carrier study area with fewer than 100,000 access lines; or

"(D) has less than 15 percent of its access lines in communities of more than 50,000 on the date of enactment of the Telecommunications Act of 1996.

"(48) Telecommunications.--The term 'telecommunications' means the transmission, between or among points specified by the user, of information of the user's choosing, without change in the form or content of the information as sent and received.

"(49) Telecommunications carrier.--The term 'telecommunications carrier' means any provider of telecommunications services, except that such term does not include aggregators of telecommunications services (as defined in section 226). A telecommunications carrier shall be treated as a common carrier under this Act only to the extent that it is engaged in providing telecommunications services, except that the

Commission shall determine whether the provision of fixed and mobile satellite service shall be treated as common carriage.

"(50) Telecommunications equipment.--The term 'telecommunications equipment' means equipment, other than customer premises equipment, used by a carrier to provide telecommunications services, and includes software integral to such equipment (including upgrades).

"(51) Telecommunications service.--The term 'telecommunications service' means the offering of telecommunications for a fee directly to the public, or to such classes of users as to be effectively available directly to the public, regardless of the facilities used."

(b) Common Terminology.--Except as otherwise provided in this Act, the terms used in this Act have the meanings provided in section 3 of the Communications Act of 1934 (47 U.S.C. 153), as amended by this section.

(c) Stylistic Consistency.--Section 3 (47 U.S.C. 153) is amended--

(1) in subsections (e) and (n), by redesignating clauses (1), (2) and (3), as clauses (A), (B), and (C), respectively;

(2) in subsection (w), by redesignating paragraphs (1) through (5) as subparagraphs (A) through (E), respectively;

(3) in subsections (y) and (z), by redesignating paragraphs (1) and (2) as subparagraphs (A) and (B), respectively;

(4) by redesignating subsections (a) through (ff) as paragraphs (1) through (32);

(5) by indenting such paragraphs 2 em spaces;

(6) by inserting after the designation of each such paragraph--

(A) a heading, in a form consistent with the form of the heading of this subsection, consisting of the term defined by such paragraph, or the first term so defined if such paragraph defines more than one term; and

(B) the words "The term";

(7) by changing the first letter of each defined term in such paragraphs from a capital to a lower case letter (except for "United States", "State", "State commission", and "Great Lakes Agreement"); and

(8) by reordering such paragraphs and the additional paragraphs added by subsection (a) in alphabetical order based on the headings of such paragraphs and renumbering such paragraphs as so reordered.

(d) Conforming Amendments.--The Act is amended--

(1) in section 225(a)(1), by striking "section 3(h)" and inserting "section 3";

(2) in section 332(d), by striking "section 3(n)" each place it appears and inserting "section 3"; and

(3) in sections 621(d)(3), 636(d), and 637(a)(2), by striking "section 3(v)" and inserting "section 3".

TITLE I–TELECOMMUNICATION SERVICES

Subtitle A–Telecommunications Services

SEC. 101. ESTABLISHMENT OF PART II OF TITLE II.

(a) Amendment.--Title II is amended by inserting after section 229 (47 U.S.C. 229) the following new part:

"PART II--DEVELOPMENT OF COMPETITIVE MARKETS

"Section 251. INTERCONNECTION.

"(a) General Duty of Telecommunications Carriers.--Each telecommunications carrier has the duty--

"(1) to interconnect directly or indirectly with the facilities and equipment of other telecommunications carriers; and

"(2) not to install network features, functions, or capabilities that do not comply with the guidelines and standards established pursuant to section 255 or 256.

"(b) Obligations of All Local Exchange Carriers.--Each local exchange carrier has the following duties:

"(1) Resale.--The duty not to prohibit, and not to impose unreasonable or discriminatory conditions or limitations on, the resale of its telecommunications services.

"(2) Number portability.--The duty to provide, to the extent technically feasible, number portability in accordance with requirements prescribed by the Commission.

"(3) Dialing parity.--The duty to provide dialing parity to competing providers of telephone exchange service and telephone toll service, and the duty to permit all such providers to have nondiscriminatory access to telephone numbers, operator services, directory assistance, and directory listing, with no unreasonable dialing delays.

"(4) Access to rights-of-way.--The duty to afford access to the poles, ducts, conduits, and rights-of-way of such carrier to competing providers of telecommunications services on rates, terms, and conditions that are consistent with section 224.

"(5) Reciprocal compensation.--The duty to establish reciprocal compensation arrangements for the transport and termination of telecommunications.

"(c) Additional Obligations of Incumbent Local Exchange Carriers.--In addition to the duties contained in subsection (b), each incumbent local exchange carrier has the following duties:

"(1) Duty to negotiate.--The duty to negotiate in good faith in accordance with section 252 the particular terms and conditions of agreements to fulfill the duties described in paragraphs (1) through (5) of subsection (b) and this subsection. The requesting telecommunications carrier also has the duty to negotiate in good faith the terms and conditions of such agreements.

"(2) Interconnection.--The duty to provide, for the facilities and equipment of any requesting telecommunications carrier, interconnection with the local exchange carrier's network--

"(A) for the transmission and routing of telephone exchange service and exchange access;

"(B) at any technically feasible point within the carrier's network;

"(C) that is at least equal in quality to that provided by the local exchange carrier to itself or to any subsidiary, affiliate, or any other party to which the carrier provides interconnection; and

"(D) on rates, terms, and conditions that are just, reasonable, and nondiscriminatory, in accordance with the terms and conditions of the agreement and the requirements of this section and section 252.

"(3) Unbundled access.--The duty to provide, to any requesting telecommunications carrier for the provision of a telecommunications service, nondiscriminatory access to network elements on an unbundled basis at any technically feasible point on rates, terms, and conditions that are just, reasonable, and nondiscriminatory in accordance with the terms and conditions of the agreement and the requirements of this section and section 252. An incumbent local exchange carrier shall provide such unbundled network elements in a manner that allows requesting carriers to combine such elements in order to provide such telecommunications service.

"(4) Resale.--The duty--

"(A) to offer for resale at wholesale rates any telecommunications service that the carrier provides at retail to subscribers who are not telecommunications carriers; and

"(B) not to prohibit, and not to impose unreasonable or discriminatory conditions or limitations on, the resale of such telecommunications service, except that a State commission may, consistent with regulations prescribed by the Commission under this section, prohibit a reseller that obtains at wholesale rates a telecommunications service that is available at retail only to a category of subscribers from offering such service to a different category of subscribers.

"(5) Notice of changes.--The duty to provide reasonable public notice of changes in the information necessary for the transmission and routing of services using that local exchange carrier's facilities or networks, as well as of any other changes that would affect the interoperability of those facilities and networks.

"(6) Collocation.--The duty to provide, on rates, terms, and conditions that are just, reasonable, and nondiscriminatory, for physical collocation of equipment necessary for interconnection or access to unbundled network elements at the premises of the local exchange carrier, except that the carrier may provide for virtual collocation if the local exchange carrier demonstrates to the State commission that physical collocation is not practical for technical reasons or because of space limitations.

"(d) Implementation.--

"(1)   In general.--Within 6 months after the date of enactment of the Telecommunications Act of 1996, the Commission shall complete all actions necessary to establish regulations to implement the requirements of this section.

"(2) Access standards.--In determining what network elements should be made available for purposes of subsection (c)(3), the Commission shall consider, at a minimum, whether--

"(A) access to such network elements as are proprietary in nature is necessary; and

"(B) the failure to provide access to such network elements would impair the ability of the telecommunications carrier seeking access to provide the services that it seeks to offer.

"(3)   Preservation of state access regulations.--In prescribing and enforcing regulations to implement the requirements of this section, the Commission shall not preclude the enforcement of any regulation, order, or policy of a State commission that--

"(A)   establishes access and interconnection obligations of local exchange carriers;

"(B) is consistent with the requirements of this section; and

"(C) does not substantially prevent implementation of the requirements of this section and the purposes of this part.

"(e) Numbering Administration.--

"(1) Commission authority and jurisdiction.--The Commission shall create or designate one or more impartial entities to administer telecommunications numbering and to make such numbers available on an equitable basis. The Commission shall have exclusive jurisdiction over those portions of the North American Numbering Plan that pertain to the United States. Nothing in this paragraph shall preclude the Commission from delegating to State commissions or other entities all or any portion of such jurisdiction.

"(2)   Costs.--The cost of establishing telecommunications numbering administration arrangements and number portability shall be borne by all telecommunications carriers on a competitively neutral basis as determined by the Commission.

"(f) Exemptions, Suspensions, and Modifications.--

"(1) Exemption for certain rural telephone companies.--

"(A) Exemption.--Subsection (c) of this section shall not apply to a rural telephone company until

"(i)   such company has received a bona fide request for interconnection, services, or network elements, and

"(ii) the State commission determines (under subparagraph (B)) that such request is not unduly economically burdensome, is technically feasible, and is consistent with section 254 (other than subsections (b)(7) and (c)(1)(D) thereof).

"(B) State termination of exemption and implementation schedule.--The party making a bona fide request of a rural telephone company for interconnection, services, or network elements shall submit a notice of its request to the State commission. The State commission shall conduct an inquiry for the purpose of determining whether to terminate the exemption under subparagraph (A). Within 120 days after the State commission receives notice of the request, the State commission shall terminate the exemption if the request is not unduly economically burdensome, is technically feasible, and is consistent with section 254 (other than subsections (b)(7) and (c)(1)(D) thereof). Upon termination of the exemption, a State commission shall establish an implementation schedule for compliance with the request that is consistent in time and manner with Commission regulations.

"(C) Limitation on exemption.--The exemption provided by this paragraph shall not apply with respect to a request under subsection (c) from a cable operator providing video programming, and seeking to provide any telecommunications service, in the area in which the rural telephone company provides video programming. The limitation contained in this subparagraph shall not apply to a rural telephone company that is providing video programming on the date of enactment of the Telecommunications Act of 1996.

"(2) Suspensions and modifications for rural carriers.--A local exchange carrier with fewer than 2 percent of the Nation's subscriber lines installed in the aggregate nationwide may petition a State commission for a suspension or modification of the application of a requirement or requirements of subsection (b) or (c) to telephone exchange service facilities specified in such petition. The State commission shall grant such petition to the extent that, and for such duration as, the State commission determines that such suspension or modification--

"(A) is necessary--

"(i)   to avoid a significant adverse economic impact on users of telecommunications services generally;

"(ii)   to avoid imposing a requirement that is unduly economically burdensome; or

"(iii)   to avoid imposing a requirement that is technically infeasible; and

"(B) is consistent with the public interest, convenience, and necessity.

The State commission shall act upon any petition filed under this paragraph within 180 days after receiving such petition. Pending such action, the State commission may suspend enforcement of the requirement or requirements to which the petition applies with respect to the petitioning carrier or carriers.

"(g) Continued Enforcement of Exchange Access and Interconnection Requirements.--On and after the date of enactment of the Telecommunications Act of 1996, each local exchange carrier, to the extent that it provides wireline services, shall provide exchange access, information access, and exchange services for such access to interexchange carriers and information service providers in accordance with the same equal access and nondiscriminatory interconnection restrictions and obligations (including receipt of compensation) that apply to such carrier on the date immediately preceding the date of enactment of the Telecommunications Act of 1996 under any court order, consent decree, or regulation, order, or policy of the Commission, until such restrictions and obligations are explicitly superseded by regulations prescribed by the Commission after such date of enactment. During the period beginning on such date of enactment and until such restrictions and obligations are so superseded, such restrictions and obligations shall be enforceable in the same manner as regulations of the Commission.

"(h) Definition of Incumbent Local Exchange Carrier.--

"(1) Definition.--For purposes of this section, the term 'incumbent local exchange carrier' means, with respect to an area, the local exchange carrier that--

"(A) on the date of enactment of the Telecommunications Act of 1996, provided telephone exchange service in such area; and

"(B)(i) on such date of enactment, was deemed to be a member of the exchange carrier association pursuant to section 69.601(b) of the Commission's regulations (47 CFR 69.601(b)); or

"(ii) is a person or entity that, on or after such date of enactment, became a successor or assign of a member described in clause (i).

"(2) Treatment of comparable carriers as incumbents.--The Commission may, by rule, provide for the treatment of a local exchange carrier (or class or category thereof) as an incumbent local exchange carrier for purposes of this section if--

"(A) such carrier occupies a position in the market for telephone exchange service within an area that is comparable to the position occupied by a carrier described in paragraph (1);

"(B) such carrier has substantially replaced an incumbent local exchange carrier described in paragraph (1); and

"(C) such treatment is consistent with the public interest, convenience, and necessity and the purposes of this section.

"(i) Savings Provision.--Nothing in this section shall be construed to limit or otherwise affect the Commission's authority under section 201.

"Section 252. PROCEDURES FOR NEGOTIATION, ARBITRATION, AND APPROVAL OF AGREEMENTS.

"(a) Agreements Arrived at Through Negotiation.--

"(1) Voluntary negotiations.--Upon receiving a request for interconnection, services, or network elements pursuant to section 251, an incumbent local exchange carrier may negotiate and enter into a binding agreement with the requesting telecommunications carrier or carriers without regard to the standards set forth in subsections (b) and (c) of section 251. The agreement shall include a detailed schedule of itemized charges for interconnection and each service or network element included in the agreement. The agreement, including any interconnection agreement negotiated before the date of enactment of the Telecommunications Act of 1996, shall be submitted to the State commission under subsection (e) of this section.

"(2) Mediation.--Any party negotiating an agreement under this section may, at any point in the negotiation, ask a State commission to participate in the negotiation and to mediate any differences arising in the course of the negotiation.

"(b) Agreements Arrived at Through Compulsory Arbitration.--

"(1) arbitration.--During the period from the 135th to the 160th day (inclusive) after the date on which an incumbent local exchange carrier receives a request for negotiation under this section, the carrier or any other party to the negotiation may petition a State commission to arbitrate any open issues.

"(2) Duty of petitioner.--

"(A) A party that petitions a State commission under paragraph (1) shall, at the same time as it submits the petition, provide the State commission all relevant documentation concerning--

"(i) the unresolved issues;

"(ii) the position of each of the parties with respect to those issues; and

"(iii) any other issue discussed and resolved by the parties.

"(B) A party petitioning a State commission under paragraph (1) shall provide a copy of the petition and any documentation to the other party or parties not later than the day on which the State commission receives the petition.

"(3) Opportunity to respond.--A non-petitioning party to a negotiation under this section may respond to the other party's petition and provide such additional information as it wishes within 25 days after the State commission receives the petition.

"(4) Action by state commission.--

"(A) The State commission shall limit its consideration of any petition under paragraph (1) (and any response thereto) to the issues set forth in the petition and in the response, if any, filed under paragraph (3).

"(B) The State commission may require the petitioning party and the responding party to provide such information as may be necessary for the State commission to reach a decision on the unresolved issues. If any party refuses or fails unreasonably to respond on a timely basis to any reasonable request from the State commission, then the State commission may proceed on the basis of the best information available to it from whatever source derived.

"(C) The State commission shall resolve each issue set forth in the petition and the response, if any, by imposing appropriate conditions as required to implement subsection (c) upon the parties to the agreement, and shall conclude the resolution of any unresolved issues not later than 9 months after the date on which the local exchange carrier received the request under this section.

"(5) Refusal to negotiate.--The refusal of any other party to the negotiation to participate further in the negotiations, to cooperate with the State commission in carrying out its function as an arbitrator, or to continue to negotiate in good faith in the presence, or with the assistance, of the State commission shall be considered a failure to negotiate in good faith.

"(c) Standards for Arbitration.--In resolving by arbitration under subsection (b) any open issues and imposing conditions upon the parties to the agreement, a State commission shall--

"(1) ensure that such resolution and conditions meet the requirements of section 251, including the regulations prescribed by the Commission pursuant to section 251;

"(2) establish any rates for interconnection, services, or network elements according to subsection (d); and

"(3) provide a schedule for implementation of the terms and conditions by the parties to the agreement.

"(d) Pricing Standards.--

"(1) Interconnection and network element charges.--Determinations by a State commission of the just and reasonable rate for the interconnection of facilities and equipment for purposes of subsection (c)(2) of section 251, and the just and reasonable rate for network elements for purposes of subsection (c)(3) of such section--

"(A) shall be--

"(i) based on the cost (determined without reference to a rate-of-return or other rate-based proceeding) of providing the interconnection or network element (whichever is applicable), and

"(ii) nondiscriminatory, and

"(B) may include a reasonable profit.

"(2) Charges for transport and termination of traffic.--

"(A) In general.--For the purposes of compliance by an incumbent local exchange carrier with section 251(b)(5), a State commission shall not consider the terms and conditions for reciprocal compensation to be just and reasonable unless--

"(i) such terms and conditions provide for the mutual and reciprocal recovery by each carrier of costs associated with the transport and termination on each carrier's network facilities of calls that originate on the network facilities of the other carrier; and

"(ii) such terms and conditions determine such costs on the basis of a reasonable approximation of the additional costs of terminating such calls.

"(B) Rules of construction.--This paragraph shall not be construed--

"(i) to preclude arrangements that afford the mutual recovery of costs through the offsetting of reciprocal obligations, including arrangements that waive mutual recovery (such as bill-and-keep arrangements); or

"(ii) to authorize the Commission or any State commission to engage in any rate regulation proceeding to establish with particularity the additional costs of transporting or terminating calls, or to require carriers to maintain records with respect to the additional costs of such calls.

"(3) Wholesale prices for telecommunications services.--For the purposes of section 251(c)(4), a State commission shall determine wholesale rates on the basis of retail rates charged to subscribers for the telecommunications service requested, excluding the portion thereof attributable to any marketing, billing, collection, and other costs that will be avoided by the local exchange carrier.

"(e) Approval by State Commission.--

"(1) Approval required.--Any interconnection agreement adopted by negotiation or arbitration shall be submitted for approval to the State commission. A State commission to which an agreement is submitted shall approve or reject the agreement, with written findings as to any deficiencies.

"(2) Grounds for rejection.--The State commission may only reject--

"(A) an agreement (or any portion thereof) adopted by negotiation under subsection (a) if it finds that--

"(i) the agreement (or portion thereof) discriminates against a telecommunications carrier not a party to the agreement; or

"(ii) the implementation of such agreement or portion is not consistent with the public interest, convenience, and necessity; or

"(B) an agreement (or any portion thereof) adopted by arbitration under subsection (b) if it finds that the agreement does not meet the requirements of section 251, including the regulations prescribed by the Commission pursuant to section 251, or the standards set forth in subsection (d) of this section.

"(3) Preservation of authority.--Notwithstanding paragraph (2), but subject to section 253, nothing in this section shall prohibit a State commission from establishing or enforcing other requirements of State law in its review of an agreement, including requiring compliance with intrastate telecommunications service quality standards or requirements.

"(4) Schedule for decision.--If the State commission does not act to approve or reject the agreement within 90 days after submission by the parties of an agreement adopted by negotiation under subsection (a), or within 30 days after submission by the parties of an agreement adopted by arbitration under subsection (b), the agreement shall be deemed approved. No State court shall have jurisdiction to review the action of a State commission in approving or rejecting an agreement under this section.

"(5) Commission to act if state will not act.--If a State commission fails to act to carry out its responsibility under this section in any proceeding or other matter under this section, then the Commission shall issue an order preempting the State commission's jurisdiction of that proceeding or matter within 90 days after being notified (or taking notice) of such failure, and shall assume the responsibility of the State commission under this section with respect to the proceeding or matter and act for the State commission.

"(6) Review of state commission actions.--In a case in which a State fails to act as described in paragraph (5), the proceeding by the Commission under such paragraph and any judicial review of the Commission's actions shall be the exclusive remedies for a State commission's failure to act. In any case in which a State commission makes a determination under this section, any party aggrieved by such determination may bring an action in an appropriate Federal district court to determine whether the agreement or statement meets the requirements of section 251 and this section.

"(f) Statements of Generally Available Terms.--

"(1) In general.--A Bell operating company may prepare and file with a State commission a statement of the terms and conditions that such company generally offers within that State to comply with the requirements of section 251 and the regulations thereunder and the standards applicable under this section.

"(2) State commission review.--A State commission may not approve such statement unless such statement complies with subsection (d) of this section and section 251 and the regulations thereunder. Except as provided in section 253, nothing in this section shall prohibit a State commission from establishing or enforcing other requirements of State law in its review of such statement, including requiring compliance with intrastate telecommunications service quality standards or requirements.

"(3) Schedule for review.--The State commission to which a statement is submitted shall, not later than 60 days after the date of such submission--

"(A) complete the review of such statement under paragraph (2) (including any reconsideration thereof), unless the submitting carrier agrees to an extension of the period for such review; or

"(B) permit such statement to take effect.

"(4) Authority to continue review.--Paragraph (3) shall not preclude the State commission from continuing to review a statement that has been permitted to take effect under subparagraph (B) of such paragraph or from approving or disapproving such statement under paragraph (2).

"(5) Duty to negotiate not affected.--The submission or approval of a statement under this subsection shall not relieve a Bell operating company of its duty to negotiate the terms and conditions of an agreement under section 251.

"(g) Consolidation of State Proceedings.--Where not inconsistent with the requirements of this Act, a State commission may, to the extent practical, consolidate proceedings under sections 214(e), 251(f), 253, and this section in order to reduce administrative burdens on telecommunications carriers, other parties to the proceedings, and the State commission in carrying out its responsibilities under this Act.

"(h) Filing Required.--A State commission shall make a copy of each agreement approved under subsection (e) and each statement approved under subsection (f) available for public inspection and copying within 10 days after the agreement or statement is approved. The State commission may charge a reasonable and nondiscriminatory fee to the parties to the agreement or to the party filing the statement to cover the costs of approving and filing such agreement or statement.

"(i) Availability to Other Telecommunications Carriers.--A local exchange carrier shall make available any interconnection, service, or network element provided under an agreement approved under this section to which it is a party to any other requesting telecommunications carrier upon the same terms and conditions as those provided in the agreement.

"(j) Definition of Incumbent Local Exchange Carrier.--For purposes of this section, the term 'incumbent local exchange carrier' has the meaning provided in section 251(h).

"Section 253. REMOVAL OF BARRIERS TO ENTRY.

"(a) In General.--No State or local statute or regulation, or other State or local legal requirement, may prohibit or have the effect of prohibiting the ability of any entity to provide any interstate or intrastate telecommunications service.

"(b) State Regulatory Authority.--Nothing in this section shall affect the ability of a State to impose, on a competitively neutral basis and consistent with section 254, requirements necessary to preserve and advance universal service, protect the public safety and welfare, ensure the continued quality of telecommunications services, and safeguard the rights of consumers.

"(c)   State and Local Government Authority.--Nothing in this section affects the authority of a State or local government to manage the public rights-of way or to require fair and reasonable compensation from telecommunications providers, on a competitively neutral and nondiscriminatory basis, for use of public rights-of-way on a nondiscriminatory basis, if the compensation required is publicly disclosed by such government.

"(d)   Preemption.--If, after notice and an opportunity for public comment, the Commission determines that a State or local government has permitted or imposed any statute, regulation, or legal requirement that violates subsection (a) or (b), the Commission shall preempt the enforcement of such statute, regulation, or legal requirement to the extent necessary to correct such violation or inconsistency.

"(e)   Commercial mobile service providers.--Nothing in this section shall affect the application of section 332(c)(3) to commercial mobile service providers.

"(f)   Rural Markets.--It shall not be a violation of this section for a State to require a telecommunications carrier that seeks to provide telephone exchange service or exchange access in a service area served by a rural telephone company to meet the requirements in section 214(e)(1) for designation as an eligible telecommunications carrier for that area before being permitted to provide such service. This subsection shall not apply--

"(1)   to a service area served by a rural telephone company that has obtained an exemption, suspension, or modification of section 251(c)(4) that effectively prevents a competitor from meeting the requirements of section 214(e)(1); and

"(2)   to a provider of commercial mobile services.

"Section 254.   UNIVERSAL SERVICE.

"(a)   Procedures to Review Universal Service Requirements.--

"(1)   Federal-state joint board on universal service.--Within one month after the date of enactment of the Telecommunications Act of 1996, the Commission shall institute and refer to a Federal-State Joint Board under section 410(c) a proceeding to recommend changes to any of its regulations in order to implement sections 214(e) and this section, including the definition of the services that are supported by Federal universal service support mechanisms and a specific timetable for completion of such recommendations. In addition to the members of the Joint Board required under section 410(c), one member of such Joint Board shall be a State-appointed utility consumer advocate nominated by a national organization of State utility consumer advocates. The Joint Board shall, after notice and opportunity for public comment, make its recommendations to the Commission 9 months after the date of enactment of the Telecommunications Act of 1996.

"(2) Commission action.--The Commission shall initiate a single proceeding to implement the recommendations from the Joint Board required by paragraph (1) and shall complete such proceeding within 15 months after the date of enactment of the Telecommunications Act of 1996. The rules established by such proceeding shall include a definition of the services that are supported by Federal universal service support mechanisms and a specific timetable for implementation. Thereafter, the Commission shall complete any proceeding to implement subsequent recommendations from any Joint Board on universal service within one year after receiving such recommendations.

"(b) Universal Service Principles.--The Joint Board and the Commission shall base policies for the preservation and advancement of universal service on the following principles:

"(1) Quality and rates.--Quality services should be available at just, reasonable, and affordable rates.

"(2) Access to advanced services.--Access to advanced telecommunications and information services should be provided in all regions of the Nation.

"(3) Access in rural and high cost areas.--Consumers in all regions of the Nation, including low-income consumers and those in rural, insular, and high cost areas, should have access to telecommunications and information services, including interexchange services and advanced telecommunications and information services, that are reasonably comparable to those services provided in urban areas and that are available at rates that are reasonably comparable to rates charged for similar services in urban areas.

"(4) Equitable and nondiscriminatory contributions.--All providers of telecommunications services should make an equitable and nondiscriminatory contribution to the preservation and advancement of universal service.

"(5) Specific and predictable support mechanisms.--There should be specific, predictable and sufficient Federal and State mechanisms to preserve and advance universal service.

"(6) Access to advanced telecommunications services for schools, health care, and libraries.--Elementary and secondary schools and classrooms, health care providers, and libraries should have access to advanced telecommunications services as described in subsection (h).

"(7) Additional principles.--Such other principles as the Joint Board and the Commission determine are necessary and appropriate for the protection of the public interest, convenience, and necessity and are consistent with this Act.

"(c) Definition.--

"(1) In general.--Universal service is an evolving level of telecommunications services that the Commission shall establish periodically under this section, taking into account advances in telecommunications and information technologies and services. The

Joint Board in recommending, and the Commission in establishing, the definition of the services that are supported by Federal universal service support mechanisms shall consider the extent to which such telecommunications services--

"(A) are essential to education, public health, or public safety;

"(B) have, through the operation of market choices by customers, been subscribed to by a substantial majority of residential customers;

"(C) are being deployed in public telecommunications networks by telecommunications carriers; and

"(D) are consistent with the public interest, convenience, and necessity.

"(2) Alterations and modifications.--The Joint Board may, from time to time, recommend to the Commission modifications in the definition of the services that are supported by Federal universal service support mechanisms.

"(3) Special services.--In addition to the services included in the definition of universal service under paragraph (1), the Commission may designate additional services for such support mechanisms for schools, libraries, and health care providers for the purposes of subsection (h).

"(d) Telecommunications Carrier Contribution.--Every telecommunications carrier that provides interstate telecommunications services shall contribute, on an equitable and nondiscriminatory basis, to the specific, predictable, and sufficient mechanisms established by the Commission to preserve and advance universal service. The Commission may exempt a carrier or class of carriers from this requirement if the carrier's telecommunications activities are limited to such an extent that the level of such carrier's contribution to the preservation and advancement of universal service would be de minimis. Any other provider of interstate telecommunications may be required to contribute to the preservation and advancement of universal service if the public interest so requires.

"(e) Universal Service Support.--After the date on which Commission regulations implementing this section take effect, only an eligible telecommunications carrier designated under section 214(e) shall be eligible to receive specific Federal universal service support. A carrier that receives such support shall use that support only for the provision, maintenance, and upgrading of facilities and services for which the support is intended. Any such support should be explicit and sufficient to achieve the purposes of this section.

"(f) State Authority.--A State may adopt regulations not inconsistent with the Commission's rules to preserve and advance universal service. Every telecommunications carrier that provides intrastate telecommunications services shall contribute, on an equitable and nondiscriminatory basis, in a manner determined by the State to the preservation and advancement of universal service in that State. A State may adopt regulations to provide for additional definitions and standards to preserve and advance universal service within that State only to the extent that such regulations adopt additional specific, predictable, and sufficient mechanisms to support such definitions or standards that do not rely on or burden Federal universal service support mechanisms.

"(g) Interexchange and Interstate Services.--Within 6 months after the date of enactment of the Telecommunications Act of 1996, the Commission shall adopt rules to require that the rates charged by providers of interexchange telecommunications services to subscribers in rural and high cost areas shall be no higher than the rates charged by each such provider to its subscribers in urban areas. Such rules shall also require that a provider of interstate interexchange telecommunications services shall provide such services to its subscribers in each State at rates no higher than the rates charged to its subscribers in any other State.

"(h) Telecommunications Services for Certain Providers.--

"(1) In general.--

"(A) Health care providers for rural areas.--A telecommunications carrier shall, upon receiving a bona fide request, provide telecommunications services which are necessary for the provision of health care services in a State, including instruction relating to such services, to any public or nonprofit health care provider that serves persons who reside in rural areas in that State at rates that are reasonably comparable to rates charged for similar services in urban areas in that State. A telecommunications carrier providing service under this paragraph shall be entitled to have an amount equal to the difference, if any, between the rates for services provided to health care providers for rural areas in a State and the rates for similar services provided to other customers in comparable rural areas in that State treated as a service obligation as a part of its obligation to participate in the mechanisms to preserve and advance universal service.

"(B) Educational providers and libraries.--All telecommunications carriers serving a geographic area shall, upon a bona fide request for any of its services that are within the definition of universal service under subsection (c)(3), provide such services to elementary schools, secondary schools, and libraries for educational purposes at rates less than the amounts charged for similar services to other parties. The discount shall be an amount that the Commission, with respect to interstate services, and the States, with respect to intrastate services, determine is appropriate and necessary to ensure affordable access to and use of such services by such entities. A telecommunications carrier providing service under this paragraph shall--

"(i) have an amount equal to the amount of the discount treated as an offset to its obligation to contribute to the mechanisms to preserve and advance universal service, or

"(ii) notwithstanding the provisions of subsection (e) of this section, receive reimbursement utilizing the support mechanisms to preserve and advance universal service.

"(2) Advanced services.--The Commission shall establish competitively neutral rules--

"(A) to enhance, to the extent technically feasible and economically reasonable, access to advanced telecommunications and information services for all public and nonprofit elementary and secondary school classrooms, health care providers, and libraries; and

"(B) to define the circumstances under which a telecommunications carrier may be required to connect its network to such public institutional telecommunications users.

"(3) Terms and conditions.--Telecommunications services and network capacity provided to a public institutional telecommunications user under this subsection may not be sold, resold, or otherwise transferred by such user in consideration for money or any other thing of value.

"(4) Eligibility of users.--No entity listed in this subsection shall be entitled to preferential rates or treatment as required by this subsection, if such entity operates as a for-profit business, is a school described in paragraph (5)(A) with an endowment of more than $50,000,000, or is a library not eligible for participation in State-based plans for funds under title III of the Library Services and Construction Act (20 U.S.C. 335c et seq.).

"(5) Definitions.--For purposes of this subsection:

"(A) Elementary and secondary schools.--The term 'elementary and secondary schools' means elementary schools and secondary schools, as defined in paragraphs (14) and (25), respectively, of section 14101 of the Elementary and Secondary Education Act of 1965 (20 U.S.C. 8801).

"(B) Health care provider.--The term 'health care provider' means--

"(i) post-secondary educational institutions offering health care instruction, teaching hospitals, and medical schools;

"(ii) community health centers or health centers providing health care to migrants;

"(iii) local health departments or agencies;

"(iv) community mental health centers;

"(v) not-for-profit hospitals;

"(vi) rural health clinics; and

"(vii) consortia of health care providers consisting of one or more entities described in clauses (i) through (vi).

"(C) Public institutional telecommunications user.--The term "public institutional telecommunications user" means an elementary or secondary school, a library, or a health care provider as those terms are defined in this paragraph.

"(i) Consumer Protection.--The Commission and the States should ensure that universal service is available at rates that are just, reasonable, and affordable.

"(j) Lifeline Assistance.--Nothing in this section shall affect the collection, distribution, or administration of the Lifeline Assistance Program provided for by the Commission under regulations set forth in section 69.117 of title 47, Code of Federal Regulations, and other related sections of such title.

"(k) Subsidy of Competitive Services Prohibited.--A telecommunications carrier may not use services that are not competitive to subsidize services that are subject to competition. The Commission, with respect to interstate services, and the States, with respect to intrastate services, shall establish any necessary cost allocation rules, accounting safeguards, and guidelines to ensure that services included in the definition of universal service bear no more than a reasonable share of the joint and common costs of facilities used to provide those services.

"Section 255. ACCESS BY PERSONS WITH DISABILITIES.

"(a) Definitions.--As used in this section--

"(1) Disability.--The term 'disability' has the meaning given to it by section 3(2)(A) of the Americans with Disabilities Act of 1990 (42 U.S.C. 12102(2)(A)).

"(2) Readily achievable.--The term "readily achievable" has the meaning given to it by section 301(9) of that Act (42 U.S.C. 12181(9)).

"(b) Manufacturing.--A manufacturer of telecommunications equipment or customer premises equipment shall ensure that the equipment is designed, developed, and fabricated to be accessible to and usable by individuals with disabilities, if readily achievable.

"(c) Telecommunications Services.--A provider of telecommunications service shall ensure that the service is accessible to and usable by individuals with disabilities, if readily achievable.

"(d) Compatibility.--Whenever the requirements of subsections (b) and (c) are not readily achievable, such a manufacturer or provider shall ensure that the equipment or service is compatible with existing peripheral devices or specialized customer premises equipment commonly used by individuals with disabilities to achieve access, if readily achievable.

"(e) Guidelines.--Within 18 months after the date of enactment of the Telecommunications Act of 1996, the Architectural and Transportation Barriers Compliance Board shall develop guidelines for accessibility of telecommunications equipment and customer premises equipment in conjunction with the Commission. The Board shall review and update the guidelines periodically.

193

"(f) No Additional Private Rights Authorized.--Nothing in this section shall be construed to authorize any private right of action to enforce any requirement of this section or any regulation thereunder. The Commission shall have exclusive jurisdiction with respect to any complaint under this section.

"Section 256. COORDINATION FOR INTERCONNECTIVITY.

"(a) Purpose.--It is the purpose of this section--

"(1) to promote nondiscriminatory accessibility by the broadest number of users and vendors of communications products and services to public telecommunications networks used to provide telecommunications service through--

"(A) coordinated public telecommunications network planning and design by telecommunications carriers and other providers of telecommunications service; and

"(B) public telecommunications network interconnectivity, and interconnectivity of devices with such networks used to provide telecommunications service; and

"(2) to ensure the ability of users and information providers to seamlessly and transparently transmit and receive information between and across telecommunications networks.

"(b) Commission Functions.--In carrying out the purposes of this section, the Commission--

"(1) shall establish procedures for Commission oversight of coordinated network planning by telecommunications carriers and other providers of telecommunications service for the effective and efficient interconnection of public telecommunications networks used to provide telecommunications service; and

"(2) may participate, in a manner consistent with its authority and practice prior to the date of enactment of this section, in the development by appropriate industry standards-setting organizations of public telecommunications network interconnectivity standards that promote access to--

"(A) public telecommunications networks used to provide telecommunications service;

"(B) network capabilities and services by individuals with disabilities; and

"(C) information services by subscribers of rural telephone companies.

"(c) Commission's Authority.--Nothing in this section shall be construed as expanding or limiting any authority that the Commission may have under law in effect before the date of enactment of the Telecommunications Act of 1996.

"(d) Definition.--As used in this section, the term 'public telecommunications network interconnectivity' means the ability of two or more public telecommunications networks used to provide telecommunications service to communicate and exchange information without degeneration, and to interact in concert with one another.

"Section 257. MARKET ENTRY BARRIERS PROCEEDING.

"(a) Elimination of Barriers.--Within 15 months after the date of enactment of the Telecommunications Act of 1996, the Commission shall complete a proceeding for the purpose of identifying and eliminating, by regulations pursuant to its authority under this Act (other than this section), market entry barriers for entrepreneurs and other small businesses in the provision and ownership of telecommunications services and information services, or in the provision of parts or services to providers of telecommunications services and information services.

"(b) National Policy.--In carrying out subsection (a), the Commission shall seek to promote the policies and purposes of this Act favoring diversity of media voices, vigorous economic competition, technological advancement, and promotion of the public interest, convenience, and necessity.

"(c) Periodic Review.--Every 3 years following the completion of the proceeding required by subsection (a), the Commission shall review and report to Congress on--

"(1) any regulations prescribed to eliminate barriers within its jurisdiction that are identified under subsection (a) and that can be prescribed consistent with the public interest, convenience, and necessity; and

"(2) the statutory barriers identified under subsection (a) that the Commission recommends be eliminated, consistent with the public interest, convenience, and necessity.

"Section 258. ILLEGAL CHANGES IN SUBSCRIBER CARRIER SELECTIONS.

"(a) Prohibition.--No telecommunications carrier shall submit or execute a change in a subscriber's selection of a provider of telephone exchange service or telephone toll service except in accordance with such verification procedures as the Commission shall prescribe. Nothing in this section shall preclude any State commission from enforcing such procedures with respect to intrastate services.

"(b) Liability for Charges.--Any telecommunications carrier that violates the verification procedures described in subsection (a) and that collects charges for telephone exchange service or telephone toll service from a subscriber shall be liable to the carrier previously selected by the subscriber in an amount equal to all charges paid by such subscriber after such violation, in accordance with such procedures as the Commission may prescribe. The remedies provided by this subsection are in addition to any other remedies available by law.

"Section 259. INFRASTRUCTURE SHARING.

"(a) Regulations Required.--The Commission shall prescribe, within one year after the date of enactment of the Telecommunications Act of 1996, regulations that require incumbent local exchange carriers (as defined in section 251(h)) to make available to any qualifying carrier such public switched network infrastructure, technology, information, and telecommunications facilities and functions as may be requested by such qualifying carrier for the purpose of enabling such qualifying carrier to provide telecommunications services, or to provide access to information services, in the service area in which such qualifying carrier has requested and obtained designation as an eligible telecommunications carrier under section 214(e).

"(b)   Terms and Conditions of Regulations.--The regulations prescribed by the Commission pursuant to this section shall--

"(1) not require a local exchange carrier to which this section applies to take any action that is economically unreasonable or that is contrary to the public interest;

"(2)   permit, but shall not require, the joint ownership or operation of public switched network infrastructure and services by or among such local exchange carrier and a qualifying carrier;

"(3) ensure that such local exchange carrier will not be treated by the Commission or any State as a common carrier for hire or as offering common carrier services with respect to any infrastructure, technology, information, facilities, or functions made available to a qualifying carrier in accordance with regulations issued pursuant to this section;

"(4)   ensure that such local exchange carrier makes such infrastructure, technology, information, facilities, or functions available to a qualifying carrier on just and reasonable terms and conditions that permit such qualifying carrier to fully benefit from the economies of scale and scope of such local exchange carrier, as determined in accordance with guidelines prescribed by the Commission in regulations issued pursuant to this section;

"(5)   establish conditions that promote cooperation between local exchange carriers to which this section applies and qualifying carriers;

"(6) not require a local exchange carrier to which this section applies to engage in any infrastructure sharing agreement for any services or access which are to be provided or offered to consumers by the qualifying carrier in such local exchange carrier's telephone exchange area; and

"(7) require that such local exchange carrier file with the Commission or State for public inspection, any tariffs, contracts, or other arrangements showing the rates, terms, and conditions under which such carrier is making available public switched network infrastructure and functions under this section.

"(c) Information Concerning Deployment of New Services and Equipment.--a local exchange carrier to which this section applies that has entered into an infrastructure sharing agreement under this section shall provide to each party to such agreement timely information on the planned deployment of telecommunications services and equipment, including any software or upgrades of software integral to the use or operation of such telecommunications equipment.

"(d) Definition.--For purposes of this section, the term "qualifying carrier" means a telecommunications carrier that--

"(1) lacks economies of scale or scope, as determined in accordance with regulations prescribed by the Commission pursuant to this section; and

"(2) offers telephone exchange service, exchange access, and any other service that is included in universal service, to all consumers without preference throughout the service area for which such carrier has been designated as an eligible telecommunications carrier under section 214(e).

"Section 260. PROVISION OF TELEMESSAGING SERVICE.

"(a) Nondiscrimination Safeguards.--Any local exchange carrier subject to the requirements of section 251(c) that provides telemessaging service--

"(1) shall not subsidize its telemessaging service directly or indirectly from its telephone exchange service or its exchange access; and

"(2) shall not prefer or discriminate in favor of its telemessaging service operations in its provision of telecommunications services.

"(b) Expedited Consideration of Complaints.--The Commission shall establish procedures for the receipt and review of complaints concerning violations of subsection (a) or the regulations thereunder that result in material financial harm to a provider of telemessaging service. Such procedures shall ensure that the Commission will make a final determination with respect to any such complaint within 120 days after receipt of the complaint. If the complaint contains an appropriate showing that the alleged violation occurred, the Commission shall, within 60 days after receipt of the complaint, order the local exchange carrier and any affiliates to cease engaging in such violation pending such final determination.

"(c) Definition.--As used in this section, the term 'telemessaging service' means voice mail and voice storage and retrieval services, any live operator services used to record, transcribe, or relay messages (other than telecommunications relay services), and any ancillary services offered in combination with these services.

197

"Section 261. EFFECT ON OTHER REQUIREMENTS.

"(a) Commission Regulations.--Nothing in this part shall be construed to prohibit the Commission from enforcing regulations prescribed prior to the date of enactment of the Telecommunications Act of 1996 in fulfilling the requirements of this part, to the extent that such regulations are not inconsistent with the provisions of this part.

"(b) Existing State Regulations.--Nothing in this part shall be construed to prohibit any State commission from enforcing regulations prescribed prior to the date of enactment of the Telecommunications Act of 1996, or from prescribing regulations after such date of enactment, in fulfilling the requirements of this part, if such regulations are not inconsistent with the provisions of this part.

"(c) Additional State Requirements.--Nothing in this part precludes a State from imposing requirements on a telecommunications carrier for intrastate services that are necessary to further competition in the provision of telephone exchange service or exchange access, as long as the State's requirements are not inconsistent with this part or the Commission's regulations to implement this part."

(b) Designation of Part I.--Title II of the Act is further amended by inserting before the heading of section 201 the following new heading:

"PART I - COMMON CARRIER REGULATION"

(c) Stylistic Consistency.--The Act is amended so that--

(1) the designation and heading of each title of the Act shall be in the form and typeface of the designation and heading of this title of this Act; and

(2) the designation and heading of each part of each title of the Act shall be in the form and typeface of the designation and heading of part I of title II of the Act, as amended by subsection (a).

SEC. 102. ELIGIBLE TELECOMMUNICATIONS CARRIERS.

(a) In General.--Section 214 (47 U.S.C. 214) is amended by adding at the end thereof the following new subsection:

"(e) Provision of Universal Service.--

"(1) Eligible telecommunications carriers.--A common carrier designated as an eligible telecommunications carrier under paragraph (2) or (3) shall be eligible to receive universal service support in accordance with section 254 and shall, throughout the service area for which the designation is received--

"(A) offer the services that are supported by Federal universal service support mechanisms under section 254(c), either using its own facilities or a combination of its own facilities and resale of another carrier's services (including the services offered by another eligible telecommunications carrier); and

"(B) advertise the availability of such services and the charges therefor using media of general distribution.

"(2) Designation of eligible telecommunications carriers.--A State commission shall upon its own motion or upon request designate a common carrier that meets the requirements of paragraph (1) as an eligible telecommunications carrier for a service area designated by the State commission. Upon request and consistent with the public interest, convenience, and necessity, the State commission may, in the case of an area served by a rural telephone company, and shall, in the case of all other areas, designate more than one common carrier as an eligible telecommunications carrier for a service area designated by the State commission, so long as each additional requesting carrier meets the requirements of paragraph (1). Before designating an additional eligible telecommunications carrier for an area served by a rural telephone company, the State commission shall find that the designation is in the public interest.

"(3) Designation of eligible telecommunications carriers for unserved areas.--If no common carrier will provide the services that are supported by Federal universal service support mechanisms under section 254(c) to an unserved community or any portion thereof that requests such service, the Commission, with respect to interstate services, or a State commission, with respect to intrastate services, shall determine which common carrier or carriers are best able to provide such service to the requesting unserved community or portion thereof and shall order such carrier or carriers to provide such service for that unserved community or portion thereof. Any carrier or carriers ordered to provide such service under this paragraph shall meet the requirements of paragraph (1) and shall be designated as an eligible telecommunications carrier for that community or portion thereof.

"(4) Relinquishment of universal service.--A State commission shall permit an eligible telecommunications carrier to relinquish its designation as such a carrier in any area served by more than one eligible telecommunications carrier. An eligible telecommunications carrier that seeks to relinquish its eligible telecommunications carrier designation for an area served by more than one eligible telecommunications carrier shall give advance notice to the State commission of such relinquishment. Prior to permitting a telecommunications carrier designated as an eligible telecommunications carrier to cease providing universal service in an area served by more than one eligible telecommunications carrier, the State commission shall require the remaining eligible telecommunications carrier or carriers to ensure that all customers served by the relinquishing carrier will continue to be served, and shall require sufficient notice to permit the purchase or construction of adequate facilities by any remaining eligible telecommunications carrier. The State commission shall establish a time, not to exceed one year after the State commission approves such relinquishment under this paragraph, within which such purchase or construction shall be completed.

"(5) Service area defined.--The term "service area" means a geographic area established by a State commission for the purpose of determining universal service obligations and support mechanisms. In the case of an area served by a rural telephone company, "service area" means such company's "study area" unless and until the Commission and the States, after taking into account recommendations of a Federal-State Joint Board instituted under section 410(c), establish a different definition of service area for such company."

SEC. 103. EXEMPT TELECOMMUNICATIONS COMPANIES.

The Public Utility Holding Company Act of 1935 (15 U.S.C. 79 and following) is amended by redesignating sections 34 and 35 as sections 35 and 36, respectively, and by inserting the following new section after section 33:

"Section 34. EXEMPT TELECOMMUNICATIONS COMPANIES.

"(a) Definitions.--For purposes of this section--

"(1) Exempt Telecommunications Company.--The term 'exempt telecommunications company' means any person determined by the Federal Communications Commission to be engaged directly or indirectly, wherever located, through one or more affiliates (as defined in section 2(a)(11)(B)), and exclusively in the business of providing--

"(A) telecommunications services;

"(B) information services;

"(C) other services or products subject to the jurisdiction of the Federal Communications Commission; or

"(D) products or services that are related or incidental to the provision of a product or service described in subparagraph (A), (B), or (C). No person shall be deemed to be an exempt telecommunications company under this section unless such person has applied to the Federal Communications Commission for a determination under this paragraph. A person applying in good faith for such a determination shall be deemed an exempt telecommunications company under this section, with all of the exemptions provided by this section, until the Federal Communications Commission makes such determination. The Federal Communications Commission shall make such determination within 60 days of its receipt of any such application filed after the enactment of this section and shall notify the Commission whenever a determination is made under this paragraph that any person is an exempt telecommunications company. Not later than 12 months after the date of enactment of this section, the Federal Communications Commission shall promulgate rules implementing the provisions of this paragraph which shall be applicable to applications filed under this paragraph after the effective date of such rules.

"(2) Other terms.--For purposes of this section, the terms 'telecommunications services' and 'information services' shall have the same meanings as provided in the Communications Act of 1934.

"(b) State Consent for Sale of Existing Rate-Based Facilities.--If a rate or charge for the sale of electric energy or natural gas (other than any portion of a rate or charge which represents recovery of the cost of a wholesale rate or charge) for, or in connection with, assets of a public utility company that is an associate company or affiliate of a registered holding company was in effect under the laws of any State as of December 19, 1995, the public utility company owning such assets may not sell such assets to an exempt telecommunications company that is an associate company or affiliate unless State commissions having jurisdiction over such public utility company approve such sale. Nothing in this subsection shall preempt the otherwise applicable authority of any State to approve or disapprove the sale of such assets. The approval of the Commission under this Act shall not be required for the sale of assets as provided in this subsection.

"(c) Ownership of ETCS by Exempt Holding Companies.--Notwithstanding any provision of this Act, a holding company that is exempt under section 3 of this Act shall be permitted, without condition or limitation under this Act, to acquire and maintain an interest in the business of one or more exempt telecommunications companies.

"(d) Ownership of ETCS by Registered Holding Companies.--Notwithstanding any provision of this Act, a registered holding company shall be permitted (without the need to apply for, or receive, approval from the Commission, and otherwise without condition under this Act) to acquire and hold the securities, or an interest in the business, of one or more exempt telecommunications companies.

"(e) Financing and Other Relationships Between ETCS and Registered Holding Companies.--The relationship between an exempt telecommunications company and a registered holding company, its affiliates and associate companies, shall remain subject to the jurisdiction of the Commission under this Act: Provided, That--

"(1) section 11 of this Act shall not prohibit the ownership of an interest in the business of one or more exempt telecommunications companies by a registered holding company (regardless of activities engaged in or where facilities owned or operated by such exempt telecommunications companies are located), and such ownership by a registered holding company shall be deemed consistent with the operation of an integrated public utility system;

"(2)   the ownership of an interest in the business of one or more exempt telecommunications companies by a registered holding company (regardless of activities engaged in or where facilities owned or operated by such exempt telecommunications companies are located) shall be considered as reasonably incidental, or economically necessary or appropriate, to the operations of an integrated public utility system;

"(3) the Commission shall have no jurisdiction under this Act over, and there shall be no restriction or approval required under this Act with respect to (A) the issue or sale of a security by a registered holding company for purposes of financing the acquisition of an exempt telecommunications company, or (B) the guarantee of a security of an exempt telecommunications company by a registered holding company; and

"(4)   except for costs that should be fairly and equitably allocated among companies that are associate companies of a registered holding company, the Commission shall have no jurisdiction under this Act over the sales, service, and construction contracts between an exempt telecommunications company and a registered holding company, its affiliates and associate companies.

"(f)   Reporting Obligations Concerning Investments and Activities of Registered Public-Utility Holding Company Systems.--

"(1)   Obligations to report information.--Any registered holding company or subsidiary thereof that acquires or holds the securities, or an interest in the business, of an exempt telecommunications company shall file with the Commission such information as the Commission, by rule, may prescribe concerning--

"(A)   investments and activities by the registered holding company, or any subsidiary thereof, with respect to exempt telecommunications companies, and

"(B)   any activities of an exempt telecommunications company within the holding company system,   that are reasonably likely to have a material impact on the financial or operational condition of the holding company system.

"(2)   Authority to require additional information.--If, based on reports provided to the Commission pursuant to paragraph (1) of this subsection or other available information, the Commission reasonably concludes that it has concerns regarding the financial or operational condition of any registered holding company or any subsidiary thereof (including an exempt telecommunications company), the Commission may require such registered holding company to make additional reports and provide additional information.

"(3)   Authority to limit disclosure of information.--Notwithstanding any other provision of law, the Commission shall not be compelled to disclose any information required to be reported under this subsection. Nothing in this subsection shall authorize the

Commission to withhold the information from Congress, or prevent the Commission from complying with a request for information from any other Federal or State department or agency requesting the information for purposes within the scope of its jurisdiction. For purposes of section 552 of title 5, United States Code, this subsection shall be considered a statute described in subsection (b)(3)(B) of such section 552.

"(g)   Assumption of Liabilities.--Any public utility company that is an associate company, or an affiliate, of a registered holding company and that is subject to the jurisdiction of a State commission with respect to its retail electric or gas rates shall not issue any security for the purpose of financing the acquisition, ownership, or operation of an exempt telecommunications company. Any public utility company that is an associate company, or an affiliate, of a registered holding company and that is subject to the jurisdiction of a State commission with respect to its retail electric or gas rates shall not assume any obligation or liability as guarantor, endorser, surety, or otherwise by the public utility company in respect of any security of an exempt telecommunications company.

"(h) Pledging or Mortgaging of Assets.--Any public utility company that is an associate company, or affiliate, of a registered holding company and that is subject to the jurisdiction of a State commission with respect to its retail electric or gas rates shall not pledge, mortgage, or otherwise use as collateral any assets of the public utility company or assets of any subsidiary company thereof for the benefit of an exempt telecommunications company.

"(i) Protection Against Abusive Affiliate Transactions.--A public utility company may enter into a contract to purchase services or products described in subsection (a)(1) from an exempt telecommunications company that is an affiliate or associate company of the public utility company only if--

"(1) every State commission having jurisdiction over the retail rates of such public utility company approves such contract; or

"(2) such public utility company is not subject to State commission retail rate regulation and the purchased services or products--

"(A) would not be resold to any affiliate or associate company; or

"(B) would be resold to an affiliate or associate company and every State commission having jurisdiction over the retail rates of such affiliate or associate company makes the determination required by subparagraph (A).

The requirements of this subsection shall not apply in any case in which the State or the State commission concerned publishes a notice that the State or State commission waives its authority under this subsection.

"(j) Nonpreemption of Rate Authority.--Nothing in this Act shall preclude the Federal Energy Regulatory Commission or a State commission from exercising its jurisdiction under otherwise applicable law to determine whether a public utility company may recover in rates the costs of products or services purchased from or sold to an associate company or affiliate that is an exempt telecommunications company, regardless of whether such costs are incurred through the direct or indirect purchase or sale of products or services from such associate company or affiliate.

"(k) Reciprocal Arrangements Prohibited.--Reciprocal arrangements among companies that are not affiliates or associate companies of each other that are entered into in order to avoid the provisions of this section are prohibited.

"(l) Books and Records.

"(1) Upon written order of a State commission, a State commission may examine the books, accounts, memoranda, contracts, and records of--

"(A) a public utility company subject to its regulatory authority under State law;

"(B) any exempt telecommunications company selling products or services to such public utility company or to an associate company of such public utility company; and

"(C) any associate company or affiliate of an exempt telecommunications company which sells products or services to a public utility company referred to in subparagraph (A), wherever located, if such examination is required for the effective discharge of the State commission's regulatory responsibilities affecting the provision of electric or gas service in connection with the activities of such exempt telecommunications company.

"(2) Where a State commission issues an order pursuant to paragraph (1), the State commission shall not publicly disclose trade secrets or sensitive commercial information.

"(3) Any United States district court located in the State in which the State commission referred to in paragraph (1) is located shall have jurisdiction to enforce compliance with this subsection.

"(4) Nothing in this section shall--

"(A) preempt applicable State law concerning the provision of records and other information; or

"(B) in any way limit rights to obtain records and other information under Federal law, contracts, or otherwise.

"(m) Independent Audit Authority for State Commissions.--

"(1) State may order audit.--Any State commission with jurisdiction over a public utility company that--

"(A) is an associate company of a registered holding company; and

"(B) transacts business, directly or indirectly, with a subsidiary company, an affiliate or an associate company that is an exempt telecommunications company, may order an independent audit to be performed, no more frequently than on an annual basis, of all matters deemed relevant by the selected auditor that reasonably relate to retail rates: Provided, That such matters relate, directly or indirectly, to transactions or transfers between the public utility company subject to its jurisdiction and such exempt telecommunications company.

"(2) Selection of firm to conduct audit.

"(A) If a State commission orders an audit in accordance with paragraph (1), the public utility company and the State commission shall jointly select, within 60 days, a firm to perform the audit. The firm selected to perform the audit shall possess demonstrated qualifications relating to--

"(i) competency, including adequate technical training and professional proficiency in each discipline necessary to carry out the audit; and

"(ii) independence and objectivity, including that the firm be free from personal or external impairments to independence, and should assume an independent position with the State commission and auditee, making certain that the audit is based upon an impartial consideration of all pertinent facts and responsible opinions.

"(B) The public utility company and the exempt telecommunications company shall cooperate fully with all reasonable requests necessary to perform the audit and the public utility company shall bear all costs of having the audit performed.

"(3) Availability of auditor's report.--The auditor's report shall be provided to the State commission not later than 6 months after the selection of the auditor, and provided to the public utility company not later than 60 days thereafter.

"(n) Applicability of Telecommunications Regulation.--Nothing in this section shall affect the authority of the Federal Communications Commission under the Communications Act of 1934, or the authority of State commissions under State laws concerning the provision of telecommunications services, to regulate the activities of an exempt telecommunications company."

SEC. 104. NONDISCRIMINATION PRINCIPLE.

Section 1 (47 U.S.C. 151) is amended by inserting after "to all the people of the United States" the following: ", without discrimination on the basis of race, color, religion, national origin, or sex,".

Subtitle B--Special Provisions Concerning Bell Operating Companies

SEC. 151. BELL OPERATING COMPANY PROVISIONS.

(a) Establishment of Part III of Title II.--Title II is amended by adding at the end of part II (as added by section 101) the following new part:

"PART III--SPECIAL PROVISIONS CONCERNING BELL OPERATING COMPANIES

"Section 271. BELL OPERATING COMPANY ENTRY INTO INTERLATA SERVICES.

"(a) General Limitation.--Neither a Bell operating company, nor any affiliate of a Bell operating company, may provide interLATA services except as provided in this section.

"(b) InterLATA Services to Which This Section Applies.--

"(1) In-region services.--A Bell operating company, or any affiliate of that Bell operating company, may provide interLATA services originating in any of its in-region States (as defined in subsection (i)) if the Commission approves the application of such company for such State under subsection (d)(3).

"(2) Out-of-region services.--A Bell operating company, or any affiliate of that Bell operating company, may provide interLATA services originating outside its in-region States after the date of enactment of the Telecommunications Act of 1996, subject to subsection (j).

"(3) Incidental interlata services.--A Bell operating company, or any affiliate of a Bell operating company, may provide incidental interLATa services (as defined in subsection (g)) originating in any State after the date of enactment of the Telecommunications Act of 1996.

"(4) Termination.--Nothing in this section prohibits a Bell operating company or any of its affiliates from providing termination for interLATa services, subject to subsection (j).

"(c) Requirements for Providing Certain In-Region InterLATA Services.--

"(1) Agreement or statement.--A Bell operating company meets the requirements of this paragraph if it meets the requirements of subparagraph (A) or subparagraph (B) of this paragraph for each State for which the authorization is sought.

"(A) Presence of a facilities-based competitor.--A Bell operating company meets the requirements of this subparagraph if it has entered into one or more binding agreements that have been approved under section 252 specifying the terms and conditions under which the Bell operating company is providing access and interconnection to its network facilities for the network facilities of one or more unaffiliated competing providers of telephone exchange service (as defined in section 3(47)(A), but excluding exchange access) to residential and business subscribers. For the purpose of this subparagraph, such telephone exchange service may be offered by such competing providers either exclusively over their own telephone exchange service facilities or predominantly over their own telephone exchange service facilities in combination with the resale of the telecommunications services of another carrier. For the purpose of this subparagraph, services provided pursuant to Subpart K of Part 22 of the Commission's regulations (47 CFR 22.901 et seq.) shall not be considered to be telephone exchange services.

"(B) Failure to request access.--A Bell operating company meets the requirements of this subparagraph if, after 10 months after the date of enactment of the Telecommunications Act of 1996, no such provider has requested the access and interconnection described in subparagraph (A) before the date which is 3 months before the date the company makes its application under subsection (d)(1), and a statement of the terms and conditions that the company generally offers to provide such access and interconnection has been approved or permitted to take effect by the State commission under section 252(f). For purposes of this subparagraph, a Bell operating company shall be considered not to have received any request for access and interconnection if the State commission of such State certifies that the only provider or providers making such a request have (i) failed to negotiate in good faith as required by section 252, or (ii) violated the terms of an agreement approved under section 252 by the provider's failure to comply, within a reasonable period of time, with the implementation schedule contained in such agreement.

"(2) Specific interconnection requirements.--

"(A) Agreement required.--A Bell operating company meets the requirements of this paragraph if, within the State for which the authorization is sought--

"(i)(I) such company is providing access and interconnection pursuant to one or more agreements described in paragraph (1)(A), or

"(II) such company is generally offering access and interconnection pursuant to a statement described in paragraph (1)(B), and

"(ii) such access and interconnection meets the requirements of subparagraph (B) of this paragraph.

"(B) Competitive checklist.--Access or interconnection provided or generally offered by a Bell operating company to other telecommunications carriers meets the requirements of this subparagraph if such access and interconnection includes each of the following:

"(i) Interconnection in accordance with the requirements of sections 251(c)(2) and 252(d)(1).

"(ii) Nondiscriminatory access to network elements in accordance with the requirements of sections 251(c)(3) and 252(d)(1).

207

"(iii) Nondiscriminatory access to the poles, ducts, conduits, and rights of-way owned or controlled by the Bell operating company at just and reasonable rates in accordance with the requirements of section 224.

"(iv) Local loop transmission from the central office to the customer's premises, unbundled from local switching or other services.

"(v) Local transport from the trunk side of a wireline local exchange carrier switch unbundled from switching or other services.

"(vi) Local switching unbundled from transport, local loop transmission, or other services.

"(vii) Nondiscriminatory access to--

"(I) 911 and E911 services;

"(II) directory assistance services to allow the other carrier's customers to obtain telephone numbers; and

"(III) operator call completion services.

"(viii) White pages directory listings for customers of the other carrier's telephone exchange service.

"(ix) Until the date by which telecommunications numbering administration guidelines, plan, or rules are established, nondiscriminatory access to telephone numbers for assignment to the other carrier's telephone exchange service customers. After that date, compliance with such guidelines, plan, or rules.

"(x) Nondiscriminatory access to databases and associated signaling necessary for call routing and completion.

"(xi) Until the date by which the Commission issues regulations pursuant to section 251 to require number portability, interim telecommunications number portability through remote call forwarding, direct inward dialing trunks, or other comparable arrangements, with as little impairment of functioning, quality, reliability, and convenience as possible. After that date, full compliance with such regulations.

"(xii) Nondiscriminatory access to such services or information as are necessary to allow the requesting carrier to implement local dialing parity in accordance with the requirements of section 251(b)(3).

"(xiii) Reciprocal compensation arrangements in accordance with the requirements of section 252(d)(2).

"(xiv) Telecommunications services are available for resale in accordance with the requirements of sections 251(c)(4) and 252(d)(3).

"(d) Administrative Provisions.--

"(1) Application to commission.--On and after the date of enactment of the Telecommunications Act of 1996, a Bell operating company or its affiliate may apply to the

Commission for authorization to provide interLATA services originating in any in-region State. The application shall identify each State for which the authorization is sought.

"(2) Consultation.--

"(A)   Consultation with the attorney general.--The Commission shall notify the Attorney General promptly of any application under paragraph (1). Before making any determination under this subsection, the Commission shall consult with the Attorney General, and if the Attorney General submits any comments in writing, such comments shall be included in the record of the Commission's decision. In consulting with and submitting comments to the Commission under this paragraph, the Attorney General shall provide to the Commission an evaluation of the application using any standard the Attorney General considers appropriate. The Commission shall give substantial weight to the Attorney General's evaluation, but such evaluation shall not have any preclusive effect on any Commission decision under paragraph (3).

"(B)   Consultation with state commissions.--Before making any determination under this subsection, the Commission shall consult with the State commission of any State that is the subject of the application in order to verify the compliance of the Bell operating company with the requirements of subsection (c).

"(3)   Determination.--Not later than 90 days after receiving an application under paragraph (1), the Commission shall issue a written determination approving or denying the authorization requested in the application for each State. The Commission shall not approve the authorization requested in an application submitted under paragraph (1) unless it finds that--

"(A)   the petitioning Bell operating company has met the requirements of subsection (c)(1) and--

"(i)   with respect to access and interconnection provided pursuant to subsection (c)(1)(A), has fully implemented the competitive checklist in subsection (c)(2)(B); or

"(ii)   with respect to access and interconnection generally offered pursuant to a statement under subsection (c)(1)(B), such statement offers all of the items included in the competitive checklist in subsection (c)(2)(B);

"(B)   the requested authorization will be carried out in accordance with the requirements of section 272; and

"(C)   the requested authorization is consistent with the public interest, convenience, and necessity.

The Commission shall state the basis for its approval or denial of the application.

"(4)   Limitation on commission.--The Commission may not, by rule or otherwise, limit or extend the terms used in the competitive checklist set forth in subsection (c)(2)(B).

"(5) Publication.--Not later than 10 days after issuing a determination under paragraph (3), the Commission shall publish in the Federal Register a brief description of the determination.

"(6) Enforcement of conditions.--

"(A) Commission authority.--If at any time after the approval of an application under paragraph (3), the Commission determines that a Bell operating company has ceased to meet any of the conditions required for such approval, the Commission may, after notice and opportunity for a hearing--

"(i) issue an order to such company to correct the deficiency;

"(ii) impose a penalty on such company pursuant to title V; or

"(iii) suspend or revoke such approval.

"(B) Receipt and review of complaints.--The Commission shall establish procedures for the review of complaints concerning failures by Bell operating companies to meet conditions required for approval under paragraph (3).
Unless the parties otherwise agree, the Commission shall act on such complaint within 90 days.

"(e) Limitations.--

"(1) Joint marketing of local and long distance services.--Until a Bell operating company is authorized pursuant to subsection (d) to provide interLATA services in an in-region State, or until 36 months have passed since the date of enactment of the Telecommunications Act of 1996, whichever is earlier, a telecommunications carrier that serves greater than 5 percent of the Nation's presubscribed access lines may not jointly market in such State telephone exchange service obtained from such company pursuant to section 251(c)(4) with interLATA services offered by that telecommunications carrier.

"(2) IntraLATA toll dialing parity.--

"(A) Provision required.--A Bell operating company granted authority to provide interLATA services under subsection (d) shall provide intraLATA toll dialing parity throughout that State coincident with its exercise of that authority.

"(B) Limitation.--Except for single-LATA States and States that have issued an order by December 19, 1995, requiring a Bell operating company to implement intraLATA toll dialing parity, a State may not require a Bell operating company to implement intraLATA toll dialing parity in that State before a Bell operating company has been granted authority under this section to provide interLATA services originating in that State or before 3 years after the date of enactment of the Telecommunications Act of 1996, whichever is earlier. Nothing in this subparagraph precludes a State from issuing an order requiring intraLATA toll dialing parity in that State prior to either such date so long as such order does not take effect until after the earlier of either such dates.

"(f) Exception for Previously Authorized Activities.--Neither subsection (a) nor section 273 shall prohibit a Bell operating company or affiliate from engaging, at any time after the date of enactment of the Telecommunications Act of 1996, in any activity to the extent authorized by, and subject to the terms and conditions contained in, an order entered by the United States District Court for the District of Columbia pursuant to section VII or VIII(C) of the AT&T Consent Decree if such order was entered on or before such date of enactment, to the extent such order is not reversed or vacated on appeal. Nothing in this subsection shall be construed to limit, or to impose terms or conditions on, an activity in which a Bell operating company is otherwise authorized to engage under any other provision of this section.

"(g) Definition of Incidental InterLATA Services.--For purposes of this section, the term "incidental interLATA services" means the interLATA provision by a Bell operating company or its affiliate--

"(1)(A) of audio programming, video programming, or other programming services to subscribers to such services of such company or affiliate;

"(B) of the capability for interaction by such subscribers to select or respond to such audio programming, video programming, or other programming services;

"(C) to distributors of audio programming or video programming that such company or affiliate owns or controls, or is licensed by the copyright owner of such programming (or by an assignee of such owner) to distribute; or

"(D) of alarm monitoring services;

"(2) of two-way interactive video services or Internet services over dedicated facilities to or for elementary and secondary schools as defined in section 254(h)(5);

"(3) of commercial mobile services in accordance with section 332(c) of this Act and with the regulations prescribed by the Commission pursuant to paragraph (8) of such section;

"(4) of a service that permits a customer that is located in one LATA to retrieve stored information from, or file information for storage in, information storage facilities of such company that are located in another LATA;

"(5) of signaling information used in connection with the provision of telephone exchange services or exchange access by a local exchange carrier; or

"(6) of network control signaling information to, and receipt of such signaling information from, common carriers offering interLATA services at any location within the area in which such Bell operating company provides telephone exchange services or exchange access.

"(h) Limitations.--The provisions of subsection (g) are intended to be narrowly construed. The interLATA services provided under subparagraph (A), (B), or (C) of subsection (g)(1) are limited to those interLATA transmissions incidental to the provision

211

by a Bell operating company or its affiliate of video, audio, and other programming services that the company or its affiliate is engaged in providing to the public. The Commission shall ensure that the provision of services authorized under subsection (g) by a Bell operating company or its affiliate will not adversely affect telephone exchange service ratepayers or competition in any telecommunications market.

"(i) Additional Definitions.--As used in this section--

"(1) In-region state.--The term 'in-region State' means a State in which a Bell operating company or any of its affiliates was authorized to provide wireline telephone exchange service pursuant to the reorganization plan approved under the AT&T Consent Decree, as in effect on the day before the date of enactment of the Telecommunications Act of 1996.

"(2) Audio programming services.--The term 'audio programming services' means programming provided by, or generally considered to be comparable to programming provided by, a radio broadcast station.

"(3) Video programming services; other programming services.--The terms 'video programming service' and 'other programming services' have the same meanings as such terms have under section 602 of this Act.

"(j) Certain Service Applications Treated as In-Region Service Applications.--For purposes of this section, a Bell operating company application to provide 800 service, private line service, or their equivalents that--

"(1) terminate in an in-region State of that Bell operating company, and

"(2) allow the called party to determine the interLATA carrier, shall be considered an in-region service subject to the requirements of subsection (b)(1).

"Section 272. SEPARATE AFFILIATE; SAFEGUARDS.

"(a) Separate Affiliate Required for Competitive Activities.--

"(1) In general.--A Bell operating company (including any affiliate) which is a local exchange carrier that is subject to the requirements of section 251(c) may not provide any service described in paragraph (2) unless it provides that service through one or more affiliates that--

"(A) are separate from any operating company entity that is subject to the requirements of section 251(c); and

"(B) meet the requirements of subsection (b).

"(2) Services for which a separate affiliate is required.--The services for which a separate affiliate is required by paragraph (1) are:

"(A) Manufacturing activities (as defined in section 273(h)).

"(B) Origination of interLATA telecommunications services, other than--

"(i) incidental interLATA services described in paragraphs (1), (2), (3), (5), and (6) of section 271(g);

"(ii) out-of-region services described in section 271(b)(2); or

"(iii) previously authorized activities described in section 271(f).

"(C) InterLATA information services, other than electronic publishing (as defined in section 274(h)) and alarm monitoring services (as defined in section 275(e)).

"(b) Structural and Transactional Requirements.--The separate affiliate required by this section--

"(1) shall operate independently from the Bell operating company;

"(2) shall maintain books, records, and accounts in the manner prescribed by the Commission which shall be separate from the books, records, and accounts maintained by the Bell operating company of which it is an affiliate;

"(3) shall have separate officers, directors, and employees from the Bell operating company of which it is an affiliate;

"(4) may not obtain credit under any arrangement that would permit a creditor, upon default, to have recourse to the assets of the Bell operating company; and

"(5) shall conduct all transactions with the Bell operating company of which it is an affiliate on an arm's length basis with any such transactions reduced to writing and available for public inspection.

"(c) Nondiscrimination Safeguards.--In its dealings with its affiliate described in subsection (a), a Bell operating company--

"(1) may not discriminate between that company or affiliate and any other entity in the provision or procurement of goods, services, facilities, and information, or in the establishment of standards; and

"(2) shall account for all transactions with an affiliate described in subsection (a) in accordance with accounting principles designated or approved by the Commission.

"(d) Biennial Audit.--

"(1) General requirement.--A company required to operate a separate affiliate under this section shall obtain and pay for a joint Federal/State audit every 2 years conducted by an independent auditor to determine whether such company has complied with this section and the regulations promulgated under this section, and particularly whether such company has complied with the separate accounting requirements under subsection (b).

"(2) Results submitted to commission; state commissions.--The auditor described in paragraph (1) shall submit the results of the audit to the Commission and to the State commission of each State in which the company audited provides service, which shall make such results available for public inspection. Any party may submit comments on the final audit report.

213

"(3) Access to documents.--For purposes of conducting audits and reviews under this subsection--

"(A) the independent auditor, the Commission, and the State commission shall have access to the financial accounts and records of each company and of its affiliates necessary to verify transactions conducted with that company that are relevant to the specific activities permitted under this section and that are necessary for the regulation of rates;

"(B) the Commission and the State commission shall have access to the working papers and supporting materials of any auditor who performs an audit under this section; and

"(C) the State commission shall implement appropriate procedures to ensure the protection of any proprietary information submitted to it under this section.

"(e) Fulfillment of Certain Requests.--A Bell operating company and an affiliate that is subject to the requirements of section 251(c)--

"(1) shall fulfill any requests from an unaffiliated entity for telephone exchange service and exchange access within a period no longer than the period in which it provides such telephone exchange service and exchange access to itself or to its affiliates;

"(2) shall not provide any facilities, services, or information concerning its provision of exchange access to the affiliate described in subsection (a) unless such facilities, services, or information are made available to other providers of interLATA services in that market on the same terms and conditions;

"(3) shall charge the affiliate described in subsection (a), or impute to itself (if using the access for its provision of its own services), an amount for access to its telephone exchange service and exchange access that is no less than the amount charged to any unaffiliated interexchange carriers for such service; and

"(4) may provide any interLATA or intraLATA facilities or services to its interLATA affiliate if such services or facilities are made available to all carriers at the same rates and on the same terms and conditions, and so long as the costs are appropriately allocated.

"(f) Sunset.--

"(1) Manufacturing and long distance.--The provisions of this section (other than subsection (e)) shall cease to apply with respect to the manufacturing activities or the interLATA telecommunications services of a Bell operating company 3 years after the date such Bell operating company or any Bell operating company affiliate is authorized to provide interLATA telecommunications services under section 271(d), unless the Commission extends such 3-year period by rule or order.

"(2) InterLATA information services.--The provisions of this section (other than subsection (e)) shall cease to apply with respect to the interLATA information services of a

Bell operating company 4 years after the date of enactment of the Telecommunications Act of 1996, unless the Commission extends such 4-year period by rule or order.

"(3) Preservation of existing authority.--Nothing in this subsection shall be construed to limit the authority of the Commission under any other section of this Act to prescribe safeguards consistent with the public interest, convenience, and necessity.

"(g) Joint Marketing.--

"(1) Affiliate sales of telephone exchange services.--A Bell operating company affiliate required by this section may not market or sell telephone exchange services provided by the Bell operating company unless that company permits other entities offering the same or similar service to market and sell its telephone exchange services.

"(2) Bell operating company sales of affiliate services.--A Bell operating company may not market or sell interLATA service provided by an affiliate required by this section within any of its in-region States until such company is authorized to provide interLATA services in such State under section 271(d).

"(3) Rule of construction.--The joint marketing and sale of services permitted under this subsection shall not be considered to violate the nondiscrimination provisions of subsection (c).

"(h) Transition.--With respect to any activity in which a Bell operating company is engaged on the date of enactment of the Telecommunications Act of 1996, such company shall have one year from such date of enactment to comply with the requirements of this section.

"Section 273. MANUFACTURING BY BELL OPERATING COMPANIES.

"(a) Authorization.--A Bell operating company may manufacture and provide telecommunications equipment, and manufacture customer premises equipment, if the Commission authorizes that Bell operating company or any Bell operating company affiliate to provide interLATA services under section 271(d), subject to the requirements of this section and the regulations prescribed thereunder, except that neither a Bell operating company nor any of its affiliates may engage in such manufacturing in conjunction with a Bell operating company not so affiliated or any of its affiliates.

"(b) Collaboration; Research and Royalty Agreements.--

"(1) Collaboration.--Subsection (a) shall not prohibit a Bell operating company from engaging in close collaboration with any manufacturer of customer premises equipment or telecommunications equipment during the design and development of hardware, software, or combinations thereof related to such equipment.

"(2) Certain research arrangements; royalty agreements.--Subsection (a) shall not prohibit a Bell operating company from--

215

"(A) engaging in research activities related to manufacturing, and

"(B) entering into royalty agreements with manufacturers of telecommunications equipment.

"(c) Information Requirements.--

"(1) Information on protocols and technical requirements.--Each Bell operating company shall, in accordance with regulations prescribed by the Commission, maintain and file with the Commission full and complete information with respect to the protocols and technical requirements for connection with and use of its telephone exchange service facilities. Each such company shall report promptly to the Commission any material changes or planned changes to such protocols and requirements, and the schedule for implementation of such changes or planned changes.

"(2) Disclosure of information.--A Bell operating company shall not disclose any information required to be filed under paragraph (1) unless that information has been filed promptly, as required by regulation by the Commission.

"(3) Access by competitors to information.--The Commission may prescribe such additional regulations under this subsection as may be necessary to ensure that manufacturers have access to the information with respect to the protocols and technical requirements for connection with and use of telephone exchange service facilities that a Bell operating company makes available to any manufacturing affiliate or any unaffiliated manufacturer.

"(4) Planning information.--Each Bell operating company shall provide, to interconnecting carriers providing telephone exchange service, timely information on the planned deployment of telecommunications equipment.

"(d) Manufacturing Limitations for Standard-Setting Organizations.--

"(1) Application to bell communications research or manufacturers.--Bell Communications Research, Inc., or any successor entity or affiliate--

"(A) shall not be considered a Bell operating company or a successor or assign of a Bell operating company at such time as it is no longer an affiliate of any Bell operating company; and

"(B) notwithstanding paragraph (3), shall not engage in manufacturing telecommunications equipment or customer premises equipment as long as it is an affiliate of more than 1 otherwise unaffiliated Bell operating company or successor or assign of any such company.

Nothing in this subsection prohibits Bell Communications Research, Inc., or any successor entity, from engaging in any activity in which it is lawfully engaged on the date of enactment of the Telecommunications Act of 1996. Nothing provided in this subsection shall render Bell Communications Research, Inc., or any successor entity, a common carrier under title II of this Act. Nothing in this subsection restricts any manufacturer from engaging in any activity in which it is lawfully engaged on the date of enactment of the Telecommunications Act of 1996.

"(2)   Proprietary information.--Any entity which establishes standards for telecommunications equipment or customer premises equipment, or generic network requirements for such equipment, or certifies telecommunications equipment or customer premises equipment, shall be prohibited from releasing or otherwise using any proprietary information, designated as such by its owner, in its possession as a result of such activity, for any purpose other than purposes authorized in writing by the owner of such information, even after such entity ceases to be so engaged.

"(3)   Manufacturing safeguards.--(A) Except as prohibited in paragraph (1), and subject to paragraph (6), any entity which certifies telecommunications equipment or customer premises equipment manufactured by an unaffiliated entity shall only manufacture a particular class of telecommunications equipment or customer premises equipment for which it is undertaking or has undertaken, during the previous 18 months, certification activity for such class of equipment through a separate affiliate.

"(B) Such separate affiliate shall--

"(i) maintain books, records, and accounts separate from those of the entity that certifies such equipment, consistent with generally acceptable accounting principles;

"(ii) not engage in any joint manufacturing activities with such entity; and

"(iii) have segregated facilities and separate employees with such entity.

"(C) Such entity that certifies such equipment shall--

"(i) not discriminate in favor of its manufacturing affiliate in the establishment of standards, generic requirements, or product certification;

"(ii) not disclose to the manufacturing affiliate any proprietary information that has been received at any time from an unaffiliated manufacturer, unless authorized in writing by the owner of the information; and

"(iii) not permit any employee engaged in product certification for telecommunications equipment or customer premises equipment to engage jointly in sales or marketing of any such equipment with the affiliated manufacturer.

"(4)   Standard-setting entities.--Any entity that is not an accredited standards development organization and that establishes industry-wide standards for telecommunications equipment or customer premises equipment, or industry-wide generic network requirements for such equipment, or that certifies telecommunications equipment or customer premises equipment manufactured by an unaffiliated entity, shall--

"(A) establish and publish any industry-wide standard for, industry-wide generic requirement for, or any substantial modification of an existing industry-wide standard or industry-wide generic requirement for, telecommunications equipment or customer premises equipment only in compliance with the following procedure:

"(i) such entity shall issue a public notice of its consideration of a proposed industry-wide standard or industry-wide generic requirement;

"(ii) such entity shall issue a public invitation to interested industry parties to fund and participate in such efforts on a reasonable and nondiscriminatory basis, administered in such a manner as not to unreasonably exclude any interested industry party;

"(iii) such entity shall publish a text for comment by such parties as have agreed to participate in the process pursuant to clause (ii), provide such parties a full opportunity to submit comments, and respond to comments from such parties;

"(iv) such entity shall publish a final text of the industry-wide standard or industry-wide generic requirement, including the comments in their entirety, of any funding party which requests to have its comments so published; and

"(v) such entity shall attempt, prior to publishing a text for comment, to agree with the funding parties as a group on a mutually satisfactory dispute resolution process which such parties shall utilize as their sole recourse in the event of a dispute on technical issues as to which there is disagreement between any funding party and the entity conducting such activities, except that if no dispute resolution process is agreed to by all the parties, a funding party may utilize the dispute resolution procedures established pursuant to paragraph (5) of this subsection;

"(B) engage in product certification for telecommunications equipment or customer premises equipment manufactured by unaffiliated entities only if--

"(i) such activity is performed pursuant to published criteria;

"(ii) such activity is performed pursuant to auditable criteria; and

"(iii) such activity is performed pursuant to available industry-accepted testing methods and standards, where applicable, unless otherwise agreed upon by the parties funding and performing such activity;

"(C) not undertake any actions to monopolize or attempt to monopolize the market for such services; and

"(D) not preferentially treat its own telecommunications equipment or customer premises equipment, or that of its affiliate, over that of any other entity in establishing and publishing industry-wide standards or industry wide generic requirements for, and in certification of, telecommunications equipment and customer premises equipment.

"(5) Alternate dispute resolution.--Within 90 days after the date of enactment of the Telecommunications Act of 1996, the Commission shall prescribe a dispute resolution process to be utilized in the event that a dispute resolution process is not agreed upon by all the parties when establishing and publishing any industry-wide standard or industry-wide generic requirement for telecommunications equipment or customer premises equipment, pursuant to paragraph (4)(A)(v). The Commission shall not establish itself as a party to the dispute resolution process. Such dispute resolution process shall permit any funding party to resolve a dispute with the entity conducting the activity that significantly affects such funding party's interests, in an open, nondiscriminatory, and unbiased fashion, within 30 days after the filing of such dispute. Such disputes may be filed within 15 days after the date the funding party receives a response to its comments from the entity conducting the activity. The Commission shall establish penalties to be assessed for delays caused by referral of frivolous disputes to the dispute resolution process.

"(6) Sunset.--The requirements of paragraphs (3) and (4) shall terminate for the particular relevant activity when the Commission determines that there are alternative sources of industry-wide standards, industry-wide generic requirements, or product certification for a particular class of telecommunications equipment or customer premises equipment available in the United States. Alternative sources shall be deemed to exist when such sources provide commercially viable alternatives that are providing such services to customers. The Commission shall act on any application for such a determination within 90 days after receipt of such application, and shall receive public comment on such application.

"(7)   Administration and enforcement authority.--For the purposes of administering this subsection and the regulations prescribed thereunder, the Commission shall have the same remedial authority as the Commission has in administering and enforcing the provisions of this title with respect to any common carrier subject to this Act.

"(8) Definitions.--For purposes of this subsection:

"(A) The term 'affiliate' shall have the same meaning as in section 3 of this Act, except that, for purposes of paragraph (1)(B)--

"(i) an aggregate voting equity interest in Bell Communications Research, Inc., of at least 5 percent of its total voting equity, owned directly or indirectly by more than 1 otherwise unaffiliated Bell operating company, shall constitute an affiliate relationship; and

"(ii) a voting equity interest in Bell Communications Research, Inc., by any otherwise unaffiliated Bell operating company of less than 1 percent of Bell Communications Research's total voting equity shall not be considered to be an equity interest under this paragraph.

"(B) The term 'generic requirement' means a description of acceptable product attributes for use by local exchange carriers in establishing product specifications for the purchase of telecommunications equipment, customer premises equipment, and software integral thereto.

"(C) The term 'industry-wide' means activities funded by or performed on behalf of local exchange carriers for use in providing wireline telephone exchange service whose combined total of deployed access lines in the United States constitutes at least 30 percent of all access lines deployed by telecommunications carriers in the United States as of the date of enactment of the Telecommunications Act of 1996.

"(D) The term 'certification' means any technical process whereby a party determines whether a product, for use by more than one local exchange carrier, conforms with the specified requirements pertaining to such product.

"(E) The term 'accredited standards development organization' means an entity composed of industry members which has been accredited by an institution vested with the responsibility for standards accreditation by the industry.

"(e) Bell Operating Company Equipment Procurement and Sales.--

"(1) Nondiscrimination standards for manufacturing.--In the procurement or awarding of supply contracts for telecommunications equipment, a Bell operating company, or any entity acting on its behalf, for the duration of the requirement for a separate subsidiary including manufacturing under this Act--

"(A) shall consider such equipment, produced or supplied by unrelated persons; and

"(B) may not discriminate in favor of equipment produced or supplied by an affiliate or related person.

"(2) Procurement standards.--Each Bell operating company or any entity acting on its behalf shall make procurement decisions and award all supply contracts for equipment, services, and software on the basis of an objective assessment of price, qualify, delivery, and other commercial factors.

"(3) Network planning and design.--A Bell operating company shall, to the extent consistent with the antitrust laws, engage in joint network planning and design with local exchange carriers operating in the same area of interest. No participant in such planning shall be allowed to delay the introduction of new technology or the deployment of facilities to provide telecommunications services, and agreement with such other carriers shall not be required as a prerequisite for such introduction or deployment.

"(4) Sales restrictions.--Neither a Bell operating company engaged in manufacturing nor a manufacturing affiliate of such a company shall restrict sales to any local exchange carrier of telecommunications equipment, including software integral to the operation of such equipment and related upgrades.

"(5) Protection of proprietary information.--A Bell operating company and any entity it owns or otherwise controls shall protect the proprietary information submitted for procurement decisions from release not specifically authorized by the owner of such information.

"(f) Administration and Enforcement Authority.--For the purposes of administering and enforcing the provisions of this section and the regulations prescribed thereunder, the Commission shall have the same authority, power, and functions with respect to any Bell operating company or any affiliate thereof as the Commission has in administering and enforcing the provisions of this title with respect to any common carrier subject to this Act.

"(g) Additional Rules and Regulations.--The Commission may prescribe such additional rules and regulations as the Commission determines are necessary to carry out the provisions of this section, and otherwise to prevent discrimination and cross-subsidization in a Bell operating company's dealings with its affiliate and with third parties.

"(h) Definition.--As used in this section, the term 'manufacturing' has the same meaning as such term has under the AT&T Consent Decree.

"Section 274. ELECTRONIC PUBLISHING BY BELL OPERATING COMPANIES.

"(a) Limitations.--No Bell operating company or any affiliate may engage in the provision of electronic publishing that is disseminated by means of such Bell operating company's or any of its affiliates' basic telephone service, except that nothing in this section shall prohibit a separated affiliate or electronic publishing joint venture operated in accordance with this section from engaging in the provision of electronic publishing.

"(b) Separated Affiliate or Electronic Publishing Joint Venture Requirements.--A separated affiliate or electronic publishing joint venture shall be operated independently from the Bell operating company. Such separated affiliate or joint venture and the Bell operating company with which it is affiliated shall--

"(1) maintain separate books, records, and accounts and prepare separate financial statements;

"(2) not incur debt in a manner that would permit a creditor of the separated affiliate or joint venture upon default to have recourse to the assets of the Bell operating company;

"(3) carry out transactions (A) in a manner consistent with such independence, (B) pursuant to written contracts or tariffs that are filed with the Commission and made publicly available, and (C) in a manner that is auditable in accordance with generally accepted auditing standards;

"(4) value any assets that are transferred directly or indirectly from the Bell operating company to a separated affiliate or joint venture, and record any transactions by which such assets are transferred, in accordance with such regulations as may be prescribed by the Commission or a State commission to prevent improper cross subsidies;

"(5) between a separated affiliate and a Bell operating company--

"(A) have no officers, directors, and employees in common after the effective date of this section; and

"(B) own no property in common;

"(6) not use for the marketing of any product or service of the separated affiliate or joint venture, the name, trademarks, or service marks of an existing Bell operating company except for names, trademarks, or service marks that are owned by the entity that owns or controls the Bell operating company;

"(7) not permit the Bell operating company--

"(A) to perform hiring or training of personnel on behalf of a separated affiliate;

"(B) to perform the purchasing, installation, or maintenance of equipment on behalf of a separated affiliate, except for telephone service that it provides under tariff or contract subject to the provisions of this section; or

"(C) to perform research and development on behalf of a separated affiliate;

"(8) each have performed annually a compliance review--

"(A) that is conducted by an independent entity for the purpose of determining compliance during the preceding calendar year with any provision of this section; and

"(B) the results of which are maintained by the separated affiliate or joint venture and the Bell operating company for a period of 5 years subject to review by any lawful authority; and

"(9) within 90 days of receiving a review described in paragraph (8), file a report of any exceptions and corrective action with the Commission and allow any person to inspect and copy such report subject to reasonable safeguards to protect any proprietary information contained in such report from being used for purposes other than to enforce or pursue remedies under this section.

"(c) Joint Marketing.--

"(1) In general.--Except as provided in paragraph (2)--

"(A) a Bell operating company shall not carry out any promotion, marketing, sales, or advertising for or in conjunction with a separated affiliate; and

"(B) a Bell operating company shall not carry out any promotion, marketing, sales, or advertising for or in conjunction with an affiliate that is related to the provision of electronic publishing.

"(2) Permissible joint activities.--

"(A) Joint telemarketing.--A Bell operating company may provide inbound telemarketing or referral services related to the provision of electronic publishing for a separated affiliate, electronic publishing joint venture, affiliate, or unaffiliated electronic publisher, provided that if such services are provided to a separated affiliate, electronic publishing joint venture, or affiliate, such services shall be made available to all electronic publishers on request, on nondiscriminatory terms.

"(B) Teaming arrangements.--A Bell operating company may engage in nondiscriminatory teaming or business arrangements to engage in electronic publishing with any separated affiliate or with any other electronic publisher if (i) the Bell operating company only provides facilities, services, and basic telephone service information as authorized by this section, and (ii) the Bell operating company does not own such teaming or business arrangement.

"(C) Electronic publishing joint ventures.--A Bell operating company or affiliate may participate on a nonexclusive basis in electronic publishing joint ventures with entities that are not a Bell operating company, affiliate, or separated affiliate to provide electronic publishing services, if the Bell operating company or affiliate has not more than a 50 percent direct or indirect equity interest (or the equivalent thereof) or the right to more than 50 percent of the gross revenues under a revenue sharing or royalty agreement in any electronic publishing joint venture. Officers and employees of a Bell operating company or affiliate participating in an electronic publishing joint venture may not have more than 50 percent of the voting control over the electronic publishing joint venture. In the case of joint ventures with small, local electronic publishers, the Commission for good cause shown may authorize the Bell operating company or affiliate to have a larger equity interest, revenue share, or voting control but not to exceed 80 percent. A Bell operating company participating in an electronic publishing joint venture may provide promotion, marketing, sales, or advertising personnel and services to such joint venture.

"(d) Bell Operating Company Requirement.--A Bell operating company under common ownership or control with a separated affiliate or electronic publishing joint venture shall provide network access and interconnections for basic telephone service to electronic publishers at just and reasonable rates that are tariffed (so long as rates for such services are subject to regulation) and that are not higher on a per-unit basis than those charged for such services to any other electronic publisher or any separated affiliate engaged in electronic publishing.

"(e) Private Right of Action.--

"(1) Damages.--Any person claiming that any act or practice of any Bell operating company, affiliate, or separated affiliate constitutes a violation of this section may file a complaint with the Commission or bring suit as provided in section 207 of this Act, and such Bell operating company, affiliate, or separated affiliate shall be liable as provided in section 206 of this Act; except that damages may not be awarded for a violation that is discovered by a compliance review as required by subsection (b)(7) of this section and corrected within 90 days.

"(2) Cease and desist orders.--In addition to the provisions of paragraph (1), any person claiming that any act or practice of any Bell operating company, affiliate, or separated affiliate constitutes a violation of this section may make application to the Commission for an order to cease and desist such violation or may make application in any district court of the United States of competent jurisdiction for an order enjoining such acts or practices or for an order compelling compliance with such requirement.

"(f)   Separated Affiliate Reporting Requirement.--Any separated affiliate under this section shall file with the Commission annual reports in a form substantially equivalent to the Form 10-K required by regulations of the Securities and Exchange Commission.

"(g)   Effective Dates.--

"(1)   Transition.--Any electronic publishing service being offered to the public by a Bell operating company or affiliate on the date of enactment of the Telecommunications Act of 1996 shall have one year from such date of enactment to comply with the requirements of this section.

"(2)   Sunset.--The provisions of this section shall not apply to conduct occurring after 4 years after the date of enactment of the Telecommunications Act of 1996.

"(h)   Definition of Electronic Publishing.--

"(1)   In general.--The term 'electronic publishing' means the dissemination, provision, publication, or sale to an unaffiliated entity or person, of any one or more of the following: news (including sports); entertainment (other than interactive games); business, financial, legal, consumer, or credit materials; editorials, columns, or features; advertising; photos or images; archival or research material; legal notices or public records; scientific, educational, instructional, technical, professional, trade, or other literary materials; or other like or similar information.

"(2)   Exceptions.--The term 'electronic publishing' shall not include the following services:

"(A) Information access, as that term is defined by the AT&T Consent Decree.

"(B) The transmission of information as a common carrier.

"(C) The transmission of information as part of a gateway to an information service that does not involve the generation or alteration of the content of information, including data transmission, address translation, protocol conversion, billing management, introductory information content, and navigational systems that enable users to access electronic publishing services, which do not affect the presentation of such electronic publishing services to users.

"(D) Voice storage and retrieval services, including voice messaging and electronic mail services.

"(E) Data processing or transaction processing services that do not involve the generation or alteration of the content of information.

"(F) Electronic billing or advertising of a Bell operating company's regulated telecommunications services.

"(G) Language translation or data format conversion.

"(H) The provision of information necessary for the management, control, or operation of a telephone company telecommunications system.

"(I) The provision of directory assistance that provides names, addresses, and telephone numbers and does not include advertising.

"(J) Caller identification services.

"(K) Repair and provisioning databases and credit card and billing validation for telephone company operations.

"(L) 911-E and other emergency assistance databases.

"(M) Any other network service of a type that is like or similar to these network services and that does not involve the generation or alteration of the content of information.

"(N) Any upgrades to these network services that do not involve the generation or alteration of the content of information.

"(O) Video programming or full motion video entertainment on demand.

"(i) Additional Definitions.--As used in this section--

"(1) The term 'affiliate' means any entity that, directly or indirectly, owns or controls, is owned or controlled by, or is under common ownership or control with, a Bell operating company. Such term shall not include a separated affiliate.

"(2) The term 'basic telephone service' means any wireline telephone exchange service, or wireline telephone exchange service facility, provided by a Bell operating company in a telephone exchange area, except that such term does not include--

"(A) a competitive wireline telephone exchange service provided in a telephone exchange area where another entity provides a wireline telephone exchange service that was provided on January 1, 1984, or

"(B) a commercial mobile service.

"(3) The term 'basic telephone service information' means network and customer information of a Bell operating company and other information acquired by a Bell operating company as a result of its engaging in the provision of basic telephone service.

"(4) The term 'control' has the meaning that it has in 17 CFR 240.12b-2, the regulations promulgated by the Securities and Exchange Commission pursuant to the Securities Exchange Act of 1934 (15 U.S.C. 78a et seq.) or any successor provision to such section.

"(5) The term 'electronic publishing joint venture' means a joint venture owned by a Bell operating company or affiliate that engages in the provision of electronic

225

publishing which is disseminated by means of such Bell operating company's or any of its affiliates' basic telephone service.

"(6)   The term 'entity' means any organization, and includes corporations, partnerships, sole proprietorships, associations, and joint ventures.

"(7)   The term 'inbound telemarketing' means the marketing of property, goods, or services by telephone to a customer or potential customer who initiated the call.

"(8)   The term 'own' with respect to an entity means to have a direct or indirect equity interest (or the equivalent thereof) of more than 10 percent of an entity, or the right to more than 10 percent of the gross revenues of an entity under a revenue sharing or royalty agreement.

"(9)   The term 'separated affiliate' means a corporation under common ownership or control with a Bell operating company that does not own or control a Bell operating company and is not owned or controlled by a Bell operating company and that engages in the provision of electronic publishing which is disseminated by means of such Bell operating company's or any of its affiliates' basic telephone service.

"(10)   The term 'Bell operating company' has the meaning provided in section 3, except that such term includes any entity or corporation that is owned or controlled by such a company (as so defined) but does not include an electronic publishing joint venture owned by such an entity or corporation.

"Section 275. ALARM MONITORING SERVICES.

"(a)   Delayed Entry Into Alarm Monitoring.--
"(1)   Prohibition.--No Bell operating company or affiliate thereof shall engage in the provision of alarm monitoring services before the date which is 5 years after the date of enactment of the Telecommunications Act of 1996.

"(2)   Existing activities.--Paragraph (1) does not prohibit or limit the provision, directly or through an affiliate, of alarm monitoring services by a Bell operating company that was engaged in providing alarm monitoring services as of November 30, 1995, directly or through an affiliate. Such Bell operating company or affiliate may not acquire any equity interest in, or obtain financial control of, any unaffiliated alarm monitoring service entity after November 30, 1995, and until 5 years after the date of enactment of the Telecommunications Act of 1996, except that this sentence shall not prohibit an exchange of customers for the customers of an unaffiliated alarm monitoring service entity.

"(b)   Nondiscrimination.--An incumbent local exchange carrier (as defined in section 251(h)) engaged in the provision of alarm monitoring services shall--

"(1) provide nonaffiliated entities, upon reasonable request, with the network services it provides to its own alarm monitoring operations, on nondiscriminatory terms and conditions; and

"(2) not subsidize its alarm monitoring services either directly or indirectly from telephone exchange service operations.

"(c) Expedited Consideration of Complaints.--The Commission shall establish procedures for the receipt and review of complaints concerning violations of subsection (b) or the regulations thereunder that result in material financial harm to a provider of alarm monitoring service. Such procedures shall ensure that the Commission will make a final determination with respect to any such complaint within 120 days after receipt of the complaint. If the complaint contains an appropriate showing that the alleged violation occurred, as determined by the Commission in accordance with such regulations, the Commission shall, within 60 days after receipt of the complaint, order the incumbent local exchange carrier (as defined in section 251(h)) and its affiliates to cease engaging in such violation pending such final determination.

"(d) Use of Data.--A local exchange carrier may not record or use in any fashion the occurrence or contents of calls received by providers of alarm monitoring services for the purposes of marketing such services on behalf of such local exchange carrier, or any other entity. Any regulations necessary to enforce this subsection shall be issued initially within 6 months after the date of enactment of the Telecommunications Act of 1996.

"(e) Definition of Alarm Monitoring service.--The term "alarm monitoring service" means a service that uses a device located at a residence, place of business, or other fixed premises--

"(1) to receive signals from other devices located at or about such premises regarding a possible threat at such premises to life, safety, or property, from burglary, fire, vandalism, bodily injury, or other emergency, and

"(2) to transmit a signal regarding such threat by means of transmission facilities of a local exchange carrier or one of its affiliates to a remote monitoring center to alert a person at such center of the need to inform the customer or another person or police, fire, rescue, security, or public safety personnel of such threat, but does not include a service that uses a medical monitoring device attached to an individual for the automatic surveillance of an ongoing medical condition.

"Section 276. PROVISION OF PAYPHONE SERVICE.

"(a) Nondiscrimination Safeguards.--After the effective date of the rules prescribed pursuant to subsection (b), any Bell operating company that provides payphone service--

227

"(1) shall not subsidize its payphone service directly or indirectly from its telephone exchange service operations or its exchange access operations; and

"(2) shall not prefer or discriminate in favor of its payphone service.

"(b) Regulations.--

"(1) Contents of regulations.--In order to promote competition among payphone service providers and promote the widespread deployment of payphone services to the benefit of the general public, within 9 months after the date of enactment of the Telecommunications Act of 1996, the Commission shall take all actions necessary (including any reconsideration) to prescribe regulations that--

"(A) establish a per call compensation plan to ensure that all payphone service providers are fairly compensated for each and every completed intrastate and interstate call using their payphone, except that emergency calls and telecommunications relay service calls for hearing disabled individuals shall not be subject to such compensation;

"(B) discontinue the intrastate and interstate carrier access charge payphone service elements and payments in effect on such date of enactment, and all intrastate and interstate payphone subsidies from basic exchange and exchange access revenues, in favor of a compensation plan as specified in subparagraph (A);

"(C) prescribe a set of nonstructural safeguards for Bell operating company payphone service to implement the provisions of paragraphs (1) and (2) of subsection (a), which safeguards shall, at a minimum, include the nonstructural safeguards equal to those adopted in the Computer Inquiry-III (CC Docket No. 90-623) proceeding;

"(D) provide for Bell operating company payphone service providers to have the same right that independent payphone providers have to negotiate with the location provider on the location provider's selecting and contracting with, and, subject to the terms of any agreement with the location provider, to select and contract with, the carriers that carry interLATA calls from their payphones, unless the Commission determines in the rulemaking pursuant to this section that it is not in the public interest; and

"(E) provide for all payphone service providers to have the right to negotiate with the location provider on the location provider's selecting and contracting with, and, subject to the terms of any agreement with the location provider, to select and contract with, the carriers that carry intraLATA calls from their payphones.

"(2) Public interest telephones.--In the rulemaking conducted pursuant to paragraph (1), the Commission shall determine whether public interest payphones, which are provided in the interest of public health, safety, and welfare, in locations where there would otherwise not be a payphone, should be maintained, and if so, ensure that such public interest payphones are supported fairly and equitably.

"(3) Existing contracts.--Nothing in this section shall affect any existing contracts between location providers and payphone service providers or interLATA or intraLATA carriers that are in force and effect as of the date of enactment of the Telecommunications Act of 1996.

"(c) State Preemption.--To the extent that any State requirements are inconsistent with the Commission's regulations, the Commission's regulations on such matters shall preempt such State requirements.

"(d) Definition.--As used in this section, the term 'payphone service' means the provision of public or semi-public pay telephones, the provision of inmate telephone service in correctional institutions, and any ancillary services."

(b) Review of Entry Decisions.--Section 402(b) (47 U.S.C. 402(b)) is amended--

(1) in paragraph (6), by striking "(3), and (4)" and inserting "(3), (4), and (9)"; and

(2) by adding at the end the following new paragraph:

"(9) By any applicant for authority to provide interLATA services under section 271 of this Act whose application is denied by the Commission."

TITLE II--BROADCAST SERVICES

SEC. 201. BROADCAST SPECTRUM FLEXIBILITY.

Title III is amended by inserting after section 335 (47 U.S.C. 335) the following new section:

"Section 336. BROADCAST SPECTRUM FLEXIBILITY.

"(a) Commission Action.--If the Commission determines to issue additional licenses for advanced television services, the Commission--

"(1) should limit the initial eligibility for such licenses to persons that, as of the date of such issuance, are licensed to operate a television broadcast station or hold a permit to construct such a station (or both); and

"(2) shall adopt regulations that allow the holders of such licenses to offer such ancillary or supplementary services on designated frequencies as may be consistent with the public interest, convenience, and necessity.

"(b) Contents of Regulations.--In prescribing the regulations required by subsection (a), the Commission shall--

"(1) only permit such licensee or permittee to offer ancillary or supplementary services if the use of a designated frequency for such services is consistent with the technology or method designated by the Commission for the provision of advanced television services;

"(2) limit the broadcasting of ancillary or supplementary services on designated frequencies so as to avoid derogation of any advanced television services, including high definition television broadcasts, that the Commission may require using such frequencies;

"(3) apply to any other ancillary or supplementary service such of the Commission's regulations as are applicable to the offering of analogous services by any other person, except that no ancillary or supplementary service shall have any rights to carriage under section 614 or 615 or be deemed a multichannel video programming distributor for purposes of section 628;

"(4) adopt such technical and other requirements as may be necessary or appropriate to assure the quality of the signal used to provide advanced television services, and may adopt regulations that stipulate the minimum number of hours per day that such signal must be transmitted; and

"(5) prescribe such other regulations as may be necessary for the protection of the public interest, convenience, and necessity.

"(c) Recovery of License.--If the Commission grants a license for advanced television services to a person that, as of the date of such issuance, is licensed to operate a television broadcast station or holds a permit to construct such a station (or both), the Commission shall, as a condition of such license, require that either the additional license or the original license held by the licensee be surrendered to the Commission for reallocation or reassignment (or both) pursuant to Commission regulation.

"(d) Public Interest Requirement.--Nothing in this section shall be construed as relieving a television broadcasting station from its obligation to serve the public interest, convenience, and necessity. In the Commission's review of any application for renewal of a broadcast license for a television station that provides ancillary or supplementary services, the television licensee shall establish that all of its program services on the existing or advanced television spectrum are in the public interest. Any violation of the Commission rules applicable to ancillary or supplementary services shall reflect upon the licensee's qualifications for renewal of its license.

"(e) Fees.--

"(1) Services to which fees apply.--If the regulations prescribed pursuant to subsection (a) permit a licensee to offer ancillary or supplementary services on a designated frequency--

"(A) for which the payment of a subscription fee is required in order to receive such services, or

"(B) for which the licensee directly or indirectly receives compensation from a third party in return for transmitting material furnished by such third party (other than commercial advertisements used to support broadcasting for which a subscription fee is not required), the Commission shall establish a program to assess and collect from the licensee for such designated frequency an annual fee or other schedule or method of payment that promotes the objectives described in subparagraphs (A) and (B) of paragraph (2).

"(2) Collection of fees.--The program required by paragraph (1) shall--

"(A) be designed (i) to recover for the public a portion of the value of the public spectrum resource made available for such commercial use, and (ii) to avoid unjust enrichment through the method employed to permit such uses of that resource;

"(B) recover for the public an amount that, to the extent feasible, equals but does not exceed (over the term of the license) the amount that would have been recovered had such services been licensed pursuant to the provisions of section 309(j) of this Act and the Commission's regulations thereunder; and

"(C) be adjusted by the Commission from time to time in order to continue to comply with the requirements of this paragraph.

"(3) Treatment of revenues.--

"(A) General rule.--Except as provided in subparagraph (B), all proceeds obtained pursuant to the regulations required by this subsection shall be deposited in the Treasury in accordance with chapter 33 of title 31, United States Code.

"(B) Retention of revenues.--Notwithstanding subparagraph (A), the salaries and expenses account of the Commission shall retain as an offsetting collection such sums as may be necessary from such proceeds for the costs of developing and implementing the program required by this section and regulating and supervising advanced television services. Such offsetting collections shall be available for obligation subject to the terms and conditions of the receiving appropriations account, and shall be deposited in such accounts on a quarterly basis.

"(4) Report.--Within 5 years after the date of enactment of the Telecommunications Act of 1996, the Commission shall report to the Congress on the implementation of the program required by this subsection, and shall annually thereafter advise the Congress on the amounts collected pursuant to such program.

"(f) Evaluation.--Within 10 years after the date the Commission first issues additional licenses for advanced television services, the Commission shall conduct an evaluation of the advanced television services program. Such evaluation shall include--

"(1) an assessment of the willingness of consumers to purchase the television receivers necessary to receive broadcasts of advanced television services;

"(2) an assessment of alternative uses, including public safety use, of the frequencies used for such broadcasts; and

"(3) the extent to which the Commission has been or will be able to reduce the amount of spectrum assigned to licensees.

"(g) Definitions.--As used in this section:

"(1) Advanced television services.--The term 'advanced television services' means television services provided using digital or other advanced technology as further defined in the opinion, report, and order of the Commission entitled Advanced Television Systems and Their Impact Upon the Existing Television Broadcast Service, MM Docket 87-268, adopted September 17, 1992, and successor proceedings.

"(2) Designated frequencies.--The term 'designated frequency' means each of the frequencies designated by the Commission for licenses for advanced television services.

"(3) High definition television.--The term 'high definition television' refers to systems that offer approximately twice the vertical and horizontal resolution of receivers generally available on the date of enactment of the Telecommunications Act of 1996, as further defined in the proceedings described in paragraph (1) of this subsection."

SEC. 202. BROADCAST OWNERSHIP.

(a) National Radio Station Ownership Rule Changes Required.--The Commission shall modify section 73.3555 of its regulations (47 CFR 73.3555) by eliminating any provisions limiting the number of AM or FM broadcast stations which may be owned or controlled by one entity nationally.

(b) Local Radio Diversity.--

(1) Applicable caps.--The Commission shall revise section 73.3555(a) of its regulations (47 CFR 73.3555) to provide that--

(A) in a radio market with 45 or more commercial radio stations, a party may own, operate, or control up to 8 commercial radio stations, not more than 5 of which are in the same service (AM or FM);

(B) in a radio market with between 30 and 44 (inclusive) commercial radio stations, a party may own, operate, or control up to 7 commercial radio stations, not more than 4 of which are in the same service (AM or FM);

(C) in a radio market with between 15 and 29 (inclusive) commercial radio stations, a party may own, operate, or control up to 6 commercial radio stations, not more than 4 of which are in the same service (AM or FM); and

(D) in a radio market with 14 or fewer commercial radio stations, a party may own, operate, or control up to 5 commercial radio stations, not more than 3 of which are in the same service (AM or FM), except that a party may not own, operate, or control more than 50 percent of the stations in such market.

(2) Exception.--Notwithstanding any limitation authorized by this subsection, the Commission may permit a person or entity to own, operate, or control, or have a cognizable interest in, radio broadcast stations if the Commission determines that such ownership,

operation, control, or interest will result in an increase in the number of radio broadcast stations in operation.

(c) Television Ownership Limitations.--

(1) National ownership limitations.--The Commission shall modify its rules for multiple ownership set forth in section 73.3555 of its regulations (47 CFR 73.3555)--

(A) by eliminating the restrictions on the number of television stations that a person or entity may directly or indirectly own, operate, or control, or have a cognizable interest in, nationwide; and

(B) by increasing the national audience reach limitation for television stations to 35 percent.

(2) Local ownership limitations.--The Commission shall conduct a rulemaking proceeding to determine whether to retain, modify, or eliminate its limitations on the number of television stations that a person or entity may own, operate, or control, or have a cognizable interest in, within the same television market.

(d) Relaxation of One-To-A-Market.--With respect to its enforcement of its one-to-a-market ownership rules under section 73.3555 of its regulations, the Commission shall extend its waiver policy to any of the top 50 markets, consistent with the public interest, convenience, and necessity.

(e) Dual Network Changes.--The Commission shall revise section 73.658(g) of its regulations (47 CFR 73.658(g)) to permit a television broadcast station to affiliate with a person or entity that maintains 2 or more networks of television broadcast stations unless such dual or multiple networks are composed of--

(1) two or more persons or entities that, on the date of enactment of the Telecommunications Act of 1996, are "networks" as defined in section 73.3613(a)(1) of the Commission's regulations (47 CFR 73.3613(a)(1)); or

(2) any network described in paragraph (1) and an English-language program distribution service that, on such date, provides 4 or more hours of programming per week on a national basis pursuant to network affiliation arrangements with local television broadcast stations in markets reaching more than 75 percent of television homes (as measured by a national ratings service).

(f) Cable Cross Ownership.--

(1) Elimination of restrictions.--The Commission shall revise section 76.501 of its regulations (47 CFR 76.501) to permit a person or entity to own or control a network of broadcast stations and a cable system.

(2) Safeguards against discrimination.--The Commission shall revise such regulations if necessary to ensure carriage, channel positioning, and nondiscriminatory treatment of nonaffiliated broadcast stations by a cable system described in paragraph (1).

(g) Local Marketing Agreements.--Nothing in this section shall be construed to prohibit the origination, continuation, or renewal of any television local marketing agreement that is in compliance with the regulations of the Commission.

(h) Further Commission Review.--The Commission shall review its rules adopted pursuant to this section and all of its ownership rules biennially as part of its regulatory reform review under section 11 of the Communications Act of 1934 and shall determine whether any of such rules are necessary in the public interest as the result of competition. The Commission shall repeal or modify any regulation it determines to be no longer in the public interest.

(i) Elimination of Statutory Restriction.--Section 613(a) (47 U.S.C. 533(a)) is amended--

(1) by striking paragraph (1);

(2) by redesignating paragraph (2) as subsection (a);

(3) by redesignating subparagraphs (A) and (B) as paragraphs (1) and (2), respectively;

(4) by striking "and" at the end of paragraph (1) (as so redesignated);

(5) by striking the period at the end of paragraph (2) (as so redesignated) and inserting "; and"; and

(6) by adding at the end the following new paragraph:

"(3) shall not apply the requirements of this subsection to any cable operator in any franchise area in which a cable operator is subject to effective competition as determined under section 623(l)."

SEC. 203. TERM OF LICENSES.

Section 307(c) (47 U.S.C. 307(c)) is amended to read as follows:

"(c) Terms of Licenses.--

"(1) Initial and renewal licenses.--Each license granted for the operation of a broadcasting station shall be for a term of not to exceed 8 years. Upon application therefor, a renewal of such license may be granted from time to time for a term of not to exceed 8 years from the date of expiration of the preceding license, if the Commission finds that public interest, convenience, and necessity would be served thereby. Consistent with the foregoing provisions of this subsection, the Commission may by rule prescribe the period or periods for which licenses shall be granted and renewed for particular classes of stations, but the Commission may not adopt or follow any rule which would preclude it, in any case involving a station of a particular class, from granting or renewing a license for a shorter period than that prescribed for stations of such class if, in its judgment, the public interest, convenience, or necessity would be served by such action.

"(2) Materials in application.--In order to expedite action on applications for renewal of broadcasting station licenses and in order to avoid needless expense to applicants for such renewals, the Commission shall not require any such applicant to file any information which previously has been furnished to the Commission or which is not directly material to the considerations that affect the granting or denial of such application, but the Commission may require any new or additional facts it deems necessary to make its findings.

"(3) Continuation pending decision.--Pending any hearing and final decision on such an application and the disposition of any petition for rehearing pursuant to section 405, the Commission shall continue such license in effect."

SEC. 204. BROADCAST LICENSE RENEWAL PROCEDURES.

(a) Renewal Procedures.--
(1) Amendment.--Section 309 (47 U.S.C. 309) is amended by adding at the end thereof the following new subsection:
"(k) Broadcast Station Renewal Procedures.--
"(1) Standards for renewal.--If the licensee of a broadcast station submits an application to the Commission for renewal of such license, the Commission shall grant the application if it finds, with respect to that station, during the preceding term of its license--
"(A) the station has served the public interest, convenience, and necessity;
"(B) there have been no serious violations by the licensee of this Act or the rules and regulations of the Commission; and
"(C) there have been no other violations by the licensee of this Act or the rules and regulations of the Commission which, taken together, would constitute a pattern of abuse.
"(2) Consequence of failure to meet standard.--If any licensee of a broadcast station fails to meet the requirements of this subsection, the Commission may deny the application for renewal in accordance with paragraph (3), or grant such application on terms and conditions as are appropriate, including renewal for a term less than the maximum otherwise permitted.
"(3) Standards for denial.--If the Commission determines, after notice and opportunity for a hearing as provided in subsection (e), that a licensee has failed to meet the requirements specified in paragraph (1) and that no mitigating factors justify the imposition of lesser sanctions, the Commission shall--
"(A) issue an order denying the renewal application filed by such licensee under section 308; and

"(B) only thereafter accept and consider such applications for a construction permit as may be filed under section 308 specifying the channel or broadcasting facilities of the former licensee.

"(4) Competitor consideration prohibited.--In making the determinations specified in paragraph (1) or (2), the Commission shall not consider whether the public interest, convenience, and necessity might be served by the grant of a license to a person other than the renewal applicant."

(2) Conforming amendment.--Section 309(d) (47 U.S.C. 309(d)) is amended by inserting after "with subsection (a)" each place it appears the following: "(or subsection (k) in the case of renewal of any broadcast station license)".

(b) Summary of Complaints on Violent Programming.--Section 308 (47 U.S.C. 308) is amended by adding at the end the following new subsection:

"(d) Summary of Complaints.--Each applicant for the renewal of a commercial or noncommercial television license shall attach as an exhibit to the application a summary of written comments and suggestions received from the public and maintained by the licensee (in accordance with Commission regulations) that comment on the applicant's programming, if any, and that are characterized by the commentor as constituting violent programming."

(c) Effective Date.--The amendments made by this section apply to applications filed after May 1, 1995.

SEC. 205. DIRECT BROADCAST SATELLITE SERVICE.

(a) DBS Signal Security.--Section 705(e)(4) (47 U.S.C. 605(e)(4)) is amended by inserting "or direct-to-home satellite services," after "programming,".

(b) FCC Jurisdiction Over Direct-to-Home Satellite Services.--Section 303 (47 U.S.C. 303) is amended by adding at the end thereof the following new subsection:

"(v) Have exclusive jurisdiction to regulate the provision of direct-to home satellite services. As used in this subsection, the term "direct-to-home satellite services" means the distribution or broadcasting of programming or services by satellite directly to the subscriber's premises without the use of ground receiving or distribution equipment, except at the subscriber's premises or in the uplink process to the satellite."

SEC. 206. AUTOMATED SHIP DISTRESS AND SAFETY SYSTEMS.

Part II of title III is amended by inserting after section 364 (47 U.S.C. 362) the following new section:

"Section 365. AUTOMATED SHIP DISTRESS AND SAFETY SYSTEMS.

"Notwithstanding any provision of this Act or any other provision of law or regulation, a ship documented under the laws of the United States operating in accordance with the Global Maritime Distress and Safety System provisions of the Safety of Life at Sea Convention shall not be required to be equipped with a radio telegraphy station operated by one or more radio officers or operators. This section shall take effect for each vessel upon a determination by the United States Coast Guard that such vessel has the equipment required to implement the Global Maritime Distress and Safety System installed and operating in good working condition."

SEC. 207. RESTRICTIONS ON OVER-THE-AIR RECEPTION DEVICES.

Within 180 days after the date of enactment of this Act, the Commission shall, pursuant to section 303 of the Communications Act of 1934, promulgate regulations to prohibit restrictions that impair a viewer's ability to receive video programming services through devices designed for over-the-air reception of television broadcast signals, multichannel multipoint distribution service, or direct broadcast satellite services.

TITLE III—CABLE SERVICES

SEC. 301. CABLE ACT REFORM.

(a) Definitions.--
(1) Definition of cable service.--Section 602(6)(B) (47 U.S.C. 522(6)(B)) is amended by inserting "or use" after "the selection".
(2) Change in definition of cable system.--Section 602(7) (47 U.S.C. 522(7)) is amended by striking "(B) a facility that serves only subscribers in 1 or more multiple unit dwellings under common ownership, control, or management, unless such facility or facilities uses any public right-of-way;" and inserting "(B) a facility that serves subscribers without using any public right-of-way;".
(b) Rate Deregulation.--
(1) Upper tier regulation.--Section 623(c) (47 U.S.C. 543(c)) is amended--
(A) in paragraph (1)(B), by striking "subscriber, franchising authority, or other relevant State or local government entity" and inserting "franchising authority (in accordance with paragraph (3))";
(B) in paragraph (1)(C), by striking "such complaint" and inserting "the first complaint filed with the franchising authority under paragraph (3)"; and

(C) by striking paragraph (3) and inserting the following:

"(3) Review of rate changes.--The Commission shall review any complaint submitted by a franchising authority after the date of enactment of the Telecommunications Act of 1996 concerning an increase in rates for cable programming services and issue a final order within 90 days after it receives such a complaint, unless the parties agree to extend the period for such review. A franchising authority may not file a complaint under this paragraph unless, within 90 days after such increase becomes effective it receives subscriber complaints.

"(4) Sunset of upper tier rate regulation.--This subsection shall not apply to cable programming services provided after March 31, 1999."

(2) Sunset of uniform rate structure in markets with effective competition.--Section 623(d) (47 U.S.C. 543(d)) is amended by adding at the end thereof the following:

"This subsection does not apply to (1) a cable operator with respect to the provision of cable service over its cable system in any geographic area in which the video programming services offered by the operator in that area are subject to effective competition, or (2) any video programming offered on a per channel or per program basis. Bulk discounts to multiple dwelling units shall not be subject to this subsection, except that a cable operator of a cable system that is not subject to effective competition may not charge predatory prices to a multiple dwelling unit. Upon a prima facie showing by a complainant that there are reasonable grounds to believe that the discounted price is predatory, the cable system shall have the burden of showing that its discounted price is not predatory."

(3) Effective competition.--Section 623(l)(1) (47 U.S.C. 543(l)(1)) is amended--

(A) by striking "or" at the end of subparagraph (B);

(B) by striking the period at the end of subparagraph (C) and inserting "; or";
and

(C) by adding at the end the following:

"(D) a local exchange carrier or its affiliate (or any multichannel video programming distributor using the facilities of such carrier or its affiliate) offers video programming services directly to subscribers by any means (other than direct-to-home satellite services) in the franchise area of an unaffiliated cable operator which is providing cable service in that franchise area, but only if the video programming services so offered in that area are comparable to the video programming services provided by the unaffiliated cable operator in that area."

(c) Greater Deregulation for Smaller Cable Companies.--Section 623 (47 U.S.C 543) is amended by adding at the end thereof the following:

"(m) Special Rules for Small Companies.--

"(1) In general.--Subsections (a), (b), and (c) do not apply to a small cable operator with respect to--

"(A) cable programming services, or

"(B) a basic service tier that was the only service tier subject to regulation as of December 31, 1994, in any franchise area in which that operator services 50,000 or fewer subscribers.

"(2) Definition of small cable operator.--For purposes of this subsection, the term 'small cable operator' means a cable operator that, directly or through an affiliate, serves in the aggregate fewer than 1 percent of all subscribers in the United States and is not affiliated with any entity or entities whose gross annual revenues in the aggregate exceed $250,000,000."

(d) Market Determinations.--

(1) Market determinations; expedited decisionmaking.--Section 614(h)(1)(C) (47 U.S.C. 534(h)(1)(C)) is amended--

(A) by striking "in the manner provided in section 73.3555(d)(3)(i) of title 47, Code of Federal Regulations, as in effect on May 1, 1991," in clause (i) and inserting "by the Commission by regulation or order using, where available, commercial publications which delineate television markets based on viewing patterns,"; and

(B) by striking clause (iv) and inserting the following:

"(iv) Within 120 days after the date on which a request is filed under this subparagraph (or 120 days after the date of enactment of the Telecommunications Act of 1996, if later), the Commission shall grant or deny the request."

(2) Application to pending requests.--The amendment made by paragraph (1) shall apply to

(A) any request pending under section 614(h)(1)(C) of the Communications Act of 1934 (47 U.S.C. 534(h)(1)(C)) on the date of enactment of this Act; and

(B) any request filed under that section after that date.

(e) Technical Standards.--Section 624(e) (47 U.S.C. 544(e)) is amended by striking the last two sentences and inserting the following: "No State or franchising authority may prohibit, condition, or restrict a cable system's use of any type of subscriber equipment or any transmission technology."

(f) Cable Equipment Compatibility.--Section 624A (47 U.S.C. 544A) is amended--

(1) in subsection (a) by striking "and" at the end of paragraph (2), by striking the period at the end of paragraph (3) and inserting "; and"; and by adding at the end the following new paragraph:

"(4) compatibility among televisions, video cassette recorders, and cable systems can be assured with narrow technical standards that mandate a minimum degree of common design and operation, leaving all features, functions, protocols, and other product and service options for selection through open competition in the market.".;

(2) in subsection (c)(1)--

(A) by redesignating subparagraphs (A) and (B) as subparagraphs (B) and (C), respectively; and

(B) by inserting before such redesignated subparagraph (B) the following new subparagraph:

"(A) the need to maximize open competition in the market for all features, functions, protocols, and other product and service options of converter boxes and other cable converters unrelated to the descrambling or decryption of cable television signals;" and

(3) in subsection (c)(2)--

(A) by redesignating subparagraphs (D) and (E) as subparagraphs (E) and (F), respectively; and

(B) by inserting after subparagraph (C) the following new subparagraph:

"(D) to ensure that any standards or regulations developed under the authority of this section to ensure compatibility between televisions, video cassette recorders, and cable systems do not affect features, functions, protocols, and other product and service options other than those specified in paragraph (1)(B), including telecommunications interface equipment, home automation communications, and computer network services;".

(g) Subscriber Notice.--Section 632 (47 U.S.C. 552) is amended--

(1) by redesignating subsection (c) as subsection (d); and

(2) by inserting after subsection (b) the following new subsection:

"(c) Subscriber Notice.--A cable operator may provide notice of service and rate changes to subscribers using any reasonable written means at its sole discretion. Notwithstanding section 623(b)(6) or any other provision of this Act, a cable operator shall not be required to provide prior notice of any rate change that is the result of a regulatory fee, franchise fee, or any other fee, tax, assessment, or charge of any kind imposed by any Federal agency, State, or franchising authority on the transaction between the operator and the subscriber."

(h) Program Access.--Section 628 (47 U.S.C. 548) is amended by adding at the end the following:

"(j) Common Carriers.--Any provision that applies to a cable operator under this section shall apply to a common carrier or its affiliate that provides video programming by any means directly to subscribers. Any such provision that applies to a satellite cable programming vendor in which a cable operator has an attributable interest shall apply to any satellite cable programming vendor in which such common carrier has an attributable interest. For the purposes of this subsection, two or fewer common officers or directors shall

240

not by itself establish an attributable interest by a common carrier in a satellite cable programming vendor (or its parent company)."

(i) Antitrafficking.--Section 617 (47 U.S.C. 537) is amended--

(1) by striking subsections (a) through (d); and

(2) in subsection (e), by striking "(e)" and all that follows through "a franchising authority" and inserting "A franchising authority".

(j) Aggregation of Equipment Costs.--Section 623(a) (47 U.S.C. 543(a)) is amended by adding at the end the following new paragraph:

"(7) Aggregation of equipment costs.--

"(A) In general.--The Commission shall allow cable operators, pursuant to any rules promulgated under subsection (b)(3), to aggregate, on a franchise, system, regional, or company level, their equipment costs into broad categories, such as converter boxes, regardless of the varying levels of functionality of the equipment within each such broad category. Such aggregation shall not be permitted with respect to equipment used by subscribers who receive only a rate regulated basic service tier.

(B) Revision to commission rules; forms.--Within 120 days of the date of enactment of the Telecommunications Act of 1996, the Commission shall issue revisions to the appropriate rules and forms necessary to implement subparagraph (A)."

(k) Treatment of Prior Year Losses.--

(1) Amendment.--Section 623 (47 U.S.C. 543) is amended by adding at the end thereof the following:

"(n) Treatment of Prior Year Losses.--Notwithstanding any other provision of this section or of section 612, losses associated with a cable system (including losses associated with the grant or award of a franchise) that were incurred prior to September 4, 1992, with respect to a cable system that is owned and operated by the original franchisee of such system shall not be disallowed, in whole or in part, in the determination of whether the rates for any tier of service or any type of equipment that is subject to regulation under this section are lawful."

(2) Effective date.--The amendment made by paragraph (1) shall take effect on the date of enactment of this Act and shall be applicable to any rate proposal filed on or after September 4, 1993, upon which no final action has been taken by December 1, 1995.

SEC. 302. CABLE SERVICE PROVIDED BY TELEPHONE COMPANIES.

(a) Provisions for Regulation of Cable Service Provided by Telephone Companies.--Title VI (47 U.S.C. 521 et seq.) is amended by adding at the end the following new part:

241

"PART V--VIDEO PROGRAMMING SERVICES PROVIDED BY TELEPHONE COMPANIES

"Section 651.   REGULATORY TREATMENT OF VIDEO PROGRAMMING SERVICES.

"(a) Limitations on Cable Regulation.--

"(1)   Radio-based systems.--To the extent that a common carrier (or any other person) is providing video programming to subscribers using radio communication, such carrier (or other person) shall be subject to the requirements of title III and section 652, but shall not otherwise be subject to the requirements of this title.

"(2)   Common carriage of video traffic.--To the extent that a common carrier is providing transmission of video programming on a common carrier basis, such carrier shall be subject to the requirements of title II and section 652, but shall not otherwise be subject to the requirements of this title.
This paragraph shall not affect the treatment under section 602(7)(C) of a facility of a common carrier as a cable system.

"(3) Cable systems and open video systems.--To the extent that a common carrier is providing video programming to its subscribers in any manner other than that described in paragraphs (1) and (2)--

"(A) such carrier shall be subject to the requirements of this title, unless such programming is provided by means of an open video system for which the Commission has approved a certification under section 653; or

"(B) if such programming is provided by means of an open video system for which the Commission has approved a certification under section 653, such carrier shall be subject to the requirements of this part, but shall be subject to parts I through IV of this title only as provided in 653(c).

"(4)   Election to operate as open video system.--A common carrier that is providing video programming in a manner described in paragraph (1) or (2), or a combination thereof, may elect to provide such programming by means of an open video system that complies with section 653.   If the Commission approves such carrier's certification under section 653, such carrier shall be subject to the requirements of this part, but shall be subject to parts I through IV of this title only as provided in 653(c).

"(b) Limitations on Interconnection Obligations.--A local exchange carrier that provides cable service through an open video system or a cable system shall not be required, pursuant to title II of this Act, to make capacity available on a nondiscriminatory basis to any other person for the provision of cable service directly to subscribers.

"(c) Additional Regulatory Relief.--A common carrier shall not be required to obtain a certificate under section 214 with respect to the establishment or operation of a system for the delivery of video programming.

"Section 652. PROHIBITION ON BUY-OUTS.

"(a) Acquisitions by Carriers.--No local exchange carrier or any affiliate of such carrier owned by, operated by, controlled by, or under common control with such carrier may purchase or otherwise acquire directly or indirectly more than a 10 percent financial interest, or any management interest, in any cable operator providing cable service within the local exchange carrier's telephone service area.

"(b) Acquisitions by Cable Operators.--No cable operator or affiliate of a cable operator that is owned by, operated by, controlled by, or under common ownership with such cable operator may purchase or otherwise acquire, directly or indirectly, more than a 10 percent financial interest, or any management interest, in any local exchange carrier providing telephone exchange service within such cable operator's franchise area.

"(c) Joint Ventures.--A local exchange carrier and a cable operator whose telephone service area and cable franchise area, respectively, are in the same market may not enter into any joint venture or partnership to provide video programming directly to subscribers or to provide telecommunications services within such market.

"(d) Exceptions.--

"(1) Rural systems.--Notwithstanding subsections (a), (b), and (c) of this section, a local exchange carrier (with respect to a cable system located in its telephone service area) and a cable operator (with respect to the facilities of a local exchange carrier used to provide telephone exchange service in its cable franchise area) may obtain a controlling interest in, management interest in, or enter into a joint venture or partnership with the operator of such system or facilities for the use of such system or facilities to the extent that--

"(A) such system or facilities only serve incorporated or unincorporated--

"(i) places or territories that have fewer than 35,000 inhabitants; and

"(ii) are outside an urbanized area, as defined by the Bureau of the Census; and

"(B) in the case of a local exchange carrier, such system, in the aggregate with any other system in which such carrier has an interest, serves less than 10 percent of the households in the telephone service area of such carrier.

"(2) Joint use.--Notwithstanding subsection (c), a local exchange carrier may obtain, with the concurrence of the cable operator on the rates, terms, and conditions, the use of that part of the transmission facilities of a cable system extending from the last multi-user

243

terminal to the premises of the end user, if such use is reasonably limited in scope and duration, as determined by the Commission.

"(3) Acquisitions in competitive markets.--Notwithstanding subsections (a) and (c), a local exchange carrier may obtain a controlling interest in, or form a joint venture or other partnership with, or provide financing to, a cable system (hereinafter in this paragraph referred to as "the subject cable system"), if--

"(A) the subject cable system operates in a television market that is not in the top 25 markets, and such market has more than 1 cable system operator, and the subject cable system is not the cable system with the most subscribers in such television market;

"(B) the subject cable system and the cable system with the most subscribers in such television market held on May 1, 1995, cable television franchises from the largest municipality in the television market and the boundaries of such franchises were identical on such date;

"(C) the subject cable system is not owned by or under common ownership or control of any one of the 50 cable system operators with the most subscribers as such operators existed on May 1, 1995; and

"(D) the system with the most subscribers in the television market is owned by or under common ownership or control of any one of the 10 largest cable system operators as such operators existed on May 1, 1995.

"(4) Exempt cable systems.--Subsection (a) does not apply to any cable system if--

"(A) the cable system serves no more than 17,000 cable subscribers, of which no less than 8,000 live within an urban area, and no less than 6,000 live within a nonurbanized area as of June 1, 1995;

"(B) the cable system is not owned by, or under common ownership or control with, any of the 50 largest cable system operators in existence on June 1, 1995; and

"(C) the cable system operates in a television market that was not in the top 100 television markets as of June 1, 1995.

"(5) Small cable systems in nonurban areas.--Notwithstanding subsections (a) and (c), a local exchange carrier with less than $100,000,000 in annual operating revenues (or any affiliate of such carrier owned by, operated by, controlled by, or under common control with such carrier) may purchase or otherwise acquire more than a 10 percent financial interest in, or any management interest in, or enter into a joint venture or partnership with, any cable system within the local exchange carrier's telephone service area that serves no more than 20,000 cable subscribers, if no more than 12,000 of those subscribers live within an urbanized area, as defined by the Bureau of the Census.

"(6) Waivers.--The Commission may waive the restrictions of subsections (a), (b), or (c) only if--

"(A) the Commission determines that, because of the nature of the market served by the affected cable system or facilities used to provide telephone exchange service--

"(i) the affected cable operator or local exchange carrier would be subjected to undue economic distress by the enforcement of such provisions;

"(ii) the system or facilities would not be economically viable if such provisions were enforced; or

"(iii) the anticompetitive effects of the proposed transaction are clearly outweighed in the public interest by the probable effect of the transaction in meeting the convenience and needs of the community to be served; and

"(B) the local franchising authority approves of such waiver.

"(e) Definition of Telephone Service Area.--For purposes of this section, the term "telephone service area" when used in connection with a common carrier subject in whole or in part to title II of this Act means the area within which such carrier provided telephone exchange service as of January 1, 1993, but if any common carrier after such date transfers its telephone exchange service facilities to another common carrier, the area to which such facilities provide telephone exchange service shall be treated as part of the telephone service area of the acquiring common carrier and not of the selling common carrier.

"Section 653. ESTABLISHMENT OF OPEN VIDEO SYSTEMS.

"(a) Open Video Systems.--

"(1) Certificates of compliance.--A local exchange carrier may provide cable service to its cable service subscribers in its telephone service area through an open video system that complies with this section. To the extent permitted by such regulations as the Commission may prescribe consistent with the public interest, convenience, and necessity, an operator of a cable system or any other person may provide video programming through an open video system that complies with this section. An operator of an open video system shall qualify for reduced regulatory burdens under subsection (c) of this section if the operator of such system certifies to the Commission that such carrier complies with the Commission's regulations under subsection (b) and the Commission approves such certification. The Commission shall publish notice of the receipt of any such certification and shall act to approve or disapprove any such certification within 10 days after receipt of such certification.

"(2) Dispute resolution.--The Commission shall have the authority to resolve disputes under this section and the regulations prescribed thereunder. Any such dispute shall be resolved within 180 days after notice of such dispute is submitted to the Commission. At that time or subsequently in a separate damages proceeding, the Commission may, in the

245

case of any violation of this section, require carriage, award damages to any person denied carriage, or any combination of such sanctions. Any aggrieved party may seek any other remedy available under this Act.

"(b) Commission Actions.--

"(1) Regulations required.--Within 6 months after the date of enactment of the Telecommunications Act of 1996, the Commission shall complete all actions necessary (including any reconsideration) to prescribe regulations that--

"(A) except as required pursuant to section 611, 614, or 615, prohibit an operator of an open video system from discriminating among video programming providers with regard to carriage on its open video system, and ensure that the rates, terms, and conditions for such carriage are just and reasonable, and are not unjustly or unreasonably discriminatory;

"(B) if demand exceeds the channel capacity of the open video system, prohibit an operator of an open video system and its affiliates from selecting the video programming services for carriage on more than one-third of the activated channel capacity on such system, but nothing in this subparagraph shall be construed to limit the number of channels that the carrier and its affiliates may offer to provide directly to subscribers;

"(C) permit an operator of an open video system to carry on only one channel any video programming service that is offered by more than one video programming provider (including the local exchange carrier's video programming affiliate), provided that subscribers have ready and immediate access to any such video programming service;

"(D) extend to the distribution of video programming over open video systems the Commission's regulations concerning sports exclusivity (47 CFR 76.67), network nonduplication (47 CFR 76.92 et seq.), and syndicated exclusivity (47 CFR 76.151 et seq.); and

"(E)(i) prohibit an operator of an open video system from unreasonably discriminating in favor of the operator or its affiliates with regard to material or information (including advertising) provided by the operator to subscribers for the purposes of selecting programming on the open video system, or in the way such material or information is presented to subscribers;

"(ii) require an operator of an open video system to ensure that video programming providers or copyright holders (or both) are able suitably and uniquely to identify their programming services to subscribers;

"(iii) if such identification is transmitted as part of the programming signal, require the carrier to transmit such identification without change or alteration; and

"(iv) prohibit an operator of an open video system from omitting television broadcast stations or other unaffiliated video programming services carried on such system from any navigational device, guide, or menu.

"(2) Consumer access.--Subject to the requirements of paragraph (1) and the regulations thereunder, nothing in this section prohibits a common carrier or its affiliate from negotiating mutually agreeable terms and conditions with over-the-air broadcast stations and other unaffiliated video programming providers to allow consumer access to their signals on any level or screen of any gateway, menu, or other program guide, whether provided by the carrier or its affiliate.

"(c) Reduced Regulatory Burdens for Open Video Systems.--

"(1) In general.--Any provision that applies to a cable operator under--

"(A) sections 613 (other than subsection (a) thereof), 616, 623(f), 628, 631, and 634 of this title, shall apply,

"(B) sections 611, 614, and 615 of this title, and section 325 of title III, shall apply in accordance with the regulations prescribed under paragraph (2), and

"(C) sections 612 and 617, and parts III and IV (other than sections 623(f), 628, 631, and 634), of this title shall not apply, to any operator of an open video system for which the Commission has approved a certification under this section.

"(2) Implementation.--

"(A) Commission action.--In the rulemaking proceeding to prescribe the regulations required by subsection (b)(1), the Commission shall, to the extent possible, impose obligations that are no greater or lesser than the obligations contained in the provisions described in paragraph (1)(B) of this subsection. The Commission shall complete all action (including any reconsideration) to prescribe such regulations no later than 6 months after the date of enactment of the Telecommunications Act of 1996.

"(B) Fees.--An operator of an open video system under this part may be subject to the payment of fees on the gross revenues of the operator for the provision of cable service imposed by a local franchising authority or other governmental entity, in lieu of the franchise fees permitted under section 622. The rate at which such fees are imposed shall not exceed the rate at which franchise fees are imposed on any cable operator transmitting video programming in the franchise area, as determined in accordance with regulations prescribed by the Commission. An operator of an open video system may designate that portion of a subscriber's bill attributable to the fee under this subparagraph as a separate item on the bill.

"(3) Regulatory streamlining.--With respect to the establishment and operation of an open video system, the requirements of this section shall apply in lieu of, and not in addition to, the requirements of title II.

"(4) Treatment as cable operator.--Nothing in this Act precludes a video programming provider making use of a open video system from being treated as an operator of a cable system for purposes of section 111 of title 17, United States Code.

"(d)   Definition of Telephone Service Area.--For purposes of this section, the term 'telephone service area' when used in connection with a common carrier subject in whole or in part to title II of this Act means the area within which such carrier is offering telephone exchange service."

(b)   Conforming and Technical Amendments.--

(1)   Repeal.--Subsection (b) of section 613 (47 U.S.C. 533(b)) is repealed.

(2)   Definitions.--Section 602 (47 U.S.C. 531) is amended--

(A)   in paragraph (7), by striking ", or (D)" and inserting the following: ", unless the extent of such use is solely to provide interactive on-demand services; (D) an open video system that complies with section 653 of this title; or (E)";

(B)   by redesignating paragraphs (12) through (19) as paragraphs (13) through (20), respectively; and

(C)   by inserting after paragraph (11) the following new paragraph:

"(12)   the term 'interactive on-demand services' means a service providing video programming to subscribers over switched networks on an on-demand, point-to-point basis, but does not include services providing video programming prescheduled by the programming provider;".

(3)   Termination of video-dialtone regulations.--The Commission's regulations and policies with respect to video dialtone requirements issued in CC Docket No. 87-266 shall cease to be effective on the date of enactment of this Act.   This paragraph shall not be construed to require the termination of any video-dialtone system that the Commission has approved before the date of enactment of this Act.

SEC. 303.   PREEMPTION OF FRANCHISING AUTHORITY REGULATION OF TELECOMMUNICATIONS SERVICES.

(a)   Provision of Telecommunications Services by a Cable Operator.--Section 621(b) (47 U.S.C. 541(b)) is amended by adding at the end thereof the following new paragraph:

"(3)(A)   If a cable operator or affiliate thereof is engaged in the provision of telecommunications services--

"(i)   such cable operator or affiliate shall not be required to obtain a franchise under this title for the provision of telecommunications services; and

"(ii)   the provisions of this title shall not apply to such cable operator or affiliate for the provision of telecommunications services.

"(B)   A franchising authority may not impose any requirement under this title that has the purpose or effect of prohibiting, limiting, restricting, or conditioning the provision of a telecommunications service by a cable operator or an affiliate thereof.

"(C) A franchising authority may not order a cable operator or affiliate thereof--

"(i) to discontinue the provision of a telecommunications service, or

"(ii) to discontinue the operation of a cable system, to the extent such cable system is used for the provision of a telecommunications service, by reason of the failure of such cable operator or affiliate thereof to obtain a franchise or franchise renewal under this title with respect to the provision of such telecommunications service.

"(D) Except as otherwise permitted by sections 611 and 612, a franchising authority may not require a cable operator to provide any telecommunications service or facilities, other than institutional networks, as a condition of the initial grant of a franchise, a franchise renewal, or a transfer of a franchise."

(b) Franchise Fees.--Section 622(b) (47 U.S.C. 542(b)) is amended by inserting "to provide cable services" immediately before the period at the end of the first sentence thereof.

SEC. 304. COMPETITIVE AVAILABILITY OF NAVIGATION DEVICES.

Part III of title VI is amended by inserting after section 628 (47 U.S.C. 548) the following new section

"Section 629. COMPETITIVE AVAILABILITY OF NAVIGATION DEVICES.

"(a) Commercial Consumer Availability of Equipment Used To Access Services Provided by Multichannel Video Programming Distributors.--The Commission shall, in consultation with appropriate industry standard-setting organizations, adopt regulations to assure the commercial availability, to consumers of multichannel video programming and other services offered over multichannel video programming systems, of converter boxes, interactive communications equipment, and other equipment used by consumers to access multichannel video programming and other services offered over multichannel video programming systems, from manufacturers, retailers, and other vendors not affiliated with any multichannel video programming distributor. Such regulations shall not prohibit any multichannel video programming distributor from also offering converter boxes, interactive communications equipment, and other equipment used by consumers to access multichannel video programming and other services offered over multichannel video programming systems, to consumers, if the system operator's charges to consumers for such devices and equipment are separately stated and not subsidized by charges for any such service.

"(b) Protection of System Security.--The Commission shall not prescribe regulations under subsection (a) which would jeopardize security of multichannel video programming and other services offered over multichannel video programming systems, or impede the legal rights of a provider of such services to prevent theft of service.

"(c) Waiver.--The Commission shall waive a regulation adopted under subsection (a) for a limited time upon an appropriate showing by a provider of multichannel video programming and other services offered over multichannel video programming systems, or an equipment provider, that such waiver is necessary to assist the development or introduction of a new or improved multichannel video programming or other service offered over multichannel video programming systems, technology, or products. Upon an appropriate showing, the Commission shall grant any such waiver request within 90 days of any application filed under this subsection, and such waiver shall be effective for all service providers and products in that category and for all providers of services and products.

"(d) Avoidance of Redundant Regulations.--

"(1) Commercial availability determinations.--Determinations made or regulations prescribed by the Commission with respect to commercial availability to consumers of converter boxes, interactive communications equipment, and other equipment used by consumers to access multichannel video programming and other services offered over multichannel video programming systems, before the date of enactment of the Telecommunications Act of 1996 shall fulfill the requirements of this section.

"(2) Regulations.--Nothing in this section affects section 64.702(e) of the Commission's regulations (47 CFR 64.702(e)) or other Commission regulations governing interconnection and competitive provision of customer premises equipment used in connection with basic common carrier communications services.

"(e) Sunset.--The regulations adopted under this section shall cease to apply when the Commission determines that--

"(1) the market for the multichannel video programming distributors is fully competitive;

"(2) the market for converter boxes, and interactive communications equipment, used in conjunction with that service is fully competitive; and

"(3) elimination of the regulations would promote competition and the public interest.

"(f) Commission's Authority.--Nothing in this section shall be construed as expanding or limiting any authority that the Commission may have under law in effect before the date of enactment of the Telecommunications Act of 1996."

SEC. 305. VIDEO PROGRAMMING ACCESSIBILITY.

Title VII is amended by inserting after section 712 (47 U.S.C. 612) the following new section:

"Section 713. VIDEO PROGRAMMING ACCESSIBILITY.

"(a)   Commission Inquiry.--Within 180 days after the date of enactment of the Telecommunications Act of 1996, the Federal Communications Commission shall complete an inquiry to ascertain the level at which video programming is closed captioned. Such inquiry shall examine the extent to which existing or previously published programming is closed captioned, the size of the video programming provider or programming owner providing closed captioning, the size of the market served, the relative audience shares achieved, or any other related factors. The Commission shall submit to the Congress a report on the results of such inquiry.

"(b)   Accountability Criteria.--Within 18 months after such date of enactment, the Commission shall prescribe such regulations as are necessary to implement this section. Such regulations shall ensure that--

"(1)   video programming first published or exhibited after the effective date of such regulations is fully accessible through the provision of closed captions, except as provided in subsection (d); and

"(2)   video programming providers or owners maximize the accessibility of video programming first published or exhibited prior to the effective date of such regulations through the provision of closed captions, except as provided in subsection (d).

"(c)   Deadlines for Captioning.--Such regulations shall include an appropriate schedule of deadlines for the provision of closed captioning of video programming.

"(d)   Exemptions.--Notwithstanding subsection (b)--

"(1)   the Commission may exempt by regulation programs, classes of programs, or services for which the Commission has determined that the provision of closed captioning would be economically burdensome to the provider or owner of such programming;

"(2)   a provider of video programming or the owner of any program carried by the provider shall not be obligated to supply closed captions if such action would be inconsistent with contracts in effect on the date of enactment of the Telecommunications Act of 1996, except that nothing in this section shall be construed to relieve a video programming provider of its obligations to provide services required by Federal law; and

"(3)   a provider of video programming or program owner may petition the Commission for an exemption from the requirements of this section, and the Commission may grant such petition upon a showing that the requirements contained in this section would result in an undue burden.

"(e) Undue Burden.--The term "undue burden" means significant difficulty or expense. In determining whether the closed captions necessary to comply with the requirements of this paragraph would result in an undue economic burden, the factors to be considered include--

> "(1) the nature and cost of the closed captions for the programming;
>
> "(2) the impact on the operation of the provider or program owner;
>
> "(3) the financial resources of the provider or program owner; and
>
> "(4) the type of operations of the provider or program owner.

"(f) Video Descriptions Inquiry.--Within 6 months after the date of enactment of the Telecommunications Act of 1996, the Commission shall commence an inquiry to examine the use of video descriptions on video programming in order to ensure the accessibility of video programming to persons with visual impairments, and report to Congress on its findings. The Commission's report shall assess appropriate methods and schedules for phasing video descriptions into the marketplace, technical and quality standards for video descriptions, a definition of programming for which video descriptions would apply, and other technical and legal issues that the Commission deems appropriate.

"(g) Video Description.--For purposes of this section, "video description" means the insertion of audio narrated descriptions of a television program's key visual elements into natural pauses between the program's dialogue.

"(h) Private Rights of Actions Prohibited.--Nothing in this section shall be construed to authorize any private right of action to enforce any requirement of this section or any regulation thereunder. The Commission shall have exclusive jurisdiction with respect to any complaint under this section."

TITLE IV--REGULATORY REFORM

SEC. 401. REGULATORY FORBEARANCE.

Title I is amended by inserting after section 9 (47 U.S.C. 159) the following new section:

"Section 10. COMPETITION IN PROVISION OF TELECOMMUNICATIONS SERVICE.

"(a) Regulatory flexibility.--Notwithstanding section 332(c)(1)(A) of this Act, the Commission shall forbear from applying any regulation or any provision of this Act to a telecommunications carrier or telecommunications service, or class of telecommunications carriers or telecommunications services, in any or some of its or their geographic markets, if the Commission determines that--

"(1) enforcement of such regulation or provision is not necessary to ensure that the charges, practices, classifications, or regulations by, for, or in connection with that telecommunications carrier or telecommunications service are just and reasonable and are not unjustly or unreasonably discriminatory;

"(2) enforcement of such regulation or provision is not necessary for the protection of consumers; and

"(3) forbearance from applying such provision or regulation is consistent with the public interest.

"(b) Competitive Effect To Be Weighed.--In making the determination under subsection (a)(3), the Commission shall consider whether forbearance from enforcing the provision or regulation will promote competitive market conditions, including the extent to which such forbearance will enhance competition among providers of telecommunications services. If the Commission determines that such forbearance will promote competition among providers of telecommunications services, that determination may be the basis for a Commission finding that forbearance is in the public interest.

"(c) Petition for Forbearance.--Any telecommunications carrier, or class of telecommunications carriers, may submit a petition to the Commission requesting that the Commission exercise the authority granted under this section with respect to that carrier or those carriers, or any service offered by that carrier or carriers. Any such petition shall be deemed granted if the Commission does not deny the petition for failure to meet the requirements for forbearance under subsection (a) within one year after the Commission receives it, unless the one-year period is extended by the Commission. The Commission may extend the initial one-year period by an additional 90 days if the Commission finds that an extension is necessary to meet the requirements of subsection (a). The Commission may grant or deny a petition in whole or in part and shall explain its decision in writing.

"(d) Limitation.--Except as provided in section 251(f), the Commission may not forbear from applying the requirements of section 251(c) or 271 under subsection (a) of this section until it determines that those requirements have been fully implemented.

"(e) State Enforcement After Commission Forbearance.--A State commission may not continue to apply or enforce any provision of this Act that the Commission has determined to forbear from applying under subsection (a)."

SEC. 402. BIENNIAL REVIEW OF REGULATIONS; REGULATORY RELIEF.

(a) Biennial Review.--Title I is amended by inserting after section 10 (as added by section 401) the following new section:

"Section 11. REGULATORY REFORM.

"(a) Biennial Review of Regulations.--In every even-numbered year (beginning with 1998), the Commission--
"(1) shall review all regulations issued under this Act in effect at the time of the review that apply to the operations or activities of any provider of telecommunications service; and
"(2) shall determine whether any such regulation is no longer necessary in the public interest as the result of meaningful economic competition between providers of such service.
"(b) Effect of Determination.--The Commission shall repeal or modify any regulation it determines to be no longer necessary in the public interest."

(b) Regulatory Relief.--
(1) Streamlined procedures for changes in charges, classifications, regulations, or practices.--
(A) Section 204(a) (47 U.S.C. 204(a)) is amended--
(i) by striking "12 months" the first place it appears in paragraph (2)(A) and inserting "5 months";
(ii) by striking "effective," and all that follows in paragraph (2)(A) and inserting "effective."; and
(iii) by adding at the end thereof the following:
"(3) A local exchange carrier may file with the Commission a new or revised charge, classification, regulation, or practice on a streamlined basis. Any such charge, classification, regulation, or practice shall be deemed lawful and shall be effective 7 days (in the case of a reduction in rates) or 15 days (in the case of an increase in rates) after the date on which it is filed with the Commission unless the Commission takes action under paragraph (1) before the end of that 7-day or 15-day period, as is appropriate."
(B) Section 208(b) (47 U.S.C. 208(b)) is amended--
(i) by striking "12 months" the first place it appears in paragraph (1) and inserting "5 months"; and
(ii) by striking "filed," and all that follows in paragraph (1) and inserting "filed."
(2) Extensions of lines under section 214; ARMIS reports.--The Commission shall permit any common carrier--
(A) to be exempt from the requirements of section 214 of the Communications Act of 1934 for the extension of any line; and
(B) to file cost allocation manuals and ARMIS reports annually, to the extent such carrier is required to file such manuals or reports.

(3)   Forbearance authority not limited.--Nothing in this subsection shall be construed to limit the authority of the Commission to waive, modify, or forbear from applying any of the requirements to which reference is made in paragraph (1) under any other provision of this Act or other law.

(4)   Effective date of amendments.--The amendments made by paragraph (1) of this subsection shall apply with respect to any charge, classification, regulation, or practice filed on or after one year after the date of enactment of this Act.

(c)   Classification of Carriers.--In classifying carriers according to section 32.11 of its regulations (47 CFR 32.11) and in establishing reporting requirements pursuant to Part 43 of its regulations (47 CFR Part 43) and section 64.903 of its regulations (47 CFR 64.903), the Commission shall adjust the revenue requirements to account for inflation as of the release date of the Commission's Report and Order in CC Docket No. 91-141, and annually thereafter. This subsection shall take effect on the date of enactment of this Act.

SEC. 403. ELIMINATION OF UNNECESSARY COMMISSION REGULATIONS AND FUNCTIONS.

(a) Modification of Amateur Radio Examination Procedures.--Section 4(f)(4) (47 U.S.C. 154(f)(4)) is amended--
(1) in subparagraph (A)--
(A) by inserting "or administering" after "for purposes of preparing";
(B) by inserting "of" after "than the class"; and
(C) by inserting "or administered" after "for which the examination is being prepared";
(2) by striking subparagraph (B);
(3) in subparagraph (H), by striking "(A), (B), and (C)" and inserting "(A) and (B)";
(4) in subparagraph (J)--
(A) by striking "or (B)"; and
(B) by striking the last sentence; and
(5) by redesignating subparagraphs (C) through (J) as subparagraphs (B) through (I), respectively.
(b) Authority To Designate Entities To Inspect.--Section 4(f)(3) (47 U.S.C. 154(f)(3)) is amended by inserting before the period at the end the following:
": And provided further, That, in the alternative, an entity designated by the Commission may make the inspections referred to in this paragraph".
(c) Expediting Instructional Television Fixed Service Processing.--Section 5(c)(1) (47 U.S.C. 155(c)(1)) is amended by striking the last sentence and inserting the following:

255

"Except for cases involving the authorization of service in the instructional television fixed service, or as otherwise provided in this Act, nothing in this paragraph shall authorize the Commission to provide for the conduct, by any person or persons other than persons referred to in paragraph (2) or (3) of section 556(b) of title 5, United States Code, of any hearing to which such section applies."

(d) Repeal Setting of Depreciation Rates.--The first sentence of section 220(b) (47 U.S.C. 220(b)) is amended by striking "shall prescribe for such carriers" and inserting "may prescribe, for such carriers as it determines to be appropriate,".

(e) Use of Independent Auditors.--Section 220(c) (47 U.S.C. 220(c)) is amended by adding at the end thereof the following:

"The Commission may obtain the services of any person licensed to provide public accounting services under the law of any State to assist with, or conduct, audits under this section. While so employed or engaged in conducting an audit for the Commission under this section, any such person shall have the powers granted the Commission under this subsection and shall be subject to subsection (f) in the same manner as if that person were an employee of the Commission."

(f) Delegation of Equipment Testing and Certification to Private Laboratories.--Section 302 (47 U.S.C. 302) is amended by adding at the end the following:

"(e) The Commission may--

"(1) authorize the use of private organizations for testing and certifying the compliance of devices or home electronic equipment and systems with regulations promulgated under this section;

"(2) accept as prima facie evidence of such compliance the certification by any such organization; and

"(3) establish such qualifications and standards as it deems appropriate for such private organizations, testing, and certification."

(g) Making License Modification Uniform.--Section 303(f) (47 U.S.C. 303(f)) is amended by striking "unless, after a public hearing," and inserting "unless".

(h) Eliminate FCC Jurisdiction Over Government-Owned Ship Radio Stations.--

(1) Section 305 (47 U.S.C. 305) is amended by striking subsection (b) and redesignating subsections (c) and (d) as (b) and (c), respectively.

(2) Section 382(2) (47 U.S.C. 382(2)) is amended by striking "except a vessel of the United States Maritime Administration, the Inland and Coastwise Waterways Service, or the Panama Canal Company,".

(i) Permit Operation of Domestic Ship and Aircraft Radios Without License.--Section 307(e) (47 U.S.C. 307(e)) is amended to read as follows:

"(e)(1) Notwithstanding any license requirement established in this Act, if the Commission determines that such authorization serves the public interest, convenience, and necessity, the Commission may by rule authorize the operation of radio stations without individual licenses in the following radio services:

"(A) the citizens band radio service;

"(B) the radio control service;

"(C) the aviation radio service for aircraft stations operated on domestic flights when such aircraft are not otherwise required to carry a radio station; and

"(D) the maritime radio service for ship stations navigated on domestic voyages when such ships are not otherwise required to carry a radio station.

"(2) Any radio station operator who is authorized by the Commission to operate without an individual license shall comply with all other provisions of this Act and with rules prescribed by the Commission under this Act.

"(3) For purposes of this subsection, the terms 'citizens band radio service', 'radio control service', 'aircraft station' and 'ship station' shall have the meanings given them by the Commission by rule."

(j) Expedited Licensing for Fixed Microwave Service.--Section 309(b)(2) (47 U.S.C. 309(b)(2)) is amended by striking subparagraph (A) and redesignating subparagraphs (B) through (G) as subparagraphs (A) through (F), respectively.

(k) Foreign Directors.--Section 310(b) (47 U.S.C. 310(b)) is amended--

(1) in paragraph (3), by striking "of which any officer or director is an alien or"; and

(2) in paragraph (4), by striking "of which any officer or more than one fourth of the directors are aliens, or".

(l)   Limitation on Silent Station Authorizations.--Section 312 (47 U.S.C. 312) is amended by adding at the end the following:

"(g) If a broadcasting station fails to transmit broadcast signals for any consecutive 12-month period, then the station license granted for the operation of that broadcast station expires at the end of that period, notwithstanding any provision, term, or condition of the license to the contrary."

(m) Modification of Construction Permit Requirement.--Section 319(d) is amended by striking the last two sentences and inserting the following:

"With respect to any broadcasting station, the Commission shall not have any authority to waive the requirement of a permit for construction, except that the Commission may by regulation determine that a permit shall not be required for minor changes in the facilities of authorized broadcast stations. With respect to any other station or class of stations, the Commission shall not waive the requirement for a construction permit unless the Commission determines that the public interest, convenience, and necessity would be served by such a waiver."

(n) Conduct of Inspections.--Section 362(b) (47 U.S.C. 362(b)) is amended to read as follows:

"(b) Every ship of the United States that is subject to this part shall have the equipment and apparatus prescribed therein inspected at least once each year by the Commission or an entity designated by the Commission. If, after such inspection, the Commission is satisfied that all relevant provisions of this Act and the station license have been complied with, the fact shall be so certified on the station license by the Commission. The Commission shall make such additional inspections at frequent intervals as the Commission determines may be necessary to ensure compliance with the requirements of this Act. The Commission may, upon a finding that the public interest could be served thereby--

"(1) waive the annual inspection required under this section for a period of up to 90 days for the sole purpose of enabling a vessel to complete its voyage and proceed to a port in the United States where an inspection can be held; or

"(2) waive the annual inspection required under this section for a vessel that is in compliance with the radio provisions of the Safety Convention and that is operating solely in waters beyond the jurisdiction of the United States, provided that such inspection shall be performed within 30 days of such vessel's return to the United States."

(o) Inspection by Other Entities.--Section 385 (47 U.S.C. 385) is amended--

(1) by inserting "or an entity designated by the Commission" after "The Commission"; and

(2) by adding at the end thereof the following:

"In accordance with such other provisions of law as apply to Government contracts, the Commission may enter into contracts with any person for the purpose of carrying out such inspections and certifying compliance with those requirements, and may, as part of any such contract, allow any such person to accept reimbursement from the license holder for travel and expense costs of any employee conducting an inspection or certification."

TITLE V--OBSCENITY AND VIOLENCE

Subtitle A--Obscene, Harassing, and Wrongful Utilization of Telecommunications Facilities

SEC. 501. SHORT TITLE.

This title may be cited as the "Communications Decency Act of 1996".

SEC. 502. OBSCENE OR HARASSING USE OF TELECOMMUNICATIONS FACILITIES UNDER THE COMMUNICATIONS ACT OF 1934.

Section 223 (47 U.S.C. 223) is amended--

(1) by striking subsection (a) and inserting in lieu thereof:

"(a) Whoever--

"(1) in interstate or foreign communications--

"(A) by means of a telecommunications device knowingly--

"(i) makes, creates, or solicits, and

"(ii) initiates the transmission of, any comment, request, suggestion, proposal, image, or other communication which is obscene, lewd, lascivious, filthy, or indecent, with intent to annoy, abuse, threaten, or harass another person;

"(B) by means of a telecommunications device knowingly--

"(i) makes, creates, or solicits, and

"(ii) initiates the transmission of, any comment, request, suggestion, proposal, image, or other communication which is obscene or indecent, knowing that the recipient of the communication is under 18 years of age, regardless of whether the maker of such communication placed the call or initiated the communication;

"(C) makes a telephone call or utilizes a telecommunications device, whether or not conversation or communication ensues, without disclosing his identity and with intent to annoy, abuse, threaten, or harass any person at the called number or who receives the communications;

"(D) makes or causes the telephone of another repeatedly or continuously to ring, with intent to harass any person at the called number; or

"(E) makes repeated telephone calls or repeatedly initiates communication with a telecommunications device, during which conversation or communication ensues, solely to harass any person at the called number or who receives the communication; or

"(2) knowingly permits any telecommunications facility under his control to be used for any activity prohibited by paragraph (1) with the intent that it be used for such activity, shall be fined under title 18, United States Code, or imprisoned not more than two years, or both.."; and

(2) by adding at the end the following new subsections:

"(d) Whoever--

"(1) in interstate or foreign communications knowingly--

"(A) uses an interactive computer service to send to a specific person or persons under 18 years of age, or

"(B) uses any interactive computer service to display in a manner available to a person under 18 years of age, any comment, request, suggestion, proposal, image, or other communication that, in context, depicts or describes, in terms patently offensive as measured by contemporary community standards, sexual or excretory activities or organs, regardless of whether the user of such service placed the call or initiated the communication; or

"(2) knowingly permits any telecommunications facility under such person's control to be used for an activity prohibited by paragraph (1) with the intent that it be used for such activity, shall be fined under title 18, United States Code, or imprisoned not more than two years, or both.

"(e) In addition to any other defenses available by law:

"(1) No person shall be held to have violated subsection (a) or (d) solely for providing access or connection to or from a facility, system, or network not under that person's control, including transmission, downloading, intermediate storage, access software, or other related capabilities that are incidental to providing such access or connection that does not include the creation of the content of the communication.

"(2) The defenses provided by paragraph (1) of this subsection shall not be applicable to a person who is a conspirator with an entity actively involved in the creation or knowing distribution of communications that violate this section, or who knowingly advertises the availability of such communications.

"(3) The defenses provided in paragraph (1) of this subsection shall not be applicable to a person who provides access or connection to a facility, system, or network engaged in the violation of this section that is owned or controlled by such person.

"(4) No employer shall be held liable under this section for the actions of an employee or agent unless the employee's or agent's conduct is within the scope of his or her employment or agency and the employer (A) having knowledge of such conduct, authorizes or ratifies such conduct, or (B) recklessly disregards such conduct.

"(5) It is a defense to a prosecution under subsection (a)(1)(B) or (d), or under subsection (a)(2) with respect to the use of a facility for an activity under subsection (a)(1)(B) that a person--

"(A) has taken, in good faith, reasonable, effective, and appropriate actions under the circumstances to restrict or prevent access by minors to a communication specified in such subsections, which may involve any appropriate measures to restrict minors from such communications, including any method which is feasible under available technology; or

"(B) has restricted access to such communication by requiring use of a verified credit card, debit account, adult access code, or adult personal identification number.

"(6) The Commission may describe measures which are reasonable, effective, and appropriate to restrict access to prohibited communications under subsection (d). Nothing in this section authorizes the Commission to enforce, or is intended to provide the Commission with the authority to approve, sanction, or permit, the use of such measures. The Commission shall have no enforcement authority over the failure to utilize such measures. The Commission shall not endorse specific products relating to such measures. The use of such measures shall be admitted as evidence of good faith efforts for purposes of paragraph (5) in any action arising under subsection (d). Nothing in this section shall be construed to treat interactive computer services as common carriers or telecommunications carriers.

"(f)(1) No cause of action may be brought in any court or administrative agency against any person on account of any activity that is not in violation of any law punishable by criminal or civil penalty, and that the person has taken in good faith to implement a defense authorized under this section or otherwise to restrict or prevent the transmission of, or access to, a communication specified in this section.

"(2) No State or local government may impose any liability for commercial activities or actions by commercial entities, nonprofit libraries, or institutions of higher education in connection with an activity or action described in subsection (a)(2) or (d) that is inconsistent with the treatment of those activities or actions under this section: Provided, however, That nothing herein shall preclude any State or local government from enacting and enforcing complementary oversight, liability, and regulatory systems, procedures, and requirements, so long as such systems, procedures, and requirements govern only intrastate services and do not result in the imposition of inconsistent rights, duties or obligations on the provision of interstate services. Nothing in this subsection shall preclude any State or local government from governing conduct not covered by this section.

"(g) Nothing in subsection (a), (d), (e), or (f) or in the defenses to prosecution under (a) or (d) shall be construed to affect or limit the application or enforcement of any other Federal law.

"(h) For purposes of this section--

"(1) The use of the term "telecommunications device" in this section--

"(A) shall not impose new obligations on broadcasting station licensees and cable operators covered by obscenity and indecency provisions elsewhere in this Act; and

"(B) does not include an interactive computer service.

"(2) The term 'interactive computer service' has the meaning provided in section 230(e)(2).

"(3) The term 'access software' means software (including client or server software) or enabling tools that do not create or provide the content of the communication but that allow a user to do any one or more of the following:

"(A) filter, screen, allow, or disallow content;

"(B) pick, choose, analyze, or digest content; or

"(C) transmit, receive, display, forward, cache, search, subset, organize, reorganize, or translate content.

"(4) The term 'institution of higher education' has the meaning provided in section 1201 of the Higher Education Act of 1965 (20 U.S.C. 1141).

"(5) The term 'library' means a library eligible for participation in State-based plans for funds under title III of the Library Services and Construction Act (20 U.S.C. 355e et seq.)."

SEC. 503. OBSCENE PROGRAMMING ON CABLE TELEVISION.

Section 639 (47 U.S.C. 559) is amended by striking "not more than $10,000" and inserting "under title 18, United States Code,"

SEC. 504. SCRAMBLING OF CABLE CHANNELS FOR NONSUBSCRIBERS.

Part IV of title VI (47 U.S.C. 551 et seq.) is amended by adding at the end the following:

"Section 640. SCRAMBLING OF CABLE CHANNELS FOR NONSUBSCRIBERS.

"(a) Subscriber Request.--Upon request by a cable service subscriber, a cable operator shall, without charge, fully scramble or otherwise fully block the audio and video programming of each channel carrying such programming so that one not a subscriber does not receive it.

"(b) Definition.--As used in this section, the term "scramble" means to rearrange the content of the signal of the programming so that the programming cannot be viewed or heard in an understandable manner."

SEC. 505. SCRAMBLING OF SEXUALLY EXPLICIT ADULT VIDEO SERVICE PROGRAMMING.

(a) Requirement.--Part IV of title VI (47 USC 551 et seq.) as amended by this Act, is further amended by adding at the end the following:

"Section 641. SCRAMBLING OF SEXUALLY EXPLICIT ADULT VIDEO SERVICE PROGRAMMING.

"(a) Requirement.--In providing sexually explicit adult programming or other programming that is indecent on any channel of its service primarily dedicated to

262

sexually-oriented programming, a multichannel video programming distributor shall fully scramble or otherwise fully block the video and audio portion of such channel so that one not a subscriber to such channel or programming does not receive it.

"(b) Implementation.--Until a multichannel video programming distributor complies with the requirement set forth in subsection (a), the distributor shall limit the access of children to the programming referred to in that subsection by not providing such programming during the hours of the day (as determined by the Commission) when a significant number of children are likely to view it.

"(c) Definition.--As used in this section, the term "scramble" means to rearrange the content of the signal of the programming so that the programming cannot be viewed or heard in an understandable manner."

(b) Effective Date.--The amendment made by subsection (a) shall take effect 30 days after the date of enactment of this Act.

SEC. 506. CABLE OPERATOR REFUSAL TO CARRY CERTAIN PROGRAMS.

(a) Public, Educational, and Governmental Channels.--Section 611(e) (47 U.S.C. 531(e)) is amended by inserting before the period the following: ", except a cable operator may refuse to transmit any public access program or portion of a public access program which contains obscenity, indecency, or nudity".

(b) Cable Channels for Commercial Use.--Section 612(c)(2) (47 U.S.C. 532(c)(2)) is amended by striking "an operator" and inserting "a cable operator may refuse to transmit any leased access program or portion of a leased access program which contains obscenity, indecency, or nudity and".

SEC. 507. CLARIFICATION OF CURRENT LAWS REGARDING COMMUNICATION OF OBSCENE MATERIALS THROUGH THE USE OF COMPUTERS.

(a) Importation or Transportation.--Section 1462 of title 18, United States Code, is amended--

(1) in the first undesignated paragraph, by inserting "or interactive computer service (as defined in section 230(e)(2) of the Communications Act of 1934)" after "carrier"; and

(2) in the second undesignated paragraph--

(A) by inserting "or receives," after "takes";

(B) by inserting "or interactive computer service (as defined in section 230(e)(2) of the Communications Act of 1934)" after "common carrier"; and

(C) by inserting "or importation" after "carriage".

(b) Transportation for Purposes of Sale or Distribution.--The first undesignated paragraph of section 1465 of title 18, United States Code, is amended--

(1) by striking "transports in" and inserting "transports or travels in, or uses a facility or means of,";

(2) by inserting "or an interactive computer service (as defined in section 230(e)(2) of the Communications Act of 1934) in or affecting such commerce" after "foreign commerce" the first place it appears;

(3) by striking ", or knowingly travels in" and all that follows through "obscene material in interstate or foreign commerce," and inserting "of".

(c) Interpretation.--The amendments made by this section are clarifying and shall not be interpreted to limit or repeal any prohibition contained in sections 1462 and 1465 of title 18, United States Code, before such amendment, under the rule established in United States v. Alpers, 338 U.S. 680 (1950).

SEC. 508. COERCION AND ENTICEMENT OF MINORS.

Section 2422 of title 18, United States Code, is amended--

(1) by inserting "(a)" before "Whoever knowingly"; and

(2) by adding at the end the following:

"(b) Whoever, using any facility or means of interstate or foreign commerce, including the mail, or within the special maritime and territorial jurisdiction of the United States, knowingly persuades, induces, entices, or coerces any individual who has not attained the age of 18 years to engage in prostitution or any sexual act for which any person may be criminally prosecuted, or attempts to do so, shall be fined under this title or imprisoned not more than 10 years, or both."

SEC. 509. ONLINE FAMILY EMPOWERMENT.

Title II of the Communications Act of 1934 (47 U.S.C. 201 et seq.) is amended by adding at the end the following new section:

"Section 230. PROTECTION FOR PRIVATE BLOCKING AND SCREENING OF OFFENSIVE MATERIAL.

"(a) Findings.--The Congress finds the following:

"(1) The rapidly developing array of Internet and other interactive computer services available to individual Americans represent an extraordinary advance in the availability of educational and informational resources to our citizens.

"(2) These services offer users a great degree of control over the information that they receive, as well as the potential for even greater control in the future as technology develops.

"(3) The Internet and other interactive computer services offer a forum for a true diversity of political discourse, unique opportunities for cultural development, and myriad avenues for intellectual activity.

"(4) The Internet and other interactive computer services have flourished, to the benefit of all Americans, with a minimum of government regulation.

"(5) Increasingly Americans are relying on interactive media for a variety of political, educational, cultural, and entertainment services.

"(b) Policy.--It is the policy of the United States--

"(1) to promote the continued development of the Internet and other interactive computer services and other interactive media;

"(2) to preserve the vibrant and competitive free market that presently exists for the Internet and other interactive computer services, unfettered by Federal or State regulation;

"(3) to encourage the development of technologies which maximize user control over what information is received by individuals, families, and schools who use the Internet and other interactive computer services;

"(4) to remove disincentives for the development and utilization of blocking and filtering technologies that empower parents to restrict their children's access to objectionable or inappropriate online material; and

"(5) to ensure vigorous enforcement of Federal criminal laws to deter and punish trafficking in obscenity, stalking, and harassment by means of computer.

"(c) Protection for "Good Samaritan" Blocking and Screening of Offensive Material.--

"(1) Treatment of publisher or speaker.--No provider or user of an interactive computer service shall be treated as the publisher or speaker of any information provided by another information content provider.

"(2) Civil liability.--No provider or user of an interactive computer service shall be held liable on account of--

"(A) any action voluntarily taken in good faith to restrict access to or availability of material that the provider or user considers to be obscene, lewd, lascivious, filthy, excessively violent, harassing, or otherwise objectionable, whether or not such material is constitutionally protected; or

"(B) any action taken to enable or make available to information content providers or others the technical means to restrict access to material described in paragraph (1).

"(d) Effect on Other Laws.--

265

"(1) No effect on criminal law.--Nothing in this section shall be construed to impair the enforcement of section 223 of this Act, chapter 71 (relating to obscenity) or 110 (relating to sexual exploitation of children) of title 18, United States Code, or any other Federal criminal statute.

"(2) No effect on intellectual property law.--Nothing in this section shall be construed to limit or expand any law pertaining to intellectual property.

"(3) State law.--Nothing in this section shall be construed to prevent any State from enforcing any State law that is consistent with this section. No cause of action may be brought and no liability may be imposed under any State or local law that is inconsistent with this section.

"(4) No effect on communications privacy law.--Nothing in this section shall be construed to limit the application of the Electronic Communications Privacy Act of 1986 or any of the amendments made by such Act, or any similar State law.

"(e) Definitions.--As used in this section:

"(1) Internet.--The term 'Internet' means the international computer network of both Federal and non-Federal interoperable packet switched data networks.

"(2) Interactive computer service.--The term 'interactive computer service' means any information service, system, or access software provider that provides or enables computer access by multiple users to a computer server, including specifically a service or system that provides access to the Internet and such systems operated or services offered by libraries or educational institutions.

"(3) Information content provider.--The term 'information content provider' means any person or entity that is responsible, in whole or in part, for the creation or development of information provided through the Internet or any other interactive computer service.

"(4) Access software provider.--The term 'access software provider' means a provider of software (including client or server software), or enabling tools that do any one or more of the following:

"(A) filter, screen, allow, or disallow content;

"(B) pick, choose, analyze, or digest content; or

"(C) transmit, receive, display, forward, cache, search, subset, organize, reorganize, or translate content."

Subtitle B—Violence

SEC. 551. PARENTAL CHOICE IN TELEVISION PROGRAMMING.

(a) Findings.--The Congress makes the following findings:

(1) Television influences children's perception of the values and behavior that are common and acceptable in society.

(2) Television station operators, cable television system operators, and video programmers should follow practices in connection with video programming that take into consideration that television broadcast and cable programming has established a uniquely pervasive presence in the lives of American children.

(3) The average American child is exposed to 25 hours of television each week and some children are exposed to as much as 11 hours of television a day.

(4) Studies have shown that children exposed to violent video programming at a young age have a higher tendency for violent and aggressive behavior later in life than children not so exposed, and that children exposed to violent video programming are prone to assume that acts of violence are acceptable behavior.

(5) Children in the United States are, on average, exposed to an estimated 8,000 murders and 100,000 acts of violence on television by the time the child completes elementary school.

(6) Studies indicate that children are affected by the pervasiveness and casual treatment of sexual material on television, eroding the ability of parents to develop responsible attitudes and behavior in their children.

(7) Parents express grave concern over violent and sexual video programming and strongly support technology that would give them greater control to block video programming in the home that they consider harmful to their children.

(8) There is a compelling governmental interest in empowering parents to limit the negative influences of video programming that is harmful to children.

(9) Providing parents with timely information about the nature of upcoming video programming and with the technological tools that allow them easily to block violent, sexual, or other programming that they believe harmful to their children is a nonintrusive and narrowly tailored means of achieving that compelling governmental interest.

(b) Establishment of Television Rating Code.--

(1) Amendment.--Section 303 (47 U.S.C. 303) is amended by adding at the end the following:

"(w) Prescribe--

"(1) on the basis of recommendations from an advisory committee established by the Commission in accordance with section 551(b)(2) of the Telecommunications Act of 1996, guidelines and recommended procedures for the identification and rating of video programming that contains sexual, violent, or other indecent material about which parents should be informed before it is displayed to children, provided that nothing in this paragraph shall be construed to authorize any rating of video programming on the basis of its political or religious content; and

267

"(2) with respect to any video programming that has been rated, and in consultation with the television industry, rules requiring distributors of such video programming to transmit such rating to permit parents to block the display of video programming that they have determined is inappropriate for their children."

(2) Advisory committee requirements.--In establishing an advisory committee for purposes of the amendment made by paragraph (1) of this subsection, the Commission shall--

(A) ensure that such committee is composed of parents, television broadcasters, television programming producers, cable operators, appropriate public interest groups, and other interested individuals from the private sector and is fairly balanced in terms of political affiliation, the points of view represented, and the functions to be performed by the committee;

(B) provide to the committee such staff and resources as may be necessary to permit it to perform its functions efficiently and promptly; and

(C) require the committee to submit a final report of its recommendations within one year after the date of the appointment of the initial members.

(c) Requirement for Manufacture of Televisions That Block Programs.--Section 303 (47 U.S.C. 303), as amended by subsection (a), is further amended by adding at the end the following:

"(x) Require, in the case of an apparatus designed to receive television signals that are shipped in interstate commerce or manufactured in the United States and that have a picture screen 13 inches or greater in size (measured diagonally), that such apparatus be equipped with a feature designed to enable viewers to block display of all programs with a common rating, except as otherwise permitted by regulations pursuant to section 330(c)(4)."

(d) Shipping of Televisions That Block Programs.--

(1) Regulations.--Section 330 (47 U.S.C. 330) is amended--

(A) by redesignating subsection (c) as subsection (d); and

(B) by adding after subsection (b) the following new subsection (c):

"(c)(1) Except as provided in paragraph (2), no person shall ship in interstate commerce or manufacture in the United States any apparatus described in section 303(x) of this Act except in accordance with rules prescribed by the Commission pursuant to the authority granted by that section.

"(2) This subsection shall not apply to carriers transporting apparatus referred to in paragraph (1) without trading in it.

"(3) The rules prescribed by the Commission under this subsection shall provide for the oversight by the Commission of the adoption of standards by industry for blocking technology. Such rules shall require that all such apparatus be able to receive the rating signals which have been transmitted by way of line 21 of the vertical blanking interval and which conform to the signal and blocking specifications established by industry under the supervision of the Commission.

"(4) As new video technology is developed, the Commission shall take such action as the Commission determines appropriate to ensure that blocking service continues to be available to consumers. If the Commission determines that an alternative blocking technology exists that--

"(A) enables parents to block programming based on identifying programs without ratings,

"(B) is available to consumers at a cost which is comparable to the cost of technology that allows parents to block programming based on common ratings, and

"(C) will allow parents to block a broad range of programs on a multichannel system as effectively and as easily as technology that allows parents to block programming based on common ratings, the Commission shall amend the rules prescribed pursuant to section 303(x) to require that the apparatus described in such section be equipped with either the blocking technology described in such section or the alternative blocking technology described in this paragraph."

(2) Conforming amendment.--Section 330(d), as redesignated by subsection (d)(1)(A), is amended by striking "section 303(s), and section 303(u)" and inserting in lieu thereof "and sections 303(s), 303(u), and 303(x)".

(e) Applicability and Effective Dates.--

(1) Applicability of rating provision.--The amendment made by subsection (b) of this section shall take effect 1 year after the date of enactment of this Act, but only if the Commission determines, in consultation with appropriate public interest groups and interested individuals from the private sector, that distributors of video programming have not, by such date--

(A) established voluntary rules for rating video programming that contains sexual, violent, or other indecent material about which parents should be informed before it is displayed to children, and such rules are acceptable to the Commission; and

(B) agreed voluntarily to broadcast signals that contain ratings of such programming.

(2) Effective date of manufacturing provision.--In prescribing regulations to implement the amendment made by subsection (c), the Federal Communications Commission shall, after consultation with the television manufacturing industry, specify the effective date for the applicability of the requirement to the apparatus covered by such amendment, which date shall not be less than two years after the date of enactment of this Act.

SEC. 552. TECHNOLOGY FUND.

It is the policy of the United States to encourage broadcast television, cable, satellite, syndication, other video programming distributors, and relevant related industries (in consultation with appropriate public interest groups and interested individuals from the private sector) to--

(1) establish a technology fund to encourage television and electronics equipment manufacturers to facilitate the development of technology which would empower parents to block programming they deem inappropriate for their children and to encourage the availability thereof to low income parents;

(2) report to the viewing public on the status of the development of affordable, easy to use blocking technology; and

(3) establish and promote effective procedures, standards, systems, advisories, or other mechanisms for ensuring that users have easy and complete access to the information necessary to effectively utilize blocking technology and to encourage the availability thereof to low income parents.

Subtitle C--Judicial Review

SEC. 561. EXPEDITED REVIEW.

(a) Three-Judge District Court Hearing.--Notwithstanding any other provision of law, any civil action challenging the constitutionality, on its face, of this title or any amendment made by this title, or any provision thereof, shall be heard by a district court of 3 judges convened pursuant to the provisions of section 2284 of title 28, United States Code.

(b) Appellate Review.--Notwithstanding any other provision of law, an interlocutory or final judgment, decree, or order of the court of 3 judges in an action under subsection (a) holding this title or an amendment made by this title, or any provision thereof, unconstitutional shall be reviewable as a matter of right by direct appeal to the Supreme Court. Any such appeal shall be filed not more than 20 days after entry of such judgment, decree, or order.

TITLE VI--EFFECT ON OTHER LAWS

SEC. 601. APPLICABILITY OF CONSENT DECREES AND OTHER LAW.

(a) Applicability of Amendments to Future Conduct.--

(1) AT&T consent decree.--Any conduct or activity that was, before the date of enactment of this Act, subject to any restriction or obligation imposed by the AT&T Consent Decree shall, on and after such date, be subject to the restrictions and obligations imposed by the Communications Act of 1934 as amended by this Act and shall not be subject to the restrictions and the obligations imposed by such Consent Decree.

(2) GTE consent decree.--Any conduct or activity that was, before the date of enactment of this Act, subject to any restriction or obligation imposed by the GTE Consent Decree shall, on and after such date, be subject to the restrictions and obligations imposed by the Communications Act of 1934 as amended by this Act and shall not be subject to the restrictions and the obligations imposed by such Consent Decree.

(3) McCaw consent decree.--Any conduct or activity that was, before the date of enactment of this Act, subject to any restriction or obligation imposed by the McCaw Consent Decree shall, on and after such date, be subject to the restrictions and obligations imposed by the Communications Act of 1934 as amended by this Act and subsection (d) of this section and shall not be subject to the restrictions and the obligations imposed by such Consent Decree.

(b) Antitrust Laws.--

(1) Savings clause.--Except as provided in paragraphs (2) and (3), nothing in this Act or the amendments made by this Act shall be construed to modify, impair, or supersede the applicability of any of the antitrust laws.

(2) Repeal.--Subsection (a) of section 221 (47 U.S.C. 221(a)) is repealed.

(3) Clayton act.--Section 7 of the Clayton Act (15 U.S.C. 18) is amended in the last paragraph by striking "Federal Communications Commission,".

(c) Federal, State, and Local Law.--

(1) No implied effect.--This Act and the amendments made by this Act shall not be construed to modify, impair, or supersede Federal, State, or local law unless expressly so provided in such Act or amendments.

(2) State tax savings provision.--Notwithstanding paragraph (1), nothing in this Act or the amendments made by this Act shall be construed to modify, impair, or supersede, or authorize the modification, impairment, or supersession of, any State or local law pertaining to taxation, except as provided in sections 622 and 653(c) of the Communications Act of 1934 and section 602 of this Act.

(d) Commercial Mobile Service Joint Marketing.--Notwithstanding section 22.903 of the Commission's regulations (47 CFR 22.903) or any other Commission regulation, a Bell operating company or any other company may, except as provided in sections 271(e)(1) and 272 of the Communications Act of 1934 as amended by this Act as they relate to wireline service, jointly market and sell commercial mobile services in conjunction with telephone exchange service, exchange access, intraLATA telecommunications service, interLATA telecommunications service, and information services.

(e) Definitions.--As used in this section:

(1) AT&T consent decree.--The term "AT&T Consent Decree" means the order entered August 24, 1982, in the antitrust action styled United States v. Western Electric, Civil Action No. 82-0192, in the United States District Court for the District of Columbia, and includes any judgment or order with respect to such action entered on or after August 24, 1982.

(2) GTE consent decree.--The term "GTE Consent Decree" means the order entered December 21, 1984, as restated January 11, 1985, in the action styled United States v. GTE Corp., Civil Action No. 83-1298, in the United States District Court for the District of Columbia, and any judgment or order with respect to such action entered on or after December 21, 1984.

(3) McCaw consent decree.--The term "McCaw Consent Decree" means the proposed consent decree filed on July 15, 1994, in the antitrust action styled United States v. AT&T Corp. and McCaw Cellular Communications, Inc., Civil Action No. 94-01555, in the United States District court for the District of Columbia. Such term includes any stipulation that the parties will abide by the terms of such proposed consent decree until it is entered and any order entering such proposed consent decree.

(4) Antitrust laws.--The term "antitrust laws" has the meaning given it in subsection (a) of the first section of the Clayton Act (15 U.S.C. 12(a)), except that such term includes the Act of June 19, 1936 (49 Stat. 1526; 15 U.S.C. 13 et seq.), commonly known as the Robinson-Patman Act, and section 5 of the Federal Trade Commission Act (15 U.S.C. 45) to the extent that such section 5 applies to unfair methods of competition.

SEC. 602. PREEMPTION OF LOCAL TAXATION WITH RESPECT TO DIRECT-TO-HOME SERVICES.

(a) Preemption.--A provider of direct-to-home satellite service shall be exempt from the collection or remittance, or both, of any tax or fee imposed by any local taxing jurisdiction on direct-to-home satellite service.

(b) Definitions.--For the purposes of this section--

(1) Direct-to-home satellite service.--The term "direct-to-home satellite service" means only programming transmitted or broadcast by satellite directly to the subscribers' premises without the use of ground receiving or distribution equipment, except at the subscribers' premises or in the uplink process to the satellite.

(2)   Provider of direct-to-home satellite service.--For purposes of this section, a "provider of direct-to-home satellite service" means a person who transmits, broadcasts, sells, or distributes direct-to-home satellite service.

(3)   Local taxing jurisdiction.--The term "local taxing jurisdiction" means any municipality, city, county, township, parish, transportation district, or assessment jurisdiction, or any other local jurisdiction in the territorial jurisdiction of the United States with the authority to impose a tax or fee, but does not include a State.

(4)   State.--The term "State" means any of the several States, the District of Columbia, or any territory or possession of the United States.

(5)   Tax or fee.--The terms "tax" and "fee" mean any local sales tax, local use tax, local intangible tax, local income tax, business license tax, utility tax, privilege tax, gross receipts tax, excise tax, franchise fees, local telecommunications tax, or any other tax, license, or fee that is imposed for the privilege of doing business, regulating, or raising revenue for a local taxing jurisdiction.

(c)   Preservation of State Authority.--This section shall not be construed to prevent taxation of a provider of direct-to-home satellite service by a State or to prevent a local taxing jurisdiction from receiving revenue derived from a tax or fee imposed and collected by a State.

TITLE VII–MISCELLANEOUS PROVISIONS

SEC. 701. PREVENTION OF UNFAIR BILLING PRACTICES FOR INFORMATION OR SERVICES PROVIDED OVER TOLL-FREE TELEPHONE CALLS.

(a)   Prevention of Unfair Billing Practices.--

(1)   In general.--Section 228(c) (47 U.S.C. 228(c)) is amended--

(A)   by striking out subparagraph (C) of paragraph (7) and inserting in lieu thereof the following:

"(C)   the calling party being charged for information conveyed during the call unless--

"(i)   the calling party has a written agreement (including an agreement transmitted through electronic medium) that meets the requirements of paragraph (8); or

"(ii)   the calling party is charged for the information in accordance with paragraph (9); or";

(B)(i)   by striking "or" at the end of subparagraph (C) of such paragraph;

(ii)   by striking the period at the end of subparagraph (D) of such paragraph and inserting a semicolon and "or"; and

(iii)   by adding at the end thereof the following:

273

"(E) the calling party being assessed, by virtue of being asked to connect or otherwise transfer to a pay-per-call service, a charge for the call."; and

(C) by adding at the end the following new paragraphs:

"(8) Subscription agreements for billing for information provided via toll free calls.--

"(A) In general.--For purposes of paragraph (7)(C)(i), a written subscription does not meet the requirements of this paragraph unless the agreement specifies the material terms and conditions under which the information is offered and includes--

"(i) the rate at which charges are assessed for the information;

"(ii) the information provider's name;

"(iii) the information provider's business address;

"(iv) the information provider's regular business telephone number;

"(v) the information provider's agreement to notify the subscriber at least one billing cycle in advance of all future changes in the rates charged for the information; and

"(vi) the subscriber's choice of payment method, which may be by direct remit, debit, prepaid account, phone bill, or credit or calling card.

"(B) Billing arrangements.--If a subscriber elects, pursuant to subparagraph (A)(vi), to pay by means of a phone bill--

"(i) the agreement shall clearly explain that the subscriber will be assessed for calls made to the information service from the subscriber's phone line;

"(ii) the phone bill shall include, in prominent type, the following disclaimer:
"Common carriers may not disconnect local or long distance telephone service for failure to pay disputed charges for information services.";
and

"(iii) the phone bill shall clearly list the 800 number dialed.

"(C) Use of pins to prevent unauthorized use.--A written agreement does not meet the requirements of this paragraph unless it--

"(i) includes a unique personal identification number or other subscriber specific identifier and requires a subscriber to use this number or identifier to obtain access to the information provided and includes instructions on its use; and

"(ii) assures that any charges for services accessed by use of the subscriber's personal identification number or subscriber-specific identifier be assessed to subscriber's source of payment elected pursuant to subparagraph (A)(vi).

"(D) Exceptions.--Notwithstanding paragraph (7)(C), a written agreement that meets the requirements of this paragraph is not required--

"(i) for calls utilizing telecommunications devices for the deaf;

274

"(ii) for directory services provided by a common carrier or its affiliate or by a local exchange carrier or its affiliate; or

"(iii) for any purchase of goods or of services that are not information services.

"(E) Termination of service.--On receipt by a common carrier of a complaint by any person that an information provider is in violation of the provisions of this section, a carrier shall--

"(i) promptly investigate the complaint; and

"(ii) if the carrier reasonably determines that the complaint is valid, it may terminate the provision of service to an information provider unless the provider supplies evidence of a written agreement that meets the requirements of this section.

"(F) Treatment of remedies.--The remedies provided in this paragraph are in addition to any other remedies that are available under title V of this Act.

"(9) Charges by credit, prepaid, debit, charge, or calling card in absence of agreement.--For purposes of paragraph (7)(C)(ii), a calling party is not charged in accordance with this paragraph unless the calling party is charged by means of a credit, prepaid, debit, charge, or calling card and the information service provider includes in response to each call an introductory disclosure message that--

"(A) clearly states that there is a charge for the call;

"(B) clearly states the service's total cost per minute and any other fees for the service or for any service to which the caller may be transferred;

"(C) explains that the charges must be billed on either a credit, prepaid, debit, charge, or calling card;

"(D) asks the caller for the card number;

"(E) clearly states that charges for the call begin at the end of the introductory message; and

"(F) clearly states that the caller can hang up at or before the end of the introductory message without incurring any charge whatsoever.

"(10) Bypass of introductory disclosure message.--The requirements of paragraph (9) shall not apply to calls from repeat callers using a bypass mechanism to avoid listening to the introductory message, provided that information providers shall disable such a bypass mechanism after the institution of any price increase and for a period of time determined to be sufficient by the Federal Trade Commission to give callers adequate and sufficient notice of a price increase.

"(11) Definition of calling card.--As used in this subsection, the term "calling card" means an identifying number or code unique to the individual, that is issued to the individual by a common carrier and enables the individual to be charged by means of a phone bill for charges incurred independent of where the call originates."

(2) Regulations.--The Federal Communications Commission shall revise its regulations to comply with the amendment made by paragraph (1) not later than 180 days after the date of enactment of this Act.

(3) Effective date.--The amendments made by paragraph (1) shall take effect on the date of enactment of this Act.

(b) Clarification of "Pay-Per-Call Services".--

(1) Telephone disclosure and dispute resolution act.--Section 204(1) of the Telephone Disclosure and Dispute Resolution Act (15 U.S.C. 5714(1)) is amended to read as follows:

"(1) The term 'pay-per-call services' has the meaning provided in section 228(i) of the Communications Act of 1934, except that the Commission by rule may, notwithstanding subparagraphs (B) and (C) of section 228(i)(1) of such Act, extend such definition to other similar services providing audio information or audio entertainment if the Commission determines that such services are susceptible to the unfair and deceptive practices that are prohibited by the rules prescribed pursuant to section 201(a)."

(2) Communications act.--Section 228(i)(2) (47 U.S.C. 228(i)(2)) is amended by striking "or any service the charge for which is tariffed,".

SEC. 702. PRIVACY OF CUSTOMER INFORMATION.

Title II is amended by inserting after section 221 (47 U.S.C. 221) the following new section:

"Section 222. PRIVACY OF CUSTOMER INFORMATION.

"(a) In General.--Every telecommunications carrier has a duty to protect the confidentiality of proprietary information of, and relating to, other telecommunication carriers, equipment manufacturers, and customers, including telecommunication carriers reselling telecommunications services provided by a telecommunications carrier.

"(b) Confidentiality of Carrier Information.--A telecommunications carrier that receives or obtains proprietary information from another carrier for purposes of providing any telecommunications service shall use such information only for such purpose, and shall not use such information for its own marketing efforts.

"(c) Confidentiality of Customer Proprietary Network Information.--

"(1) Privacy requirements for telecommunications carriers.--Except as required by law or with the approval of the customer, a telecommunications carrier that receives or obtains customer proprietary network information by virtue of its provision of a telecommunications service shall only use, disclose, or permit access to individually identifiable customer proprietary network information in its provision of (A) the telecommunications service from which such information is derived, or (B) services necessary to, or used in, the provision of such telecommunications service, including the publishing of directories.

"(2) Disclosure on request by customers.--A telecommunications carrier shall disclose customer proprietary network information, upon affirmative written request by the customer, to any person designated by the customer.

"(3) Aggregate customer information.--A telecommunications carrier that receives or obtains customer proprietary network information by virtue of its provision of a telecommunications service may use, disclose, or permit access to aggregate customer information other than for the purposes described in paragraph (1). A local exchange carrier may use, disclose, or permit access to aggregate customer information other than for purposes described in paragraph (1) only if it provides such aggregate information to other carriers or persons on reasonable and nondiscriminatory terms and conditions upon reasonable request therefor.

"(d) Exceptions.--Nothing in this section prohibits a telecommunications carrier from using, disclosing, or permitting access to customer proprietary network information obtained from its customers, either directly or indirectly through its agents--

"(1) to initiate, render, bill, and collect for telecommunications services;

"(2) to protect the rights or property of the carrier, or to protect users of those services and other carriers from fraudulent, abusive, or unlawful use of, or subscription to, such services; or

"(3) to provide any inbound telemarketing, referral, or administrative services to the customer for the duration of the call, if such call was initiated by the customer and the customer approves of the use of such information to provide such service.

"(e) Subscriber List Information.--Notwithstanding subsections (b), (c), and (d), a telecommunications carrier that provides telephone exchange service shall provide subscriber list information gathered in its capacity as a provider of such service on a timely and unbundled basis, under nondiscriminatory and reasonable rates, terms, and conditions, to any person upon request for the purpose of publishing directories in any format.

"(f) Definitions.--As used in this section:

"(1) Customer proprietary network information.--The term 'customer proprietary network information' means--

"(A) information that relates to the quantity, technical configuration, type, destination, and amount of use of a telecommunications service subscribed to by any customer of a telecommunications carrier, and that is made available to the carrier by the customer solely by virtue of the carrier-customer relationship; and

"(B) information contained in the bills pertaining to telephone exchange service or telephone toll service received by a customer of a carrier; except that such term does not include subscriber list information.

"(2) Aggregate information.--The term 'aggregate customer information' means collective data that relates to a group or category of services or customers, from which individual customer identities and characteristics have been removed.

"(3) Subscriber list information.--The term 'subscriber list information' means any information--

"(A) identifying the listed names of subscribers of a carrier and such subscribers' telephone numbers, addresses, or primary advertising classifications (as such classifications are assigned at the time of the establishment of such service), or any combination of such listed names, numbers, addresses, or classifications; and

"(B) that the carrier or an affiliate has published, caused to be published, or accepted for publication in any directory format."

SEC. 703. POLE ATTACHMENTS.

Section 224 (47 U.S.C. 224) is amended--

(1) in subsection (a)(1), by striking the first sentence and inserting the following: "The term 'utility' means any person who is a local exchange carrier or an electric, gas, water, steam, or other public utility, and who owns or controls poles, ducts, conduits, or rights-of-way used, in whole or in part, for any wire communications.";

(2) in subsection (a)(4), by inserting after "system" the following: "or provider of telecommunications service";

(3) by inserting after subsection (a)(4) the following:

"(5) For purposes of this section, the term 'telecommunications carrier' (as defined in section 3 of this Act) does not include any incumbent local exchange carrier as defined in section 251(h).";

(4) by inserting after "conditions" in subsection (c)(1) a comma and the following: "or access to poles, ducts, conduits, and rights-of-way as provided in subsection (f),";

(5) in subsection (c)(2)(B), by striking "cable television services" and inserting "the services offered via such attachments";

(6) by inserting after subsection (d)(2) the following:

"(3) This subsection shall apply to the rate for any pole attachment used by a cable television system solely to provide cable service. Until the effective date of the regulations required under subsection (e), this subsection shall also apply to the rate for any pole attachment used by a cable system or any telecommunications carrier (to the extent such carrier is not a party to a pole attachment agreement) to provide any telecommunications service."; and

(7) by adding at the end thereof the following:

"(e)(1) The Commission shall, no later than 2 years after the date of enactment of the Telecommunications Act of 1996, prescribe regulations in accordance with this subsection to govern the charges for pole attachments used by telecommunications carriers to provide telecommunications services, when the parties fail to resolve a dispute over such charges. Such regulations shall ensure that a utility charges just, reasonable, and nondiscriminatory rates for pole attachments.

"(2) A utility shall apportion the cost of providing space on a pole, duct, conduit, or right-of-way other than the usable space among entities so that such apportionment equals two-thirds of the costs of providing space other than the usable space that would be allocated to such entity under an equal apportionment of such costs among all attaching entities.

"(3) A utility shall apportion the cost of providing usable space among all entities according to the percentage of usable space required for each entity.

"(4) The regulations required under paragraph (1) shall become effective 5 years after the date of enactment of the Telecommunications Act of 1996. Any increase in the rates for pole attachments that result from the adoption of the regulations required by this subsection shall be phased in equal annual increments over a period of 5 years beginning on the effective date of such regulations.

"(f)(1) A utility shall provide a cable television system or any telecommunications carrier with nondiscriminatory access to any pole, duct, conduit, or right-of-way owned or controlled by it.

"(2) Notwithstanding paragraph (1), a utility providing electric service may deny a cable television system or any telecommunications carrier access to its poles, ducts, conduits, or rights-of-way, on a non-discriminatory basis where there is insufficient capacity and for reasons of safety, reliability and generally applicable engineering purposes.

"(g) A utility that engages in the provision of telecommunications services or cable services shall impute to its costs of providing such services (and charge any affiliate, subsidiary, or associate company engaged in the provision of such services) an equal amount to the pole attachment rate for which such company would be liable under this section.

"(h) Whenever the owner of a pole, duct, conduit, or right-of-way intends to modify or alter such pole, duct, conduit, or right-of-way, the owner shall provide written notification of such action to any entity that has obtained an attachment to such conduit or right-of-way so that such entity may have a reasonable opportunity to add to or modify its existing attachment. Any entity that adds to or modifies its existing attachment after receiving such notification shall bear a proportionate share of the costs incurred by the owner in making such pole, duct, conduit, or right-of-way accessible.

279

"(i) An entity that obtains an attachment to a pole, conduit, or right-of way shall not be required to bear any of the costs of rearranging or replacing its attachment, if such rearrangement or replacement is required as a result of an additional attachment or the modification of an existing attachment sought by any other entity (including the owner of such pole, duct, conduit, or right-of-way)."

SEC. 704. FACILITIES SITING; RADIO FREQUENCY EMISSION STANDARDS.

(a) National Wireless Telecommunications Siting Policy.--Section 332(c) (47 U.S.C. 332(c)) is amended by adding at the end the following new paragraph:

"(7) Preservation of local zoning authority.--

"(A) General authority.--Except as provided in this paragraph, nothing in this Act shall limit or affect the authority of a State or local government or instrumentality thereof over decisions regarding the placement, construction, and modification of personal wireless service facilities.

"(B) Limitations.--

"(i) The regulation of the placement, construction, and modification of personal wireless service facilities by any State or local government or instrumentality thereof--

"(I) shall not unreasonably discriminate among providers of functionally equivalent services; and

"(II) shall not prohibit or have the effect of prohibiting the provision of personal wireless services.

"(ii) A State or local government or instrumentality thereof shall act on any request for authorization to place, construct, or modify personal wireless service facilities within a reasonable period of time after the request is duly filed with such government or instrumentality, taking into account the nature and scope of such request.

"(iii) Any decision by a State or local government or instrumentality thereof to deny a request to place, construct, or modify personal wireless service facilities shall be in writing and supported by substantial evidence contained in a written record.

"(iv) No State or local government or instrumentality thereof may regulate the placement, construction, and modification of personal wireless service facilities on the basis of the environmental effects of radio frequency emissions to the extent that such facilities comply with the Commission's regulations concerning such emissions.

"(v) Any person adversely affected by any final action or failure to act by a State or local government or any instrumentality thereof that is inconsistent with this subparagraph may, within 30 days after such action or failure to act, commence an action in any court of competent jurisdiction. The court shall hear and decide such action on an expedited basis. Any person adversely affected by an act or failure to act by a State or local government or any instrumentality thereof that is inconsistent with clause (iv) may petition the Commission for relief.

"(C) Definitions.--For purposes of this paragraph--

"(i) the term 'personal wireless services' means commercial mobile services, unlicensed wireless services, and common carrier wireless exchange access services;

"(ii) the term 'personal wireless service facilities' means facilities for the provision of personal wireless services; and

"(iii) the term 'unlicensed wireless service' means the offering of telecommunications services using duly authorized devices which do not require individual licenses, but does not mean the provision of direct-to-home satellite services (as defined in section 303(v))."

(b) Radio Frequency Emissions.--Within 180 days after the enactment of this Act, the Commission shall complete action in ET Docket 93-62 to prescribe and make effective rules regarding the environmental effects of radio frequency emissions.

(c) Availability of Property.--Within 180 days of the enactment of this Act, the President or his designee shall prescribe procedures by which Federal departments and agencies may make available on a fair, reasonable, and nondiscriminatory basis, property, rights-of-way, and easements under their control for the placement of new telecommunications services that are dependent, in whole or in part, upon the utilization of Federal spectrum rights for the transmission or reception of such services. These procedures may establish a presumption that requests for the use of property, rights-of way, and easements by duly authorized providers should be granted absent unavoidable direct conflict with the department or agency's mission, or the current or planned use of the property, rights-of-way, and easements in question. Reasonable fees may be charged to providers of such telecommunications services for use of property, rights-of-way, and easements. The Commission shall provide technical support to States to encourage them to make property, rights-of-way, and easements under their jurisdiction available for such purposes.

SEC. 705. MOBILE SERVICES DIRECT ACCESS TO LONG DISTANCE CARRIERS.

Section 332(c) (47 U.S.C. 332(c)) is amended by adding at the end the following new paragraph:

"(8) Mobile services access.--A person engaged in the provision of commercial mobile services, insofar as such person is so engaged, shall not be required to provide equal access to common carriers for the provision of telephone toll services. If the Commission determines that subscribers to such services are denied access to the provider of telephone toll services of the subscribers' choice, and that such denial is contrary to the public interest, convenience, and necessity, then the Commission shall prescribe regulations to afford subscribers unblocked access to the provider of telephone toll services of the subscribers' choice through the use of a carrier identification code assigned to such provider or other mechanism. The requirements for unblocking shall not apply to mobile satellite services unless the Commission finds it to be in the public interest to apply such requirements to such services."

SEC. 706. ADVANCED TELECOMMUNICATIONS INCENTIVES.

(a) In General.--The Commission and each State commission with regulatory jurisdiction over telecommunications services shall encourage the deployment on a reasonable and timely basis of advanced telecommunications capability to all Americans (including, in particular, elementary and secondary schools and classrooms) by utilizing, in a manner consistent with the public interest, convenience, and necessity, price cap regulation, regulatory forbearance, measures that promote competition in the local telecommunications market, or other regulating methods that remove barriers to infrastructure investment.

(b) Inquiry.--The Commission shall, within 30 months after the date of enactment of this Act, and regularly thereafter, initiate a notice of inquiry concerning the availability of advanced telecommunications capability to all Americans (including, in particular, elementary and secondary schools and classrooms) and shall complete the inquiry within 180 days after its initiation. In the inquiry, the Commission shall determine whether advanced telecommunications capability is being deployed to all Americans in a reasonable and timely fashion. If the Commission's determination is negative, it shall take immediate action to accelerate deployment of such capability by removing barriers to infrastructure investment and by promoting competition in the telecommunications market.

(c) Definitions.--For purposes of this subsection:

(1) Advanced telecommunications capability.--The term "advanced telecommunications capability" is defined, without regard to any transmission media or technology, as high-speed, switched, broadband telecommunications capability that enables users to originate and receive high-quality voice, data, graphics, and video telecommunications using any technology.

(2) Elementary and secondary schools.--The term "elementary and secondary schools" means elementary and secondary schools, as defined in paragraphs (14) and (25), respectively, of section 14101 of the Elementary and Secondary Education Act of 1965 (20 U.S.C. 8801).

SEC. 707. TELECOMMUNICATIONS DEVELOPMENT FUND.

(a) Deposit and Use of Auction Escrow Accounts.--Section 309(j)(8) (47 U.S.C. 309(j)(8)) is amended by adding at the end the following new subparagraph:

"(C) Deposit and use of auction escrow accounts.--Any deposits the Commission may require for the qualification of any person to bid in a system of competitive bidding pursuant to this subsection shall be deposited in an interest bearing account at a financial institution designated for purposes of this subsection by the Commission (after consultation with the Secretary of the Treasury). Within 45 days following the conclusion of the competitive bidding--

"(i) the deposits of successful bidders shall be paid to the Treasury;

"(ii) the deposits of unsuccessful bidders shall be returned to such bidders; and

"(iii) the interest accrued to the account shall be transferred to the Telecommunications Development Fund established pursuant to section 714 of this Act."

(b) Establishment and Operation of Fund.--Title VII is amended by inserting after section 713 (as added by section 305) the following new section:

"Section 714. TELECOMMUNICATIONS DEVELOPMENT FUND.

"(a) Purpose of Section.--It is the purpose of this section--

"(1) to promote access to capital for small businesses in order to enhance competition in the telecommunications industry;

"(2) to stimulate new technology development, and promote employment and training; and

"(3) to support universal service and promote delivery of telecommunications services to underserved rural and urban areas.

"(b) Establishment of Fund.--There is hereby established a body corporate to be known as the Telecommunications Development Fund, which shall have succession until dissolved. The Fund shall maintain its principal office in the District of Columbia and shall be deemed, for purposes of venue and jurisdiction in civil actions, to be a resident and citizen thereof.

"(c) Board of Directors.--

"(1) Composition of board; chairman.--The Fund shall have a Board of Directors which shall consist of 7 persons appointed by the Chairman of the Commission. Four of such directors shall be representative of the private sector and three of such directors shall be representative of the Commission, the Small Business Administration, and the Department of the Treasury, respectively. The Chairman of the Commission shall appoint one of the representatives of the private sector to serve as chairman of the Fund within 30 days after the date of enactment of this section, in order to facilitate rapid creation and implementation of the Fund. The directors shall include members with experience in a number of the following areas: finance, investment banking, government banking, communications law and administrative practice, and public policy.

"(2) Terms of appointed and elected members.--The directors shall be eligible to serve for terms of 5 years, except of the initial members, as designated at the time of their appointment--

"(A) 1 shall be eligible to service for a term of 1 year;

"(B) 1 shall be eligible to service for a term of 2 years;

"(C) 1 shall be eligible to service for a term of 3 years;

"(D) 2 shall be eligible to service for a term of 4 years; and

"(E) 2 shall be eligible to service for a term of 5 years (1 of whom shall be the Chairman). Directors may continue to serve until their successors have been appointed and have qualified.

"(3) Meetings and functions of the board.--The Board of Directors shall meet at the call of its Chairman, but at least quarterly. The Board shall determine the general policies which shall govern the operations of the Fund. The Chairman of the Board shall, with the approval of the Board, select, appoint, and compensate qualified persons to fill the offices as may be provided for in the bylaws, with such functions, powers, and duties as may be prescribed by the bylaws or by the Board of Directors, and such persons shall be the officers of the Fund and shall discharge all such functions, powers, and duties.

"(d) Accounts of the Fund.--The Fund shall maintain its accounts at a financial institution designated for purposes of this section by the Chairman of the Board (after consultation with the Commission and the Secretary of the Treasury). The accounts of the Fund shall consist of--

"(1) interest transferred pursuant to section 309(j)(8)(C) of this Act;

"(2) such sums as may be appropriated to the Commission for advances to the Fund;

"(3) any contributions or donations to the Fund that are accepted by the Fund; and

"(4) any repayment of, or other payment made with respect to, loans, equity, or other extensions of credit made from the Fund.

"(e) Use of the Fund.--All moneys deposited into the accounts of the Fund shall be used solely for--

"(1) the making of loans, investments, or other extensions of credits to eligible small businesses in accordance with subsection (f);

"(2) the provision of financial advice to eligible small businesses;

"(3) expenses for the administration and management of the Fund (including salaries, expenses, and the rental or purchase of office space for the fund);

"(4) preparation of research, studies, or financial analyses; and

"(5) other services consistent with the purposes of this section.

"(f) Lending and Credit Operations.--Loans or other extensions of credit from the Fund shall be made available in accordance with the requirements of the Federal Credit Reform Act of 1990 (2 U.S.C. 661 et seq.) and any other applicable law to an eligible small business on the basis of--

"(1) the analysis of the business plan of the eligible small business;

"(2) the reasonable availability of collateral to secure the loan or credit extension;

"(3) the extent to which the loan or credit extension promotes the purposes of this section; and

"(4) other lending policies as defined by the Board.

"(g) Return of Advances.--Any advances appropriated pursuant to subsection (d)(2) shall be disbursed upon such terms and conditions (including conditions relating to the time or times of repayment) as are specified in any appropriations Act providing such advances.

"(h) General Corporate Powers.--The Fund shall have power--

"(1) to sue and be sued, complain and defend, in its corporate name and through its own counsel;

"(2) to adopt, alter, and use the corporate seal, which shall be judicially noticed;

"(3) to adopt, amend, and repeal by its Board of Directors, bylaws, rules, and regulations as may be necessary for the conduct of its business;

"(4) to conduct its business, carry on its operations, and have officers and exercise the power granted by this section in any State without regard to any qualification or similar statute in any State;

"(5) to lease, purchase, or otherwise acquire, own, hold, improve, use, or otherwise deal in and with any property, real, personal, or mixed, or any interest therein, wherever situated, for the purposes of the Fund;

"(6) to accept gifts or donations of services, or of property, real, personal, or mixed, tangible or intangible, in aid of any of the purposes of the Fund;

"(7) to sell, convey, mortgage, pledge, lease, exchange, and otherwise dispose of its property and assets;

"(8) to appoint such officers, attorneys, employees, and agents as may be required, to determine their qualifications, to define their duties, to fix their salaries, require bonds for them, and fix the penalty thereof; and

"(9) to enter into contracts, to execute instruments, to incur liabilities, to make loans and equity investment, and to do all things as are necessary or incidental to the proper management of its affairs and the proper conduct of its business.

"(i) Accounting, Auditing, and Reporting.--The accounts of the Fund shall be audited annually. Such audits shall be conducted in accordance with generally accepted auditing standards by independent certified public accountants. A report of each such audit shall be furnished to the Secretary of the Treasury and the Commission. The representatives of the Secretary and the Commission shall have access to all books, accounts, financial records, reports, files, and all other papers, things, or property belonging to or in use by the Fund and necessary to facilitate the audit.

"(j) Report on Audits by Treasury.--A report of each such audit for a fiscal year shall be made by the Secretary of the Treasury to the President and to the Congress not later than 6 months following the close of such fiscal year. The report shall set forth the scope of the audit and shall include a statement of assets and liabilities, capital and surplus or deficit; a statement of surplus or deficit analysis; a statement of income and expense; a statement of sources and application of funds; and such comments and information as may be deemed necessary to keep the President and the Congress informed of the operations and financial condition of the Fund, together with such recommendations with respect thereto as the Secretary may deem advisable.

"(k) Definitions.--As used in this section:

"(1) Eligible small business.--The term 'eligible small business' means business enterprises engaged in the telecommunications industry that have $50,000,000 or less in annual revenues, on average over the past 3 years prior to submitting the application under this section.

"(2) Fund.--The term 'Fund' means the Telecommunications Development Fund established pursuant to this section.

"(3) Telecommunications industry.--The term 'telecommunications industry' means communications businesses using regulated or unregulated facilities or services and includes broadcasting, telecommunications, cable, computer, data transmission, software, programming, advanced messaging, and electronics businesses."

SEC. 708. NATIONAL EDUCATION TECHNOLOGY FUNDING CORPORATION.

(a) Findings; Purpose.--

(1) Findings.--The Congress finds as follows:

(A) Corporation.--There has been established in the District of Columbia a private, nonprofit corporation known as the National Education Technology Funding Corporation which is not an agency or independent establishment of the Federal Government.

(B) Board of directors.--The Corporation is governed by a Board of Directors, as prescribed in the Corporation's articles of incorporation, consisting of 15 members, of which--

(i) five members are representative of public agencies representative of schools and public libraries;

(ii) five members are representative of State government, including persons knowledgeable about State finance, technology and education; and (iii) five members are representative of the private sector, with expertise in network technology, finance and management.

(C) Corporate purposes.--The purposes of the Corporation, as set forth in its articles of incorporation, are--

(i) to leverage resources and stimulate private investment in education technology infrastructure;

(ii) to designate State education technology agencies to receive loans, grants or other forms of assistance from the Corporation;

(iii) to establish criteria for encouraging States to--

(I) create, maintain, utilize and upgrade interactive high capacity networks capable of providing audio, visual and data communications for elementary schools, secondary schools and public libraries;

(II) distribute resources to assure equitable aid to all elementary schools and secondary schools in the State and achieve universal access to network technology; and

(III) upgrade the delivery and development of learning through innovative technology-based instructional tools and applications;

(iv) to provide loans, grants and other forms of assistance to State education technology agencies, with due regard for providing a fair balance among types of school districts and public libraries assisted and the disparate needs of such districts and libraries;

(v) to leverage resources to provide maximum aid to elementary schools, secondary schools and public libraries; and

(vi) to encourage the development of education telecommunications and information technologies through public-private ventures, by serving as a clearinghouse for information on new education technologies, and by providing technical assistance, including assistance to States, if needed, to establish State education technology agencies.

(2) Purpose.--The purpose of this section is to recognize the Corporation as a nonprofit corporation operating under the laws of the District of Columbia, and to provide authority for Federal departments and agencies to provide assistance to the Corporation.

(b) Definitions.--For the purpose of this section--

(1) the term "Corporation" means the National Education Technology Funding Corporation described in subsection (a)(1)(A);

287

(2)   the terms "elementary school" and "secondary school" have the same meanings given such terms in section 14101 of the Elementary and Secondary Education Act of 1965; and (3) the term "public library" has the same meaning given such term in section 3 of the Library Services and Construction Act.

(c) Assistance for Education Technology Purposes.--

(1) Receipt by corporation.--Notwithstanding any other provision of law, in order to carry out the corporate purposes described in subsection (a)(1)(C), the Corporation shall be eligible to receive discretionary grants, contracts, gifts, contributions, or technical assistance from any Federal department or agency, to the extent otherwise permitted by law.

(2) Agreement.--In order to receive any assistance described in paragraph (1) the Corporation shall enter into an agreement with the Federal department or agency providing such assistance, under which the Corporation agrees--

(A) to use such assistance to provide funding and technical assistance only for activities which the Board of Directors of the Corporation determines are consistent with the corporate purposes described in subsection (a)(1)(C);

(B) to review the activities of State education technology agencies and other entities receiving assistance from the Corporation to assure that the corporate purposes described in subsection (a)(1)(C) are carried out;

(C) that no part of the assets of the Corporation shall accrue to the benefit of any member of the Board of Directors of the Corporation, any officer or employee of the Corporation, or any other individual, except as salary or reasonable compensation for services;

(D) that the Board of Directors of the Corporation will adopt policies and procedures to prevent conflicts of interest;

(E) to maintain a Board of Directors of the Corporation consistent with subsection (a)(1)(B);

(F) that the Corporation, and any entity receiving the assistance from the Corporation, are subject to the appropriate oversight procedures of the Congress; and

(G) to comply with--

(i) the audit requirements described in subsection (d); and

(ii) the reporting and testimony requirements described in subsection (e).

(3) Construction.--Nothing in this section shall be construed to establish the Corporation as an agency or independent establishment of the Federal Government, or to establish the members of the Board of Directors of the Corporation, or the officers and employees of the Corporation, as officers or employees of the Federal Government.

(d) Audits.--

(1) Audits by independent certified public accountants.--

(A) In general.--The Corporation's financial statements shall be audited annually in accordance with generally accepted auditing standards by independent certified public accountants who are certified by a regulatory authority of a State or other political subdivision of the United States. The audits shall be conducted at the place or places where the accounts of the Corporation are normally kept. All books, accounts, financial records, reports, files, and all other papers, things, or property belonging to or in use by the Corporation and necessary to facilitate the audit shall be made available to the person or persons conducting the audits, and full facilities for verifying transactions with the balances or securities held by depositories, fiscal agents, and custodians shall be afforded to such person or persons.

(B) Reporting requirements.--The report of each annual audit described in subparagraph (A) shall be included in the annual report required by subsection (e)(1).

(2) Recordkeeping requirements; audit and examination of books.--

(A) Recordkeeping requirements.--The Corporation shall ensure that each recipient of assistance from the Corporation keeps--

(i) separate accounts with respect to such assistance;

(ii) such records as may be reasonably necessary to fully disclose--

(I) the amount and the disposition by such recipient of the proceeds of such assistance;

(II) the total cost of the project or undertaking in connection with which such assistance is given or used; and

(III) the amount and nature of that portion of the cost of the project or undertaking supplied by other sources; and

(iii) such other records as will facilitate an effective audit.

(B) Audit and examination of books.--The Corporation shall ensure that the Corporation, or any of the Corporation's duly authorized representatives, shall have access for the purpose of audit and examination to any books, documents, papers, and records of any recipient of assistance from the Corporation that are pertinent to such assistance. Representatives of the Comptroller General shall also have such access for such purpose.

(e) Annual Report; Testimony to the Congress.--

(1) Annual report.--Not later than April 30 of each year, the Corporation shall publish an annual report for the preceding fiscal year and submit that report to the President and the Congress. The report shall include a comprehensive and detailed evaluation of the Corporation's operations, activities, financial condition, and accomplishments under this section and may include such recommendations as the Corporation deems appropriate.

(2) Testimony before Congress.--The members of the Board of Directors, and officers, of the Corporation shall be available to testify before appropriate committees of the Congress with respect to the report described in paragraph (1), the report of any audit made

289

by the Comptroller General pursuant to this section, or any other matter which any such committee may determine appropriate.

SEC. 709. REPORT ON THE USE OF ADVANCED TELECOMMUNICATIONS SERVICES FOR MEDICAL PURPOSES.

The Secretary of Commerce, in consultation with the Secretary of Health and Human Services and other appropriate departments and agencies, shall submit a report to the Committee on Commerce of the House of Representatives and the Committee on Commerce, Science and Transportation of the Senate concerning the activities of the Joint Working Group on Telemedicine, together with any findings reached in the studies and demonstrations on telemedicine funded by the Public Health Service or other Federal agencies. The report shall examine questions related to patient safety, the efficacy and quality of the services provided, and other legal, medical, and economic issues related to the utilization of advanced telecommunications services for medical purposes. The report shall be submitted to the respective Committees by January 31, 1997.

SEC. 710. AUTHORIZATION OF APPROPRIATIONS.

(a) In General.--In addition to any other sums authorized by law, there are authorized to be appropriated to the Federal Communications Commission such sums as may be necessary to carry out this Act and the amendments made by this Act.

(b) Effect on Fees.--For the purposes of section 9(b)(2) (47 U.S.C. 159(b)(2)), additional amounts appropriated pursuant to subsection (a) shall be construed to be changes in the amounts appropriated for the performance of activities described in section 9(a) of the Communications Act of 1934.

(c) Funding Availability.--Section 309(j)(8)(B) (47 U.S.C. 309(j)(8)(B)) is amended by adding at the end the following new sentence: "Such offsetting collections are authorized to remain available until expended."

Appendix 2

The Communications Act of 1934 as amended by the Telecommunications Act of 1996

TABLE OF CONTENTS

[Editors' Note: This Table of Contents is not part of the Communications Act.]

TITLE III - PROVISIONS RELATING TO RADIO

Part I - General Provisions

AN ACT

To provide for the regulation of interstate and foreign communication by wire or radio, and for other purposes.

Be it enacted by the Senate and House of Representatives of the United States of America in Congress assembled,

TITLE I - GENERAL PROVISIONS

Section 1 [47 USC Section 151]. Purposes of Act; Creation of Federal Communications Commission.

For the purpose of regulating interstate and foreign commerce in communication by wire and radio so as to make available, so far as possible, to all the people of the United States, **without discrimination on the basis of race, color, religion, national origin, or sex,** a rapid, efficient, nationwide and world-wide wire and radio communication service with adequate facilities at reasonable charges, for the purpose of the national defense, for the purpose of promoting safety of life and property through the use of wire and radio communication, and for the purpose of securing a more effective execution of this policy by centralizing authority heretofore granted by law to several agencies and by granting additional authority with respect to interstate and foreign commerce in wire and radio communication, there is hereby created a commission to be known as the "Federal Communications Commission," which shall be constituted as hereinafter provided, and which shall execute and enforce the provisions of this Act.

Section 2 [47 USC Section 152]. Application of Act.

(a) The provisions of this Act shall apply to all interstate and foreign communication by wire or radio and all interstate and foreign transmission of energy by radio, which originates and/or is received within the United States, and to all persons engaged within the United States in such communication or such transmission of energy by radio, and to the licensing and regulating of all radio stations as hereinafter provided; but it shall not apply to persons engaged in wire or radio communication or transmission in [the Philippine Islands or] the Canal Zone, or to wire or radio communication or transmission wholly within [the Philippine Islands or] the Canal Zone. The provisions of this Act shall apply with respect to cable service, to all persons engaged within the United States in providing such service, and to the facilities of cable operators which relate to such service, as provided in Title VI.

(b) Except as provided in Sections 223 through 227, inclusive, and Section 332 and subject to the provisions of Section 301 and Title VI, nothing in this Act shall be construed to apply or to give the Commission jurisdiction with respect to (1) charges, classifications, practices, services, facilities, or regulations for or in connection with intrastate communication service by wire or radio of any carrier, or (2) any carrier engaged in interstate or foreign communication solely through physical connection with the facilities of another carrier not directly or indirectly controlling or controlled by, or under direct or indirect common control with such carrier, or (3) any carrier engaged in interstate or foreign communication solely through connection by radio, or by wire and radio, with facilities, located in an adjoining State or in Canada or Mexico (where they adjoin the State in which the carrier is doing business), or another carrier not directly or indirectly controlling or controlled by, or under direct or indirect common control with such carrier, or (4) any carrier to which clause (2) or clause (3) would be applicable except for furnishing interstate mobile radio communication service or radio communication service to mobile stations on land vehicles in Canada or Mexico; except that Sections 201 through 205 of this Act, both inclusive, shall, except as otherwise provided therein, apply to carriers described in clauses (2), (3) and (4).

Section 3 [47 USC Section 153]. Definitions.

[Editors' Note: The Telecommunications Act of 1996 alphabetized and numbered the definitions in this section, and added the definitions underlined. In addition, the phrase "the term" was added before each definition.]

For the purposes of this Act, unless the context otherwise requires.--

    (1) Affiliate.--The term "affiliate" means a person that (directly or indirectly) owns or controls, is owned or controlled by, or is under common ownership or control with, another person. For purposes of this paragraph, the term "own" means to own an equity interest (or the equivalent thereof) of more than 10 percent.

    (2) Amateur station.--The term "amateur station" means a radio station operated by a duly authorized person interested in radio technique solely with a personal aim and without pecuniary interest.

    (3) AT&T consent decree.--The term "AT&T Consent Decree" means the order entered August 24, 1982, in the antitrust action styled United States v. Western Electric, Civil Action No. 82-0192, in the United States District Court for the District of Columbia, and includes any judgment or order with respect to such action entered on or after August 24, 1982.

    (4) Bell operating company.--The term "Bell operating company"--

        (A) means any of the following companies: Bell Telephone Company of Nevada, Illinois Bell Telephone Company, Indiana Bell Telephone Company, Incorporated, Michigan Bell Telephone Company, New England Telephone and Telegraph Company, New Jersey Bell Telephone Company, New York Telephone Company, U S West Communications Company, South Central Bell Telephone Company, Southern Bell Telephone and Telegraph Company, Southwestern Bell Telephone Company, The Bell Telephone Company of Pennsylvania, The Chesapeake and Potomac Telephone Company, The Chesapeake and Potomac Telephone Company of Maryland, The Chesapeake and Potomac Telephone Company of Virginia, The Chesapeake and Potomac Telephone Company of West Virginia, The Diamond State Telephone Company, The Ohio Bell Telephone Company, The Pacific Telephone and Telegraph Company, or Wisconsin Telephone Company; and

        (B) includes any successor or assign of any such company that provides wireline telephone exchange service; but

        (C) does not include an affiliate of any such company, other than an affiliate described in subparagraph (A) or (B).

    (5) Broadcast station.--The term "broadcast station," "broadcasting station," or "radio broadcast station" means a radio station equipped to engage in broadcasting as herein defined.

(6) Broadcasting.--The term "broadcasting" means the dissemination of radio communications intended to be received by the public, directly or by the intermediary of relay stations.

(7) Cable service.--The term "cable service" has the meaning given such term in Section 602.

(8) Cable system.--The term "cable system" has the meaning given such term in Section 602.

(9) Chain broadcasting.--The term "chain broadcasting" means simultaneous broadcasting of an identical program by two or more connected stations.

(10) Common carrier.--The term "common carrier" or "carrier" means any person engaged as a common carrier for hire, in interstate or foreign communication by wire or radio or in interstate or foreign radio transmission of energy, except where reference is made to common carriers not subject to this Act; but a person engaged in radio broadcasting shall not, insofar as such person is so engaged, be deemed a common carrier.

(11) Connecting carrier.--The term "connecting carrier" means a carrier described in clauses (2), (3) or (4) of Section 2(b).

(12) Construction permit.--The term "construction permit" or "permit for construction" means that instrument of authorization required by this Act or the rules and regulations of the Commission made pursuant to this Act for the construction of a station or the installation of apparatus, for the transmission of energy, or communications, or signals by radio, by whatever name the instrument may be designated by the Commission.

(13) Corporation.--The term "corporation" includes any corporation, joint-stock company or association.

(14) Customer premises equipment.--The term "customer premises equipment" means equipment employed on the premises of a person (other than a carrier) to originate, route, or terminate telecommunications.

(15) Dialing parity.--The term "dialing parity" means that a person that is not an affiliate of a local exchange carrier is able to provide telecommunications services in such a manner that customers have the ability to route automatically, without the use of any access code, their telecommunications to the telecommunications services provider of the customer's designation from among 2 or more telecommunications services providers (including such local exchange carrier).

(16) Exchange access.--The term "exchange access" means the offering of access to telephone exchange services or facilities for the purpose of the origination or termination of telephone toll services.

(17) Foreign communication.--The term "foreign communication" or "foreign transmission" means communication or transmission from or to any place in the United States to or from a foreign country, or between a station in the United States and a mobile station located outside the United States.

(18) Great Lakes Agreement.--The term "Great Lakes Agreement" means the Agreement for the Promotion of Safety on the Great Lakes by Means of Radio in force and the regulations referred to therein.

(19) Harbor.--The term "harbor" or "port" means any place to which ships may resort for shelter or to load or unload passengers or goods, or to obtain fuel, water, or supplies. This term shall apply to such places whether proclaimed public or not and whether natural or artificial.

301

(20) Information service.--**The term "information service" means the offering of a capability for generating, acquiring, storing, transforming, processing, retrieving, utilizing, or making available information via telecommuni-cations, and includes electronic publishing, but does not include any use of any such capability for the management, control, or operation of a telecommunications system or the management of a telecommunications service.**

(21) InterLATA service.--**The term "interLATA service" means telecommunications between a point located in a local access and transport area and a point located outside such area.**

(22) Interstate communication.--The term "interstate communication" or "interstate transmission" means communication or transmission (A) from any State, Territory, or possession of the United States (other than the [Philippine Islands and] the Canal Zone), or the District of Columbia, to any other State, Territory, or possession of the United States (other than [the Philippine Islands, and] the Canal Zone), or the District of Columbia, (B) from or to the United States to or from [the Philippine Islands] or the Canal Zone, insofar as such communication or transmission takes place within the United States, or (C) between points within the United States but through a foreign country; but shall not, with respect to the provisions of Title II of this Act (other than Section 223 thereof), include wire or radio communication between points in the same State, Territory, or possession of the United States, or the District of Columbia, through any place outside thereof, if such communication is regulated by a State commission.

(23) Land station.--The term "land station" means a station, other than a mobile station, used for radio communication with mobile stations.

(24) Licensee.--The term "licensee" means the holder of a radio station license granted or continued in force under authority of this Act.

(25) Local access and transport area.--**The term "local access and transport area" or "LATA" means a contiguous geographic area--**

(A) established before the date of enactment of the Telecommunications Act of 1996 by a Bell operating company such that no exchange area includes points within more than 1 metropolitan statistical area, consolidated metropolitan statistical area, or State, except as expressly permitted under the AT&T Consent Decree; or

(B) established or modified by a Bell operating company after such date of enactment and approved by the Commission.

(26) Local exchange carrier.--**The term "local exchange carrier" means any person that is engaged in the provision of telephone exchange service or exchange access. Such term does not include a person insofar as such person is engaged in the provision of a commercial mobile service under Section 332(c), except to the extent that the Commission finds that such service should be included in the definition of such term.**

(27) Mobile service.--The term "mobile service" means a radio communication service carried on between mobile stations or receivers and land stations, and by mobile stations communicating among themselves, and includes (A) both one-way and two-way radio communication services, (B) a mobile service which provides a regularly interacting group of base, mobile, portable, and associated control and relay stations (whether licensed on an individual, cooperative, or multiple basis) for private one-way or two-way land mobile radio communications by eligible users over designated areas of operation, and (C) any service for which a license is required in a personal communications service established pursuant to the proceeding entitled "Amendment to the Commission's Rules to Establish New Personal Communications Services" (GEN Docket No. 90-314; ET Docket No. 92-100), or any successor proceeding.

(28) Mobile station.--The term "mobile station" means a radio communication station capable of being moved and which ordinarily does move.

(29) Network element.--The term "network element" means a facility or equipment used in the provision of a telecommunications service. Such term also includes features, functions, and capabilities that are provided by means of such facility or equipment, including subscriber numbers, databases, signaling systems, and information sufficient for billing and collection or used in the transmission, routing, or other provision of a telecommunications service.

(30) Number portability.--The term "number portability" means the ability of users of telecommunications services to retain, at the same location, existing telecommunications numbers without impairment of quality, reliability, or convenience when switching from one telecommunications carrier to another.

(31)(A) Operator.--The term "operator" on a ship of the United States means, for the purpose of Parts II and III of Title III of this Act, a person holding a radio operator's license of the proper class as prescribed and issued by the Commission.

(B) "operator" on a foreign ship means, for the purpose of Part II of Title III of this Act, a person holding a certificate as such of the proper class complying with the provisions of the radio regulations annexed to the International Telecommunication Convention in force, or complying with an agreement or treaty between the United States and the country in which the ship is registered.

(32) Person.--The term "person" includes an individual, partnership, association, joint-stock company, trust, or corporation.

(33) Radio communication.--The term "radio communication" or "communication by radio" means the transmission by radio of writing, signs, signals, pictures, and sounds of all kinds, including all instrumentalities, facilities, apparatus and services (among other things, the receipt, forwarding, and delivery of communications) incidental to such transmission.

(34)(A) Radio officer.--The term "radio officer" on a ship of the United States means, for the purpose of Part II of Title III of this Act, a person holding at least a first or second class radiotelegraph operator's license as prescribed and issued by the Commission. When such person is employed to operate a radiotelegraph station aboard a ship of the United States, he is also required to be licensed as a "radio officer" in accordance with the Act of May 12, 1948 (46 USC §229a-h).

(B) "Radio officer" on a foreign ship means, for the purpose of Part II of Title III of this Act, a person holding at least a first or second class radiotelegraph operator's certificate complying with the provisions of the radio regulations annexed to the International Telecommunication Convention in force.

(35) Radio station.--The term "radio station" or "station" means a station equipped to engage in radio communication or radio transmission of energy.

(36) Radiotelegraph auto alarm.--The term "radiotelegraph auto alarm" on a ship of the United States subject to the provisions of Part II of Title III of this Act means an automatic alarm receiving apparatus which responds to the radiotelegraph alarm signal and has been approved by the Commission. "Radiotelegraph auto alarm" on a foreign ship means an automatic alarm receiving apparatus which responds to the radiotelegraph alarm signal and has been approved by the government of the country in which the ship is registered: provided, that the United States and the country in which the ship is registered are parties to the same treaty, convention, or agreement prescribing the requirements for such apparatus. Nothing in this Act or in any other provision of law shall be construed to require the recognition of a radiotelegraph auto alarm as complying with Part II of Title III of this Act, on a foreign

ship subject to such part, where the country in which the ship is registered and the United States are not parties to the same treaty, convention, or agreement prescribing the requirements for such apparatus.

(37) Rural telephone company.--The term "rural telephone company" means a local exchange carrier operating entity to the extent that such entity--

(A) provides common carrier service to any local exchange carrier study area that does not include either--

(i) any incorporated place of 10,000 inhabitants or more, or any part thereof, based on the most recently available population statistics of the Bureau of the Census; or

(ii) any territory, incorporated or unincorporated, included in an urbanized area, as defined by the Bureau of the Census as of August 10, 1993;

(B) provides telephone exchange service, including exchange access, to fewer than 50,000 access lines;

(C) provides telephone exchange service to any local exchange carrier study area with fewer than 100,000 access lines; or

(D) has less than 15 percent of its access lines in communities of more than 50,000 on the date of enactment of the Telecommunications Act of 1996.

(38) Safety convention.--The term "safety convention" means the International Convention for the Safety of Life at Sea in force and the regulations referred to therein.

(39)(A) Ship.--The term "ship" or "vessel" includes every description of watercraft or other artificial contrivance, except aircraft, used or capable of being used as a means of transportation on water, whether or not it is actually afloat.

(B) A ship shall be considered a passenger ship if it carries or is licensed or certificated to carry more than twelve passengers.

(C) A cargo ship means any ship not a passenger ship.

(D) A passenger is any person carried on board a ship or vessel except (1) the officers and crew actually employed to man and operate the ship, (2) persons employed to carry on the business of the ship, and (3) persons on board a ship when they are carried, either because of the obligation laid upon the master to carry shipwrecked, distressed or other persons in like or similar situations or by reason of any circumstance over which neither the master, the owner nor the charterer (if any) has control.

(E) "Nuclear ship" means a ship provided with a nuclear power plant.

(40) State.--The term "State" includes the District of Columbia and the Territories and possessions.

(41) State commission.--The term "State commission" means the commission, board, or official (by whatever name designated) which under the laws of any state has regulatory jurisdiction with respect to intrastate operations of carriers.

(42) Station license.--The term "station license," "radio station license," or "license" means that instrument of authorization required by this Act or the rules and regulations of the Commission made pursuant to this Act, for the use or operation of apparatus for transmission of energy, or communications, or signals by radio, by whatever name the instrument may be designated by the Commission.

(43) Telecommunications.--The term "telecommunications" means the transmission, between or among points specified by the user, of information of the user's choosing, without change in the form or content of the information as sent and received.

(44) Telecommunications carrier.--The term "telecommunications carrier" means any provider of telecommunications services, except that such term does not include aggregators of telecommunications services (as defined in Section 226). A telecommunications carrier shall be treated as a common carrier under this Act only to the extent that it is engaged in providing telecommunications services, except that the Commission shall determine whether the provision of fixed and mobile satellite service shall be treated as common carriage.

(45) Telecommunications equipment.--The term "telecommunications equipment" means equipment, other than customer premises equipment, used by a carrier to provide telecommunications services, and includes software integral to such equipment (including upgrades).

(46) Telecommunications service.--The term "telecommunications means the offering of telecommunications for a fee directly to the public, or to such classes of users as to be effectively available directly to the public, regardless of the facilities used.

(47) Telephone exchange service.--The term "telephone exchange service" means (A) service within a telephone exchange, or within a connected system of telephone exchanges within the same exchange area operated to furnish to subscribers intercommunicating service of the character ordinarily furnished by a single exchange, and which is covered by the exchange service charge, or (B) comparable service provided through a system of switches, transmission equipment, or other facilities (or combination thereof) by which a subscriber can originate and terminate a telecommunications service.

(48) Telephone toll service.--The term "telephone toll service" means telephone service between stations in different exchange areas for which there is made a separate charge not included in contracts with subscribers for exchange service.

(49) Transmission of energy by radio.--The term "transmission of energy by radio" or "radio transmission of energy" includes both such transmission and all instrumentalities, facilities, and services incidental to such transmission.

(50) United States.--The term "United States" means the several States and Territories, the District of Columbia, and the possessions of the United States, but does not include [the Philippine Islands or] the Canal Zone.

(51) Wire communication.--The term "wire communication" or "communication by wire" means the transmission of writing, signs, signals, pictures, and sounds of all kinds by aid of wire, cable, or other like connection between the points of origin and reception of such transmission, including all instrumentalities, facilities, apparatus and services (among other things, the receipt, forwarding, and delivery of communications) incidental to such transmission.

Section 4 [47 USC Section 154]. Provisions Relating to the Commission.

(a) The Federal Communications Commission (in this Act referred to as the "Commission") shall be composed of five commissioners appointed by the President, by and with the advice and consent of the Senate, one of whom the President shall designated as chairman.

(b)(1) Each member of the Commission shall be a citizen of the United States.

(2)(A) No member of the Commission or person employed by the Commission shall--

(i) be financially interested in any company or other entity engaged in the manufacture or sale of telecommunications equipment which is subject to regulation by the Commission;

(ii) be financially interested in any company or other entity engaged in the business of communication by wire or radio or in the use of the electromagnetic spectrum;

(iii) be financially interested in any company or other entity which controls any company or other entity specified in clause (i) or clause (ii), or which derives a significant portion of its total income from ownership of stocks, bonds, or other securities of any such company or other entity; or

(iv) be employed by, hold any official relation to, or own any stocks, bonds, or other securities of, any person significantly regulated by the Commission under this Act; except that the prohibitions established in this subparagraph shall apply only to financial interests in any company or other entity which has a significant interest in communications, manufacturing, or sales activities which are subject to regulation by the Commission.

(B)(i) The Commission shall have authority to waive, from time to time, the application of the prohibitions established in subparagraph (A) to persons employed by the Commission if the Commission determines that the financial interests of a person which are involved in a particular case are minimal, except that such waiver authority shall be subject to the provisions of Section 208 of Title 18, United States Code. The waiver authority established in this subparagraph shall not apply with respect to members of the Commission.

(ii) In any case in which the Commission exercises the waiver authority established in this subparagraph, the Commission shall publish notice of such action in the Federal Register and shall furnish notice of such action to the appropriate committees of each House of the Congress. Each such notice shall include information regarding the identity of the person receiving the waiver, the position held by such person, and the nature of the financial interests which are the subject of the waiver.

(3) The Commission, in determining whether a company or other entity has a significant interest in communications, manufacturing, or sales activities which are subject to regulation by the Commission, shall consider (without excluding other relevant factors) --

(A) the revenues, investments, profits, and managerial efforts directed to the related communications, manufacturing, or sales activities of the company or other entity involved, as compared to the other aspects of the business of such company or other entity;

(B) the extent to which the Commission regulates and oversees the activities of such company or other entity;

(C) the degree to which the economic interests of such company or other entity may be affected by any action of the Commission; and

(D) the perceptions held by the public regarding the business activities of such company or other entity.

(4) Members of the Commission shall not engage in any other business, vocation, profession, or employment while serving as such members.

(5) The maximum number of Commissioners who may be members of the same political party shall be a number equal to the least number of Commissioners which constitutes a majority of the full membership of the Commission.

(c) Commissioners shall be appointed for terms of five years and until their successors are appointed and have been confirmed and taken the oath of office, except that they shall not continue to serve beyond the expiration of the next session of Congress subsequent to the expiration of said fixed term of office; except that any person chosen to fill a vacancy shall be appointed only for the unexpired term of the Commissioner whom he succeeds. No vacancy in the Commission shall impair the right of the remaining Commissioners to exercise all the powers of the Commission.

(d) Each Commissioner shall receive an annual salary at the annual rate payable from time to time for level IV of the Executive Schedule, payable in monthly installments. The Chairman of the Commission, during the period of his service as Chairman, shall receive an annual salary at the annual rate payable from time to time for level III of the Executive Schedule.

(e) The principal office of the Commission shall be in the District of Columbia, where its general sessions shall be held; but whenever the convenience of the public or of the parties may be promoted or delay or expense prevented thereby, the Commission may hold special sessions in any part of the United States.

(f)(1) The Commission shall have authority, subject to the provisions of the civil service laws and the Classification Act of 1949, as amended, to appoint such officers, engineers, accountants, attorneys, inspectors, examiners, and other employees as are necessary in the exercise of its functions.

(2) Without regard to the civil service laws, but subject to the Classification Act of 1949, each Commissioner may appoint three professional assistants and a secretary, each of whom shall perform such duties as such Commissioner shall direct. In addition, the Chairman of the Commission may appoint, without regard to the civil service laws, but subject to the Classification Act of 1949, an administrative assistant who shall perform such duties as the chairman shall direct.

(3) The Commission shall fix a reasonable rate of extra compensation for overtime services of engineers in charge and radio engineers of the Field Engineering and Monitoring Bureau of the Federal Communications Commission, who may be required to remain on duty between the hours of 5 o'clock postmeridian and 8 o'clock antemeridian or on Sundays or holidays to perform services in connection with the inspection of ship radio equipment and apparatus for the purposes of Part II of Title III of this Act or the Great Lakes Agreement, on the basis of one-half day's additional pay for each 2 hours or fraction thereof of at least 1 hour that the overtime extends beyond 5 o'clock postmeridian (but not to exceed 2-1/2 days' pay for the full period from 5 o'clock postmeridian to 8 o'clock antemeridian) and 2 additional days' pay for Sunday or holiday duty. The said extra compensation for overtime services shall be paid by the master, owner, or agent of such vessel to the local United States collector of customs or his representative, who shall deposit such collection into the Treasury of the United States to an appropriately designated receipt account: provided, that the amounts of such collections received by the said collector of customs or his representatives shall be covered into the Treasury as miscellaneous receipts; and the payments of such extra compensation to the several employees entitled thereto shall be made from the annual appropriations for salaries and expenses of the Commission: provided further, that to the extent that the annual appropriations which are hereby authorized to be made from the general fund of the Treasury are insufficient, there are hereby authorized to be appropriated from the general fund of the Treasury such additional amounts as may be necessary to the extent that the amounts of such receipts are in excess of the amounts appropriated: provided further, that such extra compensation shall be paid if such field employees have been ordered to report for duty and have so reported whether the actual inspection of the radio equipment or apparatus takes place or not: and provided further, that in those ports where customary working hours are other than those hereinabove mentioned, the Engineers in Charge are vested with authority to regulate the hours of such employees so as to agree with prevailing working hours in said ports where inspections are to be made, but nothing contained in this proviso shall be construed in any manner to alter the length of a working day for the engineers in charge and radio engineers or the overtime pay herein fixed: **And provided**

307

further, That, in the alternative, an entity designated by the Commission may make the inspections referred to in this paragraph.

(4)(A) The Commission, for purposes of preparing **or administering** any examination for an amateur station operator license, may accept and employ the voluntary and uncompensated services of any individual who holds an amateur station operator license of a higher class than the class **of** license for which the examination is being prepared **or administered**. In the case of examinations for the highest class of amateur station operator license, the Commission may accept and employ such services of any individual who holds such class of license.

(B)(i) ~~The Commission, for purposes of administering any examination for an amateur station operator license, may accept and employ the voluntary and uncompensated services of any individual who holds an amateur station operator license of a higher class than the class license for which the examination is being conducted. In the case of examinations for the highest class of amateur station operator license, the Commission may accept and employ such services of any individual who holds such class of license. Any person who owns a significant interest in, or is an employee of, any company or other entity which is engaged in the manufacture or distribution of equipment used in connection with amateur radio transmissions, or in the preparation or distribution of any publication used in preparation for obtaining amateur station operator licenses, shall not be eligible to render any service under this subparagraph.~~

~~(C)(i)~~ The Commission, for purposes of monitoring violations of any provision of this Act (and of any regulation prescribed by the Commission under this Act) relating to the amateur radio service, may --

(I) recruit and train any individual licensed by the Commission to operate an amateur station; and

(II) accept and employ the voluntary and uncompensated services of such individual.

(ii) The Commission, for purposes of recruiting and training individuals under clause (i) and for purposes of screening, annotating, and summarizing violation reports referred under clause (i), may accept and employ the voluntary and uncompensated services of any amateur station operator organization.

(iii) The functions of individuals recruited and trained under this subparagraph shall be limited to --

(I) the detection of improper amateur radio transmissions;

(II) the conveyance to Commission personnel of information which is essential to the enforcement of this Act (or regulations prescribed by the Commission under this Act) relating to the amateur radio service; and

(III) issuing advisory notices, under the general direction of the Commission, to persons who apparently have violated any provision of this Act (or regulations prescribed by the Commission under this Act) relating to the amateur radio service.

Nothing in this clause shall be construed to grant individuals recruited and trained under this subparagraph any authority to issue sanctions to violators or to take any enforcement action other than any action which the Commission may prescribe by rule.

~~(D)(i)~~ **(C)(i)** The Commission, for purposes of monitoring violations of any provision of this Act (and of any regulation prescribed by the Commission under this Act) relating to the citizens band radio service, may --

(I) recruit and train any citizens band radio operator; and

(II) accept and employ the voluntary and uncompensated services of such operator.

(ii) The Commission, for purposes of recruiting and training individuals under clause (i) and for purposes of screening, annotating, and summarizing violation reports referred under clause (i), may accept and employ the voluntary and uncompensated services of any citizens band radio operator organization. The Commission, in accepting and employing services of individuals under this subparagraph, shall seek to achieve a broad representation of individuals and organizations interested in citizens band radio operation.

(iii) The functions of individuals recruited and trained under this subparagraph shall be limited to --

(I) the detection of improper citizens band radio transmissions;

(II) the conveyance to Commission personnel of information which is essential to the enforcement of this Act (or regulations prescribed by the Commission under this Act) relating to the citizens band radio service; and

(III) issuing advisory notices, under the general direction of the Commission, to persons who apparently have violated any provision of this Act (or regulations prescribed by the Commission under this Act) relating to the citizens band radio service.
Nothing in this clause shall be construed to grant individuals recruited and trained under this subparagraph any authority to issue sanctions to violators or to take any enforcement action other than any action which the Commission may prescribe by rule.

<(E)>(D) The Commission shall have the authority to endorse certification of individuals to perform transmitter installation, operation, maintenance, and repair duties in the private land mobile services and fixed services (as defined by the Commission by rule) if such certification programs are conducted by organizations or committees which are representative of the users in those services and which consist of individuals who are not officers or employees of the federal government.

<(F)>(E) The authority of the Commission established in this paragraph shall not be subject to or affected by the provisions of Part III of Title 5, United States Code, or Section 3679(b) of the Revised Statutes (31 USC §665(b)).

<(G)>(F) Any person who provides services under this paragraph shall not be considered, by reason of having provided such services, a Federal employee.

<(H)>(G) The Commission, in accepting and employing services of individuals under subparagraphs (A)<,> and (B) <and (C)>, shall seek to achieve a broad representation of individuals and organizations interested in amateur station operation.

<(I)>(H) The Commission may establish rules of conduct and other regulations governing the service of individuals under this paragraph.

<(J)>(I) With respect to the acceptance of voluntary uncompensated services for the preparation, processing, or administration of examinations for amateur station operator licenses pursuant to subparagraph (A) <or (B)> of this paragraph, individuals, or organizations which provide or coordinate such authorized volunteer services may recover from examinees reimbursement for out-of-pocket costs. The total amount of allowable cost reimbursement per examinee shall not exceed $4, adjusted annually every January 1 for changes in the Department of Labor Consumer Price Index. <Such individuals and organizations shall maintain records of out-of-pocket expenditures and shall certify annually to the Commission that all costs for which reimbursement was obtained were necessarily and prudently incurred.>

309

(5)(A) The Commission, for purposes of preparing and administering any examination for a commercial radio operator license or endorsement, may accept and employ the services of persons that the Commission determines to be qualified. Any person so employed may not receive compensation for such services, but may recover from examinees such fees as the Commission permits, considering such factors as public service and cost estimates submitted by such person.

(B) The Commission may prescribe regulations to select, oversee, sanction, and dismiss any person authorized under this paragraph to be employed by the Commission.

(C) Any person who provides services under this paragraph or who provides goods in connection with such services shall not, by reason of having provided such service or goods, be considered a Federal or special government employee.

(g)(1) The Commission may make such expenditures (including expenditures for rent and personal services at the seat of government and elsewhere, for office supplies, law books, periodicals, and books of reference, for printing and binding, for land for use as sites for radio monitoring stations and related facilities, including living quarters where necessary in remote areas, for the construction of such stations and facilities, and for the improvement, furnishing, equipping and repairing of such stations and facilities and of laboratories and other related facilities (including construction of minor subsidiary buildings and structures not exceeding $25,000 in any one instance used in connection with technical research activities), as may be necessary for the execution of the functions vested in the Commission and as may be appropriated for by the Congress in accordance with the authorizations of appropriations established in Section 6. All expenditures of the Commission, including all necessary expenses for transportation incurred by the Commissioners or by their employees, under their orders, in making any investigation or upon any official business in any other places than in the city of Washington, shall be allowed and paid on the presentation of itemized vouchers therefor approved by the chairman of the Commission or by such other members or officer thereof as may be designated by the Commission for that purpose.

(2)(A) If --

(i) the necessary expenses specified in the last sentence of paragraph (1) have been incurred for the purpose of enabling commissioners or employees of the Commission to attend and participate in any convention, conference, or meeting;

(ii) such attendance and participation are in furtherance of the functions of the Commission; and

(iii) such attendance and participation are requested by the person sponsoring such convention, conference, or meeting; then the Commission shall have authority to accept direct reimbursement from such sponsor for such necessary expenses.

(B) The total amount of unreimbursed expenditures made by the Commission for travel for any fiscal year, together with the total amount of reimbursements which the Commission accepts under subparagraph (A) for such fiscal year, shall not exceed the level of travel expenses appropriated to the Commission for such fiscal year.

(C) The Commission shall submit to the appropriate committees of the Congress, and publish in the Federal Register, quarterly reports specifying reimbursements which the Commission has accepted under this paragraph.

(D) The provisions of this paragraph shall cease to have any force or effect at the end of fiscal year 1994.

(E) Funds which are received by the Commission as reimbursements under the provisions of this paragraph after the close of a fiscal year shall remain available for obligation.

(3)(A) Notwithstanding any other provision of law, in furtherance of its functions the Commission is authorized to accept, hold, administer, and use unconditional gifts, donations, and bequests of real, personal, and other property (including voluntary and uncompensated services, as authorized by section 3109 of title 5, United States Code).

(B) The Commission, for purposes of providing radio club and military-recreational call signs, may utilize the voluntary, uncompensated, and unreimbursed services of amateur radio organizations authorized by the Commission that have tax-exempt status under section 501(c)(3) of the Internal Revenue Code of 1986.

(C) For the purpose of Federal Law on income taxes, estate taxes, and gift taxes, property or services accepted under the authority of subparagraph (A) shall be deemed to be a gift, bequest, or devise to the United States.

(D) The Commission shall promulgate regulations to carry out the provisions of this paragraph. Such regulations shall include provisions to preclude the acceptance of any gift, bequest or donation that would create a conflict of interest, or the appearance of a conflict of interest.

(h) Three members of the Commission shall constitute a quorum thereof. The Commission shall have an official seal which shall be judicially noticed.

(i) The Commission may perform any and all acts, make such rules and regulations, and issue such orders, not inconsistent with this Act, as may be necessary in the execution of its functions.

(j) The Commission may conduct its proceedings in such manner as will best conduce to the proper dispatch of business and to the ends of justice. No Commissioner shall participate in any hearing or proceeding in which he has a pecuniary interest. Any party may appear before the Commission and be heard in person or by attorney. Every vote and official act of the Commission shall be entered of record and is proceedings shall be public upon the request of any party interested. The Commission is authorized to withhold publication of records or proceedings containing secret information affecting the national defense.

(k) The Commission shall make an annual report to Congress, copies of which shall be distributed as are other reports transmitted to Congress. Such report shall contain --

(1) Such information and data collected by the Commission as may be considered of value in the determination of questions connected with the regulation of interstate and foreign wire and radio communication and radio transmission of energy;

(2) Such information and data concerning the functioning of the Commission as will be of value to Congress in appraising the amount and character of the work and accomplishments of the Commission and the adequacy of its staff and equipment;

(3) An itemized statement of all funds expended during the preceding year by the Commission, of the sources of such funds, and of the authority in this Act or elsewhere under which such expenditures were made; and

(4) Specific recommendations to Congress as to additional legislation which the Commission deems necessary or desirable, including all legislative proposals submitted for approval to the Director of the Office of Management and Budget.

(l) All reports of investigations made by the Commission shall be entered of record, and a copy thereof shall be furnished to the party who may have complained, and to any common carrier or licensee that may have been complained of.

311

(m) The Commission shall provide for the publication of its reports and decisions in such form and manner as may be best adapted for public information and use, and such authorized publications shall be competent evidence of the reports and decisions of the Commission therein contained in all courts of the United States and of the several states without any further proof or authentication thereof.

(n) Rates of compensation of persons appointed under this section shall be subject to the reduction applicable to officers and employees of the federal government generally.

(o) For the purpose of obtaining maximum effectiveness from the use of radio and wire communications in connection with safety of life and property, the Commission shall investigate and study all phases of the problem and the best methods of obtaining the cooperation and coordination of these systems.

Section 5 [47 USC Section 155]. Organization and Functioning of the Commission.

(a) The member of the Commission designated by the President as Chairman shall be the chief executive officer of the Commission. It shall be his duty to preside at all meetings and sessions of the Commission, to represent the Commission in all matters relating to legislation and legislative reports, except that any Commissioner may present his own or minority views or supplemental reports, to represent the Commission in all matters requiring conferences or communications with other governmental officers, departments or agencies, and generally to coordinate and organize the work of the Commission in such manner as to promote prompt and efficient disposition of all matters within the jurisdiction of the Commission. In the case of a vacancy in the office of the Chairman of the Commission, or the absence or inability of the Chairman to serve, the Commission may temporarily designate one of its members to act as Chairman until the cause or circumstance requiring such designation shall have been eliminated or corrected.

(b) From time to time as the Commission may find necessary, the Commission shall organize its staff into (1) integrated bureaus, to function on the basis of the Commission's principal work load operations, and (2) such other divisional organizations as the Commission may deem necessary. Each such integrated bureau shall include such legal, engineering, accounting, administrative, clerical, and other personnel as the Commission may determine to be necessary to perform its functions.

(c)(1) When necessary to the proper functioning of the Commission and the prompt and orderly conduct of its business, the Commission may, by published rule or by order, delegate any of its functions (except functions granted to the Commission by this paragraph and by paragraphs (4), (5) and (6) of this subsection and except any action referred to in Sections 204(a)(2), 208(b) and 405(b) to a panel of Commissioners, an individual Commissioner, an employee board, or an individual employee, including functions with respect to hearing, determining, ordering, certifying, reporting, or otherwise acting as to any work, business, or matter; except that in delegating review functions to employees in cases of adjudication (as defined in the Administrative Procedure Act), the delegation in any such case may be made only to an employee board consisting of two or more employees referred to in paragraph (8). Any such rule or order may be adopted, amended, or rescinded only by a vote of a majority of the members of the Commission then holding office. <Nothing> **Except for cases involving the authorization of service in the instructional television fixed service, or as otherwise provided in this Act, nothing** in this paragraph shall authorize the Commission to provide for the conduct, by any person or persons other than persons referred to in <clauses> **paragraph** (2) <and> **or** (3) of Section <7(a) of the

312

~~Administrative Procedure Act~~ **556(b) of title 5, United States Code**, of any hearing to which such ~~Section 7(a)~~ **section** applies.

(2) As used in this subsection (d) the term "order, decision, report, or action" does not include an initial, tentative, or recommended decision to which exceptions may be filed as provided in Section 409(b).

(3) Any order, decision, report, or action made or taken pursuant to any such delegation, unless reviewed as provided in paragraph (4), shall have the same force and effect, and shall be made, evidenced, and enforced in the same manner, as orders, decisions, reports, or other actions of the Commission.

(4) Any person aggrieved by any such order, decision, report or action may file an application for review by the Commission within such time and in such manner as the Commission shall prescribe, and every such application shall be passed upon by the Commission. The Commission, on its own initiative, may review in whole or in part, at such time and in such manner as it shall determine any order, decision, report, or action made or taken pursuant to any delegation under paragraph (1).

(5) In passing upon applications for review, the Commission may grant in whole or in part, or deny such applications without specifying any reasons therefor. No such application for review shall rely on questions of fact or law upon which the panel of Commissioners, individual Commissioner, employee board or individual employee has been afforded no opportunity to pass.

(6) If the Commission grants the application for review, it may affirm, modify, or set aside the order, decision, report, or action, or it may order a rehearing upon such order, decision, report, or action in accordance with Section 405.

(7) The filing of an application for review under this subsection shall be a condition precedent to judicial review of any order, decision, report, or action made or taken pursuant to a delegation under paragraph (1). The time within which a petition for review must be filed in a proceeding to which Section 402(a) applies, or within which an appeal must be taken under Section 402(b), shall be computed from the date upon which public notice is given of orders disposing of all applications for review filed in any case.

(8) The employees to whom the Commission may delegate review functions in any case of adjudication (as defined in the Administrative Procedure Act) shall be qualified, by reason of their training, experience, and competence, to perform such review functions, and shall perform no duties inconsistent with such review functions. Such employees shall be in a grade classification or salary level commensurate with their important duties, and in no event less than the grade classification or salary level of the employee or employees whose actions are to be reviewed. In the performance of such review functions such employees shall be assigned to cases in rotation so far as practicable and shall not be responsible to or subject to the supervision or direction of any officer, employee, or agent engaged in the performance of investigative or prosecuting functions for any agency.

(9) The Secretary and seal of the Commission shall be the Secretary and seal of each panel of the Commission, each individual Commissioner, and each employee board or individual employee exercising functions delegated pursuant to paragraph (1) of this subsection.

(d) Meetings of the Commission shall be held at regular intervals, not less frequently than once each calendar month, at which times the functioning of the Commission and the handling of its work load shall be reviewed and such orders shall be entered and other action taken as may be necessary or appropriate to expedite the prompt and orderly conduct of the business of the Commission with the objective of rendering a final decision (1) within three months from the date of filing in all original

313

application, renewal and transfer cases in which it will not be necessary to hold a hearing, and (2) within six months from the final date of the hearing in all hearing cases.

(e) The Commission shall have a Managing Director who shall be appointed by the Chairman subject to the approval of the Commission. The Managing Director, under the supervision and direction of the Chairman, shall perform such administrative and executive functions as the Chairman shall delegate. The Managing Director shall be paid at a rate equal to the rate then payable for level V of the Executive Schedule.

Section 6 [47 USC Section 156]. Authorization of Appropriations.

(a) There are authorized to be appropriated for the administration of this Act by the Commission $109,831,000 for fiscal year 1990 and $119,831, 000 for fiscal year 1991, together with such sums as may be necessary for increases resulting from adjustments in salary, pay, retirement, other employee benefits required by law, and other nondiscretionary costs, for each of the fiscal years 1990 and 1991.

(b) In addition to the amounts authorized to be appropriated under this section, not more than 4 percent of the amount of any fees or other charges payable to the United States which are collected by the Commission during fiscal year 1990 are authorized to be made available to the Commission until expended to defray the fully distributed costs of such fees collection.

(c) Of the amounts appropriated pursuant to subsection (a) for fiscal year 1991, such sums as may be necessary not to exceed $2,000,000 shall be expended for upgrading and modernizing equipment at the Commission's electronic emissions test laboratory located in Laurel, Maryland.

(d) Of the sum appropriated in any fiscal year under this section, a portion, in an amount determined under section 9(b), shall be derived from fees authorized by section 9.

Section 7 [47 USC Section 157]. New Technologies and Services.

(a) It shall be the policy of the United States to encourage the provision of new technologies and services to the public. Any person or party (other than the Commission) who opposes a new technology or service proposed to be permitted under this Act shall have the burden to demonstrate that such proposal is inconsistent with the public interest.

(b) The Commission shall determine whether any new technology or service proposed in a petition or application is in the public interest within one year after such petition or application is filed. If the Commission initiates its own proceeding for a new technology or service, such proceeding shall be completed within 12 months after it is initiated.

Section 8 [47 USC Section 158]. Application Fees.

(a) The Commission shall assess and collect application fees at such rates as the Commission shall establish or at such modified rates as it shall establish pursuant to the provisions of subsection (b) of this section.

(b)(1) The Schedule of Application Fees established under this section shall be reviewed by the Commission every two years after October 1, 1991 and adjusted by the Commission to reflect changes in the Consumer Price Index. Increases or decreases in application fees shall apply to all categories of application fees, except that individual fees shall not be adjusted until the increase or decrease, as determined by the net change in the Consumer Price Index since the date of enactment of this section, amounts to at least $5.00 in the case of fees under $100.00, or 5 percent in the case of fees of $100.00 or more. All fees which require adjustment will be rounded upward to the next $5.00 increment. The Commission shall transmit to the Congress notification of any such adjustment not later than 90 days before the effective date of such adjustment.

(2) Increases or decreases in application fees made pursuant to this subsection shall not be subject to judicial review.

(c)(1) The Commission shall prescribe by regulation an additional application fee which shall be assessed as a penalty for late payment of application fees required by subsection (a) of this section. Such penalty shall be 25 percent of the amount of the application fee which was not paid in a timely manner.

(2) The Commission may dismiss any application or other filing for failure to pay in a timely manner any application fee or penalty under this section.

(d)(1) The application fees established under this section shall not be applicable (A) to governmental entities and nonprofit entities licensed in the following radio services: Local Government, Police, Fire, Highway Maintenance, Forestry-Conservation, Public Safety, and Special Emergency Radio, or (B) to governmental entities licensed in other services.

(2) The Commission may waive or defer payment of an application fee in any specific instance for good cause shown, where such action would promote the public interest.

(e) Moneys received from application fees established under this section shall be deposited in the general fund of the Treasury to reimburse the United States for amounts appropriated for use by the Commission in carrying out its functions under this Act.

(f) The Commission shall prescribe appropriate rules and regulations to carry out the provisions of this section.

(g) Until modified pursuant to subsection (b) of this section, the Schedule of Application Fees which the Federal Communications Commission shall prescribe pursuant to subsection (a) of this section shall be as follows:

SCHEDULE OF APPLICATION FEES

Private Radio Services

Service	Fee amount
1. Marine Coast Stations	
a. New License (per station)	$70.00
b. Modification of License (per station)	70.00
c. Renewal of License (per station)	70.00
d. Special Temporary Authority (Initial, Modifications, Extensions)	100.00
e. Assignments (per station)	70.00
f. Transfers of Control (per station)	35.00
g. Request for Waiver	
(i) Routine (per request)	105.00

		(ii) Non-Routine (per rule section/per station)	105.00
2.	Ship Stations		
	a.	New License (per application)	35.00
	b.	Modification of License (per application)	35.00
	c.	Renewal of License (per application)	35.00
	d.	Request for Waiver	
		(i) Routine (per request)	105.00
		(ii) Non-Routine (per rule section/per station)	105.00
3.	Operational Fixed Microwave Stations		
	a.	New License (per station)	155.00
	b.	Modification of License (per station)	155.00
	c.	Renewal of License (per station)	155.00
	d.	Special Temporary Authority (Initial, Modifications, Extensions)	35.00
	e.	Assignments (per station)	155.00
	f.	Transfers of Control (per station)	35.00
	g.	Request for Waiver	
		(i) Routine (per request)	105.00
		(ii) Non-Routine (per rule section/per station)	105.00
4.	Aviation (Ground Stations)		
	a.	New License (per station)	70.00
	b.	Modification of License (per station)	70.00
	c.	Renewal of License (per station)	70.00
	d.	Special Temporary Authority (Initial, Modifications, Extensions)	100.00
	e.	Assignments (per station)	70.00
	f.	Transfers of Control (per station)	35.00
	g.	Request for Waiver	
		(i) Routine (per request)	105.00
		(ii) Non-Routine (per rule section/per station)	105.00
5.	Aircraft Stations		
	a.	New License (per application)	35.00
	b.	Modification of License (per application)	35.00
	c.	Renewal of License (per application)	35.00
	d.	Request for Waiver	
		(i) Routine (per request)	105.00
		(ii) Non-Routine (per rule section/per station)	105.00
6.	Land Mobile Radio Stations (including Special Emergency and Public Safety Stations)		
	a.	New License (per call sign)	35.00
	b.	Modification of License (per call sign)	35.00
	c.	Renewal of License (per call sign)	35.00
	d.	Special Temporary Authority (Initial, Modifications, Extensions)	35.00
	e.	Assignments (per station)	35.00
	f.	Transfers of Control (per call sign)	35.00
	g.	Request for Waiver	

	(i) Routine (per request)	105.00
	(ii) Non-Routine (per rule section/per station)	105.00
h.	Reinstatement (per call sign)	35.00
i.	Specialized Mobile Radio Systems-Base Stations	
	(i) New License (per call sign)	35.00
	(ii) Modification of License (per call sign)	35.00
	(iii) Renewal of License (per call sign)	35.00
	(iv) Waiting List (annual application fee per application)	35.00
	(v) Special Temporary Authority (Initial, Modifications, Extensions)	35.00
	(vi) Assignments (per call sign)	35.00
	(vii) Transfers of Control (per call sign)	35.00
	(viii) Request for Waiver	
	(1) Routine (per request)	105.00
	(2) Non-Routine (per rule section/per station)	105.00
	(ix) Reinstatements (per call sign)	35.00
j.	Private Carrier Licenses	
	(i) New License (per call sign)	35.00
	(ii) Modification of License (per call sign)	35.00
	(iii) Renewal of License (per call sign)	35.00
	(iv) Special Temporary Authority (Initial, Modifications, Extensions)	35.00
	(v) Assignments (per call sign)	35.00
	(vi) Transfers of Control (per call sign)	35.00
	(vii) Request for Waiver	
	(1) Routine (per request)	105.00
	(2) Non-Routine (per rule section/per station)	105.00
	(viii) Reinstatements (per call sign)	35.00
7.	General Mobile Radio Service	
a.	New License (per call sign)	35.00
b.	Modifications of License (per call sign)	35.00
c.	Renewal of License (per call sign)	35.00
d.	Request for Waiver	
	(i) Routine (per request)	105.00
	(ii) Non-Routine (per rule section/per station)	105.00
e.	Special Temporary Authority (Initial, Modifications, Extensions)	35.00
f.	Transfer of control (per call sign)	35.00
8.	Restricted Radiotelephone Operator Permit	35.00
9.	Request for Duplicate Station License (all services)	35.00
10.	Hearing (Comparative, New, and Modifications)	6,760.00

Equipment Approval Services/Experimental Radio

1.   Certification

317

	a.	Receivers (except TV and FM receivers)	285.00
	b.	All Other Devices	735.00
	c.	Modifications and Class II Permissive Changes	35.00
	d.	Request for Confidentiality	105.00
2.		Type Acceptance	
	a.	All Devices	370.00
	b.	Modifications and Class II Permissive Changes	35.00
	c.	Request for Confidentiality	105.00
3.		Type Approval (all devices)	
	a.	With Testing (including Major Modifications)	1,465.00
	b.	Without Testing (including Minor Modifications)	170.00
	c.	Request for Confidentiality	105.00
4.		Notifications	115.00
5.		Advance Approval for Subscription TV System	2,255.00
	a.	Request for Confidentiality	105.00
6.		Assignment of Grantee Code for Equipment Identification	35.00
7.		Experimental Radio Service	
	a.	New Construction Permit and Station Authorization (per application)	35.00
	b.	Modification to Existing Construction Permit and Station Authorization (per application)	35.00
	c.	Renewal of Station Authorization (per application)	35.00
	d.	Assignment or Transfer of Control (per application)	35.00
	e.	Special Temporary Authority (per application)	35.00
	f.	Additional Application Fee for Applications Containing Requests to Withhold Information from Public Inspection (per application)	35.00

Mass Media Services

1.		Commercial TV Stations	
	a.	New or Major Change Construction Permits	2,535.00
	b.	Minor Change	565.00
	c.	Hearing (Major/Minor Change, Comparative New, or Comparative Renewal)	6,760.00
	d.	License	170.00
	e.	Assignment or Transfer	
		(i) Long Form (Forms 314/315)	565.00
		(ii) Short Form (Form 316)	80.00
	f.	Renewal	100.00
	g.	Call Sign (New or Modification)	55.00
	h.	Special Temporary Authority (other than to remain silent or extend an existing STA to remain silent)	100.00
	i.	Extension of Time to Construct or Replacement of CP	200.00

j.		Permit to Deliver Programs to Foreign Broadcast Stations	55.00
k.		Petition for Rulemaking for New Community of License	1,565.00
l.		Ownership Report (per report)	35.00
2.		Commercial Radio Stations	
	a.	New and Major Change Construction Permit	
		(i) AM Station	2,255.00
		(ii) FM Station	2,030.00
	b.	Minor Change	
		(i) AM Station	565.00
		(ii) FM Station	565.00
	c.	Hearing (Major/Minor Change, Comparative New, or Comparative Renewal)	6,760.00
	d.	License	
		(i) AM	370.00
		(ii) FM	115.00
		(iii) AM Directional Antenna	425.00
		(iv) FM Directional Antenna	355.00
		(v) AM Remote Control	35.00
	e.	Assignment or Transfer	
		(i) Long Form (Forms 314/315)	565.00
		(ii) Short Form (Form 316)	80.00
	f.	Renewal	100.00
	g.	Call Sign (New or Modification)	55.00
	h.	Special Temporary Authority (other than to remain silent or extend an existing STA to remain silent)	100.00
	i.	Extension of Time to Construct or Replacement of CP	200.00
	j.	Permit to Deliver Programs to Foreign Broadcast Stations	55.00
	k.	Petition for Rulemaking for New Community of License or Higher Class Channel	1,565.00
	l.	Ownership Report (per report)	35.00
3.		FM Translators	
	a.	New or Major Change Construction Permit	425.00
	b.	License	85.00
	c.	Assignment or Transfer	80.00
	d.	Renewal	35.00
	e.	Special Temporary Authority (other than to remain silent or extend an existing STA to remain silent)	100.00
4.		TV Translators and LPTV Stations	
	a.	New or Major Change Construction Permit	425.00
	b.	License	85.00
	c.	Assignment or Transfer	80.00
	d.	Renewal	35.00
	e.	Special Temporary Authority (other than to remain silent or extend an existing STA to remain silent)	100.00

5. Auxiliary Services (includes Remote Pickup Stations, TV Auxiliary Broadcast Stations, Aural Broadcast STL and Intercity Relay Stations, and Low Power Auxiliary Stations)

    a. Major Actions   85.00

    b. Renewals   35.00

    c. Special Temporary Authority (other than to remain silent or extend an existing STA to remain silent)   100.00

6. FM/TV Boosters

    a. New and Major Change Construction Permits   425.00

    b. License   85.00

    c. Special Temporary Authority (other than to remain silent or extend an existing STA to remain silent)   100.00

7. International Broadcast Station

    a. New Construction Permit and Facilities Change CP   1,705.00

    b. License   385.00

    c. Assignment or Transfer (per station)   60.00

    d. Renewal   95.00

    e. Frequency Assignment and Coordination (per frequency hour)   35.00

    f. Special Temporary Authority (other than to remain silent or extend an existing STA to remain silent)   100.00

8. Cable Television Service

    a. Cable Television Relay Service

        (i) Construction Permit   155.00

        (ii) Assignment or Transfer   155.00

        (iii) Renewal   155.00

        (iv) Modification   155.00

        (v) Special Temporary Authority (other than to remain silent or extend an existing STA to remain silent)   100.00

    b. Cable Special Relief Petition   790.00

    c. 76.12 Registration Statement (per statement)   35.00

    d. Aeronautical Frequency Usage Notifications (per notice)   35.00

    e. Aeronautical Frequency Usage Waivers (per waiver)   35.00

9. Direct Broadcast Satellite

    a. New or Major Change Construction Permit

        (i) Application for Authorization to Construct a Direct Broadcast Satellite   2,030.00

        (ii) Issuance of Construction Permit & Launch Authority   19,710.00

        (iii) License to Operate Satellite   565.00

    b. Hearing (Comparative New, Major/Minor Modifications, or Comparative Renewal)   6,760.00

    c. Special Temporary Authority (other than to remain silent or extend an existing STA to remain silent)   100.00

Common Carrier Services

1.   All Common Carrier Services
   - a.   Hearing (Comparative New or Major/Minor Modifications)   6,760.00
   - b.   Development Authority . . . Same application fee as regular authority in service unless otherwise indicated
   - c.   Formal Complaints and Pole Attachment Complaints Filing Fee   120.00
   - d.   Proceeding under Section 109(b) of the Communications Assistance for Law Enforcement Act   5,000.00
2.   Domestic Public Land Mobile Stations (includes Base, Dispatch, Control & Repeater Stations)
   - a.   New or Additional Facility (per transmitter)   230.00
   - b.   Major Modifications (per transmitter)   230.00
   - c.   Fill in Transmitters (per transmitter)   230.00
   - d.   Major Amendment to a Pending Application (per transmitter)   230.00
   - e.   Assignment or Transfer
     - (i)   First Call Sign on Application   230.00
     - (ii)   Each Additional Call Sign   35.00
   - f.   Partial Assignment (per call sign)   230.00
   - g.   Renewal (per call sign)   35.00
   - h.   Minor Modification (per transmitter)   35.00
   - i.   Special Temporary Authority (per frequency/per location)   200.00
   - j.   Extension of Time to Construct (per application)   35.00
   - k.   Notice of Completion of Construction (per application)   35.00
   - l.   Auxiliary Test Station (per transmitter)   200.00
   - m.   Subsidiary Communications Service (per request)   100.00
   - n.   Reinstatement (per application)   35.00
   - o.   Combining Call Signs (per call sign)   200.00
   - p.   Standby Transmitter (per transmitter/per location)   200.00
   - q.   900 MHz Nationwide Paging
     - (i)   Renewal
       - (1) Network Organizer   35.00
       - (2) Network Operator (per operator/per city)   35.00
   - r.   Air-Ground Individual License (per station)
     - (i)   Initial License   35.00
     - (ii)   Renewal of License   35.00
     - (iii)   Modification of License   35.00
3.   Cellular Systems (per system)
   - a.   New or Additional Facilities   230.00
   - b.   Major Modification   230.00
   - c.   Minor Modification   60.00
   - d.   Assignment or Transfer (including partial)   230.00
   - e.   License to Cover Construction
     - (i)   Initial License for Wireline Carrier   595.00

	(ii)	Subsequent License for Wireline Carrier	60.00
	(iii)	License for Nonwireline Carrier	60.00
	(iv)	Fill in License (all carriers)	60.00
f.	Renewal		35.00
g.	Extension of Time to Complete Construction		35.00
h.	Special Temporary Authority (per system)		200.00
i.	Combining Cellular Geographic Service Areas (per system)		50.00

4. Rural Radio (includes Central Office, Interoffice, or Relay Facilities)

a.	New or Additional Facility (per transmitter)	105.00
b.	Major Modification (per transmitter)	105.00
c.	Major Amendment to Pending Application (per transmitter)	105.00
d.	Minor Modification (per transmitter)	35.00
e.	Assignments or Transfers	
	(i) First Call Sign on Application	105.00
	(ii) Each Additional Call Sign	35.00
	(iii) Partial Assignment (per call sign)	105.00
f.	Renewal (per call sign)	35.00
g.	Extension of Time to Complete Construction (per application)	35.00
h.	Notice of Completion of Construction (per application)	35.00
i.	Special Temporary Authority (per frequency/per location)	200.00
j.	Reinstatement (per application)	35.00
k.	Combining Call Signs (per call sign)	200.00
l.	Auxiliary Test Station (per transmitter)	200.00
m.	Standby Transmitter (per transmitter/per location)	200.00

5. Offshore Radio Service (Mobile, Subscriber, and Central Stations; fees would also apply to any expansion of this service into coastal waters other than the Gulf of Mexico)

a.	New or Additional Facility (per transmitter)	105.00
b.	Major Modifications (per transmitter)	105.00
c.	Fill in Transmitters (per transmitter)	105.00
d.	Major Amendment to Pending Application (per transmitter)	105.00
e.	Minor Modification (per transmitter)	35.00
f.	Assignment or Transfer	
	(i) Each Additional Call Sign	35.00
	(ii) Partial Assignment (per call sign)	105.00
g.	Renewal (per call sign)	35.00
h.	Extension of Time to Complete Construction (per application)	35.00
i.	Reinstatement (per application)	35.00
j.	Notice of Completion of Construction (per application)	35.00
k.	Special Temporary Authority (per frequency/per location)	200.00
l.	Combining Call Signs (per call sign)	200.00
m.	Auxiliary Test Station (per transmitter)	200.00
n.	Standby Transmitter (per transmitter/per location)	200.00

6. Point-to-Point Microwave and Local Television Radio Service

a.	Conditional License (per station)	155.00
b.	Major Modification of Conditional License or License Authorization (per station)	155.00
c.	Certification of Completion of Construction (per station)	155.00
d.	Renewal (per licensed station)	155.00
e.	Assignment or Transfer	
	(i) First Station on Application	55.00
	(ii) Each Additional Station	35.00
f.	Extension of Construction Authorization (per station)	55.00
g.	Special Temporary Authority or Request for Waiver of Prior Construction Authorization (per request)	70.00

7. Multipoint Distribution Service (including multichannel MDS)

a.	Conditional License (per station)	155.00
b.	Major Modification of Conditional License or License Authorization (per station)	155.00
c.	Certification of Completion of Construction (per channel)	455.00
d.	Renewal (per licensed station)	155.00
e.	Assignment or Transfer	
	(i) First Station on Application	55.00
	(ii) Each Additional Station	35.00
f.	Extension of Construction Authorization (per station)	110.00
g.	Special Temporary Authority or Request for Waiver of Prior Construction Authorization (per request)	70.00

8. Digital Electronic Message Service

a.	Conditional License (per nodal station)	155.00
b.	Modification of Conditional License or License Authorization (per nodal station)	155.00
c.	Certification of Completion of Construction (per nodal station)	155.00
d.	Renewal (per licensed nodal station)	155.00
e.	Assignment or Transfer	
	(i) First Station on Application	55.00
	(ii) Each Additional Station	35.00
f.	Extension of Construction Authorization (per station)	55.00
g.	Special Temporary Authority or Request for Waiver of Prior Construction Authorization (per request)	70.00

9. International Fixed Public Radio (Public and Control Stations)

a.	Initial Construction Permit (per station)	510.00
b.	Assignment or Transfer (per application)	510.00
c.	Renewal (per license)	370.00
d.	Modification (per station)	370.00
e.	Extension of Construction Authorization (per station)	185.00
f.	Special Temporary Authority or Request for Waiver (per request)	185.00

10.	Fixed Satellite Transmit/Receive Earth Stations	
	a. Initial Application (per station)	1,525.00
	b. Modification of License (per station)	105.00
	c. Assignment or Transfer	
	(i) First Station on Application	300.00
	(ii) Each Additional Station	100.00
	d. Developmental Station (per station)	1,000.00
	e. Renewal of License (per station)	105.00
	f. Special Temporary Authority or Waivers of Prior Construction	
	Authorization (per request)	105.00
	g. Amendment of Application (per station)	105.00
	h. Extension of Construction Permit (per station)	105.00
11.	Small Transmit/Receive Earth Stations (2 meters or less and operating in the 4/6 GHz frequency band)	
	a. Lead Application	3,380.00
	b. Routine Application (per station)	35.00
	c. Modification of License (per station)	105.00
	d. Assignment or Transfer	
	(i) First Station on Application	300.00
	(ii) Each Additional Station	35.00
	e. Developmental Station (per station)	1,000.00
	f. Renewal of License (per station)	105.00
	g. Special Temporary Authority or Waivers of Prior Construction	
	Authorization (per request)	105.00
	h. Amendment of Application (per station)	105.00
	i. Extension of Construction Permit (per station)	105.00
12.	Receive Only Earth Stations	
	a. Initial Application for Registration	230.00
	b. Modification of License or Registration (per station)	105.00
	c. Assignment or Transfer	
	(i) First Station on Application	300.00
	(ii) Each Additional Station	100.00
	d. Renewal of License (per station)	105.00
	e. Amendment of Application (per station)	105.00
	f. Extension of Construction Permit (per station)	105.00
	g. Waivers (per request)	105.00
13.	Very Small Aperture Terminal (VSAT) Systems	
	a. Initial Application (per system)	5,630.00
	b. Modification of License (per system)	105.00
	c. Assignment or Transfer of System	1,505.00
	d. Developmental Station	1,000.00
	e. Renewal of License (per system)	105.00
	f. Special Temporary Authority or Waivers of Prior Construction	
	Authorization (per request)	105.00

g.	Amendment of Application (per system)		105.00
h.	Extension of Construction Permit (per system)		105.00
14.	Mobile Satellite Earth Stations		
a.	Initial Application of Blanket Authorization		5,630.00
b.	Initial Application for Individual Earth Station		1,350.00
c.	Modification of License (per system)		105.00
d.	Assignment or Transfer (per system)		1,505.00
e.	Developmental Station		1,000.00
f.	Renewal of License (per system)		105.00
g.	Special Temporary Authority or Waivers of Prior Construction Authorization (per request)		105.00
h.	Amendment of Application (per system)		105.00
i.	Extension of Construction Permit (per system)		105.00
15.	Radio Determination Satellite Earth Stations		
a.	Initial Application of Blanket Authorization		5,630.00
b.	Initial Application for Individual Earth Station		1,350.00
c.	Modification of License (per system)		105.00
d.	Assignment or Transfer (per system)		1,505.00
e.	Developmental Station		1,000.00
f.	Renewal of License (per system)		105.00
g.	Special Temporary Authority or Waivers of Prior Construction Authorization (per request)		105.00
h.	Amendment of Application (per system)		105.00
i.	Extension of Construction Permit (per system)		105.00
16.	Space Stations		
a.	Application for Authority to Construct		2,030.00
b.	Application for Authority to Launch & Operate		
	(i) Initial Application		70,000.00
	(ii) Replace Satellite		70,000.00
c.	Assignment or Transfer (per satellite)		5,000.00
d.	Modification		5,000.00
e.	Special Temporary Authority or Waiver of Prior Construction Authorization (per request)		500.00
f.	Amendment of Application		1,000.00
g.	Extension of Construction Permit/Launch Authorization (per request)		500.00
17.	Section 214 Applications		
a.	Overseas Cable Construction		9,125.00
b.	Cable Landing License		
	(i) Common Carrier		1,025.00
	(ii) Non-Common Carrier		10,150.00
c.	Domestic Cable Construction		610.00
d.	All Other 214 Applications		610.00
e.	Special Temporary Authority (all services)		610.00

f.	Assignments or Transfers (all services)	610.00
18.	Recognized Private Operating Status (per application)	610.00
19.	Telephone Equipment Registration	155.00
20.	Tariff Filings	
a.	Filing Fee	490.00
b.	Special Permission Filing (per filing)	490.00
21.	Accounting and Audits	
a.	Field Audit	62,290.00
b.	Review of Attest Audit	34,000.00
c.	Review of Depreciation Update Study (Single State)	20,685.00
	(i) Each Additional State	680.00
d.	Interpretation of Accounting Rules (per request)	2,885.00
e.	Petition for Waiver (per petition)	4,660.00
22.	Low-Earth Orbit Satellite Systems	
a.	Application for Authority to Construct (per system of technology identical satellites)	6,000.00
b.	Application for Authority to Launch and Operate (per system of technology identical satellites)	210,000.00
c.	Assignment or Transfer (per request)	6,000.00
d.	Modification (per request)	15,000.00
e.	Special Temporary Authority or Waiver of Prior Construction Authorization (per request)	1,500.00
f.	Amendment of Application (per request)	3,000.00
g.	Extension of Construction Permit/Launch Authorization (per request)	1,500.00

Miscellaneous Application Fees

1.	International Telecommunications Settlements Administrative Fee for Collections (per line item)	2.00
2.	Radio Operator Examinations	
a.	Commercial Radio Operator Examination	35.00
b.	Renewal of Commercial Radio Operator License, Permit, or Certificate	35.00
c.	Duplicate or Replacement Commercial Radio Operator License, Permit or Certificate	35.00
3.	Ship Inspections	
a.	Inspection of Oceangoing Vessels Under Title III, Part II of the Communications Act (per inspection)	620.00
b.	Inspection of Passenger Vessels Under Title III, Part III of the Communications Act (per inspection)	320.00
c.	Inspection of Vessels Under the Great Lakes Agreement (per inspection)	75.00
d.	Inspection of Foreign Vessels Under the Safety of Life at Sea	

	(SOLAS) Convention (per inspection)	540.00
e.	Temporary Waiver for Compulsorily Equipped Vessel	60.00

Section 9 [47 USC Section 159]. Regulatory Fees

(a) General Authority.

(1) Recovery of Costs. - The Commission, in accordance with this section, shall assess and collect regulatory fees to recover the costs of the following regulatory activities of the Commission: enforcement activities, policy and rulemaking activities, user information services, and international activities.

(2) Fees Contingent on Appropriations. - The fees described in paragraph (1) of this subsection shall be collected only if, and only in the total amounts, required in Appropriations Acts.

(b) Establishment and Adjustment of Regulatory Fees.

(1) In General. - The fees assessed under subsection (a) shall--

(A) be derived by determining the full-time equivalent number of employees performing the activities described in subsection (a) within the Private Radio Bureau, Mass Media Bureau, Common Carrier Bureau, and other offices of the Commission, adjusted to take into account factors that are reasonably related to the benefits provided to the payor of the fee by the Commission's activities, including such factors as service area coverage, shared use versus exclusive use, and other factors that the Commission determines are necessary in the public interest;

(B) be established at amounts that will result in collection, during each fiscal year, of an amount that can reasonably be expected to equal the amount appropriated for such fiscal year for the performance of the activities described in subsection (a); and

(C) until adjusted or amended by the Commission pursuant to paragraph (2) or (3), be the fees established by the Schedule of Regulatory Fees in subsection (g).

(2) Mandatory Adjustment of Schedule. - For any fiscal year after fiscal year 1994, the Commission shall, by rule, revise the Schedule of Regulatory Fees by proportionate increases or decreases to reflect, in accordance with paragraph (1)(B), changes in the amount appropriated for the performance of the activities described in subsection (a) for such fiscal year. Such proportionate increases or decreases shall--

(A) be adjusted to reflect, within the overall amounts described in appropriations Acts under the authority of paragraph (1)(A), unexpected increases or decreases in the number of licensees or units subject to payment of such fees; and

(B) be established at amounts that will result in collection of an aggregate amount of fees pursuant to this section that can reasonably be expected to equal the aggregate amount of fees that are required to be collected by appropriations Acts pursuant to paragraph (1)(B).

Increases or decreases in fees made by adjustments pursuant to this paragraph shall not be subject to judicial review. In making adjustments pursuant to this paragraph the Commission may round such fees to the nearest $5 in the case of fees under $1,000, or to the nearest $25 in the case of fees of $1,000 or more.

(3) Permitted Amendments. - In addition to the adjustments required by paragraph (2), the Commission shall, by regulation, amend the Schedule of Regulatory Fees if the Commission determines that the Schedule requires amendment to comply with the requirements of paragraph (1)(A). In making such amendments, the Commission shall add, delete, or reclassify services in the Schedule to reflect

additions, deletions, or changes in the nature of its services as a consequence of Commission rulemaking proceedings or changes in law. Increases or decreases in fees made by amendments pursuant to this paragraph shall not be subject to judicial review.

(4) Notice to Congress. - The Commission shall--

(A) transmit to the Congress notification of any adjustment made pursuant to paragraph (2) immediately upon the adoption of such adjustment; and

(B) transmit to the Congress notification of any amendment made pursuant to paragraph (3) not later than 90 days before the effective date of such amendment.

(c) Enforcement. -

(1) Penalties for Late Payment. - The Commission shall prescribe by regulation an additional charge which shall be assessed as a penalty for late payment of fees required by subsection (a) of this section. Such penalty shall be 25 percent of the amount of the fee which was not paid in a timely manner.

(2) Dismissal of Applications for Filings. - The Commission may dismiss any application or other filing for failure to pay in a timely manner any fee or penalty under this section.

(3) Revocations. - In addition to or in lieu of the penalties and dismissals authorized by paragraphs (1) and (2), the Commission may revoke any instrument of authorization held by any entity that has failed to make payment of a regulatory fee assessed pursuant to this section. Such revocation action may be taken by the Commission after notice of the Commission's intent to take such action is sent to the licensee by registered mail, return receipt requested, at the licensee's last known address. The notice will provide the licensee at least 30 days to either pay the fee or show cause why the fee does not apply to the licensee or should otherwise be waived or payment deferred. A hearing is not required under this subsection unless the licensee's response presents a substantial and material question of fact. In any case where a hearing is conducted pursuant to this section, the hearing shall be based on written evidence only, and the burden of proceeding with the introduction of evidence and the burden of proof shall be on the licensee. Unless the licensee substantially prevails in the hearing, the Commission may assess the licensee for the costs of such hearing. Any Commission order adopted pursuant to this subsection shall determine the amount due, if any, and provide the licensee with at least 30 days to pay that amount or have its authorization revoked. No order of revocation under this subsection shall become final until the licensee has exhausted its right to judicial review of such order under section 402(b)(5) of this title.

(d) Waiver, Reduction and Deferment. - The Commission may waive, reduce or defer payment of a fee in any specific instance for good cause shown, where such action would promote the public interest.

(e) Deposit of Collections. - Moneys received from fees established under this section shall be deposited as an offsetting collection in, and credited to, the account providing appropriations to carry out the functions of the Commission.

(f) Regulations.

(1) In General. - The Commission shall prescribe appropriate rules and regulations to carry out the provisions of this section.

(2) Installment Payments. - Such rules and regulations shall permit payment by installments in the case of fees in large amounts, and in the case of fees in small amounts, shall require the payment of the fee in advance for a number of years not to exceed the term of the license held by the payor.

(g) Schedule. - Until amended by the Commission pursuant to subsection (b), the Schedule of Regulatory Fees which the Federal Communications Commission shall, subject to subsection (a)(2), assess and collect shall be as follows:

SCHEDULE OF REGULATORY FEES

Bureau/Category	Annual Regulatory Fee (Dollars)
Private Radio Bureau	
Exclusive use services (per license)	
Land Mobile (above 470 MHz, Base Station and SMRS)	
(47 CFR Part 90)	16
Microwave (47 CFR Part 94)	16
Interactive Video Data Service (47 CFR Part 95)	16
Shared use services (per license unless otherwise noted)	7
Amateur vanity call signs	7
Mass Media Bureau (per license)	
AM radio (47 CFR Part 73)	
Class D Daytime	250
Class A Fulltime	900
Class B Fulltime	500
Class C Fulltime	200
Construction permits	100
FM radio (47 CFR Part 73)	
Classes C, C1, C2, B	900
Classes A, B1, C3	600
Construction permits	500
TV (47 CFR Part 73)	
VHF Commercial	
Markets 1 thru 10	18,000
Markets 11 thru 25	16,000
Markets 26 thru 50	12,000
Markets 51 thru 100	8,000
Remaining Markets	5,000
Construction permits	4,000
UHF Commercial	
Markets 1 thru 10	14,400
Markets 11 thru 25	12,800
Markets 26 thru 50	9,600
Markets 51 thru 100	6,400
Remaining Markets	4,000
Construction permits	3,200
Low Power TV, TV Translator, and TV Booster	
(47 CFR Part 74)	135

Broadcast Auxiliary (47 CFR Part 74)	25
International (HF) Broadcast (47 CFR Part 73)	200
Cable Antenna Relay Service (47 CFR Part 78)	220
Cable Television System (per 1,000 subscribers)	
(47 CFR Part 76)	370
Common Carrier Bureau	
Radio Facilities	
Cellular Radio (per 1,000 subscribers) (47 CFR Part 22)	60
Personal Communications (per 1,000 subscribers)	
(47 CFR Part 99)	60
Space Station (per operational station in geosynchronous	
orbit) (47 CFR Part 25)	65,000
Space Station (per system in low-earth orbit)	
(47 CFR Part 25)	90,000
Public Mobile (per 1,000 subscribers) (47 CFR Part 22)	60
Domestic Public Fixed (per call sign) (47 CFR Part 21)	55
International Public Fixed (per call sign) (47 CFR Part 23)	110
Earth Stations (47 CFR Part 25)	
VSAT and equivalent C-Band antennas (per 100 antennas)	6
Mobile satellite earth stations (per 100 antennas)	6
Earth station antennas	
Less than 9 meters (per 100 antennas)	6
9 Meters or more	
Transmit/Receive and Transmit Only (per meter)	85
Receive only (per meter)	55
Carriers	
Inter-Exchange Carrier (per 1,000 presubscribed	
access lines)	60
Local Exchange Carrier (per 1,000 access lines)	60
Competitive access provider (per 1,000 subscribers)	60
International circuits (per 100 active 64 KB circuit	
or equivalent)	220

(h) Exceptions. - The charges established under this section shall not be applicable to (1) governmental entities or non-profit entities; (2) to amateur radio operator licenses under Part 97 of the Commission's regulations (47 CFR Part 97).

(i) Accounting System. - The Commission shall develop accounting systems necessary to making the adjustments authorized by subsection (b)(3). In the Commission's annual report, the Commission shall prepare an analysis of its progress in developing such systems and shall afford interested persons the opportunity to submit comments concerning the allocation of the costs of performing the functions described in subsection (a) among the services in the Schedule.

Section 10 [47 USC Section 160]. Competition in Provision of Telecommunications Service.

(a) Regulatory flexibility.--Notwithstanding Section 332(c)(1)(A) of this Act, the Commission shall forbear from applying any regulation or any provision of this Act to a telecommunications carrier or telecommunications service, or class of telecommunications carriers or telecommunications services, in any or some of its or their geographic markets, if the Commission determines that--
(1) enforcement of such regulation or provision is not necessary to ensure that the charges, practices, classifications, or regulations by, for, or in connection with that telecommunications carrier or telecommunications service are just and reasonable and are not unjustly or unreasonably discriminatory;
(2) enforcement of such regulation or provision is not necessary for the protection of consumers; and
(3) forbearance from applying such provision or regulation is consistent with the public interest.
(b) Competitive Effect To Be Weighed.--In making the determination under subsection (a)(3), the Commission shall consider whether forbearance from enforcing the provision or regulation will promote competitive market conditions, including the extent to which such forbearance will enhance competition among providers of telecommunications services. If the Commission determines that such forbearance will promote competition among providers of telecommunications services, that determination may be the basis for a Commission finding that forbearance is in the public interest.
(c) Petition for Forbearance.--Any telecommunications carrier, or class of telecommunications carriers, may submit a petition to the Commission requesting that the Commission exercise the authority granted under this section with respect to that carrier or those carriers, or any service offered by that carrier or carriers. Any such petition shall be deemed granted if the Commission does not deny the petition for failure to meet the requirements for forbearance under subsection (a) within one year after the Commission receives it, unless the one-year period is extended by the Commission. The Commission may extend the initial one-year period by an additional 90 days if the Commission finds that an extension is necessary to meet the requirements of subsection (a). The Commission may grant or deny a petition in whole or in part and shall explain its decision in writing.
(d) Limitation.--Except as provided in Section 251(f), the Commission may not forbear from applying the requirements of Section 251(c) or 271 under subsection (a) of this section until it determines that those requirements have been fully implemented.
(e) State Enforcement After Commission Forbearance.--A State commission may not continue to apply or enforce any provision of this Act that the Commission has determined to forbear from applying under subsection (a).

Section 11 [47 USC Section 161]. Regulatory Reform.

(a) Biennial Review of Regulations.--In every even-numbered year (beginning with 1998), the Commission--

331

(1) shall review all regulations issued under this Act in effect at the time of the review that apply to the operations or activities of any provider of telecommunications service; and

(2) shall determine whether any such regulation is no longer necessary in the public interest as the result of meaningful economic competition between providers of such service.

(b) Effect of Determination.--The Commission shall repeal or modify any regulation it determines to be no longer necessary in the public interest.

TITLE II - COMMON CARRIERS

Part I - Common Carrier Regulation

Section 201 [47 USC Section 201]. Service and Charges.

(a) It shall be the duty of every common carrier engaged in interstate or foreign communication by wire or radio to furnish such communication service upon reasonable request therefor; and, in accordance with the orders of the Commission, in cases where the Commission, after opportunity for hearing, finds such action necessary or desirable in the public interest, to establish physical connections with other carriers, to establish through routes and charges applicable thereto and the divisions of such charges, and to establish and provide facilities and regulations for operating such through routes.

(b) All charges, practices, classifications, and regulations for and in connection with such communication service, shall be just and reasonable and any such charge, practice, classification, or regulation that is unjust or unreasonable is hereby declared to be unlawful: Provided, that communications by wire or radio subject to this Act may be classified into day, night, repeated, unrepeated, letter, commercial, press, government, and such other classes as the Commission may decide to be just and reasonable, and different charges may be made for the different classes of communications: Provided further, that nothing in this Act or in any other provision of law shall be construed to prevent a common carrier subject to this Act from entering into or operating under any contract with any common carrier not subject to this Act, for the exchange of their services, if the Commission is of the opinion that such contract is not contrary to the public interest: Provided further, that nothing in this Act or in any other provision of law shall prevent a common carrier subject to this Act from furnishing reports of positions of ships at sea to newspapers of general circulation, either at a nominal charge or without charge, provided the name of such common carrier is displayed along with such ship position reports. The Commission may prescribe such rules and regulations as may be necessary in the public interest to carry out the provisions of this Act.

Section 202 [47 USC Section 202]. Discrimination and Preferences.

(a) It shall be unlawful for any common carrier to make any unjust or unreasonable discrimination in charges, practices, classifications, regulations, facilities, or services for or in connection with like communication service, directly or indirectly, by any means or device, or to make or give any undue or unreasonable preference or advantage to any particular person, class of persons, or locality, or to subject any particular person, class of persons, or locality to any undue or unreasonable prejudice or disadvantage.

(b) Charges or services, whenever referred to in this Act, include charges for, or services in connection with, the use of common carrier lines of communication, whether derived from wire or radio facilities, in chain broadcasting or incidental to radio communication of any kind.

(c) Any carrier who knowingly violates the provisions of this section shall forfeit to the United States the sum of $6,000 for each such offense and $300 for each and every day of the continuance of such offense.

Section 203 [47 USC Section 203]. Schedules of Charges.

(a) Every common carrier, except connecting carriers, shall, within such reasonable time as the Commission shall designate, file with the Commission and print and keep open for public inspection schedules showing all charges for itself and its connecting carriers for interstate and foreign wire or radio communication between the different points on its own system, and between points on its own system and points on the system of its connecting carriers or points on the system of any other carrier subject to this Act when a through route has been established, whether such charges are joint or separate, and showing the classifications, practices and regulations affecting such charges. Such schedules shall contain such other information, and be printed in such form, and be posted and kept open for public inspection in such places, as the Commission may by regulation require, and each such schedule shall give notice of its effective date; and such common carrier shall furnish such schedules to each of its connecting carriers, and such connecting carriers shall keep such schedules open for inspection in such public places as the Commission may require.

(b)(1) No change shall be made in the charges, classifications, regulations, or practices which have been so filed and published except after one hundred and twenty days notice to the Commission and to the public, which shall be published in such form and contain such information as the Commission may by regulations prescribe.

(2) The Commission may, in its discretion and for good cause shown, modify any requirement made by or under the authority of this section either in particular instances or by general order applicable to special circumstances or conditions except that the Commission may not require the notice period specified in paragraph (1) to be more than one hundred and twenty days.

(c) No carrier, unless otherwise provided by or under authority of this Act, shall engage or participate in such communication unless schedules have been filed and published in accordance with the provisions of this Act and with the regulations made thereunder; and no carrier shall (1) charge, demand, collect, or receive a greater or less or different compensation for such communication, or for any service in connection therewith, between the points named in any such schedule than the charges specified in the schedule then in effect, or (2) refund or remit by any means or device any portion of the charges so specified, or (3) extend to any person any privileges or facilities in such communication, or employ or enforce any classifications, regulations, or practices affecting such charges, except as specified in such schedule.

(d) The Commission may reject and refuse to file any schedule entered for filing which does not provide and give lawful notice of its effective date. Any schedule so rejected by the Commission shall be void and its use shall be unlawful.

(e) In case of failure or refusal on the part of any carrier to comply with the provisions of this section or of any regulation or order made by the Commission thereunder, such carrier shall forfeit to the United States the sum of $6,000 for each such offense, and $300 for each and every day of the continuance of such offense.

Section 204 [47 USC Section 204]. Hearing as to Lawfulness of New Charges; Suspension

(a)(1) Whenever there is filed with the Commission any new or revised charge, classification, regulation, or practice, the Commission may either upon complaint or upon its own initiative without complaint, upon reasonable notice, enter upon a hearing concerning the lawfulness thereof; and pending such hearing and the decision thereon the Commission, upon delivering to the carrier or carriers affected thereby a statement in writing of its reasons for such suspension, may suspend the operation of such charge, classification, regulation, or practice, in whole or in part but not for a longer period than five months beyond the time when it would otherwise go into effect; and after full hearing the Commission may make such order with reference thereto as would be proper in a proceeding initiated after such charge, classification, regulation, or practice had become effective. If the proceeding has not been concluded and an order made within the period of the suspension, the proposed new or revised charge, classification, regulation, or practice shall go into effect at the end of such period; but in case of a proposed charge for a new service or a revised charge, the Commission may by order require the interested carrier or carriers to keep accurate account of all amounts received by reason of such charge for a new service or revised charge, specifying by whom and in whose behalf such amounts are paid, and upon completion of the hearing and decision may by further order require the interested carrier or carriers to refund, with interest, to the persons in whose behalf such amounts were paid, such portion of such charge for a new service or revised charges as by its decision shall be found not justified. At any hearing involving a new or revised charge, or a proposed new or revised charge, the burden of proof to show that the new or revised charge, or proposed charge, is just and reasonable shall be upon the carrier, and the Commission shall give to the hearing and decision of such questions preference over all other questions pending before it and decide the same as speedily as possible.

(2)(A) Except as provided in subparagraph (B), the Commission shall, with respect to any hearing under this section, issue an order concluding such hearing within <12> 5 months after the date that the charge, classification, regulation, or practice subject to the hearing becomes effective<, or within 15 months after such date if the hearing raises questions of fact of such extraordinary complexity that the questions cannot be resolved within 12 months>.

(B) The Commission shall, with respect to any such hearing initiated prior to the date of enactment of this paragraph, issue an order concluding the hearing not later than 12 months after such date of enactment.

(C) Any order concluding a hearing under this section shall be a final order and may be appealed under Section 402(a).

(3) A local exchange carrier may file with the Commission a new or revised charge, classification, regulation, or practice on a streamlined basis. Any such charge, classification, regulation, or practice shall be deemed lawful and shall be effective 7 days (in the case of a reduction in rates) or 15 days (in the case of an increase in rates) after the date on which it is filed with the Commission unless the Commission takes action under paragraph (1) before the end of that 7-day or 15-day period, as is appropriate.

(b) Notwithstanding the provisions of subsection (a) of this section, the Commission may allow part of a charge, classification, regulation, or practice to go into effect, based upon a written showing by the carrier or carriers affected, and an opportunity for written comment thereon by affected persons, that such partial authorization is just, fair and reasonable. Additionally, or in combination with a partial authorization, the Commission, upon a similar showing, may allow all or part of a charge, classification, regulation, or practice to go into effect on a temporary basis pending further order of the Commission. Authorizations of temporary new or increased charges may include an accounting order of the type provided for in subsection (a).

Section 205 [47 USC Section 205]. Commission Authorized to Prescribe Just and Reasonable Charges.

(a) Whenever, after full opportunity for hearing, upon a complaint or under an investigation and hearing made by the Commission on its own initiative, the Commission shall be of opinion that any charge, classification, regulation, or practice of any carrier or carriers is or will be in violation of any of the provisions of this Act, the Commission is authorized and empowered to determine and prescribe what will be the just and reasonable charge or the maximum or minimum, or maximum and minimum, charge or charges to be thereafter observed, and what classification, regulation, or practice is or will be just, fair and reasonable, to be thereafter followed, and to make an order that the carrier or carriers shall cease and desist from such violation to the extent that the Commission finds that the same does or will exist, and shall not thereafter publish, demand, or collect any charge other than the charge so prescribed, or in excess of the maximum or less than the minimum so prescribed, as the case may be, and shall adopt the classification and shall conform to and observe the regulation or practice so prescribed.

(b) Any carrier, any officer, representative, or agent of a carrier, or any receiver, trustee, lessee, or agent of either of them, who knowingly fails or neglects to obey any order made under the provisions of this section shall forfeit to the United States the sum of $12,000 for each offense. Every distinct violation shall be a separate offense, and in case of continuing violation each day shall be deemed a separate offense.

Section 206 [47 USC Section 206]. Liability of Carriers for Damages.

In case any common carrier shall do, or cause or permit to be done, any act, matter, or thing in this Act prohibited or declared to be unlawful, or shall omit to do any act, matter, or thing in this Act required to be done, such common carrier shall be liable to the person or persons injured thereby for the full amount of damages sustained in consequence of any such violation of the provisions of this Act, together with a reasonable counsel or attorney's fee, to be fixed by the court in every case of recovery, which attorney's fee shall be taxed and collected as part of the costs in the case.

Section 207 [47 USC Section 207]. Recovery of Damages.

Any person claiming to be damaged by any common carrier subject to the provisions of this Act may either make complaint to the Commission as hereinafter provided for, or may bring suit for the recovery of the damages for which such common carrier may be liable under the provisions of this Act, in any district court of the United States of competent jurisdiction; but such persons shall not have the right to pursue both such remedies.

Section 208 [47 USC Section 208]. Complaints to the Commission.

(a) Any person, any body politic or municipal organization, or state commission, complaining of anything done or omitted to be done by any common carrier subject to this Act, in contravention of the provisions thereof, may apply to said Commission by petition which shall briefly state the facts, whereupon a statement of the complaint thus made shall be forwarded by the Commission to such common carrier, who shall be called upon to satisfy the complaint or to answer the same in writing within a reasonable time to be specified by the Commission. If such common carrier within the time specified shall make reparation for the injury alleged to have been caused, the common carrier shall be relieved of liability to the complainant only for the particular violation of law thus complained of. If such carrier or carriers shall not satisfy the complaint within the time specified or there shall appear to be any reasonable ground for investigating said complaint, it shall be the duty of the Commission to investigate the matters complained of in such manner and by such means as it shall deem proper. No complaint shall at any time be dismissed because of the absence of direct damage to the complainant.

(b)(1) Except as provided in paragraph (2), the Commission shall, with respect to any investigation under this section of the lawfulness of a charge, classification, regulation, or practice, issue an order concluding such investigation within <12> 5 months after the date on which the complaint was filed<, or within 15 months after such date if the investigation raises questions of fact of such extraordinary complexity that the questions cannot be resolved within 12 months>.

(2) The Commission shall, with respect to any such investigation initiated prior to the date of enactment of this subsection, issue an order concluding the investigation not later than 12 months after such date of enactment.

(3) Any order concluding an investigation under paragraph (1) or (2) shall be a final order and may be appealed under Section 402(a).

Section 209 [47 USC Section 209]. Orders for Payment of Money.

If, after hearing on a complaint, the Commission shall determine that any party complainant is entitled to an award of damages under the provisions of this Act, the Commission shall make an order directing the carrier to pay to the complainant the sum to which he is entitled on or before a day named.

Section 210 [47 USC Section 210]. Franks and Passes.

(a) Nothing in this Act or in any other provision of law shall be construed to prohibit common carriers from issuing or giving franks to, or exchanging franks with each other for the use of, their officers, agents, employees, and their families, or, subject to such rules as the Commission may prescribe, from issuing, giving, or exchanging franks and passes to or with other common carriers not subject to the provisions of this Act, for the use of their officers, agents, employees, and their families. The term "employees," as used in this section, shall include furloughed, pensioned and superannuated employees.

(b) Nothing in this Act or in any other provision of law shall be construed to prohibit common carriers from rendering to any agency of the Government free service in connection with the preparation for the national defense: Provided, that such free service may be rendered only in accordance with such rules and regulations as the Commission may prescribe therefor.

Section 211 [47 USC Section 211]. Copies of Contracts to be Filed.

(a) Every carrier subject to this Act shall file with the Commission copies of all contracts, agreements, or arrangements with other carriers, or with common carriers not subject to the provisions of this Act, in relation to any traffic affected by the provisions of this Act to which it may be a party.

(b) The Commission shall have authority to require the filing of any other contracts of any carrier, and shall also have authority to exempt any carrier from submitting copies of such minor contracts as the Commission may determine.

Section 212 [47 USC Section 212]. Interlocking Directorates - Officials Dealing in Securities.

It shall be unlawful for any person to hold the position of officer or director of more than one carrier subject to this Act, unless such holding shall have been authorized by order of the Commission, upon due showing in form and manner prescribed by the Commission, that neither public nor private interests will be adversely affected thereby: Provided, that the Commission may authorize persons to hold the position of officer or director in more than one such carrier without regard to the requirements of this section, where it has found that one of the two or more carriers directly or indirectly owns more than 50 per centum of the stock of the other or others, or that 50 per centum or more of the stock of all such carriers is directly or indirectly owned by the same person. After this section takes effect it shall be unlawful for any officer or director of any carrier subject to this Act to receive for his own benefit, directly or indirectly, any money or thing of value in respect of negotiation, hypothecation, or sale of any securities issued or to be issued by such carrier, or to share in any of the proceeds thereof, or to participate in the making or paying of any dividends of such carriers from any funds properly included in capital account.

Section 213 [47 USC Section 213]. Valuation of Carrier Property.

(a) The Commission may from time to time, as may be necessary for the proper administration of this Act, and after opportunity for hearing, make a valuation of all or of any part of the property owned or used by any carrier subject to this Act, as of such date as the Commission may fix.

(b) The Commission may at any time require any such carrier to file with the Commission an inventory of all or of any part of the property owned or used by said carrier, which inventory shall show the units of said property classified in such detail, and in such manner, as the Commission shall direct, and shall show the estimated cost of reproduction new of said units, and their reproduction cost new less depreciation, as of such date as the Commission may direct; and such carrier shall file such inventory within such reasonable time as the Commission by order shall require.

(c) The Commission may at any time require any such carrier to file with the Commission a statement showing the original cost at the time of dedication to the public use of all or of any part of the property owned or used by said carrier. For the showing of such original cost said property shall be classified, and the original cost shall be defined, in such manner as the Commission may prescribe; and if any part of such cost cannot be determined from accounting or other records, the portion of the property for which such cost cannot be determined shall be reported to the Commission; and, if the Commission shall so direct, the original cost thereof shall be estimated in such manner as the Commission may prescribe. If the carrier owning the property at the time such original cost is reported

337

shall have paid more or less than the original cost to acquire the same, the amount of such cost of acquisition, and any facts which the Commission may require in connection therewith, shall be reported with such original cost. The report made by a carrier under this paragraph shall show the source or sources from which the original cost reported was obtained, and such other information as to the manner in which the report was prepared, as the Commission shall require.

(d) Nothing shall be included in the original cost reported for the property of any carrier under paragraph (c) of this section on account of any easement, license, or franchise granted by the United States or by any state or political subdivision thereof, beyond the reasonable necessary expense lawfully incurred in obtaining such easement, license, or franchise from the public authority aforesaid, which expense shall be reported separately from all other costs in such detail as the Commission may require; and nothing shall be included in any valuation of the property of any carrier made by the Commission on account of any such easement, license, or franchise, beyond such reasonable necessary expense lawfully incurred as aforesaid.

(e) The Commission shall keep itself informed of all new construction, extensions, improvements, retirements, or other changes in the condition, quantity, use, and classification of the property of common carriers, and of the cost of all additions and betterments thereto and of all changes in the investment therein, and may keep itself informed of current changes in costs and values of carrier properties.

(f) For the purpose of enabling the Commission to make a valuation of any of the property of any such carrier, or to find the original cost of such property, or to find any other facts concerning the same which are required for use by the Commission, it shall be the duty of each such carrier to furnish to the Commission, within such reasonable time as the Commission may order, any information with respect thereto which the Commission may by order require, including copies of maps, contracts, reports of engineers, and other data, records, and papers, and to grant to all agents of the Commission free access to its property and its accounts, records, and memoranda whenever and wherever requested by any such duly authorized agent, and to cooperate with and aid the Commission in the work of making any such valuation or finding in such manner and to such extent as the Commission may require and direct, and all rules and regulations made by the Commission for the purpose of administering this section shall have the full force and effect of law. Unless otherwise ordered by the Commission, with the reasons therefor, the records and data of the Commission shall be open to the inspection and examination of the public. The Commission, in making any such valuation, shall be free to adopt any method of valuation which shall be lawful.

(g) Nothing in this section shall impair or diminish the powers of any State commission.

Section 214 [47 USC Section 214]. Extension of Lines.

(a) No carrier shall undertake the construction of a new line or of an extension of any line, or shall acquire or operate any line, or extension thereof, or shall engage in transmission over or by means of such additional or extended line, unless and until there shall first have been obtained from the Commission a certificate that the present or future public convenience and necessity require or will require the construction, or operation, or construction and operation, of such additional or extended line: Provided, that no such certificate shall be required under this section for the construction, acquisition, or operation of (1) a line within a single State unless such line constitutes part of an interstate line, (2) local, branch, or terminal lines not exceeding ten miles in length, or (3) any line acquired under Section

221 of this Act: Provided further, that the Commission may, upon appropriate request being made, authorize temporary or emergency service, or the supplementing of existing facilities, without regard to the provisions of this section. No carrier shall discontinue, reduce or impair service to a community, or part of a community, unless and until there shall first have been obtained from the Commission a certificate that neither the present nor future public convenience and necessity will be adversely affected thereby; except that the Commission may, upon appropriate request being made, authorize temporary or emergency discontinuance, reduction, or impairment of service, or partial discontinuance, reduction, or impairment of service, without regard to the provisions of this section. As used in this section the term "line" means any channel of communication established by the use of appropriate equipment, other than a channel of communication established by the interconnection of two or more existing channels: Provided, however, that nothing in this section shall be construed to require a certificate or other authorization from the Commission for any installation, replacement, or other changes in plant, operation, or equipment, other than new construction, which will not impair the adequacy or quality of service provided.

(b) Upon receipt of an application for any such certificate, the Commission shall cause notice thereof to be given to, and shall cause a copy of such application to be filed with, the Secretary of Defense, the Secretary of State (with respect to such applications involving service to foreign points), and the Governor of each State in which such line is proposed to be constructed, extended, acquired, or operated, or in which such discontinuance, reduction, or impairment of service is proposed, with the right to those notified to be heard; and the Commission may require such published notice as it shall determine.

(c) The Commission shall have power to issue such certificate as applied for, or to refuse to issue it, or to issue it for a portion or portions of a line, or extension thereof, or discontinuance, reduction, or impairment of service, described in the application, or for the partial exercise only of such right or privilege, and may attach to the issuance of the certificate such terms and conditions as in its judgment the public convenience and necessity may require. After issuance of such certificate, and not before, the carrier may, without securing approval other than such certificate, comply with the terms and conditions contained in or attached to the issuance of such certificate and proceed with the construction, extension, acquisition, operation, or discontinuance, reduction, or impairment of service covered thereby. Any construction, extension, acquisition, operation, discontinuance, reduction, or impairment of service contrary to the provisions of this section may be enjoined by any court of competent jurisdiction at the suit of the United States, the Commission, the State commission, any State affected, or any party in interest.

(d) The Commission may, after full opportunity for hearing, in a proceeding upon complaint or upon its own initiative without complaint, authorize or require by order any carrier, party to such proceeding, to provide itself with adequate facilities for the expeditious and efficient performance of its service as a common carrier and to extend its line or to establish a public office; but no such authorization or order shall be made unless the Commission finds, as to such provision of facilities, as to such establishment of public offices, or as to such extension, that it is reasonably required in the interest of public convenience and necessity, or as to such extension or facilities that the expense involved therein will not impair the ability of the carrier to perform its duty to the public. Any carrier which refuses or neglects to comply with any order of the Commission made in pursuance of this paragraph shall forfeit to the United States $1,200 for each day during which such refusal or neglect continues.

(e) Provision of Universal Service.--

(1) Eligible telecommunications carriers.--A common carrier designated as an eligible telecommunications carrier under paragraph (2) or (3) shall be eligible to receive universal service support in accordance with Section 254 and shall, throughout the service area for which the designation is received--

(A) offer the services that are supported by Federal universal service support mechanisms under Section 254(c), either using its own facilities or a combination of its own facilities and resale of another carrier's services (including the services offered by another eligible telecommunications carrier); and

(B) advertise the availability of such services and the charges therefor using media of general distribution.

(2) Designation of eligible telecommunications carriers.--A State commission shall upon its own motion or upon request designate a common carrier that meets the requirements of paragraph (1) as an eligible telecommunications carrier for a service area designated by the State commission. Upon request and consistent with the public interest, convenience, and necessity, the State commission may, in the case of an area served by a rural telephone company, and shall, in the case of all other areas, designate more than one common carrier as an eligible telecommunications carrier for a service area designated by the State commission, so long as each additional requesting carrier meets the requirements of paragraph (1). Before designating an additional eligible telecommunications carrier for an area served by a rural telephone company, the State commission shall find that the designation is in the public interest.

(3) Designation of eligible telecommunications carriers for unserved areas.--If no common carrier will provide the services that are supported by Federal universal service support mechanisms under Section 254(c) to an unserved community or any portion thereof that requests such service, the Commission, with respect to interstate services, or a State commission, with respect to intrastate services, shall determine which common carrier or carriers are best able to provide such service to the requesting unserved community or portion thereof and shall order such carrier or carriers to provide such service for that unserved community or portion thereof. Any carrier or carriers ordered to provide such service under this paragraph shall meet the requirements of paragraph (1) and shall be designated as an eligible telecommunications carrier for that community or portion thereof.

(4) Relinquishment of universal service.--A State commission shall permit an eligible telecommunications carrier to relinquish its designation as such a carrier in any area served by more than one eligible telecommunications carrier. An eligible telecommunications carrier that seeks to relinquish its eligible telecommunications carrier designation for an area served by more than one eligible telecommunications carrier shall give advance notice to the State commission of such relinquishment. Prior to permitting a telecommunications carrier designated as an eligible telecommunications carrier to cease providing universal service in an area served by more than one eligible telecommunications carrier, the State commission shall require the remaining eligible telecommunications carrier or carriers to ensure that all customers served by the relinquishing carrier will continue to be served, and shall require sufficient notice to permit the purchase or construction of adequate facilities by any remaining eligible telecommunications carrier. The State commission shall establish a time, not to exceed one year after the State commission approves

<u>such relinquishment under this paragraph, within which such purchase or construction shall be completed.</u>

(5) Service area defined.--<u>The term "service area" means a geographic area established by a State commission for the purpose of determining universal service obligations and support mechanisms. In the case of an area served by a rural telephone company, "service area" means such company's "study area" unless and until the Commission and the States, after taking into account recommendations of a Federal-State Joint Board instituted under Section 410(c), establish a different definition of service area for such company.</u>

Section 215 [47 USC Section 215]. Transactions Relating to Services, Equipment, and so forth.

(a) The Commission shall examine into transactions entered into by any common carrier which relate to the furnishing of equipment, supplies, research, services, finances, credit, or personnel to such carrier and/or which may affect the charges made or to be made and/or the services rendered or to be rendered by such carrier, in wire or radio communication subject to this Act, and shall report to the Congress whether any such transactions have affected or are likely to affect adversely the ability of the carrier to render adequate service to the public, or may result in any undue or unreasonable increase in charges or in the maintenance or undue or unreasonable charges for such service; and in order to fully examine into such transactions the Commission shall have access to and the right of inspection and examination of all accounts, records, and memoranda, including all documents, papers, and correspondence now or hereafter existing, of persons furnishing such equipment, supplies, research, services, finances, credit, or personnel. The Commission shall include in its report its recommendations for necessary legislation in connection with such transactions, and shall report specifically whether in its opinion legislation should be enacted (1) authorizing the Commission to declare any such transactions void or to permit such transactions to be carried out subject to such modification of their terms and conditions as the Commission shall deem desirable in the public interest; and/or (2) subjecting such transactions to the approval of the Commission where the person furnishing or seeking to furnish the equipment, supplies, research, services, finances, credit, or personnel is a person directly or indirectly controlling or controlled by, or under direct or indirect common control with, such carrier; and/or (3) authorizing the Commission to require that all or any transactions of carriers involving the furnishing of equipment, supplies, research, services, finances, credit, or personnel to such carrier be upon competitive bids on such terms and conditions and subject to such regulations as it shall prescribe as necessary in the public interest.

(b) The Commission shall investigate the methods by which and the extent to which wire telephone companies are furnishing wire telegraph service and wire telegraph companies are furnishing wire telephone service, and shall report its findings to Congress, together with its recommendations as to whether additional legislation on this subject is desirable.

(c) The Commission shall examine all contracts of common carriers subject to this Act which prevent the other party thereto from dealing with another common carrier subject to this Act, and shall report its findings to Congress, together with its recommendations as to whether additional legislation on this subject is desirable.

Section 216 [47 USC Section 216].   Application of Act to Receivers and Trustees.

The provisions of this Act shall apply to all receivers and operating trustees of carriers subject to this Act to the same extent that it applies to carriers.

Section 217 [47 USC Section 217].   Liability of Carrier for Acts and Omissions of Agents.

In construing and enforcing the provisions of this Act, the act, omission, or failure of any officer, agent, or other person acting for or employed by any common carrier or user, acting within the scope of his employment, shall in every case be also deemed to be the act, omission, or failure of such carrier or user as well as that of the person.

Section 218 [47 USC Section 218].   Inquiries into Management.

The Commission may inquire into the management of the business of all carriers subject to this Act, and shall keep itself informed as to the manner and method in which the same is conducted and as to technical developments and improvements in wire and radio communication and radio transmission of energy to the end that the benefits of new inventions and developments may be made available to the people of the United States. The Commission may obtain from such carriers and from persons directly or indirectly controlling or controlled by, or under direct or indirect common control with, such carriers full and complete information necessary to enable the Commission to perform the duties and carry out the objects for which it was created.

Section 219 [47 USC Section 219].   Annual and Other Reports.

(a) The Commission is authorized to require annual reports from all carriers subject to this Act, and from persons directly or indirectly controlling or controlled by, or under direct or indirect common control with, any such carrier, to prescribe the manner in which such reports shall be made, and to require from such persons specific answers to all questions upon which the Commission may need information. Except as otherwise required by the Commission, such annual reports shall show in detail the amount of capital stock issued, the amount and privileges of each class of stock, the amounts paid therefor, and the manner of payment for the same; the dividends paid and the surplus fund, if any; the number of stockholders (and the names of the thirty largest holders of each class of stock and the amount held by each); the funded and floating debts and the interest paid thereon; the cost and value of the carrier's property, franchises, and equipment; the number of employees and the salaries paid each class; the names of all officers and directors, and the amount of salary, bonus, and all other compensation paid to each; the amounts expended for improvements each year, how expended, and the character of such improvements; the earnings and receipts from each branch of business and from all sources; the operating and other expenses; the balances of profit and loss; and a complete exhibit of the financial operations of the carrier each year, including an annual balance sheet. Such reports shall also contain such information in relation to charges or regulations concerning charges, or agreements, arrangements, or contracts affecting the same, as the Commission may require.

(b) Such reports shall be for such twelve months' period as the Commission shall designate and shall be filed with the Commission at its office in Washington within three months after the close of the year for which the report is made, unless additional time is granted in any case by the Commission; and if any person subject to the provisions of this section shall fail to make and file said annual reports within the time above specified, or within the time extended by the Commission, for making and filing the same, or shall fail to make specific answer to any question authorized by the provisions of this section within thirty days from the time it is lawfully required so to do, such persons shall forfeit to the United States the sum of $1,200 for each and every day it shall continue to be in default with respect thereto. The Commission may by general or special orders require any such carriers to file monthly reports of earnings and expenses and to file periodical and/or special reports concerning any matters with respect to which the Commission is authorized or required by law to act. If any such carrier shall fail to make and file any such periodical or special report within the time fixed by the Commission, it shall be subject to the forfeitures above provided.

Section 220 [47 USC Section 220]. Accounts, Records, and Memoranda; Depreciation Charges.

(a)(1) The Commission may, in its discretion, prescribe the forms of any and all accounts, records, and memoranda to be kept by carriers subject to this Act, including the accounts, records, and memoranda of the movement of traffic, as well as of the receipts and expenditures of moneys.

(2) The Commission shall, by rule, prescribe a uniform system of accounts for use by telephone companies. Such uniform system shall require that each common carrier shall maintain a system of accounting methods, procedures and techniques (including accounts and supporting records and memoranda) which shall ensure a proper allocation of all costs to and among telecommunications services, facilities, and products (and to and among classes of such services, facilities, and products) which are developed, manufactured, or offered by such common carrier.

(b) The Commission <del>shall</del> **may** prescribe, for such carriers **as it determines to be appropriate,** the classes of property for which depreciation charges may be properly included under operating expenses, and the percentages of depreciation which shall be charged with respect to each of such classes of property, classifying the carriers as it may deem proper for this purpose. The Commission may, when it deems necessary, modify the classes and percentages so prescribed. Such carriers shall not, after the Commission has prescribed the classes of property for which depreciation charges may be included, charge to operating expenses any depreciation charges on classes of property other than those prescribed by the Commission, or, after the Commission has prescribed percentages of depreciation, charge with respect to any class of property a percentage of depreciation other than that prescribed therefor by the Commission. No such carrier shall in any case include in any form under its operating or other expenses any depreciation or other charge or expenditure included elsewhere as a depreciation charge or otherwise under its operating or other expenses.

(c) The Commission shall at all times have access to and the right of inspection and examination of all accounts, records, and memoranda, including all documents, papers, and correspondence now or hereafter existing, and kept or required to be kept by such carriers, and the provisions of this section respecting the preservation and destruction of books, papers, and documents shall apply thereto. The burden of proof to justify every accounting entry questioned by the Commission shall be on the person making, authorizing, or requiring such entry and the Commission may suspend a charge or credit pending submission of proof by such person. Any provision of law prohibiting the disclosure of the contents of messages or communications shall not be deemed to prohibit the disclosure of any matter in accordance with the provisions of this section. **The Commission may obtain the services of any**

person licensed to provide public accounting services under the law of any State to assist with, or conduct, audits under this section. While so employed or engaged in conducting an audit for the Commission under this section, any such person shall have the powers granted the Commission under this subsection and shall be subject to subsection (f) in the same manner as if that person were an employee of the Commission.

(d) In case of failure or refusal on the part of any such carrier to keep such accounts, records, and memoranda on the books and in the manner prescribed by the Commission, or to submit such accounts, records, memoranda, documents, papers, and correspondence as are kept to the inspection of the Commission or any of its authorized agents, such carrier shall forfeit to the United States the sum of $6,000 for each day of the continuance of each such offense.

(e) Any person who shall willfully make any false entry in the accounts of any book of accounts or in any record or memoranda kept by any such carrier, or who shall willfully destroy, mutilate, alter or by any other means or device falsify any such account, record or memoranda, or who shall willfully neglect or fail to make full, true, and correct entries in such accounts, records, or memoranda of all facts and transactions appertaining to the business of the carrier, shall be deemed guilty of a misdemeanor and shall be subject, upon conviction, to a fine of not less than $1,000 nor more than $5,000 or imprisonment for a term of not less than one year nor more than three years, or both such fine and imprisonment: Provided, that the Commission may in its discretion issue orders specifying such operating, accounting, or financial papers, records, books, blanks, or documents which may, after a reasonable time, be destroyed, and prescribing the length of time such books, papers or documents shall be preserved.

(f) No member, officer, or employee of the Commission shall divulge any fact or information which may come to his knowledge during the course of examination of books or other accounts, as hereinbefore provided, except insofar as he may be directed by the Commission or by a court.

(g) After the Commission has prescribed the forms and manner of keeping of accounts, records and memoranda to be kept by any person as herein provided, it shall be unlawful for such person to keep any other accounts, records or memoranda than those so prescribed or such as may be approved by the Commission or to keep the accounts in any other manner than that prescribed or approved by the Commission. Notice of alterations by the Commission in the required manner or form of keeping accounts shall be given to such persons by the Commission at least six months before the same are to take effect.

(h) The Commission may classify carriers subject to this Act and prescribe different requirements under this section for different classes of carriers, and may, if it deems such action consistent with the public interest, except the carriers of any particular class or classes in any State from any of the requirements under this section in cases where such carriers are subject to state commission regulation with respect to matters to which this section relates.

(i) The Commission, before prescribing any requirements as to accounts, records, or memoranda, shall notify each state commission having jurisdiction with respect to any carrier involved, and shall give reasonable opportunity to each such commission to present its views, and shall receive and consider such views and recommendations.

(j) The Commission shall investigate and report to Congress as to the need for legislation to define further or harmonize the powers of the Commission and of state commissions with respect to matters to which this section relates.

Section 221 [47 USC Section 221]. Special Provisions Relating to Telephone Companies

~~(a) Upon application of one or more telephone companies for authority to consolidate their properties or a part thereof into a single company, or for authority for one or more such companies to acquire the whole or any part of the property of another telephone company or other telephone companies or the control thereof by the purchase of securities or by lease or in any other like manner, when such consolidated company would be subject to this Act, the Commission shall give reasonable notice in writing to the Governor of each of the States in which the physical property affected, or any part thereof, is situated, and to the state commission having jurisdiction over telephone companies, and to such other persons as it may deem advisable and shall afford such parties a reasonable opportunity to submit comments on the proposal. A public hearing shall be held in all cases where a request therefor is made by a telephone company, an association of telephone companies, a state commission, or local governmental authority. If the Commission finds that the proposed consolidation, acquisition or control will be of advantage to the persons to whom service is to be rendered and in the public interest, it shall certify to that effect; and thereupon any Act or Acts of Congress making the proposed transaction unlawful shall not apply. Nothing in this subsection shall be construed as in anywise limiting or restricting the powers of the several States to control and regulate telephone companies.~~ (a) [Repealed]

(b) Subject to the provision of Sections 225 and 301, nothing in this Act shall be construed to apply, or to give the Commission jurisdiction, with respect to charges, classifications, practices, services, facilities, or regulations for or in connection with wire, mobile, or point-to-point radio telephone exchange service, or any combination thereof, even though a portion of such exchange service constitutes interstate or foreign communication, in any case where such matters are subject to regulation by a state commission or by local governmental authority.

(c) For the purpose of administering this Act as to carriers engaged in wire telephone communication, the Commission may classify the property of any such carrier used for wire telephone communication, and determine what property of said carrier shall be considered as used in interstate or foreign telephone toll service. Such classification shall be made after hearing, upon notice to the carrier, the state commission (or the Governor, if the State has no state commission) of any State in which the property of said carrier is located, and such other persons as the Commission may prescribe.

(d) In making a valuation of the property of any wire telephone carrier the Commission, after making the classification authorized in this section, may in its discretion value only that part of the property of such carrier determined to be used in interstate or foreign telephone toll service.

~~§222. [Deleted]~~ **Section 222 [47 USC Section 222]. Privacy of Customer Information.**

   (a) In General.—Every telecommunications carrier has a duty to protect the confidentiality of proprietary information of, and relating to, other telecommunication carriers, equipment manufacturers, and customers, including telecommunication carriers reselling telecommunications services provided by a telecommunications carrier.

   (b) Confidentiality of Carrier Information.--A telecommunications carrier that receives or obtains proprietary information from another carrier for purposes of providing any telecommunications service shall use such information only for such purpose, and shall not use such information for its own marketing efforts.

   (c) Confidentiality of Customer Proprietary Network Information.--

(1) Privacy requirements for telecommunications carriers.--Except as required by law or with the approval of the customer, a telecommunications carrier that receives or obtains customer proprietary network information by virtue of its provision of a telecommunications service shall only use, disclose, or permit access to individually identifiable customer proprietary network information in its provision of (A) the telecommunications service from which such information is derived, or (B) services necessary to, or used in, the provision of such telecommunications service, including the publishing of directories.

(2) Disclosure on request by customers.--A telecommunications carrier shall disclose customer proprietary network information, upon affirmative written request by the customer, to any person designated by the customer.

(3) Aggregate customer information.--A telecommunications carrier that receives or obtains customer proprietary network information by virtue of its provision of a telecommunications service may use, disclose, or permit access to aggregate customer information other than for the purposes described in paragraph (1). A local exchange carrier may use, disclose, or permit access to aggregate customer information other than for purposes described in paragraph (1) only if it provides such aggregate information to other carriers or persons on reasonable and nondiscriminatory terms and conditions upon reasonable request therefor.

(d) Exceptions.--Nothing in this section prohibits a telecommunications carrier from using, disclosing, or permitting access to customer proprietary network information obtained from its customers, either directly or indirectly through its agents--

(1) to initiate, render, bill, and collect for telecommunications services;

(2) to protect the rights or property of the carrier, or to protect users of those services and other carriers from fraudulent, abusive, or unlawful use of, or subscription to, such services; or

(3) to provide any inbound telemarketing, referral, or administrative services to the customer for the duration of the call, if such call was initiated by the customer and the customer approves of the use of such information to provide such service.

(e) Subscriber List Information.--Notwithstanding subsections (b), (c), and (d), a telecommunications carrier that provides telephone exchange service shall provide subscriber list information gathered in its capacity as a provider of such service on a timely and unbundled basis, under nondiscriminatory and reasonable rates, terms, and conditions, to any person upon request for the purpose of publishing directories in any format.

(f) Definitions.--As used in this section:

(1) Customer proprietary network information.--The term "customer proprietary network information" means--

(A) information that relates to the quantity, technical configuration, type, destination, and amount of use of a telecommunications service subscribed to by any customer of a telecommunications carrier, and that is made available to the carrier by the customer solely by virtue of the carrier-customer relationship; and

(B) information contained in the bills pertaining to telephone exchange service or telephone toll service received by a customer of a carrier;
except that such term does not include subscriber list information.

346

(2) Aggregate information.--The term "aggregate customer information" means collective data that relates to a group or category of services or customers, from which individual customer identities and characteristics have been removed.

(3) Subscriber list information.--The term "subscriber list information" means any information--

(A) identifying the listed names of subscribers of a carrier and such subscribers' telephone numbers, addresses, or primary advertising classifications (as such classifications are assigned at the time of the establishment of such service), or any combination of such listed names, numbers, addresses, or classifications; and

(B) that the carrier or an affiliate has published, caused to be published, or accepted for publication in any directory format.

Section 223 [47 USC Section 223]. Obscene or Harassing Telephone Calls in the District of Columbia or in Interstate or Foreign Communications

(a) Whoever--

~~(1) in the District of Columbia or in the~~ **(1) in** interstate or foreign ~~communication~~ **communications**--

(A) by means of ~~telephone --~~ **a telecommunications device knowingly**--

~~(A) makes~~ **(i) makes, creates, or solicits, and**

(ii) initiates the transmission of, any comment, request, suggestion ~~or~~**,** proposal**, image, or other communication** which is obscene, lewd, lascivious, filthy, or indecent, **with intent to annoy, abuse, threaten, or harass another person;** ~~;~~

~~(B)~~ **(B) by means of a telecommunications device knowingly**--

(i) makes, creates, or solicits, and

(ii) initiates the transmission of, any comment, request, suggestion, proposal, image, or other communication which is obscene or indecent, knowing that the recipient of the communication is under 18 years of age, regardless of whether the maker of such communication placed the call or initiated the communication;

(C) makes a telephone call **or utilizes a telecommunications device,** whether or not conversation **or communication** ensues, without disclosing his identity and with intent to annoy, abuse, threaten, or harass any person at the called number **or who receives the communications;** ~~;~~

~~(C)~~ **(D)** makes or causes the telephone of another repeatedly or continuously to ring, with intent to harass any person at the called number; or

~~(D)~~ **(E)** makes repeated telephone calls **or repeatedly initiates communication with a telecommunications device,** during which conversation **or communication** ensues, solely to harass any person at the called number **or who receives the communication**; or

(2) knowingly permits any ~~telephone~~ **telecommunications** facility under his control to be used for any ~~purpose~~ **activity** prohibited by ~~this section~~ **paragraph (1) with the intent that it be used for such activity,** shall be fined ~~not more than $50,000~~ **under title 18, United States Code,** or imprisoned not more than ~~six months~~ **two years,** or both.

(b)(1) Whoever knowingly --

(A) within the United States, by means of telephone, makes (directly or by recording device) any obscene communication for commercial purposes to any person, regardless of whether the maker of such communication placed the call; or

(B) permits any telephone facility under such person's control to be used for an activity prohibited by subparagraph (A), shall be fined in accordance with Title 18, United States Code, or imprisoned not more than two years, or both.

(2) Whoever knowingly --

(A) within the United States, by means of telephone, makes (directly or by recording device) any indecent communication for commercial purposes which is available to any person under 18 years of age or to any other person without that person's consent, regardless of whether the maker of such communication placed the call; or

(B) permits any telephone facility under such person's control to be used for an activity prohibited by subparagraph (A), shall be fined not more than $50,000 or imprisoned not more than six months, or both.

(3) It is a defense to prosecution under paragraph (2) of this subsection that the defendant restricted access to the prohibited communication to persons 18 years of age or older in accordance with subsection (c) of this section and with such procedures as the Commission may prescribe by regulation.

(4) In addition to the penalties under paragraph (1), whoever, within the United States, intentionally violates paragraph (1) or (2) shall be subject to a fine of not more than $50,000 for each violation. For purposes of this paragraph, each day of violation shall constitute a separate violation.

(5)(A) In addition to the penalties under paragraphs (1), (2) and (5), whoever, within the United States, violates paragraph (1) or (2) shall be subject to a civil fine of not more than $50,000 for each violation. For purposes of this paragraph, each day of violation shall constitute a separate violation.

(B) A fine under this paragraph may be assessed either --

(i) by a court, pursuant to civil action by the Commission or any attorney employed by the Commission who is designated by the Commission for such purposes, or

(ii) by the Commission after appropriate administrative proceedings.

(6) The Attorney General may bring a suit in the appropriate district court of the United States to enjoin any act or practice which violates paragraph (1) or (2). An injunction may be granted in accordance with the Federal Rules of Civil Procedure.

(c)(1) A common carrier within the District of Columbia or within any State, or in interstate or foreign commerce, shall not, to the extent technically feasible, provide access to a communication specified in subsection (b) from the telephone of any subscriber who has not previously requested in writing the carrier to provide access to such communication if the carrier collects from subscribers an identifiable charge for such communication that the carrier remits, in whole or in part, to the provider of such communication.

(2) Except as provided in paragraph (3), no cause of action may be brought in any court or administrative agency against any common carrier, or any of is affiliates, including their officers, directors, employees, agents, or authorized representatives on account of --

(A) any action which the carrier demonstrates was taken in good faith to restrict access pursuant to paragraph (1) of this subsection; or

(B) any access permitted --

(i) in good faith reliance upon the lack of any representation by a provider of communications that communications provided by that provider are communications specified in subsection (b), or

(ii) because a specific representation by the provider did not allow the carrier, acting in good faith, a sufficient period to restrict access to communications described in subsection (b).

(3) Notwithstanding paragraph (2) of this subsection, a provider of communications services to which subscribers are denied access pursuant to paragraph (1) of this subsection may bring an action for a declaratory judgment or similar action in a court. Any such action shall be limited to the question of whether the communications which the provider seeks to provide fall within the category of communications to which the carrier will provide access only to subscribers who have previously requested such access.

(d) Whoever--

(1) in interstate or foreign communications knowingly--

(A) uses an interactive computer service to send to a specific person or persons under 18 years of age, or

(B) uses any interactive computer service to display in a manner available to a person under 18 years of age, any comment, request, suggestion, proposal, image, or other communication that, in context, depicts or describes, in terms patently offensive as measured by contemporary community standards, sexual or excretory activities or organs, regardless of whether the user of such service placed the call or initiated the communication; or

(2) knowingly permits any telecommunications facility under such person's control to be used for an activity prohibited by paragraph (1) with the intent that it be used for such activity, shall be fined under title 18, United States Code, or imprisoned not more than two years, or both.

(e) In addition to any other defenses available by law:

(1) No person shall be held to have violated subsection (a) or (d) solely for providing access or connection to or from a facility, system, or network not under that person's control, including transmission, downloading, intermediate storage, access software, or other related capabilities that are incidental to providing such access or connection that does not include the creation of the content of the communication.

(2) The defenses provided by paragraph (1) of this subsection shall not be applicable to a person who is a conspirator with an entity actively involved in the creation or knowing distribution of communications that violate this section, or who knowingly advertises the availability of such communications.

(3) The defenses provided in paragraph (1) of this subsection shall not be applicable to a person who provides access or connection to a facility, system, or network engaged in the violation of this section that is owned or controlled by such person.

(4) No employer shall be held liable under this section for the actions of an employee or agent unless the employee's or agent's conduct is within the scope of his or her employment or agency and the employer (A) having knowledge of such conduct, authorizes or ratifies such conduct, or (B) recklessly disregards such conduct.

(5) It is a defense to a prosecution under subsection (a)(1)(B) or (d), or under subsection (a)(2) with respect to the use of a facility for an activity under subsection (a)(1)(B) that a person--

349

(A) has taken, in good faith, reasonable, effective, and appropriate actions under the circumstances to restrict or prevent access by minors to a communication specified in such subsections, which may involve any appropriate measures to restrict minors from such communications, including any method which is feasible under available technology; or

(B) has restricted access to such communication by requiring use of a verified credit card, debit account, adult access code, or adult personal identification number.

(6) The Commission may describe measures which are reasonable, effective, and appropriate to restrict access to prohibited communications under subsection (d). Nothing in this section authorizes the Commission to enforce, or is intended to provide the Commission with the authority to approve, sanction, or permit, the use of such measures. The Commission shall have no enforcement authority over the failure to utilize such measures. The Commission shall not endorse specific products relating to such measures. The use of such measures shall be admitted as evidence of good faith efforts for purposes of paragraph (5) in any action arising under subsection (d). Nothing in this section shall be construed to treat interactive computer services as common carriers or telecommunications carriers.

(f)(1) No cause of action may be brought in any court or administrative agency against any person on account of any activity that is not in violation of any law punishable by criminal or civil penalty, and that the person has taken in good faith to implement a defense authorized under this section or otherwise to restrict or prevent the transmission of, or access to, a communication specified in this section.

(2) No State or local government may impose any liability for commercial activities or actions by commercial entities, nonprofit libraries, or institutions of higher education in connection with an activity or action described in subsection (a)(2) or (d) that is inconsistent with the treatment of those activities or actions under this section: Provided, however, That nothing herein shall preclude any State or local government from enacting and enforcing complementary oversight, liability, and regulatory systems, procedures, and requirements, so long as such systems, procedures, and requirements govern only intrastate services and do not result in the imposition of inconsistent rights, duties or obligations on the provision of interstate services. Nothing in this subsection shall preclude any State or local government from governing conduct not covered by this section.

(g) Nothing in subsection (a), (d), (e), or (f) or in the defenses to prosecution under (a) or (d) shall be construed to affect or limit the application or enforcement of any other Federal law.

(h) For purposes of this section--

(1) The use of the term "telecommunications device" in this section--

(A) shall not impose new obligations on broadcasting station licensees and cable operators covered by obscenity and indecency provisions elsewhere in this Act; and

(B) does not include an interactive computer service.

(2) The term "interactive computer service" has the meaning provided in Section 230(e)(2).

(3) The term "access software" means software (including client or server software) or enabling tools that do not create or provide the content of the communication but that allow a user to do any one or more of the following:

(A) filter, screen, allow, or disallow content;

(B) pick, choose, analyze, or digest content; or

(C) transmit, receive, display, forward, cache, search, subset, organize, reorganize, or translate content.

(4) The term "institution of higher education" has the meaning provided in Section 1201 of the Higher Education Act of 1965 (20 USC 1141).

(5) The term "library" means a library eligible for participation in State-based plans for funds under title III of the Library Services and Construction Act (20 USC 355e et seq.).

Section 224 [47 USC Section 224]. Regulation of Pole Attachments.

(a) As used in this section:

(1) The term "utility" means any person ~~whose rates or charges are regulated by the Federal Government or a State~~ who is a local exchange carrier or an electric, gas, water, steam, or other public utility, and who owns or controls poles, ducts, conduits, or rights-of-way used, in whole or in part, for any wire ~~communication~~ communications. Such term does not include any railroad, any person who is cooperatively organized, or any person owned by the Federal Government or any State;

(2) The term "Federal Government" means the Government of the United States or any agency or instrumentality thereof.

(3) The term "State" mans any State, Territory, or possession of the United States, the District of Columbia, or any political subdivision, agency, or instrumentality thereof.

(4) The term "pole attachment" means any attachment by a cable television system or provider of telecommunications service to a pole, duct, conduit, or right-of-way owner or controlled by a utility.

(5) For purposes of this section, the term "telecommunications carrier" (as defined in Section 3 of this Act) does not include any incumbent local exchange carrier as defined in Section 251(h).

(b)(1) Subject to the provisions of subsection (c) of this section, the Commission shall regulate the rates, terms, and conditions for pole attachments to provide that such rates, terms, and conditions are just and reasonable, and shall adopt procedures necessary and appropriate to hear and resolve complaints concerning such rates, terms, and conditions. For purposes of enforcing any determinations resulting from complaint procedures established pursuant to this subsection, the Commission shall take such action as it deems appropriate and necessary, including issuing cease and desist orders, as authorized by Section 312(b) of Title III of the Communications Act of 1934, as amended.

(2) The Commission shall prescribe by rule regulations to carry out the provisions of this section.

(c)(1) Nothing in this section shall be construed to apply to, or to give the Commission jurisdiction with respect to rates, terms, and conditions or access to poles, ducts, conduits, and rights-of-way as provided in subsection (f), for pole attachments in any case where such matters are regulated by a State.

(2) Each State which regulates the rates, terms, and conditions for pole attachments shall certify to the Commission that --

(A) it regulates such rates, terms, and conditions; and

351

(B) in so regulating such rates, terms, and conditions, the State has the authority to consider and does consider the interests of the subscribers of ~~cable television~~ **the** services **offered via such attachments**, as well as the interests of the consumers of the utility services.

(3) For purposes of this subsection, a State shall not be considered to regulate the rates, terms, and conditions for pole attachments --

(A) unless the State has issued and made effective rules and regulations implementing the State's regulatory authority over pole attachments; and

(B) with respect to any individual matter, unless the State takes final action on a complaint regarding such matter --

(i) within 180 days after the complaint is filed with the State or

(ii) within the applicable period prescribed for such final action in such rules and regulations of the State, if the prescribed period does not extend beyond 360 days after the filing of such complaint.

(d)(1) For purposes of subsection (b) of this section, a rate is just and reasonable if it assures a utility the recovery of not less than the additional costs of providing pole attachments, nor more than an amount determined by multiplying the percentage of the total usable space, or the percentage of the total duct or conduit capacity, which is occupied by the pole attachment by the sum of the operating expenses and actual capital costs of the utility attributable to the entire pole, duct, conduit, or right-of-way.

(2) As used in this subsection, the term "usable space" means the space above the minimum grade level which can be used for the attachment of wires, cables, and associated equipment.

(3) This subsection shall apply to the rate for any pole attachment used by a cable television system solely to provide cable service. Until the effective date of the regulations required under subsection (e), this subsection shall also apply to the rate for any pole attachment used by a cable system or any telecommunications carrier (to the extent such carrier is not a party to a pole attachment agreement) to provide any telecommunications service.

(e)(1) The Commission shall, no later than 2 years after the date of enactment of the Telecommunications Act of 1996, prescribe regulations in accordance with this subsection to govern the charges for pole attachments used by telecommunications carriers to provide telecommunications services, when the parties fail to resolve a dispute over such charges. Such regulations shall ensure that a utility charges just, reasonable, and nondiscriminatory rates for pole attachments.

(2) A utility shall apportion the cost of providing space on a pole, duct, conduit, or right-of-way other than the usable space among entities so that such apportionment equals two-thirds of the costs of providing space other than the usable space that would be allocated to such entity under an equal apportionment of such costs among all attaching entities.

(3) A utility shall apportion the cost of providing usable space among all entities according to the percentage of usable space required for each entity.

(4) The regulations required under paragraph (1) shall become effective 5 years after the date of enactment of the Telecommunications Act of 1996. Any increase in the rates for pole attachments that result from the adoption of the regulations required by this subsection shall be phased in equal annual increments over a period of 5 years beginning on the effective date of such regulations.

(f)(1) A utility shall provide a cable television system or any telecommunications carrier with nondiscriminatory access to any pole, duct, conduit, or right-of-way owned or controlled by it.

(2) Notwithstanding paragraph (1), a utility providing electric service may deny a cable television system or any telecommunications carrier access to its poles, ducts, conduits, or rights-of-way, on a non-discriminatory basis where there is insufficient capacity and for reasons of safety, reliability and generally applicable engineering purposes.

(g) A utility that engages in the provision of telecommunications services or cable services shall impute to its costs of providing such services (and charge any affiliate, subsidiary, or associate company engaged in the provision of such services) an equal amount to the pole attachment rate for which such company would be liable under this section.

(h) Whenever the owner of a pole, duct, conduit, or right-of-way intends to modify or alter such pole, duct, conduit, or right-of-way, the owner shall provide written notification of such action to any entity that has obtained an attachment to such conduit or right-of-way so that such entity may have a reasonable opportunity to add to or modify its existing attachment. Any entity that adds to or modifies its existing attachment after receiving such notification shall bear a proportionate share of the costs incurred by the owner in making such pole, duct, conduit, or right-of-way accessible.

(i) An entity that obtains an attachment to a pole, conduit, or right-of way shall not be required to bear any of the costs of rearranging or replacing its attachment, if such rearrangement or replacement is required as a result of an additional attachment or the modification of an existing attachment sought by any other entity (including the owner of such pole, duct, conduit, or right-of-way).

Section 225 [47 USC Section 225]. Telecommunications Services for Hearing-Impaired and Speech-Impaired Individuals.

(a) Definitions. As used in this section --

(1) Common carrier or carrier. - The term "common carrier" or "carrier" includes any common carrier engaged in interstate communication by wire or radio as defined in Section 3<(h)> and any common carrier engaged in intrastate communication by wire or radio, notwithstanding Sections 2(b) and 221(b).

(2) TDD.- The term "TDD" means a Telecommunications Device for the Deaf, which is a machine that employs graphic communication in the transmission of coded signals through a wire or radio communication system.

(3) Telecommunications relay services. - The term "telecommunications relay services" means telephone transmission services that provide the ability for an individual who has a hearing impairment or speech impairment to engage in communication by wire or radio with a hearing individual in a manner that is functionally equivalent to the ability of an individual who does not have a hearing impairment or speech impairment to communicate using voice communication services by wire or radio. Such term includes services that enable two-way communication between an individual who uses a TDD or other nonvoice terminal device and an individual who does not use such a device.

(b) Availability of telecommunications relay services. -

(1) In general. - In order to carry out the purposes established under Section 1, to make available to all individuals in the United States a rapid, efficient nationwide communication service, and to increase the utility of the telephone system of the Nation, the Commission shall ensure that interstate and intrastate telecommunications relay services are available, to the extent possible and in the most efficient manner, to hearing-impaired and speech-impaired individuals in the United States.

(2) Use of general authority and remedies. - For the purposes of administering and enforcing the provisions of this section and the regulations prescribed thereunder, the Commission shall have the same authority, power, and functions with respect to common carriers engaged in intrastate communication as the Commission has in administering and enforcing the provisions of this title with respect to any common carrier engaged in interstate communication. Any violation of this section by any common carrier engaged in intrastate communication shall be subject to the same remedies, penalties, and procedures as are applicable to a violation of this Act by a common carrier engaged in interstate communication.

(c) Provision of services. - Each common carrier providing telephone voice transmission services shall, not later than 3 years after the date of enactment of this section, provide in compliance with the regulations prescribed under this section, throughout the area in which it offers service, telecommunications relay services, individually, through designees, through a competitively selected vendor, or in concert with other carriers. A common carrier shall be considered to be in compliance with such regulations --

(1) with respect to intrastate telecommunications relay services in any State that does not have a certified program under subsection (f) and with respect to interstate telecommunications relay services, if such common carrier (or other entity through which the carrier is providing such relay services) is in compliance with the Commission's regulations under subsection (d); or

(2) with respect to intrastate telecommunications relay services in any State that has a certified program under subsection (f) for such State, if such common carrier (or other entity through which the carrier is providing such relay services) is in compliance with the program certified under subsection (f) for such State.

(d) Regulations. -

(1) In general. - The Commission shall, not later than 1 year after the date of enactment of this section, prescribe regulations to implement this section, including regulations that --

(A) establish functional requirements, guidelines, and operations procedures for telecommunications relay services;

(B) establish minimum standards that shall be met in carrying out subsection (c);

(C) require that telecommunications relay services operate every day for 24 hours per day;

(D) require that users of telecommunications relay services pay rates no greater than the rates paid for functionally equivalent voice communication services with respect to such factors as the duration of the call, the time of day, and the distance from point of origination to point of termination;

(E) prohibit relay operators from failing to fulfill the obligation of common carriers by refusing calls or limiting the length of calls that use telecommunications relay services;

(F) prohibit relay operators from disclosing the content of any relayed conversation and from keeping records of the content of any such conversation beyond the duration of the call; and

(G) prohibit relay operators from intentionally altering a relayed conversation.

(2) Technology. - The Commission shall ensure that regulations prescribed to implement this section encourage, consistent with Section 7(a) of this Act, the use of existing technology and do not discourage or impair the development of improved technology.

(3) Jurisdictional separation of costs. -

(A) In general. - Consistent with the provisions of Section 410 of this Act, the Commission shall prescribe regulations governing the jurisdictional separation of costs for the services provided pursuant to this section.

(B) Recovery costs. - Such regulations shall generally provide that costs caused by interstate telecommunications relay services shall be recovered from all subscribers for every interstate service and costs caused by intrastate telecommunications relay services shall be recovered from the intrastate jurisdiction. In a State that has a certified program under subsection (f), a State commission shall permit a common carrier to recover the costs incurred in providing intrastate telecommunications relay services by a method consistent with the requirements of this section.

(e) Enforcement. -

(1) In general. - Subject to subsections (f) and (g), the Commission shall enforce this section.

(2) Complaint. - The Commission shall resolve, by final order, a complaint alleging a violation of this section within 180 days after the date such complaint is filed.

(f) Certification. -

(1) State documentation. - Any State desiring to establish a State program under this section shall submit documentation to the Commission that describes the program of such State for implementing intrastate telecommunications relay services and the procedures and remedies available for enforcing any requirements imposed by the State program.

(2) Requirements for certification. - After review of such documentation, the Commission shall certify the State program if the Commission determines that --

(A) the program makes available to hearing-impaired and speech-impaired individuals, either directly, through designees, through a competitively selected vendor, or through regulation of intrastate common carriers, intrastate telecommunications relay services in such State in a manner that meets or exceeds the requirements of regulations prescribed by the Commission under subsection (d); and

(B) the program makes available adequate procedures and remedies for enforcing the requirements of the State program.

(3) Method of funding. - Except as provided in subsection (d), the Commission shall not refuse to certify a State program based solely on the method such State will implement for funding intrastate telecommunications relay services.

(4) Suspension or revocation of certification. - The Commission may suspend or revoke such certification if, after notice and opportunity for hearing, the Commission determines that such certification is no longer warranted. In a State whose program has been suspended or revoked, the Commission shall take such steps as may be necessary, consistent with this section, to ensure continuity of telecommunications relay services.

(g) Complaint. -

(1) Referral of complaint. - If a complaint to the Commission alleges a violation of this section with respect to intrastate telecommunications relay services within a State and certification of

the program of such State under subsection (f) is in effect, the Commission shall refer such complaint to such State.

(2) Jurisdiction of Commission. - After referring a complaint to a State under paragraph (1), the Commission shall exercise jurisdiction over such complaint only if --

(A) final action under such State program has not been taken on such complaint by such State --

(i) within 180 days after the complaint is filed with such State; or

(ii) within a shorter period as prescribed by the regulations of such State; or

(B) the Commission determines that such State program is no longer qualified for certification under subsection (f).

Section 226 [47 USC Section 226]. Telephone Operator Services.

(a) Definitions. As used in this section --

(1) The term "access code" means a sequence of numbers that, when dialed, connect the caller to the provider of operator services associated with that sequence.

(2) The term "aggregator" means any person that, in the ordinary course of its operations, makes telephones available to the public or to transient users of its premises, for interstate telephone calls using a provider of operator services.

(3) The term "call splashing" means the transfer of a telephone call from one provider of operator services to another such provider in such a manner that the subsequent provider is unable or unwilling to determine the location of the origination of the call and, because of such inability or unwillingness, is prevented from billing the call on the basis of such location.

(4) The term "consumer" means a person initiating any interstate telephone call using operator services.

(5) The term "equal access" has the meaning given that term in Appendix B of the Modification of Final Judgment entered August 24, 1982, in United States v. Western Electric, Civil Action No. 82-0192 (United States District Court, District of Columbia), as amended by the court in its orders issued prior to the enactment of this section.

(6) The term "equal access code" means an access code that allows the public to obtain an equal access connection to the carrier associated with that code.

(7) The term "operator services" means any interstate telecommunications service initiated from an aggregator location that includes, as a component, any automatic or live assistance to a consumer to arrange for billing or completion, or both, of an interstate telephone call through a method other than --

(A) automatic completion with billing to the telephone from which the call originated; or

(B) completion through an access code used by the consumer, with billing to an account previously established with the carrier by the consumer.

(8) The term "presubscribed provider of operator services" means the interstate provider of operator services to which the consumer is connected when the consumer places a call using a provider of operator services without dialing an access code.

(9) The term "provider of operator services" means any common carrier that provides operator services or any other person determined by the Commission to be providing operator services.

(b) Requirements for providers of operator services --

(1) In general. - Beginning not later than 90 days after the date of enactment of this section, each provider of operator services shall, at a minimum --

(A) identify itself, audibly and distinctly, to the consumer at the beginning of each telephone call and before the consumer incurs any charge for the call;

(B) permit the consumer to terminate the telephone call at no charge before the call is connected;

(C) disclose immediately to the consumer, upon request and at no charge to the consumer --

(i) a quote of its rates or charges for the call;

(ii) the methods by which such rates or charges will be collected; and

(iii) the methods by which complaints concerning such rates, charges, or collection practices will be resolved;

(D) ensure, by contract or tariff, that each aggregator for which such provider is the presubscribed provider of operator services is in compliance with the requirements of subsection (c) and, if applicable, subsection (e)(1);

(E) withhold payment (on a location-by-location basis) of any compensation, including commissions, to aggregators if such provider reasonably believes that the aggregator (i) is blocking access by means of "950" or "800" numbers to interstate common carriers in violation of subsection (c)(1)(B) or (ii) is blocking access to equal access codes in violation of rules the Commission may prescribe under subsection (e)(1);

(F) not bill for unanswered telephone calls in areas where equal access is available;

(G) not knowingly bill for unanswered telephone calls where equal access is not available;

(H) not engage in call splashing, unless the consumer requests to be transferred to another provider of operator services, the consumer is informed prior to incurring any charges that the rates for the call may not reflect the rates from the actual originating location of the call, and the consumer then consents to be transferred; and

(I) except as provided in subparagraph (H), not bill for a call that does not reflect the location of the origination of the call.

(2) Additional requirements for first 3 years. - In addition to meeting the requirements of paragraph (1), during the 3-year period beginning on the date that is 90 days after the date of enactment of this section, each presubscribed provider of operator services shall identify itself audibly and distinctly to the consumer, not only as required in paragraph (1)(A), but also for a second time before connecting the call and before the consumer incurs any charge.

(c) Requirements for aggregations --

(1) In general. - Each aggregator, beginning not later than 90 days after the date of enactment of this section, shall --

(A) post on or near the telephone instrument, in plain view of consumers --

(i) the name, address, and toll-free telephone number of the provider of operator services;

(ii) a written disclosure that the rates for all operator-assisted calls are available on request, and that consumers have a right to obtain access to the interstate common carrier of their

357

choice and may contact their preferred interstate common carriers for information on accessing that carrier's service using that telephone; and

(iii) the name and address of the enforcement division of the Common Carrier Bureau of the Commission, to which the consumer may direct complaints regarding operator services; and

(B) ensure that each of its telephones presubscribed to a provider of operator services allows the consumer to use "800" and "950" access code numbers to obtain access to the provider of operator services desired by the consumer; and

(C) ensure that no charge by the aggregator to the consumer for using an "800" or "950" access code number, or any other access code number, is greater than the amount the aggregator charges for calls placed using the presubscribed provider of operator services.

(2) Effect of State law or regulation. - The requirements of paragraph (1)(A) shall not apply to an aggregator in any case in which State law or State regulation requires the aggregator to take actions that are substantially the same as those required in paragraph (1)(A).

(d) General rulemaking required --

(1) Rulemaking proceeding. - The Commission shall conduct a rulemaking proceeding pursuant to this title to prescribe regulations to --

(A) protect consumers from unfair and deceptive practices relating to their use of operator services to place interstate telephone calls; and

(B) ensure that consumers have the opportunity to make informed choices in making such calls.

(2) Contents of regulations. - The regulations prescribed under this section shall --

(A) contain provisions to implement each of the requirements of this section, other than the requirements established by the rulemaking under subsection (e) on access and compensation; and

(B) contain such other provisions as the Commission determines necessary to carry out this section and the purposes and policies of this section.

(3) Additional requirements to be implemented by regulations. - The regulations prescribed under this section shall, at a minimum --

(A) establish minimum standards for providers of operator services and aggregators to use in the routing and handling of emergency telephone calls; and

(B) establish a policy for requiring providers of operator services to make public information about recent changes in operator services and choices available to consumers in that market.

(e) Separate rulemaking on access and compensation --

(1) Access. - The Commission shall require --

(A) that each aggregator ensure within a reasonable time that each of its telephones presubscribed to a provider of operator services allows the consumer to obtain access to the provider of operator services desired by the consumer through the use of an equal access code; or

(B) that all providers of operator services, within a reasonable time, make available to their customers a "950" or "800" access code number for use in making operator services calls from anywhere in the United States; or

(C) that the requirements described under both subparagraphs (A) and (B) apply.

(2) Compensation. - The Commission shall consider the need to prescribe compensation (other than advance payment by consumers) for owners of competitive public pay telephones for calls

routed to providers of operator services that are other than the presubscribed provider of operator services for such telephones. Within 9 months after the date of enactment of this section, the Commission shall reach a final decision on whether to prescribe such compensation.

(f) Technological capability of equipment. - Any equipment and software manufactured or imported more than 18 months after the date of enactment of this section and installed by any aggregator shall be technologically capable of providing consumers with access to interstate providers of operator services through the use of equal access codes.

(g) Fraud. - In any proceeding to carry out the provisions of this section, the Commission shall require such actions or measures as are necessary to ensure that aggregators are not exposed to undue risk of fraud.

(h) Determinations of rate compliance. --

(1) Filing of informational tariff. --

(A) In general. - Each provider of operator services shall file, within 90 days after the date of enactment of this section, and shall maintain, update regularly, and keep open for public inspection, an informational tariff specifying rates, terms, and conditions, and including commissions, surcharges, any fees which are collected from consumers, and reasonable estimates of the amount of traffic priced at each rate, with respect to calls for which operator services are provided. Any changes in such rates, terms, or conditions shall be filed no later than the first day on which the changed rates, terms, or conditions are in effect.

(B) Waiver authority. - The Commission may, after 4 years following the date of enactment of this section, waive the requirements of this paragraph only if --

(i) the findings and conclusions of the Commission in the final report issued under paragraph (3)(B)(iii) state that the regulatory objectives specified in subsection (d)(1)(A) and (B) have been achieved; and

(ii) the Commission determines that such waiver will not adversely affect the continued achievement of such regulatory objectives.

(2) Review of informational tariffs. - If the rates and charges filed by any provider of operator services under paragraph (1) appear upon review by the Commission to be unjust or unreasonable, the Commission may require such provider of operator services to do either or both of the following:

(A) demonstrate that its rates and charges are just and reasonable, and

(B) announce that its rates are available on request at the beginning of each call.

(3) Proceeding required. --

(A) In general. - Within 60 days after the date of enactment of this section, the Commission shall initiate a proceeding to determine whether the regulatory objectives specified in subsection (d)(1)(A) and (B) are being achieved. The proceeding shall --

(i) monitor operator service rates;

(ii) determine the extent to which offerings made by providers of operator services are improvements, in terms of service quality, price, innovation, and other factors, over those available before the entry of new providers of operator services into the market;

(iii) report on (in the aggregate and by individual provider) operator service rates, incidence of service complaints, and service offerings;

(iv) consider the effect that commissions and surcharges, billing and validation costs, and other costs of doing business have on the overall rates charged to consumers; and

(v) monitor compliance with the provisions of this section, including the periodic placement of telephone calls from aggregator locations.

(B) Reports. - (i) The Commission shall, during the pendency of such proceeding and not later than 5 months after its commencement, provide the Congress with an interim report on the Commission's activities and progress to date.

(ii) Not later than 11 months after the commencement of such proceeding, the Commission shall report to the Congress on its interim findings as a result of the proceeding.

(iii) Not later than 23 months after the commencement of such proceeding, the Commission shall submit a final report to the Congress on its findings and conclusions.

(4) Implementing regulations. --

(A) In general. - Unless the Commission makes the determination described in subparagraph (B), the Commission shall, within 180 days after submission of the report required under paragraph (3)(B)(iii), complete a rulemaking proceeding pursuant to this title to establish regulations for implementing the requirements of this title (and paragraphs (1) and (2) of this subsection) that rates and charges for operator services be just and reasonable. Such regulations shall include limitations on the amount of commissions or any other compensation given to aggregators by providers of operator service.

(B) Limitation. - The requirement of subparagraph (A) shall not apply if, on the basis of the proceeding under paragraph (3)(A), the Commission makes (and includes in the report required by paragraph (3)(B)(iii)) a factual determination that market forces are securing rates and charges that are just and reasonable, as evidenced by rate levels, costs, complaints, service quality, and other relevant factors.

(i) Statutory construction. - Nothing in this section shall be construed to alter the obligations, powers, or duties of common carriers or the Commission under the other sections of this Act.

Section 227 [47 USC Section 227]. Restrictions on the Use of Telephone Equipment.

(a) Definitions. - As used in this section --

(1) The term "automatic telephone dialing system" means equipment which has the capacity --

(A) to store or produce telephone numbers to be called, using a random or sequential number generator; and

(B) to dial such numbers.

(2) The term "telephone facsimile machine" means equipment which has the capacity (A) to transcribe text or images, or both, from paper into an electronic signal and to transmit that signal over a regular telephone line, or (B) to transcribe text or images (or both) from an electronic signal received over a regular telephone line onto paper.

(3) The term "telephone solicitation" means the initiation of a telephone call or message for the purpose of encouraging the purchase or rental of, or investment in, property, goods, or services, which is transmitted to any person, but such term does not include a call or message (A) to any person with that person's prior express invitation or permission, (B) to any person with whom the caller has an established business relationship, or (C) by a tax exempt nonprofit organization.

(4) The term "unsolicited advertisement" means any material advertising the commercial availability or quality of any property, goods, or services which is transmitted to any person without that person's prior express invitation or permission.

(b) Restrictions on the use of automated telephone equipment. --

(1) Prohibitions. - It shall be unlawful for any person within the United States --

(A) to make any call (other than a call made for emergency purposes or made with the prior express consent of the called party) using any automatic telephone dialing system or an artificial or prerecorded voice --

(i) to any emergency telephone line (including any "911" line and any emergency line of a hospital, medical physician or service office, health care facility, poison control center, or fire protection or law enforcement agency);

(ii) to the telephone line of any guest room or patient room of a hospital, health care facility, elderly home, or similar establishment; or

(iii) to any telephone number assigned to a paging service, cellular telephone service, specialized mobile radio service, or other radio common carrier service, or any service for which the called party is charged for the call;

(B) to initiate any telephone call to any residential telephone line using an artificial or prerecorded voice to deliver a message without the prior express consent of the called party, unless the call is initiated for emergency purposes or is exempted by rule or order by the Commission under paragraph (2)(B);

(C) to use any telephone facsimile machine, computer, or other device to send an unsolicited advertisement to a telephone facsimile machine; or

(D) to use an automatic telephone dialing system in such a way that two or more telephone lines of a multi-line business are engaged simultaneously.

(2) Regulations; exemptions and other provisions. - The Commission shall prescribe regulations to implement the requirements of this subsection. In implementing the requirements of this subsection, the Commission --

(A) shall consider prescribing regulations to allow businesses to avoid receiving calls made using an artificial or prerecorded voice to which they have not given their prior express consent;

(B) may, by rule or order, exempt from the requirements of paragraph (1)(B) of this subsection, subject to such conditions as the Commission may prescribe --

(i) calls that are not made for a commercial purpose; and

(ii) such classes or categories of calls made for commercial purposes as the Commission determines --

(I) will not adversely affect the privacy rights that this section is intended to protect; and

(II) do not include the transmission of any unsolicited advertisement;

(C) may, by rule or order, exempt from the requirements of paragraph (1)(A)(iii) of this subsection calls to a telephone number assigned to a cellular telephone service that are not charged to the called party, subject to such conditions as the Commission may prescribe as necessary in the interest of the privacy rights this section is intended to protect.

(3) Private right of action. - A person or entity may, if otherwise permitted by the laws or rules of court of a State, bring in an appropriate court of that State --

(A) an action based on a violation of this subsection or the regulations prescribed under this subsection to enjoin such violation,

(B) an action to recover for actual monetary loss from such a violation, or to receive $500 in damages for each such violation, whichever is greater, or

(C) both such actions.

If the court finds that the defendant willfully or knowingly violated this subsection or the regulations prescribed under this subsection, the court may, in its discretion, increase the amount of the award to an amount equal to not more than 3 times the amount available under subparagraph (B) of this paragraph.

(c) Protection of subscriber privacy rights. --

(1) Rulemaking proceeding required. - Within 120 days after the date of enactment of this section, the Commission shall initiate a rulemaking proceeding concerning the need to protect residential telephone subscribers' privacy rights to avoid receiving telephone solicitations to which they object. The proceeding shall --

(A) compare and evaluate alternative methods and procedures (including the use of electronic databases, telephone network technologies, special directory markings, industry-based or company-specific "do not call" systems, and any other alternatives, individually or in combination) for their effectiveness in protecting such privacy rights, and in terms of their cost and other advantages and disadvantages;

(B) evaluate the categories of public and private entities that would have the capacity to establish and administer such methods and procedures;

(C) consider whether different methods and procedures may apply for local telephone solicitations, such as local telephone solicitations of small businesses or holders of second class mail permits;

(D) consider whether there is a need for additional Commission authority to further restrict telephone solicitations, including those calls exempted under subsection (a)(3) of this section, and, if such a finding is made and supported by the record, propose specific restrictions to the Congress; and

(E) develop proposed regulations to implement the methods and procedures that the Commission determines are most effective and efficient to accomplish the purposes of this section.

(2) Regulations. - Not later than 9 months after the date of enactment of this section, the Commission shall conclude the rulemaking proceeding initiated under paragraph (1) and shall prescribe regulations to implement methods and procedures for protecting the privacy rights described in such paragraph in an efficient, effective, and economic manner and without the imposition of any additional charge to telephone subscribers.

(3) Use of database permitted. - The regulations required by paragraph (2) may require the establishment and operation of a single national database to compile a list of telephone numbers of residential subscribers who object to receiving telephone solicitations, and to make that compiled list and parts thereof available for purchase. If the Commission determines to require such a database, such regulations shall --

(A) specify a method by which the Commission will select an entity to administer such database;

(B) require each common carrier providing telephone exchange service, in accordance with regulations prescribed by the Commission, to inform subscribers for telephone exchange service of the opportunity to provide notification, in accordance with regulations established under this paragraph, that such subscriber objects to receiving telephone solicitations;

(C) specify the methods by which each telephone subscriber shall be informed, by the common carrier that provides local exchange service to that subscriber, of (i) the subscriber's right to give or revoke a notification of an objection under subparagraph (A), and (ii) the methods by which such right may be exercised by the subscriber;

(D) specify the methods by which such objections shall be collected and added to the database;

(E) prohibit any residential subscriber from being charged for giving or revoking such notification or for being included in a database compiled under this section;

(F) prohibit any person from making or transmitting a telephone solicitation to the telephone number of any subscriber included in such database;

(G) specify (i) the methods by which any person desiring to make or transmit telephone solicitations will obtain access to the database, by area code or local exchange prefix, as required to avoid calling the telephone numbers of subscribers included in such database; and (ii) the costs to be recovered from such persons;

(H) specify the methods for recovering, from persons accessing such database, the costs involved in identifying, collecting, updating, disseminating, and selling, and other activities relating to, the operations of the database that are incurred by the entities carrying out those activities;

(I) specify the frequency with which such database will be updated and specify the method by which such updating will take effect for purposes of compliance with the regulations prescribed under this subsection;

(J) be designed to enable States to use the database mechanism selected by the Commission for purposes of administering or enforcing State law;

(K) prohibit the use of such database for any purpose other than compliance with the requirements of this section and any such State law and specify methods for protection of the privacy rights of persons whose numbers are included in such database; and

(L) require each common carrier providing services to any person for the purpose of making telephone solicitations to notify such person of the requirements of this section and the regulations thereunder.

(4) Considerations required for use of database method. - If the Commission determines to require the database mechanism described in paragraph (3), the Commission shall --

(A) in developing procedures for gaining access to the database, consider the different needs of telemarketers conducting business on a national, regional, State, or local level;

(B) develop a fee schedule or price structure for recouping the cost of such database that recognizes such differences and --

(i) reflect the relative costs of providing a national, regional, State, or local list of phone numbers of subscribers who object to receiving telephone solicitations;

(ii) reflect the relative costs of providing such lists on paper or electronic media; and

(iii) not place an unreasonable financial burden on small businesses; and

(C) consider (i) whether the needs of telemarketers operating on a local basis could be met through special markings of area white pages directories, and (ii) if such directories are needed as an adjunct to database lists prepared by area code and local exchange prefix.

(5) Private right of action. - A person who has received more than one telephone call within any 12-month period by or on behalf of the same entity in violation of the regulations prescribed under this subsection may, if otherwise permitted by the laws or rules of court of a State bring in an appropriate court of that State --

(A) an action based on a violation of the regulations prescribed under this subsection to enjoin such violation,

(B) an action to recover for actual monetary loss from such a violation, or to receive up to $500 in damages for each such violation, whichever is greater, or

(C) both such actions.

It shall be an affirmative defense in any action brought under this paragraph that the defendant has established an implemented, with due care, reasonable practices and procedures to effectively prevent telephone solicitations in violation of the regulations prescribed under this subsection. If the court finds that the defendant willfully or knowingly violated the regulations prescribed under this subsection, the court may, in its discretion, increase the amount of the award to an amount equal to not more than 3 times the amount available under subparagraph (B) of this paragraph.

(6) Relation to subsection (B). - The provisions of this subsection shall not be construed to permit a communication prohibited by subsection (b).

(d) Technical and procedural standards. --

(1) Prohibition. - It shall be unlawful for any person within the United States --

(A) to initiate any communication using a telephone facsimile machine, or to make any telephone call using any automatic telephone dialing system, that does not comply with the technical and procedural standards prescribed under this subsection, or to use any telephone facsimile machine or automatic telephone dialing system in a manner that does not comply with such standards; or

(B) to use a computer or other electronic device to send any message via a telephone facsimile machine unless such person clearly marks, in a margin at the top or bottom of each transmitted page of the message or on the first page of the transmission, the date and time it is sent and an identification of the business, other entity, or individual sending the message and the telephone number of the sending machine or of such business, other entity, or individual.

(2) Telephone facsimile machines. - The Commission shall revise the regulations setting technical and procedural standards for telephone facsimile machines to require that any such machine which is manufactured after one year after the date of enactment of this section clearly marks, in a margin at the top or bottom of each transmitted page or on the first page of each transmission, the date and time sent, an identification of the business, other entity, or individual sending the message, and the telephone number of the sending machine or of such business, other entity, or individual.

(3) Artificial or prerecorded voice systems. - The Commission shall prescribe technical and procedural standards for systems that are used to transmit any artificial or prerecorded voice message via telephone. Such standards shall require that --

(A) all artificial or prerecorded telephone messages (i) shall, at the beginning of the message, state clearly the identity of the business, individual, or other entity initiating the call, and (ii) shall, during or after the message, state clearly the telephone number or address of such business, other entity, or individual; and

(B) any such system will automatically release the called party's line within 5 seconds of the time notification is transmitted to the system that the called party has hung up, to allow the called party's line to be used to make or receive other calls.

364

(e) Effect on State law. --

    (1) State law not preempted. - Except for the standards prescribed under subsection (d) and subject to paragraph (2) of this subsection, nothing in this section or in the regulations prescribed under this section shall preempt any State law that imposes more restrictive intrastate requirements or regulations on, or which prohibits --

    (A) the use of telephone facsimile machines or other electronic devices to send unsolicited advertisements;

    (B) the use of automatic telephone dialing systems;

    (C) the use of artificial or prerecorded voice messages; or

    (D) the making of telephone solicitations.

    (2) State use of databases. - If, pursuant to subsection (c)(3), the Commission requires the establishment of a single national database of telephone numbers of subscribers who object to receiving telephone solicitations, a State or local authority may not, in its regulation of telephone solicitations, require the use of any database, list, or listing system that does not include the part of such single national database that relates to such State.

(f) Actions by States. --

    (1) Authority of States. - Whenever the attorney general of a State, or an official or agency designated by a State, has reason to believe that any person has engaged or is engaging in a pattern or practice of telephone calls or other transmissions to residents of that State in violation of this section or the regulations prescribed under this section, the State may bring a civil action on behalf of its residents to enjoin such calls, an action to recover for actual monetary loss or receive $500 in damages for each violation, or both such actions. If the court finds the defendant willfully or knowingly violated such regulations, the court may, in its discretion, increase the amount of the award to an amount equal to not more than 3 times the amount available under the preceding sentence.

    (2) Exclusive jurisdiction of federal courts. - The district courts of the United States, the United States courts of any territory, and the District Court of the United States for the District of Columbia shall have exclusive jurisdiction over all civil actions brought under this subsection. Upon proper application, such courts shall also have jurisdiction to issue writs of mandamus, or orders affording like relief, commanding the defendant to comply with the provisions of this section or regulations prescribed under this section, including the requirement that the defendant take such action as is necessary to remove the danger of such violation. Upon a proper showing, a permanent or temporary injunction or restraining order shall be granted without bond.

    (3) Rights of Commission. - The State shall serve prior written notice of any such civil action upon the Commission and provide the Commission with a copy of its complaint, except in any case where such prior notice is not feasible, in which case the State shall serve such notice immediately upon instituting such action. The Commission shall have the right (A) to intervene in the action, (B) upon so intervening, to be heard on all matters arising therein, and (C) to file petitions for appeal.

    (4) Venue; service of process. - Any civil action brought under this subsection in a district court of the United States may be brought in the district wherein the defendant is found or is an inhabitant or transacts business or wherein the violation occurred or is occurring, and process in such cases may be served in any district in which the defendant is an inhabitant or where the defendant may be found.

    (5) Investigatory powers. - For purposes of bringing any civil action under this subsection, nothing in this section shall prevent the attorney general of a State, or an official or agency designated

by a State, from exercising the powers conferred on the attorney general or such official by the laws of such State to conduct investigations or to administer oaths or affirmations or to compel the attendance of witnesses or the production of documentary and other evidence.

(6) Effect on State court proceedings. - Nothing contained in this subsection shall be construed to prohibit an authorized State official from proceeding in State court on the basis of an alleged violation of any general civil or criminal statute of such State.

(7) Limitation. - Whenever the Commission has instituted a civil action for violation of regulations prescribed under this section, no State may, during the pendency of such action instituted by the Commission, subsequently institute a civil action against any defendant named in the Commission's complaint for any violation as alleged in the Commission's complaint.

(8) Definition. - As used in this subsection, the term "attorney general" means the chief legal officer of a State.

Section 228 [47 USC Section 228]. Regulation of Carrier Offering of Pay-Per-Call Services.

(a) Purpose. -- It is the purpose of this section-

(1) to put into effect a system of national regulation and review that will oversee interstate pay-per-call services; and

(2) to recognize the Commission's authority to prescribe regulations and enforcement procedures and conduct oversight to afford reasonable protection to consumers of pay-per-call services and to assure that violations of Federal law do not occur.

(b) General Authority For Regulations. -- The Commission by regulation shall, within 270 days after the date of enactment this section, establish a system for oversight and regulation of pay-per-call services in order to provide for the protection of consumers in accordance with this Act and other applicable Federal statutes and regulations. The Commission's final rules shall--

(1) include measures that provide a consumer of pay-per-call services with adequate and clear descriptions of the rights of the caller;

(2) define the obligations of common carriers with respect to the provision of pay-per-call services;

(3) include requirements on such carriers to protect against abusive practices by providers of pay-per-call services;

(4) identify procedures by which common carriers and providers of pay-per-call services may take affirmative steps to protect against nonpayment of legitimate charges; and

(5) require that any service described in subparagraphs (A) and (B) of subsection (i)(1) be offered only through the use of certain telephone number prefixes and area codes.

(c) Common Carrier Obligations. -- Within 270 days after the date of enactment of this section, the Commission shall, by regulation, establish the following requirements for common carriers:

(1) Contractual Obligations To Comply. -- Any common carrier assigning to a provider of pay-per-call services a telephone number with a prefix or area code designated by the Commission in accordance with subsection (b)(5) shall require by contract or tariff that such provider comply with the provisions of titles II and III of the Telephone Disclosure and Dispute Resolution Act and the regulations prescribed by the Federal Trade Commission pursuant to those titles.

(2) Information Availability. -- A common carrier that by tariff or contract assigns a telephone number with a prefix or area code designated by the Commission in accordance with

subsection (b)(5) to a provider of a pay-per-call service shall make readily available on request to Federal and State agencies and other interested persons --

(A) a list of the telephone numbers for each of the pay-per-call services it carries;

(B) a short description of each such service;

(C) a statement of the total cost or the cost per minute and any other fees for each such service;

(D) a statement of the pay-per-call service's name, business address, and business telephone; and

(E) such other information as the Commission considers necessary for the enforcement of this section and other applicable Federal statutes and regulations.

(3) Compliance Procedures. -- A common carrier that by contract or tariff assigns a telephone number with a prefix or area code designated by the Commission in accordance with subsection (b)(5) to a provider of pay-per-call services shall terminate, in accordance with procedures specified in such regulations, the offering of a pay-per-call service of a provider if the carrier knows or reasonably should know that such service is not provided in compliance with title II or III of the Telephone Disclosure and Dispute Resolution Act or the regulations prescribed by the Federal Trade Commission pursuant to such titles.

(4) Subscriber Disconnection Prohibited. -- A common carrier shall not disconnect or interrupt a subscriber's local exchange telephone service or long distance telephone service because of nonpayment of charges for any pay-per-call service.

(5) Blocking And Presubscription. -- A common carrier that provides local exchange service shall--

(A) offer telephone subscribers (where technically feasible) the option of blocking access from their telephone number to all, or to certain specific, prefixes or area codes used by pay-per-call services, which option--

(i) shall be offered at no charge (I) to all subscribers for a period of 60 days after the issuance of the regulations under subsection (b), and (II) to any subscriber who subscribes to a new telephone number until 60 days after the time the new telephone number is effective; and

(ii) shall otherwise be offered at a reasonable fee; and

(B) offer telephone subscribers (where the Commission determines it is technically and economically feasible), in combination with the blocking option described under subparagraph (A), the option of presubscribing to or blocking only specific pay-per-call services for a reasonable one-time charge.

The regulations prescribed under subparagraph (A)(i) of this paragraph may permit the costs of such blocking to be recovered by contract or tariff, but such costs may not be recovered from local or long-distance ratepayers. Nothing in this subsection precludes a common carrier from filing its rates and regulations regarding blocking and presubscription in its interstate tariffs.

(6) Verification of Charitable Status. -- A common carrier that assigns by contract or tariff a telephone number with a prefix or area code designated by the Commission in accordance with subsection (b)(5) to a provider of pay-per-call services that the carrier knows or reasonably should know is engaged in soliciting charitable contributions shall obtain from such provider proof of the tax exempt status of any person or organization for which contributions are solicited.

(7) Billing For 800 Calls. -- A common carrier shall prohibit by tariff or contract the use of any 800 telephone number, or other telephone number advertised or widely understood to be toll free, in a manner that would result in--

(A) the calling party being assessed, by virtue of completing the call, a charge for the call;

(B) the calling party being connected to a pay-per-call service;

(C) the calling party being charged for information conveyed during the call unless--

(i) the calling party has a <preexisting> **written** agreement <to be> **(including an agreement transmitted through electronic medium) that meets the requirements of paragraph (8); or**

(ii) **the calling party is** charged for the information <or discloses a credit or charge card number during the call; or> **in accordance with paragraph (9);**

(D) the calling party being called back collect for the provision of audio information services or simultaneous voice conversation services**; or**

(E) **the calling party being assessed, by virtue of being asked to connect or otherwise transfer to a pay-per-call service, a charge for the call.**

(8) Subscription agreements for billing for information provided via toll free calls.--

(A) In general.--For purposes of paragraph (7)(C)(i), a written subscription does not meet the requirements of this paragraph unless the agreement specifies the material terms and conditions under which the information is offered and includes--

(i) the rate at which charges are assessed for the information;

(ii) the information provider's name;

(iii) the information provider's business address;

(iv) the information provider's regular business telephone number;

(v) the information provider's agreement to notify the subscriber at least one billing cycle in advance of all future changes in the rates charged for the information; and

(vi) the subscriber's choice of payment method, which may be by direct remit, debit, prepaid account, phone bill, or credit or calling card.

(B) Billing arrangements.--If a subscriber elects, pursuant to subparagraph (A)(vi), to pay by means of a phone bill--

(i) the agreement shall clearly explain that the subscriber will be assessed for calls made to the information service from the subscriber's phone line;

(ii) the phone bill shall include, in prominent type, the following disclaimer: Common carriers may not disconnect local or long distance telephone service for failure to pay disputed charges for information services.
and

(iii) the phone bill shall clearly list the 800 number dialed.

(C) Use of pins to prevent unauthorized use.--A written agreement does not meet the requirements of this paragraph unless it--

(i) includes a unique personal identification number or other subscriber specific identifier and requires a subscriber to use this number or identifier to obtain access to the information provided and includes instructions on its use; and

(ii) assures that any charges for services accessed by use of the subscriber's personal identification number or subscriber-specific identifier be assessed to subscriber's source of payment elected pursuant to subparagraph (A)(vi).

(D) Exceptions.--Notwithstanding paragraph (7)(C), a written agreement that meets the requirements of this paragraph is not required--

(i) for calls utilizing telecommunications devices for the deaf;

(ii) for directory services provided by a common carrier or its affiliate or by a local exchange carrier or its affiliate; or

(iii) for any purchase of goods or of services that are not information services.

(E) Termination of service.--On receipt by a common carrier of a complaint by any person that an information provider is in violation of the provisions of this section, a carrier shall--

(i) promptly investigate the complaint; and

(ii) if the carrier reasonably determines that the complaint is valid, it may terminate the provision of service to an information provider unless the provider supplies evidence of a written agreement that meets the requirements of this section.

(F) Treatment of remedies.--The remedies provided in this paragraph are in addition to any other remedies that are available under title V of this Act.

(9) Charges by credit, prepaid, debit, charge, or calling card in absence of agreement.--For purposes of paragraph (7)(C)(ii), a calling party is not charged in accordance with this paragraph unless the calling party is charged by means of a credit, prepaid, debit, charge, or calling card and the information service provider includes in response to each call an introductory disclosure message that

(A) clearly states that there is a charge for the call;

(B) clearly states the service's total cost per minute and any other fees for the service or for any service to which the caller may be transferred;

(C) explains that the charges must be billed on either a credit, prepaid, debit, charge, or calling card;

(D) asks the caller for the card number;

(E) clearly states that charges for the call begin at the end of the introductory message; and

(F) clearly states that the caller can hang up at or before the end of the introductory message without incurring any charge whatsoever.

(10) Bypass of introductory disclosure message.--The requirements of paragraph (9) shall not apply to calls from repeat callers using a bypass mechanism to avoid listening to the introductory message, provided that information providers shall disable such a bypass mechanism after the institution of any price increase and for a period of time determined to be sufficient by the Federal Trade Commission to give callers adequate and sufficient notice of a price increase.

(11) Definition of calling card.--As used in this subsection, the term "calling card" means an identifying number or code unique to the individual, that is issued to the individual by a common carrier and enables the individual to be charged by means of a phone bill for charges incurred independent of where the call originates.

(d) Billing and Collection Practices. -- The regulations required by this section shall require that any common carrier that by tariff or contract assigns a telephone number with a prefix or area code designated by the Commission in accordance with subsection (b)(5) to a provider of a pay-per-call service and that offers billing and collection services to such provider--

(1) ensure that a subscriber is not billed--

(A) for pay-per-call services that such carrier knows or reasonably should know was provided in violation of the regulations issued pursuant to title II of the Telephone Disclosure and Dispute Resolution Act; or

(B) under such other circumstances as the Commission determines necessary in order to protect subscribers from abusive practices;

(2) establish a local or a tell-free telephone number to answer questions and provide information on subscribers' rights and obligations with regard to their use of pay-per-call services and to provide to callers the name and mailing address of any provider of pay-per-call services offered by the common carrier;

(3) within 60 days after the issuance of final regulations pursuant to subsection (b), provide, either directly or through contract with any local exchange carrier that provides billing or collection services to the common carrier, to all of such common carrier's telephone subscribers, to all new subscribers, and to all subscribers requesting service at a new location, a disclosure statement that sets forth all rights and obligations of the subscriber and the carrier with respect to the use and payment for pay-per-call services, including the right of a subscriber not to be billed and the applicable blocking option; and

(4) in any billing to telephone subscribers that includes charges for any pay-per-call service--

(A) display any charges for pay-per-call services in a part of the subscriber's bill that is identified as not being related to local and long distance telephone charges;

(B) for each charge so displayed, specify, at a minimum, the type of service, the amount of the charge, and the date, time, and duration of the call; and

(C) identify the toll-free number established pursuant to paragraph (2).

(e) Liability. --

(1) Common Carriers Not Liable For Transmission or Billing. -- No common carrier shall be liable for a criminal or civil sanction or penalty solely because the carrier, provided transmission or billing and collection for a pay-per-call service unless the carrier knew or reasonably should have known that such service was provided in violation of a provision of, or regulation prescribed pursuant to, title II or III of the Telephone Disclosure and Dispute Resolution Act or any other Federal law. This paragraph shall not prevent the Commission from imposing a sanction or penalty on a common carrier for a violation by that carrier of a regulation prescribed under this section.

(2) Civil Liability. -- No cause of action may be brought in any court or administrative agency against any common carrier or any of its affiliates on account of any act of the carrier or affiliate to terminate any pay-per-call service in order to comply with the regulations prescribed under this section, title II or III of the Telephone Disclosure and Dispute Resolution Act, or any other Federal law unless the complainant demonstrates that the carrier or affiliate did not act in good faith.

(f) Special Provisions. --

(1) Consumer Refund Requirements. -- The regulations required by subsection (d) shall establish procedures, consistent with the provisions of titles II and III of the Telephone Disclosure and

Dispute Resolution Act, to ensure that carriers and other parties providing billing and collection services with respect to pay-per-call services provide appropriate refunds to subscribers who have been billed for pay-per-call services pursuant to programs that have been found to have violated this section or such regulations, any provision of, or regulations prescribed pursuant to, title II or III of the Telephone Disclosure and Dispute Resolution Act, or any other Federal law.

(2) Recovery of Costs. -- The regulations prescribed by the Commission under this section shall permit a common carrier to recover its cost of complying with such regulations from providers of pay-per-call services, but shall not permit such costs to be recovered from local or long distance ratepayers.

(3) Recommendations on Data Pay-Per-Call. -- The Commission, within one year after the date of enactment of this section, shall submit to the Congress the Commission's recommendations with respect to the extension of regulations under this section to persons that provide, for a per-call charge, data services that are not pay-per-call services.

(g) Effect on Other Law. --

(1) No Preemption of Election Law. -- Nothing in this section shall relieve any provider of pay-per-call services, common carrier, local exchange carrier, or any other person from the obligation to comply with Federal, State, and local election statutes and regulations.

(2) Consumer Protection Laws. -- Nothing in this section shall relieve any provider of pay-per-call services, common carrier, local exchange carrier, or any other person from the obligation to comply with any Federal, State, or local statute or regulation relating to consumer protection or unfair trade.

(3) Gambling Laws. -- Nothing in this section shall preclude any State from enforcing its statutes and regulations with regard to lotteries, wagering, betting, and other gambling activities.

(4) State Authority. -- Nothing in this section shall preclude any State from enacting and enforcing additional and complementary oversight and regulatory systems or procedures, or both, so long as such systems and procedures govern intrastate services and do not significantly impede the enforcement of this section or other Federal statutes.

(5) Enforcement of Existing Regulations. -- Nothing in this section shall be construed to prohibit the Commission from enforcing regulations prescribed prior to the date of enactment of this section in fulfilling the requirements of this section to the extent that such regulations are consistent with the provisions of this section.

(h) Effect on Dial-A-Porn Prohibitions. -- Nothing in this section shall affect the provisions of section 223 of this Act.

(i) Definition of Pay-Per-Call Services. -- For purposes of this section--

(1) The term "pay-per-call services" means any service--

(A) in which any person provides or purports to provide--

(i) audio information or audio entertainment produced or packaged by such person;

(ii) access to simultaneous voice conversation services; or

(iii) any service, including the provision of a product, the charges for which are assessed on the basis of the completion of the call;

(B) for which the caller pays a per-call or per-time-interval charge that is greater than, or in addition to, the charge for transmission of the call; and

371

(C) which is accessed through use of a 900 telephone number or other prefix or area code designated by the Commission in accordance with subsection (b)(5).

(2) Such term does not include directory services provided by a common carrier or its affiliate or by a local exchange carrier or its affiliate, ~~or any service the charge for which is tariffed,~~ or any service for which users are assessed charges only after entering into a presubscription or comparable arrangement with the provider of such service.

Section 229 [47 USC Section 229]. Communications Assistance for Law Enforcement Act Compliance.

(a) In General. - The Commission shall prescribe such rules as are necessary to implement the requirements of the Communications Assistance for Law Enforcement Act.

(b) Systems Security and Integrity. - The rules prescribed pursuant to subsection (a) shall include rules to implement Section 105 of the Communications Assistance for Law Enforcement Act that require common carriers--

(1) to establish appropriate policies and procedures for the supervision and control of its officers and employees--

(A) to require appropriate authorization to activate interception of communications or access to call-identifying information; and

(B) to prevent any such interception or access without such authorization;

(2) to maintain secure and accurate records of any interception or access with or without such authorization; and

(3) to submit to the Commission the policies and procedures adopted to comply with the requirements established under paragraphs (1) and (2).

(c) Commission Review of Compliance. - The Commission shall review the policies and procedures submitted under subsection (b)(3) and shall order a common carrier to modify any such policy or procedure that the Commission determines does not comply with Commission regulations. The Commission shall conduct such investigations as may be necessary to insure compliance by common carriers with the requirements of the regulations prescribed under this section.

(d) Penalties. - For purposes of this Act, a violation by an officer or employee of any policy or procedure adopted by a common carrier pursuant to subsection (b), or of a rule prescribed by the Commission pursuant to subsection (a), shall be considered to be a violation by the carrier of a rule prescribed by the Commission pursuant to this Act.

(e) Cost Recovery for Communications Assistance for Law Enforcement Act Compliance.--

(1) Petitions Authorized. - A common carrier may petition the Commission to adjust charges, practices, classifications, and regulations to recover costs expended for making modifications to equipment, facilities, or services pursuant to the requirements of Section 103 of the Communications Assistance for Law Enforcement Act.

(2) Commission Authority. - The Commission may grant, with or without modification, a petition under paragraph (1) if the Commission determines that such costs are reasonable and that permitting recovery is consistent with the public interest. The Commission may, consistent with maintaining just and reasonable charges, practices, classifications, and regulations in connection with the provision of interstate or foreign communication by wire or radio by a common carrier, allow carriers

to adjust such charges, practices, classifications, and regulations in order to carry out the purposes of this Act.

(3) Joint Board. - The Commission shall convene a Federal-State joint board to recommend appropriate changes to Part 36 of the Commission's rules with respect to recovery of costs pursuant to charges, practices, classifications, and regulations under the jurisdiction of the Commission.

Section 230 [47 USC Section 230]. Protection for Private Blocking and Screening of Offensive Material.

(a) Findings.--The Congress finds the following:

(1) The rapidly developing array of Internet and other interactive computer services available to individual Americans represent an extraordinary advance in the availability of educational and informational resources to our citizens.

(2) These services offer users a great degree of control over the information that they receive, as well as the potential for even greater control in the future as technology develops.

(3) The Internet and other interactive computer services offer a forum for a true diversity of political discourse, unique opportunities for cultural development, and myriad avenues for intellectual activity.

(4) The Internet and other interactive computer services have flourished, to the benefit of all Americans, with a minimum of government regulation.

(5) Increasingly Americans are relying on interactive media for a variety of political, educational, cultural, and entertainment services.

(b) Policy.--It is the policy of the United States--

(1) to promote the continued development of the Internet and other interactive computer services and other interactive media;

(2) to preserve the vibrant and competitive free market that presently exists for the Internet and other interactive computer services, unfettered by Federal or State regulation;

(3) to encourage the development of technologies which maximize user control over what information is received by individuals, families, and schools who use the Internet and other interactive computer services;

(4) to remove disincentives for the development and utilization of blocking and filtering technologies that empower parents to restrict their children's access to objectionable or inappropriate online material; and

(5) to ensure vigorous enforcement of Federal criminal laws to deter and punish trafficking in obscenity, stalking, and harassment by means of computer.

(c) Protection for "Good Samaritan" Blocking and Screening of Offensive Material.--

(1) Treatment of publisher or speaker.--No provider or user of an interactive computer service shall be treated as the publisher or speaker of any information provided by another information content provider.

(2) Civil liability.--No provider or user of an interactive computer service shall be held liable on account of--

(A) any action voluntarily taken in good faith to restrict access to or availability of material that the provider or user considers to be obscene, lewd, lascivious, filthy, excessively violent, harassing, or otherwise objectionable, whether or not such material is constitutionally protected; or

(B) any action taken to enable or make available to information content providers or others the technical means to restrict access to material described in paragraph (1).

(d) Effect on Other Laws.--

(1) No effect on criminal law.--Nothing in this section shall be construed to impair the enforcement of Section 223 of this Act, chapter 71 (relating to obscenity) or 110 (relating to sexual exploitation of children) of title 18, United States Code, or any other Federal criminal statute.

(2) No effect on intellectual property law.--Nothing in this section shall be construed to limit or expand any law pertaining to intellectual property.

(3) State law.--Nothing in this section shall be construed to prevent any State from enforcing any State law that is consistent with this section. No cause of action may be brought and no liability may be imposed under any State or local law that is inconsistent with this section.

(4) No effect on communications privacy law.--Nothing in this section shall be construed to limit the application of the Electronic Communications Privacy Act of 1986 or any of the amendments made by such Act, or any similar State law.

(e) Definitions.--As used in this section:

(1) Internet.--The term "Internet" means the international computer network of both Federal and non-Federal interoperable packet switched data networks.

(2) Interactive computer service.--The term "interactive computer service" means any information service, system, or access software provider that provides or enables computer access by multiple users to a computer server, including specifically a service or system that provides access to the Internet and such systems operated or services offered by libraries or educational institutions.

(3) Information content provider.--The term "information content provider" means any person or entity that is responsible, in whole or in part, for the creation or development of information provided through the Internet or any other interactive computer service.

(4) Access software provider.--The term "access software provider" means a provider of software (including client or server software), or enabling tools that do any one or more of the following:

(A) filter, screen, allow, or disallow content;

(B) pick, choose, analyze, or digest content; or

(C) transmit, receive, display, forward, cache, search, subset, organize, reorganize, or translate content.

Part II - Development of Competitive Markets

Section 251 [47 USC Section 251]. Interconnection.

(a) General Duty of Telecommunications Carriers.--Each telecommunications carrier has the duty--

(1) to interconnect directly or indirectly with the facilities and equipment of other telecommunications carriers; and

(2) not to install network features, functions, or capabilities that do not comply with the guidelines and standards established pursuant to Section 255 or 256.

(b) **Obligations of All Local Exchange Carriers.**--Each local exchange carrier has the following duties:

(1) **Resale.**--The duty not to prohibit, and not to impose unreasonable or discriminatory conditions or limitations on, the resale of its telecommunications services.

(2) **Number portability.**--The duty to provide, to the extent technically feasible, number portability in accordance with requirements prescribed by the Commission.

(3) **Dialing parity.**--The duty to provide dialing parity to competing providers of telephone exchange service and telephone toll service, and the duty to permit all such providers to have nondiscriminatory access to telephone numbers, operator services, directory assistance, and directory listing, with no unreasonable dialing delays.

(4) **Access to rights-of-way.**--The duty to afford access to the poles, ducts, conduits, and rights-of-way of such carrier to competing providers of telecommunications services on rates, terms, and conditions that are consistent with Section 224.

(5) **Reciprocal compensation.**--The duty to establish reciprocal compensation arrangements for the transport and termination of telecommunications.

(c) **Additional Obligations of Incumbent Local Exchange Carriers.**--In addition to the duties contained in subsection (b), each incumbent local exchange carrier has the following duties:

(1) **Duty to negotiate.**--The duty to negotiate in good faith in accordance with Section 252 the particular terms and conditions of agreements to fulfill the duties described in paragraphs (1) through (5) of subsection (b) and this subsection. The requesting telecommunications carrier also has the duty to negotiate in good faith the terms and conditions of such agreements.

(2) **Interconnection.**--The duty to provide, for the facilities and equipment of any requesting telecommunications carrier, interconnection with the local exchange carrier's network--

(A) for the transmission and routing of telephone exchange service and exchange access;

(B) at any technically feasible point within the carrier's network;

(C) that is at least equal in quality to that provided by the local exchange carrier to itself or to any subsidiary, affiliate, or any other party to which the carrier provides interconnection; and

(D) on rates, terms, and conditions that are just, reasonable, and nondiscriminatory, in accordance with the terms and conditions of the agreement and the requirements of this section and Section 252.

(3) **Unbundled access.**--The duty to provide, to any requesting telecommunications carrier for the provision of a telecommunications service, nondiscriminatory access to network elements on an unbundled basis at any technically feasible point on rates, terms, and conditions that are just, reasonable, and nondiscriminatory in accordance with the terms and conditions of the agreement and the requirements of this section and Section 252. An incumbent local exchange carrier shall provide such unbundled network elements in a manner that allows requesting carriers to combine such elements in order to provide such telecommunications service.

(4) **Resale.**--The duty--

(A) to offer for resale at wholesale rates any telecommunications service that the carrier provides at retail to subscribers who are not telecommunications carriers; and

(B) not to prohibit, and not to impose unreasonable or discriminatory conditions or limitations on, the resale of such telecommunications service, except that a State commission may, consistent with regulations prescribed by the Commission under this section, prohibit a reseller that obtains at wholesale rates a telecommunications service that is available at retail only to a category of subscribers from offering such service to a different category of subscribers.

(5) Notice of changes.--The duty to provide reasonable public notice of changes in the information necessary for the transmission and routing of services using that local exchange carrier's facilities or networks, as well as of any other changes that would affect the interoperability of those facilities and networks.

(6) Collocation.--The duty to provide, on rates, terms, and conditions that are just, reasonable, and nondiscriminatory, for physical collocation of equipment necessary for interconnection or access to unbundled network elements at the premises of the local exchange carrier, except that the carrier may provide for virtual collocation if the local exchange carrier demonstrates to the State commission that physical collocation is not   practical for technical reasons or because of space limitations.

(d) Implementation.--

(1)   In general.--Within 6 months after the date of enactment of the Telecommunications Act of 1996, the Commission shall complete all actions necessary to establish regulations to implement the requirements of this section.

(2)   Access standards.--In determining what network elements should be made available for purposes of subsection (c)(3), the Commission shall consider, at a minimum, whether--

(A)   access to such network elements as are proprietary in nature is necessary; and

(B)   the failure to provide access to such network elements would impair the ability of the telecommunications carrier seeking access to provide the services that it seeks to offer.

(3) Preservation of state access regulations.--In prescribing and enforcing regulations to implement the requirements of this section, the Commission shall not preclude the enforcement of any regulation, order, or policy of a State commission that--

(A)   establishes access and interconnection obligations of local exchange carriers;

(B)   is consistent with the requirements of this section; and

(C)   does not substantially prevent implementation of the requirements of this section and the purposes of this part.

(e) Numbering Administration.--

(1) Commission authority and jurisdiction.--The Commission shall create or designate one or more impartial entities to administer telecommunications numbering and to make such numbers available on an equitable basis. The Commission shall have exclusive jurisdiction over those portions of the North American Numbering Plan that pertain to the United States. Nothing in this paragraph shall preclude the Commission from delegating to State commissions or other entities all or any portion of such jurisdiction.

(2) Costs.--The cost of establishing telecommunications numbering administration arrangements and number portability shall be borne by all telecommunications carriers on a competitively neutral basis as determined by the Commission.

(f) Exemptions, Suspensions, and Modifications.--

(1) Exemption for certain rural telephone companies.--

(A) Exemption.--Subsection (c) of this section shall not apply to a rural telephone company until

(i) such company has received a bona fide request for interconnection, services, or network elements, and

(ii) the State commission determines (under subparagraph (B)) that such request is not unduly economically burdensome, is technically feasible, and is consistent with Section 254 (other than subsections (b)(7) and (c)(1)(D) thereof).

(B) State termination of exemption and implementation schedule.--The party making a bona fide request of a rural telephone company for interconnection, services, or network elements shall submit a notice of its request to the State commission. The State commission shall conduct an inquiry for the purpose of determining whether to terminate the exemption under subparagraph (A). Within 120 days after the State commission receives notice of the request, the State commission shall terminate the exemption if the request is not unduly economically burdensome, is technically feasible, and is consistent with Section 254 (other than subsections (b)(7) and (c)(1)(D) thereof). Upon termination of the exemption, a State commission shall establish an implementation schedule for compliance with the request that is consistent in time and manner with Commission regulations.

(C) Limitation on exemption.--The exemption provided by this paragraph shall not apply with respect to a request under subsection (c) from a cable operator providing video programming, and seeking to provide any telecommunications service, in the area in which the rural telephone company provides video programming. The limitation contained in this subparagraph shall not apply to a rural telephone company that is providing video programming on the date of enactment of the Telecommunications Act of 1996.

(2) Suspensions and modifications for rural carriers.--A local exchange carrier with fewer than 2 percent of the Nation's subscriber lines installed in the aggregate nationwide may petition a State commission for a suspension or modification of the application of a requirement or requirements of subsection (b) or (c) to telephone exchange service facilities specified in such petition. The State commission shall grant such petition to the extent that, and for such duration as, the State commission determines that such suspension or modification--

(A) is necessary--

(i) to avoid a significant adverse economic impact on users of telecommunications services generally;

(ii) to avoid imposing a requirement that is unduly economically burdensome; or

(iii) to avoid imposing a requirement that is technically infeasible; and

(B) is consistent with the public interest, convenience, and necessity.

The State commission shall act upon any petition filed under this paragraph within 180 days after receiving such petition. Pending such action, the State commission may suspend enforcement of the requirement or requirements to which the petition applies with respect to the petitioning carrier or carriers.

(g) Continued Enforcement of Exchange Access and Interconnection Requirements.--On and after the date of enactment of the Telecommunications Act of 1996, each local exchange carrier, to the extent that it provides wireline services, shall provide exchange access, information access, and exchange services for such access to interexchange carriers and information service providers in accordance with the same equal access and nondiscriminatory interconnection restrictions and obligations (including receipt of compensation) that apply to such carrier on the date immediately preceding the date of enactment of the Telecommunications Act of 1996 under any court order, consent decree, or regulation, order, or policy of the Commission, until such restrictions and obligations are explicitly superseded by regulations prescribed by the Commission after such date of enactment. During the period beginning on such date of enactment and until such restrictions and obligations are so superseded, such restrictions and obligations shall be enforceable in the same manner as regulations of the Commission.

(h) Definition of Incumbent Local Exchange Carrier.--

(1) Definition.--For purposes of this section, the term "incumbent local exchange carrier" means, with respect to an area, the local exchange carrier that--

(A) on the date of enactment of the Telecommunications Act of 1996, provided telephone exchange service in such area; and

(B)(i) on such date of enactment, was deemed to be a member of the exchange carrier association pursuant to Section 69.601(b) of the Commission's regulations (47 CFR §69.601(b)); or

(ii) is a person or entity that, on or after such date of enactment, became a successor or assign of a member described in clause (i).

(2) Treatment of comparable carriers as incumbents.--The Commission may, by rule, provide for the treatment of a local exchange carrier (or class or category thereof) as an incumbent local exchange carrier for purposes of this section if--

(A) such carrier occupies a position in the market for telephone exchange service within an area that is comparable to the position occupied by a carrier described in paragraph (1);

(B) such carrier has substantially replaced an incumbent local exchange carrier described in paragraph (1); and

(C) such treatment is consistent with the public interest, convenience, and necessity and the purposes of this section.

(i) Savings Provision.--Nothing in this section shall be construed to limit or otherwise affect the Commission's authority under Section 201.

Section 252 [47 USC Section 252]. Procedures For Negotiation, Arbitration, and Approval of Agreements.

(a) Agreements Arrived at Through Negotiation.--

(1) Voluntary negotiations.--Upon receiving a request for interconnection, services, or network elements pursuant to Section 251, an incumbent local exchange carrier may negotiate and enter into a binding agreement with the requesting telecommunications carrier or carriers without regard to the standards set forth in subsections (b) and (c) of Section 251. The agreement

shall include a detailed schedule of itemized charges for interconnection and each service or network element included in the agreement. The agreement, including any interconnection agreement negotiated before the date of enactment of the Telecommunications Act of 1996, shall be submitted to the State commission under subsection (e) of this section.

(2) Mediation.--Any party negotiating an agreement under this section may, at any point in the negotiation, ask a State commission to participate in the negotiation and to mediate any differences arising in the course of the negotiation.

(b) Agreements Arrived at Through Compulsory Arbitration.--

(1) arbitration.--During the period from the 135th to the 160th day (inclusive) after the date on which an incumbent local exchange carrier receives a request for negotiation under this section, the carrier or any other party to the negotiation may petition a State commission to arbitrate any open issues.

(2) Duty of petitioner.--

(A) A party that petitions a State commission under paragraph (1) shall, at the same time as it submits the petition, provide the State commission all relevant documentation concerning--

(i) the unresolved issues;

(ii) the position of each of the parties with respect to those issues; and

(iii) any other issue discussed and resolved by the parties.

(B) A party petitioning a State commission under paragraph (1) shall provide a copy of the petition and any documentation to the other party or parties not later than the day on which the State commission receives the petition.

(3) Opportunity to respond.--A non-petitioning party to a negotiation under this section may respond to the other party's petition and provide such additional information as it wishes within 25 days after the State commission receives the petition.

(4) Action by state commission.--

(A) The State commission shall limit its consideration of any petition under paragraph (1) (and any response thereto) to the issues set forth in the petition and in the response, if any, filed under paragraph (3).

(B) The State commission may require the petitioning party and the responding party to provide such information as may be necessary for the State commission to reach a decision on the unresolved issues. If any party refuses or fails unreasonably to respond on a timely basis to any reasonable request from the State commission, then the State commission may proceed on the basis of the best information available to it from whatever source derived.

(C) The State commission shall resolve each issue set forth in the petition and the response, if any, by imposing appropriate conditions as required to implement subsection (c) upon the parties to the agreement, and shall conclude the resolution of any unresolved issues not later than 9 months after the date on which the local exchange carrier received the request under this section.

(5) Refusal to negotiate.--The refusal of any other party to the negotiation to participate further in the negotiations, to cooperate with the State commission in carrying out its function as an arbitrator, or to continue to negotiate in good faith in the presence, or with the assistance, of the State commission shall be considered a failure to negotiate in good faith.

(c) Standards for Arbitration.--In resolving by arbitration under subsection (b) any open issues and imposing conditions upon the parties to the agreement, a State commission shall--

(1) ensure that such resolution and conditions meet the requirements of Section 251, including the regulations prescribed by the Commission pursuant to Section 251;

(2) establish any rates for interconnection, services, or network elements according to subsection (d); and

(3) provide a schedule for implementation of the terms and conditions by the parties to the agreement.

(d) Pricing Standards.--

(1) Interconnection and network element charges.--Determinations by a State commission of the just and reasonable rate for the interconnection of facilities and equipment for purposes of subsection (c)(2) of Section 251, and the just and reasonable rate for network elements for purposes of subsection (c)(3) of such section--

(A) shall be--

(i) based on the cost (determined without reference to a rate-of-return or other rate-based proceeding) of providing the interconnection or network element (whichever is applicable), and

(ii) nondiscriminatory, and

(B) may include a reasonable profit.

(2) Charges for transport and termination of traffic.--

(A) In general.--For the purposes of compliance by an incumbent local exchange carrier with Section 251(b)(5), a State commission shall not consider the terms and conditions for reciprocal compensation to be just and reasonable unless--

(i) such terms and conditions provide for the mutual and reciprocal recovery by each carrier of costs associated with the transport and termination on each carrier's network facilities of calls that originate on the network facilities of the other carrier; and

(ii) such terms and conditions determine such costs on the basis of a reasonable approximation of the additional costs of terminating such calls.

(B) Rules of construction.--This paragraph shall not be construed--

(i) to preclude arrangements that afford the mutual recovery of costs through the offsetting of reciprocal obligations, including arrangements that waive mutual recovery (such as bill-and-keep arrangements); or

(ii) to authorize the Commission or any State commission to engage in any rate regulation proceeding to establish with particularity the additional costs of transporting or terminating calls, or to require carriers to maintain records with respect to the additional costs of such calls.

(3) Wholesale prices for telecommunications services.--For the purposes of Section 251(c)(4), a State commission shall determine wholesale rates on the basis of retail rates charged to subscribers for the telecommunications service requested, excluding the portion thereof attributable to any marketing, billing, collection, and other costs that will be avoided by the local exchange carrier.

(e) Approval by State Commission.--

(1) Approval required.--Any interconnection agreement adopted by negotiation or arbitration shall be submitted for approval to the State commission. A State commission to which

an agreement is submitted shall approve or reject the agreement, with written findings as to any deficiencies.

(2) Grounds for rejection.--The State commission may only reject--

(A) an agreement (or any portion thereof) adopted by negotiation under subsection (a) if it finds that--

(i) the agreement (or portion thereof) discriminates against a telecommunications carrier not a party to the agreement; or

(ii) the implementation of such agreement or portion is not consistent with the public interest, convenience, and necessity; or

(B) an agreement (or any portion thereof) adopted by arbitration under subsection (b) if it finds that the agreement does not meet the requirements of Section 251, including the regulations prescribed by the Commission pursuant to Section 251, or the standards set forth in subsection (d) of this section.

(3) Preservation of authority.--Notwithstanding paragraph (2), but subject to Section 253, nothing in this section shall prohibit a State commission from establishing or enforcing other requirements of State law in its review of an agreement, including requiring compliance with intrastate telecommunications service quality standards or requirements.

(4) Schedule for decision.--If the State commission does not act to approve or reject the agreement within 90 days after submission by the parties of an agreement adopted by negotiation under subsection (a), or within 30 days after submission by the parties of an agreement adopted by arbitration under subsection (b), the agreement shall be deemed approved. No State court shall have jurisdiction to review the action of a State commission in approving or rejecting an agreement under this section.

(5) Commission to act if state will not act.--If a State commission fails to act to carry out its responsibility under this section in any proceeding or other matter under this section, then the Commission shall issue an order preempting the State commission's jurisdiction of that proceeding or matter within 90 days after being notified (or taking notice) of such failure, and shall assume the responsibility of the State commission under this section with respect to the proceeding or matter and act for the State commission.

(6) Review of state commission actions.--In a case in which a State fails to act as described in paragraph (5), the proceeding by the Commission under such paragraph and any judicial review of the Commission's actions shall be the exclusive remedies for a State commission's failure to act. In any case in which a State commission makes a determination under this section, any party aggrieved by such determination may bring an action in an appropriate Federal district court to determine whether the agreement or statement meets the requirements of Section 251 and this section.

(f) Statements of Generally Available Terms.--

(1) In general.--A Bell operating company may prepare and file with a State commission a statement of the terms and conditions that such company generally offers within that State to comply with the requirements of Section 251 and the regulations thereunder and the standards applicable under this section.

(2) State commission review.--A State commission may not approve such statement unless such statement complies with subsection (d) of this section and Section 251 and the regulations thereunder. Except as provided in Section 253, nothing in this section shall prohibit

381

a State commission from establishing or enforcing other requirements of State law in its review of such statement, including requiring compliance with intrastate telecommunications service quality standards or requirements.

(3) Schedule for review.--The State commission to which a statement is submitted shall, not later than 60 days after the date of such submission--

(A) complete the review of such statement under paragraph (2) (including any reconsideration thereof), unless the submitting carrier agrees to an extension of the period for such review; or

(B) permit such statement to take effect.

(4) Authority to continue review.--Paragraph (3) shall not preclude the State commission from continuing to review a statement that has been permitted to take effect under subparagraph (B) of such paragraph or from approving or disapproving such statement under paragraph (2).

(5) Duty to negotiate not affected.--The submission or approval of a statement under this subsection shall not relieve a Bell operating company of its duty to negotiate the terms and conditions of an agreement under Section 251.

(g) Consolidation of State Proceedings.--Where not inconsistent with the requirements of this Act, a State commission may, to the extent practical, consolidate proceedings under Sections 214(e), 251(f), 253, and this section in order to reduce administrative burdens on telecommunications carriers, other parties to the proceedings, and the State commission in carrying out its responsibilities under this Act.

(h) Filing Required.--A State commission shall make a copy of each agreement approved under subsection (e) and each statement approved under subsection (f) available for public inspection and copying within 10 days after the agreement or statement is approved. The State commission may charge a reasonable and nondiscriminatory fee to the parties to the agreement or to the party filing the statement to cover the costs of approving and filing such agreement or statement.

(i) Availability to Other Telecommunications Carriers.--A local exchange carrier shall make available any interconnection, service, or network element provided under an agreement approved under this section to which it is a party to any other requesting telecommunications carrier upon the same terms and conditions as those provided in the agreement.

(j) Definition of Incumbent Local Exchange Carrier.--For purposes of this section, the term "incumbent local exchange carrier" has the meaning provided in Section 251(h).

Section 253 [47 USC Section 253]. Removal of Barriers to Entry.

(a) In General.--No State or local statute or regulation, or other State or local legal requirement, may prohibit or have the effect of prohibiting the ability of any entity to provide any interstate or intrastate telecommunications service.

(b) State Regulatory Authority.--Nothing in this section shall affect the ability of a State to impose, on a competitively neutral basis and consistent with Section 254, requirements necessary to preserve and advance universal service, protect the public safety and welfare, ensure the continued quality of telecommunications services, and safeguard the rights of consumers.

(c) State and Local Government Authority.--Nothing in this section affects the authority of a State or local government to manage the public rights-of way or to require fair and reasonable compensation from telecommunications providers, on a competitively neutral and nondiscriminatory basis, for use of public rights-of-way on a nondiscriminatory basis, if the compensation required is publicly disclosed by such government.

(d) Preemption.--If, after notice and an opportunity for public comment, the Commission determines that a State or local government has permitted or imposed any statute, regulation, or legal requirement that violates subsection (a) or (b), the Commission shall preempt the enforcement of such statute, regulation, or legal requirement to the extent necessary to correct such violation or inconsistency.

(e) Commercial mobile service providers.--Nothing in this section shall affect the application of Section 332(c)(3) to commercial mobile service providers.

(f) Rural Markets.--It shall not be a violation of this section for a State to require a telecommunications carrier that seeks to provide telephone exchange service or exchange access in a service area served by a rural telephone company to meet the requirements in Section 214(e)(1) for designation as an eligible telecommunications carrier for that area before being permitted to provide such service. This subsection shall not apply--

(1) to a service area served by a rural telephone company that has obtained an exemption, suspension, or modification of Section 251(c)(4) that effectively prevents a competitor from meeting the requirements of Section 214(e)(1); and

(2) to a provider of commercial mobile services.

Section 254 [47 USC Section 254]. Universal Service

(a) Procedures to Review Universal Service Requirements.--

(1) Federal-state joint board on universal service.--Within one month after the date of enactment of the Telecommunications Act of 1996, the Commission shall institute and refer to a Federal-State Joint Board under Section 410(c) a proceeding to recommend changes to any of its regulations in order to implement Section 214(e) and this section, including the definition of the services that are supported by Federal universal service support mechanisms and a specific timetable for completion of such recommendations. In addition to the members of the Joint Board required under Section 410(c), one member of such Joint Board shall be a State-appointed utility consumer advocate nominated by a national organization of State utility consumer advocates. The Joint Board shall, after notice and opportunity for public comment, make its recommendations to the Commission 9 months after the date of enactment of the Telecommunications Act of 1996.

(2) Commission action.--The Commission shall initiate a single proceeding to implement the recommendations from the Joint Board required by paragraph (1) and shall complete such proceeding within 15 months after the date of enactment of the Telecommunications Act of 1996. The rules established by such proceeding shall include a definition of the services that are supported by Federal universal service support mechanisms and a specific timetable for implementation. Thereafter, the Commission shall complete any proceeding to implement subsequent recommendations from any Joint Board on universal service within one year after receiving such recommendations.

383

(b) Universal Service Principles.--The Joint Board and the Commission shall base policies for the preservation and advancement of universal service on the following principles:

(1) Quality and rates.--Quality services should be available at just, reasonable, and affordable rates.

(2) Access to advanced services.--Access to advanced telecommunications and information services should be provided in all regions of the Nation.

(3) Access in rural and high cost areas.--Consumers in all regions of the Nation, including low-income consumers and those in rural, insular, and high cost areas, should have access to telecommunications and information services, including interexchange services and advanced telecommunications and information services, that are reasonably comparable to those services provided in urban areas and that are available at rates that are reasonably comparable to rates charged for similar services in urban areas.

(4) Equitable and nondiscriminatory contributions.--All providers of telecommunications services should make an equitable and nondiscriminatory contribution to the preservation and advancement of universal service.

(5) Specific and predictable support mechanisms.--There should be specific, predictable and sufficient Federal and State mechanisms to preserve and advance universal service.

(6) Access to advanced telecommunications services for schools, health care, and libraries.--Elementary and secondary schools and classrooms, health care providers, and libraries should have access to advanced telecommunications services as described in subsection (h).

(7) Additional principles.--Such other principles as the Joint Board and the Commission determine are necessary and appropriate for the protection of the public interest, convenience, and necessity and are consistent with this Act.

(c) Definition.

(1) In general.--Universal service is an evolving level of telecommunications services that the Commission shall establish periodically under this section, taking into account advances in telecommunications and information technologies and services. The Joint Board in recommending, and the Commission in establishing, the definition of the services that are supported by Federal universal service support mechanisms shall consider the extent to which such telecommunications services--

(A) are essential to education, public health, or public safety;

(B) have, through the operation of market choices by customers, been subscribed to by a substantial majority of residential customers;

(C) are being deployed in public telecommunications networks by telecommunications carriers; and

(D) are consistent with the public interest, convenience, and necessity.

(2) Alterations and modifications.--The Joint Board may, from time to time, recommend to the Commission modifications in the definition of the services that are supported by Federal universal service support mechanisms.

(3) Special services.--In addition to the services included in the definition of universal service under paragraph (1), the Commission may designate additional services for such support mechanisms for schools, libraries, and health care providers for the purposes of subsection (h).

(d) Telecommunications Carrier Contribution.--Every telecommunications carrier that provides interstate telecommunications services shall contribute, on an equitable and nondiscriminatory basis, to the specific, predictable, and sufficient mechanisms established by the Commission to preserve and advance universal service. The Commission may exempt a carrier or class of carriers from this requirement if the carrier's telecommunications activities are limited to such an extent that the level of such carrier's contribution to the preservation and advancement of universal service would be de minimis. Any other provider of interstate telecommunications may be required to contribute to the preservation and advancement of universal service if the public interest so requires.

(e) Universal Service Support.--After the date on which Commission regulations implementing this section take effect, only an eligible telecommunications carrier designated under Section 214(e) shall be eligible to receive specific Federal universal service support. A carrier that receives such support shall use that support only for the provision, maintenance, and upgrading of facilities and services for which the support is intended. Any such support should be explicit and sufficient to achieve the purposes of this section.

(f) State Authority.--A State may adopt regulations not inconsistent with the Commission's rules to preserve and advance universal service. Every telecommunications carrier that provides intrastate telecommunications services shall contribute, on an equitable and nondiscriminatory basis, in a manner determined by the State to the preservation and advancement of universal service in that State. A State may adopt regulations to provide for additional definitions and standards to preserve and advance universal service within that State only to the extent that such regulations adopt additional specific, predictable, and sufficient mechanisms to support such definitions or standards that do not rely on or burden Federal universal service support mechanisms.

(g) Interexchange and Interstate Services.--Within 6 months after the date of enactment of the Telecommunications Act of 1996, the Commission shall adopt rules to require that the rates charged by providers of interexchange telecommunications services to subscribers in rural and high cost areas shall be no higher than the rates charged by each such provider to its subscribers in urban areas. Such rules shall also require that a provider of interstate interexchange telecommunications services shall provide such services to its subscribers in each State at rates no higher than the rates charged to its subscribers in any other State.

(h) Telecommunications Services for Certain Providers.--

(1) In general.--

(A) Health care providers for rural areas.--A telecommunications carrier shall, upon receiving a bona fide request, provide telecommunications services which are necessary for the provision of health care services in a State, including instruction relating to such services, to any public or nonprofit health care provider that serves persons who reside in rural areas in that State at rates that are reasonably comparable to rates charged for similar services in urban areas in that State. A telecommunications carrier providing service under this paragraph shall be entitled to have an amount equal to the difference, if any, between the rates for services provided to health care providers for rural areas in a State and the rates for similar services provided to other customers in comparable rural areas in that State treated as a service obligation as a part of its obligation to participate in the mechanisms to preserve and advance universal service.

(B)   Educational providers and libraries.--All telecommunications carriers serving a geographic area shall, upon a bona fide request for any of its services that are within the definition of universal service under subsection (c)(3), provide such services to elementary schools, secondary schools, and libraries for educational purposes at rates less than the amounts charged for similar services to other parties. The discount shall be an amount that the Commission, with respect to interstate services, and the States, with respect to intrastate services, determine is appropriate and necessary to ensure affordable access to and use of such services by such entities. A telecommunications carrier providing service under this paragraph shall--

(i) have an amount equal to the amount of the discount treated as an offset to its obligation to contribute to the mechanisms to preserve and advance universal service, or

(ii) notwithstanding the provisions of subsection (e) of this section, receive reimbursement utilizing the support mechanisms to preserve and advance universal service.

(2) Advanced services.--The Commission shall establish competitively neutral rules--

(A) to enhance, to the extent technically feasible and economically reasonable, access to advanced telecommunications and information services for all public and nonprofit elementary and secondary school classrooms, health care providers, and libraries; and

(B) to define the circumstances under which a telecommunications carrier may be required to connect its network to such public institutional telecommunications users.

(3)   Terms and conditions.--Telecommunications services and network capacity provided to a public institutional telecommunications user under this subsection may not be sold, resold, or otherwise transferred by such user in consideration for money or any other thing of value.

(4)   Eligibility of users.--No entity listed in this subsection shall be entitled to preferential rates or treatment as required by this subsection, if such entity operates as a for-profit business, is a school described in paragraph (5)(A) with an endowment of more than $50,000,000, or is a library not eligible for participation in State-based plans for funds under title III of the Library Services and Construction Act (20 USC 335c et seq.).

(5) Definitions.--For purposes of this subsection:

(A) Elementary and secondary schools.--The term "elementary and secondary schools" means elementary schools and secondary schools, as defined in paragraphs (14) and (25), respectively, of Section 14101 of the Elementary and Secondary Education Act of 1965 (20 USC 8801).

(B) Health care provider.--The term "health care provider" means--

(i) post-secondary educational institutions offering health care instruction, teaching hospitals, and medical schools;

(ii)   community health centers or health centers providing health care to migrants;

(iii) local health departments or agencies;

(iv) community mental health centers;

(v) not-for-profit hospitals;

(vi) rural health clinics; and

(vii)   consortia of health care providers consisting of one or more entities described in clauses (i) through (vi).

(C) Public institutional telecommunications user.--The term "public institutional telecommunications user" means an elementary or secondary school, a library, or a health care provider as those terms are defined in this paragraph.

(i) Consumer Protection.--The Commission and the States should ensure that universal service is available at rates that are just, reasonable, and affordable.

(j) Lifeline Assistance.--Nothing in this section shall affect the collection, distribution, or administration of the Lifeline Assistance Program provided for by the Commission under regulations set forth in Section 69.117 of title 47, Code of Federal Regulations, and other related sections of such title.

(k) Subsidy of Competitive Services Prohibited.--A telecommunications carrier may not use services that are not competitive to subsidize services that are subject to competition. The Commission, with respect to interstate services, and the States, with respect to intrastate services, shall establish any necessary cost allocation rules, accounting safeguards, and guidelines to ensure that services included in the definition of universal service bear no more than a reasonable share of the joint and common costs of facilities used to provide those services.

Section 255 [47 USC Section 255]. Access by Persons with Disabilities.

(a) Definitions.--As used in this section--

(1) Disability.--The term "disability" has the meaning given to it by Section 3(2)(A) of the Americans with Disabilities Act of 1990 (42 USC 12102(2)(A)).

(2) Readily achievable.--The term "readily achievable" has the meaning given to it by Section 301(9) of that Act (42 USC 12181(9)).

(b) Manufacturing.--A manufacturer of telecommunications equipment or customer premises equipment shall ensure that the equipment is designed, developed, and fabricated to be accessible to and usable by individuals with disabilities, if readily achievable.

(c) Telecommunications Services.--A provider of telecommunications service shall ensure that the service is accessible to and usable by individuals with disabilities, if readily achievable.

(d) Compatibility.--Whenever the requirements of subsections (b) and (c) are not readily achievable, such a manufacturer or provider shall ensure that the equipment or service is compatible with existing peripheral devices or specialized customer premises equipment commonly used by individuals with disabilities to achieve access, if readily achievable.

(e) Guidelines.--Within 18 months after the date of enactment of the Telecommunications Act of 1996, the Architectural and Transportation Barriers Compliance Board shall develop guidelines for accessibility of telecommunications equipment and customer premises equipment in conjunction with the Commission. The Board shall review and update the guidelines periodically.

(f) No Additional Private Rights Authorized.--Nothing in this section shall be construed to authorize any private right of action to enforce any requirement of this section or any regulation thereunder. The Commission shall have exclusive jurisdiction with respect to any complaint under this section.

Section 256 [47 USC Section 256]. Coordination for Interconnectivity.

(a) Purpose.--It is the purpose of this section--

(1) to promote nondiscriminatory accessibility by the broadest number of users and vendors of communications products and services to public telecommunications networks used to provide telecommunications service through--

(A) coordinated public telecommunications network planning and design by telecommunications carriers and other providers of telecommunications service; and

(B) public telecommunications network interconnectivity, and interconnectivity of devices with such networks used to provide telecommunications service; and

(2) to ensure the ability of users and information providers to seamlessly and transparently transmit and receive information between and across telecommunications networks.

(b) Commission Functions.--In carrying out the purposes of this section, the Commission--

(1) shall establish procedures for Commission oversight of coordinated network planning by telecommunications carriers and other providers of telecommunications service for the effective and efficient interconnection of public telecommunications networks used to provide telecommunications service; and

(2) may participate, in a manner consistent with its authority and practice prior to the date of enactment of this section, in the development by appropriate industry standards-setting organizations of public telecommunications network interconnectivity standards that promote access to--

(A) public telecommunications networks used to provide telecommunications service;

(B) network capabilities and services by individuals with disabilities; and

(C) information services by subscribers of rural telephone companies.

(c) Commission's Authority.--Nothing in this section shall be construed as expanding or limiting any authority that the Commission may have under law in effect before the date of enactment of the Telecommunications Act of 1996.

(d) Definition.--As used in this section, the term "public telecommunications network interconnectivity" means the ability of two or more public telecommunications networks used to provide telecommunications service to communicate and exchange information without degeneration, and to interact in concert with one another.

Section 257 [47 USC Section 257]. Market Entry Barriers Proceeding.

(a) Elimination of Barriers.--Within 15 months after the date of enactment of the Telecommunications Act of 1996, the Commission shall complete a proceeding for the purpose of identifying and eliminating, by regulations pursuant to its authority under this Act (other than this section), market entry barriers for entrepreneurs and other small businesses in the provision and ownership of telecommunications services and information services, or in the provision of parts or services to providers of telecommunications services and information services.

(b) National Policy.--In carrying out subsection (a), the Commission shall seek to promote the policies and purposes of this Act favoring diversity of media voices, vigorous economic competition, technological advancement, and promotion of the public interest, convenience, and necessity.

(c) Periodic Review.--Every 3 years following the completion of the proceeding required by subsection (a), the Commission shall review and report to Congress on--

(1) any regulations prescribed to eliminate barriers within its jurisdiction that are identified under subsection (a) and that can be prescribed consistent with the public interest, convenience, and necessity; and

(2) the statutory barriers identified under subsection (a) that the Commission recommends be eliminated, consistent with the public interest, convenience, and necessity.

Section 258 [47 USC Section 258]. Illegal Changes in Subscriber Carrier Selections.

(a) Prohibition.--No telecommunications carrier shall submit or execute a change in a subscriber's selection of a provider of telephone exchange service or telephone toll service except in accordance with such verification procedures as the Commission shall prescribe. Nothing in this section shall preclude any State commission from enforcing such procedures with respect to intrastate services.

(b) Liability for Charges.--Any telecommunications carrier that violates the verification procedures described in subsection (a) and that collects charges for telephone exchange service or telephone toll service from a subscriber shall be liable to the carrier previously selected by the subscriber in an amount equal to all charges paid by such subscriber after such violation, in accordance with such procedures as the Commission may prescribe. The remedies provided by this subsection are in addition to any other remedies available by law.

Section 259 [47 USC Section 259]. Infrastructure Sharing.

(a) Regulations Required.--The Commission shall prescribe, within one year after the date of enactment of the Telecommunications Act of 1996, regulations that require incumbent local exchange carriers (as defined in Section 251(h)) to make available to any qualifying carrier such public switched network infrastructure, technology, information, and telecommunications facilities and functions as may be requested by such qualifying carrier for the purpose of enabling such qualifying carrier to provide telecommunications services, or to provide access to information services, in the service area in which such qualifying carrier has requested and obtained designation as an eligible telecommunications carrier under Section 214(e).

(b) Terms and Conditions of Regulations.--The regulations prescribed by the Commission pursuant to this section shall--

(1) not require a local exchange carrier to which this section applies to take any action that is economically unreasonable or that is contrary to the public interest;

(2) permit, but shall not require, the joint ownership or operation of public switched network infrastructure and services by or among such local exchange carrier and a qualifying carrier;

(3) ensure that such local exchange carrier will not be treated by the Commission or any State as a common carrier for hire or as offering common carrier services with respect to any

infrastructure, technology, information, facilities, or functions made available to a qualifying carrier in accordance with regulations issued pursuant to this section;

(4) ensure that such local exchange carrier makes such infrastructure, technology, information, facilities, or functions available to a qualifying carrier on just and reasonable terms and conditions that permit such qualifying carrier to fully benefit from the economies of scale and scope of such local exchange carrier, as determined in accordance with guidelines prescribed by the Commission in regulations issued pursuant to this section;

(5) establish conditions that promote cooperation between local exchange carriers to which this section applies and qualifying carriers;

(6) not require a local exchange carrier to which this section applies to engage in any infrastructure sharing agreement for any services or access which are to be provided or offered to consumers by the qualifying carrier in such local exchange carrier's telephone exchange area; and

(7) require that such local exchange carrier file with the Commission or State for public inspection, any tariffs, contracts, or other arrangements showing the rates, terms, and conditions under which such carrier is making available public switched network infrastructure and functions under this section.

(c) Information Concerning Deployment of New Services and Equipment.--a local exchange carrier to which this section applies that has entered into an infrastructure sharing agreement under this section shall provide to each party to such agreement timely information on the planned deployment of telecommunications services and equipment, including any software or upgrades of software integral to the use or operation of such telecommunications equipment.

(d) Definition.--For purposes of this section, the term "qualifying carrier" means a telecommunications carrier that--

(1) lacks economies of scale or scope, as determined in accordance with regulations prescribed by the Commission pursuant to this section; and

(2) offers telephone exchange service, exchange access, and any other service that is included in universal service, to all consumers without preference throughout the service area for which such carrier has been designated as an eligible telecommunications carrier under Section 214(e).

Section 260 [47 USC Section 260]. Provision of Telemessaging Service.

(a) Nondiscrimination Safeguards.--Any local exchange carrier subject to the requirements of Section 251(c) that provides telemessaging service--

(1) shall not subsidize its telemessaging service directly or indirectly from its telephone exchange service or its exchange access; and

(2) shall not prefer or discriminate in favor of its telemessaging service operations in its provision of telecommunications services.

(b) Expedited Consideration of Complaints.--The Commission shall establish procedures for the receipt and review of complaints concerning violations of subsection (a) or the regulations thereunder that result in material financial harm to a provider of telemessaging service. Such procedures shall ensure that the Commission will make a final determination with respect to any such complaint within 120 days after receipt of the complaint. If the complaint contains an appropriate showing that the alleged violation occurred, the Commission shall, within 60 days after receipt of the complaint, order the local exchange carrier and any affiliates to cease engaging in such violation pending such final determination.

(c) Definition.--As used in this section, the term "telemessaging service" means voice mail and voice storage and retrieval services, any live operator services used to record, transcribe, or relay messages (other than telecommunications relay services), and any ancillary services offered in combination with these services.

Section 261 [47 USC Section 261]. Effect on Other Requirements.

(a) Commission Regulations.--Nothing in this part shall be construed to prohibit the Commission from enforcing regulations prescribed prior to the date of enactment of the Telecommunications Act of 1996 in fulfilling the requirements of this part, to the extent that such regulations are not inconsistent with the provisions of this part.

(b) Existing State Regulations.--Nothing in this part shall be construed to prohibit any State commission from enforcing regulations prescribed prior to the date of enactment of the Telecommunications Act of 1996, or from prescribing regulations after such date of enactment, in fulfilling the requirements of this part, if such regulations are not inconsistent with the provisions of this part.

(c) Additional State Requirements.--Nothing in this part precludes a State from imposing requirements on a telecommunications carrier for intrastate services that are necessary to further competition in the provision of telephone exchange service or exchange access, as long as the State's requirements are not inconsistent with this part or the Commission's regulations to implement this part.

Part III - Special Provisions Concerning Bell Operating Companies

Section 271 [47 USC Section 271]. Bell Operating Company Entry Into InterLATA Services.

(a) General Limitation.--Neither a Bell operating company, nor any affiliate of a Bell operating company, may provide interLATA services except as provided in this section.

(b) InterLATA Services to Which This Section Applies.--

(1) In-region services.--A Bell operating company, or any affiliate of that Bell operating company, may provide interLATA services originating in any of its in-region States (as defined in subsection (i)) if the Commission approves the application of such company for such State under subsection (d)(3).

(2) Out-of-region services.--A Bell operating company, or any affiliate of that Bell operating company, may provide interLATA services originating outside its in-region States after the date of enactment of the Telecommunications Act of 1996, subject to subsection (j).

(3) Incidental interlata services.--A Bell operating company, or any affiliate of a Bell operating company, may provide incidental interLATa services (as defined in subsection (g)) originating in any State after the date of enactment of the Telecommunications Act of 1996.

(4) Termination.--Nothing in this section prohibits a Bell operating company or any of its affiliates from providing termination for interLATa services, subject to subsection (j).

391

(c) Requirements for Providing Certain In-Region InterLATA Services.--

(1) Agreement or statement.--A Bell operating company meets the requirements of this paragraph if it meets the requirements of subparagraph (A) or subparagraph (B) of this paragraph for each State for which the authorization is sought.

(A) Presence of a facilities-based competitor.--A Bell operating company meets the requirements of this subparagraph if it has entered into one or more binding agreements that have been approved under Section 252 specifying the terms and conditions under which the Bell operating company is providing access and interconnection to its network facilities for the network facilities of one or more unaffiliated competing providers of telephone exchange service (as defined in Section 3(47)(A), but excluding exchange access) to residential and business subscribers. For the purpose of this subparagraph, such telephone exchange service may be offered by such competing providers either exclusively over their own telephone exchange service facilities or predominantly over their own telephone exchange service facilities in combination with the resale of the telecommunications services of another carrier. For the purpose of this subparagraph, services provided pursuant to Subpart K of Part 22 of the Commission's regulations (47 CFR §22.901 et seq.) shall not be considered to be telephone exchange services.

(B) Failure to request access.--A Bell operating company meets the requirements of this subparagraph if, after 10 months after the date of enactment of the Telecommunications Act of 1996, no such provider has requested the access and interconnection described in subparagraph (A) before the date which is 3 months before the date the company makes its application under subsection (d)(1), and a statement of the terms and conditions that the company generally offers to provide such access and interconnection has been approved or permitted to take effect by the State commission under Section 252(f). For purposes of this subparagraph, a Bell operating company shall be considered not to have received any request for access and interconnection if the State commission of such State certifies that the only provider or providers making such a request have (i) failed to negotiate in good faith as required by Section 252, or (ii) violated the terms of an agreement approved under Section 252 by the provider's failure to comply, within a reasonable period of time, with the implementation schedule contained in such agreement.

(2) Specific interconnection requirements.--

(A) Agreement required.--A Bell operating company meets the requirements of this paragraph if, within the State for which the authorization is sought--

(i)(I) such company is providing access and interconnection pursuant to one or more agreements described in paragraph (1)(A), or

(II) such company is generally offering access and interconnection pursuant to a statement described in paragraph (1)(B), and

(ii) such access and interconnection meets the requirements of subparagraph (B) of this paragraph.

(B) Competitive checklist.--Access or interconnection provided or generally offered by a Bell operating company to other telecommunications carriers meets the requirements of this subparagraph if such access and interconnection includes each of the following:

(i) Interconnection in accordance with the requirements of Sections 251(c)(2) and 252(d)(1).

(ii) Nondiscriminatory access to network elements in accordance with the requirements of Sections 251(c)(3) and 252(d)(1).

(iii) Nondiscriminatory access to the poles, ducts, conduits, and rights of-way owned or controlled by the Bell operating company at just and reasonable rates in accordance with the requirements of Section 224.

(iv) Local loop transmission from the central office to the customer's premises, unbundled from local switching or other services.

(v) Local transport from the trunk side of a wireline local exchange carrier switch unbundled from switching or other services.

(vi) Local switching unbundled from transport, local loop transmission, or other services.

(vii) Nondiscriminatory access to--

(I) 911 and E911 services;

(II) directory assistance services to allow the other carrier's customers to obtain telephone numbers; and

(III) operator call completion services.

(viii) White pages directory listings for customers of the other carrier's telephone exchange service.

(ix) Until the date by which telecommunications numbering administration guidelines, plan, or rules are established, nondiscriminatory access to telephone numbers for assignment to the other carrier's telephone exchange service customers. After that date, compliance with such guidelines, plan, or rules.

(x) Nondiscriminatory access to databases and associated signaling necessary for call routing and completion.

(xi) Until the date by which the Commission issues regulations pursuant to Section 251 to require number portability, interim telecommunications number portability through remote call forwarding, direct inward dialing trunks, or other comparable arrangements, with as little impairment of functioning, quality, reliability, and convenience as possible. After that date, full compliance with such regulations.

(xii) Nondiscriminatory access to such services or information as are necessary to allow the requesting carrier to implement local dialing parity in accordance with the requirements of Section 251(b)(3).

(xiii) Reciprocal compensation arrangements in accordance with the requirements of Section 252(d)(2).

(xiv) Telecommunications services are available for resale in accordance with the requirements of Sections 251(c)(4) and 252(d)(3).

(d) Administrative Provisions.--

(1) Application to commission.--On and after the date of enactment of the Telecommunications Act of 1996, a Bell operating company or its affiliate may apply to the Commission for authorization to provide interLATA services originating in any in-region State. The application shall identify each State for which the authorization is sought.

(2) Consultation.--

(A) Consultation with the attorney general.--The Commission shall notify the Attorney General promptly of any application under paragraph (1). Before making any

393

determination under this subsection, the Commission shall consult with the Attorney General, and if the Attorney General submits any comments in writing, such comments shall be included in the record of the Commission's decision. In consulting with and submitting comments to the Commission under this paragraph, the Attorney General shall provide to the Commission an evaluation of the application using any standard the Attorney General considers appropriate. The Commission shall give substantial weight to the Attorney General's evaluation, but such evaluation shall not have any preclusive effect on any Commission decision under paragraph (3).

(B) Consultation with state commissions.--Before making any determination under this subsection, the Commission shall consult with the State commission of any State that is the subject of the application in order to verify the compliance of the Bell operating company with the requirements of subsection (c).

(3) Determination.--Not later than 90 days after receiving an application under paragraph (1), the Commission shall issue a written determination approving or denying the authorization requested in the application for each State. The Commission shall not approve the authorization requested in an application submitted under paragraph (1) unless it finds that--

(A) the petitioning Bell operating company has met the requirements of subsection (c)(1) and--

(i) with respect to access and interconnection provided pursuant to subsection (c)(1)(A), has fully implemented the competitive checklist in subsection (c)(2)(B); or

(ii) with respect to access and interconnection generally offered pursuant to a statement under subsection (c)(1)(B), such statement offers all of the items included in the competitive checklist in subsection (c)(2)(B);

(B) the requested authorization will be carried out in accordance with the requirements of Section 272; and

(C) the requested authorization is consistent with the public interest, convenience, and necessity.

The Commission shall state the basis for its approval or denial of the application.

(4) Limitation on commission.--The Commission may not, by rule or otherwise, limit or extend the terms used in the competitive checklist set forth in subsection (c)(2)(B).

(5) Publication.--Not later than 10 days after issuing a determination under paragraph (3), the Commission shall publish in the Federal Register a brief description of the determination.

(6) Enforcement of conditions.--

(A) Commission authority.--If at any time after the approval of an application under paragraph (3), the Commission determines that a Bell operating company has ceased to meet any of the conditions required for such approval, the Commission may, after notice and opportunity for a hearing--

(i) issue an order to such company to correct the deficiency;

(ii) impose a penalty on such company pursuant to title V; or

(iii) suspend or revoke such approval.

(B) Receipt and review of complaints.--The Commission shall establish procedures for the review of complaints concerning failures by Bell operating companies to meet conditions required for approval under paragraph (3).

Unless the parties otherwise agree, the Commission shall act on such complaint within 90 days.

(e) Limitations.--

(1) Joint marketing of local and long distance services.--Until a Bell operating company is authorized pursuant to subsection (d) to provide interLATA services in an in-region State, or until 36 months have passed since the date of enactment of the Telecommunications Act of 1996, whichever is earlier, a telecommunications carrier that serves greater than 5 percent of the Nation's presubscribed access lines may not jointly market in such State telephone exchange service obtained from such company pursuant to Section 251(c)(4) with interLATA services offered by that telecommunications carrier.

(2) IntraLATA toll dialing parity.--

(A) Provision required.--A Bell operating company granted authority to provide interLATA services under subsection (d) shall provide intraLATA toll dialing parity throughout that State coincident with its exercise of that authority.

(B) Limitation.--Except for single-LATA States and States that have issued an order by December 19, 1995, requiring a Bell operating company to implement intraLATA toll dialing parity, a State may not require a Bell operating company to implement intraLATA toll dialing parity in that State before a Bell operating company has been granted authority under this section to provide interLATA services originating in that State or before 3 years after the date of enactment of the Telecommunications Act of 1996, whichever is earlier. Nothing in this subparagraph precludes a State from issuing an order requiring intraLATA toll dialing parity in that State prior to either such date so long as such order does not take effect until after the earlier of either such dates.

(f) Exception for Previously Authorized Activities.--Neither subsection (a) nor Section 273 shall prohibit a Bell operating company or affiliate from engaging, at any time after the date of enactment of the Telecommunications Act of 1996, in any activity to the extent authorized by, and subject to the terms and conditions contained in, an order entered by the United States District Court for the District of Columbia pursuant to section VII or VIII(C) of the AT&T Consent Decree if such order was entered on or before such date of enactment, to the extent such order is not reversed or vacated on appeal. Nothing in this subsection shall be construed to limit, or to impose terms or conditions on, an activity in which a Bell operating company is otherwise authorized to engage under any other provision of this section.

(g) Definition of Incidental InterLATA Services.--For purposes of this section, the term "incidental interLATA services" means the interLATA provision by a Bell operating company or its affiliate--

(1)(A) of audio programming, video programming, or other programming services to subscribers to such services of such company or affiliate;

(B) of the capability for interaction by such subscribers to select or respond to such audio programming, video programming, or other programming services;

(C) to distributors of audio programming or video programming that such company or affiliate owns or controls, or is licensed by the copyright owner of such programming (or by an assignee of such owner) to distribute; or

(D) of alarm monitoring services;

(2) of two-way interactive video services or Internet services over dedicated facilities to or for elementary and secondary schools as defined in Section 254(h)(5);

(3) of commercial mobile services in accordance with Section 332(c) of this Act and with the regulations prescribed by the Commission pursuant to paragraph (8) of such section;

(4) of a service that permits a customer that is located in one LATA to retrieve stored information from, or file information for storage in, information storage facilities of such company that are located in another LATA;

(5) of signaling information used in connection with the provision of telephone exchange services or exchange access by a local exchange carrier; or

(6) of network control signaling information to, and receipt of such signaling information from, common carriers offering interLATA services at any location within the area in which such Bell operating company provides telephone exchange services or exchange access.

(h) Limitations.--The provisions of subsection (g) are intended to be narrowly construed. The interLATA services provided under subparagraph (A), (B), or (C) of subsection (g)(1) are limited to those interLATA transmissions incidental to the provision by a Bell operating company or its affiliate of video, audio, and other programming services that the company or its affiliate is engaged in providing to the public. The Commission shall ensure that the provision of services authorized under subsection (g) by a Bell operating company or its affiliate will not adversely affect telephone exchange service ratepayers or competition in any telecommunications market.

(i) Additional Definitions.--As used in this section--

(1) In-region state.--The term "in-region State" means a State in which a Bell operating company or any of its affiliates was authorized to provide wireline telephone exchange service pursuant to the reorganization plan approved under the AT&T Consent Decree, as in effect on the day before the date of enactment of the Telecommunications Act of 1996.

(2) Audio programming services.--The term "audio programming services" means programming provided by, or generally considered to be comparable to programming provided by, a radio broadcast station.

(3) Video programming services; other programming services.--The terms "video programming service" and "other programming services" have the same meanings as such terms have under Section 602 of this Act.

(j) Certain Service Applications Treated as In-Region Service Applications.--For purposes of this section, a Bell operating company application to provide 800 service, private line service, or their equivalents that--

(1) terminate in an in-region State of that Bell operating company, and

(2) allow the called party to determine the interLATA carrier, shall be considered an in-region service subject to the requirements of subsection (b)(1).

Section 272 [47 USC Section 272]. Separate Affiliate; Safeguards.

(a) Separate Affiliate Required for Competitive Activities.--

(1) In general.--A Bell operating company (including any affiliate) which is a local exchange carrier that is subject to the requirements of Section 251(c) may not provide any service described in paragraph (2) unless it provides that service through one or more affiliates that--

(A) are separate from any operating company entity that is subject to the requirements of Section 251(c); and

(B) meet the requirements of subsection (b).

(2) Services for which a separate affiliate is required.--The services for which a separate affiliate is required by paragraph (1) are:

(A) Manufacturing activities (as defined in Section 273(h)).

(B) Origination of interLATA telecommunications services, other than--

(i) incidental interLATA services described in paragraphs (1), (2), (3), (5), and (6) of Section 271(g);

(ii) out-of-region services described in Section 271(b)(2); or

(iii) previously authorized activities described in Section 271(f).

(C) InterLATA information services, other than electronic publishing (as defined in Section 274(h)) and alarm monitoring services (as defined in Section 275(e)).

(b) Structural and Transactional Requirements.--The separate affiliate required by this section--

(1) shall operate independently from the Bell operating company;

(2) shall maintain books, records, and accounts in the manner prescribed by the Commission which shall be separate from the books, records, and accounts maintained by the Bell operating company of which it is an affiliate;

(3) shall have separate officers, directors, and employees from the Bell operating company of which it is an affiliate;

(4) may not obtain credit under any arrangement that would permit a creditor, upon default, to have recourse to the assets of the Bell operating company; and

(5) shall conduct all transactions with the Bell operating company of which it is an affiliate on an arm's length basis with any such transactions reduced to writing and available for public inspection.

(c) Nondiscrimination Safeguards.--In its dealings with its affiliate described in subsection (a), a Bell operating company--

(1) may not discriminate between that company or affiliate and any other entity in the provision or procurement of goods, services, facilities, and information, or in the establishment of standards; and

(2) shall account for all transactions with an affiliate described in subsection (a) in accordance with accounting principles designated or approved by the Commission.

(d) Biennial Audit.--

(1) General requirement.--A company required to operate a separate affiliate under this section shall obtain and pay for a joint Federal/State audit every 2 years conducted by an independent auditor to determine whether such company has complied with this section and the regulations promulgated under this section, and particularly whether such company has complied with the separate accounting requirements under subsection (b).

(2) Results submitted to commission; state commissions.--The auditor described in paragraph (1) shall submit the results of the audit to the Commission and to the State commission of each State in which the company audited provides service, which shall make such results available for public inspection. Any party may submit comments on the final audit report.

(3) Access to documents.--For purposes of conducting audits and reviews under this subsection--

(A) the independent auditor, the Commission, and the State commission shall have access to the financial accounts and records of each company and of its affiliates necessary to verify transactions conducted with that company that are relevant to the specific activities permitted under this section and that are necessary for the regulation of rates;

(B) the Commission and the State commission shall have access to the working papers and supporting materials of any auditor who performs an audit under this section; and

(C) the State commission shall implement appropriate procedures to ensure the protection of any proprietary information submitted to it under this section.

(e) Fulfillment of Certain Requests.--A Bell operating company and an affiliate that is subject to the requirements of Section 251(c)--

(1) shall fulfill any requests from an unaffiliated entity for telephone exchange service and exchange access within a period no longer than the period in which it provides such telephone exchange service and exchange access to itself or to its affiliates;

(2) shall not provide any facilities, services, or information concerning its provision of exchange access to the affiliate described in subsection (a) unless such facilities, services, or information are made available to other providers of interLATA services in that market on the same terms and conditions;

(3) shall charge the affiliate described in subsection (a), or impute to itself (if using the access for its provision of its own services), an amount for access to its telephone exchange service and exchange access that is no less than the amount charged to any unaffiliated interexchange carriers for such service; and

(4) may provide any interLATA or intraLATA facilities or services to its interLATA affiliate if such services or facilities are made available to all carriers at the same rates and on the same terms and conditions, and so long as the costs are appropriately allocated.

(f) Sunset.--

(1) Manufacturing and long distance.--The provisions of this section (other than subsection (e)) shall cease to apply with respect to the manufacturing activities or the interLATA telecommunications services of a Bell operating company 3 years after the date such Bell operating company or any Bell operating company affiliate is authorized to provide interLATA telecommunications services under Section 271(d), unless the Commission extends such 3-year period by rule or order.

(2) InterLATA information services.--The provisions of this section (other than subsection (e)) shall cease to apply with respect to the interLATA information services of a Bell operating company 4 years after the date of enactment of the Telecommunications Act of 1996, unless the Commission extends such 4-year period by rule or order.

(3) Preservation of existing authority.--Nothing in this subsection shall be construed to limit the authority of the Commission under any other section of this Act to prescribe safeguards consistent with the public interest, convenience, and necessity.

(g) Joint Marketing.--

(1) Affiliate sales of telephone exchange services.--A Bell operating company affiliate required by this section may not market or sell telephone exchange services provided by the Bell operating company unless that company permits other entities offering the same or similar service to market and sell its telephone exchange services.

(2) Bell operating company sales of affiliate services.--A Bell operating company may not market or sell interLATA service provided by an affiliate required by this section within any of its in-region States until such company is authorized to provide interLATA services in such State under Section 271(d).

(3) Rule of construction.--The joint marketing and sale of services permitted under this subsection shall not be considered to violate the nondiscrimination provisions of subsection (c).

(h) Transition.--With respect to any activity in which a Bell operating company is engaged on the date of enactment of the Telecommunications Act of 1996, such company shall have one year from such date of enactment to comply with the requirements of this section.

Section 273 [47 USC Section 273]. Manufacturing by Bell Operating Companies.

(a) Authorization.--A Bell operating company may manufacture and provide telecommunications equipment, and manufacture customer premises equipment, if the Commission authorizes that Bell operating company or any Bell operating company affiliate to provide interLATA services under Section 271(d), subject to the requirements of this section and the regulations prescribed thereunder, except that neither a Bell operating company nor any of its affiliates may engage in such manufacturing in conjunction with a Bell operating company not so affiliated or any of its affiliates.

(b) Collaboration; Research and Royalty Agreements.--

(1) Collaboration.--Subsection (a) shall not prohibit a Bell operating company from engaging in close collaboration with any manufacturer of customer premises equipment or telecommunications equipment during the design and development of hardware, software, or combinations thereof related to such equipment.

(2) Certain research arrangements; royalty agreements.--Subsection (a) shall not prohibit a Bell operating company from--

(A) engaging in research activities related to manufacturing, and

(B) entering into royalty agreements with manufacturers of telecommunications equipment.

(c) Information Requirements.--

(1) Information on protocols and technical requirements.--Each Bell operating company shall, in accordance with regulations prescribed by the Commission, maintain and file with the Commission full and complete information with respect to the protocols and technical requirements for connection with and use of its telephone exchange service facilities. Each such company shall report promptly to the Commission any material changes or planned changes to such protocols and requirements, and the schedule for implementation of such changes or planned changes.

(2) Disclosure of information.--A Bell operating company shall not disclose any information required to be filed under paragraph (1) unless that information has been filed promptly, as required by regulation by the Commission.

(3) Access by competitors to information.--The Commission may prescribe such additional regulations under this subsection as may be necessary to ensure that manufacturers have access to the information with respect to the protocols and technical requirements for connection with and use of telephone exchange service facilities that a Bell operating company makes available to any manufacturing affiliate or any unaffiliated manufacturer.

(4)   Planning information.--Each Bell operating company shall provide, to interconnecting carriers providing telephone exchange service, timely information on the planned deployment of telecommunications equipment.

(d) Manufacturing Limitations for Standard-Setting Organizations.--

(1)   Application to bell communications research or manufacturers.--Bell Communications Research, Inc., or any successor entity or affiliate--

(A) shall not be considered a Bell operating company or a successor or assign of a Bell operating company at such time as it is no longer an affiliate of any Bell operating company; and

(B)   notwithstanding paragraph (3), shall not engage in manufacturing telecommunications equipment or customer premises equipment as long as it is an affiliate of more than 1 otherwise unaffiliated Bell operating company or successor or assign of any such company. Nothing in this subsection prohibits Bell Communications Research, Inc., or any successor entity, from engaging in any activity in which it is lawfully engaged on the date of enactment of the Telecommunications Act of 1996. Nothing provided in this subsection shall render Bell Communications Research, Inc., or any successor entity, a common carrier under title II of this Act. Nothing in this subsection restricts any manufacturer from engaging in any activity in which it is lawfully engaged on the date of enactment of the Telecommunications Act of 1996.

(2)   Proprietary information.--Any entity which establishes standards for telecommunications equipment or customer premises equipment, or generic network requirements for such equipment, or certifies telecommunications equipment or customer premises equipment, shall be prohibited from releasing or otherwise using any proprietary information, designated as such by its owner, in its possession as a result of such activity, for any purpose other than purposes authorized in writing by the owner of such information, even after such entity ceases to be so engaged.

(3)   Manufacturing safeguards.--(A) Except as prohibited in paragraph (1), and subject to paragraph (6), any entity which certifies telecommunications equipment or customer premises equipment manufactured by an unaffiliated entity shall only manufacture a particular class of telecommunications equipment or customer premises equipment for which it is undertaking or has undertaken, during the previous 18 months, certification activity for such class of equipment through a separate affiliate.

(B) Such separate affiliate shall--

(i) maintain books, records, and accounts separate from those of the entity that certifies such equipment, consistent with generally acceptable accounting principles;

(ii) not engage in any joint manufacturing activities with such entity; and

(iii) have segregated facilities and separate employees with such entity.

(C) Such entity that certifies such equipment shall--

(i)   not discriminate in favor of its manufacturing affiliate in the establishment of standards, generic requirements, or product certification;

(ii) not disclose to the manufacturing affiliate any proprietary information that has been received at any time from an unaffiliated manufacturer, unless authorized in writing by the owner of the information; and

(iii) not permit any employee engaged in product certification for telecommunications equipment or customer premises equipment to engage jointly in sales or marketing of any such equipment with the affiliated manufacturer.

(4) Standard-setting entities.--Any entity that is not an accredited standards development organization and that establishes industry-wide standards for telecommunications equipment or customer premises equipment, or industry-wide generic network requirements for such equipment, or that certifies telecommunications equipment or customer premises equipment manufactured by an unaffiliated entity, shall--

(A) establish and publish any industry-wide standard for, industry-wide generic requirement for, or any substantial modification of an existing industry-wide standard or industry-wide generic requirement for, telecommunications equipment or customer premises equipment only in compliance with the following procedure:

(i) such entity shall issue a public notice of its consideration of a proposed industry-wide standard or industry-wide generic requirement;

(ii) such entity shall issue a public invitation to interested industry parties to fund and participate in such efforts on a reasonable and nondiscriminatory basis, administered in such a manner as not to unreasonably exclude any interested industry party;

(iii) such entity shall publish a text for comment by such parties as have agreed to participate in the process pursuant to clause (ii), provide such parties a full opportunity to submit comments, and respond to comments from such parties;

(iv) such entity shall publish a final text of the industry-wide standard or industry-wide generic requirement, including the comments in their entirety, of any funding party which requests to have its comments so published; and

(v) such entity shall attempt, prior to publishing a text for comment, to agree with the funding parties as a group on a mutually satisfactory dispute resolution process which such parties shall utilize as their sole recourse in the event of a dispute on technical issues as to which there is disagreement between any funding party and the entity conducting such activities, except that if no dispute resolution process is agreed to by all the parties, a funding party may utilize the dispute resolution procedures established pursuant to paragraph (5) of this subsection;

(B) engage in product certification for telecommunications equipment or customer premises equipment manufactured by unaffiliated entities only if--

(i) such activity is performed pursuant to published criteria;

(ii) such activity is performed pursuant to auditable criteria; and

(iii) such activity is performed pursuant to available industry-accepted testing methods and standards, where applicable, unless otherwise agreed upon by the parties funding and performing such activity;

(C) not undertake any actions to monopolize or attempt to monopolize the market for such services; and

(D) not preferentially treat its own telecommunications equipment or customer premises equipment, or that of its affiliate, over that of any other entity in establishing and publishing industry-wide standards or industry wide generic requirements for, and in certification of, telecommunications equipment and customer premises equipment.

401

(5) Alternate dispute resolution.--Within 90 days after the date of enactment of the Telecommunications Act of 1996, the Commission shall prescribe a dispute resolution process to be utilized in the event that a dispute resolution process is not agreed upon by all the parties when establishing and publishing any industry-wide standard or industry-wide generic requirement for telecommunications equipment or customer premises equipment, pursuant to paragraph (4)(A)(v). The Commission shall not establish itself as a party to the dispute resolution process. Such dispute resolution process shall permit any funding party to resolve a dispute with the entity conducting the activity that significantly affects such funding party's interests, in an open, nondiscriminatory, and unbiased fashion, within 30 days after the filing of such dispute. Such disputes may be filed within 15 days after the date the funding party receives a response to its comments from the entity conducting the activity. The Commission shall establish penalties to be assessed for delays caused by referral of frivolous disputes to the dispute resolution process.

(6) Sunset.--The requirements of paragraphs (3) and (4) shall terminate for the particular relevant activity when the Commission determines that there are alternative sources of industry-wide standards, industry-wide generic requirements, or product certification for a particular class of telecommunications equipment or customer premises equipment available in the United States. Alternative sources shall be deemed to exist when such sources provide commercially viable alternatives that are providing such services to customers. The Commission shall act on any application for such a determination within 90 days after receipt of such application, and shall receive public comment on such application.

(7) Administration and enforcement authority.--For the purposes of administering this subsection and the regulations prescribed thereunder, the Commission shall have the same remedial authority as the Commission has in administering and enforcing the provisions of this title with respect to any common carrier subject to this Act.

(8) Definitions.--For purposes of this subsection:

(A) The term "affiliate" shall have the same meaning as in Section 3 of this Act, except that, for purposes of paragraph (1)(B)--

(i) an aggregate voting equity interest in Bell Communications Research, Inc., of at least 5 percent of its total voting equity, owned directly or indirectly by more than 1 otherwise unaffiliated Bell operating company, shall constitute an affiliate relationship; and

(ii) a voting equity interest in Bell Communications Research, Inc., by any otherwise unaffiliated Bell operating company of less than 1 percent of Bell Communications Research's total voting equity shall not be considered to be an equity interest under this paragraph.

(B) The term "generic requirement" means a description of acceptable product attributes for use by local exchange carriers in establishing product specifications for the purchase of telecommunications equipment, customer premises equipment, and software integral thereto.

(C) The term "industry-wide" means activities funded by or performed on behalf of local exchange carriers for use in providing wireline telephone exchange service whose combined total of deployed access lines in the United States constitutes at least 30 percent of all access lines deployed by telecommunications carriers in the United States as of the date of enactment of the Telecommunications Act of 1996.

(D) The term "certification" means any technical process whereby a party determines whether a product, for use by more than one local exchange carrier, conforms with the specified requirements pertaining to such product.

(E) The term "accredited standards development organization" means an entity composed of industry members which has been accredited by an institution vested with the responsibility for standards accreditation by the industry.

(e) Bell Operating Company Equipment Procurement and Sales.--

(1) Nondiscrimination standards for manufacturing.--In the procurement or awarding of supply contracts for telecommunications equipment, a Bell operating company, or any entity acting on its behalf, for the duration of the requirement for a separate subsidiary including manufacturing under this Act--

(A) shall consider such equipment, produced or supplied by unrelated persons; and

(B) may not discriminate in favor of equipment produced or supplied by an affiliate or related person.

(2) Procurement standards.--Each Bell operating company or any entity acting on its behalf shall make procurement decisions and award all supply contracts for equipment, services, and software on the basis of an objective assessment of price, qualify, delivery, and other commercial factors.

(3) Network planning and design.--A Bell operating company shall, to the extent consistent with the antitrust laws, engage in joint network planning and design with local exchange carriers operating in the same area of interest. No participant in such planning shall be allowed to delay the introduction of new technology or the deployment of facilities to provide telecommunications services, and agreement with such other carriers shall not be required as a prerequisite for such introduction or deployment.

(4) Sales restrictions.--Neither a Bell operating company engaged in manufacturing nor a manufacturing affiliate of such a company shall restrict sales to any local exchange carrier of telecommunications equipment, including software integral to the operation of such equipment and related upgrades.

(5) Protection of proprietary information.--A Bell operating company and any entity it owns or otherwise controls shall protect the proprietary information submitted for procurement decisions from release not specifically authorized by the owner of such information.

(f) Administration and Enforcement Authority.--For the purposes of administering and enforcing the provisions of this section and the regulations prescribed thereunder, the Commission shall have the same authority, power, and functions with respect to any Bell operating company or any affiliate thereof as the Commission has in administering and enforcing the provisions of this title with respect to any common carrier subject to this Act.

(g) Additional Rules and Regulations.--The Commission may prescribe such additional rules and regulations as the Commission determines are necessary to carry out the provisions of this section, and otherwise to prevent discrimination and cross-subsidization in a Bell operating company's dealings with its affiliate and with third parties.

(h) Definition.--As used in this section, the term "manufacturing" has the same meaning as such term has under the AT&T Consent Decree.

Section 274 [47 USC Section 274]. Electronic Publishing by Bell Operating Companies.

(a) Limitations.--No Bell operating company or any affiliate may engage in the provision of electronic publishing that is disseminated by means of such Bell operating company's or any of its affiliates' basic telephone service, except that nothing in this section shall prohibit a separated affiliate or electronic publishing joint venture operated in accordance with this section from engaging in the provision of electronic publishing.

(b) Separated Affiliate or Electronic Publishing Joint Venture Requirements.--A separated affiliate or electronic publishing joint venture shall be operated independently from the Bell operating company. Such separated affiliate or joint venture and the Bell operating company with which it is affiliated shall--

(1) maintain separate books, records, and accounts and prepare separate financial statements;

(2) not incur debt in a manner that would permit a creditor of the separated affiliate or joint venture upon default to have recourse to the assets of the Bell operating company;

(3) carry out transactions (A) in a manner consistent with such independence, (B) pursuant to written contracts or tariffs that are filed with the Commission and made publicly available, and (C) in a manner that is auditable in accordance with generally accepted auditing standards;

(4) value any assets that are transferred directly or indirectly from the Bell operating company to a separated affiliate or joint venture, and record any transactions by which such assets are transferred, in accordance with such regulations as may be prescribed by the Commission or a State commission to prevent improper cross subsidies;

(5) between a separated affiliate and a Bell operating company--

(A) have no officers, directors, and employees in common after the effective date of this section; and

(B) own no property in common;

(6) not use for the marketing of any product or service of the separated affiliate or joint venture, the name, trademarks, or service marks of an existing Bell operating company except for names, trademarks, or service marks that are owned by the entity that owns or controls the Bell operating company;

(7) not permit the Bell operating company--

(A) to perform hiring or training of personnel on behalf of a separated affiliate;

(B) to perform the purchasing, installation, or maintenance of equipment on behalf of a separated affiliate, except for telephone service that it provides under tariff or contract subject to the provisions of this section; or

(C) to perform research and development on behalf of a separated affiliate;

(8) each have performed annually a compliance review--

(A) that is conducted by an independent entity for the purpose of determining compliance during the preceding calendar year with any provision of this section; and

(B) the results of which are maintained by the separated affiliate or joint venture and the Bell operating company for a period of 5 years subject to review by any lawful authority; and

(9) within 90 days of receiving a review described in paragraph (8), file a report of any exceptions and corrective action with the Commission and allow any person to inspect and copy such report subject to reasonable safeguards to protect any proprietary information contained in such report from being used for purposes other than to enforce or pursue remedies under this section.

(c) Joint Marketing.--

(1) In general.--Except as provided in paragraph (2)--

(A) a Bell operating company shall not carry out any promotion, marketing, sales, or advertising for or in conjunction with a separated affiliate; and

(B) a Bell operating company shall not carry out any promotion, marketing, sales, or advertising for or in conjunction with an affiliate that is related to the provision of electronic publishing.

(2) Permissible joint activities.--

(A) Joint telemarketing.--A Bell operating company may provide inbound telemarketing or referral services related to the provision of electronic publishing for a separated affiliate, electronic publishing joint venture, affiliate, or unaffiliated electronic publisher, provided that if such services are provided to a separated affiliate, electronic publishing joint venture, or affiliate, such services shall be made available to all electronic publishers on request, on nondiscriminatory terms.

(B) Teaming arrangements.--A Bell operating company may engage in nondiscriminatory teaming or business arrangements to engage in electronic publishing with any separated affiliate or with any other electronic publisher if (i) the Bell operating company only provides facilities, services, and basic telephone service information as authorized by this section, and (ii) the Bell operating company does not own such teaming or business arrangement.

(C) Electronic publishing joint ventures.--A Bell operating company or affiliate may participate on a nonexclusive basis in electronic publishing joint ventures with entities that are not a Bell operating company, affiliate, or separated affiliate to provide electronic publishing services, if the Bell operating company or affiliate has not more than a 50 percent direct or indirect equity interest (or the equivalent thereof) or the right to more than 50 percent of the gross revenues under a revenue sharing or royalty agreement in any electronic publishing joint venture. Officers and employees of a Bell operating company or affiliate participating in an electronic publishing joint venture may not have more than 50 percent of the voting control over the electronic publishing joint venture. In the case of joint ventures with small, local electronic publishers, the Commission for good cause shown may authorize the Bell operating company or affiliate to have a larger equity interest, revenue share, or voting control but not to exceed 80 percent. A Bell operating company participating in an electronic publishing joint venture may provide promotion, marketing, sales, or advertising personnel and services to such joint venture.

(d) Bell Operating Company Requirement.--A Bell operating company under common ownership or control with a separated affiliate or electronic publishing joint venture shall provide network access and interconnections for basic telephone service to electronic publishers at just and reasonable rates that are tariffed (so long as rates for such services are subject to regulation) and that are not higher on a per-unit basis than those charged for such services to any other electronic publisher or any separated affiliate engaged in electronic publishing.

(e) Private Right of Action.--

(1) Damages.--Any person claiming that any act or practice of any Bell operating company, affiliate, or separated affiliate constitutes a violation of this section may file a complaint with the Commission or bring suit as provided in Section 207 of this Act, and such Bell operating company, affiliate, or separated affiliate shall be liable as provided in Section 206 of this Act; except that damages may not be awarded for a violation that is discovered by a compliance review as required by subsection (b)(7) of this section and corrected within 90 days.

(2) Cease and desist orders.--In addition to the provisions of paragraph (1), any person claiming that any act or practice of any Bell operating company, affiliate, or separated affiliate constitutes a violation of this section may make application to the Commission for an order to cease and desist such violation or may make application in any district court of the United States of competent jurisdiction for an order enjoining such acts or practices or for an order compelling compliance with such requirement.

(f) Separated Affiliate Reporting Requirement.--Any separated affiliate under this section shall file with the Commission annual reports in a form substantially equivalent to the Form 10-K required by regulations of the Securities and Exchange Commission.

(g) Effective Dates.--

(1) Transition.--Any electronic publishing service being offered to the public by a Bell operating company or affiliate on the date of enactment of the Telecommunications Act of 1996 shall have one year from such date of enactment to comply with the requirements of this section.

(2) Sunset.--The provisions of this section shall not apply to conduct occurring after 4 years after the date of enactment of the Telecommunications Act of 1996.

(h) Definition of Electronic Publishing.--

(1) In general.--The term "electronic publishing" means the dissemination, provision, publication, or sale to an unaffiliated entity or person, of any one or more of the following: news (including sports); entertainment (other than interactive games); business, financial, legal, consumer, or credit materials; editorials, columns, or features; advertising; photos or images; archival or research material; legal notices or public records; scientific, educational, instructional, technical, professional, trade, or other literary materials; or other like or similar information.

(2) Exceptions.--The term "electronic publishing" shall not include the following services:

(A) Information access, as that term is defined by the AT&T Consent Decree.

(B) The transmission of information as a common carrier.

(C) The transmission of information as part of a gateway to an information service that does not involve the generation or alteration of the content of information, including data transmission, address translation, protocol conversion, billing management, introductory information content, and navigational systems that enable users to access electronic publishing services, which do not affect the presentation of such electronic publishing services to users.

(D) Voice storage and retrieval services, including voice messaging and electronic mail services.

(E) Data processing or transaction processing services that do not involve the generation or alteration of the content of information.

(F) Electronic billing or advertising of a Bell operating company's regulated telecommunications services.

(G) Language translation or data format conversion.

(H) The provision of information necessary for the management, control, or operation of a telephone company telecommunications system.

(I) The provision of directory assistance that provides names, addresses, and telephone numbers and does not include advertising.

(J) Caller identification services.

(K) Repair and provisioning databases and credit card and billing validation for telephone company operations.

(L) 911-E and other emergency assistance databases.

(M) Any other network service of a type that is like or similar to these network services and that does not involve the generation or alteration of the content of information.

(N) Any upgrades to these network services that do not involve the generation or alteration of the content of information.

(O) Video programming or full motion video entertainment on demand.

(i) Additional Definitions.--As used in this section--

(1) The term "affiliate" means any entity that, directly or indirectly, owns or controls, is owned or controlled by, or is under common ownership or control with, a Bell operating company. Such term shall not include a separated affiliate.

(2) The term "basic telephone service" means any wireline telephone exchange service, or wireline telephone exchange service facility, provided by a Bell operating company in a telephone exchange area, except that such term does not include--

(A) a competitive wireline telephone exchange service provided in a telephone exchange area where another entity provides a wireline telephone exchange service that was provided on January 1, 1984, or

(B) a commercial mobile service.

(3) The term "basic telephone service information" means network and customer information of a Bell operating company and other information acquired by a Bell operating company as a result of its engaging in the provision of basic telephone service.

(4) The term "control" has the meaning that it has in 17 CFR §240.12b-2, the regulations promulgated by the Securities and Exchange Commission pursuant to the Securities Exchange Act of 1934 (15 USC 78a et seq.) or any successor provision to such section.

(5) The term "electronic publishing joint venture" means a joint venture owned by a Bell operating company or affiliate that engages in the provision of electronic publishing which is disseminated by means of such Bell operating company's or any of its affiliates' basic telephone service.

(6) The term "entity" means any organization, and includes corporations, partnerships, sole proprietorships, associations, and joint ventures.

(7) The term "inbound telemarketing" means the marketing of property, goods, or services by telephone to a customer or potential customer who initiated the call.

(8) The term "own" with respect to an entity means to have a direct or indirect equity interest (or the equivalent thereof) of more than 10 percent of an entity, or the right to more than 10 percent of the gross revenues of an entity under a revenue sharing or royalty agreement.

(9) The term "separated affiliate" means a corporation under common ownership or control with a Bell operating company that does not own or control a Bell operating company and is not owned or controlled by a Bell operating company and that engages in the provision of

electronic publishing which is disseminated by means of such Bell operating company's or any of its affiliates' basic telephone service.

(10) The term "Bell operating company" has the meaning provided in Section 3, except that such term includes any entity or corporation that is owned or controlled by such a company (as so defined) but does not include an electronic publishing joint venture owned by such an entity or corporation.

Section 275 [47 USC Section 275]. Alarm Monitoring Services.

(a) Delayed Entry Into Alarm Monitoring.--

(1) Prohibition.--No Bell operating company or affiliate thereof shall engage in the provision of alarm monitoring services before the date which is 5 years after the date of enactment of the Telecommunications Act of 1996.

(2) Existing activities.--Paragraph (1) does not prohibit or limit the provision, directly or through an affiliate, of alarm monitoring services by a Bell operating company that was engaged in providing alarm monitoring services as of November 30, 1995, directly or through an affiliate. Such Bell operating company or affiliate may not acquire any equity interest in, or obtain financial control of, any unaffiliated alarm monitoring service entity after November 30, 1995, and until 5 years after the date of enactment of the Telecommunications Act of 1996, except that this sentence shall not prohibit an exchange of customers for the customers of an unaffiliated alarm monitoring service entity.

(b) Nondiscrimination.--An incumbent local exchange carrier (as defined in Section 251(h)) engaged in the provision of alarm monitoring services shall--

(1) provide nonaffiliated entities, upon reasonable request, with the network services it provides to its own alarm monitoring operations, on nondiscriminatory terms and conditions; and

(2) not subsidize its alarm monitoring services either directly or indirectly from telephone exchange service operations.

(c) Expedited Consideration of Complaints.--The Commission shall establish procedures for the receipt and review of complaints concerning violations of subsection (b) or the regulations thereunder that result in material financial harm to a provider of alarm monitoring service. Such procedures shall ensure that the Commission will make a final determination with respect to any such complaint within 120 days after receipt of the complaint. If the complaint contains an appropriate showing that the alleged violation occurred, as determined by the Commission in accordance with such regulations, the Commission shall, within 60 days after receipt of the complaint, order the incumbent local exchange carrier (as defined in Section 251(h)) and its affiliates to cease engaging in such violation pending such final determination.

(d) Use of Data.--A local exchange carrier may not record or use in any fashion the occurrence or contents of calls received by providers of alarm monitoring services for the purposes of marketing such services on behalf of such local exchange carrier, or any other entity. Any regulations necessary to enforce this subsection shall be issued initially within 6 months after the date of enactment of the Telecommunications Act of 1996.

(e) Definition of Alarm Monitoring service.--The term "alarm monitoring service" means a service that uses a device located at a residence, place of business, or other fixed premises--

(1) to receive signals from other devices located at or about such premises regarding a possible threat at such premises to life, safety, or property, from burglary, fire, vandalism, bodily injury, or other emergency, and

(2) to transmit a signal regarding such threat by means of transmission facilities of a local exchange carrier or one of its affiliates to a remote monitoring center to alert a person at such center of the need to inform the customer or another person or police, fire, rescue, security, or public safety personnel of such threat, but does not include a service that uses a medical monitoring device attached to an individual for the automatic surveillance of an ongoing medical condition.

Section 276 [47 USC Section 276]. Provision of Payphone Service.

(a) Nondiscrimination Safeguards.–After the effective date of the rules prescribed pursuant to subsection (b), any Bell operating company that provides payphone service--

(1) shall not subsidize its payphone service directly or indirectly from its telephone exchange service operations or its exchange access operations; and

(2) shall not prefer or discriminate in favor of its payphone service.

(b) Regulations.--

(1) Contents of regulations.–In order to promote competition among payphone service providers and promote the widespread deployment of payphone services to the benefit of the general public, within 9 months after the date of enactment of the Telecommunications Act of 1996, the Commission shall take all actions necessary (including any reconsideration) to prescribe regulations that--

(A) establish a per call compensation plan to ensure that all payphone service providers are fairly compensated for each and every completed intrastate and interstate call using their payphone, except that emergency calls and telecommunications relay service calls for hearing disabled individuals shall not be subject to such compensation;

(B) discontinue the intrastate and interstate carrier access charge payphone service elements and payments in effect on such date of enactment, and all intrastate and interstate payphone subsidies from basic exchange and exchange access revenues, in favor of a compensation plan as specified in subparagraph (A);

(C) prescribe a set of nonstructural safeguards for Bell operating company payphone service to implement the provisions of paragraphs (1) and (2) of subsection (a), which safeguards shall, at a minimum, include the nonstructural safeguards equal to those adopted in the Computer Inquiry-III (CC Docket No. 90-623) proceeding;

(D) provide for Bell operating company payphone service providers to have the same right that independent payphone providers have to negotiate with the location provider on the location provider's selecting and contracting with, and, subject to the terms of any agreement with the location provider, to select and contract with, the carriers that carry interLATA calls from their payphones, unless the Commission determines in the rulemaking pursuant to this section that it is not in the public interest; and

(E) provide for all payphone service providers to have the right to negotiate with the location provider on the location provider's selecting and contracting with, and, subject to the terms of any agreement with the location provider, to select and contract with, the carriers that carry intraLATA calls from their payphones.

(2) Public interest telephones.--In the rulemaking conducted pursuant to paragraph (1), the Commission shall determine whether public interest payphones, which are provided in the interest of public health, safety, and welfare, in locations where there would otherwise not be a payphone, should be maintained, and if so, ensure that such public interest payphones are supported fairly and equitably.

(3) Existing contracts.--Nothing in this section shall affect any existing contracts between location providers and payphone service providers or interLATA or intraLATA carriers that are in force and effect as of the date of enactment of the Telecommunications Act of 1996.

(c) State Preemption.--To the extent that any State requirements are inconsistent with the Commission's regulations, the Commission's regulations on such matters shall preempt such State requirements.

(d) Definition.--As used in this section, the term "payphone service" means the provision of public or semi-public pay telephones, the provision of inmate telephone service in correctional institutions, and any ancillary services.

TITLE III - PROVISIONS RELATING TO RADIO

Part I - General Provisions

Section 301 [47 USC Section 301]. License for Radio Communication or Transmission of Energy

It is the purpose of this Act, among other things, to maintain the control of the United States over all the channels of radio transmission; and to provide for the use of such channels, but not the ownership thereof, by persons for limited periods of time, under licenses granted by Federal authority, and no such license shall be construed to create any right, beyond the terms, conditions, and periods of the license. No person shall use or operate any apparatus for the transmission of energy or communications or signals by radio (a) from one place in any State, territory, or possession of the United States or in the District of Columbia to another place in the same State, territory, possession, or district; or (b) from any State, territory, or possession of the United States, or from the District of Columbia to any other State, territory, or possession of the United States; or (c) from any place in any State, territory, or possession of the United States, or in the District of Columbia, to any place in any foreign country or to any vessel; or (d) within any State when the effects of such use extend beyond the borders of said State, or when interference is caused by such use or operation with the transmission of such energy, communications, or signals from within said State to any place beyond its borders, or from any place beyond its borders to any place within said State, or with the transmission or reception of such energy, communications, or signals from and/or to places beyond the borders of said State; or (e) upon any vessel or aircraft of the United States (except as provided in Section 303(t)); or (f) upon any other mobile stations within the jurisdiction of the United States, except under and in accordance with this Act and with a license in that behalf granted under the provisions of this Act.

Section 302 [47 USC Section 302]. Devices which Interfere with Radio Reception.

(a) The Commission may, consistent with the public interest, convenience, and necessity, make reasonable regulations (1) governing the interference potential of devices which in their operation are capable of emitting radio frequency energy by radiation, conduction, or other means in sufficient degree to cause harmful interference to radio communications; and (2) establishing minimum performance standards for home electronic equipment and systems to reduce their susceptibility to interference from radio frequency energy. Such regulations shall be applicable to the manufacture, import, sale, offer for sale or shipment of such devices and home electronic equipment and systems, and to the use of such devices.

(b) No person shall manufacture, import, sell, offer for sale, or ship devices or home electronic equipment and systems, or use devices which fail to comply with regulations promulgated pursuant to this section.

(c) The provisions of this section shall not be applicable to carriers transporting such devices or home electronic equipment and systems without trading in them, to devices or home electronic equipment and systems manufactured solely for export, to the manufacture, assembly, or installation of devices or home electronic equipment and systems for its own use by a public utility engaged in providing electric service, or to devices or home electronic equipment and systems for use by the Government of the United States or any agency thereof. Devices and home electronic equipment and systems for use by the Government of the United States or any agency thereof shall be developed, procured, or otherwise acquired, including offshore procurement, under United States Government criteria, standards, or specifications designed to achieve the objectives of reducing interference to radio reception and to home electronic equipment and systems, taking into account the unique needs of a national defense and security.

(d)(1) Within 180 days after the date of enactment of this subsection, the Commission shall prescribe and make effective regulations denying equipment authorization (under Part 15 of title 47, Code of Federal Regulations, or any other part of that title) for any scanning receiver that is capable of --

(A) receiving transmissions in the frequencies allocated to the domestic cellular radio telecommunications service,

(B) readily being altered by the user to receive transmissions in such frequencies, or

(C) being equipped with decoders that convert digital cellular transmissions to analog voice audio.

(2) Beginning 1 year after the effective date of the regulations adopted pursuant to paragraph (1), no receiver having the capabilities described in subparagraph (A), (B), or (c) of paragraph (1), as such capabilities are defined in such regulations, shall be manufactured in the United States or imported for use in the United States.

(e) The Commission may--(1) authorize the use of private organizations for testing and certifying the compliance of devices or home electronic equipment and systems with regulations promulgated under this section;

(2) accept as prima facie evidence of such compliance the certification by any such organization; and

(3) establish such qualifications and standards as it deems appropriate for such private organizations, testing, and certification.

Section 303 [47 USC Section 303]. General Powers of Commission.

Except as otherwise provided in this Act, the Commission from time to time, as public convenience, interest, or necessity requires, shall --

(a) Classify radio stations;

(b) Prescribe the nature of the service to be rendered by each class of licensed stations and each station within any class;

(c) Assign bands of frequencies to the various classes of stations; and assign frequencies for each individual station and determine the power which each station shall use and the time during which it may operate;

(d) Determine the location of classes of stations or individual stations;

(e) Regulate the kind of apparatus to be used with respect to its external effects and the purity and sharpness of the emissions from each station and from the apparatus therein;

(f) Make such regulations not inconsistent with law as it may deem necessary to prevent interference between stations and to carry out the provisions of this Act: Provided, however, that changes in the frequencies, authorized power, or in the times of operation of any station, shall not be made without the consent of the station licensee unless~~, after a public hearing,~~ the Commission shall determine that such changes will promote public convenience or interest or will serve public necessity, or the provisions of this Act will be more fully complied with;

(g) Study new uses for radio, provide for experimental uses of frequencies, and generally encourage the larger and more effective use of radio in the public interest;

(h) Have authority to establish areas or zones to be served by any station;

(i) Have authority to make special regulations applicable to radio stations engaged in chain broadcasting;

(j) Have authority to make general rules and regulations requiring stations to keep such records of programs, transmissions of energy, communications, or signals as it may deem desirable;

(k) Have authority to exclude from the requirements of any regulations in whole or in part any radio station upon railroad rolling stock, or to modify such regulations in its discretion;

(l)(1) Have authority to prescribe the qualifications of station operators, to classify them according to the duties to be performed, to fix the forms of such licenses, and to issue them to persons who are found to be qualified by the Commission and who otherwise are legally eligible for employment in the United States, except that such requirement relating to eligibility for employment in the United States shall not apply in the case of licenses issued by the Commission to (A) persons holding United States pilot certificates; or (B) persons holding foreign aircraft pilot certificates which are valid in the United States, if the foreign government involved has entered into a reciprocal agreement under which such foreign government does not impose any similar requirement relating to eligibility for employment upon citizens of the United States.

(2) Notwithstanding paragraph (1) of this subsection, an individual to whom a radio station is licensed under the provisions of this Act may be issued an operator's license to operate that station.

(3) In addition to amateur operator licenses which the Commission may issue to aliens pursuant to paragraph (2) of this subsection, and notwithstanding Section 301 of this Act and paragraph (1) of this subsection, the Commission may issue authorizations, under such conditions and terms as it may prescribe, to permit an alien licensed by his government as an amateur radio operator to operate his amateur radio station licensed by his government in the United States, its possessions, and the

412

Commonwealth of Puerto Rico provided there is in effect a multilateral or bilateral agreement, to which the United States and the alien's government are parties, for such operation on a reciprocal basis by United States amateur radio operators. Other provisions of this Act and of the Administrative Procedure Act shall not be applicable to any request or application for or modification, suspension, or cancellation of any such authorization.

(m)(1) Have authority to suspend the license of any operator upon proof sufficient to satisfy the Commission that the licensee --

(A) Has violated, or caused, aided or abetted the violation of, any provision of the Act, treaty or convention binding on the United States, which the Commission is authorized to administer, or by regulation made by the Commission under any such Act, treaty, or convention; or

(B) Has failed to carry out a lawful order of the master or person lawfully in charge of the ship or aircraft on which he is employed; or

(C) Has willfully damaged or permitted radio apparatus or installations to be damaged; or

(D) Has transmitted superfluous radio communications or signals or communications containing profane or obscene words, language or meaning, or has knowingly transmitted --

(1) False or deceptive signals or communications, or

(2) A call signal or letter which has not been assigned by proper authority to the station he is operating; or

(E) Has willfully or maliciously interfered with any other radio communications or signals; or

(F) Has obtained or attempted to obtain, or has assisted another to obtain or attempt to obtain, an operator's license by fraudulent means.

(2) No order of suspension of any operator's license shall take effect until fifteen days' notice in writing thereof, stating the cause for the proposed suspension, has been given to the operator licensee who may make written application to the Commission at any time within said fifteen days for a hearing upon such order. The notice to the operator licensee shall not be effective until actually received by him and from that time he shall have fifteen days in which to mail the said application. In the event that physical conditions prevent mailing of the application at the expiration of the fifteen-day period, the application shall then be mailed as soon as possible thereafter, accompanied by a satisfactory explanation of the delay. Upon receipt by the Commission of such application for hearing, said order of suspension shall be held in abeyance until the conclusion of the hearing, which shall be conducted under such rules as the Commission may prescribe. Upon the conclusion of said hearing the Commission may affirm, modify, or revoke said order of suspension.

(n) Have authority to inspect all radio installations associated with stations required to be licensed by any Act, or which the Commission by rule has authorized to operate without a license under Section 307(e)(1), or which are subject to the provisions of any Act, treaty, or convention binding on the United States, to ascertain whether in construction, installation, and operation they conform to the requirements of the rules and regulations of the Commission, the provisions of any Act, the terms of any treaty or convention binding on the United States, and the conditions of the license or other instrument of authorization under which they are constructed, installed, or operated;

(o) Have authority to designate call letters of all stations;

413

(p) Have authority to cause to be published such call letters and such other announcements and data as in the judgment of the Commission may be required for the efficient operation of radio stations subject to the jurisdiction of the United States and for the proper enforcement of this Act;

(q) Have authority to require the painting and/or illumination of radio towers if and when in its judgment such towers constitute, or there is a reasonable possibility that they may constitute, a menace to air navigation. The permittee or licensee, and the tower owner in any case in which the owner is not the permittee or licensee, shall maintain the painting and/or illumination of the tower as prescribed by the Commission pursuant to this section. In the event that the tower ceases to be licensed by the Commission for the transmission of radio energy, the owner of the tower shall maintain the prescribed painting and/or illumination of such tower until it is dismantled, and the Commission may require the owner to dismantle and remove the tower when the Administrator of the Federal Aviation Agency determines that there is a reasonable possibility that it may constitute a menace to air navigation;

(r) Make such rules and regulations and prescribe such restrictions and conditions, not inconsistent with law, as may be necessary to carry out the provisions of this Act, or any international radio or wire communications treaty or convention, or regulations annexed thereto, including any treaty or convention insofar as it relates to the use of radio, to which the United States is or may hereafter become a party;

(s) Have authority to require that apparatus designed to receive television pictures broadcast simultaneously with sound be capable of adequately receiving all frequencies allocated by the Commission to television broadcasting when such apparatus is shipped in interstate commerce, or is imported from any foreign country into the United States, for sale or resale to the public.

(t) Notwithstanding the provisions of Section 301(e), have authority, in any case in which an aircraft registered in the United States is operated (pursuant to a lease, charter, or similar arrangement) by an aircraft operator who is subject to regulation by the government of a foreign nation, to enter into an agreement with such government under which the Commission shall recognize and accept any radio station licenses and radio operator licenses issued by such government with respect to such aircraft.

(u) Require that apparatus designed to receive television pictures broadcast simultaneously with sound be equipped with built-in decoder circuitry designed to display closed-captioned television transmissions when such apparatus is manufactured in the United States or imported for use in the United States, and its television picture screen is 13 inches or greater in size.

(v) Have exclusive jurisdiction to regulate the provision of direct-to home satellite services. As used in this subsection, the term "direct-to-home satellite services" means the distribution or broadcasting of programming or services by satellite directly to the subscriber's premises without the use of ground receiving or distribution equipment, except at the subscriber's premises or in the uplink process to the satellite.

(w) Prescribe--

(1) on the basis of recommendations from an advisory committee established by the Commission in accordance with Section 551(b)(2) of the Telecommunications Act of 1996, guidelines and recommended procedures for the identification and rating of video programming that contains sexual, violent, or other indecent material about which parents should be informed before it is displayed to children, provided that nothing in this paragraph shall be construed to authorize any rating of video programming on the basis of its political or religious content; and

(2) with respect to any video programming that has been rated, and in consultation with the television industry, rules requiring distributors of such video programming to transmit

<u>such rating to permit parents to block the display of video programming that they have determined is inappropriate for their children.</u>

<u>(x) Require, in the case of an apparatus designed to receive television signals that are shipped in interstate commerce or manufactured in the United States and that have a picture screen 13 inches or greater in size (measured diagonally), that such apparatus be equipped with a feature designed to enable viewers to block display of all programs with a common rating, except as otherwise permitted by regulations pursuant to Section 330(c)(4).</u>

Section 303a [47 USC Section 303a]. Standards for Children's Television Programming.

(a) The Commission shall, within 30 days after the date of enactment of this Act [enacted Oct. 18, 1990], initiate a rulemaking proceeding to prescribe standards applicable to commercial television broadcast licensees with respect to the time devoted to commercial matter in conjunction with children's television programming. The Commission shall, within 180 days after the date of enactment [enacted Oct. 18, 1990], complete the rulemaking proceeding and prescribe final standards that meet the requirements of subsection (b).

(b) Except as provided in subsection (c), the standards prescribed under subsection (a) shall include the requirement that each commercial television broadcast licensee shall limit the duration of advertising in children's television programming to not more than 10.5 minutes per hour on weekends and not more than 12 minutes per hour on weekdays.

(c) After January 1, 1993, the Commission --

(1) May review and evaluate the advertising duration limitations required by subsection (b); and

(2) May, after notice and public comment and a demonstration of the need for modification of such limitations, modify such limitations in accordance with the public interest.

(d) As used in this section, the term "commercial television broadcast licensee" includes a cable operator, as defined in section 602 of the Communications Act of 1934 (47 USC 522).

Section 303b [47 USC Section 303b]. Consideration of Children's Television Service in Broadcast License Renewal.

(a) After the standards required by section 102 <~~[47 USCS §303a]~~> are in effect, the Commission shall, in its review of any application for renewal of a commercial or noncommercial television broadcast license, consider the extent to which the licensee --

(1) Has complied with such standards; and

(2) Has served the educational and informational needs of children through the licensee's overall programming, including programming specifically designed to serve such needs.

(b) In addition to consideration of the licensee's programming as required under subsection (a), the Commission may consider --

(1) Any special nonbroadcast efforts by the licensee which enhance the educational and informational value of such programming to children; and

(2) Any special efforts by the licensee to produce or support programming broadcast by another station in the licensee's marketplace which is specifically designed to serve the educational and informational needs of children.

Section 303c [47 USC Section 303c]. Television Program Improvement.

(a) Short title. This section may be cited as the "Television Program Improvement Act of 1990."

(b) Definitions. For purposes of this section --

(1) The term "antitrust laws" has the meaning given it in subsection (a) of the first section of the Clayton Act (15 USC <§12(a)), except that such term includes section 5 of the Federal Trade Commission Act (15 USC §45) to the extent that such section 5 applies to unfair methods of competition;

(2) The term "person in the television industry" means a television network, any entity which produces programming (including theatrical motion pictures) for telecasting or telecasts programming, the National Cable Television Association, the Association of Independent Television Stations, Incorporated, the National Association of Broadcasters, the Motion Picture Association of America, the Community Antenna Television Association, and each of the networks' affiliate organizations, and shall include any individual acting on behalf of such person; and

(3) The term "telecast" means --

(A) To broadcast by a television broadcast station; or

(B) To transmit by a cable television system or a satellite television distribution service.

(c) Exemption. The antitrust laws shall not apply to any joint discussion, consideration, review, action or agreement by or among persons in the television industry for the purpose of, and limited to, developing and disseminating voluntary guidelines designed to alleviate the negative impact of violence in telecast material.

(d) Limitations. (1) The exemption provided in subsection (c) shall not apply to any joint discussion, consideration, review, action or agreement which results in a boycott of any person.

(2) The exemption provided in subsection (c) shall apply only to any joint discussion, consideration, review, action or agreement engaged in only during the 3-year period beginning on the date of the enactment of this section.

Section 304 [47 USC Section 304]. Waiver by Licensee.

No station license shall be granted by the Commission until the applicant therefor shall have waived any claim to the use of any particular frequency or of the electromagnetic spectrum as against the regulatory power of the United States because of the previous use of the same, whether by license or otherwise.

Section 305 [47 USC Section 305]. Government-Owned Stations.

(a) Radio stations belonging to and operated by the United States shall not be subject to the provisions of Sections 301 and 303 of this Act. All such government stations shall use such frequencies as shall be assigned to each or to each class by the President. All such stations, except stations on board naval and other government vessels while at sea or beyond the limits of the continental United States, when transmitting any radio communication or signal other than a communication or signal relating to government business, shall conform to such rules and regulations designed to prevent interference with other radio stations and the rights of others as the Commission may prescribe.

(b)~~Radio stations on board vessels of the Maritime Administration of the Department of Transportation or the Inland and Coastwise Waterways Service shall be subject to the provisions of this title.~~

~~(c)~~ All stations owned and operated by the United States, except mobile stations of the Army of the United States, and all other stations on land and sea, shall have special call letters designated by the Commission.

~~(d)~~(c) The provisions of Sections 301 and 303 of this Act notwithstanding, the President may, provided he determines it to be consistent with and in the interest of national security, authorize a foreign government, under such terms and conditions as he may prescribe, to construct and operate at the seat of government of the United States a low-power radio station in the fixed service at or near the site of the embassy or legation of such foreign government for transmission of its messages to points outside the United States, but only (1) where he determines that the authorization would be consistent with the national interest of the United States and (2) where such foreign government has provided reciprocal privileges to the United States to construct and operate radio stations within territories subject to its jurisdiction. Foreign government stations authorized pursuant to the provisions of this subsection shall conform to such rules and regulations as the President may prescribe. The authorization of such stations, and the renewal, modification, suspension, revocation, or other termination of such authority shall be in accordance with such procedures as may be established by the President and shall not be subject to the other provisions of this Act or of the Administrative Procedure Act.

Section 306 [47 USC Section 306]. Foreign Ships.

Section 301 of this Act shall not apply to any person sending radio communications or signals on a foreign ship while the same is within the jurisdiction of the United States, but such communications or signals shall be transmitted only in accordance with such regulations designed to prevent interference as may be promulgated under the authority of this Act.

Section 307 [47 USC Section 307]. Allocation of Facilities; ~~Terms~~ Term of Licenses.

(a) The Commission, if public convenience, interest or necessity will be served thereby, subject to the limitations of this Act, shall grant to any applicant therefor a station license provided for by this Act.

(b) In considering applications for licenses, and modifications and renewals thereof, when and insofar as there is demand for the same, the Commission shall make such distribution of licenses, frequencies, hours of operation, and of power among the several states and communities as to provide a fair, efficient, and equitable distribution of radio service to each of the same.

(c) ~~No~~ **Terms of Licenses.--**

(1) Initial and renewal licenses.--Each license granted for the operation of a ~~television~~ broadcasting station shall be for a ~~longer term than five years and no~~ **term of not to exceed 8 years. Upon application therefor, a renewal of such** license ~~so granted for any other class of station (other than a radio broadcasting station) shall be for a longer term than ten years, and any license granted may be revoked as hereinafter provided. Each license granted for the operation of a radio broadcasting station shall be~~ **may be granted from time to time** for a term of not to exceed ~~seven years. The term of any license for the operation of any auxiliary broadcast station or equipment which can be used only in~~

417

~~conjunction with a primary radio, television or translator station shall be concurrent with the term of the license for such primary radio, television, or transfer station. Upon the expiration of any license, upon application therefor, a renewal of such license may be granted from time to time for a term of not to exceed five years in the case of television broadcasting licenses, for a term of not to exceed seven years in the case of radio broadcasting station licenses and for a term of not to exceed ten years in the case of other licenses,~~ **8 years from the date of expiration of the preceding license,** if the Commission finds that public interest, convenience, and necessity would be served thereby. ~~In order to expedite action on applications for renewal of broadcasting station licenses and in order to avoid needless expense to applicants for such renewals, the Commission shall not require any such applicant to file any information which previously has been furnished to the Commission or which is not directly material to the considerations that affect the granting or denial of such application, but the Commission may require any new or additional facts it deems necessary to make its findings. Pending any hearing and final decision on such an application and the disposition of any petition for rehearing pursuant to Section 405, the Commission shall continue such license in effect. Consistently~~ **Consistent** with the foregoing provisions of this subsection, the Commission may by rule prescribe the period or periods for which licenses shall be granted and renewed for particular classes of stations, but the Commission may not adopt or follow any rule which would preclude it, in any case involving a station of a particular class, from granting or renewing a license for a shorter period than that prescribed for stations of such class if, in its judgment, **the** public interest, convenience, or necessity would be served by such action.

    (2) Materials in application.--In order to expedite action on applications for renewal of broadcasting station licenses and in order to avoid needless expense to applicants for such renewals, the Commission shall not require any such applicant to file any information which previously has been furnished to the Commission or which is not directly material to the considerations that affect the granting or denial of such application, but the Commission may require any new or additional facts it deems necessary to make its findings.

    (3) Continuation pending decision.--Pending any hearing and final decision on such an application and the disposition of any petition for rehearing pursuant to Section 405, the Commission shall continue such license in effect.

    (d) No renewal of an existing station license in the broadcast or the common carrier services shall be granted more than thirty days prior to the expiration of the original license.

    (e)(1) Notwithstanding any ~~licensing~~ **license** requirement established in this Act, **if the Commission determines that such authorization serves the public interest, convenience, and necessity,** the Commission may by rule authorize the operation of radio stations without individual licenses in the **following** radio ~~control service and~~ **services:**

        (A) the citizens band radio service ~~if the Commission determines that such authorization serves the public interest, convenience, and necessity.~~**;**

        (B) the radio control service;

        (C) the aviation radio service for aircraft stations operated on domestic flights when such aircraft are not otherwise required to carry a radio station; and

        (D) the maritime radio service for ship stations navigated on domestic voyages when such ships are not otherwise required to carry a radio station.

    (2) Any radio station operator who is authorized by the Commission ~~under paragraph (1)~~ to operate without an individual license shall comply with all other provisions of this Act and with rules prescribed by the Commission under this Act.

(3) For purposes of this subsection, the terms ~~"radio control service" and~~ "citizens band radio service", **"radio control service", "aircraft station" and "ship station"** shall have the meanings given them by the Commission by rule.

Section 308 [47 USC Section 308]. Applications for Licenses; Conditions in License for Foreign Communication.

(a) The Commission may grant construction permits and station licenses, or modifications or renewals thereof, only upon written application therefor received by it: Provided, that (1) in cases of emergency found by the Commission involving danger to life or property or due to damage to equipment, or (2) during a national emergency proclaimed by the President or declared by the Congress and during the continuance of any war in which the United States is engaged and when such action is necessary for the national defense or security or otherwise in furtherance of the war effort, or (3) in cases of emergency where the Commission finds, in the nonbroadcast services, that it would not be feasible to secure renewal application from existing licensees or otherwise to follow normal licensing procedure, the Commission may grant construction permits and station licenses, or modifications or renewals thereof, during the emergency so found by the Commission or during the continuance of any such national emergency or war, in such manner and upon such terms and conditions as the Commission shall by regulation prescribe, and without the filing of a formal application, but no authorization so granted shall continue in effect beyond the period of the emergency or war requiring it: Provided further, that the Commission may issue by cable, telegraph, or radio a permit for the operation of a station on a vessel of the United States at sea, effective in lieu of a license until said vessel shall return to a port of the continental United States.

(b) All applications for station licenses, or modifications or renewals thereof, shall set forth such facts as the Commission by regulation may prescribe as to the citizenship, character, and financial, technical and other qualifications of the applicant to operate the station; the ownership and location of the proposed station and of the stations, if any, with which it is proposed to communicate; the frequencies and the power desired to be used; the hours of the day or other periods of time during which it is proposed to operate the station; the purposes for which the station is to be used; and such other information as it may require. The Commission, at any time after the filing of such original application and during the term of any such license, may require from an applicant or licensee further written statements of fact to enable it to determine whether such original application should be granted or denied or such license revoked. Such application and/or such statement of fact shall be signed by the applicant and/or licensee in any manner or form, including by electronic means, as the Commission may prescribe by regulation.

(c) The Commission in granting any license for a station intended or used for commercial communication between the United States or any territory or possession, continental or insular, subject to the jurisdiction of the United States, and any foreign country, may impose any terms, conditions or restrictions authorized to be imposed with respect to submarine-cable licenses by Section 2 of an Act entitled "An Act relating to the landing and the operation of submarine cables in the United States," approved May 27, 1921.

(d) **Summary of Complaints.**--**Each applicant for the renewal of a commercial or noncommercial television license shall attach as an exhibit to the application a summary of written comments and suggestions received from the public and maintained by the licensee (in accordance**

<u>with Commission regulations) that comment on the applicant's programming, if any, and that are</u> <u>characterized by the commentor as constituting violent programming.</u>

Section 309 [47 USC Section 309]. Action upon Applications; Form of and Conditions Attached to Licenses.

(a) Subject to the provisions of this section, the Commission shall determine, in the case of each application filed with it to which Section 308 applies, whether the public interest, convenience, and necessity will be served by the granting of such application, and, if the Commission, upon examination of such application and upon consideration of such other matters as the Commission may officially notice, shall find that public interest, convenience and necessity would be served by the granting thereof, it shall grant such application.

(b) Except as provided in subsection (c) of this section, no such application --

(1) for an instrument of authorization in the case of a station in the broadcasting or common carrier services, or

(2) for an instrument of authorization in the case of a station in any of the following categories:

(A)< fixed point-to-point microwave stations (exclusive of control and relay stations used as integral parts of mobile radio systems),

(B)> industrial radio positioning stations for which frequencies are assigned on an exclusive basis,

(B) aeronautical en route stations,

(C) aeronautical <en route> **advisory** stations,

(D) <aeronautical advisory> **airdrome control** stations,

(E) <airdrome control stations,

(F)> aeronautical fixed stations, and

<(G)>(F) such other stations or classes of stations, not in the broadcasting or common carrier services, as the Commission shall by rule prescribe, shall be granted by the Commission earlier than thirty days following issuance of public notice by the Commission of the acceptance for filing of such application or of any substantial amendment thereof.

(c) Subsection (b) of this section shall not apply --

(1) to any minor amendment of an application to which such subsection is applicable, or

(2) to any application for --

(A) a minor change in the facilities of an authorized station,

(B) consent to a involuntary assignment or transfer under Section 310(b) or to an assignment or transfer thereunder which does not involve a substantial change in ownership or control,

(C) a license under Section 319(c) or, pending application for or grant of such license, any special or temporary authorization to permit interim operation to facilitate completion of authorized construction or to provide substantially the same service as would be authorized by such license,

(D) extension of time to complete construction of authorized facilities,

(E) an authorization of facilities for remote pickups, studio links and similar facilities for use in the operation of a broadcast station,

(F) authorizations pursuant to Section 325(c) where the programs to be transmitted are special events not of a continuing nature,

(G) a special temporary authorization for nonbroadcast operation not to exceed thirty days where no application for regular operation is contemplated to be filed or not to exceed sixty days pending the filing of an application for such regular operation, or

(H) an authorization under any of the proviso clauses of Section 308(a).

(d)(1) Any party in interest may file with the Commission a petition to deny any application (whether as originally filed or as amended) to which subsection (b) of this section applies at any time prior to the day of Commission grant thereof without hearing or the day of formal designation thereof for hearing; except that with respect to any classification of applications, the Commission from time to time by rule may specify a shorter period (no less than thirty days following the issuance of public notice by the Commission of the acceptance for filing of such application or of any substantial amendment thereof), which shorter period shall be reasonably related to the time when the applications would normally be reached for processing. The petitioner shall serve a copy of such petition on the applicant. The petition shall contain specific allegations of fact sufficient to show that the petitioner is a party in interest and that a grant of the application would be prima facie inconsistent with subsection (a) **(or subsection (k) in the case of renewal of any broadcast station license)**. Such allegations of fact shall, except for those of which official notice may be taken, be supported by affidavit of a person or persons with personal knowledge thereof. The applicant shall be given the opportunity to file a reply in which allegations of fact or denials thereof shall similarly be supported by affidavit.

(2) If the Commission finds on the basis of the application, the pleadings filed, or other matters which it may officially notice that there are no substantial and material questions of fact and that a grant of the application would be consistent with subsection (a) **(or subsection (k) in the case of renewal of any broadcast station license)**, it shall make the grant, deny the petition, and issue a concise statement of the reasons for denying the petition, which statement shall dispose of all substantial issues raised by the petition. If a substantial and material question of fact is presented or if the Commission for any reason is unable to find that grant of the application would be consistent with subsection (a) **(or subsection (k) in the case of renewal of any broadcast station license)**, it shall proceed as provided in subsection (e).

(e) If, in the case of any application to which subsection (a) of this section applies, a substantial and material question of fact is presented or the Commission for any reason is unable to make the finding specified in such subsection, it shall formally designate the application for hearing on the ground or reasons then obtaining and shall forthwith notify the applicant and all other known parties in interest of such action and the grounds and reasons therefor, specifying with particularity the matters and things in issue but not including issues or requirements phrased generally. When the Commission has so designated an application for hearing the parties in interest, if any, who are not notified by the Commission of such action may acquire the status of a party to the proceeding thereon by filing a petition for intervention showing the basis for their interest not more than thirty days after publication of the hearing issues or any substantial amendment thereto in the Federal Register. Any hearing subsequently held upon such application shall be a full hearing in which the applicant and all other parties in interest shall be permitted to participate. The burden of proceeding with the introduction of evidence and the burden of proof shall be upon the applicant, except that with respect to any issue presented by a petition to deny or a petition to enlarge the issues, such burdens shall be as determined by the Commission.

(f) When an application subject to subsection (b) has been filed, the Commission, notwithstanding the requirements of such subsection, may, if the grant of such application is otherwise authorized by law and if it finds that there are extraordinary circumstances requiring temporary operations in the public interest and that delay in the institution of such temporary operations would seriously prejudice the public interest, grant a temporary authorization, accompanied by a statement of its reasons therefor, to permit such temporary operations for a period not exceeding 180 days, and upon making like findings may extend such temporary authorization for additional periods not to exceed 180 days. When any such grant of a temporary authorization is made, the Commission shall give expeditious treatment to any timely filed petition to deny such application and to any petition for rehearing of such grant filed under Section 405.

(g) The Commission is authorized to adopt reasonable classifications of applications and amendments in order to effectuate the purposes of this section.

(h) Such station licenses as the Commission may grant shall be in such general form as it may prescribe, but each license shall contain, in addition to other provisions, a statement of the following conditions to which such license shall be subject:

(1) the station license shall not vest in the licensee any right to operate the station nor any right in the use of the frequencies designated in the license beyond the term thereof nor in any other manner than authorized therein;

(2) neither the license nor the right granted thereunder shall be assigned or otherwise transferred in violation of this Act;

(3) every license issued under this Act shall be subject in terms to the right of use or control conferred by Section 706 of this Act.

(i) Random Selection. - (1) General Authority. - If--

(A) there is more than one application for any initial license or construction permit which will involve a use of the electromagnetic spectrum; and

(B) the Commission has determined that the use is not described in subsection (j)(2)(A);

then the Commission shall have authority to grant such license or permit to a qualified applicant through the use of a system of random selection.

(2) No license or construction permit shall be granted to an applicant selected pursuant to paragraph (1) unless the Commission determines the qualifications of such applicant pursuant to subsection (a) and Section 308(b). When substantial and material questions of fact exist concerning such qualifications, the Commission shall conduct a hearing in order to make such determinations. For the purpose of making such determinations, the Commission may, by rule, and notwithstanding any other provision of law --

(A) adopt procedures for the submission of all or part of the evidence in written form;

(B) delegate the function of presiding at the taking of written evidence to Commission employees other than administrative law judges; and

(C) omit the determination required by subsection (a) with respect to any application other than the one selected pursuant to paragraph (1).

(3)(A) The Commission shall establish rules and procedures to ensure that, in the administration of any system of random selection under this subsection, used for granting licenses or construction permits for any media of mass communications, significant preferences will be granted to applicants or groups of applicants, the grant to which of the license or permit would increase the diversification of ownership of the media of mass communications. To further diversify the ownership of the media of mass communications, an additional significant preference shall be granted to any applicant controlled by a member or members of a minority group.

(B) The Commission shall have authority to require each qualified applicant seeking a significant preference under subparagraph (A) to submit to the Commission such information as may be necessary to enable the Commission to make a determination regarding whether such applicant shall be granted such preference. Such information shall be submitted in such form, at such times, and in accordance with such procedures, as the Commission may require.

(C) For purposes of this paragraph:

(i) The term "media of mass communications" includes television, radio, cable television, multipoint distribution service, direct broadcast satellite service, and other services, the licensed facilities of which may be substantially devoted toward providing programming or other information services within the editorial control of the licensee.

(ii) The term "minority group" includes Blacks, Hispanics, American Indians, Alaska Natives, Asians, and Pacific Islanders.

(4)(A) The Commission shall, after notice and opportunity for hearing, prescribe rules establishing a system of random selection for use by the Commission under this subsection in any instance in which the Commission, in its discretion, determines that such use is appropriate for the granting of any license or permit in accordance with paragraph (1).

(B) The Commission shall have authority to amend such rules from time to time to the extent necessary to carry out the provisions of this subsection. Any such amendment shall be made after notice and opportunity for hearing.

(C) Not later than 180 days after the date of enactment of this subparagraph, the Commission shall prescribe such transfer disclosures and antitrafficking restrictions and payment schedules as are necessary to prevent the unjust enrichment of recipients of licenses or permits as a result of the methods employed to issue licenses under this subsection.

(j) Use of Competitive Bidding. -

(1) General Authority. - If mutually exclusive applications are accepted for filing for any initial license or construction permit which will involve a use of the electromagnetic spectrum described in paragraph (2), then the Commission shall have the authority, subject to paragraph (10), to grant such license or permit to a qualified applicant through the use of a system of competitive bidding that meets the requirements of this subsection.

(2) Uses To Which Bidding May Apply. - A use of the electromagnetic spectrum is described in this paragraph if the Commission determines that --

(A) the principal use of such spectrum will involve, or is reasonably likely to involve, the licensee receiving compensation from subscribers in return for which the licensee --

(i) enables those subscribers to receive communications signals that are transmitted utilizing frequencies on which the licensee is licensed to operate; or

(ii) enables those subscribers to transmit directly communications signals utilizing frequencies on which the licensee is licensed to operate; and

(B) a system of competitive bidding will promote the objectives described in paragraph (3).

(3) Design of Systems of Competitive Bidding. - For each class of licenses or permits that the Commission grants through the use of a competitive bidding system, the Commission shall, by regulation, establish a competitive bidding methodology. The Commission shall seek to design and test

423

multiple alternative methodologies under appropriate circumstances. In identifying classes of licenses and permits to be issued by competitive bidding, in specifying eligibility and other characteristics of such licenses and permits, and in designing the methodologies for use under this subsection, the Commission shall include safeguards to protect the public interest in the use of the spectrum and shall seek to promote the purposes specified in Section 1 of this Act and the following objectives:

(A) the development and rapid deployment of new technologies, products, and services for the benefit of the public, including those residing in rural areas, without administrative or judicial delays;

(B) promoting economic opportunity and competition and ensuring that new and innovative technologies are readily accessible to the American people by avoiding excessive concentration of licenses and by disseminating licenses among a wide variety of applicants, including small businesses, rural telephone companies, and businesses owned by members of minority groups and women;

(C) recovery for the public of a portion of the value of the public spectrum resource made available for commercial use and avoidance of unjust enrichment through the methods employed to award uses of that resource; and

(D) efficient and intensive use of the electromagnetic spectrum.

(4) Contents of Regulations. - In prescribing regulations pursuant to paragraph (3), the Commission shall --

(A) consider alternative payment schedules and methods of calculation, including lump sums or guaranteed installment payments, with or without royalty payments, or other schedules or methods that promote the objectives described in paragraph(3)(B), and combinations of such schedules and methods;

(B) include performance requirements, such as appropriate deadlines and penalties for performance failures, to ensure prompt delivery of service to rural areas, to prevent stockpiling or warehousing of spectrum by licensees or permittees, and to promote investment in and rapid deployment of new technologies and services;

(C) consistent with the public interest, convenience, and necessity, the purposes of this Act, and the characteristics of the proposed service, prescribe area designations and bandwidth assignments that promote (i) an equitable distribution of licenses and services among geographic areas, (ii) economic opportunity for a wide variety of applicants, including small businesses, rural telephone companies, and businesses owned by members of minority groups and women, and (iii) investment in and rapid deployment of new technologies and services;

(D) ensure that small businesses, rural telephone companies, and businesses owned by members of minority groups and women are given the opportunity to participate in the provision of spectrum-based services, and, for such purposes, consider the use of tax certificates, bidding preferences, and other procedures; and

(E) require such transfer disclosures and antitrafficking restrictions and payment schedules as may be necessary to prevent unjust enrichment as a result of the methods employed to issue licenses and permits.

(5) Bidder and Licensee Qualification. - No person shall be permitted to participate in a system of competitive bidding pursuant to this subsection unless such bidder submits such information and assurances as the Commission may require to demonstrate that such bidder's application is acceptable for filing. No license shall be granted to an applicant selected pursuant to this subsection

424

unless the Commission determines that the applicant is qualified pursuant to subsection (a) and Sections 308(b) and 310. Consistent with the objectives described in paragraph (3), the Commission shall, by regulation, prescribe expedited procedures consistent with the procedures authorized by subsection (i)(2) for the resolution of any substantial and material issues of fact concerning qualifications.

(6) Rules of Construction. - Nothing in this subsection, or in the use of competitive bidding, shall --

(A) alter spectrum allocation criteria and procedures established by the other provisions of this Act;

(B) limit or otherwise affect the requirements of subsection (h) of this section, Sections 301, 304, 307, 310, or 706, or any other provision of this Act (other than subsections (d)(2) and (e) of this section);

(C) diminish the authority of the Commission under the other provisions of this Act to regulate or reclaim spectrum licenses;

(D) be construed to convey any rights, including any expectation of renewal of a license, that differ from the rights that apply to other licenses within the same service that were not issued pursuant to this subsection;

(E) be construed to relieve the Commission of the obligation in the public interest to continue to use engineering solutions, negotiation, threshold qualifications, service regulations, and other means in order to avoid mutual exclusivity in application and licensing proceedings;

(F) be construed to prohibit the Commission from issuing nationwide, regional, or local licenses or permits;

(G) be construed to prevent the Commission from awarding licenses to those persons who make significant contributions to the development of a new telecommunications service or technology; or

(H) be construed to relieve any applicant for a license or permit of the obligation to pay charges imposed pursuant to Section 8 of this Act.

(7) Consideration of Revenues in Public Interest Determinations. --

(A) Consideration Prohibited. - In making a decision pursuant to Section 303(c) to assign a band of frequencies to a use for which licenses or permits will be issued pursuant to this subsection, and in prescribing regulations pursuant to paragraph (4)(C) of this subsection, the Commission may not base a finding of public interest, convenience, and necessity on the expectation of Federal revenues from the use of a system of competitive bidding under this subsection.

(B) Consideration Limited. - In prescribing regulations pursuant to paragraph (4)(A) of this subsection, the Commission may not base a finding of public interest, convenience, and necessity solely or predominantly on the expectation of Federal revenues from the use of a system of competitive bidding under this subsection.

(C) Consideration of Demand for Spectrum Not Affected. - Nothing in this paragraph shall be construed to prevent the Commission from continuing to consider consumer demand for spectrum-based services.

(8) Treatment of Revenues. -

(A) General Rule. - Except as provided in subparagraph (B), all proceeds from the use of a competitive bidding system under this subsection shall be deposited in the Treasury in accordance with Chapter 33 of Title 31, United States Code.

(B)   Retention of Revenues. - Notwithstanding subparagraph (A), the salaries and expenses account of the Commission shall retain as an offsetting collection such sums as may be necessary from such proceeds for the costs of developing and implementing the program required by this subsection. Such offsetting collections shall be available for obligation subject to the terms and conditions of the receiving appropriations account, and shall be deposited in such accounts on a quarterly basis. Any funds appropriated to the Commission for fiscal years 1994 through 1998 for the purpose of assigning licenses using random selection under subsection (i) shall be used by the Commission to implement this subsection. **Such offsetting collections are authorized to remain available until expended.**

(C)   Deposit and use of auction escrow accounts.--Any deposits the Commission may require for the qualification of any person to bid in a system of competitive bidding pursuant to this subsection shall be deposited in an interest bearing account at a financial institution designated for purposes of this subsection by the Commission (after consultation with the Secretary of the Treasury). Within 45 days following the conclusion of the competitive bidding--

(i) the deposits of successful bidders shall be paid to the Treasury;

(ii) the deposits of unsuccessful bidders shall be returned to such bidders; and

(iii)   the interest accrued to the account shall be transferred to the Telecommunications Development Fund established pursuant to Section 714 of this Act.

(9) Use of Former Government Spectrum. - The Commission shall, not later than 5 years after the date of enactment of this subsection, issue licenses and permits pursuant to this subsection for the use of bands of frequencies that --

(A) in the aggregate span not less than 10 megahertz; and

(B) have been reassigned from Government use pursuant to Part B of the National Telecommunications and Information Administration Organization Act.

(10) Authority Contingent on Availability of Additional Spectrum. --

(A) Initial Conditions. - The Commission's authority to issue licenses or permits under this subsection shall not take effect unless --

(i) the Secretary of Commerce has submitted to the Commission the report required by Section 113(d)(1) of the National Telecommunications and Information Administration Organization Act;

(ii) such report recommends for immediate reallocation bands of frequencies that, in the aggregate, span not less than 50 megahertz;

(iii) such bands of frequencies meet the criteria required by Section 113(a) of such Act; and

(iv) the Commission has completed the rulemaking required by Section 332(c)(1)(D) of this Act.

(B) Subsequent Conditions. - The Commission's authority to issue licenses or permits under this subsection on and after 2 years after the date of the enactment of this subsection shall cease to be effective if --

(i) the Secretary of Commerce has failed to submit the report required by Section 113(a) of the National Telecommunications and Information Administration Organization Act;

(ii) the President has failed to withdraw and limit assignments of frequencies as required by paragraphs (1) and (2) of Section 114(a) of such Act;

426

(iii) the Commission has failed to issue the regulations required by Section 115(a) of such Act;

(iv) the Commission has failed to complete and submit to Congress, not later than 18 months after the date of enactment of this subsection, a study of current and future spectrum needs of State and local government public safety agencies through the year 2010, and a specific plan to ensure that adequate frequencies are made available to public safety licensees; or

(v) the Commission has failed under Section 332(c)(3) to grant or deny within the time required by such section any petition that a State has filed within 90 days after the date of enactment of this subsection;

until such failure has been corrected.

(11) Termination. - The authority of the Commission to grant a license or permit under this subsection shall expire September 30, 1998.

(12) Evaluation. - Not later than September 30, 1997, the Commission shall conduct a public inquiry and submit to the Congress a report --

(A) containing a statement of the revenues obtained, and a projection of the future revenues, from the use of competitive bidding systems under this subsection;

(B) describing the methodologies established by the Commission pursuant to paragraphs (3) and (4);

(C) comparing the relative advantages and disadvantages of such methodologies in terms of attaining the objectives described in such paragraphs;

(D) evaluating whether and to what extent --

(i) competitive bidding significantly improved the efficiency and effectiveness of the process for granting radio spectrum licenses;

(ii) competitive bidding facilitated the introduction of new spectrum-based technologies and the entry of new companies into the telecommunications market;

(iii) competitive bidding methodologies have secured prompt delivery of service to rural areas and have adequately addressed the needs of rural spectrum users; and

(iv) small businesses, rural telephone companies, and businesses owned by members of minority groups and women were able to participate successfully in the competitive bidding process; and

(E) recommending any statutory changes that are needed to improve the competitive bidding process.

(13) Recovery of value of public spectrum in connection with pioneer preferences.

(A) In general. - Notwithstanding paragraph 6(G), the Commission shall not award licenses pursuant to a preferential treatment accorded by the Commission to persons who make significant contributions to the development of a new telecommunications service or technology, except in accordance with the requirements of this paragraph.

(B) Recovery of value. - The Commission shall recover for the public a portion of the value of the public spectrum resource made available to such person by requiring such person, as a condition for receipt of the license, to agree to pay a sum determined by--

(i) identifying the winning bids for the licenses that the Commission determines are most reasonably comparable in terms of bandwidth, scope of service area, usage restrictions, and other technical characteristics to the license awarded to such person, and excluding licenses that the Commission determines are subject to bidding anomalies due to the award of preferential treatment;

(ii) dividing each winning bid by the population of its service area (hereinafter referred to as the per capita bid amount);

(iii) computing the average of the per capita bid amounts for the licenses identified under clause (i);

(iv) reducing such average amount by 15 percent; and

(v) multiplying the amount determined under clause (iv) by the population of the service area of the license obtained by such person.

(C) Installments permitted. - The Commission shall require such person to pay the sum required by subparagraph (B) in a lump sum or in guaranteed installment payments, with or without royalty payments, over a period of not more than 5 years.

(D) Rulemaking on Pioneer Preferences. - Except with respect to pending applications described in clause (IV) of this subparagraph, the Commission shall prescribe regulations specifying the procedures and criteria by which the Commission will evaluate applications for preferential treatment in its licensing processes (by precluding the filing of mutually exclusive applications) for persons who make significant contributions to the development of a new service or to the development of new technologies that substantially enhance an existing service. Such regulations shall--

(i) specify the procedures and criteria by which the significance of such contributions will be determined, after an opportunity for review and verification by experts in the radio sciences drawn from among persons who are not employees of the Commission or by any applicant for such preferential treatment;

(ii) include such other procedures as may be necessary to prevent unjust enrichment by ensuring that the value of any such contribution justifies any reduction in the amounts paid for comparable licenses under this subsection;

(iii) be prescribed not later than 6 months after the date of enactment of this paragraph;

(iv) not apply to applications that have been accepted for filing on or before September 1, 1994; and

(v) cease to be effective on the date of the expiration of the Commission's authority under subparagraph (F).

(E) Implementation with respect to pending applications. - In applying this paragraph to any broadband licenses in the personal communications service awarded pursuant to the preferential treatment accorded by the Federal Communications Commission in the Third Report and Order in General Docket 90-314 (FCC 93-550, released February 3, 1994)--

(i) the Commission shall not reconsider the award of preferences in such Third Report and Order, and the Commission shall not delay the grant of licenses based on such awards more than 15 days following the date of enactment of this paragraph, and the award of such preferences and the licenses shall not be subject to administrative review;

(ii) the Commission shall not alter the bandwidth or service areas designated for such licenses in such Third Report and Order;

(iii) except as provided in clause (v), the Commission shall use, as the most reasonably comparable licenses for purposes of subparagraph (B)(i), the broadband licenses in the personal communications service for blocks A and B for the 20 largest markets (ranked by population) in which no applicant has obtained preferential treatment;

(iv) for purposes of subparagraph (C), the Commission shall permit guaranteed installment payments over a period of 5 years, subject to--

(I) the payment only of interest on unpaid balances during the first two years, commencing not later than 30 days after the award of the license (including any preferential treatment used in making such award) is final and no longer subject to administrative and judicial review, except that no such payment shall be required prior to the date of completion of the auction of the comparable licenses described in clause (iii); and

(II) payment of the unpaid balance and interest thereon after the end of such 2 years in accordance with the regulations prescribed by the Commission; and

(v) the Commission shall recover with respect to broadband licenses in the personal communications service an amount under this paragraph that is equal to not less than $400,000,000, and if such amount is less than $400,000,000, the Commission shall recover an amount equal to $400,000,000 by allocating such amount among the holders of such licenses based on the population of the license areas held by each licensee.

The Commission shall not include in any amounts required to be collected under clause (v) the interest on unpaid balances required to be collected under clause (iv).

(F) Expiration. - The authority of the Commission to provide preferential treatment in licensing procedures (by precluding the filing of mutually exclusive applications) to persons who make significant contributions to the development of a new service or to the development of new technologies that substantially enhance an existing service shall expire on September 30, 1998.

(G) Effective date. - This paragraph shall be effective on the date of its enactment and apply to any licenses issued on or after August 1, 1994, by the Federal Communications Commission pursuant to any licensing procedure that provides preferential treatment (by precluding the filing of mutually exclusive applications) to persons who make significant contributions to the development of a new service or to the development of new technologies that substantially enhance an existing service.

(k) Broadcast Station Renewal Procedures.--

(1) Standards for renewal.--If the licensee of a broadcast station submits an application to the Commission for renewal of such license, the Commission shall grant the application if it finds, with respect to that station, during the preceding term of its license--

(A) the station has served the public interest, convenience, and necessity;

(B) there have been no serious violations by the licensee of this Act or the rules and regulations of the Commission; and

(C) there have been no other violations by the licensee of this Act or the rules and regulations of the Commission which, taken together, would constitute a pattern of abuse.

(2) Consequence of failure to meet standard.--If any licensee of a broadcast station fails to meet the requirements of this subsection, the Commission may deny the application for renewal in accordance with paragraph (3), or grant such application on terms and conditions as are appropriate, including renewal for a term less than the maximum otherwise permitted.

(3) Standards for denial.--If the Commission determines, after notice and opportunity for a hearing as provided in subsection (e), that a licensee has failed to meet the requirements specified in paragraph (1) and that no mitigating factors justify the imposition of lesser sanctions, the Commission shall--

(A) issue an order denying the renewal application filed by such licensee under Section 308; and

(B) only thereafter accept and consider such applications for a construction permit as may be filed under Section 308 specifying the channel or broadcasting facilities of the former licensee.

(4) Competitor consideration prohibited.--In making the determinations specified in paragraph (1) or (2), the Commission shall not consider whether the public interest, convenience, and necessity might be served by the grant of a license to a person other than the renewal applicant.

Section 310 [47 USC Section 310]. Limitation on Holding and Transfer of Licenses.

(a) The station license required under this Act shall not be granted to or held by any foreign government or the representative thereof.

(b) No broadcast or common carrier or aeronautical en route or aeronautical fixed radio station license shall be granted to or held by --

(1) any alien or the representative of any alien;

(2) any corporation organized under the laws of any foreign government;

(3) any corporation <del>of which any officer or director is an alien or</del> of which more than one-fifth of the capital stock is owned of record or voted by aliens or their representatives or by a foreign government or representative thereof or by any corporation organized under the laws of a foreign country;

(4) any corporation directly or indirectly controlled by any other corporation <del>of which any officer or more than one-fourth of the directors are aliens, or</del> of which more than one-fourth of the capital stock is owned of record or voted by aliens, their representatives, or by a foreign government or representative thereof, or by any corporation organized under the laws of a foreign country, if the Commission finds that the public interest will be served by the refusal or revocation of such license.

(c) In addition to amateur station licenses which the Commission may issue to aliens pursuant to this Act, the Commission may issue authorizations, under such conditions and terms as it may prescribe, to permit an alien licensed by his government as an amateur radio operator to operate his amateur radio station licensed by his government in the United States, its possessions, and the Commonwealth of Puerto Rico provided there is in effect a multilateral or bilateral agreement, to which the United States and the alien's government are parties, for such operation on a reciprocal basis by United States amateur radio operators. Other provisions of this Act and of the Administrative Procedure Act shall not be applicable to any request or application for or modification, suspension, or cancellation of any such authorization.

(d) No construction permit or station license, or any rights thereunder, shall be transferred, assigned, or disposed of in any manner, voluntarily or involuntarily, directly or indirectly, or by transfer of control of any corporation holding such permit or license, to any person except upon application to the Commission and upon finding by the Commission that the public interest, convenience and necessity will be served thereby. Any such application shall be disposed of as if the proposed transferee or assignee were making application under Section 308 for the permit or license in question; but in acting thereon the Commission may not consider whether the public interest, convenience and necessity might be served by the transfer, assignment, or disposal of the permit or license to a person other than the proposed transferee or assignee.

(e)(1) In the case of any broadcast station, and any ownership interest therein, which is excluded from the regional concentration rules by reason of the savings provision for existing facilities provided by the First Report and Order adopted March 9, 1977 (Docket No. 20548; 42 FR 16145), the exclusion shall not terminate solely by reason of changes made in the technical facilities of the station to improve its service.

(2) For purposes of this subsection, the term "regional concentration rules" means the provisions of §§73.35, 73.240, and 73.636 of Title 47, Code of Federal Regulations (as in effect June 1, 1983), which prohibit any party from directly or indirectly owning, operating, or controlling three broadcast stations in one or several services where any two of such stations are within 100 miles of the third (measured city-to-city), and where there is a primary service contour overlap of any of the stations.

Section 311 [47 USC Section 311]. Special Requirements with Respect to Certain Applications in the Broadcasting Service.

(a) When there is filed with the Commission any application to which Section 309(b)(1) applies, for an instrument of authorization for a station in the broadcasting service the applicant --

(1) shall give notice of such filing in the principal area which is served or is to be served by the station; and

(2) if the application is formally designated for hearing in accordance with Section 309, shall give notice of such hearings in such area at least ten days before commencement of such hearing. The Commission shall by rule prescribe the form and content of the notices to be given in compliance with this subsection, and the manner and frequency with which such notices shall be given.

(b) Hearings referred to in subsection (a) may be held at such places as the Commission shall determine to be appropriate, and in making such determination in any case the Commission shall consider whether the public interest, convenience or necessity will be served by conducting the hearing at a place in, or in the vicinity of, the principal area to be served by the station involved.

(c)(1) If there are pending before the Commission two or more applications for a permit for construction of a broadcasting station, only one of which can be granted, it shall be unlawful, without approval of the Commission, for the applicants or any of them to effectuate an agreement whereby one or more of such applicants withdraws his or their application or applications.

(2) The request for Commission approval in any such case shall be made in writing jointly by all parties to the agreement. Such request shall contain or be accompanied by full information with respect to the agreement, set forth in such detail, form and manner as the Commission shall by rule require.

(3) The Commission shall approve the agreement only if it determines that (A) the agreement is consistent with the public interest, convenience or necessity; and (B) no party to the agreement filed its application for the purpose of reaching or carrying out such agreement.

(4) For the purposes of this subsection an application shall be deemed to be "pending" before the Commission from the time such application is filed with the Commission until an order of the Commission granting or denying it is no longer subject to rehearing by the Commission or to review by any court.

(d)(1) If there are pending before the Commission an application for the renewal of a license granted for the operation of a broadcasting station and one or more applications for a construction permit relating to such station, only one of which can be granted, it shall be unlawful, without approval of the

431

Commission, for the applicants or any of them to effectuate an agreement whereby one or more of such applicants withdraws his or their application or applications in exchange for the payment of money, or the transfer of assets or any other thing of value by the remaining applicant or applicants.

(2) The request for Commission approval in any such case shall be made in writing jointly by all the parties to the agreement. Such request shall contain or be accompanied by full information with respect to the agreement, set forth in such detail, form, and manner as the Commission shall require.

(3) The Commission shall approve the agreement only if it determines that (A) the agreement is consistent with the public interest, convenience, or necessity; and (B) no party to the agreement filed its application for the purpose of reaching or carrying out such agreement.

(4) For purposes of this subsection, an application shall be deemed to be pending before the Commission from the time such application is filed with the Commission until an order of the Commission granting or denying it is no longer subject to rehearing by the Commission or to review by any court.

Section 312 [47 USC Section 312]. Administrative Sanctions.

(a) The Commission may revoke any station license or construction permit --

(1) for false statements knowingly made either in the application or in any statement of fact which may be required pursuant to Section 308;

(2) because of conditions coming to the attention of the Commission which would warrant it in refusing to grant a license or permit on an original application;

(3) for willful or repeated failure to operate substantially as set forth in the license;

(4) for willful or repeated violation of, or willful or repeated failure to observe, any provision of this Act or any rule or regulation of the Commission authorized by this Act or by a treaty ratified by the United States;

(5) for violation of or failure to observe any final cease and desist order issued by the Commission under this section;

(6) for violation of Sections 1304, 1343, or 1464 of Title 18 of the United States Code; or

(7) for willful or repeated failure to allow reasonable access to or to permit purchase of reasonable amounts of time for the use of a broadcasting station by a legally qualified candidate for Federal elective office on behalf of his candidacy.

(b) Where any person (a) has failed to operate substantially as set forth in a license, (2) has violated or failed to observe any of the provisions of this Act, or Sections 1304, 1343, or 1464 of Title 18 of the United States Code, or (3) has violated or failed to observe any rule or regulation of the Commission authorized by this Act or by a treaty ratified by the United States, the Commission may order such person to cease and desist from such action.

(c) Before revoking a license or permit pursuant to subsection (a), or issuing a cease and desist order pursuant to subsection (b), the Commission shall serve upon the licensee, permittee or person involved an order to show cause why an order of revocation or a cease and desist order should not be issued. Any such order to show cause shall contain a statement of the matters with respect to which the Commission is inquiring and shall call upon said licensee, permittee or person to appear before the Commission at a time and place stated in the order, but in no event less than thirty days after the receipt of such order, and give evidence upon the matter specified therein; except that where safety or life or property is involved, the Commission may provide in the order for a shorter period. If after hearing, or

432

a waiver thereof, the Commission determines that an order of revocation or a cease and desist order should issue, it shall issue such order, which shall include a statement of the findings of the Commission and the grounds and reasons therefor, and specify the effective date of the order, and shall cause the same to be served on said licensee, permittee, or person.

(d) In any case where a hearing is conducted pursuant to the provisions of this section, both the burden of proceeding with the introduction of evidence and the burden of proof shall be upon the Commission.

(e) The provisions of Section 9(b) of the Administrative Procedure Act which apply with respect to the institution of any proceeding for the revocation of a license or permit shall apply also with respect to the institution, under this section, of any proceeding for the issuance of a cease and desist order.

(f) For purposes of this section:

(1) The term "willful," when used with reference to the commission or omission of any act, means the conscious and deliberate commission or omission of such act, irrespective of any intent to violate any provision of this Act or any rule or regulation of the Commission authorized by this Act or by a treaty ratified by the United States.

(2) The term "repeated," when used with reference to the commission or omission of any act, means the commission or omission of such act more than once or, if such commission or omission is continuous, for more than one day.

(g) If a broadcasting station fails to transmit broadcast signals for any consecutive 12-month period, then the station license granted for the operation of that broadcast station expires at the end of that period, notwithstanding any provision, term, or condition of the license to the contrary.

Section 313 [47 USC Section 313]. Application of Antitrust Laws; Refusal of Licenses and Permits in Certain Cases

(a) All laws of the United States relating to unlawful restraints and monopolies and to combinations, contracts, or agreements in restraint of trade are hereby declared to be applicable to the manufacture and sale of and to trade in radio apparatus and devices entering into or affecting interstate or foreign commerce and to interstate or foreign radio communications. Whenever in any suit, action, or proceeding, civil or criminal, brought under the provisions of any of said laws or in any proceedings brought to enforce or to review findings and orders of the Federal Trade Commission or other governmental agency in respect of any matters as to which said Commission or other governmental agency is by law authorized to act, any licensee shall be found guilty of the violation of the provisions of such laws or any of them, the court, in addition to the penalties imposed by said laws, may adjudge, order, and/or decree that the license of such licensee shall, as of the date the decree or judgment becomes finally effective or as of such other date as the said decree shall fix, be revoked and that all rights under such license shall thereupon cease: Provided, however, that such licensee shall have the same right of appeal or review as is provided by law in respect of other decrees and judgments of said court.

(b) The Commission is hereby directed to refuse a station license and/or the permit hereinafter required for the construction of the station to any person (or to any person directly or indirectly controlled by such person) whose license has been revoked by a court under this section.

Section 314 [47 USC Section 314]. Preservation of Competition in Commerce.

After the effective date of this Act no person engaged directly, or indirectly, through any person directly or indirectly controlling or controlled by, or under direct or indirect common control with, such person, or through an agent, or otherwise, in the business of transmitting and/or receiving for hire energy, communications, or signals by radio in accordance with the terms of the license issued under this Act, shall by purchase, lease, construction, or otherwise, directly or indirectly, acquire, own, control, or operate any cable or wire telegraph or telephone line or system between any place in any state, territory, or possession of the United States or in the District of Columbia, and any place in any foreign country, or shall acquire, own, or control any part of the stock or other capital share or any interest in the physical property and/or other assets of any such cable, wire, telegraph, or telephone line or system, if in either case the purpose is and/or the effect thereof may be to substantially lessen competition or to restrain commerce between any place in any state, territory, or possession of the United States, or in the District of Columbia, and any place in any foreign country, or unlawfully to create monopoly in any line of commerce; nor shall any person engaged directly, or indirectly through any person directly or indirectly controlling or controlled by, or under direct or indirect common control with, such person, or through an agent, or otherwise, in the business of transmitting and/or receiving for hire messages by any cable, wire, telegraph or telephone line or system (a) between any place in any state, territory, or possession of the United States, or in the District of Columbia, and any place in any other state, territory, or possession of the United States; or (b) between any place in any state, territory, or possession of the United States, or the District of Columbia, and any place in any foreign country, by purchase, lease, construction, or otherwise, directly or indirectly acquire, own, control, or operate any station or the apparatus therein, or any system for transmitting and/or receiving radio communications or signals between any place in any state, territory, or possession of the United States, or in the District of Columbia, and any place in any foreign country, or shall acquire, own, or control any part of the stock or other capital share or any interest in the physical property and/or other assets of any such radio station, apparatus, or system, if in either case the purpose is and/or the effect thereof may be to substantially lessen competition or to restrain commerce between any place in any state, territory, or possession of the United States, or in the District of Columbia, and any place in any foreign country, or unlawfully to create monopoly in any line of commerce.

Section 315 [47 USC Section 315]. Facilities for Candidates for Public Office.

(a) If any licensee shall permit any person who is a legally qualified candidate for any public office to use a broadcasting station, he shall afford equal opportunities to all other such candidates for that office in the use of such broadcasting station: Provided, that such licensee shall have no power of censorship over the material broadcast under the provisions of this section. No obligation is imposed under this subsection upon any licensee to allow the use of its station by any such candidate. Appearance by a legally qualified candidate on any --

(1) bona fide newscast,

(2) bona fide news interview,

(3) bona fide news documentary (if the appearance of the candidate is incidental to the presentation of the subject or subjects covered by the news documentary), or

(4) on-the-spot coverage of bona fide news events (including but not limited to political conventions and activities incidental thereto), shall not be deemed to be use of a broadcasting station within the meaning of this subsection. Nothing in the foregoing sentence shall be construed as relieving broadcasters, in connection with the presentation of newscasts, news interviews, news documentaries, and on-the-spot coverage of news events, from the obligation imposed upon them under this Act to operate in the public interest and to afford reasonable opportunity for the discussion of conflicting views on issues of public importance.

(b) The charges made for the use of any broadcasting station by any person who is a legally qualified candidate for any public office in connection with his campaign for nomination for election, or election, to such office shall not exceed --

(1) during the forty-five days preceding the date of a primary or primary runoff election and during the sixty days preceding the date of a general or special election in which such person is a candidate, the lowest unit charge of the station for the same class and amount of time for the same period; and

(2) at any other time, the charges made for comparable use of such station by other users thereof.

(c) For the purposes of this section:

(1) The term "broadcasting station" includes a community antenna television system; and

(2) The terms "licensee" and "station licensee" when used with respect to a community antenna television system, mean the operator of such system.

(d) The Commission shall prescribe appropriate rules and regulations to carry out the provisions of this section.

Section 316 [47 USC Section 316]. Modification by Commission of Construction Permits or Licenses.

(a)(1) Any station license or construction permit may be modified by the Commission either for a limited time or for the duration of the term thereof, if in the judgment of the Commission such action will promote the public interest, convenience and necessity, or the provisions of this Act or of any treaty ratified by the United States will be more fully complied with. No such order of modification shall become final until the holder of the license or permit shall have been notified in writing of the proposed action and the grounds and reasons therefor, and shall be given reasonable opportunity, of at least thirty days, to protest such proposed order of modification; except that, where safety of life or property is involved, the Commission may by order provide for a shorter period of notice.

(2) Any other licensee or permittee who believes its license or permit would be modified by the proposed action may also protest the proposed action before its effective date.

(3) A protest filed pursuant to this subsection shall be subject to the requirements of Section 309 for petitions to deny.

(b) In any case where a hearing is conducted pursuant to the provisions of this section, both the burden of proceeding with the introduction of evidence and the burden of proof shall be upon the Commission; except that, with respect to any issue that addresses the question of whether the proposed action would modify the license or permit of a person described in subsection (a)(2), such burdens shall be as determined by the Commission.

435

Section 317 [47 USC Section 317]. Announcement with Respect to Certain Matter Broadcast.

(a)(1) All matter broadcast by any radio station for which any money, service, or other valuable consideration is directly or indirectly paid, or promised to or charged or accepted by, the station so broadcasting, from any person, shall, at the time the same is so broadcast, be announced as paid for or furnished, as the case may be, by such person: Provided, that "service or other valuable consideration" shall not include any service or property furnished without charge or at a nominal charge for use on, or in connection with, a broadcast unless it is so furnished in consideration for an identification in a broadcast of any person, product, service, trademark or brand name beyond an identification which is reasonably related to the use of such service or property on the broadcast.

(2) Nothing in this section shall preclude the Commission from requiring that an appropriate announcement shall be made at the time of the broadcast in the case of any political program or any program involving the discussion of any controversial issue for which any films, records, transcriptions, talent, scripts, or other material or service of any kind have been furnished, without charge or at a nominal charge, directly or indirectly, as an inducement to the broadcast of such program.

(b) In any case where a report has been made to a radio station, as required by Section 507 of this Act, of circumstances which would have required an announcement under this section had the consideration been received by such radio station, an appropriate announcement shall be made by such radio station.

(c) The licensee of each radio station shall exercise reasonable diligence to obtain from its employees, and from other persons with whom it deals directly in connection with any program or program matter for broadcast, information to enable such licensee to make the announcement required by this section.

(d) The Commission may waive the requirement of an announcement as provided in this section in any case or class of cases with respect to which it determines that the public interest, convenience or necessity does not require the broadcasting of such announcement.

(e) The Commission shall prescribe appropriate rules and regulations to carry out the provisions of this section.

Section 318 [47 USC Section 318]. Operation of Transmitting Apparatus.

The actual operation of all transmitting apparatus in any radio station for which a station license is required by this Act shall be carried on only by a person holding an operator's license issued hereunder, and no person shall operate any such apparatus in such station except under and in accordance with an operator's license issued to him by the Commission: Provided, however, that the Commission if it shall find that the public interest, convenience or necessity will be served thereby may waive or modify the foregoing provisions of this section for the operation of any station except (1) stations for which licensed operators are required by international agreement, (2) stations for which licensed operators are required for safety purposes, (3) stations operated as common carriers on frequencies below thirty thousand kilocycles: Provided further, that the Commission shall have power to make special regulations governing the granting of licenses for the use of automatic radio devices and for the operation of such devices.

Section 319 [47 USC Section 319]. Construction Permits.

(a) No license shall be issued under the authority of this Act for the operation of any station unless a permit for its construction had been granted by the Commission. The application for a construction permit shall set forth such facts as the Commission by regulation may prescribe as to the citizenship, character, and the financial, technical and other ability of the applicant to construct and operate the station, the ownership and location of the proposed station and of the station or stations with which it is proposed to communicate, the frequencies desired to be used, the hours of the day or other periods of time during which it is proposed to operate the station, the purpose for which the station is to be used, the type of transmitting apparatus to be used, the power to be used, the date upon which the station is expected to be completed and in operation, and such other information as the Commission may require. Such application shall be signed by the applicant in any manner or form, including by electronic means, as the Commission may prescribe by regulation.

(b) Such permit for construction shall show specifically the earliest and latest dates between which the actual operation of such station is expected to begin, and shall provide that said permit will be automatically forfeited if the station is not ready for operation within the time specified or within such further time as the Commission may allow, unless prevented by causes not under the control of the grantee.

(c) Upon the completion of any station for the construction or continued construction of which a permit has been granted, and upon it being made to appear to the Commission that all the terms, conditions and obligations set forth in the application and permit have been fully met, and that no cause or circumstance arising or first coming to the knowledge of the Commission since the granting of the permit would, in the judgment of the Commission, make the operation of such station against the public interest, the Commission shall issue a license to the lawful holder of said permit for the operation of said station. Said license shall conform generally to the terms of said permit. The provisions of Section 309(a), (b), (c), (d), (e), (f), and (g), shall not apply with respect to any station license the issuance of which is provided for and governed by the provisions of this subsection.

(d) A permit for construction shall not be required for Government stations, amateur stations, or mobile stations. A permit for construction shall not be required for public coast stations, privately owned fixed microwave stations, or stations licensed to common carriers, unless the Commission determines that the public interest, convenience, and necessity would be served by requiring such permits for any such stations. With respect to any broadcasting station, the Commission shall not have any authority to waive the requirement of a permit for construction, **except that the Commission may by regulation determine that a permit shall not be required for minor changes in the facilities of authorized broadcast stations**. With respect to any other station or class of stations, the Commission shall not waive <del>such</del> **the** requirement **for a construction permit** unless the Commission determines that the public interest, convenience, and necessity would be served by such a waiver.

Section 320 [47 USC Section 320]. Designation of Stations Liable to Interfere with Distress Signals.

The Commission is authorized to designate from time to time radio stations the communications or signals of which, in its opinion, are liable to interference with the transmission or reception of distress signals of ships. Such stations are required to keep a licensed radio operator listening in on the frequencies designated for signals of distress and radio communications relating thereto during the entire period the transmitter of such station is in operation.

Section 321 [47 USC Section 321]. Distress Signals and Communications.

(a) The transmitting set in a radio station on shipboard may be adjusted in such a manner as to produce a maximum radiation, irrespective of the amount of interference which may thus be caused, when such station is sending radio communications or signals of distress and radio communications relating thereto.

(b) All radio stations, including government stations and stations on board foreign vessels when within the territorial waters of the United States, shall give absolute priority to radio communications or signals relating to ships in distress; shall cease all sending on frequencies which will interfere with hearing a radio communication or signal of distress, and, except when engaged in answering or aiding the ship in distress, shall refrain from sending any radio communications or signals until there is assurance that no interference will be caused with the radio communications or signals relating thereto, and shall assist the vessel in distress, so far as possible, by complying with its instructions.

Section 322 [47 USC Section 322]. Intercommunication in Mobile Service.

Every land station open to general public service between the coast and vessels or aircraft at sea shall, within the scope of its normal operations, be bound to exchange radio communications or signals with any ship or aircraft station at sea; and each station on shipboard or aircraft at sea shall, within the scope of its normal operations, be bound to exchange radio communications or signals with any other station on shipboard or aircraft at sea or with any land station open to general public service between the coast and vessels or aircraft at sea: Provided, that such exchange of radio communication shall be without distinction as to radio systems or instruments adopted by each station.

Section 323 [47 USC Section 323]. Interference Between Government and Commercial Stations.

(a) At all places where government and private or commercial radio stations on land operate in such close proximity that interference with the work of government stations cannot be avoided when they are operating simultaneously, such private or commercial stations as do interfere with the transmission or reception of radio communications or signals by the government stations concerned shall not use their transmitters during the first fifteen minutes of each hour, local standard time.

(b) The government stations for which the above-mentioned division of time is established shall transmit radio communications or signals only during the first fifteen minutes of each hour, local standard time, except in case of signals or radio communications relating to vessels in distress and vessel requests for information as to course, location or compass direction.

Section 324 [47 USC Section 324]. Use of Minimum Power.

In all circumstances, except in case of radio communications or signals relating to vessels in distress, all radio stations, including those owned and operated by the United States, shall use the minimum amount of power necessary to carry out the communication desired.

Section 325 [47 USC Section 325]. False Distress Signals; Rebroadcasting; Studios of Foreign Stations.

(a) No person within the jurisdiction of the United States shall knowingly utter or transmit, or cause to be uttered or transmitted, any false or fraudulent signal of distress, or communication relating thereto, nor shall any broadcasting station rebroadcast the program or any part thereof of another broadcasting station without the express authority of the originating station.

(b)(1) Following the date that is one year after the date of enactment of the Cable Television Consumer Protection and Competition Act of 1992, no cable system or other multichannel video programming distributor shall retransmit the signal of a broadcasting station, or any part thereof, except --

(A) with the express authority of the originating station; or

(B) pursuant to Section 614, in the case of a station electing, in accordance with this subsection, to assert the right to carriage under such section.

(2) The provisions of this subsection shall not apply to --

(A) retransmission of the signal of a noncommercial broadcasting station;

(B) retransmission directly to a home satellite antenna of the signal of a broadcasting station that is not owned or operated by, or affiliated with, a broadcasting network, if such signal was retransmitted by a satellite carrier on May 1, 1991;

(C) retransmission of the signal of a broadcasting station that is owned or operated by, or affiliated with, a broadcasting network directly to a home satellite antenna, if the household receiving the signal is an unserved household; or

(D) retransmission by a cable operator or other multichannel video programming distributor of the signal of a superstation if such signal was obtained from a satellite carrier and the originating station was a superstation on May 1, 1991.

For purposes of this paragraph, the terms "satellite carrier," "superstation," and "unserved household" have the meanings given those terms, respectively, in Section 119(d) of Title 17, United States Code, as in effect on the date of enactment of the Cable Television Consumer Protection and Competition Act of 1992.

(3)(A) Within 45 days after the date of enactment of the Cable Television Consumer Protection and Competition Act of 1992, the Commission shall commence a rulemaking proceeding to establish regulations to govern the exercise by television broadcast stations of the right to grant retransmission consent under this subsection and of the right to signal carriage under Section 614, and such other regulations as are necessary to administer the limitations contained in paragraph (2). The Commission shall consider in such proceeding the impact that the grant of retransmission consent by television stations may have on the rates for the basic service tier and shall ensure that the regulations prescribed under this subsection do not conflict with the Commission's obligation under Section 623(b)(1) to ensure that the rates for the basic service tier are reasonable. Such rulemaking proceeding shall be completed within 180 days after the date of enactment of the Cable Television Consumer Protection and Competition Act of 1992.

(B) The regulations required by subparagraph (A) shall require that television stations, within one year after the date of enactment of the Cable Television Consumer Protection and Competition Act of 1992 and every three years thereafter, make an election between the right to grant retransmission consent under this subsection and the right to signal carriage under Section 614. If there

439

is more than one cable system which services the same geographic area, a station's election shall apply to all such cable systems.

(4) If an originating television station elects under paragraph (3)(B) to exercise its right to grant retransmission consent under this subsection with respect to a cable system, the provisions of Section 614 shall not apply to the carriage of the signal of such station by such cable system.

(5) The exercise by a television broadcast station of the right to grant retransmission consent under this subsection shall not interfere with or supersede the rights under Section 614 or 615 of any station electing to assert the right to signal carriage under that section.

(6) Nothing in this section shall be construed as modifying the compulsory copyright license established in Section 111 of Title 17, United States Code, or as affecting existing or future video programming licensing agreements between broadcasting stations and video programmers.

(c) No person shall be permitted to locate, use, or maintain a radio broadcast studio or other place or apparatus from which or whereby sound waves are converted into electrical energy, or mechanical or physical reproduction of sound waves produced, and caused to be transmitted or delivered to a radio station in a foreign country for the purpose of being broadcast from any radio station there having a power output of sufficient intensity and/or being so located geographically that its emissions may be received consistently in the United States, without first obtaining a permit from the Commission upon proper application therefor.

(d) Such application shall contain such information as the Commission may by regulation prescribe, and the granting or refusal thereof shall be subject to the requirements of Section 309 hereof with respect to applications for station licenses or renewal or modification thereof, and the license or permission so granted shall be revocable for false statements in the application so required or when the Commission, after hearings, shall find its continuation no longer in the public interest.

Section 326 [47 USC Section 326]. Censorship; Indecent Language.

Nothing in this Act shall be understood or construed to give the Commission the power of censorship over the radio communications or signals transmitted by any radio station, and no regulation or condition shall be promulgated or fixed by the Commission which shall interfere with the right of free speech by means of radio communication.

Section 327 [47 USC Section 327]. Use of Naval Stations for Commercial Messages.

The Secretary of the Navy is hereby authorized, unless restrained by international agreement, under the terms and conditions and at rates prescribed by him, which rates shall be just and reasonable, and which, upon complaint, shall be subject to review and revision by the Commission, to use all radio stations and apparatus, wherever located, owned by the United States and under the control of the Navy Department, (a) for the reception and transmission of press messages offered by any newspaper published in the United States, its territories or possessions, or published by citizens of the United States in foreign countries, or by any press association of the United States, and (b) for the reception and transmission of private commercial messages between ships, between ship and shore, between localities in Alaska and between Alaska and the continental United States: Provided, that the rates fixed for the reception and transmission of all such messages, other than press messages between the Pacific coast of the United States, Hawaii, Alaska, Guam, American Samoa, the Philippine Islands, and the Orient, and between the

United States and the Virgin Islands, shall not be less than the rates charged by privately owned and operated stations for like messages and service: Provided further, that the right to use such stations for any of the purposes named in this section shall terminate and cease as between any countries or localities or between any locality and privately operated ships whenever privately owned and operated stations are capable of meeting the normal communication requirements between such countries or localities or between any locality and privately operated ships, and the Commission shall have notified the Secretary of the Navy thereof.

Section 328 [47 USC Section 328]. [Deleted]

Section 329 [47 USC Section 329]. Administration of Radio Laws in Territories and Possessions.

The Commission is authorized to designate any officer or employee of any other department of the Government on duty in any Territory or possession of the United States to render therein such service in connection with the administration of this Act as the Commission may prescribe, and also to designate any officer or employee of any other department of the Government to render such services at any place within the United States in connection with the administration of Title III of this Act as may be necessary: Provided, that such designation shall be approved by the head of the department in which such person is employed.

Section 330 [47 USC Section 330]. Prohibition Against Shipment of Certain Television Receivers.

(a) No person shall ship in interstate commerce, or import from any foreign country into the United States, for sale or resale to the public, apparatus described in paragraph(s) of Section 303 unless it complies with rules prescribed by the Commission pursuant to the authority granted by that paragraph: Provided, that this section shall not apply to carriers transporting such apparatus without trading in it.

(b) No person shall ship in interstate commerce, manufacture, assemble, or import from any foreign country into the United States, any apparatus described in Section 303(u) of this Act except in accordance with rules prescribed by the Commission pursuant to the authority granted by that section. Such rules shall provide performance and display standards for such built-in decoder circuitry. Such rules shall further require that all such apparatus be able to receive and display closed captioning which have been transmitted by way of line 21 of the vertical blanking interval and which conform to the signal and display specifications set forth in the Public Broadcasting System engineering report numbered E-7709-C dated May 1980, as amended by the Telecaption II Decoder Module Performance Specification published by the National Captioning Institute, November 1985. As new video technology is developed, the Commission shall take such action as the Commission determines appropriate to ensure that closed-captioning service continues to be available to consumers. This subsection shall not apply to carriers transporting such apparatus without trading it.

(c)**(1) Except as provided in paragraph (2), no person shall ship in interstate commerce or manufacture in the United States any apparatus described in Section 303(x) of this Act except in accordance with rules prescribed by the Commission pursuant to the authority granted by that section.**

(2) This subsection shall not apply to carriers transporting apparatus referred to in paragraph (1) without trading in it.

441

(3) The rules prescribed by the Commission under this subsection shall provide for the oversight by the Commission of the adoption of standards by industry for blocking technology. Such rules shall require that all such apparatus be able to receive the rating signals which have been transmitted by way of line 21 of the vertical blanking interval and which conform to the signal and blocking specifications established by industry under the supervision of the Commission.

(4) As new video technology is developed, the Commission shall take such action as the Commission determines appropriate to ensure that blocking service continues to be available to consumers. If the Commission determines that an alternative blocking technology exists that--

(A) enables parents to block programming based on identifying programs without ratings,

(B) is available to consumers at a cost which is comparable to the cost of technology that allows parents to block programming based on common ratings, and

(C) will allow parents to block a broad range of programs on a multichannel system as effectively and as easily as technology that allows parents to block programming based on common ratings, the Commission shall amend the rules prescribed pursuant to Section 303(x) to require that the apparatus described in such section be equipped with either the blocking technology described in such section or the alternative blocking technology described in this paragraph.

(d) For the purposes of this section, <del>Section</del> **and Sections** 303(s) <del>and Section</del>, 303(u)<del>,</del>, **and 303(x)--**

(1) The term "interstate commerce" means (A) commerce between any State, the District of Columbia, the Commonwealth of Puerto Rico, or any possession of the United States and any place outside thereof which is within the United States, (B) commerce between points in the same State, the District of Columbia, the Commonwealth of Puerto Rico, or possession of the United States but through any place outside thereof, or (C) commerce wholly within the District of Columbia or any possession of the United States.

(2) The term "United States" means the several States, the District of Columbia, the Commonwealth of Puerto Rico, and the possessions of the United States, but does not include the Canal Zone.

Section 331 [47 USC Section 331]. Very High Frequency Stations and AM Radio Stations.

(a) Very high frequency stations. - It shall be the policy of the Federal Communications Commission to allocate channels for very high frequency commercial television broadcasting in a manner which ensures that not less than one such channel shall be allocated to each State, if technically feasible. In any case in which a licensee of a very high frequency commercial television broadcast station notifies the Commission to the effect that such licensee will agree to the reallocation of its channel to a community within a State in which there is allocated no very high frequency commercial television broadcast channel at the time of such notification, the Commission shall, notwithstanding any other provision of law, order such reallocation and issue a license to such licensee for that purpose pursuant to such notification for a term of not to exceed 5 years as provided in Section 307(d) of the Communications Act of 1934.

(b) AM radio stations. - It shall be the policy of the Commission, in any case in which the licensee of an existing AM daytime-only station located in a community with a population of more than 100,000 persons that lacks a local full-time aural station licensed to that community and that is located within a Class I station primary service area notifies the Commission that such licensee seeks to provide full-time service, to ensure that such a licensee is able to place a principal community contour signal over its entire community of license 24 hours a day, if technically feasible. The Commission shall report to the appropriate committees of Congress within 30 days after the date of enactment of this Act on how it intends to meet this policy goal.

Section 332 [47 USC Section 332]. Mobile Services.

(a) In taking actions to manage the spectrum to be made available for use by the private mobile services, the Commission shall consider, consistent with Section 1 of this Act, whether such actions will --

(1) promote the safety of life and property;

(2) improve the efficiency of spectrum use and reduce the regulatory burden upon spectrum users, based upon sound engineering principles, user operational requirements, and marketplace demands;

(3) encourage competition and provide services to the largest feasible number of users; or

(4) increase interservice sharing opportunities between private mobile services and other services.

(b)(1) The Commission, in coordinating the assignment of frequencies to stations in the private mobile services and in the fixed services (as defined by the Commission by rule), shall have authority to utilize assistance furnished by advisory coordinating committees consisting of individuals who are not officers or employees of the Federal Government.

(2) The authority of the Commission established in this subsection shall not be subject to or affected by the provisions of Part III of Title 5, United States Code, or Section 3679(b) of the Revised Statutes (31 USC §665(b)).

(3) Any person who provides assistance to the Commission under this subsection shall not be considered, by reason of having provided such assistance, a Federal employee.

(4) Any advisory coordinating committee which furnishes assistance to the Commission under this subsection shall not be subject to the provisions of the Federal Advisory Committee Act.

(c) Regulatory Treatment of Mobile Services.

(1) Common Carrier Treatment of Commercial Mobile Services.

(A) A person engaged in the provision of service that is a commercial mobile service shall, insofar as such person is so engaged, be treated as a common carrier for purposes of this Act, except for such provisions of Title II as the Commission may specify by regulation as inapplicable to that service or person. In prescribing or amending any such regulation, the Commission may not specify any provision of Section 201, 202, or 208, and may specify any other provision only if the Commission determines that--

(i) enforcement of such provision is not necessary in order to ensure that the charges, practices, classifications, or regulations for or in connection with that service are just and reasonable and are not unjustly or unreasonably discriminatory;

443

(ii) enforcement of such provision is not necessary for the protection of consumers; and

(iii) specifying such provision is consistent with the public interest.

(B) Upon reasonable request of any person providing commercial mobile service, the Commission shall order a common carrier to establish physical connections with such service pursuant to the provisions of Section 201 of this Act. Except to the extent that the Commission is required to respond to such a request, this subparagraph shall not be construed as a limitation or expansion of the Commission's authority to order interconnection pursuant to this Act.

(C) The Commission shall review competitive market conditions with respect to commercial mobile services and shall include in its annual report an analysis of those conditions. Such analysis shall include an identification of the number of competitors in various commercial mobile services, an analysis of whether or not there is effective competition, an analysis of whether any of such competitors have a dominant share of the market for such services, and a statement of whether additional providers or classes of providers in those services would be likely to enhance competition. As a part of making a determination with respect to the public interest under subparagraph (A)(iii), the Commission shall consider whether the proposed regulation (or amendment thereof) will promote competitive market conditions, including the extent to which such regulation (or amendment) will enhance competition among providers of commercial mobile services. If the Commission determines that such regulation (or amendment) will promote competition among providers of commercial mobile services, such determination may be the basis for a Commission finding that such regulation (or amendment) is in the public interest.

(D) The Commission shall, not later than 180 days after the date of enactment of this subparagraph, complete a rulemaking required to implement this paragraph with respect to the licensing of personal communications services, including making any determinations required by subparagraph (C).

(2) Non-Common Carrier Treatment of Private Mobile Services. -- A person engaged in the provision of a service that is a private mobile service shall not, insofar as such person is so engaged, be treated as a common carrier for any purpose under this Act. A common carrier (other than a person that was treated as a provider of a private land mobile service prior to the enactment of the Omnibus Budget Reconciliation Act of 1993) shall not provide any dispatch service on any frequency allocated for common carrier service, except to the extent that such dispatch service is provided on stations licensed in the domestic public land mobile radio service before January 1, 1982. The Commission may by regulation terminate, in whole or in part, the prohibition contained in the preceding sentence if the Commission determines that such termination will serve the public interest.

(3) State Preemption. -- (A) Notwithstanding Sections 2(b) and 221(b), no State or local government shall have any authority to regulate the entry of or the rates charged by any commercial mobile service or any private mobile service, except that this paragraph shall not prohibit a State from regulating the other terms and conditions of commercial mobile services. Nothing in this subparagraph shall exempt providers of commercial mobile services (where such services are a substitute for land line telephone exchange service for a substantial portion of the communications within such State) from requirements imposed by a State commission on all providers of telecommunications services necessary to ensure the universal availability of telecommunications service at affordable rates. Notwithstanding the first sentence of this subparagraph, a State may petition the Commission for authority to regulate the

rates for any commercial mobile service and the Commission shall grant such petition if such State demonstrates that--

(i) market conditions with respect to such services fail to protect subscribers adequately from unjust and unreasonable rates or rates that are unjustly or unreasonably discriminatory; or

(ii) such market conditions exist and such service is a replacement for land line telephone exchange service for a substantial portion of the telephone land line exchange service within such State.

The Commission shall provide reasonable opportunity for public comment in response to such petition, and shall, within 9 months after the date of its submission, grant or deny such petition. If the Commission grants such petition, the Commission shall authorize the State to exercise under State law such authority over rates, for such periods of time, as the Commission deems necessary to ensure that such rates are just and reasonable and not unjustly or unreasonably discriminatory.

(B) If a State has in effect on June 1, 1993, any regulation concerning the rates for any commercial mobile service offered in such State on such date, such State may, no later than 1 year after the date of enactment of the Omnibus Budget Reconciliation Act of 1993, petition the Commission requesting that the State be authorized to continue exercising authority over such rates. If a State files such a petition, the State's existing regulation shall, notwithstanding subparagraph (A), remain in effect until the Commission completes all action (including any reconsideration) on such petition. The Commission shall review such petition in accordance with the procedures established in such subparagraph, shall complete all action (including any reconsideration) within twelve months after such petition is filed, and shall grant such petition if the State satisfies the showing required under subparagraph (A)(i) or (A)(ii). If the Commission grants such petition, the Commission shall authorize the State to exercise under State law such authority over rates, for such period of time, as the Commission deems necessary to ensure that such rates are just and reasonable and not unjustly or unreasonably discriminatory. After a reasonable period of time, as determined by the Commission, has elapsed from the issuance of an order under subparagraph (A) or this subparagraph, any interested party may petition the Commission for an order that the exercise of authority by a State pursuant to such subparagraph is no longer necessary to ensure that the rates for commercial mobile services are just and reasonable and not unjustly or unreasonably discriminatory. The Commission shall provide reasonable opportunity for public comment in response to such petition, and shall, within 9 months after the date of its submission, grant or deny such petition in whole or in part.

(4) Regulatory Treatment of Communications Satellite Corporation. -- Nothing in this subsection shall be construed to alter or affect the regulatory treatment required by title IV of the Communications Satellite Act of 1962 of the corporation authorized by title III of such Act.

(5) Space Segment Capacity. -- Nothing in this section shall prohibit the Commission from continuing to determine whether the provision of space segment capacity by satellite systems to providers of commercial mobile services shall be treated as common carriage.

(6) Foreign Ownership. -- The Commission, upon a petition for waiver filed within 6 months after the date of enactment of the Omnibus Budget Reconciliation Act of 1993, may waive the application of Section 310(b) to any foreign ownership that lawfully existed before May 24, 1993, of any provider of a private land mobile service that will be treated as a common carrier as a result of the enactment of the Omnibus Budget Reconciliation Act of 1993, but only upon the following conditions:

(A) The extent of foreign ownership interest shall not be increased above the extent which existed on May 24, 1993.

(B) Such waiver shall not permit the subsequent transfer of ownership to any other person in violation of Section 310(b).

(7) Preservation of local zoning authority.--

(A) General authority.--Except as provided in this paragraph, nothing in this Act shall limit or affect the authority of a State or local government or instrumentality thereof over decisions regarding the placement, construction, and modification of personal wireless service facilities.

(B) Limitations.--

(i) The regulation of the placement, construction, and modification of personal wireless service facilities by any State or local government or instrumentality thereof--

(I) shall not unreasonably discriminate among providers of functionally equivalent services; and

(II) shall not prohibit or have the effect of prohibiting the provision of personal wireless services.

(ii) A State or local government or instrumentality thereof shall act on any request for authorization to place, construct, or modify personal wireless service facilities within a reasonable period of time after the request is duly filed with such government or instrumentality, taking into account the nature and scope of such request.

(iii) Any decision by a State or local government or instrumentality thereof to deny a request to place, construct, or modify personal wireless service facilities shall be in writing and supported by substantial evidence contained in a written record.

(iv) No State or local government or instrumentality thereof may regulate the placement, construction, and modification of personal wireless service facilities on the basis of the environmental effects of radio frequency emissions to the extent that such facilities comply with the Commission's regulations concerning such emissions.

(v) Any person adversely affected by any final action or failure to act by a State or local government or any instrumentality thereof that is inconsistent with this subparagraph may, within 30 days after such action or failure to act, commence an action in any court of competent jurisdiction. The court shall hear and decide such action on an expedited basis. Any person adversely affected by an act or failure to act by a State or local government or any instrumentality thereof that is inconsistent with clause (iv) may petition the Commission for relief.

(C) Definitions.--For purposes of this paragraph--

(i) the term "personal wireless services" means commercial mobile services, unlicensed wireless services, and common carrier wireless exchange access services;

(ii) the term "personal wireless service facilities" means facilities for the provision of personal wireless services; and

(iii) the term "unlicensed wireless service" means the offering of telecommunications services using duly authorized devices which do not require individual licenses, but does not mean the provision of direct-to-home satellite services (as defined in Section 303(v)).

(8) Mobile services access.--A person engaged in the provision of commercial mobile services, insofar as such person is so engaged, shall not be required to provide equal access to

common carriers for the provision of telephone toll services. **If the Commission determines that subscribers to such services are denied access to the provider of telephone toll services of the subscribers' choice, and that such denial is contrary to the public interest, convenience, and necessity, then the Commission shall prescribe regulations to afford subscribers unblocked access to the provider of telephone toll services of the subscribers' choice through the use of a carrier identification code assigned to such provider or other mechanism. The requirements for unblocking shall not apply to mobile satellite services unless the Commission finds it to be in the public interest to apply such requirements to such services.**

(d) Definitions. -- For purposes of this section--

(1) the term "commercial mobile service" means any mobile service (as defined in Section 3 ~~(n))~~) that is provided for profit and makes interconnected service available (A) to the public or (B) to such classes of eligible users as to be effectively available to a substantial portion of the public, as specified by regulation by the Commission;

(2) the term "interconnected service" means service that is interconnected with the public switched network (as such terms are defined by regulation by the Commission) or service for which a request for interconnection is pending pursuant to subsection (c)(1)(B); and

(3) the term "private mobile service" means any mobile service (as defined in Section 3 ~~(n))~~) that is not a commercial mobile service or the functional equivalent of a commercial mobile service, as specified by regulation by the Commission.

Section 333 [47 USC Section 333]. Willful or Malicious Interference.

No person shall willfully or maliciously interfere with or cause interference to any radio communications of any station licensed or authorized by or under this Act or operated by the United States Government.

Section 334 [47 USC Section 334]. Limitation on Revision of Equal Employment Opportunity Regulations.

(a) Limitation. - Except as specifically provided in this section, the Commission shall not revise --

(1) the regulations concerning equal employment opportunity as in effect on September 1, 1992 (47 CFR §73.2080) as such regulations apply to television broadcast station licensees and permittees; or

(2) the forms used by such licensees and permittees to report pertinent employment data to the Commission.

(b) Midterm Review. - The Commission shall revise the regulations described in subsection (a) to require a midterm review of television broadcast station licensees' employment practices and to require the Commission to inform such licensees of necessary improvements in recruitment practices identified as a consequence of such review.

(c) Authority to Make Technical Revisions. - The Commission may revise the regulations described in subsection (a) to make nonsubstantive technical or clerical revisions in such regulations as necessary to reflect changes in technology, terminology, or Commission organization.

447

Section 335 [47 USC Section 335]. Direct Broadcast Satellite Service Obligations.

(a) Proceeding required to review DBS responsibilities. - The Commission shall, within 180 days after the date of enactment of this section, initiate a rulemaking proceeding to impose, on providers of direct broadcast satellite service, public interest or other requirements for providing video programming. Any regulations prescribed pursuant to such rulemaking shall, at a minimum, apply the access to broadcast time requirement of Section 312(a)(7) and the use of facilities requirements of Section 315 to providers of direct broadcast satellite service providing video programming. Such proceeding also shall examine the opportunities that the establishment of direct broadcast satellite service provides for the principle of localism under this Act, and the methods by which such principle may be served through technological and other developments in, or regulation of, such service.

(b) Carriage obligations for noncommercial, educational, and informational programming.--

(1) Channel capacity required. - The Commission shall require, as a condition of any provision, initial authorization, or authorization renewal for a provider of direct broadcast satellite service providing video programming, that the provider of such service reserve a portion of its channel capacity, equal to not less than 4 percent nor more than 7 percent, exclusively for noncommercial programming of an educational or informational nature.

(2) Use of unused channel capacity. - A provider of such service may utilize for any purpose any unused channel capacity required to be reserved under this subsection pending the actual use of such channel capacity for noncommercial programming of an educational or informational nature.

(3) Prices, terms, and conditions; editorial control. - A provider of direct broadcast satellite service shall meet the requirements of this subsection by making channel capacity available to national educational programming suppliers, upon reasonable prices, terms, and conditions, as determined by the Commission under paragraph (4). The provider of direct broadcast satellite service shall not exercise any editorial control over any video programming provided pursuant to this subsection.

(4) Limitations. - In determining reasonable prices under paragraph (3) -

(A) the Commission shall take into account the nonprofit character of the programming provider and any Federal funds used to support such programming;

(B) the Commission shall not permit such prices to exceed, for any channel made available under this subsection, 50 percent of the total direct costs of making such channel available; and

(C) in the calculation of total direct costs, the Commission shall exclude --

(i) marketing costs, general administrative costs, and similar overhead costs of the provider of direct broadcast satellite service; and

(ii) the revenue that such provider might have obtained by making such channel available to a commercial provider of video programming.

(5) Definitions. - For purposes of this subsection --

(A) The term "provider of direct broadcast satellite service" means --

(i) a licensee for a Ku-band satellite system under Part 100 of Title 47 of the Code of Federal Regulations; or

(ii) any distributor who controls a minimum number of channels (as specified by Commission regulation) using a Ku-band fixed service satellite system for the provision of video programming directly to the home and licensed under Part 25 of Title 47 of the Code of Federal Regulations.

(B) The term "national educational programming supplier" includes any qualified noncommercial educational television station. other public telecommunications entities, and public or private educational institutions.

Section 336 [47 USC Section 336]. Broadcast Spectrum Flexibility.

(a) Commission Action.--If the Commission determines to issue additional licenses for advanced television services, the Commission--

(1) should limit the initial eligibility for such licenses to persons that, as of the date of such issuance, are licensed to operate a television broadcast station or hold a permit to construct such a station (or both); and

(2) shall adopt regulations that allow the holders of such licenses to offer such ancillary or supplementary services on designated frequencies as may be consistent with the public interest, convenience, and necessity.

(b) Contents of Regulations.--In prescribing the regulations required by subsection (a), the Commission shall--

(1) only permit such licensee or permittee to offer ancillary or supplementary services if the use of a designated frequency for such services is consistent with the technology or method designated by the Commission for the provision of advanced television services;

(2) limit the broadcasting of ancillary or supplementary services on designated frequencies so as to avoid derogation of any advanced television services, including high definition television broadcasts, that the Commission may require using such frequencies;

(3) apply to any other ancillary or supplementary service such of the Commission's regulations as are applicable to the offering of analogous services by any other person, except that no ancillary or supplementary service shall have any rights to carriage under Section 614 or 615 or be deemed a multichannel video programming distributor for purposes of Section 628;

(4) adopt such technical and other requirements as may be necessary or appropriate to assure the quality of the signal used to provide advanced television services, and may adopt regulations that stipulate the minimum number of hours per day that such signal must be transmitted; and

(5) prescribe such other regulations as may be necessary for the protection of the public interest, convenience, and necessity.

(c) Recovery of License.--If the Commission grants a license for advanced television services to a person that, as of the date of such issuance, is licensed to operate a television broadcast station or holds a permit to construct such a station (or both), the Commission shall, as a condition of such license, require that either the additional license or the original license held by the licensee be surrendered to the Commission for reallocation or reassignment (or both) pursuant to Commission regulation.

(d) Public Interest Requirement.--Nothing in this section shall be construed as relieving a television broadcasting station from its obligation to serve the public interest, convenience, and necessity. In the Commission's review of any application for renewal of a broadcast license for a television station that provides ancillary or supplementary services, the television licensee shall establish that all of its program services on the existing or advanced television spectrum are in the public interest. Any violation of the Commission rules applicable to ancillary or supplementary services shall reflect upon the licensee's qualifications for renewal of its license.

(e) Fees.--

(1) Services to which fees apply.--If the regulations prescribed pursuant to subsection (a) permit a licensee to offer ancillary or supplementary services on a designated frequency--

(A) for which the payment of a subscription fee is required in order to receive such services, or

(B) for which the licensee directly or indirectly receives compensation from a third party in return for transmitting material furnished by such third party (other than commercial advertisements used to support broadcasting for which a subscription fee is not required), the Commission shall establish a program to assess and collect from the licensee for such designated frequency an annual fee or other schedule or method of payment that promotes the objectives described in subparagraphs (A) and (B) of paragraph (2).

(2) Collection of fees.--The program required by paragraph (1) shall--

(A) be designed (i) to recover for the public a portion of the value of the public spectrum resource made available for such commercial use, and (ii) to avoid unjust enrichment through the method employed to permit such uses of that resource;

(B) recover for the public an amount that, to the extent feasible, equals but does not exceed (over the term of the license) the amount that would have been recovered had such services been licensed pursuant to the provisions of Section 309(j) of this Act and the Commission's regulations thereunder; and

(C) be adjusted by the Commission from time to time in order to continue to comply with the requirements of this paragraph.

(3) Treatment of revenues.--

(A) General rule.--Except as provided in subparagraph (B), all proceeds obtained pursuant to the regulations required by this subsection shall be deposited in the Treasury in accordance with chapter 33 of title 31, United States Code.

(B) Retention of revenues.--Notwithstanding subparagraph (A), the salaries and expenses account of the Commission shall retain as an offsetting collection such sums as may be necessary from such proceeds for the costs of developing and implementing the program required by this section and regulating and supervising advanced television services. Such offsetting collections shall be available for obligation subject to the terms and conditions of the receiving appropriations account, and shall be deposited in such accounts on a quarterly basis.

(4) Report.--Within 5 years after the date of enactment of the Telecommunications Act of 1996, the Commission shall report to the Congress on the implementation of the program required by this subsection, and shall annually thereafter advise the Congress on the amounts collected pursuant to such program.

(f) Evaluation.--Within 10 years after the date the Commission first issues additional licenses for advanced television services, the Commission shall conduct an evaluation of the advanced television services program. Such evaluation shall include--

(1) an assessment of the willingness of consumers to purchase the television receivers necessary to receive broadcasts of advanced television services;

(2) an assessment of alternative uses, including public safety use, of the frequencies used for such broadcasts; and

(3) the extent to which the Commission has been or will be able to reduce the amount of spectrum assigned to licensees.

(g) Definitions.--As used in this section:

(1) Advanced television services.--The term "advanced television services" means television services provided using digital or other advanced technology as further defined in the opinion, report, and order of the Commission entitled Advanced Television Systems and Their Impact Upon the Existing Television Broadcast Service, MM Docket 87-268, adopted September 17, 1992, and successor proceedings.

(2) Designated frequencies.--The term "designated frequency" means each of the frequencies designated by the Commission for licenses for advanced television services.

(3) High definition television.--The term "high definition television" refers to systems that offer approximately twice the vertical and horizontal resolution of receivers generally available on the date of enactment of the Telecommunications Act of 1996, as further defined in the proceedings described in paragraph (1) of this subsection.

Part II - Radio Equipment and Radio Operators on Board Ship

Section 351 [47 USC Section 351]. Ship Radio Stations and Operations

(a) Except as provided in Section 352 hereof it shall be unlawful --

(1) For any ship of the United States, other than a cargo ship of less than three hundred gross tons, to be navigated in the open sea outside of a harbor or port, or for any ship of the United States or any foreign country, other than a cargo ship of less than three hundred gross tons, to leave or attempt to leave any harbor or port of the United States for a voyage in the open sea, unless such ship is equipped with an efficient radio station in operating condition, as specified by subparagraphs (A) and (B) of this paragraph, in charge of and operated by one or more radio officers or operators, adequately installed and protected so as to insure proper operation, and so as not to endanger the ship and radio station as hereinafter provided, and in the case of a ship of the United States, unless there is on board a valid station license issued in accordance with this Act.

(A) Passenger ships irrespective of size and cargo ships of one thousand six hundred gross tons and upward shall be equipped with a radiotelegraph station complying with the provisions of this part;

(B) Cargo ships of three hundred gross tons and upward but less than one thousand six hundred gross tons, unless equipped with a radiotelegraph station complying with the provisions of this part, shall be equipped with a radiotelephone station complying with the provisions of this part.

(2) For any ship of the United States of one thousand six hundred gross tons and upward to be navigated in the open sea outside of a harbor or port, or for any such ship of the United States or any foreign country to leave or attempt to leave any harbor or port of the United States for a voyage in the open sea, unless such ship is equipped with efficient radio direction finding apparatus approved by the Commission, properly adjusted in operating condition as hereinafter provided.

(b) A ship which is not subject to the provisions of this part at the time of its departure on a voyage shall not become subject to such provisions on account of any deviation from its intended voyage due to stress of weather or any other cause over which neither the master, the owner, nor the charterer (if any) has control.

451

Section 352 [47 USC Section 352]. Exceptions.

(a) The provisions of this part shall not apply to --

(1) A ship of war;

(2) A ship of the United States belonging to and operated by the Government, except a ship of the Maritime Administration of the Department of Transportation, the Inland and Coastwise Waterways Service, or the Panama Canal Company;

(3) A foreign ship belonging to a country which is a party to any Safety Convention in force between the United States and that country which ship carries a valid certificate exempting said ship from the radio provisions of that Convention, or which ship conforms to the radio requirements of such Convention or Regulations and has on board a valid certificate to that effect, or which ship is not subject to the radio provisions of any such convention;

(4) Yachts of less than six hundred gross tons not subject to the radio provisions of the Safety Convention;

(5) Vessels in tow;

(6) A ship navigating solely on any bays, sounds, rivers, or protected waters within the jurisdiction of the United States, or to a ship leaving or attempting to leave any harbor or port of the United States for a voyage solely on any bays, sounds, rivers, or protected waters within the jurisdiction of the United States;

(7) A ship navigating solely on the Great Lakes of North America and the River Saint Lawrence as far east as a straight line drawn from Cap des Rosiers to West Point, Anticosti Island, and, on the north side of Anticosti Island, the sixty-third meridian, or to a ship leaving or attempting to leave any harbor or port of the United States for a voyage solely on such waters and within such area;

(8) A ship which is navigated during the course of a voyage both on the Great Lakes of North America and in the open sea, during the period while such ship is being navigated within the Great Lakes of North America and their connecting and tributary waters as far east as the lower exit of the Saint Lambert lock at Montreal in the Province of Quebec, Canada;

(b) Except for nuclear ships, the Commission may, if it considers that the route or the conditions of the voyage or other circumstances are such as to render a radio station unreasonable or unnecessary for the purposes of this part, exempt from the provisions of this part any ship, or any class of ships, which falls within any of the following descriptions:

(1) Passenger ships which in the course of their voyage do not go more than twenty nautical miles from the nearest land or, alternatively, do not go more than two hundred nautical miles between two consecutive ports;

(2) Cargo ships which in the course of their voyage do not go more than one hundred and fifty nautical miles from the nearest land;

(3) Passenger vessels of less than one hundred gross tons not subject to the radio provisions of the Safety Convention;

(4) Sailing ships.

(c) If because of unforeseeable failure of equipment, a ship is unable to comply with the equipment requirements of this part without undue delay of the ship, the mileage limitations set forth in paragraphs (1) and (2) of subsection (b) shall not apply: Provided, that exemption of the ship is found to be reasonable or necessary in accordance with subsection (b) to permit the ship to proceed to a port where the equipment deficiency may be remedied.

452

(d) Except for nuclear ships, and except for ships of five thousand gross tons and upward which are subject to the Safety Convention, the Commission may exempt from the requirements, for radio direction finding apparatus, of this part and of the Safety Convention, any ship which falls within the descriptions set forth in paragraphs (1), (2), (3) and (4) of subsection (b) of this section, if it considers that the route or conditions of the voyage or other circumstances are such as to render such apparatus unreasonable or unnecessary.

Section 353 [47 USC Section 353]. Radio Officers, Watches, Auto Alarm-Radiotelegraph Equipped Ships.

(a) Each cargo ship which in accordance with this part is equipped with a radiotelegraph station and which is not equipped with a radiotelegraph auto alarm, and each passenger ship required by this part to be equipped with a radiotelegraph station, shall, for safety purposes, carry at least two radio officers.

(b) A cargo which in accordance with this part is equipped with a radiotelegraph station, which is equipped with a radiotelegraph auto alarm, shall, for safety purposes, carry at least one radio officer who shall have had at least six months' previous service in the aggregate as a radio officer in a station on board a ship or ships of the United States.

(c) Each ship of the United States which in accordance with this part is equipped with a radiotelegraph station shall, while being navigated in the open sea outside of a harbor or port, keep a continuous watch by means of radio officers whenever the station is not being used for authorized traffic: Provided, that, in lieu thereof, on a cargo ship equipped with a radiotelegraph auto alarm in proper operating condition, a watch of at least eight hours per day, in the aggregate, shall be maintained by means of a radio officer.

(d) The Commission shall, when it finds it necessary for safety purposes, have authority to prescribe the particular hours of watch on a ship of the United States which in accordance with this part is equipped with a radiotelegraph station.

(e) On all ships of the United States equipped with a radiotelegraph auto alarm, said apparatus shall be in operation at all times while the ship is being navigated in the open sea outside of a harbor or port when the radio officer is not on watch.

Section 354 [47 USC Section 353a]. Operators, Watches <—>— Radiotelephone Equipped Ships.

(a) Each cargo ship which in accordance with this part is equipped with a radiotelephone station shall, for safety purposes, carry at least one operator who may be the master, an officer, or a member of the crew.

(b) Each cargo ship of the United States which in accordance with this part is equipped with a radiotelephone station shall, while being navigated in the open sea outside of a harbor or port, maintain continuous watch whenever the station is not being used for authorized traffic.

Section 355 [47 USC Section 354]. Technical Requirements - Radiotelegraph Equipped Ships.

The radiotelegraph station and the radio direction finding apparatus required by Section 351 of this part shall comply with the following requirements:

(a) The radiotelegraph station shall include a main installation and a reserve installation, electrically separate and electrically independent of each other: Provided, that, in installations on cargo ships of three hundred gross tons and upward but less than one thousand six hundred gross tons, and in installations on cargo ships of one thousand six hundred gross tons and upward installed prior to November 19, 1952, if the main transmitter complies with all the requirements for the reserve transmitter, the latter may be omitted.

(b) The radiotelegraph station shall be so located that no harmful interference from extraneous mechanical or other noise will be caused to the proper reception of radio signals, and shall be placed in the upper part of the ship in a position of the greatest possible safety and as high as practicable above the deepest load waterline. The location of the radiotelegraph operating room or rooms shall be approved by the Commandant of the Coast Guard. The radiotelegraph installation shall be installed, in such a position that it will be protected against the harmful effects of water or extremes of temperature, and shall be readily accessible both for immediate use in case of distress and for repair.

(c) The radiotelegraph operating room shall be of sufficient size and of adequate ventilation to enable the main and reserve radiotelegraph installations to be operated efficiently, and shall not be used for any purpose which will interfere with the operation of the radiotelegraph station. The sleeping accommodation of at least one radio officer shall be situated as near as practicable to the radiotelegraph operating room. In ships the keels of which are laid on or after May 26, 1965, this sleeping accommodation shall not be within the radiotelegraph operating room.

(d) The main and reserve installations shall be capable of transmitting and receiving on the frequencies, and using the classes of emission, designated by the Commission pursuant to law for the purposes of distress and safety of navigation.

(e) The main and reserve installations shall, when connected to the main antenna, have a minimum normal range of two hundred nautical miles and one hundred nautical miles, respectively; that is, they must be capable of transmitting and receiving clearly perceptible signals from ship to ship by day and under normal conditions and circumstances over the specified ranges.

(f) Sufficient electrical energy shall be available at all times to operate the main installation over the normal range required by subsection (e) of this section as well as for the purpose of charging any batteries forming part of the radiotelegraph station.

(g) The reserve installation shall include a source of electrical energy independent of the propelling power of the ship and of any other electrical system and shall be capable of being put into operation rapidly and of working for at least six continuous hours. The reserve source of energy and its switchboard shall be as high as practicable in the ship and readily accessible to the radio officer.

(h) There shall be provided between the bridge of the ship and the radiotelegraph operating room, and between the bridge and the location of the radio direction finding apparatus, when such apparatus is not located on the bridge, an efficient two-way system for calling and voice communication which shall be independent of any other communication system in the ship.

(i) The radio direction finding apparatus shall be efficient and capable of receiving signals with the minimum of receiver noise and of taking bearings from which the true bearing and direction may be determined. It shall be capable of receiving signals on the radiotelegraph frequencies assigned by the radio regulations annexed to the International Telecommunication Convention in force for the purposes of distress, direction finding, and maritime radio beacons, and, in installations made after May 26, 1965, such other frequencies as the Commission may for safety purposes designate.

Section 356 [47 USC Section 354a]. Technical Requirements -- Radiotelephone Equipped Ships.

Cargo ships of three hundred gross tons and upward but less than one thousand six hundred gross tons may, in lieu of the radiotelegraph station prescribed by Section 355, be equipped with a radiotelephone station complying with the following requirements:

(a) The radiotelephone station shall be in the upper part of the ship, so located that it is sheltered to the greatest possible extent from noise which might impair the correct reception of messages and signals, and, unless such station is situated on the bridge, there shall be efficient communication with the bridge.

(b) The radiotelephone station shall be capable of transmitting and receiving on the frequencies, and using the classes of emission, designated by the Commission pursuant to law for the purpose of distress and safety of navigation.

(c) The radiotelephone installation shall have a minimum normal range of one hundred and fifty nautical miles; that is, it shall be capable of transmitting and receiving clearly perceptible signals from ship to ship by day and under normal conditions and circumstances over this range.

(d) There shall be available at all times a main source of electrical energy sufficient to operate the installation over the normal range required by subsection (c) of this section. If batteries are provided they shall have sufficient capacity to operate the transmitter and receiver for at least six continuous hours under normal working conditions. In installations made on or after November 19, 1952, a reserve source of electrical energy shall be provided in the upper part of the ship unless the main source of energy is so situated.

Section 357 [47 USC Section 355]. Survival Craft.

Every ship required to be provided with survival craft radio by treaty to which the United States is a party, by statute, or by regulation made in conformity with a treaty, convention, or statute, shall be fitted with efficient radio equipment appropriate to such requirement under such rules and regulations as the Commission may find necessary for safety of life. For purposes of this section "radio equipment" shall include portable as well as nonportable apparatus.

Section 358 [47 USC Section 356]. Approval of Installations.

Insofar as is necessary to carry out the purposes and requirements of this part, the Commission shall have authority, for any ship subject to this part --

(1) To approve the details as to the location and manner of installations of the equipment required by this part or of equipment necessitated by reason of the purposes and requirements of this part;

(2) To approve installations, apparatus, and spare parts necessary to comply with the purposes and requirements of this part;

(3) To prescribe such additional equipment as may be determined to be necessary to supplement that specified herein, for the proper functioning of the radio installation installed in accordance with this part or for the proper conduct of radio communication in time of emergency or distress.

Section 359 [47 USC Section 357]. Transmission of Information.

(a) The master of every ship of the United States, equipped with radio transmitting apparatus, which meets with dangerous ice, a dangerous derelict, a tropical storm, or any other direct danger to navigation, or encounters subfreezing air temperatures associated with gale force winds causing severe ice accretion on superstructures, or winds of force 10 or above on the Beaufort scale for which no storm warning has been received, shall cause to be transmitted all pertinent information relating thereto to ships in the vicinity and to the appropriate authorities on land, in accordance with rules and regulations issued by the Commission. When they consider it necessary, such authorities of the United States shall promptly bring the information received by them to the knowledge of those concerned, including interested foreign authorities.

(b) No charge shall be made by any ship or station in the mobile service of the United States for the transmission, receipt, or relay of the information designated in subsection (a) originating on a ship of the United States or of a foreign country.

(c) The transmission by any ship of the United States, made in compliance with subsection (a), to any station which imposes a charge for the reception, relay, or forwarding of the required information, shall be free of cost to the ship concerned and any communication charges incurred by the ship for transmission, relay, or forwarding of the information may be certified to the Commission for reimbursement out of moneys appropriated to the Commission for that purpose.

(d) No charge shall be made by any ship or station in the mobile service of the United States for the transmission of distress messages and replies thereto in connection with situations involving the safety of life and property at sea.

(e) Notwithstanding any other provision of law, any station or carrier may render free service in connection with situations involving the safety of life and property, including hydrographic reports, weather reports, reports regarding aids to navigation and medical assistance to injured or sick persons or ships and aircraft at sea. All free service permitted by this subsection shall be subject to such rules and regulations as the Commission may prescribe, which rules may limit such free service to the extent which the Commission finds desirable in the public interest.

Section 360 [47 USC Section 358]. Authority of Master.

The radio installation, the operators, the regulation of their watches, the transmission and receipt of messages, and the radio service of the ship except as they may be regulated by law or international agreement or by rules and regulations made in pursuance thereof, shall in the case of a ship of the United States be under the supreme control of the master.

Section 361 [47 USC Section 359]. Certificates.

(a) Each vessel of the United States to which the Safety Convention applies shall comply with the radio and communication provisions of said Convention at all times while the vessel is in use, in addition to all other requirements of law, and shall have on board an appropriate certificate as prescribed by the Safety Convention.

(b) Appropriate certificates concerning the radio particulars provided for in said Convention shall be issued upon proper request to any vessel which is subject to the radio provisions of the Safety

Convention and is found by the Commission to comply therewith. Cargo ship safety radio telegraphy certificates, cargo ship safety radiotelephony certificates, and exemption certificates, with respect to radio particulars shall be issued by the Commission. Other certificates concerning the radio particulars provided for in the said Convention shall be issued by the Commandant of the Coast Guard or whatever other agency is authorized by law to do so upon request of the Commission made after proper inspection or determination of the facts. If the holder of a certificate violates the radio provisions of the Safety Convention or the provisions of this Act, or the rules, regulations or conditions prescribed by the Commission, and if the effective administration of the Safety Convention or of this part so requires, the Commission, after hearing in accordance with law, is authorized to modify or cancel a certificate which it has issued, or to request the modification or cancellation of a certificate which has been issued by another agency upon the Commission's request. Upon receipt of such request for modification or cancellation, the Commandant of the Coast Guard, or whatever agency is authorized by law to do so, shall modify or cancel the certificate in accordance therewith.

Section 362 [47 USC Section 360]. Inspection.

(a) In addition to any other provisions required to be included in a radio station license, the station license of each ship of the United States subject to this title shall include particulars with reference to the items specifically required by this title.

(b) Every ship of the United States <s><,></s> **that is** subject to this part <s><,></s> shall have the equipment and apparatus prescribed therein inspected at least once each year by the Commission **or an entity designated by the Commission**. If, after such inspection, the Commission is satisfied that all relevant provisions of this Act and the station license have been complied with, <s><that></s> **the** fact shall be **so** certified <s><to></s> on the station license by the Commission. The Commission shall make such additional inspections at frequent intervals as **the Commission determines** may be necessary to <s><insure></s> **ensure** compliance with the requirements of this Act. The Commission may, upon a finding that the public interest <s><would></s> **could** be served thereby<s><.></s>**—**

(1) waive the annual inspection required under this section <s><from the time of first arrival at a United States port from a foreign port,></s> **for a period of up to 90 days** for the sole purpose of enabling <s><the></s> **a** vessel to **complete its voyage and** proceed <s><coastwise to another></s> **to a** port in the United States where an inspection can be held<s><: Provided, that such waiver may not exceed a period of thirty days.></s>**; or**

(2) waive the annual inspection required under this section for a vessel that is in compliance with the radio provisions of the Safety Convention and that is operating solely in waters beyond the jurisdiction of the United States, provided that such inspection shall be performed within 30 days of such vessel's return to the United States.

Section 363 [47 USC Section 361]. Control by Commission.

Nothing in this title shall be interpreted as lessening in any degree the control of the Commission over all matters connected with the radio equipment and its operation on shipboard and its decision and determination in regard to the radio requirements, installations, or exemptions from prescribed radio requirements shall be final, subject only to review in accordance with law.

Section 364 [47 USC Section 362]. Forfeitures.

The following forfeitures shall apply to this part, in addition to the penalties and forfeitures provided by Title V of this Act:

(a) Any ship that leaves or attempts to leave any harbor or port of the United States in violation of the provisions of this part, or the rules and regulations of the Commission made in pursuance thereof, or any ship of the United States that is navigated outside of any harbor or port in violation of any of the provisions of this part, or the rules and regulations of the Commission made in pursuance thereof, shall forfeit to the United States the sum of $5,000, recoverable by way of suit or libel. Each such departure or attempted departure and in the case of a ship of the United States each day during which such navigation occurs shall constitute a separate offense.

(b) Every willful failure on the part of the master of a ship of the United States to enforce or to comply with the provisions of this Act or the rules and regulations of the Commission as to equipment, operators, watches, or radio service shall cause him to forfeit to the United States the sum of $1,000.

Section 365 [47 USC Section 363]. Automated Ship Distress and Safety Systems.

Notwithstanding any provision of this Act or any other provision of law or regulation, a ship documented under the laws of the United States operating in accordance with the Global Maritime Distress and Safety System provisions of the Safety of Life at Sea Convention shall not be required to be equipped with a radio telegraphy station operated by one or more radio officers or operators. This section shall take effect for each vessel upon a determination by the United States Coast Guard that such vessel has the equipment required to implement the Global Maritime Distress and Safety System installed and operating in good working condition.

Part III - Radio Installations on Vessels Carrying Passengers for Hire

Section 381 [47 USC Section 381]. Vessels Transporting More Than Six Passengers for Hire Required to <Be> be Equipped <with Radio Telephone.> With Radiotelephone

Except as provided in Section 382, it shall be unlawful for any vessel of the United States, transporting more than six passengers for hire, to be navigated in the open sea or any tidewater within the jurisdiction of the United States adjacent or contiguous to the open sea, unless such vessel is equipped with an efficient radiotelephone installation in operating condition.

Section 382 [47 USC Section 382]. Vessels Excepted from Radiotelephone Requirement.

The provisions of this part shall not apply to --

(1) vessels which are equipped with a radio installation in accordance with the provisions of Part II of Title III of this Act, or in accordance with the radio requirements of the Safety Convention; and

(2) vessels of the United States belonging to and operated by the Government<, except a vessel of the United States Maritime Administration, the Inland and Coastwise Waterways Service, or the Panama Canal Company>; and

(3) vessels navigating on the Great Lakes.

Section 383 [47 USC Section 383]. Exemptions by Commission

The Commission shall exempt from the provisions of this part any vessel, or class of vessels, in the case of which the route or conditions of the voyage, or other conditions or circumstances, are such as to render a radio installation unreasonable, unnecessary, or ineffective, for the purposes of this Act.

Section 384 [47 USC Section 384]. Authority of Commission; Operations, Installations, and Additional Equipment.

The Commission shall have authority with respect to any vessel subject to this part --

(1) to specify operating and technical conditions and characteristics including frequencies, emissions, power, communication capability and range, of installations required by reason of this part;

(2) to approve the details as to the locations and manner of installation of the equipment required by this part or of equipment necessitated by reason of the purposes and requirements of this part;

(3) to approve installations, apparatus and spare parts necessary to comply with the purposes and requirements of this part;

(4) to prescribe such additional equipment as may be determined to be necessary to supplement that specified herein for the proper functioning of the radio installation installed in accordance with this part or for the proper conduct of radio communication in time of emergency or distress.

Section 385 [47 USC Section 385]. Inspections

<The> **The Commission or an entity designated by the** Commission shall make such inspections as may be necessary to insure compliance with the requirements of this part. **In accordance with such other provisions of law as apply to Government contracts, the Commission may enter into contracts with any person for the purpose of carrying out such inspections and certifying compliance with those requirements, and may, as part of any such contract, allow any such person to accept reimbursement from the license holder for travel and expense costs of any employee conducting an inspection or certification.**

Section 386 [47 USC Section 386]. Forfeitures.

The following forfeitures shall apply to this part in addition to penalties and forfeitures provided by Title V of this Act:

(a) Any vessel of the United States that is navigated in violation of the provisions of this part or of the rules and regulations of the Commission made in pursuance thereof shall forfeit to the United States the sum of $5,000 recoverable by way of suit or libel. Each day during which such navigation occurs shall constitute a separate offense.

459

(b) Every willful failure on the part of the master of a vessel of the United States to enforce or to comply with the provisions of this part or the rules and regulations of the Commission made in pursuance thereof shall cause him to forfeit to the United States the sum of $1,000.

Part IV - Assistance for Public Telecommunications Facilities; Telecommunications Demonstrations; Corporation for Public Broadcasting

Subpart A - Assistance for Public Telecommunications Facilities

Section 390 [47 USC Section 390]. Declaration of Purpose.

The purpose of this subpart is to assist, through matching grants, in the planning and construction of public telecommunications facilities in order to achieve the following objectives: (1) extend delivery of public telecommunications services to as many citizens of the United States as possible by the most efficient and economical means, including the use of broadcast and nonbroadcast technologies; (2) increase public telecommunications services and facilities available to, operated by, and owned by minorities and women; and (3) strengthen the capability of existing public television and radio stations to provide public telecommunications service to the public.

Section 391 [47 USC Section 391]. Authorization of Appropriations.

There are authorized to be appropriated $42,000,000 for each of the fiscal years 1992, 1993, and 1994, to be used by the Secretary of Commerce to assist in the planning and construction of public telecommunications facilities as provided in this subpart. Sums appropriated under this subpart for any fiscal year shall remain available until expended for payment of grants for projects for which applications approved by the Secretary pursuant to this subpart have been submitted within such fiscal year. Sums appropriated under this subpart may be used by the Secretary to cover the cost of administering the provisions of this subpart.

Section 392 [47 USC Section 392]. Grants for Construction and Planning.

(a) For each project for the construction of public telecommunications facilities there shall be submitted to the Secretary an application for a grant containing such information with respect to such project as the Secretary may require, including the total cost of such project, the amount of the grant requested for such project, and a 5-year plan outlining the applicant's projected facilities requirements and the projected costs of such facilities requirements. Each applicant shall also provide assurances satisfactory to the Secretary that --

(1) the applicant is (A) a public broadcast station; (B) a noncommercial telecommunications entity; (C) a system of public telecommunications entities; (D) a nonprofit foundation, corporation, institution, or association organized primarily for educational or cultural purposes; or (E) a State or local government (or any agency thereof), or a political or special purpose subdivision of a State;

(2) the operation of such public telecommunications facilities will be under the control of the applicant;

460

(3) necessary funds to construct, operate, and maintain such public telecommunications facilities will be available when needed;

(4) such public telecommunications facilities will be primarily for the provision of public telecommunications services and that the use of such public telecommunications facilities for purposes other than the provision of public telecommunications services will not interfere with the provision of such public telecommunications services as required in this part;

(5) the applicant has participated in comprehensive planning for such public telecommunications facilities in the area which the applicant proposes to serve, and such planning has included an evaluation of alternate technologies and coordination with State educational television and radio agencies, as appropriate; and

(6) the applicant will make the most efficient use of the grant.

(b) Upon approving any application under this section with respect to any project for the construction of public telecommunications facilities, the Secretary shall make a grant to the applicant in an amount determined by the Secretary, except that such amount shall not exceed 75 percent of the amount determined by the Secretary to be the reasonable and necessary cost of such project.

(c) The Secretary may provide such funds as the Secretary deems necessary for the planning of any project for which construction funds may be obtained under this section. An applicant for a planning grant shall provide such information with respect to such project as the Secretary may require and shall provide assurances satisfactory to the Secretary that the applicant meets the eligible requirements of subsection (a) to receive construction assistance.

(d) Any studies conducted by or for any grant recipient under this section shall be provided to the Secretary, if such studies are conducted through the use of funds received under this section.

(e) The Secretary shall establish such rules and regulations as may be necessary to carry out this subpart, including rules and regulations relating to the order of priority in approving applications for construction projects and relating to determining the amount of each grant for such projects.

(f) In establishing criteria for grants pursuant to Section 393 and in establishing procedures relating to the order of priority established in subsection (e) in approving applications for grants, the Secretary shall give special consideration to applications which would increase minority and women's ownership of, operation of, and participation in public telecommunications entities. The Secretary shall take affirmative steps to inform minorities and women of the availability of funds under this subpart, and the localities where new public telecommunications facilities are needed, and to provide such other assistance and information as may be appropriate.

(g) If, within 10 years after completion of any project for construction of public telecommunications facilities with respect to which a grant has been made under this section --

(1) the applicant or other owner of such facilities ceases to be an agency, institution, foundation, corporation, association, or other entity described in subsection (a)(1); or

(2) such facilities cease to be used only for the provision of public telecommunications services (or the use of such public telecommunications facilities for purposes other than the provision of public telecommunications services interferes with the provision of such public telecommunications services as required in this part) the United States shall be entitled to recover from the applicant or other owner of such facilities the amount bearing the same ratio to the value of such facilities at the time the applicant ceases to be such an entity or at the time of such determination (as determined by agreement of the parties or by action brought in the United States district court for the district in which such

461

facilities are situated), as the amount of the Federal participation bore to the cost of construction of such facilities.

(h) Each recipient of assistance under this subpart shall keep such records as may be reasonably necessary to enable the Secretary to carry out the functions of the Secretary under this subpart, including a complete and itemized inventory of all public telecommunications facilities under the control of such recipient, and records which fully disclose the amount and the disposition by such recipient of the proceeds of such assistance, the total cost of the project in connection with which assistance is given or used, the amount and nature of that portion of the cost of the project supplied by other sources, and such other records as will facilitate an effective audit.

(i) The Secretary and the Comptroller General of the United States, or any of their duly authorized representatives, shall have access for the purpose of audit and examination to any books, documents, papers, and records of any recipient of assistance under this subpart that are pertinent to assistance received under this subpart.

Section 393 [47 USC Section 393]. Criteria for Approval and Expenditures by Secretary of Commerce.

(a) The Secretary, in consultation with the Corporation, public telecommunications entities, and as appropriate with others, shall establish criteria for making construction and planning grants. Such criteria shall be consistent with the objectives and provisions set forth in this subpart, and shall be made available to interested parties upon request.

(b) The Secretary shall base determinations of whether to approve applications for grants under this subpart, and the amount of such grants, on criteria developed pursuant to subsection (a) and designed to achieve --

(1) the provision of new telecommunications facilities to extend service to areas currently not receiving public telecommunications services;

(2) the expansion of the service areas of existing public telecommunications entities;

(3) the development of public telecommunications facilities owned by, operated by, and available to minorities and women; and

(4) the improvement of the capabilities of existing public broadcast stations to provide public telecommunications services, including services to underserved audiences such as deaf and hearing impaired individuals and blind and visually impaired individuals.

(c) Of the sums appropriated pursuant to Section 391 for any fiscal year, a substantial amount shall be available for the expansion and development of noncommercial radio broadcast station facilities.

Section 393A [47 USC Section 393A]. Long-Range Planning for Facilities.

(a) The Secretary, in consultation with the Corporation, public telecommunications entities, and as appropriate with other parties, shall develop a long-range plan to accomplish the objectives set forth in Section 390. Such plan shall include a detailed 5-year projection of the broadcast and nonbroadcast public telecommunications facilities required to meet such objectives, and the expenditures necessary to provide such facilities.

(b) The plan required in subsection (a) shall be updated annually, and a summary of the activities of the Secretary in implementing the plan, shall be submitted concurrently to the President and the Congress not later than the 31st day of December of each year.

Subpart B - National Endowment for Children's Educational Television

Section 394 [47 USC Section 394]. Establishment of National Endowment.

(a) It is the purpose of this section to enhance the education of children through the creation and production of television programming specifically directed toward the development of fundamental intellectual skills.

(b)(1) There is established, under the direction of the Secretary, a National Endowment for Children's Educational Television. In administering the National Endowment, the Secretary is authorized to --

(A) contract with the Corporation for the production of educational television programming for children; and

(B) make grants directly to persons proposing to create and produce educational television programming for children.

The Secretary shall consult with the Advisory Council on Children's Educational Television in the making of the grants or the awarding of contracts for the purpose of making the grants.

(2) Contracts and grants under this section shall be made on the condition that the programming shall --

(A) during the first two years after its production, be made available only to public television licensees and permittees and noncommercial television licensees and permittees; and

(B) thereafter be made available to any commercial television licensee or permittee or cable television system operator, at a charge established by the Secretary that will assure the maximum practicable distribution of such programming, so long as such licensee, permittee, or operator does not interrupt the programming with commercial advertisements. The Secretary may, consistent with the purpose and provisions of this section, permit the programming to be distributed to persons using other media, establish conditions relating to such distribution, and apply those conditions to any contract or grant made under this section. The Secretary may waive the requirements of subparagraph (A) if the Secretary finds that neither public television licensees and permittees nor noncommercial television licensees and permittees will have an opportunity to air such programming in the first two years after its production.

(c)(1) The Secretary, with the advice of the Advisory Council on Children's Educational Television, shall establish criteria for making contracts and grants under this section. Such criteria shall be consistent with the purpose and provisions of this section and shall be made available to interested parties upon request. Such criteria shall include --

(A) criteria to maximize the amount of programming that is produced with the funds made available by the Endowment;

(B) criteria to minimize the costs of --

(i) selection of grantees,

(ii) administering the contracts and grants, and

(iii) the administrative costs of the programming production; and

(C) criteria to otherwise maximize the proportion of funds made available by the Endowment that are expended for the cost of programming production.

(2) Applications for grants under this section shall be submitted to the Secretary in such form and containing such information as the Secretary shall require by regulation.

(d) Upon approving any application for a grant under subsection (b)(1)(B), the Secretary shall make a grant to the applicant in an amount determined by the Secretary, except that such amounts shall not exceed 75 percent of the amount determined by the Secretary to be the reasonable and necessary cost of the project for which the grant is made.

(e)(1) The Secretary shall establish an Advisory Council on Children's Educational Television. The Secretary shall appoint ten individuals as members of the Council and designate one of such members to serve as Chairman.

(2) Members of the Council shall have terms of two years, and no member shall serve for more than three consecutive terms. The members shall have expertise in the fields of education, psychology, child development, or television programming, or related disciplines. Officers and employees of the United States shall not be appointed as members.

(3) While away from their homes or regular places of business in the performance of duties for the Council, the members of the Council shall serve without compensation but shall be allowed travel expenses, including per diem in lieu of subsistence, in accordance with 5703 of Title 5, United States Code.

(4) The Council shall meet at the call of the Chairman and shall advise the Secretary concerning the making of contracts and grants under this section.

(f)(1) Each recipient of a grant under this section shall keep such records as may be reasonably necessary to enable the Secretary to carry out the Secretary's functions under this section, including records which fully disclose the amount and the disposition by such recipient of the proceeds of such grant, the total cost of the project, the amount and nature of that portion of the cost of the project supplied by other sources, and such other records as will facilitate an effective audit.

(2) The Secretary and the Comptroller General of the United States, or any of their duly authorized representatives, shall have access for the purposes of audit and examination to any books, documents, papers, and records of the recipient that are pertinent to a grant received under this section.

(g) The Secretary is authorized to make such rules and regulations as may be necessary to carry out this section, including those relating to the order of priority in approving applications for projects under this section or to determining the amounts of contracts and grants for such projects.

(h) There are authorized to be appropriated $2,000,000 for fiscal year 1991, $4,000,000 for fiscal year 1992, $5,000,000 for fiscal year 1993, and $6,000,000 for fiscal year 1994 to be used by the Secretary to carry out the provisions of this section. Sums appropriated under this subsection for any fiscal year shall remain available for contracts and grants for projects for which applications approved under this section have been submitted within one year after the last day of such fiscal year.

(i) For purposes of this section --

(1) the term "educational television programming for children" means any television program which is directed to an audience of children who are 16 years of age or younger and which is designed for the intellectual development of those children, except that such term does not include any television program which is directed to a general audience but which might also be viewed by a significant number of children; and

(2) the term "person" means an individual, partnership, association, joint stock company, trust, corporation, or State or local governmental entity.

Subpart C- Telecommunications Demonstrations

Section 395 [47 USC Section 395]. Assistance for Demonstration Projects.

(a) It is the purpose of this subpart to promote the development of nonbroadcast telecommunications facilities and services for the transmission, distribution, and delivery of health, education, and public or social service information. The Secretary is authorized, upon receipt of an application in such form and containing such information as he may by regulation require, to make grants to, and enter into contracts with, public and private nonprofit agencies, organizations, and institutions for the purpose of carrying out telecommunications demonstrations.

(b) The Secretary may approve an application submitted under subsection (a) if he determines that --

(1) the project for which application is made will demonstrate innovative methods or techniques of utilizing nonbroadcast telecommunications equipment or facilities to satisfy the purpose of this subpart;

(2) demonstrations and related activities assisted under this subpart will remain under the administration and control of the applicant;

(3) the applicant has the managerial and technical capability to carry out the project for which the application is made; and

(4) the facilities and equipment acquired or developed pursuant to the application will be used substantially for the transmission, distribution, and delivery of health, education, or public or social service information.

(c) Upon approving any application under this subpart with respect to any project, the Secretary shall make a grant to or enter into a contract with the applicant in an amount determined by the Secretary not to exceed the reasonable and necessary cost of such project. The Secretary shall pay such amount from the sums available therefor, in advance or by way of reimbursement, and in such installments consistent with established practice, as he may determine.

(d) Funds made available pursuant to this subpart shall not be available for the construction, remodeling, or repair of structures to house the facilities or equipment acquired or developed with such funds, except that such funds may be used for minor remodeling which is necessary for and incidental to the installation of such facilities or equipment.

(e) For purposes of this section, the term "nonbroadcast telecommunications facilities" includes, but is not limited to, cable television systems, communications satellite systems and related terminal equipment, and other modes of transmitting, emitting, or receiving images and sounds or intelligence by means of wire, radio, optical, electromagnetic, or other means.

(f) The funding of any demonstration pursuant to this subpart shall continue for not more than 3 years from the date of the original grant or contract.

(g) The Secretary shall require that the recipient of a grant or contract under this subpart submit a summary and evaluation of the results of the demonstration at least annually for each year in which funds are received pursuant to this section.

(h)(1) Each recipient of assistance under this subpart shall keep such records as may be reasonably necessary to enable the Secretary to carry out the Secretary's functions under this subpart, including records which fully disclose the amount and the disposition by such recipient of the proceeds of such assistance, the total cost of the project or undertaking in connection with which such assistance is given or used, the amount and nature of that portion of the cost of the project or undertaking supplied by other sources, and such other records as will facilitate an effective audit.

(2) The Secretary and the Comptroller General of the United States, or any of their duly authorized representatives, shall have access for the purposes of audit and examination to any books, documents, papers, and records of the recipient that are pertinent to assistance received under this subpart.

(i) The Secretary is authorized to make such rules and regulations as may be necessary to carry out this subpart, including regulations relating to the order of priority in approving applications for projects under this subpart or to determining the amounts of grants for such projects.

(j) The Commission is authorized to provide such assistance in carrying out the provisions of this subpart as may be requested by the Secretary. The Secretary shall provide for close coordination with the Commission in the administration of the Secretary's functions under this subpart which are of interest to or affect the functions of the Commission. The Secretary shall provide for close coordination with the Corporation in the administration of the Secretary's functions under this subpart which are of interest to or affect the functions of the Corporation.

(k) There are authorized to be appropriated $1,000,000 for each of the fiscal years 1979, 1980 and 1981, to be used by the Secretary to carry out the provisions of this subpart. Sums appropriated under this subsection for any fiscal year shall remain available for payment of grants or contracts for projects for which applications approved under this subpart have been submitted within one year after the last day of such fiscal year.

Subpart D - Corporation for Public Broadcasting

Section 396 [47 USC Section 396]. Declaration of Policy.

(a) The Congress hereby finds and declares that --

(1) it is in the public interest to encourage the growth and development of public radio and television broadcasting, including the use of such media for instructional, educational, and cultural purposes;

(2) it is in the public interest to encourage the growth and development of nonbroadcast telecommunications technologies for the delivery of public telecommunications services;

(3) expansion and development of public telecommunications and of diversity of its programming depend on freedom, imagination, and initiative on both local and national levels;

(4) the encouragement and support of public telecommunications, while matters of importance for private and local development, are also of appropriate and important concern to the Federal Government;

(5) it furthers the general welfare to encourage public telecommunications services which will be responsive to the interests of people both in particular localities and throughout the United States, which will constitute an expression of diversity and excellence; and which will constitute a source of alternative telecommunications services for all the citizens of the Nation.

466

(6) it is in the public interest to encourage the development of programming that involves creative risks and that addresses the needs of unserved and underserved audiences, particularly children and minorities;

(7) it is necessary and appropriate for the Federal Government to complement, assist, and support a national policy that will most effectively make public telecommunications services available to all citizens of the United States; and

(8) public television and radio stations and public telecommunications services constitute valuable local community resources for utilizing electronic media to address national concerns and solve local problems through community programs and outreach programs;

(9) it is in the public interest for the Federal Government to ensure that all citizens of the United States have access to public telecommunications services through all appropriate available telecommunications distribution technologies; and

(10) a private corporation should be created to facilitate the development of public telecommunications and to afford maximum protection from extraneous interference and control.

Corporation Established

(b) There is authorized to be established a nonprofit corporation, to be known as the "Corporation for Public Broadcasting," which will not be an agency or establishment of the United States Government. The Corporation shall be subject to the provisions of this section, and, to the extent consistent with this section, to the District of Columbia Nonprofit Corporation Act.

Board of Directors

(c)(1) The Corporation for Public Broadcasting shall have a Board of Directors (hereinafter in this section referred to as the "Board"), consisting of 9 members appointed by the President, by and with the advice and consent of the Senate. No more than 5 members of the Board appointed by the President may be members of the same political party.

(2) The 9 members of the Board appointed by the President (A) shall be selected from among citizens of the United States (not regular full-time employees of the United States) who are eminent in such fields as education, cultural and civic affairs, or the arts, including radio and television; and (B) shall be selected so as to provide as nearly as practicable a broad representation of various regions of the Nation, various professions and occupations, and various kinds of talent and experience appropriate to the functions and responsibilities of the Corporation.

(3) Of the members of the Board appointed by the President under paragraph (1), one member shall be selected from among individuals who represent the licensees and permittees of public television stations, and one member shall be selected from among individuals who represent the licensees and permittees of public radio stations.

(4) The members of the initial Board of Directors shall serve as incorporators and shall take whatever actions are necessary to establish the Corporation under the District of Columbia Nonprofit Corporation Act.

(5) The term of office of each member of the Board appointed by the President shall be 6 years, except as provided in section 5(c) of the Public Telecommunications Act of 1992. Any member whose term has expired may serve until such member's successor has taken office, or until the end of the calendar year in which such member's term has expired, whichever is earlier. Any member appointed to fill a vacancy occurring prior to the expiration of the term for which such member's predecessor was appointed shall be appointed for the remainder of such term. No member of the Board shall be eligible to serve in excess of 2 consecutive full terms.

467

(6) Any vacancy in the Board shall not affect its power, but shall be filled in the manner consistent with this Act.

(7) Members of the Board shall attend not less than 50 percent of all duly convened meetings of the Board in any calendar year. A member who fails to meet the requirement of the preceding sentence shall forfeit membership and the President shall appoint a new member to fill such vacancy not later than 30 days after such vacancy is determined by the Chairman of the Board.

Election of Chairman and Vice Chairman; Compensation

(d)(1) Members of the Board shall annually elect one of their members to be Chairman and elect one or more of their members as a Vice Chairman or Vice Chairmen.

(2) The members of the Board shall not, by reason of such membership, be deemed to be officers or employees of the United States. They shall, while attending meetings of the Board or while engaged in duties related to such meetings or other activities of the Board pursuant to this subpart, be entitled to receive compensation at the rate of $150 per day, including travel time. No Board member shall receive compensation of more than $10,000 in any fiscal year. While away from their homes or regular places of business, Board members shall be allowed travel and actual, reasonable, and necessary expenses.

Compensation of Officers and Employees

(e)(1) The Corporation shall have a President, and such other officers as may be named and appointed by the Board for terms and at rates of compensation fixed by the Board. No officer or employee of the Corporation may be compensated by the Corporation at an annual rate of pay which exceeds the rate of basic pay in effect from time to time for level I of the Executive Schedule under Section 5312 of Title 5, United States Code. No individual other than a citizen of the United States may be an officer of the Corporation. No officer of the Corporation, other than the Chairman or a Vice Chairman, may receive any salary or other compensation (except for compensation for services on boards of directors of other organizations that do not receive funds from the Corporation, on committees of such boards, and in similar activities for such organizations) from any sources other than the Corporation for services rendered during the period of his or her employment by the Corporation. Service by any officer on boards of directors of other organizations, on committees of such boards, and in similar activities for such organizations shall be subject to annual advance approval by the Board and subject to the provisions of the Corporation's Statement of Ethical Conduct. All officers shall serve at the pleasure of the Board.

(2) Except as provided in the second sentence of subsection (c)(1) of this section, no political test or qualification shall be used in selecting, appointing, promoting, or taking other personnel actions with respect to officers, agents, and employees of the Corporation.

Nonprofit and Nonpolitical Nature of the Corporation

(f)(1) The Corporation shall have no power to issue any shares of stock, or to declare or pay any dividends.

(2) No part of the income or assets of the Corporation shall inure to the benefit of any director, officer, employee, or any other individual except as salary or reasonable compensation for services.

(3) The Corporation may not contribute to or otherwise support any political party or candidate for elective public office.

Purposes and Activities of the Corporation

(g)(1) In order to achieve the objectives and to carry out the purposes of this subpart, as set out in subsection (a), the Corporation is authorized to --

(A) facilitate the full development of public telecommunications in which programs of high quality, diversity, creativity, excellence, and innovation, which are obtained from diverse sources, will be made available to public telecommunications entities, with strict adherence to objectivity and balance in all programs or series of programs of a controversial nature;

(B) assist in the establishment and development of one or more interconnection systems to be used for the distribution of public telecommunications services so that all public telecommunications entities may disseminate such services at times chosen by the entities;

(C) assist in the establishment and development of one or more systems of public telecommunications entities throughout the United States; and

(D) carry out its purposes and functions and engage in its activities in ways that will most effectively assure the maximum freedom of the public telecommunications entities and systems from interference with, or control of, program content or other activities.

(2) In order to carry out the purposes set forth in subsection (a), the Corporation is authorized to --

(A) obtain grants from and make contracts with individuals and with private, State, and Federal agencies, organizations, and institutions;

(B) contract with or make grants to public telecommunications entities, national, regional, and other systems of public telecommunications entities, and independent producers and production entities, for the production or acquisition of public telecommunications services to be made available for use by public telecommunications entities, except that --

(i) to the extent practicable, proposals for the provision of assistance by the Corporation in the production or acquisition of programs or series of programs shall be evaluated on the basis of comparative merit by panels of outside experts, representing diverse interests and perspectives, appointed by the Corporation; and

(ii) nothing in this subparagraph shall be construed to prohibit the exercise by the Corporation of its prudent business judgment with respect to any grant to assist in the production or acquisition of any program or series of programs recommended by any such panel;

(C) make payments to existing and new public telecommunications entities to aid in financing the production or acquisition of public telecommunications services by such entities, particularly innovative approaches to such services, and other costs of operation of such entities;

(D) establish and maintain, or contribute to, a library and archives of noncommercial educational and cultural radio and television programs and related materials and develop public awareness of, and disseminate information about, public telecommunications services by various means, including the publication of a journal;

(E) arrange, by grant to or contract with appropriate public or private agencies, organizations, or institutions, for interconnection facilities suitable for distribution and transmission of public telecommunications services to public telecommunications entities;

(F) hire or accept the voluntary services of consultants, experts, advisory boards, and panels to aid the Corporation in carrying out the purposes of this subpart;

(G) conduct (directly or through grants or contracts) research, demonstrations, or training in matters related to public television or radio broadcasting and the use of nonbroadcast communications technologies for the dissemination of noncommercial educational and cultural television or radio programs;

(H) make grants or contracts for the use of nonbroadcast telecommunications technologies for the dissemination to the public of public telecommunications services; and

(I) take such other actions as may be necessary to accomplish the purposes set forth in subsection (a).

Nothing contained in this paragraph shall be construed to commit the Federal Government to provide any sums for the payment of any obligation of the Corporation which exceeds amounts provided in advance in appropriation Acts.

(3) To carry out the foregoing purposes and engage in the foregoing activities, the Corporation shall have the usual powers conferred upon a nonprofit corporation by the District of Columbia Nonprofit Corporation Act (DC Code, §29-1001 et seq.), except that the Corporation is prohibited from --

(A) owning or operating any television or radio broadcast station system or network community antenna television system, interconnection system or facility, program production facility, or any public telecommunications entity, system or network; and

(B) producing programs, scheduling programs for dissemination, or disseminating programs to the public.

(4) All meetings of the Board of Directors of the Corporation, including any committee of the Board, shall be open to the public under such terms, conditions, and exceptions as are set forth in subsection (k)(4).

(5) The Corporation, in consultation with interested parties, shall create a 5-year plan for the development of public telecommunications services. Such plan shall be updated annually by the Corporation.

Interconnection Service

(h)(1) Nothing in this Act, or in any other provision of law, shall be construed to prevent United States communications common carriers from rendering free or reduced rate communications interconnection services for public television or radio services, subject to such rules and regulations as the Commission may prescribe.

(2) Subject to such terms and conditions as may be established by public telecommunications entities receiving space satellite interconnection facilities or services purchased or arranged for, in whole or in part, with funds authorized under this part, other public telecommunications entities shall have reasonable access to such facilities or services for the distribution of educational and cultural programs to public telecommunications entities. Any remaining capacity shall be made available to other persons for the transmission of noncommercial educational and cultural programs and program information relating to such programs, to public telecommunications entities, at a charge or charges comparable to the charge or charges, if any, imposed upon a public telecommunications entity for the distribution of noncommercial educational and cultural programs to public telecommunications entities. No such person shall be denied such access whenever sufficient capacity is available.

Report to Congress

(i)(1) The Corporation shall submit an annual report for the preceding fiscal year ending September 30 to the President for transmittal to the Congress on or before the 15th day of May of each year. The report shall include --

(A) a comprehensive and detailed report of the Corporation's operations, activities, financial condition, and accomplishments under this subpart and such recommendations as the Corporation deems appropriate;

(B) a comprehensive and detailed inventory of funds distributed by Federal agencies to public telecommunications entities during the preceding fiscal years;

(C) a listing of each organization that receives a grant from the Corporation to produce programming, the name of the producer of any programming produced under each such grant, the title or description of any program so produced, and the amount of each such grant;

(D) the summary of the annual report provided to the Secretary pursuant to Section 398(b)(4).

(2) The officers and directors of the Corporation shall be available to testify before appropriate committees of the Congress with respect to such report, the report of any audit made by the Comptroller General pursuant to subsection (1), or any other matter which such committees may determine.

Right to Repeal, Alter, or Amend

(j) The right to repeal, alter, or amend this section at any time is expressly reserved.

Financing; Open Meetings and Financial Records

(k)(1)(A) There is hereby established in the Treasury a fund which shall be known as the Public Broadcasting Fund (hereinafter in this subsection referred to as the "Fund"), to be administered by the Secretary of the Treasury.

(B) There is authorized to be appropriated to the Fund, for each of the fiscal years 1978, 1979 and 1980, an amount equal to 40 percent of the total amount of non-Federal financial support received by public broadcasting entities during the fiscal year second preceding each such fiscal year, except that the amount so appropriated shall not exceed $121,000,000 for fiscal year 1978, $140,000,000 for fiscal year 1979, and $160,000,000 for fiscal year 1980.

(C) There is authorized to be appropriated to the Fund, for each of the fiscal years 1981, 1982, 1983, 1984, 1985, 1986, 1987, 1988, 1989, 1990, 1991, 1992 and 1993 an amount equal to 40 percent of the total amount of non-Federal financial support received by public broadcasting entities during the fiscal year second preceding each such fiscal year, except that the amount so appropriated shall not exceed $265,000,000 for fiscal year 1992, $285,000,000 for fiscal year 1993, $310,000,000 for fiscal year 1994, $375,000,000 for fiscal year 1995, and $425,000,000 for fiscal year 1996..

(D) Funds appropriated under this subsection shall remain available until expended.

(E) In recognition of the importance of educational programs and services, and the expansion of public radio services, to unserved and underserved audiences, the Corporation, after consultation with the system of public telecommunications entities, shall prepare and submit to the Congress an annual report for each of the fiscal years 1994, 1995, and 1996 on the Corporation's activities and expenditures relating to those programs and services.

(2)(A) The funds authorized to be appropriated in this subsection shall be used by the Corporation, in a prudent and financially responsible manner, solely for its grants, contracts, and administrative costs, except that the Corporation may not use any funds appropriated under this subpart for purposes of conducting any reception, or providing any other entertainment, for any officer or employee of the Federal Government or any State or local government. The Corporation shall determine the amount of non-Federal financial support received by public broadcasting entities during each of the

471

fiscal years referred to in paragraph (1) for the purpose of determining the amount of each authorization, and shall certify such amount to the Secretary of the Treasury, except that the Corporation may include in its certification non-Federal financial support received by a public broadcasting entity during its most recent fiscal year ending before September 30 of the year for which certification is made. Upon receipt of such certification, the Secretary of the Treasury shall make available to the Corporation, from such funds as may be appropriated to the Fund, the amount authorized for each of the fiscal years pursuant to the provisions of this subsection.

(B) Funds appropriated and made available under this subsection shall be disbursed by the Secretary of the Treasury on a fiscal year basis.

(3)(A)(i) The Corporation shall establish an annual budget for use in allocating amounts from the Fund. Of the amounts appropriated into the Fund available for allocation for any fiscal year --

(I) $10,200,000 shall be available for the administrative expenses of the Corporation for fiscal year 1989, and for each succeeding fiscal year the amount which shall be available for such administrative expenses shall be the sum of the amount made available to the Corporation under this subclause for such expenses in the preceding fiscal year plus the greater of 4 percent of such amount or a percentage of such amount equal to the percentage change in the Consumer Price Index, except that none of the amounts allocated under subclauses (II), (III) and (IV) and clause (v) shall be used for any administrative expenses of the Corporation and not more than 5 percent of all the amounts appropriated into the Fund available for allocation for any fiscal year shall be available for such administrative expenses;

(II) 6 percent of such amounts shall be available for expenses incurred by the Corporation for capital costs relating to telecommunications satellites, the payment of programming royalties and other fees, the costs of interconnection facilities and operations (as provided in clause (iv)(I), and grants which the Corporation may make for assistance to stations that broadcast programs in languages other than English, or for assistance in the provision of affordable training programs for employees at public broadcast stations and if the available funding level permits, for projects and activities that will enhance public broadcasting; and

(III) 75 percent of the remainder (after allocations are made under subclause (I) and subclause (II) shall be allocated in accordance with clause (ii); and

(IV) 25 percent of such remainder shall be allocated in accordance with clause (iii).

(ii) Of the amounts allocated under clause (i)(III) for any fiscal year --

(I) 75 percent of such amounts shall be available for distribution among the licensees and permittees of public television stations pursuant to paragraph (6)(B); and

(II) 25 percent of such amounts shall be available for distribution under subparagraph (B)(i) and in accordance with any plan implemented under paragraph (6)(A), for national public television programming.

(iii) Of the amounts allocated under clause (i)(IV) for any fiscal year --

(I) 70 percent of such amounts shall be available for distribution among the licensees and permittees of public radio stations pursuant to paragraph (6)(B);

(II) 7 percent of such amounts shall be available for distribution under subparagraph (B)(i) for public radio programming; and

(III) 23 percent of such amounts shall be available for distribution among the licensees and permittees of public radio stations pursuant to paragraph (6)(B), solely to be used for acquiring or producing programming that is to be distributed nationally and is designed to serve the needs of a national audience.

(iv)(I) From the amount provided pursuant to clause (i)(II), the Corporation shall defray an amount equal to 50 percent of the total costs of interconnection facilities and operations to facilitate the availability of public television and radio programs among public broadcast stations.

(II) Of the amounts received as the result of any contract, lease agreement, or any other arrangement under which the Corporation directly or indirectly makes available interconnection facilities, 50 percent of such amounts shall be distributed to the licensees and permittees of public television stations and public radio stations. The Corporation shall not have any authority to establish any requirements, guidelines, or limitations with respect to the use of such amounts by such licensees and permittees.

(v) Of the interest on the amounts appropriated into the Fund which is available for allocation for any fiscal year --

(I) 75 percent shall be available for distribution for the purposes referred to in clause (ii)(II); and

(II) 25 percent shall be available for distribution for the purposes referred to in clause (iii)(II) and (III).

(B)(i) The Corporation shall utilize the funds allocated pursuant to subparagraph (A)(ii)(II) and subparagraph (A)(iii)(II) to make grants for production of public television or radio programs by independent producers and production entities and public telecommunications entities, producers of national children's educational programming, and producers of programs addressing the needs and interests of minorities, and for acquisition of such programs by public telecommunications entities. The Corporation may make grants to public telecommunications entities and producers for the production of programs in languages other than English. Of the funds utilized pursuant to this clause, a substantial amount shall be distributed to independent producers and production entities, producers of national children's educational programming, and producers of programming addressing the needs and interests of minorities for the production of programs.

(ii) All funds available for distribution under clause (i) shall be distributed to entities outside the Corporation and shall not be used for the general administrative costs of the Corporation, the salaries or related expenses of Corporation personnel and members of the Board, or for expenses of consultants and advisers to the Corporation.

(iii)(I) For fiscal year 1990 and succeeding fiscal years, the Corporation shall, in carrying out its obligations under clause (i) with respect to public television programming, provide adequate funds for an independent production service.

(II) Such independent production service shall be separate from the Corporation and shall be incorporated under the laws of the District of Columbia for the purpose of contracting with the Corporation for the expenditure of funds for the production of public television programs by independent producers and independent production entities.

(III) The Corporation shall work with organizations or associations of independent producers or independent production entities to develop a plan and budget for the operation of such service that is acceptable to the Corporation.

(IV) The Corporation shall ensure that the funds provided to such independent production service shall be used exclusively in pursuit of the Corporation's obligation to expand the diversity and innovativeness of programming available to public broadcasting.

(V) The Corporation shall report annually to Congress regarding the activities and expenditures of the independent production service, including carriage and viewing information for programs produced or acquired with funds provided pursuant to subclause I. At the end of fiscal years 1992, 1993, 1994 and 1995, the Corporation shall submit a report to Congress evaluating the performance of the independent production service in light of its mission to expand the diversity and innovativeness of programming available to public broadcasting.

(VI) The Corporation shall not contract to provide funds to any such independent production service, unless that service agrees to comply with public inspection requirements established by the Corporation within 3 months after the date of enactment of this subclause. Under such requirements the service shall maintain at its offices a public file, updated regularly, containing information relating to the service's award of funds for the production of programming. The information shall be available for public inspection and copying for at least 3 years and shall be of the same kind as the information required to be maintained by the Corporation under subsection (l)(4)(B).

(4) Funds may not be distributed pursuant to this subsection to the Public Broadcasting Service or National Public Radio (or any successor organization), or to the licensee or permittee of any public broadcast station, unless the governing body of any such organization, any committee of such governing body, or any advisory body of any such organization, holds open meetings preceded by reasonable notice to the public. All persons shall be permitted to attend any meeting of the board or of any such committee or body, and no person shall be required, as a condition to attendance at any such meeting, to register such person's name or to provide any other information. Nothing contained in this paragraph shall be construed to prevent any such board, committee, or body from holding closed sessions to consider matters relating to individual employees, proprietary information, litigation and other matters requiring the confidential advice of counsel, commercial or financial information obtained from a person on a privileged or confidential basis, or the purchase of property or services whenever the premature exposure of such purchase would compromise the business interest of any such organization. If any such meeting is closed pursuant to the provisions of this paragraph, the organization involved shall thereafter (within a reasonable period of time) make available to the public a written statement containing an explanation of the reasons for closing the meeting.

(5) Funds may not be distributed pursuant to this subsection to any public telecommunications entity that does not maintain for public examination copies of the annual financial and audit reports, or other information regarding finances, submitted to the Corporation pursuant to subsection (1)(3)(B).

(6)(A) The Corporation shall conduct a study and prepare a plan, in consultation with public television licensees (or designated representatives of those licensees) and the Public Broadcasting Service, on how funds available to the Corporation under paragraph (3)(A)(ii)(II) can be best allocated to meet the objectives of this Act with regard to national public television programming. The plan, which shall be based on the conclusions resulting from the study, shall be submitted by the Corporation to the Congress not later than January 31, 1990. Unless directed otherwise by an Act of Congress, the Corporation shall implement the plan during the first fiscal year beginning after the fiscal year in which the plan is submitted to Congress.

(B) The Corporation shall make a basic grant from the portion reserved for television stations under paragraph (3)(A)(ii)(I) to each licensee and permittee of a public television station that is on the air. The Corporation shall assist radio stations to maintain and improve their service where public radio is the only broadcast service available. The balance of the portion reserved for television

474

stations and the total portion reserved for radio stations under paragraph (3)(A)(iii)(I) shall be distributed to licensees and permittees of such stations in accordance with eligibility criteria (which the Corporation shall review periodically in consultation with public radio and television licensees or permittees, or their designated representatives) that promote the public interest in public broadcasting, and on the basis of a formula designed to --

(i) provide for the financial needs and requirements of stations in relation to the communities and audiences such stations undertake to serve;

(ii) maintain existing, and stimulate new, sources of non-federal financial support for stations by providing incentives for increases in such support; and

(iii) assure that each eligible licensee and permittee of a public radio station receives a basic grant.

(7) The funds distributed pursuant to paragraph (3)(A)(ii)(I) and (iii)(I) may be used at the discretion of the recipient for purposes related primarily to the production or acquisition of programming.

(8)(A) Funds may not be distributed pursuant to this subpart to any public broadcast station (other than any station which is owned and operated by a State, a political or special purpose subdivision of a State, or a public agency) unless such station establishes a community advisory board. Any such station shall undertake good faith efforts to assure that (i) its advisory board meet at regular intervals; (ii) the members of its advisory board regularly attend the meetings of the advisory board; and (iii) the composition of its advisory board is reasonably representative of the diverse needs and interests of the communities served by such station.

(B) The board shall be permitted to review the programming goals established by the station, the service provided by the station, and the significant policy decisions rendered by the station. The board may also be delegated any other responsibilities, as determined by the governing body of the station. The board shall advise the governing body of the station with respect to whether the programming and other policies of such station are meeting the specialized educational and cultural needs of the communities served by the station, and may make such recommendations as it considers appropriate to meet such needs.

(C) The role of the board shall be solely advisory in nature, except to the extent other responsibilities are delegated to the board by the governing body of the station. In no case shall the board have any authority to exercise any control over the daily management or operation of the station.

(D) In the case of any public broadcast station (other than any station which is owned and operated by a State, a political or special purpose subdivision of a State, or a public agency) in existence on the effective date of this paragraph, such station shall comply with the requirements of this paragraph with respect to the establishment of a community advisory board not later than 180 days after such effective date.

(E) The provision of subparagraph (A) prohibiting the distribution of funds to any public broadcast station (other than any station which is owned and operated by a State, a political or special purpose subdivision of a State, or a public agency) - unless such station establishes a community advisory board - shall be the exclusive remedy for the enforcement of the provisions of this paragraph.

(9) Funds may not be distributed to this subsection to the Public Broadcasting Service or National Public Radio (or any successor organization) unless assurances are provided to the Corporation that no officer or employee of the Public Broadcasting Service or National Public Radio (or any successor organization), as the case may be, will be compensated at an annual rate of pay which exceeds

the rate of basic pay in effect from time to time for level I of the Executive Schedule under Section 5312 of Title 5, United States Code, and unless further assurances are provided to the Corporation that no officer or employee of such an entity will be loaned money by that entity on an interest-free basis.

(10)(A) There is hereby established in the Treasury a fund which shall be known as the Public Broadcasting Satellite Interconnection Fund (hereinafter in this subsection referred to as the Satellite Interconnection Fund), to be administered by the Secretary of the Treasury.

(B) There is authorized to be appropriated to the Satellite Interconnection Fund, for fiscal year 1991, the amount of $200,000,000. If such amount is not appropriated in full for fiscal year 1991, the portion of such amount not yet appropriated is authorized to be appropriated for fiscal years 1992 and 1993. Funds appropriated to the Satellite Interconnection Fund shall remain available until expended.

(C) The Secretary of the Treasury shall make available and disburse to the Corporation, at the beginning of fiscal year 1991 and of each succeeding fiscal year thereafter, such funds as have been appropriated to the Satellite Interconnection Fund for the fiscal year in which such disbursement is to be made.

(D) Notwithstanding any other provision of this subsection except paragraphs (4), (5), (8) and (9), all funds appropriated to the Satellite Interconnection Fund and interest thereon --

(i) shall be distributed by the Corporation to the licensees and permittees of noncommercial educational television broadcast stations providing public telecommunications services or the national entity they designate for satellite interconnection purposes and to those public telecommunications entities participating in the public radio satellite interconnection system or the national entity they designate for satellite interconnection purposes, exclusively for the capital costs of the replacement, refurbishment, or upgrading of their national satellite interconnection systems and associated maintenance of such systems; and

(ii) shall not be used for the administrative costs of the Corporation, the salaries or related expenses of Corporation personnel and members of the Board, or for expenses of consultants and advisers to the Corporation.

(11)(A) Funds may not be distributed pursuant to this subsection for any fiscal year to the licensee or permittee of any public broadcast station if such licensee or permittee --

(i) fails to certify to the Corporation that such licensee or permittee complies with the Commission's regulations concerning equal employment opportunity as published under section 73.2080 of title 47, Code of Federal Regulations, or any successor regulations thereto; or

(ii) fails to submit to the Corporation the report required by subparagraph (B) for the preceding calendar year.

(B) A licensee or permittee of any public broadcast station with more than five full-time employees to file annually with the Corporation a statistical report, consistent with reports required by Commission regulation, identifying by race and sex the number of employees in each of the following full-time and part-time job categories:

(i) Officials and managers.
(ii) Professionals.
(iii) Technicians.
(iv) Semiskilled operatives.
(v) Skilled craft persons.
(vi) Clerical and office personnel.

(vii) Unskilled operatives.

(viii) Service workers.

(C) In addition, such report shall state the number of job openings occurring during the course of the year. Where the job openings were filled in accordance with the regulations described in subparagraph (A)(i), the report shall so certify, and where the job openings were not filled in accordance with such regulations, the report shall contain a statement providing reasons therefor. The statistical report shall be available to the public at the central office and at every location where more than five full-time employees are regularly assigned to work.

Financial Management and Records

(l)(1)(A) The accounts of the Corporation shall be audited annually in accordance with generally accepted auditing standards by independent certified public accountants or independent licensed public accountants certified or licensed by a regulatory authority of a State or other political subdivision of the United States, except that such requirement shall not preclude shared auditing arrangements between any public telecommunications entity and its licensee where such licensee is a public or private institution. The audits shall be conducted at the place or places where the accounts of the Corporation are normally kept. All books, accounts, financial records, reports, files, and all other papers, things, or property belonging to or in use by the Corporation and necessary to facilitate the audits shall be made available to the person or persons conducting the audits; and full facilities for verifying transactions with the balances or securities held by depositories, fiscal agents and custodians shall be afforded to such person or persons.

(B) The report of each such independent audit shall be included in the annual report required by subsection (i) of this section. The audit report shall set forth the scope of the audit and include such statements as are necessary to present fairly the Corporation's assets and liabilities, surplus or deficit, with an analysis of the changes therein during the year, supplemented in reasonable detail by a statement of the Corporation's income and expenses during the year, and a statement of the sources and application of funds, together with the independent auditor's opinion of those statements.

(2)(A) The financial transactions of the Corporation for any fiscal year during which Federal funds are available to finance any portion of its operations may be audited by the General Accounting Office in accordance with the principles and procedures applicable to commercial corporate transactions and under such rules and regulations as may be prescribed by the Comptroller General of the United States. Any such audit shall be conducted at the place or places where accounts of the Corporation are normally kept. The representative of the General Accounting Office shall have access to all books, accounts, records, reports, files, and all other papers, things, or property belonging to or in use by the Corporation pertaining to its financial transactions and necessary to facilitate the audit, and they shall be afforded full facilities for verifying transactions with the balances or securities held by depositories, fiscal agents, and custodians. All such books, accounts, records, reports, files, papers and property of the Corporation shall remain in possession and custody of the Corporation.

(B) A report of each such audit shall be made by the Comptroller General to the Congress. The report to the Congress shall contain such comments and information as the Comptroller General may deem necessary to inform Congress of the financial operations and condition of the Corporation, together with such recommendations with respect thereto as he may deem advisable. The report shall also show specifically any program, expenditure, or other financial transaction or undertaking observed in the course of audit, which, in the opinion of the Comptroller General, has been carried on or made without authority or law. A copy of each report shall be furnished to the President, to the Secretary, and to the Corporation at the time submitted to the Congress.

(3)(A) Not later than 1 year after the effective date of this paragraph, the Corporation, in consultation with the Comptroller General, and as appropriate with others, shall develop accounting principles which shall be used uniformly by all public telecommunications entities receiving funds under this subpart, taking into account organizational differences among various categories of such entities. Such principles shall be designed to account fully for all funds received and expended for public telecommunications purposes by such entities.

(B) Each public telecommunications entity receiving funds under this subpart shall be required --

(i) to kept its books, records, and accounts in such form as may be required by the Corporation;

(ii)(I) to undergo a biennial audit by independent certified public accountants or independent licensed public accountants certified or licensed by a regulatory authority of a State, which audit shall be in accordance with auditing standards developed by the Corporation, in consultation with the Comptroller General; or

(II) to submit a financial statement in lieu of the audit required by subclause (I) if the Corporation determines that the cost burden of such audit on such entity is excessive in light of the financial condition of such entity; and

(iii) to furnish biennially to the Corporation a copy of the audit report required pursuant to clause (ii), as well as such other information regarding finances (including an annual financial report) as the Corporation may require.

(C) Any recipient of assistance by grant or contract under this section, other than a fixed price contract awarded pursuant to competitive bidding procedures, shall keep such records as may be reasonably necessary to disclose fully the amount and the disposition by such recipient of such assistance, the total cost of the project or undertaking in connection with which such assistance is given or used, and the amount and nature of that portion of the cost of the project or undertaking by other sources, and such other records as will facilitate an effective audit.

(D) The Corporation or any of its duly authorized representatives shall have access to any books, documents, papers, and records of any recipient of assistance for the purpose of auditing and examining all funds received or expended for public telecommunications purposes by the recipient. The Comptroller General of the United States or any of his duly authorized representatives also shall have access to such books, documents, papers, and records for the purpose of auditing and examining all funds received or expended for public telecommunications purposes during any fiscal year for which Federal funds are available to the Corporation.

(4)(A) The Corporation shall maintain the information described in subparagraphs (B), (C), and (D) at its offices for public inspection and copying for at least three years, according to such reasonable guidelines as the Corporation may issue. This public file shall be updated regularly. This paragraph shall be effective upon its enactment and shall apply to all grants awarded after January 1, 1993.

(B) Subsequent to any award of funds by the Corporation for the production or acquisition of national broadcasting programming pursuant to subsection (k)(3)(A)(ii)(II) or (iii)(II), the Corporation shall make available for public inspection the following:

(i) Grant and solicitation guidelines for proposals for such programming.

(ii) The reasons for selecting the proposal for which the award was made.

(iii) Information on each program for which the award was made, including the names of the awardee and producer (and if the awardee or producer is a corporation or partnership, the principals of such corporation or partnership), the monetary amount of the award, and the title and description of the program (and of each program in a series of programs).

(iv) A report based on the final audit findings resulting from any audit of the award by the Corporation or the Comptroller General.

(v) Reports which the Corporation shall require to be provided by the awardee relating to national public broadcasting programming funded, produced, or acquired by the awardee with such funds. Such reports shall include, where applicable, the information described in clauses (i), (ii), and (iii), but shall exclude proprietary, confidential, or privileged information.

(C) The Corporation shall make available for public inspection the final report required by the Corporation on an annual basis from each recipient of funds under subsection (k)(3)(A)(iii)(III), excluding proprietary, confidential, or privileged information.

(D) The Corporation shall make available for public inspection an annual list of national programs distributed by public broadcasting entities that receive funds under subsection (k)(3)(A)(ii)(II) or (iii)(II) and are engaged primarily in the national distribution of public television or radio programs. Such list shall include the names of the programs (or program series), producers, and providers of funding.

(m)(1) Prior to July 1, 1989, and every three years thereafter, the Corporation shall compile an assessment of the needs of minority and diverse audiences, the plans of public broadcasting entities and public telecommunications entities to address such needs, the ways radio and television can be used to help these underrepresented groups, and projections concerning minority employment by public broadcasting entities and public telecommunications entities. Such assessment shall address the needs of racial and ethnic minorities, new immigrant populations, people for whom English is a second language, and adults who lack basic reading skills.

(2) Commencing July 1, 1989, the Corporation shall prepare an annual report on the provision by public broadcasting entities and public telecommunications entities of service to the audiences described in paragraph (1). Such report shall address programming (including that which is produced by minority producers), training, minority employment, and efforts by the Corporation to increase the number of minority public radio and television stations eligible for financial support from the Corporation. Such report shall include a summary of the statistical reports received by the Corporation pursuant to subsection (k)(11), and a comparison of the information submitted by the Corporation in the previous year's annual report.

(3) As soon as they have been prepared, each assessment and annual report required under paragraphs (1) and (2) shall be submitted to Congress.

Subpart E - General

Section 397 [47 USC Section 397]. Definitions.

For the purposes of this part --

(1) The term "construction" (as applied to public telecommunications facilities) means acquisition (including acquisition by lease), installation, and modernization of public

479

telecommunications facilities and planning and preparatory steps incidental to any such acquisition, installation, or modernization.

(2) The term "Corporation" means the Corporation for Public Broadcasting authorized to be established in Subpart D.

(3) The term "interconnection" means the use of microwave equipment, boosters, translators, repeaters, communication space satellites, or other apparatus or equipment for the transmission and distribution of television or radio programs to public telecommunications entities.

(4) The term "interconnection system" means any system of interconnection facilities used for distribution of programs to public telecommunications entities.

(5) The term "meeting" means the deliberations of at least the number of members of a governing or advisory body, or any committee thereof, required to take action on behalf of such body or committee where such deliberations determine or result in the joint conduct or disposition of the governing of advisory body's business, or the committee's business, as the case may be, but only to the extent that such deliberations relate to public broadcasting.

(6) The terms "noncommercial educational broadcast station" and "public broadcast station" mean a television or radio broadcast station which --

(A) under the rules and regulations of the Commission in effect on the effective date of this paragraph, is eligible to be licensed by the Commission as a noncommercial educational radio or television broadcast station and which is owned and operated by a public agency or nonprofit private foundation, corporation, or association; or

(B) is owned and operated by a municipality and which transmits only noncommercial programs for educational purposes.

(7) The term "noncommercial telecommunications entity" means any enterprise which --

(A) is owned and operated by a State, a political or special purpose subdivision of a State, a public agency, or a nonprofit private foundation, corporation, or association; and

(B) has been organized primarily for the purpose of disseminating audio or video noncommercial educational and cultural programs to the public by means other than a primary television or radio broadcast station, including, but not limited to, coaxial cable, optical fiber, broadcast translators, cassettes, discs, microwave, or laser transmission through the atmosphere.

(8) The term "nonprofit" (as applied to any foundation, corporation, or association) means a foundation, corporation, or association, no part of the net earnings of which inures, or may lawfully inure, to the benefit of any private shareholder or individual.

(9) The term "non-Federal financial support" means the total value of cash and the fair market value of property and services (including, to the extent provided in the second sentence of this paragraph, the personal services of volunteers), received --

(A) as gifts, grants, bequests, donations, or other contributions for the construction or operation of noncommercial educational broadcast stations, or for the production, acquisition, distribution, or dissemination of educational television or radio programs, and related activities, from any source other than (i) the United States or any agency or instrumentality of the United States; or (ii) any public broadcasting entity; or

(B) as gifts, grants, donations, contributions, or payments from any State, or any educational institution, for the construction or operation of noncommercial educational broadcast stations or for the production, acquisition, distribution, or dissemination of educational television or

480

radio programs, or payments in exchange for services or materials with respect to the provision of educational or instructional television or radio programs.

Such term includes the fair market value of personal services or volunteers, as computed using the valuation standards established by the Corporation and approved by the Comptroller General pursuant to Section 396(g)(5), but only with respect to such services provided to public telecommunications entities after such standards are approved by the Comptroller General and only, with respect to such an entity in a fiscal year, to the extent that the value of the services does not exceed 5 percent of the total non-Federal financial support of the entity in such fiscal year.

(10) The term "preoperational expenses" means all nonconstruction costs incurred by new telecommunications entities before the date on which they begin providing service to the public, and all nonconstruction costs associated with expansion of existing entities before the date on which such expanded capacity is activated, except that such expenses shall not include any portion of the salaries of any personnel employed by an operating public telecommunications entity.

(11) The term "public broadcasting entity" means the Corporation, any licensee or permittee of a public broadcast station, or any nonprofit institution engaged primarily in the production, acquisition, distribution, or dissemination of educational and cultural television or radio programs.

(12) The term "public telecommunications entity" means any enterprise which --

(A) is a public broadcast station or a noncommercial telecommunications entity; and

(B) disseminates public telecommunications services to the public.

(13) The term "public telecommunications facilities" means apparatus necessary for production, interconnection, captioning, broadcast, or other distribution of programming, including, but not limited to, studio equipment, cameras, microphones, audio and video storage or reproduction equipment, or both, signal processors and switchers, towers, antennas, transmitters, translators, microwave equipment, mobile equipment, satellite communications equipment, instructional television fixed service equipment, subsidiary communications authorization transmitting and receiving equipment, cable television equipment, video and audio cassettes and discs, optical fiber communications equipment, and other means of transmitting, emitting, storing, and receiving images and sounds, or intelligence, except that such term does not include the buildings to house such apparatus (other than small equipment shelters which are part of satellite earth stations, translators, microwave interconnection facilities, and similar facilities).

(14) The term "public telecommunications services" means noncommercial educational and cultural radio and television programs, and related noncommercial instructional or informational material that may be transmitted by means of electronic communications.

(15) The term "Secretary" means the Secretary of Commerce when such term is used in Subpart A and Subpart B, and the Secretary of Health and Human Services when such term is used in Subpart C, Subpart D and this subpart.

(16) The term "State" includes the District of Columbia, the Commonwealth of Puerto Rico, the Virgin Islands, Guam, American Samoa, the Northern Mariana Islands, and the Trust Territory of the Pacific Islands.

(17) The term "system of public telecommunications entities" means any combination of public telecommunications entities acting cooperatively to produce, acquire, or distribute programs, or to undertake related activities.

Section 398 [47 USC Section 398]. Federal Interference or Control Prohibited; Equal Employment Opportunity.

(a) Nothing contained in this part shall be deemed (1) to amend any other provision of, or requirement under, this Act; or (2) except to the extent authorized in subsection (b), to authorize any department, agency, officer, or employee of the United States to exercise any direction, supervision, or control over public telecommunications, or over the Corporation or any of its grantees or contractors, or over the charter or bylaws of the Corporation, or over the curriculum, program of instruction, or personnel of any educational institution, school system, or public telecommunications entity.

(b)(1) Equal opportunity in employment shall be afforded to all persons by the Public Broadcasting Service and National Public Radio (or any successor organization) and by all public telecommunications entities receiving funds pursuant to Subpart C (hereinafter in this subsection referred to as "recipients") in accordance with the equal employment opportunity regulations of the Commission, and no person shall be subjected to discrimination in employment by any recipient on the grounds of race, color, religion, national origin, or sex.

(2)(A) The Secretary is authorized and directed to enforce this subsection and to prescribe such rules and regulations as may be necessary to carry out the functions of the Secretary under this subsection.

(B) The Secretary shall provide for close coordination with the Commission in the administration of the responsibilities of the Secretary under this subsection which are of interest to or affect the functions of the Commission so that, to the maximum extent possible consistent with the enforcement responsibilities of each, the reporting requirements of public telecommunications entities shall be uniformly based upon consistent definitions and categories of information.

(3)(A) The Corporation shall incorporate into each grant agreement or contract with any recipient entered into on or after the effective date of the rules and regulations prescribed by the Secretary pursuant to paragraph (2)(A), a statement indicating that, as a material part of the terms and conditions of the grant agreement or contract, the recipient will comply with the provisions of paragraph (1) and the rules and regulations prescribed pursuant to paragraph (2)(A). Any person which desires to be a recipient (within the meaning of paragraph (1)) of funds under Subpart C shall, before receiving any such funds, provide to the Corporation any information which the Corporation may require to satisfy itself that such person is affording equal opportunity in employment in accordance with the requirements of this subsection. Determinations made by the Corporation in accordance with the preceding sentence shall be based upon guidelines relating to equal opportunity in employment which shall be established by rule by the Secretary.

(B) If the Corporation is not satisfied that any such person is affording equal opportunity in employment in accordance with the requirements of this subsection, the Corporation shall notify the Secretary, and the Secretary shall review the matter and make a final determination regarding whether such person is affording equal opportunity in employment. In any case in which the Secretary conducts a review under the preceding sentence, the Corporation shall make funds available to the person involved pursuant to the grant application of such person (if the Corporation would have approved such application but for the finding of the Corporation under this paragraph) pending a final determination of the Secretary upon completion of such review. The Corporation shall monitor the equal employment opportunity practices of each recipient throughout the duration of the grant or contract.

(C) The provisions of subparagraph (A) and subparagraph (B) shall take effect on the effective date of the rules and regulations prescribed by the Secretary pursuant to paragraph (2)(A).

(4) Based upon its responsibilities under paragraph (3), the Corporation shall provide an annual report for the preceding fiscal year ending September 30 to the Secretary on or before the 15th Day of February of each year. The report shall contain information in the form required by the Secretary. The Corporation shall submit a summary of such report to the President and the Congress as part of the report required in Section 396(i). The Corporation shall provide other information in the form which the Secretary may require in order to carry out the functions of the Secretary under this subsection.

(5) Whenever the Secretary makes a final determination, pursuant to the rules and regulations which the Secretary shall prescribe, that a recipient is not in compliance with paragraph (1), the Secretary shall, within 10 days after such determination, notify the recipient in writing of such determination and request the recipient to secure compliance. Unless the recipient within 120 days after receipt of such written notice --

(A) demonstrates to the Secretary that the violation has been corrected; or

(B) enters into a compliance agreement approved by the Secretary;

the Secretary shall direct the Corporation to reduce or suspend any further payments of funds under this part to the recipient and the Corporation shall comply with such directive. Resumption of payments shall take place only when the Secretary certifies to the Corporation that the recipient has entered into a compliance agreement approved by the Secretary. A recipient whose funds have been reduced or suspended under this paragraph may apply at any time to the Secretary for such certification.

(c) Nothing in this section shall be construed to authorize any department, agency, officer, or employee of the United States to exercise any direction, supervision, or control over the content or distribution of public telecommunications programs and services, or over the curriculum or program of instruction of any educational institution or school system.

Section 399 [47 USC Section 399]. Support of Political Candidates Prohibited.

No noncommercial educational broadcasting station may support or oppose any candidate for political office.

Section 399A [47 USC Section 399a]. Use of Business or Institutional Logograms.

(a) For purposes of this section, the term "business or institutional logogram" means any aural or visual letters or words, or any symbol or sign, which is used for the exclusive purpose of identifying any corporation, company, or other organization, and which is not used for the purpose of promoting the products, services, or facilities of such corporation, company, or other organization.

(b) Each public television station and each public radio station shall be authorized to broadcast announcements which include the use of any business or institutional logogram and which include a reference to the location of the corporation, company, or other organization involved, except that such announcements may not interrupt regular programming.

(c) The provisions of this section shall not be construed to limit the authority of the Commission to prescribe regulations relating to the manner in which logograms may be used to identify corporations, companies, or other organizations.

483

Section 399B [47 USC Section 399b]. Offering of Certain Services, Facilities, or Products by Public Broadcast Stations.

(a) For purposes of this section, the term "advertisement" means any message or other programming material which is broadcast or otherwise transmitted in exchange for any remuneration, and which is intended --

(1) to promote any service, facility, or product offered by any person who is engaged in such offering for profit;

(2) to express the views of any person with respect to any matter of public importance or interest; or

(3) to support or oppose any candidate for political office.

(b)(1) Except as provided in paragraph (2), each public broadcast station shall be authorized to engage in the offering of services, facilities, or products in exchange for remuneration.

(2) No public broadcast station may make its facilities available to any person for the broadcasting of any advertisement.

(c) Any public broadcast station which engages in any offering specified in subsection (b)(1) may not use any funds distributed by the corporation under Section 396(k) to defray any costs associated with such offering. Any such offering by a public broadcast station shall not interfere with the provision of public telecommunications services by such station.

(d) Each public broadcast station which engages in the activity specified in subsection (b)(1) shall, in consultation with the corporation, develop an accounting system which is designed to identify any amounts received as remuneration for, or cost related to, such activities under this section, and to account for such amounts separately from any other amounts received by such station from any source.

Title IV - Procedural and Administrative Provisions

Section 401 [47 USC Section 401]. Jurisdiction to Enforce Act and Orders of Commission.

(a) The district courts of the United States shall have jurisdiction, upon application of the Attorney General of the United States at the request of the Commission, alleging a failure to comply with or a violation of any of the provisions of this Act by any person, to issue a writ or writs of mandamus commanding such person to comply with the provisions of this Act.

(b) If any person fails or neglects to obey any order of the Commission other than for the payment of money, while the same is in effect, the Commission or any party injured thereby, or the United States, by its Attorney General, may apply to the appropriate district court of the United States for the enforcement of such order. If, after hearing, that court determines that the order was regularly made and duly served, and that the person is in disobedience of the same, the court shall enforce obedience to such order by writ of injunction or other proper process, mandatory or otherwise, to restrain such person or the officers, agents, or representatives of such person, from further disobedience of such order, or to enjoin upon it or them obedience to the same.

(c) Upon the request of the Commission it shall be the duty of any district attorney of the United States to whom the Commission may apply to institute in the proper court and to prosecute under the direction of the Attorney General of the United States all necessary proceedings for the enforcement of the provisions of this Act and for the punishment of all violations thereof, and the costs and expenses of such prosecutions shall be paid out of the appropriations for the expenses of the courts of the United States.

Section 402 [47 USC Section 402]. Proceedings to Enjoin, Set Aside, Annul or Suspend Orders of the Commission.

(a) Any proceeding to enjoin, set aside, annul or suspend any order of the Commission under this Act (except those appealable under subsection (b) of this section) shall be brought as provided by and in the manner prescribed in Chapter 158 of Title 28, United States Code.

(b) Appeals may be taken from decisions and orders of the Commission to the United States Court of Appeals for the District of Columbia in any of the following cases:

(1) By any applicant for a construction permit or station license, whose application is denied by the Commission.

(2) By any applicant for the renewal or modification of any such instrument of authorization whose application is denied by the Commission.

(3) By any party to an application for authority to transfer, assign or dispose of any such instrument of authorization, or any rights thereunder, whose application is denied by the Commission.

(4) By any applicant for the permit required by Section 325 of this Act whose application has been denied by the Commission, or by any permittee under said section whose permit has been revoked by the Commission.

(5) By the holder of any construction permit or station license which has been modified or revoked by the Commission.

(6) By any other person who is aggrieved or whose interests are adversely affected by any order of the Commission granting or denying any application described in paragraphs (1), (2), (3) ~~and~~, (4) **and (9)** hereof.

(7) By any person upon whom an order to cease and desist has been served under Section 312 of this Act.

(8) By any radio operator whose license has been suspended by the Commission.

(9) By any applicant for authority to provide interLATA services under Section 271 of this Act whose application is denied by the Commission.

(c) Such appeal shall be taken by filing a notice of appeal with the court within thirty days from the date upon which public notice is given of the decision or order complained of. Such notice of appeal shall contain a concise statement of the nature of the proceedings as to which the appeal is taken; a concise statement of the reasons on which the appellant intends to rely, separately stated and numbered; and proof of service of a true copy of said notice and statement upon the Commission. Upon filing of such notice, the court shall have jurisdiction of the proceedings and of the questions determined therein and shall have power, by order, directed to the Commission or any other party to the appeal, to grant such temporary relief as it may deem just and proper. Orders granting temporary relief may be either affirmative or negative in their scope and application so as to permit either the maintenance of the status quo in the matter in which the appeal is taken or the restoration of a position or status terminated or adversely affected by the order appealed from and shall, unless otherwise ordered by the court, be effective pending hearing and determination of said appeal and compliance by the Commission with the final judgment of the court rendered in said appeal.

(d) Notice to interested parties: filing of record. Upon the filing of any such notice of appeal the appellant shall, not later than five days after the filing of such notice, notify each person shown by the records of the Commission to be interested in said appeal of the filing and pendency of the same. The Commission shall file with the court the record upon which the order complained of was entered, as provided in Section 2112 of Title 28, United States Code<[28 USCS §2112]>.

(e) Within thirty days after the filing of any such appeal any interested person may intervene and participate in the proceedings had upon said appeal by filing with the court a notice of intention to intervene and a verified statement showing the nature of the interest of such party, together with proof of service of true copies of said notice and statement, both upon appellant and upon the Commission. Any person who would be aggrieved or whose interest would be adversely affected by a reversal or modification of the order of the Commission complained of shall be considered an interested party.

(f) The record and briefs upon which any such appeal shall be heard and determined by the court shall contain such information and material, and shall be prepared within such time and in such manner as the court may by rule prescribe.

(g) The court shall hear and determine the appeal upon the record before it in the manner prescribed by Section 706 of Title 5, United States Code.

(h) In the event that the court shall render a decision and enter an order reversing the order of the Commission, it shall remand the case to the Commission to carry out the judgment of the court and it shall be the duty of the Commission, in the absence of the proceedings to renew such judgment, to forthwith give effect thereto, and unless otherwise ordered by the court, to do so upon the basis of the proceedings already had and the record upon which said appeal was heard and determined.

(i) The court may, in its discretion, enter judgment for costs in favor of or against an appellant, or other interested parties intervening in said appeal, but not against the Commission, depending upon the nature of the issues involved upon said appeal and the outcome thereof.

(j) The court's judgment shall be final, subject, however, to review by the Supreme Court of the United States upon writ of certiorari on petition therefor under Section 1254 of Title 28 of the United States Code, by the appellant, by the Commission, or by any interested party intervening in the appeal, or by certification by the court pursuant to the provisions of that section.

Section 403 [47 USC Section 403]. Inquiry by Commission on Its Own Motion.

The Commission shall have full authority and power at any time to institute an inquiry, on its own motion, in any case and as to any matter or thing concerning which complaint is authorized to be made, to or before the Commission by any provision of this Act, or concerning which any question may arise under any of the provisions of this Act, or relating to the enforcement of any of the provisions of this Act. The Commission shall have the same powers and authority to proceed with any inquiry instituted on its own motion as though it had been appealed to by complaint or petition under any of the provisions of this Act, including the power to make and enforce any order or orders in the case, or relating to the matter or thing concerning which the inquiry is had, excepting orders for the payment of money.

Section 404 [47 USC Section 404]. Reports of Investigations.

Whenever an investigation shall be made by the Commission it shall be its duty to make a report in writing in respect thereto, which shall state the conclusions of the Commission, together with its decision, order, or requirement in the premises; and in case damages are awarded such report shall include the findings of fact on which the award is made.

Section 405 [47 USC Section 405]. Reconsiderations.

(a) After an order, decision, report, or action has been made or taken in any proceeding by the Commission, or by any designated authority within the Commission pursuant to a delegation under Section 5(c)(1), any party thereto, or any other person aggrieved or whose interests are adversely affected thereby, may petition for reconsideration only to the authority, making or taking the order, decision, report, or action; and it shall be lawful for such authority, whether it be the Commission or other authority designated under Section 5(c)(1), in its discretion, to grant such a reconsideration if sufficient reason therefor be made to appear. A petition for reconsideration must be filed within thirty days from the date upon which public notice is given of the order, decision, report, or action complained of. No such application shall excuse any person from complying with or obeying any order, decision, report, or action of the Commission, or operate in any manner to stay or postpone the enforcement thereof, without the special order of the Commission. The filing of a petition for reconsideration shall not be a condition precedent to judicial review of any such order, decision, report, or action, except where the party seeking such review (1) was not a party to the proceedings resulting in such order, decision, report, or action, or (2) relies on questions of fact or law upon which the Commission, or designated authority within the Commission, has been afforded no opportunity to pass. The Commission, or designated authority within the Commission, shall enter an order, with a concise statement of the reasons therefor, denying a petition for reconsideration or granting such petition, in whole or in part, and ordering such further proceedings as may be appropriate: provided, that in any case where such petition relates to an instrument of authorization granted without a hearing, the Commission, or designated authority within the Commission shall take such action within ninety days of the filing of such petition. Reconsiderations shall be governed by such general rules as the Commission may establish, except that no evidence other than newly discovered evidence, evidence which has become available only since the original taking of evidence, or evidence which the Commission or designated authority within the Commission believes should have been taken in the original proceeding shall be taken on any reconsideration. The time within which a petition for review must be filed in a proceeding to which Section 402(a) applies, or within which an appeal must be taken under Section 402(b) in any case, shall be computed from the date upon which the Commission gives public notice of the order, decision, report, or action complained of.

(b)(1) Within 90 days after receiving a petition for reconsideration of an order concluding a hearing under Section 204(a) or concluding an investigation under Section 208(b), the Commission shall issue an order granting or denying such petition.

(2) Any order issued under paragraph (1) shall be a final order and may be appealed under Section 402(a).

Section 406 [47 USC Section 406]. Mandamus to Compel Furnishing of Facilities

The district courts of the United States shall have jurisdiction upon the relation of any person alleging any violation, by a carrier subject to this Act, of any of the provisions of this Act which prevent the relator from receiving service in interstate or foreign communication by wire or radio, or in interstate or foreign transmission of energy by radio, from said carrier at the same charges, or upon terms or conditions as favorable as those given by said carrier for like communication or transmission under similar conditions to any other person, to issue a writ or writs of mandamus against such carrier commanding such carrier to furnish facilities for such communication or transmission to the party applying for the writ: provided, that if any question of fact as to the proper compensation to the carrier for the service to be enforced by the writ is raised by the pleadings, the writ of peremptory mandamus may issue, notwithstanding such question of fact is undetermined, upon such terms as to security, payment of money into the court, or otherwise, as the court may think proper pending the determination of the question of fact: provided further, that the remedy hereby given by writ of mandamus shall be cumulative and shall not be held to exclude or interfere with other remedies provided by this Act.

Section 407 [47 USC Section 407]. Petition for Enforcement of Order for Payment of Money.

If a carrier does not comply with an order for the payment of money within the time limit in such order, the complainant, or any person for whose benefit such order was made, may file in the district court of the United States for the district in which he resides or in which is located the principal operating office of the carrier, or through which the line of the carrier runs, or in any state court of general jurisdiction having jurisdiction of the parties, a petition setting forth briefly the causes for which he claims damages, and the order of the Commission in the premises. Such suit in the district court of the United States shall proceed in all respects like other civil suits for damages, except that on the trial of such suits the findings and order of the Commission shall be prima facie evidence of the facts therein stated, except that the petitioner shall not be liable for costs in the district court nor for costs at any subsequent stage of the proceedings unless they accrue upon his appeal. If the petitioner shall finally prevail, he shall be allowed a reasonable attorney's fee, to be taxed and collected as a part of the costs of the suit.

Section 408 [47 USC Section 408]. Orders Not for Payment of Money -- When Effective.

Except as otherwise provided in this Act, all orders of the Commission, other than orders for the payment of money, shall take effect thirty calendar days from the date upon which public notice of the order is given, unless the Commission designates a different effective date. All such orders shall continue in force for the period of time specified in the order or until the Commission or a court of competent jurisdiction issues a superseding order.

Section 409 [47 USC Section 409]. General Provisions Relating to Proceedings -- Witnesses and Depositions.

(a) In every case of adjudication (as defined in the Administrative Procedure Act) which has been designated by the Commission for hearing, the person or persons conducting the hearing shall prepare and file an initial, tentative, or recommended decision, except where such person or persons become unavailable to the Commission or where the Commission finds upon the record that due and timely execution of its functions imperatively and unavoidably require that the record be certified to the Commission for initial or final decision.

(b) In every case of adjudication (as defined in the Administrative Procedure Act) which has been designated by the Commission for hearing, any party to the proceeding shall be permitted to file exceptions and memoranda in support thereof to the initial, tentative, or recommended decision, which shall be passed upon by the Commission or by the authority within the Commission, if any, to whom the function of passing upon the exceptions is delegated under Section 5(d)(1): provided, however, that such authority shall not be the same authority which made the decision to which the exception is taken.

(c)(1) In any case of adjudication (as defined in the Administrative Procedure Act) which has been designated by the Commission for a hearing, no person who has participated in the presentation or preparation for presentation of such case at the hearing or upon review shall (except to the extent required for the disposition of ex parte matters as authorized by law) directly or indirectly make any additional presentation respecting such case to the hearing officer or officers or to the Commission, or to any authority within the Commission to whom, in such case, review functions have been delegated by the Commission under Section 5(d)(1), unless upon notice and opportunity for all parties to participate.

(2) The provision in subsection (c) of Section 5 of the Administrative Procedure Act which states that such subsection shall not apply in determining applications for initial licenses, shall not be applicable hereafter in the case of applications for initial licenses before the Federal Communications Commission.

(d) To the extent that the foregoing provisions of this section and Section 5(d) are in conflict with the provisions of the Administrative Procedure Act, such provisions of this section and Section 5(d) shall be held to supersede and modify the provisions of that Act.

(e) For the purposes of this Act the Commission shall have the power to require by subpoena the attendance and testimony of witnesses and the production of all books, papers, schedules of charges, contracts, agreements, and documents relating to any matter under investigation. Witnesses summoned before the Commission shall be paid the same fees and mileage that are paid witnesses in the courts of the United States.

(f) Such attendance of witnesses, and the production of such documentary evidence, may be required from any place in the United States, at any designated place of hearing. And in case of disobedience to a subpoena the Commission, or any party to a proceeding before the Commission, may invoke the aid of any court of the United States in requiring the attendance and testimony of witnesses and the production of books, papers and documents under the provisions of this section.

(g) Any of the district courts of the United States within the jurisdiction of which such inquiry is carried on may, in case of contumacy or refusal to obey a subpoena issued to any common carrier or licensee or other person, issue an order requiring such common carrier, licensee, or other person to appear before the Commission (and produce books and papers if so ordered) and give evidence touching the matter in question; and any failure to obey such order of the court may be punished by such court as a contempt thereof.

(h) The testimony of any witness may be taken, at the instance of a party, in any proceeding or investigation pending before the Commission, by deposition, at any time after a cause or proceeding is at issue on petition and answer. The Commission may also order testimony to be taken by deposition in any proceeding or investigation pending before it, at any stage of such proceeding or investigation. Such depositions may be taken before any judge of any court of the United States, or any United States commissioner, or any clerk of a district court, or any chancellor, justice, or judge of a supreme or superior court, mayor, or chief magistrate of a city, judge of a county court, or court of common pleas of any of the United States, or any notary public, not being of counsel or attorney to either of the parties, nor interested in the event of the proceeding or investigation. Reasonable notice must first be given in writing by the party or his attorney proposing to take such deposition to the opposite party or his attorney of record, as either may be nearest, which notice shall state the name of the witness and the time and place of the taking of his deposition. Any person may be compelled to appear and depose, and to produce documentary evidence, in the same manner as witnesses may be compelled to appear and testify and produce documentary evidence before the Commission, as herein before provided.

(i) Every person deposing as herein provided shall be cautioned and sworn (or affirm, if he so request) to testify the whole truth, and shall be carefully examined. His testimony shall be reduced to writing by the magistrate taking the deposition, or under his direction, and shall, after it has been reduced to writing, be subscribed by the deponent.

(j) If a witness whose testimony may be desired to be taken by deposition be in a foreign country, the deposition may be taken before an officer or person designated by the Commission, or agreed upon by the parties by stipulation in writing to be filed with the Commission. All depositions must be promptly filed with the Commission.

(k) Witnesses whose depositions are taken as authorized in this Act, and the magistrate or other officer taking the same, shall severally be entitled to the same fees as are paid for like services in the courts of the United States.

(l) [Repealed] [No person shall be excused from attending and testifying or from producing books, papers, schedules of charges, contracts, agreements, and documents before the Commission, or in obedience to the subpoena of the Commission, whether such subpoena be signed or issued by one or more commissioners or in any cause or proceeding, criminal or otherwise, based upon or growing out of an alleged violation of this Act, or of any amendments thereto, on the ground or for the reason that the testimony or evidence, documentary or otherwise, required of him may tend to incriminate him or subject him to a penalty or forfeiture; but no individual shall be prosecuted or subjected to any penalty or forfeiture for or on account of any transaction, matter or thing concerning which he is compelled, after having claimed his privilege against self-incrimination, to testify or produce evidence, documentary or otherwise, except that any individual so testifying shall not be exempt from prosecution and punishment for perjury committed in so testifying.]

(m) Any person who shall neglect or refuse to attend and testify, or to answer any lawful inquiry, or to produce books, papers, schedules of charges, contracts, agreements, and documents, if in his power to do so, in obedience to the subpoena or lawful requirement of the Commission, shall be guilty of a misdemeanor and upon conviction thereof by a court of competent jurisdiction shall be punished by a fine of not less than $100 nor more than $5,000 or by imprisonment for not more than one year, or by both such fine and imprisonment.

Section 410 [47 USC Section 410]. Use of Joint Boards -- Cooperation with State Commissions.

(a) Except as provided in Section 409, the Commission may refer any matter arising in the administration of this Act to a joint board to be composed of a member, or of an equal number of members, as determined by the Commission, from each of the states in which the wire or radio communication affected by or involved in the proceeding takes place or is proposed. For purposes of acting upon such matter any such board shall have all the jurisdiction and powers conferred by law upon an examiner provided for in Section 11 of the Administrative Procedure Act, designated by the Commission, and shall be subject to the same duties and obligations. The action of a joint board shall have such force and effect and its proceedings shall be conducted in such manner as the Commission shall by regulations prescribe. The joint board member or members of each state shall be nominated by the state commission of the state or by the governor if there is no state commission, and appointed by the Federal Communications Commission. The Commission shall have discretion to reject any nominee. Joint board members shall receive such allowances for expenses as the Commission shall provide.

(b) The Commission may confer with any state commission having regulatory jurisdiction with respect to carriers, regarding the relationship between rate structures, accounts, charges, practices, classifications and regulations of carriers subject to the jurisdiction of such state commission and of the Commission; and the Commission is authorized under such rules and regulations as it shall prescribe to hold joint hearings with any state commission in connection with any matter with respect to which the Commission is authorized to act. The Commission is authorized in the administration of this Act to avail itself of such cooperation, services, records and facilities as may be afforded by any state commission.

(c) The Commission shall refer any proceeding regarding the jurisdictional separation of common carrier property and expenses between interstate and intrastate operations, which it institutes pursuant to a notice of proposed rulemaking and, except as provided in Section 409 of this Act, may refer any other matter, relating to common carrier communications of joint Federal-State concern, to a Federal-State Joint Board. The Joint Board shall possess the same jurisdiction, powers, duties, and obligations as a joint board established under subsection (a) of this section, and shall prepare a recommended decision for prompt review and action by the Commission. In addition, the State members of the Joint Board shall sit with the Commission en banc at any oral argument that may be scheduled in the proceeding. The Commission shall also afford the State members of the Joint Board an opportunity to participate in its deliberations, but not vote, when it has under consideration the recommended decision of the Joint Board or any further decisional action that may be required in the proceeding. The Joint Board shall be composed of three Commissioners of the Commission and of four State commissioners nominated by the national organization of the State commissions and approved by the Commission. The Chairman of the Commission, or another Commissioner designated by the Commission, shall serve as Chairman of the Joint Board.

Section 411 [47 USC Section 411]. Joinder of Parties.

(a) In any proceeding for the enforcement of the provisions of this Act, whether such proceeding be instituted before the Commission or be begun originally in any district court of the United States, it shall be lawful to include as parties, in addition to the carrier, all persons interested in or affected by the charge, regulation or practice under consideration, and inquiries, investigations, orders, and decrees may be made with reference to and against such additional parties in the same manner, to the same extent, and subject to the same provisions as are or shall be authorized by law with respect to carriers.

(b) In any suit for the enforcement of an order for the payment of money all parties in whose favor the Commission may have made an award for damages by a single order may be joined as plaintiffs, and all of the carriers parties to such order awarding such damages may be joined as defendants, and such suit may be maintained by such joint plaintiffs and against such joint defendants in any district where any one of such joint plaintiffs could maintain such suit against any one of such joint defendants; and service of process against any one of such defendants as may not be found in the district where the suit is brought may be made in any district where such defendant carrier has its principal operating office. In case of such joint suit, the recovery, if any, may be by judgment in favor of any one of such plaintiffs, against the defendant found to be liable to such plaintiff.

Section 412 [47 USC Section 412]. Documents Filed to be Public Records -- Use in Proceedings.

The copies of schedules of charges, classifications, and of all contracts, agreements, and arrangements between common carriers filed with the Commission as herein provided, and the statistics, tables, and figures contained in the annual or other reports of carriers and other persons made to the Commission as required under the provisions of this Act shall be preserved as public records in the custody of the secretary of the Commission, and shall be received as prima facie evidence of what they purport to be for the purpose of investigations by the Commission and in all judicial proceedings; and copies of and extracts from any of said schedules, classifications, contracts, agreements, arrangements, or reports, made public records as aforesaid, certified by the Secretary, under the Commission's seal, shall be received in evidence with like effect as the originals; provided, that the Commission may, if the public interest will be served thereby, keep confidential any contract, agreement, or arrangement relating to foreign wire or radio communication when the publication of such contract, agreement, or arrangement would place American communications companies at a disadvantage in meeting the competition of foreign communication companies.

Section 413 [47 USC Section 413]. Designation of Agent for Service.

It shall be the duty of every carrier subject to this Act to designate in writing an agent in the District of Columbia, upon whom service of all notices and process and all orders, decisions, and requirements of the Commission may be made for and on behalf of said carrier in any proceeding or suit pending before the Commission, and to file such designation in the Office of the Secretary of the Commission, which designation may from time to time be changed by like writing similarly filed; and thereupon service of all notices and process and orders, decisions, and requirements of the Commission may be made upon such carrier by leaving a copy thereof with such designated agent at his office or usual place of residence in the District of Columbia, with like effect as if made personally upon such carrier, and in default of such designation of such agent, service of any notice or other process in any proceeding before said Commission, or of any order, decision, or requirement of the Commission, may be made by posting such notice, process, order, requirement, or decision in the Office of the Secretary of the Commission.

Section 414 [47 USC Section 414]. Remedies in this Act not Exclusive.

Nothing in this Act contained shall in any way abridge or alter the remedies now existing at common law or by statute, but the provisions of this Act are in addition to such remedies.

Section 415 [47 USC Section 415]. Limitations as to Actions.

(a) All actions at law by carriers for recovery of their lawful charges, or any part thereof, shall be begun within two years from the time the cause of action accrues, and not after.

(b) All complaints against carriers for the recovery of damages not based on overcharges shall be filed with the Commission within two years from the time the cause of action accrues, and not after, subject to subsection (d) of this section.

(c) For recovery of overcharges action at law shall be begun or complaint filed with the Commission against carriers within two years from the time the cause of action accrues, and not after, subject to subsection (d) of this section, except that if claim for overcharge has been presented in writing to the carrier within the two-year period of limitation said period shall be extended to include two years from the time notice in writing is given by the carrier to the claimant of disallowance of the claim, or any part or parts thereof, specified in the notice.

(d) If on or before expiration of the period of limitation in subsection (b) or (c) a carrier begins action under subsection (a) for recovery of lawful charges in respect of the same service, or, without beginning action, collects charges in respect of that service, said period of limitation shall be extended to include ninety days from the time such action is begun or such charges are collected by the carrier.

(e) The cause of action in respect of the transmission of a message shall, for the purpose of this section, be deemed to accrue upon delivery or tender of delivery thereof by the carrier, and not after.

(f) A petition for the enforcement of an order of the Commission for the payment of money shall be filed in the district court or the state court within one year from the date of the order, and not after.

(g) The term "overcharges" as used in this section shall be deemed to mean charges for services in excess of those applicable thereto under the schedules of charges lawfully on file with the Commission.

Section 416 [47 USC Section 416]. Provisions Relating to Orders

(a) Every order of the Commission shall be forthwith served upon the designated agent of the carrier in the city of Washington or in such other manner as may be provided by law.

(b) Except as otherwise provided in this Act, the Commission is hereby authorized to suspend or modify its orders upon such notice and in such manner as it shall deem proper.

(c) It shall be the duty of every person, its agents and employees and any receiver or trustee thereof, to observe and comply with such orders so long as the same shall remain in effect.

Title V - Penal Provisions -- Forfeitures

Section 501 [47 USC Section 501]. General Penalty.

Any person who willfully and knowingly does or causes or suffers to be done any act, matter, or thing, in this Act prohibited or declared to be unlawful, or who willfully and knowingly, omits or fails to do any act, matter, or thing in this Act required to be done, or willfully and knowingly causes or suffers such omission or failure, shall, upon conviction thereof, be punished for such offense, for which no penalty (other than a forfeiture) is provided in this Act, by a fine of not more than $10,000 or by imprisonment for a term not exceeding one year, or both; except that any person, having been once convicted of an offense punishable under this section, who is subsequently convicted of violating any provision of this Act punishable under this section, shall be punished by a fine of not more than $10,000 or by imprisonment for a term not exceeding two years, or both.

Section 502 [47 USC Section 502]. Violations of Rules, Regulations, and So Forth.

Any person who willfully and knowingly violates any rule, regulation, restriction, or condition made or imposed by the Commission under authority of this Act, or any rule, regulation, restriction, or condition made or imposed by any international radio or wire communications treaty or convention, or regulations annexed thereto, to which the United States is or may hereafter become a party, shall, in addition to any other penalties provided by law, be punished, upon conviction thereof, by a fine of not more than $500 for each and every day during which such offense occurs.

Section 503 [47 USC Section 503]. Forfeitures in Cases of Rebates and Offsets.

(a) Any person who shall deliver messages for interstate or foreign transmission to any carrier, or for whom as sender or receiver, any such carrier shall transmit any interstate or foreign wire or radio communication, who shall knowingly by employee, agent, officer, or otherwise, directly or indirectly, by or through any means or device whatsoever, receive or accept from such common carrier any sum of money or any other valuable consideration as a rebate or offset against the regular charges for transmission of such messages as fixed by the schedules of charges provided for in this Act, shall in addition to any other penalty provided by this Act forfeit to the United States a sum of money three times the amount of money so received or accepted and three times the value of any other consideration so received or accepted, to be ascertained by the trial court; and in the trial of said action all such rebates or other considerations so received or accepted for a period of six years prior to the commencement of the action, may be included therein, and the amount recovered shall be three time the total amount of money, or three times the total value of such consideration, so received or accepted, or both, as the case my be.

(b)(1) Any person who is determined by the Commission, in accordance with paragraph (3) or (4) of this subsection, to have --

(A) willfully or repeatedly failed to comply substantially with the terms and conditions of any license, permit, certificate, or other instrument or authorization issued by the Commission;

(B) willfully or repeatedly failed to comply with any of the provisions of this Act or of any rule, regulation, or order issued by the Commission under this Act or under any treaty convention, or other agreement to which the United States is a party and which is binding upon the United States;

(C) violated any provision of Section 317(c) or 508(a) of this Act; or

(D) violate any provision of Sections 1304; 1343, or 1464 of Title 18, United States Code;

shall be liable to the United States for a forfeiture penalty. A forfeiture penalty under this subsection shall be in addition to any other penalty provided for by this Act; except that this subsection shall not apply to any conduct which is subject to forfeiture under Title II, Part II or III of Title III, or Section 506 of this Act.

(2)(A) If the violator is (i) a broadcast station licensee or permittee, (ii) a cable television operator, or (iii) an applicant for any broadcast or cable television operator license, permit, certificate, or other instrument or authorization issued by the Commission, the amount of any forfeiture penalty determined under this section shall not exceed $25,000 for each violation or each day of a continuing violation, except that the amount assessed for any continuing violation shall not exceed a total of $250,000 for any single act or failure to act described in paragraph (1) of this subsection.

(B) If the violator is a common carrier subject to the provisions of this Act or an applicant for any common carrier license, permit, certificate, or other instrument of authorization issued by the Commission, the amount of any forfeiture penalty determined under this subsection shall not exceed $100,000 for each violation or each day of a continuing violation, except that the amount assessed for any continuing violation shall not exceed a total of $1,000,000 for any single act or failure to act described in paragraph (1) of this subsection.

(C) In any case not covered in subparagraph (A) or (B), the amount of any forfeiture penalty determined under this subsection shall not exceed $10,000 for each violation or each day of a continuing violation, except that the amount assessed for any continuing violation shall not exceed a total of $75,000 for any single act or failure to act described in paragraph (1) of this subsection.

(D) The amount of such forfeiture penalty shall be assessed by the Commission, or its designee, by written notice, In determining the amount of such a forfeiture penalty, the Commission or its designee shall take into account the nature, circumstances, extent, and gravity of the violation and, with respect to the violator, the degree of culpability, any history of prior offenses, ability to pay, and such other matters as justice may require.

(3)(A) At the discretion of the Commission, a forfeiture penalty may be determined against a person under this subsection after notice and an opportunity for a hearing before the Commission or an administrative law judge thereof in accordance with Section 554 of Title 5, United States Code. Any person against whom a forfeiture penalty is determined under this paragraph may obtain review thereof pursuant to Section 402(a).

(B) If any person fails to pay an assessment of a forfeiture penalty determined under subparagraph (A) of this paragraph, after it has become a final and unappealable order or after the appropriate court has entered final judgment in favor of the Commission, the Commission shall refer the matter to the Attorney General of the United States, who shall recover the amount assessed in any appropriate district court of the United States. In such action, the validity and appropriateness of the final order imposing the forfeiture penalty shall not be subject to review.

(4) Except as provided in paragraph (3) of this subsection, no forfeiture penalty shall be imposed under this subsection against any person unless and until --

(A) the Commission issues a notice of apparent liability, in writing, with respect to such person;

(B) such notice has been received by such person, or until the Commission has sent such notice to the last known address of such person, by registered or certified mail; and

(C) such person is granted an opportunity to show, in writing, within such reasonable period of time as the Commission prescribes by rule or regulation, why no such forfeiture penalty should be imposed.

Such a notice shall (i) identify each specific provision, term, and condition of any Act, rule, regulation, order, treaty, convention, or other agreement, license, permit, certificate, instrument, or authorization which such person apparently violated or with which such person apparently failed to comply; (ii) set forth the nature of the act or omission charged against such person and the facts upon which such charge is based; and (iii) state the date on which such conduct occurred. Any forfeiture penalty determined under this paragraph shall be recoverable pursuant to Section 504(a) of this Act.

(5) No forfeiture liability shall be determined under this subsection against any person, is such person does not hold a license, permit, certificate, or other authorization issued by the Commission and if such person is not an applicant for a license, permit, certificate, or other authorization issued by the Commission, unless, prior to the notice required by paragraph (3) of this subsection or the notice of apparent liability required by paragraph (4) of this subsection, such person (A) is sent a citation of the violation charged; (B) is given a reasonable opportunity for a personal interview with an official of the Commission, at the field office of the Commission which is nearest to such person's place of residence; and (C) subsequently engages in conduct of the type described in such citation. The provisions of this paragraph shall not apply, however, if the person involved is engaging in activities for which a license, permit, certificate, or other authorization is required, or is a cable television system operator, if the person involved is transmitting on frequencies assigned for use in a service in which individual station operation is authorized by rule pursuant to Section 307(e) or in the case of violations of section 303(q), if the person involved is a nonlicensee tower owner who has previously received notice of the obligations imposed by section 303(q) from the Commission or the permittee or licensee who uses that tower. Whenever the requirements of this paragraph are satisfied with respect to a particular person, such person shall not be entitled to receive any additional citation of the violation charged, with respect to any conduct of the type described in the citation sent under this paragraph.

(6) No forfeiture penalty shall be determined or imposed against any person under this subsection if --

(A) such person holds a broadcast station license issued under Title III of this Act and if the violation charged occurred --

(i) more than 1 year prior to the date of issuance of the required notice or notice of apparent liability, or

(ii) prior to the date of commencement of the current term of such license, whichever is earlier; or

(B) such person does not hold a broadcast station license issued under Title III of this Act and if the violation charged occurred more than 1 year prior to the date of issuance of the required notice or notice of apparent liability.

For purposes of this paragraph, "date of commencement of the current term of such license" means the date of commencement of the last term of license for which the licensee has been granted a license by the Commission. A separate license term shall not be deemed to have commenced as a result of continuing a license in effect under section 307(c) pending decision on an application for renewal of the license.

Section 504 [47 USC Section 504]. Provisions Relating to Forfeitures.

(a) The forfeitures provided for in this Act shall be payable into the Treasury of the United States, and shall be recoverable, except as otherwise provided with respect to a forfeiture penalty determined under Section 503(b)(3) of this Act, in a civil suit in the name of the United States brought in the district where the person or carrier has its principal operating office or in any district through which the line or system of the carrier runs; provided, that any suit for the recovery of a forfeiture imposed pursuant to the provisions of this Act shall be a trial de novo; provided further, that in the case of forfeiture by a ship, said forfeiture may also be recoverable by way of libel in any district in which such ship shall arrive or depart. Such forfeiture shall be in addition to any other general or specific penalties herein provided. It shall be the duty of the various district attorneys, under the direction of the Attorney General of the United States, to prosecute for the recovery of forfeitures under this Act. The costs and expenses of such prosecutions shall be paid from the appropriation for the expenses of the courts of the United States.

(b) The forfeitures imposed by Title II, Parts II and III of Title III and Sections 503(b) and 506 of this Act shall be subject to remission or mitigation by the Commission under such regulations and methods of ascertaining the facts as may seem to it advisable, and, if suit has been instituted, the Attorney General, upon request of the Commission, shall direct the discontinuance of any prosecution to recover such forfeitures: provided, however, that no forfeiture shall be remitted or mitigated after determination by a court of competent jurisdiction.

(c) In any case where the Commission issues a notice of apparent liability looking toward the imposition of a forfeiture under this Act, that fact shall not be used, in other proceeding before the Commission, to the prejudice of the person to whom such notice was issued, unless (i) the forfeiture has been paid, or (ii) a court of competent jurisdiction has ordered payment of such forfeiture, and such order has become final.

Section 505 [47 USC Section 505]. Venue of Offenses.

The trial of any offense under this Act shall be in the district in which it is committed; or if the offense is committed upon the high seas, or out of the jurisdiction of any particular state or district, the trial shall be in the district where the offender may be found or into which he shall be first brought. Whenever the offense is begun in one jurisdiction and completed in another it may be dealt with, inquired of, tried, determined, and punished in either jurisdiction in the same manner as if the offense had been actually and wholly committed therein.

Section 506 [47 USC Section 506]. Violation of Great Lakes Agreement.

(a) Any vessel of the United States that is navigated in violation of the provisions of the Great Lakes Agreement or the rules and regulations of the Commission made in pursuance thereof and any vessel of a foreign country that is so navigated on waters under the jurisdiction of the United States shall forfeit to the United States the sum of $500 recoverable by way of suit or libel. Each day during which such navigation occurs shall constitute a separate offense.

(b) Every willful failure on the part of the master of a vessel of the United States to enforce or to comply with the provisions of the Great Lakes Agreement or the rules and regulations of the Commission made in pursuance thereof shall cause him to forfeit to the United States the sum of $100.

Section 507 [47 USC Section 507]. Disclosure of Certain Payments.

(a) Subject to subsection (d), any employee of a radio station who accepts or agrees to accept from any person (other than such station), or any person (other than such station) who pays or agrees to pay such employee, any money, service or other valuable consideration for the broadcast of any matter over such station shall, in advance of such broadcast, disclose the fact of such acceptance or agreement to such station.

497

(b) Subject to subsection (d), any person who, in connection with the production or preparation of any program or program matter which is intended for broadcasting over any radio station, accepts or agrees to accept, or pays or agrees to pay, ay money, service or other valuable consideration for the inclusion of any matter as a part of such program or program matter, shall, in advance of such broadcast, disclose the fact of such acceptance or payment or agreement to the payee's employer, or to the person for whom such program or program matter is being produced, or to the licensee of such station over which such program is broadcast.

(c) Subject to subsection (d), any person who supplies to any other person any program or program matter which is intended for broadcasting over any radio station shall, in advance of such broadcast, disclose to such other person any information of which he has knowledge, or which has been disclosed to him, as to any money, service or other valuable consideration which any person has paid or accepted, or has agreed to pay or accept, for the inclusion of any matter as a part of such program or program matter.

(d) The provisions of this section requiring the disclosure of information shall not apply in any case where, because of a waiver made by the Commission under Section 317(d), an announcement is not required to be made under Section 317.

(e) The inclusion in the program of the announcement required by Section 317 shall constitute the disclosure required by this section.

(f) The term "service or other valuable consideration" as used in this section shall not include any service or property furnished without charge or at a nominal charge for use on, or in connection with, a broadcast, or for use on a program which is intended for broadcasting over any radio station, unless it is so furnished in consideration for an identification in such broadcast or in such program of any person, product, service, trademark, or brand name beyond an identification which is reasonably related to the use of such service or property in such broadcast or such program.

(g) Any person who violates any provision of this section shall, for each such violation, be fined not more than $10,000 or imprisoned not more than one year, or both.

Section 508 [47 USC Section 508]. Prohibited Practices in Case of Contests of Intellectual Knowledge, Intellectual Skill, or Chance.

(a) It shall be unlawful for any person, with intent to deceive the listening or viewing public --

(1) to supply to any contestant in a purportedly bona fide contest of intellectual knowledge or intellectual skill any special and secret assistance whereby the outcome of such contest will be in whole or in part prearranged or predetermined:

(2) by means of persuasion, bribery, intimidation, or otherwise, to induce or cause any contestant in a purportedly bona fide contest of intellectual knowledge or intellectual skill to refrain in any manner from using or displaying his knowledge or skill in such contest, whereby the outcome thereof will be in whole or in part prearranged or predetermined;

(3) to engage in any artifice or scheme for the purpose of prearranging or predetermining in whole or in part to the outcome of a purportedly bona fide contest of intellectual knowledge, intellectual skill, or chance;

(4) to produce or participate in the production for broadcasting of, to broadcast or participate in the broadcasting of, to offer to a licensee for broadcasting, or to sponsor, any radio program knowing or having reasonable ground for believing that, in connection with a purportedly bona

fide contest of intellectual knowledge, intellectual skill, or chance constituting any part of such program, any person has done or is going to do any act or thing referred to in paragraph (1), (2) or (3) of this subsection;

(5) to conspire with any other person or persons to do any act or thing prohibited by paragraph (1), (2), (3), or (4) of this subsection, if one or more of such persons do any act to effect the object of such conspiracy.

(b) For the purposes of this section --

(1) the term "contest" means any contest broadcast by a radio station in connection with which any money or any other thing of value is offered as a prize or prizes to be paid or presented by the program sponsor or by any other person or persons, as announced in the course of the broadcast;

(2) the term "the listening or viewing public" means those members of the public who, with the aid of radio receiving sets, listen to or view programs broadcast by radio stations.

(c) Whoever violates subsection (a) shall be fined not more than $10,000 or imprisoned not more than one year, or both.

Section 510 [47 USC Section 510]. Forfeiture of Communications Devices.

(a) Any electronic, electromagnetic, radio frequency, or similar device, or component thereof, used, sent, carried, manufactured, assembled, possessed, offered for sale, sold, or advertised with willful and knowing intent to violate Section 301 or 302, or rules prescribed by the Commission under such sections, may be seized and forfeited to the United States.

(b) Any property subject to forfeiture to the United States under this section may be seized by the Attorney General of the United States upon process issued pursuant to the supplemental rules for certain admiralty and maritime claims by any district court of the United States having jurisdiction over the property, except that seizure without such process may be made if the seizure is incident to a lawful arrest or search.

(c) All provisions of law relating to --

(1) the seizure, summary and judicial forfeiture, and condemnation of property for violation of the customs laws;

(2) the disposition of such property or the proceeds from the sale thereof;

(3) the remission or mitigation of such forfeitures; and

(4) the compromise of claims with respect to such forfeitures;

shall apply to seizures and forfeitures incurred, or alleged to have been incurred, under the provisions of this section, insofar as applicable and not inconsistent with the provisions of this section, except that such seizures and forfeitures shall be limited to the communications device, devices, or components thereof.

(d) Whenever property is forfeited under this section, the Attorney General of the United States may forward it to the Commission or sell any forfeited property which is not harmful to the public. The proceeds from any such sale shall be deposited in the general fund of the Treasury of the United States.

Title VI - Cable Communications

Part I - General Provisions

Section 601 [47 USC Section 521]. Purposes.

The purposes of this title are to --
    (1) establish a national policy concerning cable communications;
    (2) establish franchise procedures and standards which encourage the growth and development of cable systems and which assure that cable systems are responsive to the needs and interests of the local community;
    (3) establish guidelines for the exercise of Federal, State, and local authority with respect to the regulation of cable systems;
    (4) assure that cable communications provide and are encouraged to provide the widest possible diversity of information sources and services to the public;
    (5) establish an orderly process for franchise renewal which protects cable operators against unfair denials of renewal where the operator's past performance and proposal for future performance meet the standards established by this title; and
    (6) promote competition in cable communications and minimize unnecessary regulation that would impose an undue economic burden on cable systems.

Section 602 [47 USC Section 522]. Definitions.

For purposes of this title --
    (1) the term "activated channels" means those channels engineered at the headend of a cable system for the provision of services generally available to residential subscribers of the cable system, regardless of whether such services actually are provided, including any channel designated for public, educational, or governmental use;
    (2) the term "affiliate," when used in relation to any person, means another person who owns or controls, is owned or controlled by, or is under common ownership or control with, such person;
    (3) the term "basic cable service" means any service tier which includes the retransmission of local television broadcast signals;
    (4) the term "cable channel" or "channel" means a portion of the electromagnetic frequency spectrum which is used in a cable system and which is capable of delivering a television channel (as television channel is defined by the Commission by regulation);
    (5) the term "cable operator" means any person or group of persons (A) who provides cable service over a cable system and directly or through one or more affiliates owns a significant interest in such cable system, or (B) who otherwise controls or is responsible for, through any arrangement, the management and operation of such a cable systems;
    (6) the term "cable service" means --
        (A) the one-way transmission to subscribers of (i) video programming, or (ii) other programming service, and
        (B) subscriber interaction, if any, which is required for the selection **or use** of such video programming or other programming service;

(7) the term "cable system" means a facility, consisting of a set of closed transmission paths and associated signal generation, reception, and control equipment that is designed to provide cable service which includes video programming and which is provided to multiple subscribers within a community, but such term does not include (A) a facility that serves only to retransmit the television signals of 1 or more television broadcast stations; (B) a facility that serves <only> subscribers <in 1 or more multiple unit dwellings under common ownership, control, or management, unless such facility or facilities uses> **without using** any public right-of-way; (C) a facility of a common carrier which is subject, in whole or in part, to the provisions of Title II of this Act, except that such facility shall be considered a cable system (other than for purposes of Section 621(c)) to the extent such facility is used in the transmission of video programming directly to subscribers<; or (D)>**, unless the extent of such use is solely to provide interactive on-demand services; (D) an open video system that complies with Section 653 of this title; or (E)** any facilities of any electric utility used solely for operating its electric utility systems;

(8) the term "Federal agency" means any agency of the United States, including the Commission;

(9) the term "franchise" means an initial authorization, or renewal thereof (including a renewal of an authorization which has been granted subject to Section 626), issued by a franchising authority, whether such authorization is designated as a franchise, permit, license, resolution, contract, certificate, agreement, or otherwise, which authorizes the construction or operation of a cable system;

(10) the term "franchising authority" means any governmental entity empowered by Federal, State, or local law to grant a franchise;

(11) the term "grade B contour" means the field strength of a television broadcast station computed in accordance with regulations promulgated by the Commission;

(12) **the term "interactive on-demand services" means a service providing video programming to subscribers over switched networks on an on-demand, point-to-point basis, but does not include services providing video programming prescheduled by the programming provider;**

(13) the term "multichannel video programming distributor" means a person such as, but not limited to, a cable operator, a multichannel multipoint distribution service, a direct broadcast satellite service, or a television receive-only satellite program distributor, who makes available for purchase, by subscribers or customers, multiple channels of video programming;

<(13)>**(14)** the term "other programming service" means information that a cable operator makes available to all subscribers generally;

<(14)>**(15)** the term "person" means an individual, partnership, association, joint stock company, trust, corporation, or governmental entity;

<(15)>**(16)** the term "public, educational, or governmental access facilities" means --

(A) channel capacity designated for public, educational, or governmental use; and

(B) facilities and equipment for the use of such channel capacity;

<(16)>**(17)** the term "service tier" means a category of cable service or other services provided by a cable operator and for which a separate rate is charged by the cable operator;

<(17)>**(18)** the term "State" means any State, or political subdivision, or agency thereof; and

~~(18)~~ **(19)** the term "usable activated channels" means activated channels of a cable system, except those channels whose use for the distribution of broadcast signals would conflict with technical and safety regulations as determined by the Commission; and

~~(19)~~ **(20)** the term "video programming" means programming provided by, or generally considered comparable to programming provided by, a television broadcast station.

Part II - Use of Cable Channels and Cable Ownership Restrictions

Section 611 [47 USC Section 531]. Cable Channels for Public, Educational, or Governmental Use.

(a) A franchising authority may establish requirements in a franchise with respect to the designation or use of channel capacity for public, educational, or governmental use only to the extent provided in this section.

(b) A franchising authority may in its request for proposals require as part of a franchise, and may require as part of a cable operator's proposal for a franchise renewal, subject to Section 626, that channel capacity be designated for public, educational, or governmental use, and channel capacity on institutional networks be designated for educational or governmental use, and may require rules and procedures for the use of the channel capacity designated pursuant to this section.

(c) A franchising authority may enforce any requirement in any franchise regarding the providing or use of such channel capacity. Such enforcement authority includes the authority to enforce any provisions of the franchise for services, facilities, or equipment proposed by the cable operator which relate to public, educational, or governmental use of channel capacity, whether or not required by the franchising authority pursuant to subsection (b).

(d) In the case of any franchise under which channel capacity is designated under subsection (b), the franchising authority shall prescribe --

(1) rules and procedures under which the cable operator is permitted to use such channel capacity for the provision of other services if such channel capacity is not being used for the purposes designated, and

(2) rules and procedures under which such permitted use shall cease.

(e) Subject to Section 624(d), a cable operator shall not exercise any editorial control over any public, educational, or governmental use of channel capacity provided pursuant to this section**, except a cable operator may refuse to transmit any public access program or portion of a public access program which contains obscenity, indecency, or nudity**.

(f) For purposes of this section, the term "institutional network" means a communication network which is constructed or operated by the cable operator and which is generally available only to subscribers who are not residential subscribers.

Section 612 [47 USC Section 532]. Cable Channels for Commercial Use.

(a) The purpose of this section is to promote competition in the delivery of diverse sources of video programming and to assure that the widest possible diversity of information sources are made available to the public from cable systems in a manner consistent with growth and development of cable systems.

(b)(1) A cable operator shall designate channel capacity for commercial use by persons unaffiliated with the operator in accordance with the following requirements:

(A) An operator of any cable system with 36 or more (but not more than 54) activated channels shall designate 10 percent of such channels which are not otherwise required for use (or the use of which is not prohibited) by Federal law or regulation.

(B) An operator of any cable system with 55 or more (but not more than 100) activated channels shall designate 15 percent of such channels which are not otherwise required for use (or the use of which is not prohibited) by Federal law or regulation.

(C) An operator of any cable system with more than 100 activated channels shall designate 15 percent of all such channels.

(D) An operator of any cable system with fewer than 36 activated channels shall not be required to designate channel capacity for commercial use by persons unaffiliated with the operator, unless the cable system is required to provide such channel capacity under the terms of a franchise in effect on the date of the enactment of this title.

(E) An operator of any cable system in operation on the date of the enactment of this title shall not be required to remove any service actually being provided on July 1, 1984, in order to comply with this section, but shall make channel capacity available for commercial use as such capacity becomes available until such time as the cable operator is in full compliance with this section.

(2) Any Federal agency, State, or franchising authority may not require any cable system to designate channel capacity for commercial use by unaffiliated persons in excess of the capacity specified in ~~<para.>~~ **paragraph** (1), except as otherwise provided in this section.

(3) A cable operator may not be required, as part of a request for proposals or as part of a proposal for renewal, subject to Section 626, to designate channel capacity for any use (other than commercial use by unaffiliated persons under this section) except as provided in Sections 611 and 637, but a cable operator may offer in a franchise, or proposal for renewal thereof, to provide, consistent with applicable law, such capacity for other than commercial use by such persons.

(4) A cable operator may use any unused channel capacity designated pursuant to this section until the use of such channel capacity is obtained, pursuant to a written agreement, by a person unaffiliated with the operator.

(5) For the purposes of this section, the term "commercial use" means the provision of video programming, whether or not for profit.

(6) Any channel capacity which has been designated for public, educational, or governmental use may not be considered as designated under this section for commercial use for the purpose of this section.

(c)(1) If a person unaffiliated with the cable operator seeks to use channel capacity designated pursuant to subsection (b) for commercial use, the cable operator shall establish, consistent with the purpose of this section, and with rules prescribed by the Commission under paragraph (4), the price, terms, and conditions of such use which are at least sufficient to assure that such use will not adversely affect the operation, financial condition, or market development of the cable system.

(2) A cable operator shall not exercise any editorial control over any video programming provided pursuant to this section, or in any other way consider the content of such programming, except that ~~<an>~~ **a cable** operator **may refuse to transmit any leased access program or portion of a leased access program which contains obscenity, indecency, or nudity and** may consider such content to

the minimum extent necessary to establish a reasonable price for the commercial use of designated channel capacity by an unaffiliated person.

(3) Any cable system channel designated in accordance with this section shall not be used to provide a cable service that is being provided over such system on the date of the enactment of this title, if the provision of such programming is intended to avoid the purpose of this section.

(4)(A) The Commission shall have the authority to --

(i) determine the maximum reasonable rates that a cable operator may establish pursuant to paragraph (1) for commercial use of designated channel capacity, including the rate charged for the billing of rates to subscribers and for the collection of revenue from subscribers by the cable operator for such use;

(ii) establish reasonable terms and conditions for such use, including those for billing and collection; and

(iii) establish procedures for the expedited resolution of disputes concerning rates or carriage under this section.

(B) Within 180 days after the date of enactment of this paragraph, the Commission shall establish rules for determining maximum reasonable rates under subparagraph (A)(i), for establishing terms and conditions under subparagraph (A)(ii), and for providing procedures under subparagraph (A)(iii).

(d) Any person aggrieved by the failure or refusal of a cable operator to make channel capacity available for use pursuant to this section may bring an action in the district court of the United States for the judicial district in which the cable system is located to compel that such capacity be made available. If the court finds that the channel capacity sought by such person has not been made available in accordance with this section, or finds that the price, terms, or conditions, established by the cable operator are unreasonable, the court may order such system to make available to such person the channel capacity sought, and further determine the appropriate price, terms, or conditions, for such use consistent with subsection (c), and may award actual damages if it deems such relief appropriate. In any such action, the court shall not consider any price, term, or condition established between an operator and an affiliate for comparable services.

(e)(1) Any person aggrieved by the failure or refusal of a cable operator to make channel capacity available pursuant to this section may petition the Commission for relief under this subsection upon a showing of prior adjudicated violations of this section. Records of previous adjudications resulting in a court determination that the operator has violated this section shall be considered as sufficient for the showing necessary under this subsection. If the Commission finds that the channel capacity sought by such person has not been made available in accordance with this section, or that the price, terms, or conditions established by such system are unreasonable under subsection (c), the Commission shall, by rule or order, require such operator to make available such channel capacity under price, terms, and conditions consistent with subsection (c).

(2) In any case in which the Commission finds that the prior adjudicated violations of this section constitute a pattern or practice of violations by an operator, the Commission may also establish any further rule or order necessary to assure that the operator provides the diversity of information sources required by this section.

(3) In any case in which the Commission finds that the prior adjudicated violations of this section constitute a pattern or practice of violations by any person who is an operator of more than one

cable system, the Commission may also establish any further rule or order necessary to assure that such person provides the diversity of information sources required by this section.

(f) In any action brought under this section in any Federal district court or before the Commission, there shall be a presumption that the price, terms, and conditions for use of channel capacity designated pursuant to subsection (b) are reasonable and in good faith unless shown by clear and convincing evidence to the contrary.

(g) Notwithstanding Sections 621(c) and 623(a), at such time as cable systems with 36 or more activated channels are available to 70 percent of households within the United States and are subscribed to by 70 percent of the households to which such systems are available, the Commission may promulgate any additional rules necessary to provide diversity of information sources. Any rules promulgated by the Commission pursuant to this subsection shall not preempt authority expressly granted to franchising authorities under this title.

(h) Any cable service offered pursuant to this section shall not be provided, or shall be provided subject to conditions, if such cable service in the judgment of the franchising authority or the cable operator is obscene, or is in conflict with community standards in that it is lewd, lascivious, filthy, or indecent or is otherwise unprotected by the Constitution of the United States. This subsection shall permit a cable operator to enforce prospectively a written and published policy of prohibiting programming that the cable operator reasonably believes describes or depicts sexual or excretory activities or organs in a patently offensive manner as measured by contemporary community standards.

(i)(1) Notwithstanding the provisions of subsections (b) and (c), a cable operator required by this section to designate channel capacity for commercial use may use any such channel capacity for the provision of programming from a qualified minority programming source or from any qualified educational programming source, whether or not such source is affiliated with the cable operator. The channel capacity used to provide programming from a qualified minority programming source or from any qualified educational programming source pursuant to this subsection may not exceed 33 percent of the channel capacity designated pursuant to this section. No programming provided over a cable system on July 1, 1990, may qualify as minority programming or educational programming on that cable system under this subsection.

(2) For purposes of this subsection, the term "qualified minority programming source" means a programming source which devotes substantially all of its programming to coverage of minority viewpoints, or to programming directed at members of minority groups, and which is over 50 percent minority-owned, as the term "minority" is defined in Section 309(i)(3)(C)(ii).

(3) For purposes of this subsection, the term "qualified educational programming source" means a programming source which devotes substantially all of its programming to educational or instructional programming that promotes public understanding of mathematics, the sciences, the humanities, and the arts and has a documented annual expenditure on programming exceeding $15,000,000. The annual expenditure on programming means all annual costs incurred by the programming source to produce or acquire programs which are scheduled to be televised, and specifically excludes marketing, promotion, satellite transmission and operational costs, and general administrative costs.

(4) Nothing in this subsection shall substitute for the requirements to carry qualified noncommercial educational television stations as specified under Section 615.

(j)(1) Within 120 days following the date of the enactment of this subsection, the Commission shall promulgate regulations designed to limit the access of children to indecent programming, as

505

defined by Commission regulations, and which cable operators have not voluntarily prohibited under subsection (h) by --

    (A) requiring cable operators to place on a single channel all indecent programs, as identified by program providers, intended for carriage on channels designated for commercial use under this section;

    (B) requiring cable operators to block such single channel unless the subscriber requests access to such channel in writing; and

    (C) requiring programmers to inform cable operators if the program would be indecent as defined by Commission regulations.

    (2) Cable operators shall comply with the regulations promulgated pursuant to paragraph (1).

Section 613 [47 USC Section 533]. Ownership Restrictions.

(a)(1) It shall be unlawful for any person to be a cable operator if such person, directly or through one or more affiliates, owns or controls, the licensee of a television broadcast station and the predicted grade B contour of such station covers any portion of the community served by such operator's cable system.

(2)>**(a)** It shall be unlawful for a cable operator to hold a license for multichannel multipoint distribution service, or to offer satellite master antenna television service separate and apart from any franchised cable service, in any portion of the franchise area served by that cable operator's cable system. The Commission --

    ~~(A)>~~**(1)** shall waive the requirements of this paragraph for all existing multichannel multipoint distribution services and satellite master antenna television services which are owned by a cable operator on the date of enactment of this paragraph;

    ~~and~~

~~(B)>~~**(2)** may waive the requirements of this paragraph to the extent the Commission determines is necessary to ensure that all significant portions of a franchise area are able to obtain video programming**;** **and**.

    ~~(b)(1) It shall be unlawful for any common carrier, subject in whole or in part to Title II of this Act, to provide video programming directly in subscribers in its telephone service area, either directly or indirectly through an affiliate owned by, operated by, controlled by, or under common control with the common carrier.~~

~~(2) It shall be unlawful for any common carrier, subject in whole or in part to Title II of this Act, to provide channels of communications or pole, line, conduit space, or other rental arrangements, to any entity which is directly or indirectly owned by, operated by, controlled by, or under common control with such common carrier, if such facilities or arrangements are to be used for, or in connection with, the provision of video programming directly to subscribers in the telephone service area of the common carrier.~~

~~(3) This subsection>~~**(3)** shall not apply **the requirements** ~~to any common carrier to the extent such carrier provides telephone exchange service in any rural area (as defined by the Commission).~~

~~(4) In those areas where the provision of video programming directly to subscribers through a cable system demonstrably could not exist except through a cable system owned by, operated by, controlled by, or affiliated with the common carrier involved, or upon other showing of good cause, the Commission may, on petition for waiver, waive the applicability of paras. (1) and (2)>~~ of this subsection~~. Any such waiver shall be made in accordance with §63.56 of Title 47, Code of Federal Regulations (as in effect Sept. 20, 1984) and shall be granted by the Commission upon a finding that the issuance of such waiver is justified by the particular circumstances demonstrated by the petitioner, taking into account the policy of this subsection.~~ **to any cable operator in any franchise area in which a cable operator is subject to effective competition as determined under Section 623(l).**

(b) [Repealed]

(c) The Commission may prescribe rules with respect to the ownership or control of cable systems by persons who own or control other media of mass communications which serve the same community served by a cable system.

(d) Any State or franchising authority may not prohibit the ownership or control of a cable system by any person because of such person's ownership or control of any other media of mass communications or other media interests. Nothing in this section shall be construed to prevent any State or franchising authority from prohibiting the ownership or control of a cable system in a jurisdiction by any person (1) because of such person's ownership or control of any other cable system in such jurisdiction; or (2) in circumstances in which the State or franchising authority determines that the acquisition of such a cable system may eliminate or reduce competition in the delivery of cable service in such jurisdiction.

(e)(1) Subject to ~~para.~~ **paragraph** (2), a State or franchising authority may hold any ownership interest in any cable system.

(2) Any State or franchising authority shall not exercise any editorial control regarding the content of any cable service on a cable system in which such governmental entity holds ownership interest (other than programming on any channel designated for educational or governmental use), unless such control is exercised through an entity separate from the franchising authority.

(f)(1) In order to enhance effective competition, the Commission shall, within one year after the date of enactment of the Cable Television Consumer Protection and Competition Act of 1992, conduct a proceeding --

(A) to prescribe rules and regulations establishing reasonable limits on the number of cable subscribers a person is authorized to reach through cable systems owned by such person, or in which such person has an attributable interest;

(B) to prescribe rules and regulations establishing reasonable limits on the number of channels on a cable system that can be occupied by a video programmer in which a cable operator has an attributable interest; and

(C) to consider the necessary and appropriateness of imposing limitations on the degree to which multichannel video programming distributors may engage in the creation or production of video programming.

(2) In prescribing rules and regulations under paragraph (1), the Commission shall, among other public interest objectives --

(A) ensure that no cable operator or group of cable operators can unfairly impede, either because of the size of any individual operator or because of joint actions by a group of operators of sufficient size, the flow of video programming from the video programmer to the consumer;

(B) ensure that cable operators affiliated with video programmers do not favor such programmers in determining carriage on their cable systems or do not unreasonably restrict the flow of the video programming of such programmers to other video distributors;

507

(C) take particular account of the market structure, ownership patterns, and other relationships of the cable television industry, including the nature and market power of the local franchise, the joint ownership of cable systems and video programmers, and the various types of non-equity controlling interests;

(D) account for any efficiencies and other benefits that might be gained through increased ownership or control;

(E) make such rules and regulations reflect the dynamic nature of the communications marketplace;

(F) not impose limitations which would bar cable operators from serving previously unserved rural areas; and

(G) not impose limitations which would impair the development of diverse and high quality video programming.

(g) This section shall not apply to prohibit any combination of any interests held by any person on July 1, 1984, to the extent of the interests so held as of such date, if the holding of such interests was not inconsistent with any applicable Federal or State law or regulations in effect on that date.

(h) For purposes of this section, the term "media of mass communications" shall have the meaning given such term under Section 309(i)(3)(C)(i) of this Act.

Section 614 [47 USC Section 534]. Carriage of Local Commercial Television Signals.

(a) Carriage Obligations. - Each cable operator shall carry, on the cable system of that operator, the signals of local commercial television stations and qualified low power stations as provided by this section. Carriage of additional broadcast television signals on such system shall be at the discretion of such operator, subject to Section 325(b).

(b) Signals Required. --

(1) In general. - (A) A cable operator of a cable system with 12 or fewer usable activated channels shall carry the signals of at least three local commercial television stations, except that if such a system has 300 or fewer subscribers, it shall not be subject to any requirements under this section so long as such system does not delete from carriage by that system any signal of a broadcast television station.

(B) A cable operator of a cable system with more than 12 usable activated channels shall carry the signals of local commercial television stations, up to one-third of the aggregate number of usable activated channels of such system.

(2) Selection of signals. - Whenever the number of local commercial television stations exceeds the maximum number of signals a cable system is required to carry under paragraph (1), the cable operator shall have discretion in selecting which such stations shall be carried on its cable system, except that --

(A) under no circumstances shall a cable operator carry a qualified low power station in lieu of a local commercial television station; and

(B) if the cable operator elects to carry an affiliate of a broadcast network (as such term is defined by the Commission by regulation), such cable operator shall carry the affiliate of such broadcast network whose city of license reference point, as defined in §76.53 of Title 47, Code of Federal Regulations (in effect on January 1, 1991), or any successor regulation thereto, is closest to the principal headend of the cable system.

508

(3) Content to be carried. - (A) A cable operator shall carry in its entirety, on the cable system of that operator, the primary video, accompanying audio, and line 21 closed caption transmission of each of the local commercial television stations carried on the cable system and, to the extent technically feasible, program-related material carried in the vertical blanking interval or on subcarriers. Retransmission of other material in the vertical blanking internal or other nonprogram-related material (including teletext and other subscription and advertiser-supported information services) shall be at the discretion of the cable operator. Where appropriate and feasible, operators may delete signal enhancements, such as ghost-canceling, from the broadcast signal and employ such enhancements at the system headend or headends.

(B) The cable operator shall carry the entirety of the program schedule of any television station carried on the cable system unless carriage of specific programming is prohibited, and other programming authorized to be substituted, under §76.67 or Subpart F of Part 76 of Title 47, Code of Federal Regulations (as in effect on January 1, 1991), or any successor regulations thereto.

(4) Signal quality. --

(A) Nondegradation; technical specifications. - The signals of local commercial television stations that a cable operator carries shall be carried without material degradation. The Commission shall adopt carriage standards to ensure that, to the extent technically feasible, the quality of signal processing and carriage provided by a cable system for the carriage of local commercial television stations will be no less than that provided by the system for carriage of any other type of signal.

(B) Advanced television. - At such time as the Commission prescribes modifications of the standards for television broadcast signals, the Commission shall initiate a proceeding to establish any changes in the signal carriage requirements of cable television systems necessary to ensure cable carriage of such broadcast signals of local commercial television stations which have been changed to conform with such modified standards.

(5) Duplication not required. - Notwithstanding paragraph (1), a cable operator shall not be required to carry the signal of any local commercial television station that substantially duplicates the signal of another local commercial television station which is carried on its cable system, or to carry the signals of more than one local commercial television station affiliated with a particular broadcast network (as such term is defined by regulation). If a cable operator elects to carry on its cable system a signal which substantially duplicates the signal of another local commercial television station carried on the cable system, or to carry on its system the signals of more than one local commercial television station affiliated with a particular broadcast network, all such signals shall be counted toward the number of signals the operator is required to carry under paragraph (1).

(6) Channel positioning. - Each signal carried in fulfillment of the carriage obligations of a cable operator under this section shall be carried on the cable system channel number on which the local commercial television station is broadcast over the air, or on the channel on which it was carried on July 19, 1985, or on the channel on which it was carried on January 1, 1992, at the election of the station, or on such other channel number as is mutually agreed upon by the station and the cable operator. Any dispute regarding the positioning of a local commercial television station shall be resolved by the Commission.

(7) Signal availability. - Signals carried in fulfillment of the requirements of this section shall be provided to every subscriber of a cable system. Such signals shall be viewable via cable on all television receivers of a subscriber which are connected to a cable system by a cable operator or for

which a cable operator provides a connection. If a cable operator authorizes subscribers to install additional receiver connections, but does not provide the subscriber with such connections, or with the equipment and materials for such connections, the operator shall notify such subscribers of all broadcast stations carried on the cable system which cannot be viewed via cable without a converter box and shall offer to sell or lease such a converter box to such subscribers at rates in accordance with Section 623(b)(3).

(8) Identification of signals carried. - A cable operator shall identify, upon request by any person, the signals carried on its system in fulfillment of the requirements of this section.

(9) Notification. - A cable operator shall provide written notice to a local commercial television station at least 30 days prior to either deleting from carriage or repositioning that station. No deletion or repositioning of a local commercial television station shall occur during a period in which major television ratings services measure the size of audiences of local television stations. The notification provisions of this paragraph shall not be used to undermine or evade the channel positioning or carriage requirements imposed upon cable operators under this section.

(10) Compensation for carriage. - A cable operator shall not accept or request monetary payment or other valuable consideration in exchange either for carriage of local commercial television stations in fulfillment of the requirements of this section or for the channel positioning rights provided to such stations under this section, except that --

(A) any such station may be required to bear the costs associated with delivering a good quality signal or a baseband video signal to the principal headend of the cable system;

(B) a cable operator may accept payments from stations which would be considered distant signals under Section 111 of Title 17, United States Code, as indemnification for any increased copyright liability resulting from carriage of such signal; and

(C) a cable operator may continue to accept monetary payment or other valuable consideration in exchange for carriage or channel positioning of the signal of any local commercial television station carried in fulfillment of the requirements of this section, through, but not beyond, the date of expiration of an agreement thereon between a cable operator and a local commercial television station entered into prior to June 26, 1990.

(c) Low Power Station Carriage Obligation. --

(1) Requirement. - If there are not sufficient signals of full power local commercial television stations to fill the channels set aside under subsection (b) --

(A) a cable operator of a cable system with a capacity of 35 or fewer usable activated channels shall be required to carry one qualified low power station; and

(B) a cable operator of a cable system with a capacity of more than 35 usable activated channels shall be required to carry two qualified low power stations.

(2) Use of public, educational, or governmental channels. - A cable operator required to carry more than one signal of a qualified low power station under this subsection may do so, subject to approval by the franchising authority pursuant to Section 611, by placing such additional station on public, educational, or governmental channels not in use for their designated purposes.

(d) Remedies. --

(1) Complaints by broadcast stations. - Whenever a local commercial television station believes that a cable operator has failed to meet its obligations under this section, such station shall notify the operator, in writing, of the alleged failure and identify its reasons for believing that the cable operator is obligated to carry the signal of such station or has otherwise failed to comply with the

channel positioning or repositioning or other requirements of this section. The cable operator shall, within 30 days of such written notification, respond in writing to such notification and either commence to carry the signal of such station in accordance with the terms requested or state its reasons for believing that it is not obligated to carry such signal or is in compliance with the channel positioning and repositioning and other requirements of this section. A local commercial television station that is denied carriage or channel positioning or repositioning in accordance with this section by a cable operator may obtain review of such denial by filing a complaint with the Commission. Such complaint shall allege the manner in which such cable operator has failed to meet its obligations and the basis for such allegations.

(2) Opportunity to respond. - The Commission shall afford such cable operator an opportunity to present data and arguments to establish that there has been no failure to meet its obligations under this section.

(3) Remedial actions; dismissal. - Within 120 days after the date a complaint is filed, the Commission shall determine whether the cable operator has met its obligations under this section. If the Commission determines that the cable operator has failed to meet such obligations, the Commission shall order the cable operator to reposition the complaining station or, in the case of an obligation to carry a station, to commence carriage of the station and to continue such carriage for at least 12 months. If the Commission determines that the cable operator has fully met the requirements of this section, it shall dismiss the complaint.

(e) Input Selector Switch Rules Abolished. - No cable operator shall be required --

(1) to provide or make available any input selector switch as defined in §76.5(mm) of Title 47, Code of Federal Regulations, or any comparable device; or

(2) to provide information to subscribers about input selector switches or comparable devices.

(f) Regulations by Commission. - Within 180 days after the date of enactment of this section, the Commission shall, following a rulemaking proceeding, issue regulations implementing the requirements imposed by this section. Such implementing regulations shall include necessary revisions to update §76.51 of Title 47 of the Code of Federal Regulations.

(g) Sales Presentations and Program Length Commercials. --

(1) Carriage pending proceeding. - Pending the outcome of the proceeding under paragraph (2), nothing in this Act shall require a cable operator to carry on any tier, or prohibit a cable operator from carrying on any tier, the signal of any commercial television station or video programming service that is predominantly utilized for the transmission of sales presentations or program length commercials.

(2) Proceeding concerning certain stations. - Within 270 days after the date of enactment of this section, the Commission, notwithstanding prior proceedings to determine whether broadcast television stations that are predominantly utilized for the transmission of sales presentations or program length commercials are serving the public interest, convenience, and necessity, shall complete a proceeding in accordance with this paragraph to determine whether broadcast television stations that are predominantly utilized for the transmission of sales presentations or program length commercials are serving the public interest, convenience, and necessity. In conducting such proceeding, the Commission shall provide appropriate notice and opportunity for public comment. The Commission shall consider the viewing of such stations, the level of competing demands for the spectrum allocated to such stations, and the role of such stations in providing competition to nonbroadcast services offering similar programming. In the event that the Commission concludes that one or more of such stations are serving

the public interest, convenience, and necessity, the Commission shall qualify such stations as local commercial television stations for purposes of subsection (a). In the event that the Commission concludes that one or more of such stations are not serving the public interest, convenience, and necessity, the Commission shall allow the licensees of such stations a reasonable period within which to provide different programming, and shall not deny such stations a renewal expectancy solely because their programming consisted predominantly of sales presentations or program length commercials.

(h) Definitions. --

(1) Local commercial television station. --

(A) In general. - For purposes of this section, the term "local commercial television station" means any full power television broadcast station, other than a qualified noncommercial educational television station within the meaning of Section 615(l)(1), licensed and operating on a channel regularly assigned to its community by the Commission that, with respect to a particular cable system, is within the same television market as the cable system.

(B) Exclusions. - The term "local commercial television station" shall not include --

(i) low power television stations, television translator stations, and passive repeaters which operate pursuant to Part 74 of Title 47, Code of Federal Regulations, or any successor regulations thereto;

(ii) a television broadcast station that would be considered a distant signal under Section 111 of Title 17, United States Code, if such station does not agree to indemnify the cable operator for any increased copyright liability resulting from carriage on the cable system; or

(iii) a television broadcast station that does not deliver to the principal headend of a cable system either a signal level of -45 dBm for UHF signals or -49 dBm for VHF signals at the input terminals of the signal processing equipment, if such station does not agree to be responsible for the costs of delivering to the cable system a signal of good quality or a baseband video signal.

(C) Market determinations. - (i) For purposes of this section, a broadcasting station's market shall be determined ~~in the manner provided in §73.3555(d)(3)(i) of Title 47, Code of Federal Regulations, as in effect on May 1, 1991~~ **by the Commission by regulation or order using, where available, commercial publications which delineate television markets based on viewing patterns,** except that, following a written request, the Commission may, with respect to a particular television broadcast station, include additional communities within its television market or exclude communities from such station's television market to better effectuate the purposes of this section. In considering such requests, the Commission may determine that particular communities are part of more than one television market.

(ii) In considering requests filed pursuant to clause (i), the Commission shall afford particular attention to the value of localism by taking into account such factors as --

(I) whether the station, or other stations located in the same area, have been historically carried on the cable system or systems within such community;

(II) whether the television station provides coverage or other local service to such community;

(III) whether any other television station that is eligible to be carried by a cable system in such community in fulfillment of the requirements of this section provides news coverage of issues of concern to such community or provides carriage or coverage of sporting and other events of interest to the community; and

(IV) evidence of viewing patterns in cable and noncable households within the areas served by the cable system or systems in such community.

(iii) A cable operator shall not delete from carriage the signal of a commercial television station during the pendency of any proceeding pursuant to this subparagraph.

(iv) ~~In the rulemaking proceeding required by subsection (f), the Commission shall provide for expedited consideration of requests~~ Within 120 days after the date on which a request is filed under this subparagraph (or 120 days after the date of enactment of the Telecommunications Act of 1996, if later), the Commission shall grant or deny the request.

(2) Qualified low power station. - The term "qualified low power station" means any television broadcast station conforming to the rules established for Low Power Television Stations contained in Part 74 of Title 47, Code of Federal Regulations, only if --

(A) such station broadcasts for at least the minimum number of hours of operation required by the Commission for television broadcast stations under Part 73 of Title 47, Code of Federal Regulations;

(B) such station meets all obligations and requirements applicable to television broadcast stations under Part 73 of Title 47, Code of Federal Regulations, with respect to the broadcast of nonentertainment programming; programming and rates involving political candidates, election issues, controversial issues of public importance, editorials, and personal attacks; programming for children; and equal employment opportunity; and the Commission determines that the provision of such programming by such station would address local news and informational needs which are not being adequately served by full power television broadcast stations because of the geographic distance of such full power stations from the low power station's community of license;

(C) such station complies with interference regulations consistent with its secondary status pursuant to Part 74 of Title 47, Code of Federal Regulations;

(D) such station is located no more than 35 miles from the cable system's headend, and delivers to the principal headend of the cable system an over-the-air signal of good quality, as determined by the Commission;

(E) the community of license of such station and the franchise area of the cable system are both located outside of the largest 160 Metropolitan Statistical Areas, ranked by population, as determined by the Office of Management and Budget on June 30, 1990, and the population of such community of license on such date did not exceed 35,000; and

(F) there is no full power television broadcast station licensed to any community within the county or other political subdivision (of a State) served by the cable system.

Nothing in this paragraph shall be construed to change the secondary status of any low power station as provided in Part 74 of Title 47, Code of Federal Regulations, as in effect on the date of enactment of this section.

Section 615 [47 USC Section 535]. Carriage of Noncommercial Educational Television.

(a) Carriage obligations. - In addition to the carriage requirements set forth in Section 614, each cable operator of a cable system shall carry the signals of qualified noncommercial educational television stations in accordance with the provisions of this section.

(b) Requirements to carry qualified stations. --

(1) General requirement to carry each qualified station. - Subject to paragraphs (2) and (3) and subsection (e), each cable operator shall carry, on the cable system of that cable operator, any qualified local noncommercial educational television station requesting carriage.

(2)(A) Systems with 12 or fewer channels. - Notwithstanding paragraph (1), a cable operator of a cable system with 12 or fewer usable activated channels shall be required to carry the signal of one qualified local noncommercial educational television station; except that a cable operator of such a system shall comply with subsection (c) and may, in its discretion, carry the signals of other qualified noncommercial educational television stations.

(B) In the case of a cable system described in subparagraph (A) which operates beyond the presence of any qualified local noncommercial educational television station --

(i) the cable operator shall import and carry on that system the signal of one qualified noncommercial educational television station;

(ii) the selection for carriage of such a signal shall be at the election of the cable operator; and

(iii) in order to satisfy the requirements for carriage specified in this subsection, the cable operator of the system shall not be required to remove any other programming service actually provided to subscribers on March 29, 1990; except that such cable operator shall use the first channel available to satisfy the requirements of this subparagraph.

(3) Systems with 13 to 36 channels. - (A) Subject to subsection (c), a cable operator of a cable system with 13 to 36 usable activated channels --

(i) shall carry the signal of at least one qualified local noncommercial educational television station but shall not be required to carry the signals of more than three such stations, and

(ii) may, in its discretion, carry additional such stations.

(B) In the case of a cable system described in this paragraph which operates beyond the presence of any qualified local noncommercial educational television station, the cable operator shall import and carry on that system the signal of at least one qualified noncommercial educational television station to comply with subparagraph (A)(i).

(C) Th cable operator of a cable system described in this paragraph which carries the signal of a qualified local noncommercial educational station affiliated with a State public television network shall not be required to carry the signal of any additional qualified local noncommercial educational television stations affiliated with the same network if the programming of such additional stations is substantially duplicated by the programming of the qualified local noncommercial educational television station receiving carriage.

(D) A cable operator of a system described in this paragraph which increases the usable activated channel capacity of the system to more than 36 channels on or after March 29, 1990, shall, in accordance with the other provisions of this section, carry the signal of each qualified local noncommercial educational television station requesting carriage, subject to subsection (e).

(c) Continued carriage of existing stations. - Notwithstanding any other provision of this section, all cable operators shall continue to provide carriage to all qualified local noncommercial educational television stations whose signals were carried on their systems as of March 29, 1990. The requirements of this subsection may be waived with respect to a particular cable operator and a particular such station, upon the written consent of the cable operator and the station.

514

(d) Placement of additional signals. - a cable operator required to add the signals of qualified local noncommercial educational television stations to a cable system under this section may do so, subject to approval by the franchising authority pursuant to Section 611, by placing such additional stations on public, educational, or governmental channels not in use for their designated purposes.

(e) Systems with more than 36 channels. - A cable operator of a cable system with a capacity of more than 36 usable activated channels which is required to carry the signals of three qualified local noncommercial educational television stations shall not be required to carry the signals of additional such stations the programming of which substantially duplicates the programming broadcast by another qualified local noncommercial educational television station requesting carriage. Substantial duplication shall be defined by the Commission in a manner that promotes access to distinctive noncommercial educational television services.

(f) Waiver of nonduplication rights. - A qualified local noncommercial educational television station whose signal is carried by a cable operator shall not assert any network nonduplication rights it may have pursuant to §76.92 of Title 47, Code of Federal Regulations, to require the deletion of programs aired on other qualified local noncommercial educational television stations whose signals are carried by that cable operator.

(g) Conditions of carriage. --

(1) Content to be carried. - A cable operator shall retransmit in its entirety the primary video, accompanying audio, and line 21 closed caption transmission of each qualified local noncommercial educational television station whose signal is carried on the cable system, and, to the extent technically feasible, program-related material carried in the vertical blanking interval, or on subcarriers, that may be necessary for receipt of programming by handicapped persons or for educational or language purposes. Retransmission of other material in the vertical blanking interval or on subcarriers shall be within the discretion of the cable operator.

(2) Bandwidth and technical quality. - A cable operator shall provide each qualified local noncommercial educational television station whose signal is carried in accordance with this section with bandwidth and technical capacity equivalent to that provided to commercial television broadcast stations carried on the cable system and shall carry the signal of each qualified local noncommercial educational television station without material degradation.

(3) Changes in carriage. - The signal of a qualified local noncommercial educational television station shall not be repositioned by a cable operator unless the cable operator, at least 30 days in advance of such repositioning, has provided written notice to the station and all subscribers of the cable system. For purposes of this paragraph, repositioning includes (A) assignment of a qualified local noncommercial educational television station to a cable system channel number different from the cable system channel number to which the station was assigned as of March 29, 1990, and (B) deletion of the station from the cable system. The notification provisions of this paragraph shall not be used to undermine or evade the channel positioning or carriage requirements imposed upon cable operators under this section.

(4) Good quality signal required. - Notwithstanding the other provisions of this section, a cable operator shall not be required to carry the signal of any qualified local noncommercial educational television station which does not deliver to the cable system's principal headend a signal of good quality or a baseband video signal, as may be defined by the Commission.

(5) Channel positioning. - Each signal carried in fulfillment of the carriage obligations of a cable operator under this section shall be carried on the cable system channel number on which the

qualified local noncommercial educational television station is broadcast over the air, or on the channel on which it was carried on July 19, 1985, at the election of the station, or on such other channel number as is mutually agreed upon by the station and the cable operator. Any dispute regarding the positioning of a qualified local noncommercial educational television station shall be resolved by the Commission.

(h) Availability of signals. - Signals carried in fulfillment of the carriage obligations of a cable operator under this section shall be available to every subscriber as part of the cable system's lowest priced service tier that includes the retransmission of local commercial television broadcast signals.

(i) Payment for carriage prohibited. --

(1) In general. - A cable operator shall not accept monetary payment or other valuable consideration in exchange for carriage of the signal of any qualified local noncommercial educational television station carried in fulfillment of the requirements of this section, except that such a station may be required to bear the cost associated with delivering a good quality signal or a baseband video signal to the principal headend of the cable system.

(2) Distant signal exception. - Notwithstanding the provisions of this section, a cable operator shall not be required to add the signal of a qualified local noncommercial educational television station not already carried under the provision of subsection (c), where such signal would be considered a distant signal for copyright purposes unless such station indemnifies the cable operator for any increased copyright costs resulting from carriage of such signal.

(j) Remedies. --

(1) Complaint. - Whenever a qualified local noncommercial educational television station believes that a cable operator of a cable system has failed to comply with the signal carriage requirements of this section, the station may file a complaint with the Commission. Such complaint shall allege the manner in which such cable operator has failed to comply with such requirements and state the basis for such allegations.

(2) Opportunity to respond. - The Commission shall afford such cable operator an opportunity to present data, views, and arguments to establish that the cable operator has complied with the signal carriage requirements of this section.

(3) Remedial actions; dismissal. - Within 120 days after the date a complaint is filed under this subsection, the Commission shall determine whether the cable operator has complied with the requirements of this section. If the Commission determines that the cable operator has failed to comply with such requirements, the Commission shall state with particularity the basis for such findings and order the cable operator to take such remedial action as is necessary to meet such requirements. If the Commission determines that the cable operator has fully complied with such requirements, the Commission shall dismiss the complaint.

(k) Identification of signals. - A cable operator shall identify, upon request by any person, those signals carried in fulfillment of the requirements of this section.

(l) Definitions. - For purposes of this section --

(1) Qualified noncommercial educational television station. - The term "qualified noncommercial educational television station" means any television broadcast station which --

(A)(i) under the rules and regulations of the Commission in effect on March 29, 1990, is licensed by the Commission as a noncommercial educational television broadcast station and which is owned and operated by a public agency, nonprofit foundation, corporation, or association; and

(ii) has as its licensee an entity which is eligible to receive a community service grant, or any successor grant thereto, from the Corporation for Public Broadcasting, or any successor organization thereto, on the basis of the formula set forth in Section 396(k)(6)(B); or

(B) is owned and operated by a municipality and transmits predominantly noncommercial programs for educational purposes.

Such term includes (I) the translator of any noncommercial educational television station with five watts or higher power serving the franchise area, (II) a full-service station or translator if such station or translator is licensed to a channel reserved for noncommercial educational use pursuant to §73.606 of Title 47, Code of Federal Regulations, or any successor regulations thereto, and (III) such stations and translators operating on channels not so reserved as the Commission determines are qualified as noncommercial educational stations.

(2) Qualified local noncommercial educational television station. - The term "qualified local noncommercial educational television station" means a qualified noncommercial educational television station --

(A) which is licensed to a principal community whose reference point, as defined in §76.53 of Title 47, Code of Federal Regulations (as in effect on March 29, 1990), or any successor regulations thereto, is within 50 miles of the principal headend of the cable system; or

(B) whose Grade B service contour, as defined in §73.683(a) of such title (as in effect on March 29, 1990), or any successor regulations thereto, encompasses the principal headend of the cable system.

Section 616 [47 USC Section 536]. Regulation of Carriage Agreements.

(a) Regulations. - Within one year after the date of enactment of this section, the Commission shall establish regulations governing program carriage agreements and related practices between cable operators or other multichannel video programming distributors and video programming vendors. Such regulations shall --

(1) include provisions designed to prevent a cable operator or other multichannel video programming distributor from requiring a financial interest in a program service as a condition for carriage on one or more of such operator's systems;

(2) include provisions designed to prohibit a cable operator or other multichannel video programming distributor from coercing a video programming vendor to provide, and from retaliating against such a vendor for failing to provide, exclusive rights against other multichannel video programming distributors as a condition of carriage on a system;

(3) contain provisions designed to prevent a multichannel video programming distributor from engaging in conduct the effect of which is to unreasonably restrain the ability of an unaffiliated video programming vendor to compete fairly by discriminating in video programming distribution on the basis of affiliation or nonaffiliation of vendors in the selection, terms, or conditions for carriage of video programming provided by such vendors;

(4) provide for expedited review of any complaints made by a video programming vendor pursuant to this section;

(5) provide for appropriate penalties and remedies for violations of this subsection, including carriage; and

517

(6) provide penalties to be assessed against any person filing a frivolous complaint pursuant to this section.

(b) Definition. - As used in this section, the term "video programming vendor" means a person engaged in the production, creation, or wholesale distribution of video programming for sale.

Section 617 [47 USC Section 537]. Sales of Cable Systems.

~~<(a) 3-year holding period required. - Except as provided in this section, no cable operator may sell or otherwise transfer ownership in a cable system within a 36-month period following either the acquisition or initial construction of such system by such operator.~~

~~(b) Treatment of multiple transfers. - In the case of a sale of multiple systems, if the terms of the sale require the buyer to subsequently transfer ownership of one or more such systems to one or more third parties, such transfers shall be considered a part of the initial transaction.~~

~~(c) Exceptions. - Subsection (a) shall not apply to --~~

~~(1) any transfer of ownership interest in any cable system which is not subject to Federal income tax liability;~~

~~(2) any sale required by operation of any law or any act of any Federal agency, any State or political subdivision thereof, or any franchising authority; or~~

~~(3) any sale, assignment, or transfer, to one or more purchasers, assignees, or transferees controlled by, controlling, or under common control with, the seller, assignor, or transferor.~~

~~(d) Waiver authority. - The Commission may, consistent with the public interest, waive the requirement of subsection (a), except that, if the franchise requires franchise authority approval of a transfer, the Commission shall not waive such requirements unless the franchise authority has approved the transfer. The Commission shall use its authority under this subsection to permit appropriate transfers in the cases of default, foreclosure, or other financial distress.~~

~~(e) Limitation on duration of franchising authority power to disapprove transfers. - In the case of any sale or transfer of ownership of any cable system after the 36-month period following acquisition of such system, a>~~ A franchising authority shall, if the franchise requires franchising authority approval of a sale or transfer, have 120 days to act upon any request for approval of such sale or transfer that contains or is accompanied by such information as is required in accordance with Commission regulations and by the franchising authority. If the franchising authority fails to render a final decision on the request within 120 days, such request shall be deemed granted unless the requesting party and the franchising authority agree to an extension of time.

Part III - Franchising and Regulation

Section 621 [47 USC Section 541]. General Franchise Requirements.

(a)(1) A franchising authority may award, in accordance with the provisions of this title, one or more franchises within its jurisdiction; except that a franchising authority may not grant an exclusive franchise and may not unreasonably refuse to award an additional competitive franchise. Any applicant whose application for a second franchise has been denied by a final decision of the franchising authority may appeal such final decision pursuant to the provisions of Section 635 for failure to comply with this subsection.

(2) Any franchise shall be construed to authorize the construction of a cable system over public rights-of-way, and through easements, which are within the area to be served by the cable system and which have been dedicated for compatible uses, except that in using such easements the cable operator shall ensure --

(A) that the safety, functioning, and appearance of the property and the convenience and safety of other persons not be adversely affected by the installation or construction of facilities necessary for a cable system;

(B) that the cost of the installation, construction, operation, or removal of such facilities be borne by the cable operator or subscriber, or a combination of both; and

(C) that the owner of the property be justly compensated by the cable operator for any damages caused by the installation, construction, operation, or removal of such facilities by the cable operator.

(3) In awarding a franchise or franchises, a franchising authority shall assure that access to cable service is not denied to any group of potential residential cable subscribers because of the income of the residents of the local area in which such group resides.

(4) In awarding a franchise, the franchising authority --

(A) shall allow the applicant's cable system a reasonable period of time to become capable of providing cable service to all households in the franchise area;

(B) may require adequate assurance that the cable operator will provide adequate public, educational, and governmental access channel capability, facilities, or financial support; and

(C) may require adequate assurance that the cable operator has the financial, technical, or legal qualifications to provide cable service.

(b)(1) Except to the extent provided in ~~\<para.\>~~ **paragraph** (2) and subsection (f), a cable operator may not provide cable service without a franchise.

(2) Paragraph (1) shall not require any person lawfully providing cable service without a franchise on July 1, 1984, to obtain a franchise unless the franchising authority so requires.

(3)(A) If a cable operator or affiliate thereof is engaged in the provision of telecommunications services--

(i) such cable operator or affiliate shall not be required to obtain a franchise under this title for the provision of telecommunications services; and

(ii) the provisions of this title shall not apply to such cable operator or affiliate for the provision of telecommunications services.

(B) A franchising authority may not impose any requirement under this title that has the purpose or effect of prohibiting, limiting, restricting, or conditioning the provision of a telecommunications service by a cable operator or an affiliate thereof.

(C) A franchising authority may not order a cable operator or affiliate thereof--

(i) to discontinue the provision of a telecommunications service, or

(ii) to discontinue the operation of a cable system, to the extent such cable system is used for the provision of a telecommunications service, by reason of the failure of such cable operator or affiliate thereof to obtain a franchise or franchise renewal under this title with respect to the provision of such telecommunications service.

(D) Except as otherwise permitted by Sections 611 and 612, a franchising authority may not require a cable operator to provide any telecommunications service or facilities,

other than institutional networks, as a condition of the initial grant of a franchise, a franchise renewal, or a transfer of a franchise.

(c) Any cable system shall not be subject to regulations as a common carrier or utility by reason of providing any cable service.

(d)(1) A State or the Commission may require the filing of informational tariffs for any intrastate communications service provided by a cable system, other than cable service, that would be subject to regulation by the Commission or any State if offered by a common carrier subject, in whole or in part, to Title II of this Act. Such informational tariffs shall specify the rates, terms, and conditions for the provision of such service, including whether it is made available to all subscribers generally, and shall take effect on the date specified therein.

(2) Nothing in this title shall be construed to affect the authority of any State to regulate any cable operator to the extent that such operator provides any communication service other than cable service, whether offered on a common carrier or private contract basis.

(3) For purposes of this subsection, the term "State" has the meaning given it in Section 3<(v)>.

(e) Nothing in this title shall be construed to affect the authority of any State to license or otherwise regulate any facility or combination of facilities which serves only subscribers in one or more multiple unit dwellings under common ownership, control, or management and which does not use any public right-of-way.

(f) No provision of this Act shall be construed to --

(1) prohibit a local or municipal authority that is also, or is affiliated with, a franchising authority from operating as a multichannel video programming distributor in the franchise area, notwithstanding the granting of one or more franchises by such franchising authority; or

(2) require such local or municipal authority to secure a franchise to operate as a multichannel video programming distributor.

Section 622 [47 USC Section 542]. Franchise Fees.

(a) Subject to the limitation of subsection (b), any cable operator may be required under the terms of any franchise to pay a franchise fee.

(b) For any 12-month period, the franchise fees paid by a cable operator with respect to any cable system shall not exceed 5 percent of such cable operator's gross revenues derived in such period from the operation of the cable system **to provide cable services**. For purposes of this section, the 12-month period shall be the 12-month period applicable under the franchise for accounting purposes. Nothing in this subsection shall prohibit a franchising authority and a cable operator from agreeing that franchise fees which lawfully could be collected for any such 12-month period shall be paid on a prepaid or deferred basis; except that the sum of the fees paid during the term of the franchise may not exceed the amount, including the time value of money, which would have lawfully been collected if such fees had been paid per annum.

(c) Each cable operator may identify, consistent with the regulations prescribed by the Commission pursuant to Section 623, as a separate line item on each regular bill of each subscriber, each of the following:

(1) The amount of the total bill assessed as a franchise fee and the identity of the franchising authority to which the fee is paid.

(2) The amount of the total bill assessed to satisfy any requirements imposed on the cable operator by the franchise agreement to support public, educational, or governmental channels or the use of such channels.

(3) The amount of any other fee, tax, assessment, or charge of any kind imposed by any governmental authority on the transaction between the operator and the subscriber.

(d) In any court action under subsection (c), the franchising authority shall demonstrate that the rate structure reflects all costs of the franchise fees.

(e) Any cable operator shall pass through to subscribers the amount of any decrease in a franchise fee.

(f) A cable operator may designate that portion of a subscriber's bill attributable to the franchise fee as a separate item on the bill.

(g) For the purposes of this section --

(1) the term "franchisee fee" includes any tax, fee, or assessment of any kind imposed by a franchising authority or other government entity on a cable operator or cable subscriber, or both, solely because of their status as such;

(2) the term "franchisee fee" does not include --

(A) any tax, fee, or assessment of general applicability (including any such tax, fee, or assessment imposed on both utilities and cable operators or their services but not including a tax, fee, or assessment which is unduly discriminatory against cable operators or cable subscribers);

(B) in the case of any franchise in effect on the date of the enactment of this title, payments which are required by the franchise to be made by the cable operator during the term of such franchise for, or in support of the use of, public, educational, or governmental access facilities;

(C) in the case of any franchise granted after such date of enactment, capital costs which are required by the franchise to be incurred by the cable operator for public, educational, or governmental access facilities;

(D) requirements or charges incidental to the awarding or enforcing of the franchise, including payments for bonds, security funds, letters of credit, insurance, indemnification, penalties, or liquidated damages; or

(E) any fee imposed under Title 17, United States Code.

(h)(1) Nothing in this Act shall be construed to limit any authority of a franchising authority to impose a tax, fee, or other assessment of any kind on any person (other than a cable operator) with respect to cable service or other communications service provided by such person over a cable system for which charges are assessed to subscribers but not received by the cable operator.

(2) For any 12-month period, the fees paid by such person with respect to any such cable service or other communications service shall not exceed 5 percent of such person's gross revenues derived in such period from the provision of such service over the cable system.

(i) Any Federal agency may not regulate the amount of the franchise fees paid by a cable operator, or regulate the use of funds derived from such fees, except as provided in this section.

Section 623 [47 USC Section 543]. Regulation of Rates.

(a) Competition preference; local and Federal regulation. --

(1) In general. - No Federal agency or State may regulate the rates for the provision of cable service except to the extent provided under this section and Section 612. Any franchising authority may

regulate the rates for the provision of cable service, or any other communications service provided over a cable system to cable subscribers, but only to the extent provided under this section. No Federal agency, State, or franchising authority may regulate the rates for cable service of a cable system that is owned or operated by a local government or franchising authority within whose jurisdiction that cable system is located and that is the only cable system located within such jurisdiction.

(2) Preference for competition. - If the Commission finds that a cable system is subject to effective competition, the rates for the provision of cable service by such system shall not be subject to regulation by the Commission or by a State or franchising authority under this section. If the Commission finds that a cable system is not subject to effective competition --

(A) the rates for the provision of basic cable service shall be subject to regulation by a franchising authority, or by the Commission if the Commission exercises jurisdiction pursuant to paragraph (6), in accordance with the regulations prescribed by the Commission under subsection (b); and

(B) the rates for cable programming services shall be subject to regulation by the Commission under subsection (c).

(3) Qualification of franchising authority. - A franchising authority that seeks to exercise the regulatory jurisdiction permitted under paragraph (2)(A) shall file with the Commission a written certification that --

(A) the franchising authority will adopt and administer regulations with respect to the rates subject to regulation under this section that are consistent with the regulations prescribed by the Commission under subjection (b);

(B) the franchising authority has the legal authority to adopt, and the personnel to administer, such regulations; and

(C) procedural laws and regulations applicable to rate regulation proceedings by such authority provide a reasonable opportunity for consideration of the views of interested parties.

(4) Approval by Commission. - A certification filed by a franchising authority under paragraph (3) shall be effective 30 days after the date on which it is filed unless the Commission finds, after notice to the authority and a reasonable opportunity for the authority to comment, that --

(A) the franchising authority has adopted or is administering regulations with respect to the rates subject to regulation under this section that are not consistent with the regulations prescribed by the Commission under subsection (b);

(B) the franchising authority does not have the legal authority to adopt, or the personnel to administer, such regulations; or

(C) procedural laws and regulations applicable to rate regulation proceedings by such authority do not provide a reasonable opportunity for consideration of the views of interested parties.
If the Commission disapproves a franchising authority's certification, the Commission shall notify the franchising authority of any revisions or modifications necessary to obtain approval.

(5) Revocation of jurisdiction. - Upon petition by a cable operator or other interested party, the Commission shall review the regulation of cable system rates by a franchising authority under this subsection. A copy of the petition shall be provided to the franchising authority by the person filing the petition. If the Commission finds that the franchising authority has acted inconsistently with the requirements of this subsection, the Commission shall grant appropriate relief. If the Commission, after the franchising authority has had a reasonable opportunity to comment, determines that the State and

local laws and regulations are not in conformance with the regulations prescribed by the Commission under subsection (b), the Commission shall revoke the jurisdiction of such authority.

(6) Exercise of jurisdiction by Commission. - If the Commission disapproves a franchising authority's certification under paragraph (4), or revokes such authority's jurisdiction under paragraph (5), the Commission shall exercise the franchising authority's regulatory jurisdiction under paragraph (2)(A) until the franchising authority has qualified to exercise that jurisdiction by filing a new certification that meets the requirements of paragraph (3). Such new certification shall be effective upon approval by the Commission. The Commission shall act to approve or disapprove any such new certification within 90 days after the date it is filed.

(7) Aggregation of equipment costs.--

(A) In general.--The Commission shall allow cable operators, pursuant to any rules promulgated under subsection (b)(3), to aggregate, on a franchise, system, regional, or company level, their equipment costs into broad categories, such as converter boxes, regardless of the varying levels of functionality of the equipment within each such broad category. Such aggregation shall not be permitted with respect to equipment used by subscribers who receive only a rate regulated basic service tier.

(B) Revision to commission rules; forms.--Within 120 days of the date of enactment of the Telecommunications Act of 1996, the Commission shall issue revisions to the appropriate rules and forms necessary to implement subparagraph (A).

(b) Establishment of basic service tier rate regulations --

(1) Commission obligation to subscribers. - The Commission shall, by regulation, ensure that the rates for the basic service tier are reasonable. Such regulations shall be designed to achieve the goal of protecting subscribers of any cable system that is not subject to effective competition from rates for the basic service tier that exceed the rates that would be charged for the basic service tier if such cable system were subject to effective competition.

(2) Commission regulations. - Within 180 days after the date of enactment of the Cable Television Consumer Protection and Competition Act of 1992, the Commission shall prescribe, and periodically thereafter revise, regulations to carry out its obligations under paragraph (1). In prescribing such regulations, the Commission --

(A) shall seek to reduce the administrative burdens on subscribers, cable operators, franchising authorities, and the Commission;

(B) may adopt formulas or other mechanisms and procedures in complying with the requirements of subparagraph (A); and

(C) shall take into account the following factors:

(i) the rates for cable systems, if any, that are subject to effective competition;

(ii) the direct costs (if any) of obtaining, transmitting, and otherwise providing signals carried on the basic service tier, including signals and services carried on the basic service tier pursuant to paragraph (7)(B), and changes in such costs;

(iii) only such portion of the joint and common costs (if any) of obtaining, transmitting, and otherwise providing such signals as is determined, in accordance with regulations prescribed by the Commission, to be reasonably and properly allocable to the basic service tier, and changes in such costs;

(iv) the revenues (if any) received by a cable operator from advertising from programming that is carried as part of the basic service tier or from other consideration obtained in connection with the basic service tier;

(v) the reasonably and properly allocable portion of any amount assessed as a franchise fee, tax, or charge of any kind imposed by any State or local authority on the transactions between cable operators and cable subscribers or any other fee, tax, or assessment of general applicability imposed by a governmental entity applied against cable operators or cable subscribers;

(vi) any amount required, in accordance with paragraph (4), to satisfy franchise requirements to support public, educational, or governmental channels or the use of such channels or any other services required under the franchise; and

(vii) a reasonable profit, as defined by the Commission consistent with the Commission's obligations to subscribers under paragraph (1).

(3) Equipment. - The regulations prescribed by the Commission under this subsection shall include standards to establish, on the basis of actual cost, the price or rate for --

(A) installation and lease of the equipment used by subscribers to receive the basic service tier, including a converter box and a remote control unit and, if requested by the subscriber, such addressable converter box or other equipment as is required to access programming described in paragraph (8); and

(B) installation and monthly use of connections for additional television receivers.

(4) Costs of franchise requirements. - The regulations prescribed by the Commission under this subsection shall include standards to identify costs attributable to satisfying franchise requirements to support public, educational, and governmental channels or the use of such channels or any other services required under the franchise.

(5) Implementation and enforcement. - The regulations prescribed by the Commission under this subsection shall include additional standards, guidelines, and procedures concerning the implementation and enforcement of such regulations, which shall include --

(A) procedures by which cable operators may implement and franchising authorities may enforce the regulations prescribed by the Commission under this subsection;

(B) procedures for the expeditious resolution of disputes between cable operators and franchising authorities concerning the administration of such regulations;

(C) standards and procedures to prevent unreasonable charges for changes in the subscriber's selection of services or equipment subject to regulation under this section, which standards shall require that charges for changing the service tier selected shall be based on the cost of such change and shall not exceed nominal amounts when the system's configuration permits changes in service tier selection to be effected solely by coded entry on a computer terminal or by other similarly simple method; and

(D) standards and procedures to assure that subscribers receive notice of the availability of the basic service tier required under this section.

(6) Notice. - The procedures prescribed by the Commission pursuant to paragraph (5)(A) shall require a cable operator to provide 30 days' advance notice to a franchising authority of any increase proposed in the price to be charged for the basic service tier.

(7) Components of basic tier subject to rate regulation. --

(A) Minimum contents. - Each cable operator of a cable system shall provide its subscribers a separately available basic service tier to which subscription is required for access to any other tier of service. Such basic service tier shall, at a minimum, consist of the following:

(i) All signals carried in fulfillment of the requirements of Sections 614 and 615.

(ii) Any public, educational, and governmental access programming required by the franchise of the cable system to be provided to subscribers.

(iii) Any signal of any television broadcast station that is provided by the cable operator to any subscriber, except a signal which is secondarily transmitted by a satellite carrier beyond the local service area of such station.

(B) Permitted additions to basic tier. - A cable operator may add additional video programming signals or services to the basic service tier. Any such additional signals or services provided on the basic service tier shall be provided to subscribers at rates determined under the regulations prescribed by the Commission under this subsection.

(8) Buy-through of other tiers prohibited. --

(A) Prohibition. - A cable operator may not require the subscription to any tier other than the basic service tier required by paragraph (7) as a condition of access to video programming offered on a per channel or per program basis. A cable operator may not discriminate between subscribers to the basic service tier and other subscribers with regard to the rates charged for video programming offered on a per channel or per program basis.

(B) Exception; limitation. - The prohibition in subparagraph (A) shall not apply to a cable system that, by reason of the lack of addressable converter boxes or other technological limitations, does not permit the operator to offer programming on a per channel or per program basis in the same manner required by subparagraph (A). This subparagraph shall not be available to any cable operator after --

(i) the technology utilized by the cable system is modified or improved in a way that eliminates such technological limitation; or

(ii) 10 years after the date of enactment of the Cable Television Consumer Protection and Competition Act of 1992, subject to subparagraph (C).

(C) Waiver. - If, in any proceeding initiated at the request of any cable operator, the Commission determines that compliance with the requirements of subparagraph (A) would require the cable operator to increase its rates, the Commission may, to the extent consistent with the public interest, grant such cable operator a waiver from such requirements for such specified period as the Commission determines reasonable and appropriate.

(c) Regulation of unreasonable rates. --

(1) Commission regulations. - Within 180 days after the date of enactment of the Cable Television Consumer Protection and Competition Act of 1992, the Commission shall, by regulation, establish the following:

(A) criteria prescribed in accordance with paragraph (2) for identifying, in individual cases, rates for cable programming services that are unreasonable;

(B) fair and expeditious procedures for the receipt, consideration, and resolution of complaints from any ~~subscriber,~~ franchising authority ~~, or other relevant State or local government entity~~ **(in accordance with paragraph (3))** alleging that a rate for cable programming services charged by a cable operator violates the criteria prescribed under subparagraph (A), which procedures shall

525

include the minimum showing that shall be required for a complaint to obtain Commission consideration and resolution of whether the rate in question is unreasonable; and

(C) the procedures to be used to reduce rates for cable programming services that are determined by the Commission to be unreasonable and to refund such portion of the rates or charges that were paid by subscribers after the filing of <~~such~~> **the first** complaint **filed with the franchising authority under paragraph (3)** and that are determined to be unreasonable.

(2) Factors to be considered. - In establishing the criteria for determining in individual cases whether rates for cable programming services are unreasonable under paragraph (1)(A), the Commission shall consider, among other factors --

(A) the rates for similarly situated cable systems offering comparable cable programming services, taking into account similarities in facilities, regulatory and governmental costs, the number of subscribers and other relevant factors;

(B) the rates for cable systems, if any, that are subject to effective competition;

(C) the history of the rates for cable programming services of the system, including the relationship of such rates to changes in general consumer prices;

(D) the rates, as a whole, for all the cable programming, cable equipment, and cable services provided by the system, other that programming provided on a per channel or per program basis;

(E) capital and operating costs of the cable system, including the quality and costs of the customer service provided by the cable system; and

(F) the revenues (if any) received by a cable operator from advertising from programming that is carried as part of the service for which a rate is being established, and changes in such revenues, or from other consideration, obtained in connection with the cable programming services concerned.

(3) <~~Limitation on complaints concerning existing rates. - Except during the 180-day period following the effective date of the regulations prescribed by the~~> **Review of rate changes.--The** Commission <~~under paragraph (1), the procedures established under subparagraph (B) of such paragraph shall be available only with respect to complaints filed within a reasonable period of time following a change~~> **shall review any complaint submitted by a franchising authority after the date of enactment of the Telecommunications Act of 1996 concerning an increase** in rates <~~that is initiated after that effective date, including a change in rates that results from a change in that system's service tiers.~~> **for cable programming services and issue a final order within 90 days after it receives such a complaint, unless the parties agree to extend the period for such review. A franchising authority may not file a complaint under this paragraph unless, within 90 days after such increase becomes effective it receives subscriber complaints.**

(4) Sunset of upper tier rate regulation.--This subsection shall not apply to cable programming services provided after March 31, 1999.

(d) Uniform rate structure required. - A cable operator shall have a rate structure, for the provision of cable service, that is uniform throughout the geographic area in which cable service is provided over its cable system. **This subsection does not apply to (1) a cable operator with respect to the provision of cable service over its cable system in any geographic area in which the video programming services offered by the operator in that area are subject to effective competition, or (2) any video programming offered on a per channel or per program basis. Bulk discounts to multiple dwelling units shall not be subject to this subsection, except that a cable operator of a**

cable system that is not subject to effective competition may not charge predatory prices to a multiple dwelling unit. Upon a prima facie showing by a complainant that there are reasonable grounds to believe that the discounted price is predatory, the cable system shall have the burden of showing that its discounted price is not predatory.

(e) Discrimination; services for the hearing impaired. - Nothing in this title shall be construed as prohibiting any Federal agency, State, or a franchising authority from --

(1) prohibiting discrimination among subscribers and potential subscribers to cable service, except that no Federal agency, State, or franchising authority may prohibit a cable operator from offering reasonable discounts to senior citizens or other economically disadvantaged group discounts; or

(2) requiring and regulating the installation or rental of equipment which facilitates the reception of cable service by hearing impaired individuals.

(f) Negative option billing prohibited. - A cable operator shall not charge a subscriber for any service or equipment that the subscriber has not affirmatively requested by name. For purposes of this subsection, a subscriber's failure to refuse a cable operator's proposal to provide such service or equipment shall not be deemed to be an affirmative request for such service or equipment.

(g) Collection of information. - The Commission shall, by regulation, require cable operators to file with the Commission or a franchising authority, as appropriate, within one year after the date of enactment of the Cable Television Consumer Protection and Competition Act of 1992 and annually thereafter, such financial information as may be needed for purposes of administering and enforcing this section.

(h) Prevention of evasions. - Within 180 days after the date of enactment of the Cable Television Consumer Protection and Competition Act of 1992, the Commission shall, by regulation, establish standards, guidelines, and procedures to prevent evasions, including evasions that result from retiering, of the requirements of this section and shall, thereafter, periodically review and revise such standards, guidelines, and procedures.

(i) Small system burdens. - In developing and prescribing regulations pursuant to this section, the Commission shall design such regulations to reduce the administrative burdens and cost of compliance for cable systems that have 1,000 or fewer subscribers.

(j) Rate regulation agreements. - During the term of an agreement made before July 1, 1990, by a franchising authority and a cable operator providing for the regulation of basic cable service rates, where there was not effective competition under Commission rules in effect on that date, nothing in this section (or the regulations thereunder) shall abridge the ability of such franchising authority to regulate rates in accordance with such an agreement.

(k) Reports on average prices. - The Commission shall annually publish statistical reports on the average rates for basic cable service and other cable programming, and for converter boxes, remote control units, and other equipment, of --

(1) cable systems that the Commission has found are subject to effective competition under subsection (a)(2), compared with

(2) cable systems that the Commission has found are not subject to such effective competition.

(l) Definitions. - As used in this section --

(1) The term "effective competition" means that --

(A) fewer than 30 percent of the households in the franchise area subscribe to the cable service of a cable system;

(B) the franchise area is --

(i) served by at least two unaffiliated multichannel video programming distributors each of which offers comparable video programming to at least 50 percent of the households in the franchise area; and

(ii) the number of households subscribing to programming services offered by multichannel video programming distributors other than the largest multichannel video programming distributor exceeds 15 percent of the households in the franchise area; ~~or~~

➤

(C) a multichannel video programming distributor operated by the franchising authority for that franchise area offers video programming to at least 50 percent of the households in that franchise area; **or**

(D) a local exchange carrier or its affiliate (or any multichannel video programming distributor using the facilities of such carrier or its affiliate) offers video programming services directly to subscribers by any means (other than direct-to-home satellite services) in the franchise area of an unaffiliated cable operator which is providing cable service in that franchise area, but only if the video programming services so offered in that area are comparable to the video programming services provided by the unaffiliated cable operator in that area.

(2) The term "cable programming service" means any video programming provided over a cable system, regardless of service tier, including installation or rental of equipment used for the receipt of such video programming, other than (A) video programming carried on the basic service tier, and (B) video programming offered on a per channel or per program basis.

(m) Special Rules for Small Companies.--

(1) In general.--Subsections (a), (b), and (c) do not apply to a small cable operator with respect to--

(A) cable programming services, or

(B) a basic service tier that was the only service tier subject to regulation as of December 31, 1994, in any franchise area in which that operator services 50,000 or fewer subscribers.

(2) Definition of small cable operator.--For purposes of this subsection, the term "small cable operator" means a cable operator that, directly or through an affiliate, serves in the aggregate fewer than 1 percent of all subscribers in the United States and is not affiliated with any entity or entities whose gross annual revenues in the aggregate exceed $250,000,000.

(n) Treatment of Prior Year Losses.--Notwithstanding any other provision of this section or of Section 612, losses associated with a cable system (including losses associated with the grant or award of a franchise) that were incurred prior to September 4, 1992, with respect to a cable system that is owned and operated by the original franchisee of such system shall not be disallowed, in whole or in part, in the determination of whether the rates for any tier of service or any type of equipment that is subject to regulation under this section are lawful.

Section 624 [47 USC Section 544]. Regulation of Services, Facilities, and Equipment.

(a) Any franchising authority may not regulate the services, facilities, and equipment provided by a cable operator except to the extent consistent with this title.

(b) In the case of any franchise granted after the effective date of this title, the franchising authority, to the extent related to the establishment or operation of a cable system --

(1) in its request for proposals for a franchise (including requests for renewal proposals, subject to Section 626), may establish requirements for facilities and equipment, but may not, except as provided in subsection (h), establish requirements for video programming or other information services; and

(2) subject to Section 625, may enforce any requirements contained within the franchise --

(A) for facilities and equipment; and

(B) for broad categories of video programming or other services.

(c) In the case of any franchise in effect on the effective date of this title, the franchising authority may, subject to Section 625, enforce requirements contained within the franchise for the provision of services, facilities, and equipment, whether or not related to the establishment or operation of a cable system.

(d)(1) Nothing in this title shall be construed as prohibiting a franchising authority and a cable operator from specifying, in a franchise or renewal thereof, that certain cable services shall not be provided or shall be provided subject to conditions, if such cable services are obscene or are otherwise unprotected by the Constitution of the United States.

(2) In order to restrict the viewing of programming which is obscene or indecent, upon the request of a subscriber, a cable operator shall provide (by sale or lease) a device by which the subscriber can prohibit viewing of a particular cable service during periods selected by that subscriber.

(3)(A) If a cable operator provides a premium channel without charge to cable subscribers who do not subscribe to such premium channel, the cable operator shall, not later than 30 days before such premium channel is provided without charge --

(i) notify all cable subscribers that the cable operator plans to provide a premium channel without charge;

(ii) notify all cable subscribers when the cable operator plans to offer a premium channel without charge;

(iii) notify all cable subscribers that they have a right to request that the channel carrying the premium channel be blocked; and

(iv) block the channel carrying the premium channel upon the request of a subscriber.

(B) For the purpose of this section, the term "premium channel" shall mean any pay service offered on a per channel or per program basis, which offers movies rated by the Motion Picture Association of America as X, NC-17, or R.

(e) Within one year after the date of enactment of the Cable Television Consumer Protection and Competition Act of 1992, the Commission shall prescribe regulations which establish minimum technical standards relating to cable systems' technical operation and signal quality. The Commission shall update such standards periodically to reflect improvements in technology. <A> **No State or** franchising authority may <del>require as part of a franchise (including a modification, renewal, or transfer thereof) provisions for the enforcement of the standards prescribed under this subsection. A franchising authority may apply to the Commission for a waiver to impose standards that are more stringent than the standards prescribed by the Commission under this subsection.</del>> **prohibit, condition, or restrict a cable system's use of any type of subscriber equipment or any transmission technology.**

(f)(1) Any Federal agency, State, or franchising authority may not impose requirements regarding the provision or content of cable services, except as expressly provided in this title.

(2) Paragraph (1) shall not apply to --

(A) any rule, regulation, or order issued under any Federal law, as such rule, regulation, or order (i) was in effect on Sept. 21, 1983, or (ii) may be amended after such date if the rule, regulation, or order as amended is not inconsistent with the express provisions of this title; and

(B) any rule, regulation, or order under Title 17, United States Code.

(g) Notwithstanding any such rule, regulation, or order, each cable operator shall comply with such standards as the Commission shall prescribe to ensure that viewers of video programming on cable systems are afforded the same emergency information as is afforded by the emergency broadcasting system pursuant to Commission regulations in Subpart G of Part 73, Title 47, Code of Federal Regulations.

(h) A franchising authority may require a cable operator to do any one or more of the following:

(1) Provide 30 days' advance written notice of any change in channel assignment or in the video programming service provided over any such channel.

(2) Inform subscribers, via written notice, that comments on programming and channel position changes are being recorded by a designated office of the franchising authority.

(i) Within 120 days after the date of enactment of this subsection, the Commission shall prescribe rules concerning the disposition, after a subscriber to a cable system terminates service, of any cable installed by the cable operator within the premises of such subscriber.

Section 624A [47 USC Section 544a]. Consumer Electronics Equipment Compatibility.

(a) Findings. - The Congress finds that --

(1) new and recent models of television receivers and video cassette recorders often contain premium features and functions that are disabled or inhibited because of cable scrambling, encoding, or encryption technologies and devices, including converter boxes and remote control devices required by cable operators to receive programming;

(2) if these problems are allowed to persist, consumers will be less likely to purchase, and electronics equipment manufacturers will be less likely to develop, manufacture, or offer for sale, television receivers and video cassette recorders with new and innovative features and functions; ~~and~~ ~~>~~

(3) cable operators should use technologies that will prevent signal thefts while permitting consumers to benefit from such features and functions in such receivers and recorders; **and**

(4) compatibility among televisions, video cassette recorders, and cable systems can be assured with narrow technical standards that mandate a minimum degree of common design and operation, leaving all features, functions, protocols, and other product and service options for selection through open competition in the market.;.

(b) Compatible interfaces. --

(1) Report; regulations. - Within 1 year after the date of enactment of this section, the Commission, in consultation with representatives of the cable industry and the consumer electronics industry, shall report to Congress on means of assuring compatibility between televisions and video cassette recorders and cable systems, consistent with the need to prevent theft of cable service, so that cable subscribers will be able to enjoy the full benefit of both the programming available on cable

systems and the functions available on their televisions and video cassette recorders. Within 180 days after the date of submission of the report required by this subsection, the Commission shall issue such regulations as are necessary to assure such compatibility.

(2) Scrambling and encryption. - In issuing the regulations referred to in paragraph (1), the Commission shall determine whether and, if so, under what circumstances to permit cable systems to scramble or encrypt signals or to restrict cable systems in the manner in which they encrypt or scramble signals, except that the Commission shall not limit the use of scrambling or encryption technology where the use of such technology does not interfere with the functions of subscribers' television receivers or video cassette recorders.

(c) Rulemaking requirements. --

(1) Factors to be considered. - In prescribing the regulations required by this section, the Commission shall consider --

~~(A)~~ **(A) the need to maximize open competition in the market for all features, functions, protocols, and other product and service options of converter boxes and other cable converters unrelated to the descrambling or decryption of cable television signals; and**

(B) the costs and benefits to consumers of imposing compatibility requirements on cable operators and television manufacturers in a manner that, while providing effective protection against theft or unauthorized reception of cable service, will minimize interference with or nullification of the special functions of subscribers' television receivers or video cassette recorders, including functions that permit the subscriber --

(i) to watch a program on one channel while simultaneously using a video cassette recorder to tape a program on another channel;

(ii) to use a video cassette recorder to tape two consecutive programs that appear on different channels; and

(iii) to use advanced television picture generation and display features; and

~~(B)~~ **(C)** the need for cable operators to protect the integrity of the signals transmitted by the cable operator against theft or to protect such signals against unauthorized reception.

(2) Regulations required. - The regulations prescribed by the Commission under this section shall include such regulations as are necessary --

(A) to specify the technical requirements with which a television receiver or video cassette recorder must comply in order to be sold as "cable compatible" or "cable ready";

(B) to require cable operators offering channels whose reception requires a converter box --

(i) to notify subscribers that they may be unable to benefit from the special functions of their television receivers and video cassette recorders, including functions that permit subscribers --

(I) to watch a program on one channel while simultaneously using a video cassette recorder to tape a program on another channel;

(II) to use a video cassette recorder to tape two consecutive programs that appear on different channels; and

(III) to use advanced television picture generation and display features; and

(ii) to the extent technically and economically feasible, to offer subscribers the option of having all other channels delivered directly to the subscribers' television receivers or video cassette recorders without passing through the converter box;

(C) to promote the commercial availability, from cable operators and retail vendors that are not affiliated with cable systems, of converter boxes and of remote control devices compatible with converter boxes;

(D) **to ensure that any standards or regulations developed under the authority of this section to ensure compatibility between televisions, video cassette recorders, and cable systems do not affect features, functions, protocols, and other product and service options other than those specified in paragraph (1)(B), including telecommunications interface equipment, home automation communications, and computer network services;**

(E) to require a cable operator who offers subscribers the option of renting a remote control unit --

(i) to notify subscribers that they may purchase a commercially available remote control device from any source that sells such devices rather than renting it from the cable operator; and

(ii) to specify the types of remote control units that are compatible with the converter box supplied by the cable operator; and

~~(E)~~ (F) to prohibit a cable operator from taking any action that prevents or in any way disables the converter box supplied by the cable operator from operating compatibly with commercially available remote control units.

(d) Review of regulations. - The Commission shall periodically review and, if necessary, modify the regulations issued pursuant to this section in light of any actions taken in response to such regulations and to reflect improvements and changes in cable systems, television receivers, video cassette recorders, and similar technology.

Section 625 [47 USC Section 545]. Modification of Franchise Obligations.

(a)(1) During the period a franchise is in effect, the cable operator may obtain from the franchising authority modifications of the requirements in such franchise --

(A) in the case of any such requirement for facilities or equipment, including public, educational, or governmental access facilities or equipment, if the cable operator demonstrates that (i) it is commercially impracticable for the operator to comply with such requirement, and (ii) the proposal by the cable operator for modification of such requirement is appropriate because of commercial impracticability; or

(B) in the case of any such requirement for services, if the cable operator demonstrates that the mix, quality, and level of services required by the franchise at the time it was granted will be maintained after such modification.

(2) Any final decision by a franchising authority under this subsection shall be made in a public proceeding. Such decision shall be made within 120 days after receipt of such request by the franchising authority, unless such 120-day period is extended by mutual agreement of the cable operator and the franchising authority.

(b)(1) Any cable operator whose request for modification under subsection (a) has been denied by a final decision of a franchising authority may obtain modification of such franchise requirements pursuant to the provisions of Section 635.

(2) In the case of any proposed modification of a requirement for facilities or equipment, the court shall grant such modification only if the cable operator demonstrates to the court that --

(A) it is commercially impracticable for the operator to comply with such requirement; and

(B) the terms of the modification requested are appropriate because of commercial impracticability.

(3) In the case of any proposed modification of a requirement for services, the court shall grant such modification only if the cable operator demonstrates to the court that the mix, quality, and level of services required by the franchise at the time it was granted will be maintained after such modification.

(c) Notwithstanding subsections (a) and (b), a cable operator may, upon 30 days' advance notice to the franchising authority, rearrange, replace, or remove a particular cable service required by the franchise if --

(1) such service is no longer available to the operator; or

(2) such service is available to the operator only upon the payment of a royalty required under Section 801(b)(2) of Title 17, United States Code, which the cable operator can document --

(A) is substantially in excess of the amount of such payment required on the date of the operator's offer to provide such service; and

(B) has not been specifically compensated for through a rate increase or other adjustment.

(d) Notwithstanding subsections (a) and (b), a cable operator may take such actions to rearrange a particular service from one service to another, or otherwise offer the service, if the rates for all of the service tiers involved in such actions are not subject to regulation under Section 623.

(e) A cable operator may not obtain modification under this section of any requirement for services relating to public, educational, or governmental access.

(f) For purposes of this section, the term "commercially impracticable" means, with respect to any requirement applicable to a cable operator, that it is commercially impracticable for the operator to comply with such requirement as a result of a change in conditions which is beyond the control of the operator and the nonoccurrence of which was a basic assumption on which the requirement was based.

Section 626 [47 USC Section 546]. Renewal.

(a)(1) A franchising authority may, on its own initiative during the 6-month period which begins with the 36th month before the franchise expiration, commence a proceeding which affords the public in the franchise area appropriate notice and participation for the purpose of (A) identifying the future cable-related community needs and interests, and (B) reviewing the performance of the cable operator under the franchise during the then current franchise term. If the cable operator submits, during such 6-month period, a written renewal notice requesting the commencement of such a proceeding, the franchising authority shall commence such a proceeding not later than 6 months after the date such notice is submitted.

(2) The cable operator may not invoke the renewal procedures set forth in subsections (b) through (g) unless --

(A) such a proceeding is requested by the cable operator by timely submission of such notice; or

(B) such a proceeding is commenced by the franchising authority on its own initiative.

(b)(1) Upon completion of a proceeding under subsection (a), a cable operator seeking renewal of a franchise may, on its own initiative or at the request of a franchising authority, submit a proposal for renewal.

(2) Subject to Section 624, any such proposal shall contain such material as the franchising authority may require, including proposals for an upgrade of the cable system.

(3) The franchising authority may establish a date by which such proposal shall be submitted.

(c)(1) Upon submittal by a cable operator of a proposal to the franchising authority for the renewal of a franchise, pursuant to subsection (b) the franchising authority shall provide prompt public notice of such proposal and, during the 4-month period which begins on the date of the submission of the cable operator's proposal pursuant to subsection (b), renew the franchise or, issue a preliminary assessment that the franchise should not be renewed and, at the request of the operator or on its own initiative, commence an administrative proceeding, after providing prompt public notice of such proceeding, in accordance with ~~<para.>~~ **paragraph** (2) to consider whether --

(A) the cable operator has substantially complied with the material terms of the existing franchise with applicable law;

(B) the quality of the operator's service, including signal quality, response to consumer complaints, and billing practices, but without regard to the mix or quality of cable services or other services provided over the system, has been reasonable in light of community needs;

(C) the operator has the financial, legal, and technical ability to provide the services, facilities, and equipment as set forth in the operator's proposal; and

(D) the operator's proposal is reasonable to meet the future cable-related community needs and interests, taking into account the cost of meeting such needs and interests.

(2) In any proceeding under ~~<para.>~~ **paragraph** (1), the cable operator shall be afforded adequate notice and the cable operator and the franchise authority, or its designee, shall be afforded fair opportunity for full participation, including the right to introduce evidence (including evidence related to issues raised in the proceeding under subsection (a)), to require the production of evidence, and to question witnesses. a transcript shall be made of any such proceeding.

(3) At the completion of a proceeding under this subsection, the franchising authority shall issue a written decision granting or denying the proposal for renewal based upon the record of such proceeding, and transmit a copy of such decision to the cable operator. Such decision shall state the reasons therefor.

(d) Any denial of a proposal for renewal that has been submitted in compliance with subsection (b) shall be based on one or more adverse findings made with respect to the factors described in subparagraphs (A) through (D) of subsection (c)(1), pursuant to the record of the proceeding under subsection (c). A franchising authority may not base a denial of renewal on a failure to substantially comply with the material terms of the franchise under subsection (c)(1)(A) or on events considered under subsection (c)(1)(B) in any case in which a violation of the franchise or the events considered under subsection (c)(1)(B) occur after the effective date of this title unless the franchising authority has provided the operator with notice and the opportunity to cure, or in any case in which it is documented that the franchising authority has waived its right to object, or the cable operator gives written notice of a failure or inability to cure and the franchising authority fails to object within a reasonable time after receipt of such notice.

(e)(1) Any cable operator whose proposal for renewal has been denied by a final decision of a franchising authority made pursuant to this section, or has been adversely affected by a failure of the franchising authority to act in accordance with the procedural requirements of this section, may appeal such final decision or failure pursuant to the provisions of Section 635.

(2) The court shall grant appropriate relief if the court finds that --

(A) any action of the franchising authority, other than harmless error, is not in compliance with the procedural requirements of this section; or

(B) in the event of a final decision of the franchising authority denying the renewal proposal, the operator has demonstrated that the adverse finding of the franchising authority with respect to each of the factors described in subparagraphs (A) through (D) of subsection (c)(1) on which the denial is based is not supported by a preponderance of the evidence, based on the record of the proceeding conducted under subsection (c).

(f) Any decision of a franchising authority on a proposal for renewal shall not be considered final unless all administrative review by the State has occurred or the opportunity therefor has lapsed.

(g) For purposes of this section, the term "franchise expiration" means the date of the expiration of the term of the franchise, as provided under the franchise, as it was in effect on the date of the enactment of this title.

(h) Notwithstanding the provisions of subsections (a) through (g) of this section, a cable operator may submit a proposal for the renewal of a franchise pursuant to this subsection at any time, and a franchising authority may, after affording the public adequate notice and opportunity for comment, grant or deny such proposal at any time (including after proceedings pursuant to this section have commenced). The provisions of subsections (a) through (g) of this section shall not apply to a decision to grant or deny a proposal under this subsection. The denial of a renewal pursuant to this subsection shall not affect action on a renewal proposal that is submitted in accordance with subsections (a) through (g).

(i) Notwithstanding the provisions of subsections (a) through (h), any lawful action to revoke a cable operator's franchise for cause shall not be negated by the subsequent initiation of renewal proceedings by the cable operator under this section.

Section 627 [47 USC Section 547]. Conditions of Sale.

(a) If a renewal of a franchise held by a cable operator is denied and the franchising authority acquires ownership of the cable system or effects a transfer of ownership of the system to another person, any such acquisition or transfer shall be --

(1) at fair market value, determined on the basis of the cable system valued as a going concern but with no value allocated to the franchise itself, or

(2) in the case of any franchise existing on the effective date of this title, at a price determined in accordance with the franchise if such franchise contains provisions applicable to such an acquisition or transfer.

(b) If a franchise held by a cable operator is revoked for cause and the franchising authority acquires ownership of the cable system or effects a transfer of ownership of the system to another person, any such acquisition or transfer shall be --

535

(1) at an equitable price, or

(2) in the case of any franchise existing on the effective date of this title, at a price determined in accordance with the franchise if such franchise contains provisions applicable to such an acquisition or transfer.

Section 628 [47 USC Section 548]. Development of Competition and Diversity in Video Programming Distribution.

(a) Purpose. - The purpose of this section is to promote the public interest, convenience, and necessity by increasing competition and diversity in the multichannel video programming market, to increase the availability of satellite cable programming and satellite broadcast programming to persons in rural and other areas not currently able to receive such programming, and to spur the development of communications technologies.

(b) Prohibition. - It shall be unlawful for a cable operator, a satellite cable programming vendor in which a cable operator has an attributable interest, or a satellite broadcast programming vendor to engage in unfair methods of competition or unfair or deceptive acts or practices, the purpose or effect of which is to hinder significantly or to prevent any multichannel video programming distributor from providing satellite cable programming or satellite broadcast programming to subscribers or consumers.

(c) Regulations required. --

(1) Proceeding required. - Within 180 days after the date of enactment of this section, the Commission shall, in order to promote the public interest, convenience, and necessity by increasing competition and diversity in the multichannel video programming market and the continuing development of communications technologies, prescribe regulations to specify particular conduct that is prohibited by subsection (b).

(2) Minimum contents of regulations. - The regulations to be promulgated under this section shall --

(A) establish effective safeguards to prevent a cable operator which has an attributable interest in a satellite cable programming vendor or a satellite broadcast programming vendor from unduly or improperly influencing the decision of such vendor to sell, or the prices, terms, and conditions of sale of, satellite cable programming or satellite broadcast programming to any unaffiliated multichannel video programming distributor;

(B) prohibit discrimination by a satellite cable programming vendor in which a cable operator has an attributable interest or by a satellite broadcast programming vendor in the prices, terms, and conditions of sale or delivery of satellite cable programming or satellite broadcast programming among or between cable systems, cable operators, or other multichannel video programming distributors, or their agents or buying groups; except that such a satellite cable programming vendor in which a cable operator has an attributable interest or such a satellite broadcast programming vendor shall not be prohibited from --

(i) imposing reasonable requirements for creditworthiness, offering of service, and financial stability and standards regarding character and technical quality;

(ii) establishing different prices, terms, and conditions to take into account actual and reasonable differences in the cost of creation, sale, delivery, or transmission of satellite cable programming or satellite broadcast programming;

536

(iii) establishing different prices, terms, and conditions which take into account economies of scale, cost savings, or other direct and legitimate economic benefits reasonably attributable to the number of subscribers served by the distributor; or

(iv) entering into an exclusive contract that is permitted under subparagraph (D);

(C) prohibit practices, understandings, arrangements, and activities, including exclusive contracts for satellite cable programming or satellite broadcast programming between a cable operator an a satellite cable programming vendor or satellite broadcast programming vendor, that prevent a multichannel video programming distributor from obtaining such programming from any satellite cable programming vendor in which a cable operator has an attributable interest or any satellite broadcast programming vendor in which a cable operator has an attributable interest for distribution to persons in areas not served by a cable operator as of the date of enactment of this section; and

(D) with respect to distribution to persons in areas served by a cable operator, prohibit exclusive contracts for satellite cable programming or satellite broadcast programming between a cable operator and a satellite cable programming vendor in which a cable operator has an attributable interest or a satellite broadcast programming vendor in which a cable operator has an attributable interest, unless the Commission determines (in accordance with paragraph (4)) that such contract is in the public interest.

(3) Limitations. --

(A) Geographic limitations. - Nothing in this section shall require any person who is engaged in the national or regional distribution of video programming to make such programming available in any geographic area beyond which such programming has been authorized or licensed for distribution.

(B) Applicability to satellite retransmissions. - Nothing in this section shall apply (i) to the signal of any broadcast affiliate of a national television network or other television signal that is retransmitted by satellite but that is not satellite broadcast programming, or (ii) to any internal satellite communication of any broadcast network or cable network that is not satellite broadcast programming.

(4) Public interest determinations on exclusive contracts. - In determining whether an exclusive contract is in the public interest for purposes of paragraph (2)(D), the Commission shall consider each of the following factors with respect to the effect of such contract on the distribution of video programming in areas that are served by a cable operator;

(A) the effect of such exclusive contract on the development of competition in local and national multichannel video programming distribution markets;

(B) the effect of such exclusive contract on competition from multichannel video programming distribution technologies other than cable;

(C) the effect of such exclusive contract on the attraction of capital investment in the production and distribution of new satellite cable programming;

(D) the effect of such exclusive contract on diversity of programming in the multichannel video programming distribution market; and

(E) the duration of the exclusive contract.

(5) Sunset provision. - The prohibition required by paragraph (2)(D) shall cease to be effective 10 years after the date of enactment of this section, unless the Commission finds, in a proceeding conducted during the last year of such 10-year period, that such prohibition continues to be necessary to preserve and protect competition and diversity in the distribution of video programming.

537

(d) Adjudicatory proceeding. - Any multichannel video programming distributor aggrieved by conduct that it alleges constitutes a violation of subsection (b), or the regulations of the Commission under subsection (c), may commence an adjudicatory proceeding at the Commission.

(e) Remedies for violations. --

(1) Remedies authorized. - Upon completion of such adjudicatory proceeding, the Commission shall have the power to order appropriate remedies, including, if necessary, the power to establish prices, terms, and conditions of sale of programming to the aggrieved multichannel video programming distributor.

(2) Additional remedies. - The remedies provided in paragraph (1) are in addition to and not in lieu of the remedies available under Title V or any other provision of this Act.

(f) Procedures. - The Commission shall prescribe regulations to implement this section. The Commission's regulations shall --

(1) provide for an expedited review of any complaints made pursuant to this section;

(2) establish procedures for the Commission to collect such data, including the right to obtain copies of all contracts and documents reflecting arrangements and understandings alleged to violate this section, as the Commission requires to carry out this section; and

(3) provide for penalties to be assessed against any person filing a frivolous complaint pursuant to this section.

(g) Reports. - The Commission shall, beginning not later than 18 months after promulgation of the regulations required by subsection (c), annually report to Congress on the status of competition in the market for the delivery of video programming.

(h) Exemptions for prior contracts. --

(1) In general. - Nothing in this section shall affect any contract that grants exclusive distribution rights to any person with respect to satellite cable programming and that was entered into on or before June 1, 1990, except that the provisions of subsection (c)(2)(C) shall apply for distribution to persons in areas not served by a cable operator.

(2) Limitation on renewals. - A contract that was entered into on or before June 1, 1990, but that is renewed or extended after the date of enactment of this section shall not be exempt under paragraph (1).

(i) Definitions. - As used in this section:

(1) The term "satellite cable programming" has the meaning provided under Section 705 of this Act, except that such term does not include satellite broadcast programming.

(2) The term "satellite cable programming vendor" means a person engaged in the production, creation, or wholesale distribution for sale of satellite cable programming, but does not include a satellite broadcast programming vendor.

(3) The term "satellite broadcast programming" means broadcast video programming when such programming is retransmitted by satellite and the entity retransmitting such programming is not the broadcaster or an entity performing such retransmission on behalf of and with the specific consent of the broadcaster.

(4) The term "satellite broadcast programming vendor" means a fixed service satellite carrier that provides service pursuant to Section 119 of Title 17, United States Code, with respect to satellite broadcast programming.

(j) Common Carriers.--Any provision that applies to a cable operator under this section shall apply to a common carrier or its affiliate that provides video programming by any means

538

directly to subscribers. Any such provision that applies to a satellite cable programming vendor in which a cable operator has an attributable interest shall apply to any satellite cable programming vendor in which such common carrier has an attributable interest. For the purposes of this subsection, two or fewer common officers or directors shall not by itself establish an attributable interest by a common carrier in a satellite cable programming vendor (or its parent company).

Section 629 [47 USC Section 549]. Competitive Availability of Navigation Devices.

(a) Commercial Consumer Availability of Equipment Used To Access Services Provided by Multichannel Video Programming Distributors.--The Commission shall, in consultation with appropriate industry standard-setting organizations, adopt regulations to assure the commercial availability, to consumers of multichannel video programming and other services offered over multichannel video programming systems, of converter boxes, interactive communications equipment, and other equipment used by consumers to access multichannel video programming and other services offered over multichannel video programming systems, from manufacturers, retailers, and other vendors not affiliated with any multichannel video programming distributor. Such regulations shall not prohibit any multichannel video programming distributor from also offering converter boxes, interactive communications equipment, and other equipment used by consumers to access multichannel video programming and other services offered over multichannel video programming systems, to consumers, if the system operator's charges to consumers for such devices and equipment are separately stated and not subsidized by charges for any such service.

(b) Protection of System Security.--The Commission shall not prescribe regulations under subsection (a) which would jeopardize security of multichannel video programming and other services offered over multichannel video programming systems, or impede the legal rights of a provider of such services to prevent theft of service.

(c) Waiver.--The Commission shall waive a regulation adopted under subsection (a) for a limited time upon an appropriate showing by a provider of multichannel video programming and other services offered over multichannel video programming systems, or an equipment provider, that such waiver is necessary to assist the development or introduction of a new or improved multichannel video programming or other service offered over multichannel video programming systems, technology, or products. Upon an appropriate showing, the Commission shall grant any such waiver request within 90 days of any application filed under this subsection, and such waiver shall be effective for all service providers and products in that category and for all providers of services and products.

(d) Avoidance of Redundant Regulations.--

(1) Commercial availability determinations.--Determinations made or regulations prescribed by the Commission with respect to commercial availability to consumers of converter boxes, interactive communications equipment, and other equipment used by consumers to access multichannel video programming and other services offered over multichannel video programming systems, before the date of enactment of the Telecommunications Act of 1996 shall fulfill the requirements of this section.

(2) **Regulations.--Nothing in this section affects Section 64.702(e) of the Commission's regulations (47 CFR §64.702(e)) or other Commission regulations governing interconnection and competitive provision of customer premises equipment used in connection with basic common carrier communications services.**

(e) **Sunset.--The regulations adopted under this section shall cease to apply when the Commission determines that--**

(1) **the market for the multichannel video programming distributors is fully competitive;**

(2) **the market for converter boxes, and interactive communications equipment, used in conjunction with that service is fully competitive; and**

(3) **elimination of the regulations would promote competition and the public interest.**

(f) **Commission's Authority.--Nothing in this section shall be construed as expanding or limiting any authority that the Commission may have under law in effect before the date of enactment of the Telecommunications Act of 1996.**

Part IV - Miscellaneous Provisions

Section 631 [47 USC Section 551]. Protection of Subscriber Privacy.

(a)(1) At the time of entering into an agreement to provide any cable service or other service to a subscriber and at least once a year thereafter, a cable operator shall provide notice in the form of a separate, written statement to such subscriber which clearly and conspicuously informs the subscriber of --

(A) the nature of personally identifiable information collected or to be collected with respect to the subscriber and the nature of the use of such information;

(B) the nature, frequency, and purpose of any disclosure which may be made of such information, including an identification of the types of persons to whom the disclosure may be made;

(C) the period during which such information will be maintained by the cable operator;

(D) the times and place at which the subscriber may have access to such information in accordance with subsection (d); and

(E) the limitations provided by this section with respect to the collection and disclosure of information by a cable operator and the right of the subscriber under subsections (f) and (h) to enforce such limitations.

In the case of subscribers who have entered into such an agreement before the effective date of this section, such notice shall be provided within 180 days of such date and at least once a year thereafter.

(2) For purposes of this section, other than subsection (h) --

(A) the term "personally identifiable information" does not include any record of aggregate data which does not identify particular persons;

(B) the term "other service" includes any wire or radio communications service provided using any of the facilities of a cable operator that are used in the provision of cable service; and

(C) the term "cable operator" includes, in addition to persons within the definition of cable operator in Section 602, any person who (i) is owned or controlled by, or under common ownership or control with a cable operator, and (ii) provides any wire or radio communications service.

(b)(1) Except as provided in <del>para.</del> **paragraph** (2), a cable operator shall not use the cable system to collect personally identifiable information concerning any subscriber without the prior written or electronic consent of the subscriber concerned.

(2) A cable operator may use the cable system to collect such information in order to --

(A) obtain information necessary to render a cable service or other service provided by the cable operator to the subscriber; or

(B) detect unauthorized reception of cable communications.

(c)(1) Except as provided in <del>para.</del> **paragraph** (2), a cable operator shall not disclose personally identifiable information concerning any subscriber without the prior written or electronic consent of the subscriber concerned and shall take such actions as are necessary to prevent unauthorized access to such information by a person other than the subscriber or cable operator.

(2) A cable operator may disclose such information if the disclosure is --

(A) necessary to render, or conduct a legitimate business activity related to, a cable service or other service provided by the cable operator to the subscriber;

(B) subject to subsection (h), made pursuant to a court order authorizing such disclosure, if the subscriber is notified of such order by the person to whom the order is directed; or

(C) a disclosure of the names and addresses of subscribers to any cable service or other service, if --

(i) the cable operator has provided the subscriber the opportunity to prohibit or limit such disclosure, and

(ii) the disclosure does not reveal, directly or indirectly, the --

(I) extent of any viewing or other use by the subscriber of a cable service or other service provided by the cable operator, or

(II) the nature of any transaction made by the subscriber over the cable system of the cable operator.

(d) A cable subscriber shall be provided access to all personally identifiable information regarding that subscriber which is collected and maintained by a cable operator. Such information shall be made available to the subscriber at reasonable times and at a convenient place designated by such cable operator. A cable subscriber shall be provided reasonable opportunity to correct any error in such information.

(e) A cable operator shall destroy personally identifiable information if the information is no longer necessary for the purpose for which it was collected and there are no pending requests or orders for access to such information under subsection (d) or pursuant to a court order.

(f)(1) Any person aggrieved by any act of a cable operator in violation of this section may bring a civil action in a United States district court.

(2) The court may award --

(A) actual damages but not less than liquidated damages computed at the rate of $100 a day for each day of violation or $1,000, whichever is higher;

(B) punitive damages; and

(C) reasonable attorney's fees and other litigation costs reasonably incurred.

(3) The remedy provided by this section shall be in addition to any other lawful remedy available to a cable subscriber.

(g) Nothing in this title shall be construed to prohibit any State or any franchising authority from enacting or enforcing laws consistent with this section for the protection of subscriber privacy.

(h) A governmental entity may obtain personally identifiable information concerning a cable subscriber pursuant to a court order only if, in the court proceeding relevant to such court order --

(1) such entity offers clear and convincing evidence that the subject of the information is reasonably suspected of engaging in criminal activity and that the information sought would be material evidence in the case; and

(2) the subject of the information is afforded the opportunity to appear and contest such entity's claim.

Section 632 [47 USC Section 552]. Consumer Protection and Customer Service.

(a) Franchising authority enforcement. - A franchising authority may establish and enforce --

(1) customer service requirements of the cable operator; and

(2) construction schedules and other construction-related requirements, including construction-related performance requirements, of the cable operator.

(b) Commission standards. - The Commission shall, within 180 days of enactment of the Cable Television Consumer Protection and Competition Act of 1992, establish standards by which cable operators may fulfill their customer service requirements. Such standards shall include, at a minimum, requirements governing --

(1) cable system office hours and telephone availability;

(2) installations, outages, and service calls; and

(3) communications between the cable operator and the subscriber (including standards governing bills and refunds).

(c) **Subscriber Notice.--A cable operator may provide notice of service and rate changes to subscribers using any reasonable written means at its sole discretion. Notwithstanding Section 623(b)(6) or any other provision of this Act, a cable operator shall not be required to provide prior notice of any rate change that is the result of a regulatory fee, franchise fee, or any other fee, tax, assessment, or charge of any kind imposed by any Federal agency, State, or franchising authority on the transaction between the operator and the subscriber.**

(d) Consumer protection laws and customer service agreements. --

(1) Consumer protection laws. - Nothing in this title shall be construed to prohibit any State or any franchising authority from enacting or enforcing any consumer protection law, to the extent not specifically preempted by this title.

(2) Customer service requirement agreements. - Nothing in this section shall be construed to preclude a franchising authority and a cable operator from agreeing to customer service requirements that exceed the standards established by the Commission under subsection (b). Nothing in this title shall be construed to prevent the establishment or enforcement of any municipal law or regulation, or any State law, concerning customer service that imposes customer service requirements that exceed the standards set by the Commission under this section, or that addresses matters not addressed by the standards set by the Commission under this section.

Section 633 [47 USC Section 553]. Unauthorized Reception of Cable Service.

(a)(1)   No person shall intercept or receive or assist in intercepting or receiving any communications service offered over a cable system, unless specifically authorized to do so by a cable operator or as may otherwise be specifically authorized by law.

(2)   For the purpose of this section, the term "assist in intercepting or receiving" shall include the manufacture or distribution of equipment intended by the manufacturer or distributor (as the case may be) for unauthorized reception or any communications service offered over a cable system in violation of subparagraph (1).

(b)(1)   Any person who willfully violates subsection (a)(1) shall be fined not more than $1,000 or imprisoned for not more than 6 months, or both.

(2)   Any person who violates subsection (a)(1) willfully and for purposes of commercial advantage or private financial gain shall be fined not more than $50,000 or imprisoned for not more than 2 years, or both, for the first offense and shall be fined not more than $100,000 or imprisoned for not more than 5 years, or both, for any subsequent offense.

(3)   For purposes of all penalties and remedies established for violations of subsection (a)(1), the prohibited activity established herein as it applies to each such device shall be deemed a separate violation.

(c)(1)   Any person aggrieved by any violation of subsection (a)(1) may bring a civil action in a United States district court or in any other court of competent jurisdiction.

(2)   The court may --

(A)   grant temporary and final injunctions on such terms as it may deem reasonable to prevent or restrain violations of subsection (a)(1);

(B)   award damages as described in ~~<para.>~~ **paragraph** (3); and

(C)   direct the recovery of full costs, including awarding reasonable attorneys' fees to an aggrieved party who prevails.

(3)(A) Damages awarded by any court under this section shall be computed in accordance with either of the following clauses:

(i)   the party aggrieved may recover the actual damages suffered by him as a result of the violation and any profits of the violator that are attributable to the violation which are not taken into account in computing the actual damages; in determining the violator's profits, the party aggrieved shall be required to prove only the violator's gross revenue, and the violator shall be required to prove his deductible expenses and the elements of profit attributable to factors other than the violation; or

(ii)   the party aggrieved may recover an award of statutory damages for all violations involved in the action, in a sum of not less than $250 or more than $10,000 as the court considers just.

(B)   In any case in which the court finds that the violation was committed willfully and for purposes of commercial advantage or private financial gain, the court in its discretion may increase the award of damages, whether actual or statutory under ~~<subpara.>~~ **subparagraph** (A), by an amount of not more than $50,000.

(C)   In any case where the court finds that the violator was not aware and had no reason to believe that his acts constituted a violation of this section, the court in its discretion may reduce the aware of damages to a sum of not less than $100.

(D) Nothing in this title shall prevent any State or franchising authority from enacting or enforcing laws, consistent with this section, regarding the unauthorized interception or reception of any cable service or other communications service.

Section 634 [47 USC Section 554]. Equal Employment Opportunity.

(a) This section shall apply to any corporation, partnership, association, joint-stock company, or trust engaged primarily in the management or operation of any cable system.

(b) Equal opportunity in employment shall be afforded by each entity specified in subsection (a), and no person shall be discriminated against in employment by such entity because of race, color, religion, national origin, age or sex.

(c) Any entity specified in subsection (a) shall establish, maintain, and execute a positive continuing program of specific practices designed to ensure equal opportunity in every aspect of its employment policies and practices. Under the terms of its program, each such entity shall --

(1) define the responsibility of each level of management to ensure a positive application and vigorous enforcement of its policy of equal opportunity, and establish a procedure to review and control managerial and supervisory performance;

(2) inform its employees and recognized employee organizations of the equal employment opportunity policy and program and enlist their cooperation;

(3) communicate its equal employment opportunity policy and program and its employment needs to sources of qualified applicants without regard to race, color, religion, national origin, age, or sex, and solicit their recruitment assistance on a continuing basis;

(4) conduct a continuing program to exclude every form of prejudice or discrimination based on race, color, religion, national origin, age, or sex, from its personnel policies and practices and working conditions; and

(5) conduct a continuing review of job structure and employment practices and adopt positive recruitment, training, job design, and other measures needed to ensure genuine equality of opportunity to participate fully in all its organizational units, occupations, and levels of responsibility.

(d)(1) Not later than 270 days after the date of enactment of the Cable Television Consumer Protection and Competition Act of 1992, and after notice and opportunity for hearing, the Commission shall prescribe revisions in the rules under this section in order to implement the amendments made to this section by such Act. Such revisions shall be designed to promote equality of employment opportunities for females and minorities in each of the job categories itemized in paragraph (3).

(2) Such rules shall specify the terms under which an entity specified in subsection (a) shall, to the extent possible --

(A) disseminate its equal opportunity program to job applicants, employees, and those with whom it regularly does business;

(B) use minority organizations, organizations for women, media, educational institutions, and other potential sources of minority and female applicants, to supply referrals whenever jobs are available in its operation;

(C) evaluate its employment profile and job turnover against the availability of minorities and women in its franchise area;

(D) undertake to offer promotions of minorities and women to positions of greater responsibility;

544

(E) encourage minority and female entrepreneurs to conduct business with all parts of its operation; and

(F) analyze the results of its efforts to recruit, hire, promote, and use the services of minorities and women and explain any difficulties encountered in implementing its equal employment opportunity program.

(3)(A) Such rules also shall require an entity specified in subsection (a) with more than 5 full-time employees to file with the Commission an annual statistical report identifying by race, sex, and job title the number of employees in each of the following full-time and part-time job categories:

(i) Corporate officers.

(ii) General Manager.

(iii) Chief Technician.

(iv) Comptroller.

(v) General Sales Manager.

(vi) Production Manager.

(vii) Managers.

(viii) Professionals.

(ix) Technicians.

(x) Sales Personnel.

(xi) Office and Clerical Personnel.

(xii) Skilled Craftspersons.

(xiii) Semiskilled Operatives.

(xiv) Unskilled Laborers.

(xv) Service Workers.

(B) The report required by subparagraph (A) shall be made on separate forms, provided by the Commission, for full-time and part-time employees. The Commission's rules shall sufficiently define the job categories listed in clauses (i) through (vi) of such subparagraph so as to ensure that only employees who are principal decisionmakers and who have supervisory authority are reported for such categories. The Commission shall adopt rules that define the job categories listed in clauses (vii) through (xv) in a manner that is consistent with the Commission policies in effect on June 1, 1990. The Commission shall prescribe the method by which entities shall be required to compute and report the number of minorities and women in the job categories listed in clauses (i) through (x) and the number of minorities and women in the job categories listed in clauses (i) through (xv) in proportion to the total number of qualified minorities and women in the relevant labor market. The report shall include information on hiring, promotion, and recruitment practices necessary for the Commission to evaluate the efforts of entities to comply with the provisions of paragraph (2) of this subsection. The report shall be available for public inspection at the entity's central location and at every location where 5 or more full-time employees are regularly assigned to work. Nothing in this subsection shall be construed as prohibiting the Commission from collecting or continuing to collect statistical or other employment information in a manner that it deems appropriate to carry out this section.

(4) The Commission may amend such rules from time to time to the extent necessary to carry out the provisions of this section. Any such amendment shall be made after notice and opportunity for comment.

(e)(1) On an annual basis, the Commission shall certify each entity described in subsection (a) as in compliance with this section if, on the basis of information in the possession of the Commission, including the report filed pursuant to subsection (d)(3), such entity was in compliance, during the annual period involved, with the requirements of subsections (b), (c), and (d).

(2) The Commission shall, periodically but not less frequently than every five years, investigate the employment practices of each entity described in subsection (a), in the aggregate, as well as in individual job categories, and determine whether such entity is in compliance with the requirements of subsections (b), (c), and (d), including whether such entity's employment practices deny or abridge women's and minorities' equal employment opportunities. As part of such investigation, the Commission shall review whether the entity's reports filed pursuant to subsection (d)(3) accurately reflect employee responsibilities in the reported job classifications.

(f)(1) If the Commission finds after notice and hearing that the entity involved has willfully or repeatedly without good cause failed to comply with the requirements of this section, such failure shall constitute a substantial failure to comply with this title. The failure to obtain certification under subsection (e) shall not itself constitute the basis for a determination of substantial failure to comply with this title. For purposes of this paragraph, the term "repeatedly," when used with respect to failures to comply, refers to three or more failures during any 7-year period.

(2) Any person who is determined by the Commission, through an investigation pursuant to subsection (e) or otherwise, to have failed to meet or failed to make best efforts to meet the requirements of this section, or rules under this section, shall be liable to the United States for a forfeiture penalty of $500 for each violation. Each day of a continuing violation shall constitute a separate offense. Any entity defined in subsection (a) shall not be liable for more than 180 days of forfeitures which accrued prior to notification by the Commission of a potential violation. Nothing in this paragraph shall limit the forfeiture imposed on any person as a result of any violation that continues subsequent to such notification. In addition, any person liable for such penalty may also have any license under this Act for cable auxiliary relay service suspended until the Commission determines that the failure involved has been corrected. Whoever knowingly makes any false statement or submits documentation which he knows to be false, pursuant to an application for certification under this section shall be in violation of this section.

(3) The provisions of ~~<paras.>~~ **paragraphs** (3) and 4), and the last 2 sentences of ~~<para.>~~ **paragraph** (2), of Section 503(b) shall apply to forfeitures under this subsection.

(4) The Commission shall provide for notice to the public and appropriate franchising authorities of any penalty imposed under this section.

(g) Employees or applicants for employment who believe they have been discriminated against in violation of the requirements of this section, or rules under this section, or any other interested person, may file a complaint with the Commission. A complaint by any such person shall be in writing, and shall be signed and sworn to by that person. The regulations under subsection (d)(1) shall specify a program, under authorities otherwise available to the Commission, for the investigation of complaints and violations, and for the enforcement of this section.

(h)(1) For purposes of this section, the term "cable operator" includes any operator of any satellite master antenna television system, including a system described in Section 602(7)(A) and any multichannel video programming distributor.

(2) Such term does not include any operator of a system which, in the aggregate, serves fewer than 50 subscribers.

(3) In any case in which a cable operator is the owner of a multiple unit dwelling, the requirements of this section shall only apply to such cable operator with respect to its employees who are primarily engaged in cable telecommunications.

(i)(1) Nothing in this section shall affect the authority of any State or any franchising authority --

(A) to establish or enforce any requirement which is consistent with the requirements of this section, including any requirement which affords equal employment opportunity protection for employees;

(B) to establish or enforce any provision requiring or encouraging any cable operator to conduct business with enterprises which are owned or controlled by members of minorities groups (as defined in Section 309(i)(3)(C)(ii) or which have their principal operations located within the community served by the cable operator; or

(C) to enforce any requirement of a franchise in effect on the effective date of this title.

(2) The remedies and enforcement provisions of this section are in addition to, and not in lieu of, those available under this or any other law.

(3) The provisions of this section shall apply to any cable operator, whether operating pursuant to a franchise granted before, on, or after the date of the enactment of this section.

Section 635 [47 USC Section 555]. Judicial Proceedings.

(a) Any cable operator adversely affected by any final determination made by a franchising authority under Section 621(a)(1), 625 or 626 may commence an action within 120 days after receiving notice of such determination, which may be brought in --

(1) the district court of the United States for any judicial district in which the cable system is located; or

(2) in any State court of general jurisdiction having jurisdiction over the parties.

(b) The court may award any appropriate relief consistent with the provisions of the relevant section described in subsection (a) and with the provisions of subsection (a).

(c)(1) Notwithstanding any other provision of law, any civil action challenging the constitutionality of Section 614 or 615 of this Act or any provision thereof shall be heard by a district court of three judges convened pursuant to the provisions of Section 2284 of Title 28, United States Code.

(2) Notwithstanding any other provision of law, an interlocutory or final judgment, decree, or order of the court of three judges in an action under paragraph (1) holding Section 614 or 615 of this Act or any provision thereof unconstitutional shall be reviewable as a matter of right by direct appeal to the Supreme Court. Any such appeal shall be filed not more than 20 days after entry of such judgment, decree, or order.

Section 635A [47 USC Section 555a]. Limitation of Franchising Authority Liability.

(a) Suits for damages prohibited. - In any court proceeding pending on or initiated after the date of enactment of this section involving any claim against a franchising authority or other governmental entity, or any official, member, employee, or agent of such authority or entity, arising from the regulation of cable service or from a decision of approval or disapproval with respect to a grant, renewal, transfer, or amendment of a franchise, any relief, to the extent such relief is required by any other provision of Federal, State, or local law, shall be limited to injunctive relief and declaratory relief.

(b) Exception for completed cases. - The limitation contained in subsection (a) shall not apply to actions that, prior to such violation, have been determined by a final order of a court of binding jurisdiction, no longer subject to appeal, to be in violation of a cable operator's rights.

(c) Discrimination claims permitted. - Nothing in this section shall be construed as limiting the relief authorized with respect to any claim against a franchising authority or other governmental entity, or any official, member, employee, or agent of such authority or entity, to the extent such claim involves discrimination on the basis of race, color, sex, age, religion, national origin, or handicap.

(d) Rule of construction. - Nothing in this section shall be construed as creating or authorizing liability of any kind, under any law, for any action or failure to act relating to cable service or the granting of a franchise by any franchising authority or other governmental entity, or any official, member, employee, or agent of such authority or entity.

Section 636 [47 USC Section 556]. Coordination of Federal, State, and Local Authority.

(a) Nothing in this title shall be construed to affect any authority of any State, political subdivision, or agency thereof, or franchising authority, regarding matters of public health, safety, and welfare, to the extent consistent with the express provisions of this title.

(b) Nothing in this title shall be construed to restrict a State from exercising jurisdiction with regard to cable services consistent with this title.

(c) Except as provided in Section 637, any provision of law of any State, political subdivision, or agency thereof, or franchising authority, or any provision of any franchise granted by such authority, which is inconsistent with this Act shall be deemed to be preempted and superseded.

(d) For purposes of this section, the term "State" has the meaning given such term in Section 3⫷(v)⫸.

Section 637 [47 USC Section 557]. Existing Franchises.

(a) The provisions of --

(1) any franchise in effect on the effective date of this title, including any such provisions which relate to the designation, use, or support for the use of channel capacity for public, educational, or governmental use; and

(2) any law or any State (as defined in Section 3⫷(v)⫸) in effect on the date of the enactment of this section, or any regulation promulgated pursuant to such law, which relates to such designation, use or support of such channel capacity, shall remain in effect, subject to the express provisions of this title, and for not longer than the current remaining term of the franchise as such franchise existed on such effective date.

(b) For purposes of subsection (a) and other provisions of this title, a franchise shall be considered in effect on the effective date of this title if such franchise was granted on or before such effective date.

Section 638 [47 USC Section 558]. Criminal and Civil Liability.

Nothing in this title shall be deemed to affect the criminal or civil liability of cable programmers or cable operators pursuant to the Federal, State, or local law of libel, slander, obscenity, incitement, invasions of privacy, false or misleading advertising, or other similar laws, except that cable operators shall not incur any such liability for any program carried on any channel designated for public, educational, governmental use or on any other channel obtained under Section 612 or under similar arrangements unless the program involves obscene material.

Section 639 [47 USC Section 559]. Obscene Programming.

Whoever transmits over any cable system any matter which is obscene or otherwise unprotected by the Constitution of the United States shall be fined <del>not more than $10,000</del> **under Title 18, United States Code** or imprisoned not more than 2 years, or both.

Section 640 [47 USC Section 560]. Scrambling of Cable Channels for Nonsubscribers.

(a) Subscriber Request.–Upon request by a cable service subscriber, a cable operator shall, without charge, fully scramble or otherwise fully block the audio and video programming of each channel carrying such programming so that one not a subscriber does not receive it.

(b) Definition.–As used in this section, the term "scramble" means to rearrange the content of the signal of the programming so that the programming cannot be viewed or heard in an understandable manner.

Section 641 [47 USC Section 561]. Scrambling of Sexually Explicit Adult Video Service Programming.

(a) Requirement.–In providing sexually explicit adult programming or other programming that is indecent on any channel of its service primarily dedicated to sexually-oriented programming, a multichannel video programming distributor shall fully scramble or otherwise fully block the video and audio portion of such channel so that one not a subscriber to such channel or programming does not receive it.

(b) Implementation.--Until a multichannel video programming distributor complies with the requirement set forth in subsection (a), the distributor shall limit the access of children to the programming referred to in that subsection by not providing such programming during the hours of the day (as determined by the Commission) when a significant number of children are likely to view it.

(c) Definition.–As used in this section, the term "scramble" means to rearrange the content of the signal of the programming so that the programming cannot be viewed or heard in an understandable manner.

Part V - Video Programming Services Provided by Telephone Companies

Section 651 [47 USC Section 571]. Regulatory Treatment of Video Programming Services.

(a) Limitations on Cable Regulation.--

(1) Radio-based systems.--To the extent that a common carrier (or any other person) is providing video programming to subscribers using radio communication, such carrier (or other person) shall be subject to the requirements of title III and Section 652, but shall not otherwise be subject to the requirements of this title.

(2) Common carriage of video traffic.--To the extent that a common carrier is providing transmission of video programming on a common carrier basis, such carrier shall be subject to the requirements of title II and Section 652, but shall not otherwise be subject to the requirements of this title.
This paragraph shall not affect the treatment under Section 602(7)(C) of a facility of a common carrier as a cable system.

(3) Cable systems and open video systems.--To the extent that a common carrier is providing video programming to its subscribers in any manner other than that described in paragraphs (1) and (2)--

(A) such carrier shall be subject to the requirements of this title, unless such programming is provided by means of an open video system for which the Commission has approved a certification under Section 653; or

(B) if such programming is provided by means of an open video system for which the Commission has approved a certification under Section 653, such carrier shall be subject to the requirements of this part, but shall be subject to parts I through IV of this title only as provided in 653(c).

(4) Election to operate as open video system.--A common carrier that is providing video programming in a manner described in paragraph (1) or (2), or a combination thereof, may elect to provide such programming by means of an open video system that complies with Section 653. If the Commission approves such carrier's certification under Section 653, such carrier shall be subject to the requirements of this part, but shall be subject to parts I through IV of this title only as provided in 653(c).

(b) Limitations on Interconnection Obligations.--A local exchange carrier that provides cable service through an open video system or a cable system shall not be required, pursuant to title II of this Act, to make capacity available on a nondiscriminatory basis to any other person for the provision of cable service directly to subscribers.

(c) Additional Regulatory Relief.--A common carrier shall not be required to obtain a certificate under Section 214 with respect to the establishment or operation of a system for the delivery of video programming.

Section 652 [47 USC Section 572]. Prohibition on Buy-Outs

(a) Acquisitions by Carriers.--No local exchange carrier or any affiliate of such carrier owned by, operated by, controlled by, or under common control with such carrier may purchase or otherwise acquire directly or indirectly more than a 10 percent financial interest, or any management interest, in any cable operator providing cable service within the local exchange carrier's telephone service area.

(b) Acquisitions by Cable Operators.--No cable operator or affiliate of a cable operator that is owned by, operated by, controlled by, or under common ownership with such cable operator may purchase or otherwise acquire, directly or indirectly, more than a 10 percent financial interest, or any management interest, in any local exchange carrier providing telephone exchange service within such cable operator's franchise area.

(c) Joint Ventures.--A local exchange carrier and a cable operator whose telephone service area and cable franchise area, respectively, are in the same market may not enter into any joint venture or partnership to provide video programming directly to subscribers or to provide telecommunications services within such market.

(d) Exceptions.--

(1) Rural systems.--Notwithstanding subsections (a), (b), and (c) of this section, a local exchange carrier (with respect to a cable system located in its telephone service area) and a cable operator (with respect to the facilities of a local exchange carrier used to provide telephone exchange service in its cable franchise area) may obtain a controlling interest in, management interest in, or enter into a joint venture or partnership with the operator of such system or facilities for the use of such system or facilities to the extent that--

(A) such system or facilities only serve incorporated or unincorporated--

(i) places or territories that have fewer than 35,000 inhabitants; and

(ii) are outside an urbanized area, as defined by the Bureau of the Census; and

(B) in the case of a local exchange carrier, such system, in the aggregate with any other system in which such carrier has an interest, serves less than 10 percent of the households in the telephone service area of such carrier.

(2) Joint use.--Notwithstanding subsection (c), a local exchange carrier may obtain, with the concurrence of the cable operator on the rates, terms, and conditions, the use of that part of the transmission facilities of a cable system extending from the last multi-user terminal to the premises of the end user, if such use is reasonably limited in scope and duration, as determined by the Commission.

(3) Acquisitions in competitive markets.--Notwithstanding subsections (a) and (c), a local exchange carrier may obtain a controlling interest in, or form a joint venture or other partnership with, or provide financing to, a cable system (hereinafter in this paragraph referred to as "the subject cable system"), if--

(A) the subject cable system operates in a television market that is not in the top 25 markets, and such market has more than 1 cable system operator, and the subject cable system is not the cable system with the most subscribers in such television market;

(B) the subject cable system and the cable system with the most subscribers in such television market held on May 1, 1995, cable television franchises from the largest municipality in the television market and the boundaries of such franchises were identical on such date;

(C) the subject cable system is not owned by or under common ownership or control of any one of the 50 cable system operators with the most subscribers as such operators existed on May 1, 1995; and

(D) the system with the most subscribers in the television market is owned by or under common ownership or control of any one of the 10 largest cable system operators as such operators existed on May 1, 1995.

(4) Exempt cable systems.--Subsection (a) does not apply to any cable system if--

(A) the cable system serves no more than 17,000 cable subscribers, of which no less than 8,000 live within an urban area, and no less than 6,000 live within a nonurbanized area as of June 1, 1995;

(B) the cable system is not owned by, or under common ownership or control with, any of the 50 largest cable system operators in existence on June 1, 1995; and

(C) the cable system operates in a television market that was not in the top 100 television markets as of June 1, 1995.

(5) Small cable systems in nonurban areas.--Notwithstanding subsections (a) and (c), a local exchange carrier with less than $100,000,000 in annual operating revenues (or any affiliate of such carrier owned by, operated by, controlled by, or under common control with such carrier) may purchase or otherwise acquire more than a 10 percent financial interest in, or any management interest in, or enter into a joint venture or partnership with, any cable system within the local exchange carrier's telephone service area that serves no more than 20,000 cable subscribers, if no more than 12,000 of those subscribers live within an urbanized area, as defined by the Bureau of the Census.

(6) Waivers.--The Commission may waive the restrictions of subsections (a), (b), or (c) only if--

(A) the Commission determines that, because of the nature of the market served by the affected cable system or facilities used to provide telephone exchange service--

(i) the affected cable operator or local exchange carrier would be subjected to undue economic distress by the enforcement of such provisions;

(ii) the system or facilities would not be economically viable if such provisions were enforced; or

(iii) the anticompetitive effects of the proposed transaction are clearly outweighed in the public interest by the probable effect of the transaction in meeting the convenience and needs of the community to be served; and

(B) the local franchising authority approves of such waiver.

(e) Definition of Telephone Service Area.--For purposes of this section, the term "telephone service area" when used in connection with a common carrier subject in whole or in part to title II of this Act means the area within which such carrier provided telephone exchange service as of January 1, 1993, but if any common carrier after such date transfers its telephone exchange service facilities to another common carrier, the area to which such facilities provide telephone exchange service shall be treated as part of the telephone service area of the acquiring common carrier and not of the selling common carrier.

Section 653 [47 USC Section 573]. Establishment of Open Video Systems.

(a) Open Video Systems.--

(1) Certificates of compliance.--A local exchange carrier may provide cable service to its cable service subscribers in its telephone service area through an open video system that

552

complies with this section. To the extent permitted by such regulations as the Commission may prescribe consistent with the public interest, convenience, and necessity, an operator of a cable system or any other person may provide video programming through an open video system that complies with this section. An operator of an open video system shall qualify for reduced regulatory burdens under subsection (c) of this section if the operator of such system certifies to the Commission that such carrier complies with the Commission's regulations under subsection (b) and the Commission approves such certification. The Commission shall publish notice of the receipt of any such certification and shall act to approve or disapprove any such certification within 10 days after receipt of such certification.

(2) Dispute resolution.--The Commission shall have the authority to resolve disputes under this section and the regulations prescribed thereunder. Any such dispute shall be resolved within 180 days after notice of such dispute is submitted to the Commission. At that time or subsequently in a separate damages proceeding, the Commission may, in the case of any violation of this section, require carriage, award damages to any person denied carriage, or any combination of such sanctions. Any aggrieved party may seek any other remedy available under this Act.

(b) Commission Actions.--

(1) Regulations required.--Within 6 months after the date of enactment of the Telecommunications Act of 1996, the Commission shall complete all actions necessary (including any reconsideration) to prescribe regulations that--

(A) except as required pursuant to Section 611, 614, or 615, prohibit an operator of an open video system from discriminating among video programming providers with regard to carriage on its open video system, and ensure that the rates, terms, and conditions for such carriage are just and reasonable, and are not unjustly or unreasonably discriminatory;

(B) if demand exceeds the channel capacity of the open video system, prohibit an operator of an open video system and its affiliates from selecting the video programming services for carriage on more than one-third of the activated channel capacity on such system, but nothing in this subparagraph shall be construed to limit the number of channels that the carrier and its affiliates may offer to provide directly to subscribers;

(C) permit an operator of an open video system to carry on only one channel any video programming service that is offered by more than one video programming provider (including the local exchange carrier's video programming affiliate), provided that subscribers have ready and immediate access to any such video programming service;

(D) extend to the distribution of video programming over open video systems the Commission's regulations concerning sports exclusivity (47 CFR §76.67), network nonduplication (47 CFR §76.92 et seq.), and syndicated exclusivity (47 CFR §76.151 et seq.); and

(E)(i) prohibit an operator of an open video system from unreasonably discriminating in favor of the operator or its affiliates with regard to material or information (including advertising) provided by the operator to subscribers for the purposes of selecting programming on the open video system, or in the way such material or information is presented to subscribers;

(ii) require an operator of an open video system to ensure that video programming providers or copyright holders (or both) are able suitably and uniquely to identify their programming services to subscribers;

(iii) if such identification is transmitted as part of the programming signal, require the carrier to transmit such identification without change or alteration; and

(iv) prohibit an operator of an open video system from omitting television broadcast stations or other unaffiliated video programming services carried on such system from any navigational device, guide, or menu.

(2) Consumer access.--Subject to the requirements of paragraph (1) and the regulations thereunder, nothing in this section prohibits a common carrier or its affiliate from negotiating mutually agreeable terms and conditions with over-the-air broadcast stations and other unaffiliated video programming providers to allow consumer access to their signals on any level or screen of any gateway, menu, or other program guide, whether provided by the carrier or its affiliate.

(c) Reduced Regulatory Burdens for Open Video Systems.--

(1) In general.--Any provision that applies to a cable operator under--

(A) Sections 613 (other than subsection (a) thereof), 616, 623(f), 628, 631, and 634 of this title, shall apply,

(B) Sections 611, 614, and 615 of this title, and Section 325 of title III, shall apply in accordance with the regulations prescribed under paragraph (2), and

(C) Sections 612 and 617, and parts III and IV (other than Sections 623(f), 628, 631, and 634), of this title shall not apply, to any operator of an open video system for which the Commission has approved a certification under this section.

(2) Implementation.--

(A) Commission action.--In the rulemaking proceeding to prescribe the regulations required by subsection (b)(1), the Commission shall, to the extent possible, impose obligations that are no greater or lesser than the obligations contained in the provisions described in paragraph (1)(B) of this subsection. The Commission shall complete all action (including any reconsideration) to prescribe such regulations no later than 6 months after the date of enactment of the Telecommunications Act of 1996.

(B) Fees.--An operator of an open video system under this part may be subject to the payment of fees on the gross revenues of the operator for the provision of cable service imposed by a local franchising authority or other governmental entity, in lieu of the franchise fees permitted under Section 622. The rate at which such fees are imposed shall not exceed the rate at which franchise fees are imposed on any cable operator transmitting video programming in the franchise area, as determined in accordance with regulations prescribed by the Commission. An operator of an open video system may designate that portion of a subscriber's bill attributable to the fee under this subparagraph as a separate item on the bill.

(3) Regulatory streamlining.--With respect to the establishment and operation of an open video system, the requirements of this section shall apply in lieu of, and not in addition to, the requirements of title II.

(4) Treatment as cable operator.--Nothing in this Act precludes a video programming provider making use of a open video system from being treated as an operator of a cable system for purposes of Section 111 of title 17, United States Code.

(d) Definition of Telephone Service Area.--For purposes of this section, the term "telephone service area" when used in connection with a common carrier subject in whole or in part to title II of this Act means the area within which such carrier is offering telephone exchange service.

Title VII - Miscellaneous Provisions

Section 701 [47 USC Section 601]. Transfer to Commission of Duties, Powers, and Functions Under Existing Law.

(a) All duties, powers, and functions of the Interstate Commerce Commission under the Act of August 7, 1888 (25 Stat 382), relating to operation of telegraph lines by railroad and telegraph companies granted government aid in the construction of their lines, are hereby imposed upon and vested in the Commission: provided, that such transfer of duties, powers, and functions shall not be construed to affect the duties, powers, functions, or jurisdiction of the Interstate Commerce Commission under, or to interfere with or prevent the enforcement of, the Interstate Commerce Act and all acts amendatory thereof or supplemental thereto.

(b) All duties, powers, and functions of the Postmaster General with respect to telegraph companies and telegraph lines under any existing provision of law are hereby imposed upon and vested in the Commission.

Section 702 [47 USC Section 602]. [Deleted]

Section 703 [47 USC Section 603]. [Deleted]

Section 704 [47 USC Section 604]. Effect of Transfers, Repeals, and Amendments.

(a) All orders, determinations, rules, regulations, permits, contracts, licenses, and privileges which have been issued, made, or granted by the Interstate Commerce Commission, the Federal Radio Commission, or the Postmaster General, under any provision of law repealed or amended by this Act or in the exercise of duties, powers, or functions transferred to the Commission by this Act, and which are in effect at the time this section takes effect, shall continue in effect until modified, terminated, superseded, or repealed by the Commission or by operation of law.

(b) All records transferred to the Commission under this Act shall be available for use by the Commission to the same extent as if such records were originally records of the Commission. All final valuations and determinations of depreciation charges by the Interstate Commerce Commission with respect to common carriers engaged in radio or wire communication, and all orders of the Interstate Commerce Commission with respect to such valuations and determinations, shall have the same force and effect as though made by the Commission under this Act.

Section 705 [47 USC Section 605]. Unauthorized Publication <del>or Use></del> of Communications.

(a) Except as authorized by Chapter 119, Title 18, no person receiving, assisting in receiving, transmitting, or assisting in transmitting, any interstate or foreign communication by wire or radio shall divulge or publish the existence, contents, substance, purport, effect, or meaning thereof, except through authorized channels of transmission or reception, (1) to any person other than the addressee, his agent, or attorney, (2) to a person employed or authorized to forward such communication to its destination, (3) to proper accounting or distributing officers of the various communicating centers over which the communication may be passed, (4) to the master of a ship under whom he is serving, (5) in response to a subpoena issued by a court of competent jurisdiction, or (6) on demand of other lawful authority. No person not being authorized by the sender shall intercept any radio communication and divulge or publish the existence, contents, substance, purport, effect, or meaning of such intercepted communication to any person. No person not being entitled thereto shall receive or assist in receiving any interstate or foreign communication by radio and use such communication (or any information therein contained) for his own benefit or for the benefit of another not entitled thereto. No person having received any intercepted radio communication or having become acquainted with the contents, substance, purport, effect, or meaning of such communication (or any part thereof) knowing that such communication was intercepted, shall divulge or publish the existence, contents, substance, purport, effect, or meaning of such communication (or any part thereof) or use such communication (or any information therein contained) for his own benefit or for the benefit of another not entitled thereto. This section shall not apply to the receiving, divulging, publishing, or utilizing the contents of any radio communication which is transmitted by any station for the use of the general public, which relates to ships, aircraft, vehicles or persons in distress, or which is transmitted by an amateur radio station operator or by a citizens band radio operator.

(b) The provisions of subsection (a) shall not apply to the interception or receipt by any individual, or the assisting (including the manufacture or sale) of such interception or receipt, of any satellite cable programming for private viewing if --

(1) the programming involved is not encrypted; and

(2)(A) a marketing system is not established under which --

(i) an agent or agents have been lawfully designated for the purpose of authorizing private viewing by individuals, and

(ii) such authorization is available to the individual involved from the appropriate agent or agents; or

(B) a marketing system described in subparagraph (A) is established and the individuals receiving such programming have obtained authorization for private viewing under that system.

(c) No person shall encrypt or continue to encrypt satellite delivered programs included in the National Program Service of the Public Broadcasting Service and intended for public viewing by retransmission by television broadcast stations; except that as long as at least one unencrypted satellite transmission of any program subject to this subsection is provided, this subsection shall not prohibit additional encrypted satellite transmissions of the same program.

(d) For purposes of this section --

(1) the term "satellite cable programming" means video programming which is transmitted via satellite and which is primarily intended for the direct receipt by cable operators for their retransmission to cable subscribers;

(2) the term "agent," with respect to any person, includes an employee of such person;

(3) the term "encrypt," when used with respect to satellite cable programming, means to transmit such programming in a form whereby the aural and visual characteristics (or both) are modified or altered for the purpose of preventing the unauthorized receipt of such programming by persons without authorized equipment which is designed to eliminate the effects of such modification or alteration;

(4) the term "private viewing" means the viewing for private use in an individual's dwelling unit by means of equipment, owned or operated by such individual, capable of receiving satellite cable programming directly from a satellite; and

(5) the term "private financial gain" shall not include the gain resulting to any individual for the private use in such individual's dwelling unit of any programming for which the individual has not obtained authorization for that use; and

(6) the term "any person aggrieved" shall include any person with proprietary rights in the intercepted communication by wire or radio, including wholesale or retail distributors of satellite cable programming, and, in the case of a violation of paragraph (4) of subsection (e), shall also include any person engaged in the lawful manufacture, distribution, or sale of equipment necessary to authorize or receive satellite cable programming.

(e)(1) Any person who willfully violates subsection (a) shall be fined not more than $2,000 or imprisoned for not more than 6 months or both.

(2) Any person who violates subsection (a) willfully and for purposes of direct or indirect commercial advantage or private financial gain shall be fined not more than $50,000 or imprisoned for not more than 2 years, or both, for the first such conviction and shall be fined not more than $100,000 or imprisoned for not more than 5 years, or both, for any subsequent conviction.

(3)(A) Any person aggrieved by any violation of subsection (a) or paragraph (4) of this subsection may bring a civil action in a United States district court or in any other court of competent jurisdiction.

(B) The court --

(i) may grant temporary and final injunctions on such terms as it may deem reasonable to prevent or restrain violations of subsection (a);

(ii) may award damages as described in subparagraph (C); and

(iii) shall direct the recovery of full costs, including awarding reasonable attorneys' fees to an aggrieved party who prevails.

(C)(i) Damages awarded by any court under this section shall be computed, at the election of the aggrieved party, in accordance with either of the following subclauses;

(I) the party aggrieved may recover the actual damages suffered by him as a result of the violation and any profits of the violator that are attributable to the violation which are not taken into account in computing the actual damages; in determining the violator's profits, the party aggrieved shall be required to prove only the violator's gross revenue, and the violator shall be required to prove his deductible expenses and the elements of profit attributable to factors other than the violation; or

(II) the party aggrieved may recover an award of statutory damages for each violation of subsection (a) involved in the action in a sum of not less than $1,000 or more than $10,000 as the court considers just and for each violation of paragraph (4) if this subsection involved in the action an aggrieved party may recover statutory damages in a sum not less than $10,000, or more than $100,000, as the court considers just.

(ii) In any case in which the court finds that the violation was committed willfully and for purposes of direct or indirect commercial advantage or private financial gain, the court in its discretion may increase the award of damages, whether actual or statutory, by an amount of not more than $100,000 for each violation of subsection (a).

(iii) In any case where the court finds that the violator was not aware and had no reason to believe that his acts constituted a violation of this section, the court in its discretion may reduce the award of damages to a sum of not less than $250.

(4) Any person who manufactures, assembles, modifies, imports, exports, sells, or distributes any electronic, mechanical, or other device or equipment, knowing or having reason to know that the device or equipment is primarily of assistance in the unauthorized decryption of satellite cable programming, **or direct-to-home satellite services,** or is intended for any other activity prohibited by subsection (a), shall be fined not more than $500,000 for each violation, or imprisoned for not more than 5 years for each violation, or both. For purposes of all penalties and remedies established for violations of this paragraph, the prohibited activity established herein as it applies to each such device shall be deemed a separate violation.

(5) The penalties under this subsection shall be in addition to those prescribed under any other provision of this title.

(6) Nothing in this subsection shall prevent any State, or political subdivision thereof, from enacting or enforcing any laws with respect to the importation, sale, manufacture, or distribution of equipment by any person with the intent of is use to assist in the interception or receipt of radio communications prohibited by subsection (a).

(f) Nothing in this section shall affect any right, obligation or liability under Title 17, United States Code, any rule, regulation, or order thereunder, or any other applicable Federal, State, or local law.

(g) The Commission shall initiate an inquiry concerning the need for a universal encryption standard that permits decryption of satellite cable programming intended for private viewing. In conducting such inquiry, the Commission shall take into account --

(1) consumer costs and benefits of any such standard, including consumer investment in equipment in operation;

(2) incorporation of technological enhancements, including advanced television formats;

(3) whether any such standard would effectively prevent present and future unauthorized decryption of satellite cable programming;

(4) the costs and benefits of any such standard on other authorized users of encrypted satellite cable programming, including cable systems and satellite master antenna television systems;

(5) the effect of any such standard on competition in the manufacture of decryption equipment; and

(6) the impact of the time delay associated with the Commission procedures necessary for establishment of such standards.

(h) If the Commission finds, based on the information gathered from the inquiry required by subsection (g), that a universal encryption standard is necessary and in the public interest, the Commission shall initiate a rulemaking to establish such a standard.

Section 706 [47 USC Section 606]. War Emergency -- Powers of President.

(a) During the continuance of a war in which the United States is engaged, the President is authorized, if he finds it necessary for the national defense and security, to direct that such communications as in his judgment may be essential to the national defense and security shall have preference or priority with any carrier subject to this Act. He may give these directions at and for such times as he may determine, and may modify, change, suspend, or annul them and for any such purpose he is hereby authorized to issue orders directly, or through such person or persons as he designates for the purpose, or through the Commission. Any carrier complying with any such order or direction for preference or priority herein authorized shall be exempt from any and all provisions in existing law imposing civil or criminal penalties, obligations, or liabilities upon carriers by reason of giving preference or priority in compliance with such order or direction.

(b) It shall be unlawful for any person during any war in which the United States is engaged to knowingly or willfully, by physical force or intimidation by threats or physical force, obstruct or retard or aid in obstructing or retarding interstate or foreign communication by radio or wire. The President is hereby authorized, whenever in his judgment the public interest requires, to employ the armed forces of the United States to prevent any such obstruction or retardation of communication: provided, that nothing in this section shall be construed to repeal, modify, or affect either Section 6 or Section 20 of an Act entitled "An Act to Supplement Existing Laws Against Unlawful Restraints and Monopolies, and for Other Purposes," approved October 15, 1914.

(c) Upon proclamation by the President that there exists war or a threat of war, or a state of public peril or disaster or other national emergency, or in order to preserve the neutrality of the United States, the President, if he deems it necessary in the interest of national security or defense, may suspend or amend, for such time as he may see fit, the rules and regulations applicable to any or all stations or devices capable of emitting electromagnetic radiations within the jurisdiction of the United States as prescribed by the Commission, and may cause the closing of any station for radio communication, or any device capable of emitting electromagnetic radiations between 10 kilocycles and 100,000 megacycles, which is suitable for use as a navigational aid beyond 5 miles, and the removal therefrom of its apparatus and equipment, or he may authorize the use or control of any such station or device and/or its apparatus and equipment, by any department of the Government under such regulations as he may prescribe upon just compensation to the owners. The authority granted to the President, under this subsection, to cause the closing of any station or device and the removal therefrom of its apparatus and equipment, or to authorize the use or control of any station or device and/or its equipment, may be exercised in the Canal Zone.

(d) Upon proclamation by the President that there exists a state or threat of war involving the United States, the President, if he deems it necessary in the interest of the national security and defense, may, during a period ending not later than six months after the termination of such state or threat of war and not later than such earlier date as the Congress by concurrent resolution may designate, (1) suspend or amend the rules and regulations applicable to any or all facilities or stations for wire communication within the jurisdiction of the United States as prescribed by the Commission, (2) cause the closing of any facility or station for wire communication and the removal therefrom of its apparatus and equipment, or (3) authorize the use or control of any such facility or station and its apparatus and equipment by any department of the Government under such regulations as he may prescribe, upon just compensation to the owners.

(e) The President shall ascertain the just compensation for such use or control and certify the amount ascertained to Congress for appropriation and payment to the person entitled thereto. If the amount so certified is unsatisfactory to the person entitled thereto, such person shall be paid only 75 per centum of the amount and shall be entitled to sue the United States to recover such further sum as added to such payment of 75 per centum will make such amount as will be just compensation for the use and control. Such suit shall be brought in the manner provided by paragraph 20 of Section 24, or by Section 145, of the Judicial Code, as amended.

(f) Nothing in subsections (c) or (d) shall be construed to amend, repeal, impair, or affect existing laws or powers of the states in relation to taxation or the lawful police regulations of the several states, except wherein such laws, powers, or regulations may affect the transmission of government communications, or the issue of stocks and bonds by any communication system or systems.

(g) Nothing in subsections (c) or (d) shall be construed to authorize the President to make any amendment to the rules and regulations of the Commission which the Commission would not be authorized by law to make; and nothing in subsection (d) shall be construed to authorize the President to take any action the force and effect of which shall continue beyond the date after which taking of such action would not have been authorized.

(h) Any person who willfully does or causes or suffers to be done any act prohibited pursuant to the exercise of the President's authority under this section, or who willfully fails to do any act which he is required to do pursuant to the exercise of the President's authority under this section, or who willfully causes or suffers such failure, shall, upon conviction thereof, be punished for such offense by a fine of not more than $1,000 or by imprisonment for not more than 1 year, or both, and, if a firm, partnership, association, or corporation, by fine of not more than $5,000, except that any person who commits such an offense with intent to injure the United States or with intent to secure an advantage to any foreign nation, shall, upon conviction thereof, be punished by a fine or not more than $20,000 or by imprisonment for not more than 20 years, or both.

Section 707 [47 USC Section 607]. Effective Date of Act.

This Act shall take effect upon the organization of the Commission, except that this section and Sections 1 and 4 shall take effect July 1, 1934. The Commission shall be deemed to be organized upon such date as four members of the Commission have taken office.

Section 708 [47 USC Section 608]. Separability Clause.

If any provision of this Act or the application thereof to any person or circumstance is held invalid, the remainder of the Act and the application of such provision to other persons or circumstances shall not be affected thereby.

Section 709 [47 USC Section 609]. Short Title.

This Act may be cited as the "Communications Act of 1934."

Section 710 [47 USC Section 610]. Telephone Service for the Disabled.

(a) The Commission shall establish such regulations as are necessary to ensure reasonable access to telephone service by persons with impaired hearing.

(b)(1) Except as provided in paragraphs (2) and (3), the Commission shall require that --

(A) all essential telephones, and

(B) all telephones manufactured in the United States (other than for export) more than one year after the date of enactment of the Hearing Aid Compatibility Act of 1988 or imported for use in the United States more than one year after such date, provide internal means for effective use with hearing aids that are designed to be compatible with telephones which meet established technical standards for hearing aid compatibility.

(2)(A) The initial regulations prescribed by the Commission under paragraph (1) of this subsection after the date of enactment of the Hearing Aid Compatibility Act of 1988 shall exempt from the requirements established pursuant to paragraph (1)(B) of this subsection only--

(i) telephones used with public mobile services;

(ii) telephones used with private radio services;

(iii) cordless telephones; and

(iv) secure telephones.

(B) The exemption provided by such regulations for cordless telephones shall not apply with respect to cordless telephones manufactured or imported more than three years after the date of enactment of the Hearing Aid Compatibility Act of 1988.

(C) The Commission shall periodically assess the appropriateness of continuing in effect the exemptions provided by such regulations for telephones used with public mobile services and telephones used with private radio services. The Commission shall revoke or otherwise limit any such exemption if the Commission determines that --

(i) such revocation or limitation is in the public interest;

(ii) continuation of the exemption without such revocation or limitation would have an adverse effect on hearing-impaired individuals;

(iii) compliance with the requirements of paragraph (1)(B) is technologically feasible for the telephones to which the exemption applies; and

(iv) compliance with the requirements of paragraph (1)(B) would not increase costs to such an extent that the telephones to which the exemption applies could not be successfully marketed.

(3) The Commission may, upon the application of any interested person, initiate a proceeding to waive the requirements of paragraph (1)(B) of this subsection with respect to new telephones, or telephones associated with a new technology or service. The Commission shall not grant such a waiver unless the Commission determines, on the basis of evidence in the record of such proceeding, that such telephones, or such technology or service, are in the public interest, and that (A) compliance with the requirements of paragraph (1)(B) is technologically infeasible, or (B) compliance with such requirements would increase the costs of the telephones, or of the technology or service, to such an extent that such telephones, technology, or service could not be successfully marketed. In any proceeding under this paragraph to grant a waiver from the requirements of paragraph (1)(B), the Commission shall consider the effect on hearing-impaired individuals of granting the waiver. The Commission shall periodically review and determine the continuing need for any waiver granted pursuant to this paragraph.

(4) For purposes of this subsection --

(A) the term "essential telephones" means only coin-operated telephones, telephones provided for emergency use, and other telephones frequently needed for use by persons using such hearing aids;

561

(B) the term "public mobile services" means air-to-ground radiotelephone services, cellular radio telecommunications services, offshore radio, rural radio service, public land mobile telephone service, and other common carrier radio communication services covered by Part 22 of Title 47 of the Code of Federal Regulations;

(C) the term "private radio services" means private land mobile radio services and other communications services characterized by the Commission in its rules as private radio services; and

(D) the term "secure telephones" means telephones that are approved by the United States Government for the transmission of classified or sensitive voice communications.

(c) The Commission shall establish or approve such technical standards as are required to enforce this section.

(d) The Commission shall establish such requirements for the labeling of packaging materials for equipment as are needed to provide adequate information to consumers on the compatibility between telephones and hearing aids.

(e) In any rulemaking to implement the provisions of this section the Commission shall specifically consider the costs and benefits to all telephone users, including persons with and without hearing impairments. The Commission shall ensure that regulations adopted to implement this section encourage the use of currently available technology and do not discourage or impair the development of improved technology.

(f) The Commission shall periodically review the regulations established pursuant to this section. Except for coin-operated telephones and telephones provided for emergency use, the Commission may not require the retrofitting of equipment to achieve the purposes of this section.

(g) Any common carrier or connecting carrier may provide specialized terminal equipment needed by persons whose hearing, speech, vision, or mobility is impaired. The State commission may allow the carrier to recover in its tariffs for regulated service reasonable and prudent costs not charged directly to users of such equipment.

(h) The Commission shall delegate to each State commission the authority to enforce within such State compliance with the specific regulations that the Commission issues under subsections (a) and (b), conditioned upon the adoption and enforcement of such regulations by the State commission.

Section 711 [47 USC Section 611]. Closed-Captioning of Public Service Announcements.

Any television public service announcement that is produced or funded in whole or in part by any agency or instrumentality of Federal Government shall include closed captioning of the verbal content of such announcement. A television broadcast station licensee --

(1) shall not be required to supply closed captioning for any such announcement that fails to include it; and

(2) shall not be liable for broadcasting any such announcement without transmitting a closed caption unless the licensee intentionally fails to transmit the closed caption that was included with the announcement.

Section 712 [47 USC Section 612]. Syndicated Exclusivity.

(a) The Federal Communications Commission shall initiate a combined inquiry and rulemaking proceeding for the purpose of --

(1) determining the feasibility of imposing syndicated exclusivity rules with respect to the delivery of syndicated programming (as defined by the Commission) for private home viewing of secondary transmissions by satellite of broadcast station signals similar to the rules issued by the Commission with respect to syndicated exclusivity and cable television; and

(2) adopting such rules if the Commission considers the imposition of such rules to be feasible.

(b) In the event that the Commission adopts such rules, any willful and repeated secondary transmission made by a satellite carrier to the public of a primary transmission embodying the performance or display of a work which violates such Commission rules shall be subject to the remedies, sanctions, and penalties provided by Title V and Section 705 of this Act.

~~**< Section 713 [47 USC Section 613]. [Deleted]>**~~ **Section 713 [47 USC Section 613]. Video Programming Accessibility.**

(a) Commission Inquiry.--Within 180 days after the date of enactment of the Telecommunications Act of 1996, the Federal Communications Commission shall complete an inquiry to ascertain the level at which video programming is closed captioned. Such inquiry shall examine the extent to which existing or previously published programming is closed captioned, the size of the video programming provider or programming owner providing closed captioning, the size of the market served, the relative audience shares achieved, or any other related factors. The Commission shall submit to the Congress a report on the results of such inquiry.

(b) Accountability Criteria.--Within 18 months after such date of enactment, the Commission shall prescribe such regulations as are necessary to implement this section. Such regulations shall ensure that--

(1) video programming first published or exhibited after the effective date of such regulations is fully accessible through the provision of closed captions, except as provided in subsection (d); and

(2) video programming providers or owners maximize the accessibility of video programming first published or exhibited prior to the effective date of such regulations through the provision of closed captions, except as provided in subsection (d).

(c) Deadlines for Captioning.--Such regulations shall include an appropriate schedule of deadlines for the provision of closed captioning of video programming.

(d) Exemptions.--Notwithstanding subsection (b)--

(1) the Commission may exempt by regulation programs, classes of programs, or services for which the Commission has determined that the provision of closed captioning would be economically burdensome to the provider or owner of such programming;

(2) a provider of video programming or the owner of any program carried by the provider shall not be obligated to supply closed captions if such action would be inconsistent with contracts in effect on the date of enactment of the Telecommunications Act of 1996, except that

nothing in this section shall be construed to relieve a video programming provider of its obligations to provide services required by Federal law; and

(3) a provider of video programming or program owner may petition the Commission for an exemption from the requirements of this section, and the Commission may grant such petition upon a showing that the requirements contained in this section would result in an undue burden.

(e) Undue Burden.--The term "undue burden" means significant difficulty or expense. In determining whether the closed captions necessary to comply with the requirements of this paragraph would result in an undue economic burden, the factors to be considered include--

(1) the nature and cost of the closed captions for the programming;

(2) the impact on the operation of the provider or program owner;

(3) the financial resources of the provider or program owner; and

(4) the type of operations of the provider or program owner.

(f) Video Descriptions Inquiry.--Within 6 months after the date of enactment of the Telecommunications Act of 1996, the Commission shall commence an inquiry to examine the use of video descriptions on video programming in order to ensure the accessibility of video programming to persons with visual impairments, and report to Congress on its findings. The Commission's report shall assess appropriate methods and schedules for phasing video descriptions into the marketplace, technical and quality standards for video descriptions, a definition of programming for which video descriptions would apply, and other technical and legal issues that the Commission deems appropriate.

(g) Video Description.--For purposes of this section, "video description" means the insertion of audio narrated descriptions of a television program's key visual elements into natural pauses between the program's dialogue.

(h) Private Rights of Actions Prohibited.--Nothing in this section shall be construed to authorize any private right of action to enforce any requirement of this section or any regulation thereunder. The Commission shall have exclusive jurisdiction with respect to any complaint under this section.

Section 714 [47 USC Section 614]. Telecommunications Development Fund.

(a) Purpose of Section.--It is the purpose of this section--

(1) to promote access to capital for small businesses in order to enhance competition in the telecommunications industry;

(2) to stimulate new technology development, and promote employment and training; and

(3) to support universal service and promote delivery of telecommunications services to underserved rural and urban areas.

(b) Establishment of Fund.--There is hereby established a body corporate to be known as the Telecommunications Development Fund, which shall have succession until dissolved. The Fund shall maintain its principal office in the District of Columbia and shall be deemed, for purposes of venue and jurisdiction in civil actions, to be a resident and citizen thereof.

(c) Board of Directors.--

(1) Composition of board; chairman.--The Fund shall have a Board of Directors which shall consist of 7 persons appointed by the Chairman of the Commission. Four of such directors shall be representative of the private sector and three of such directors shall be representative of the Commission, the Small Business Administration, and the Department of the Treasury, respectively. The Chairman of the Commission shall appoint one of the representatives of the private sector to serve as chairman of the Fund within 30 days after the date of enactment of this section, in order to facilitate rapid creation and implementation of the Fund. The directors shall include members with experience in a number of the following areas: finance, investment banking, government banking, communications law and administrative practice, and public policy.

(2) Terms of appointed and elected members.--The directors shall be eligible to serve for terms of 5 years, except of the initial members, as designated at the time of their appointment--

(A) 1 shall be eligible to service for a term of 1 year;

(B) 1 shall be eligible to service for a term of 2 years;

(C) 1 shall be eligible to service for a term of 3 years;

(D) 2 shall be eligible to service for a term of 4 years; and

(E) 2 shall be eligible to service for a term of 5 years (1 of whom shall be the Chairman). Directors may continue to serve until their successors have been appointed and have qualified.

(3) Meetings and functions of the board.--The Board of Directors shall meet at the call of its Chairman, but at least quarterly. The Board shall determine the general policies which shall govern the operations of the Fund. The Chairman of the Board shall, with the approval of the Board, select, appoint, and compensate qualified persons to fill the offices as may be provided for in the bylaws, with such functions, powers, and duties as may be prescribed by the bylaws or by the Board of Directors, and such persons shall be the officers of the Fund and shall discharge all such functions, powers, and duties.

(d) Accounts of the Fund.--The Fund shall maintain its accounts at a financial institution designated for purposes of this section by the Chairman of the Board (after consultation with the Commission and the Secretary of the Treasury). The accounts of the Fund shall consist of--

(1) interest transferred pursuant to Section 309(j)(8)(C) of this Act;

(2) such sums as may be appropriated to the Commission for advances to the Fund;

(3) any contributions or donations to the Fund that are accepted by the Fund; and

(4) any repayment of, or other payment made with respect to, loans, equity, or other extensions of credit made from the Fund.

(e) Use of the Fund.--All moneys deposited into the accounts of the Fund shall be used solely for--

(1) the making of loans, investments, or other extensions of credits to eligible small businesses in accordance with subsection (f);

(2) the provision of financial advice to eligible small businesses;

(3) expenses for the administration and management of the Fund (including salaries, expenses, and the rental or purchase of office space for the fund);

(4) preparation of research, studies, or financial analyses; and

(5) other services consistent with the purposes of this section.

565

(f) Lending and Credit Operations.--Loans or other extensions of credit from the Fund shall be made available in accordance with the requirements of the Federal Credit Reform Act of 1990 (2 USC 661 et seq.) and any other applicable law to an eligible small business on the basis of--

(1) the analysis of the business plan of the eligible small business;

(2) the reasonable availability of collateral to secure the loan or credit extension;

(3) the extent to which the loan or credit extension promotes the purposes of this section; and

(4) other lending policies as defined by the Board.

(g) Return of Advances.--Any advances appropriated pursuant to subsection (d)(2) shall be disbursed upon such terms and conditions (including conditions relating to the time or times of repayment) as are specified in any appropriations Act providing such advances.

(h) General Corporate Powers.--The Fund shall have power--

(1) to sue and be sued, complain and defend, in its corporate name and through its own counsel;

(2) to adopt, alter, and use the corporate seal, which shall be judicially noticed;

(3) to adopt, amend, and repeal by its Board of Directors, bylaws, rules, and regulations as may be necessary for the conduct of its business;

(4) to conduct its business, carry on its operations, and have officers and exercise the power granted by this section in any State without regard to any qualification or similar statute in any State;

(5) to lease, purchase, or otherwise acquire, own, hold, improve, use, or otherwise deal in and with any property, real, personal, or mixed, or any interest therein, wherever situated, for the purposes of the Fund;

(6) to accept gifts or donations of services, or of property, real, personal, or mixed, tangible or intangible, in aid of any of the purposes of the Fund;

(7) to sell, convey, mortgage, pledge, lease, exchange, and otherwise dispose of its property and assets;

(8) to appoint such officers, attorneys, employees, and agents as may be required, to determine their qualifications, to define their duties, to fix their salaries, require bonds for them, and fix the penalty thereof; and

(9) to enter into contracts, to execute instruments, to incur liabilities, to make loans and equity investment, and to do all things as are necessary or incidental to the proper management of its affairs and the proper conduct of its business.

(i) Accounting, Auditing, and Reporting.--The accounts of the Fund shall be audited annually. Such audits shall be conducted in accordance with generally accepted auditing standards by independent certified public accountants. A report of each such audit shall be furnished to the Secretary of the Treasury and the Commission. The representatives of the Secretary and the Commission shall have access to all books, accounts, financial records, reports, files, and all other papers, things, or property belonging to or in use by the Fund and necessary to facilitate the audit.

(j) Report on Audits by Treasury.--A report of each such audit for a fiscal year shall be made by the Secretary of the Treasury to the President and to the Congress not later than 6 months following the close of such fiscal year. The report shall set forth the scope of the audit and shall include a statement of assets and liabilities, capital and surplus or deficit; a statement of surplus or deficit analysis; a statement of income and expense; a statement of sources and application of funds; and such comments and information as may be deemed necessary to keep the President and the Congress informed of the operations and financial condition of the Fund, together with such recommendations with respect thereto as the Secretary may deem advisable.

(k) Definitions.--As used in this section:

(1) Eligible small business.--The term "eligible small business" means business enterprises engaged in the telecommunications industry that have $50,000,000 or less in annual revenues, on average over the past 3 years prior to submitting the application under this section.

(2) Fund.--The term "Fund" means the Telecommunications Development Fund established pursuant to this section.

(3) Telecommunications industry.--The term "telecommunications industry" means communications businesses using regulated or unregulated facilities or services and includes broadcasting, telecommunications, cable, computer, data transmission, software, programming, advanced messaging, and electronics businesses.

Appendix 3

Status of Local Switched Competition

State	Competitors Have Applied? (*=approved)	Competitive Operations Have Begun?	Notes on the status of local switched access competition
Alabama	yes		Workshops in progress. Public Utility Commission to prepare price regulation and local-competition plan.
Alaska	yes		Rules not yet in place.
Arizona	yes*		Rules established.
Arkansas	yes*		Rules not yet in place.
California	yes	yes	Interim rules through 1996 may become permanent 1/97. Interim number portability. Permanent implementation details and universal service in separate dockets at Public Utilities Commission. Interconnection agreement approved. Of 66 companies that have applied to compete, 31 have been approved.
Colorado	yes		Rules in committee at Public Utilities Commission. Competition set to begin 7/96. Some rules adopted.

State	Competitors Have Applied? (*=approved)	Competitive Operations Have Begun?	Notes on the status of local switched access competition
Connecticut	yes*		Interim rules set rates for unbundled service and interconnection. Guidelines established. Three companies have contracts with Southern New England Telephone. None is yet operating. Interim resale rates filed.
Delaware	yes		Rulemakings in progress.
District of Columbia	yes		Legislation pending.
Florida	yes*		Rulemaking in process at Public Service Commission. Companies must negotiate. Three agreements reached setting rules for universal service, interconnection, temporary number portability, unbundling, and resale.
Georgia	yes*		Temporary rules in place. Workshops and hearings in progress. Number portability ordered to be in palce by 9/97.
Hawaii	yes		Companies must negotiate. Open docket on rules to be completed 12/96. Legislation addresses rules and requires incumbent local exchange carrier to comply.

State	Competitors Have Applied? (*=approved)	Competitive Operations Have Begun?	Notes on the status of local switched access competition
Idaho	yes		Rules not yet in place.
Illinois	yes	yes	Rules in place. Competition began 9/1/95. Number portability solution adopted, resale tariffs filed. Two competitors have reciprocal compensation co-carrier agreement with Ameritech in Chicago.
Indiana	yes		Hearings on local competition issues. Workshops in progress.
Iowa	yes*		Rulemaking in progress. Local service offered through resale of Centrex services. U S WEST tariffs disputed.
Kansas	yes*		Rulemakings and workshops in progress. One new entrant in operation, bought facilities from United but faces no competition. One other carrier certified for area but not yet operational.
Kentucky	yes		Docket in progress. Generic proceeding under way at public utilities commission. Hearing scheduled 3/96.

571

State	Competitors Have Applied? (*=approved)	Competitive Operations Have Begun?	Notes on the status of local switched access competition
Louisiana	yes		Public service commission has adopted rules.
Maine	yes		Rules not yet in place.
Maryland	yes	yes	911 and interconnection rules in place. Interim rules on number portability. Competition in test period.
Massach-usetts	yes	yes	Docket regarding rules suspended pending federal action. Contracts between firms. MFS actively marketing service sand serving a handful of customers.
Michigan	yes	yes	Interconnection contracts in place between firms.
Minnesota	yes		Rules docket to be complete 8/97 for companies serving >50,000 lines. Rules for smaller companies by 1/98. Task forces considering interconnection, number portability, etc.
Mississippi	yes		Rules not yet in place. Docket established, no dates set.
Missouri	yes		Rules not yet in place.
Montana	yes*		Rules not yet in place.

State	Competitors Have Applied? (*=approved)	Competitive Operations Have Begun?	Notes on the status of local switched access competition
Nebraska	yes		Rules not yet in place. To be certified, potential competitor must prove incumbent is inadequate.
Nevada	yes		Contracts must be developed between firms.
New Hampshire	yes		Public Utilities Commission has rules docket in progress. Rules must be completed by end of 1996.
New Jersey	yes		Rulemaking in progress — comment/reply stage.
New Mexico	yes		Rulemakings in progress. Companies serving <100,000 lines exempt.
New York	yes	yes	Rules in place. 23 competitive companies are certified. Competition limited to NYC and Rochester.
North Carolina	yes*		Interim rules in place. Parties to negotiate in "good faith," after 90 days can petition Public Utility Commission for determination. Companies serving <200,000 lines exempt. Competition to begin 7/96.
North Dakota	yes		Rules not yet in place.

State	Competitors Have Applied? (*=approved)	Competitive Operations Have Begun?	Notes on the status of local switched access competition
Ohio	yes*		Interim interconnection agreement in place for two companies. Public Utility Commission has proosed generic local competition rules.
Oklahoma	yes		Rules not yet in place. Rulemaking in progress. Bill introduced.
Oregon	yes*		Public Utilities Commission adopted temporary number portability, bill-and-keep rules for two years. Working on permanent number portability solution.
Pennsylvan- ia	yes*		Rules not yet in place. Rulemakings in progress.
Rhode Island	yes		Rules not yet in place. Public Utilities Commission has open docket and is following the progress of Massachusetts and Connecticut.
South Carolina	yes		Rules not yet in place.
South Dakota	yes		Rules not yet in place. Public Utilities Commission has legal authority. No other actions have been taken.

State	Competitors Have Applied? (*=approved)	Competitive Operations Have Begun?	Notes on the status of local switched access competition
Tennessee	yes*		Rules approved by Public Service Commission and need to be approved by Attorney General.
Texas	yes*		Proposed rules in hearing stage. Universal service provisions in state law. Competitors began filing 9/95.
Utah	yes*		Contracts must be developed between firms. Interconnection hearings delayed pending federal action. Interim number portability agreement. Compensation on bill-and-keep basis.
Vermont	yes		Rules not yet in place. Public Utilities Commission has an open docket.
Virginia	yes		Generic rules in place, detailed to be worked out between firms.
Washington	yes	yes	Interconnection rules in place. Six companies authorized to compete with incumbents, serving a handful of customers.
West Virginia	yes		Rules not yet in place. Public Utilities Commission continuing general investigation, which began 11/94.

State	Competitors Have Applied? (*=approved)	Competitive Operations Have Begun?	Notes on the status of local switched access competition
Wisconsin	yes*		Rules are in a pending docket at the Public Utilities Commission. Discussions concerned with interconnection, number portability, reciprocal compensation.
Wyoming	yes*		Rules not yet in place.

Source: FCC

Date: April, 1996

Appendix 4

Proposed Schedule of FCC Rulemakings

LEGEND

BUREAUS/OFFICES

CSB	Cable Services Bureau
CCB	Common Carrier Bureau
CIB	Compliance and Information Bureau
DTF	Disabilities Task Force
IB	International Bureau
MMB	Mass Media Bureau
OCBO	Office of Communications Business Opportunities
OET	Office of Engineering and Technology
OGC	Office of General Counsel
OPP	Office of Plans and Policy
WTB	Wireless Telecommunications Bureau

Boldface	Indicates Bureau/Office with primary responsibility
[ ]	Indicates Bureau/Office with secondary responsibility

FCC PROCEEDINGS

NOI	Notice of Inquiry
NPRM	Notice of Proposed Rulemaking
Order	Report and Order
Recon.	Reconsideration Order

FCC CAVEAT

This chart is a working document that reflects the FCC staff's current plans regarding implementation of the Telecommunications Act of 1996 but does not constitute an interpretation of the Act by the staff or the Commission. It is being released for the convenience of the public. It is **not** intended to be binding in any way and it is subject to change without any notice.

[Editors' Note: The full text of the FCC's implementation schedule is available on the internet at http://www.fcc.gov. The FCC periodically updates the chart.]

ISSUES/ FCC BUREAUS	FCC PROCEEDINGS	TIMETABLE
1. Interconnection **CCB** [WTB] [CSB]	Interconnection Proceeding	NPRM April 1996 Order August 1996
WTB [CCB]	LEC-CMRS Interconnection Docket 94-54 and 95-185	Order Third Quarter 1996
CCB	Numbering Administration	Complete
CCB [WTB]	Number Portability (CC Docket 95-116)	Order May 1996
CCB [WTB]	Intelligent Network (CC Docket 91-346)	Order March 1996
2. Negotiation, Arbitration, and Approval of Agreements **CCB** [WTB]	Interconnection Proceeding	NPRM April 1996 Order August 1996

ISSUES/ FCC BUREAUS	FCC PROCEEDINGS	TIMETABLE
3. Universal Service **CCB** [WTB]	Joint Board (Definition of Universal Service; Support Mechanisms)	NPRMs March 1996 Joint Board Recommendation November 1996 FCC Order May 1997
OPP **CCB** **WTB** **CSB** **IB**	Advanced Services	NPRM Second Quarter 1996
CCB	Interexchange Carrier Proceeding	NPRM March 1996 Order August 1996
CCB	Accounting Safeguards	NPRM March 1996 Order July 1997
4. Access by Persons **w/Disabilities** **DTF** **CCB** [WTB] [CSB]	Equipment Accessibility Rules Service Accessibility Rules Wireline HAC Proceeding (CC Docket 87-124) Telecommunications Relay Service	Notice August 1996 Order August 1997 Notice October 1996 Order August 1997 Order May 1996 NOI June 1996

ISSUES/ FCC BUREAUS	FCC PROCEEDINGS	TIMETABLE
5. Interconnectivity **WTB** **OET** **CCB**	Amend Network Reliability Council Charter -------------------------- Network Planning	March 1996 -------------------------- Notice Third Quarter 1996 Order First Quarter 1997
6. Market Entry **Barriers** **OCBO** **OGC** **WTB**	Market Entry Barriers	NOI March 1996 Policy Statement November 1996 NPRMs Fourth Quarter 1996 Orders May 1997
7. Illegal Changes in **Subscriber Carrier** **Selection (Slamming)** **CCB**	Policies and Rules Concerning Unauthorized Changes of Consumers' Long Distance Carriers CC Docket 94-129	NPRM Second Quarter 1996 Order Fourth Quarter 1996
8. Infrastructure **Sharing** **WTB** [CCB]	Infrastructure Sharing	Notice July 1996 Order January 1997

ISSUES/ FCC BUREAUS	FCC PROCEEDINGS	TIMETABLE
9. Telemessaging **CCB**	Telemessaging	NPRM Third Quarter 1996 Order Fourth Quarter 1996
10. Eligible Telecom. Carriers **CCB** [WTB]	Joint Board (Definition of Universal Service; Support Mechanisms)	NPRMs March 1996 Joint Board Recommendation November 1996 FCC Order May 1997
11. Service Area Definition **CCB** [WTB]	Joint Board (Definition of Universal Service; Support Mechanisms)	NPRMs March 1996 Joint Board Recommendation November 1996 FCC Order May 1997
12. Exempt Telecom. Companies **OGC**	Utility Company Entry	NPRM April 1996 Order December 1996
13. BOC Entry into InterLATA Services **CCB**	InterLATA Complaint Procedures	NPRM Second Quarter 1996 Order Fourth Quarter 1996

ISSUES/ FCC BUREAUS	FCC PROCEEDINGS	TIMETABLE
CCB	Accounting Systems and Other Safeguards	NPRM April 1996 (Interim Rules) Order August 1996 NPRM September 1996 (Final Rules - Affiliates) Order March 1997 NPRM September 1996 (Final Rules - Cost Allocations) Order March 1997
	Price Caps-Long Term Plan (CC Docket 94-1) (NPRM September 1995)	Order September 1996
CCB	Dialing Parity	Notice/Order Second Quarter 1996 2nd Order Fourth Quarter 1996
14. Manufacturing by BOCs **CCB**	BOC Manufacturing Protocols	NPRM April 1996 (Interim Rules) Order August 1996 NPRM October 1996 (Final Rules) Order March 1997
OGC [CCB] [OET]	ADR for Manufacturing	NPRM March 1996 Order May 1996

ISSUES/ FCC BUREAUS	FCC PROCEEDINGS	TIMETABLE
CCB	Accounting Systems and Other Safeguards	NPRM April 1996 (Interim Rules) Order August 1996 NPRM Sept. 1996 (Final Rules-Affiliates) Order March 1997 NPRM Sept. 1996 (Final Rules - Cost Allocations) Order March 1997
	Price Caps-Long Term Plan (CC Docket 94-1) (Notice September 1995)	Order September 1996
15. Electronic Publishing by BOCs **CCB**	Accounting Systems and Other Safeguards	NPRM April 1996 (Interim Rules) Order August 1996 NPRM Sept. 1996 (Final Rules-Affiliates) Order March 1997 NPRM Sept. 1996 (Final Rules - Cost Allocations) Order March 1997
	Price Caps-Long Term Plan (CC Docket 94-1) (Notice September 1995)	Order September 1996

583

ISSUES/ FCC BUREAUS	FCC PROCEEDINGS	TIMETABLE
16. Alarm Monitoring Services **CCB**	Alarm Monitoring Complaint Procedures	Notice Third Quarter 1996 Order Fourth Quarter 1996
CCB	Data Safeguards	NPRM April 1996 Order August 1996
17. Pay Phone Services **CCB**	Pay Phone Proceeding (Per Call)	NPRM May 1996 Order September 1996 Recon. Order November 1996
18. Broadcast Spectrum Flexibility **MMB** **OET** [OPP]	DTV Standards NPRM DTV Allotment NPRM	To Be Determined To Be Determined
MMB [OPP]	Fees for Ancillary or Supplementary Services	To Be Determined
19. Broadcast Ownership **MMB**	Omnibus Order Omnibus Order	Order March 1996 Order March 1996

ISSUES/ FCC BUREAUS	FCC PROCEEDINGS	TIMETABLE
MMB	Local Radio Ownership	NPRM Third Quarter 1996 Order Fourth Quarter 1996
MMB **CSB**	TV Ownership	NPRM Second Quarter 1996 Order Fourth Quarter 1996
CSB [MMB]	TV Network-Cable Cross Ownership	Order March 1996
MMB	Biennial Review	
CSB [MMB]	Cable/MDS Cross-Ownership	Order March 1996
20. Terms of Broadcast Licenses **MMB**	Broadcast License Terms	NPRM March 1996 Order Third Quarter 1996
21. Broadcast License Renewals **MMB**	Comparative Renewal Reform	NPRM Second Quarter 1996 Order Fourth Quarter 1996

ISSUES/ FCC BUREAUS	FCC PROCEEDINGS	TIMETABLE
MMB	Omnibus Order	March 1996
22. Over-the-Air Reception Devices **IB** (DBS) ------------------------ **CSB** (Other)	DBS -------------------------- Other Over-the-Air Reception Devices	NPRM March 1996 Order August 1996 ---------------------------- NPRM March 1996 Order August 1996
23. Cable Reform **CSB**	Cable Reform	NPRM Second Quarter 1996 Order Fourth Quarter 1996
CSB	Market Definition NPRM, CS Docket No. 95-178 (Adopted December 8, 1995)	Order First Quarter 1996
CSB	Cable Equipment Averaging	NPRM March 1996 Order June 1996
24. Open Video System **CSB** [CCB]	Eliminating Section 214 Rules	Notice or Order March 1996 Order Third Quarter 1996

ISSUES/ FCC BUREAUS	FCC PROCEEDINGS	TIMETABLE
CSB	Cable Drops	NPRM Second Quarter 1996 Order Fourth Quarter 1996
CSB	Open Video Systems	NPRM March 1996 Order June 1996 Recon. Order August 1996
CSB [CCB]	Responsible Accounting Officer (RAO) 25; VDT Reporting Requirements Repeal of Existing Video Dialtone Rules	Order Revoking RAO letter and VDT Reporting Requirements March 1996 Action Second Quarter 1996
25. Competitive Availability of Navigation Devices **CSB** [OET] [IB]	Wiring NPRM, CS Docket No. 95-184 (Released January 26, 1996) Competitive Navigation Devices	NPRM Second Quarter 1996 Order First Quarter 1997

ISSUES/ FCC BUREAUS	FCC PROCEEDINGS	TIMETABLE
26. Video **Programming** **Accessibility** **CSB** [MMB] [DTF]	Video Programming Accessibility (Hearing Impaired)	Further NOI in MM Docket No. 95-176 March 1996 Report August 1996 NPRM December 1996 Order August 1997
CSB [MMB] [DTF]	Video Programming Accessibility (Sight Impaired)	Further NOI in MM Docket No. 95-176 March 1996 Report August 1996
27. Regulatory **Reform: Biennial** **Review** **CCB**	Tariff Procedures	NPRM Third Quarter 1996 Order First Quarter 1997
CCB	Complaint Procedures	NPRM Third Quarter 1996 Order Fourth Quarter 1996
CCB	Section 214 Proceeding	NPRM March 1996 Order July 1996

ISSUES/ FCC BUREAUS	FCC PROCEEDINGS	TIMETABLE
CCB	Accounting Reports	NPRM May 1996 Order September 1996
27. Regulatory Reform: Elimination of Unnecessary FCC Regulations and Functions **CCB**	Depreciation	NPRM February 1997 Order Fourth Quarter 1997
WTB	Streamlining of Amateur Rules	Order February 1996
MMB	ITFS Delegation Order	Order March 1996
OET	Digital Equipment Deregulation	Order March 1996
WTB [CIB]	Delicensing	NPRM Second Quarter Order Third Quarter
MMB	Silent Station Expiration	NPRM Third Quarter Order Fourth Quarter

589

ISSUES/ FCC BUREAUS	FCC PROCEEDINGS	TIMETABLE
MMB	Construction Permits	NPRM Second Quarter 1996 Order Third Quarter 1996
WTB [CIB]	GMDSS	Order March 1996
WTB	Delete Public Notice Requirement	Order February 1996 Completed
28. Obscene or Harassing Use of Telecom. Facilities **CCB** [OGC]	Section 223 Measures	NOI Third Quarter 1996 Policy Statement First Quarter 1997
29. Scrambling of Sexually Explicit Adult Video Service Programming **CSB** [MMB] [OGC]	Scrambling of Sexually Explicit Programming	Order and NPRM March 1996 Order Fourth Quarter 1996

ISSUES/ FCC BUREAUS	FCC PROCEEDINGS	TIMETABLE
30. Parental Choice in TV Programming "V-Chip" **OGC** [CSB] [MMB]	V-Chip	NOI Second Quarter 1996
OGC **OET** [CSB] [MMB]	V-Chip Blocking Technology Rulemaking	NOI Second Quarter 1996 NPRM Third Quarter 1996 Order First Quarter 1997
31. Effect on Other Laws **WTB**	LEC-CMRS Safeguards Remand in Gen. Docket 90-314, and Reconsideration in Gen. Docket 93-252	NPRM March 1996 Order July 1996
32. Unfair Billing Practices for Information or Services Provided Over Toll-Free Telephone Calls **CCB**	Unfair Billing Practices	NPRM April 1996 Order August 1996

ISSUES/ FCC BUREAUS	FCC PROCEEDINGS	TIMETABLE
33. Privacy of Customer Information **CCB**	Privacy	To Be Determined
34. Pole Attachments **CSB**	Pole Attachments	NPRM June 1996 Order March 1997
35. Facilities Siting; Radio Frequency Emission Standards **OET**	RF Emissions Effects	Order April 1996
36. Mobile Services Direct Access to Long Distance Carriers **WTB**	CMRS Unblocking Proceeding Docket 94-54	Supplemental Notice Second Quarter 1996 Order Third Quarter 1996
37. Advanced Telecom. Incentives **CCB WTB CSB OPP IB**	Advanced Services	NOI Second Quarter 1996 Report Fourth Quarter 1996

ISSUES/ FCC BUREAUS	FCC PROCEEDINGS	TIMETABLE
38. Telecom **Development Fund** **OCBO** **OGC** **WTB**	Letter from Chairman Appointing Directors Letter from Chairman Appointing Development Fund Chairman	March 1996

Glossary

access: *see exchange access.*

basic exchange telephone radio systems (BETRS): A class of radio service, initially authorized by the Federal Communications Commission in 1988, which allows telephone companies to use digital radio instead of copper wire in situations were it is more cost effective. BETRS was an historic first step by the FCC toward recognizing radio as a fully equivalent alternative access technology for conventional telephone customers (*i.e.*, not just for mobile telephones).

Bell Operating Company (BOC): One of the local exchange carrier telephone companies that were part of the Bell System prior to divestiture. As listed in the Telecom Act, these are Bell Telephone Company of Nevada, Illinois Bell Telephone Company, Indiana Bell Telephone Company, Incorporated, Michigan Bell Telephone Company, New England Telephone and Telegraph Company, New Jersey Bell Telephone Company, New York Telephone Company, U S West Communications Company, South Central Bell Telephone Company, Southern Bell Telephone and Telegraph Company, Southwestern Bell Telephone Company, The Bell Telephone Company of Pennsylvania, The Chesapeake and Potomac Telephone Company, The Chesapeake and Potomac Telephone Company of Maryland, The Chesapeake and Potomac Telephone Company of Virginia, The Chesapeake and Potomac Telephone Company of West Virginia, The Diamond State Telephone Company, The Ohio Bell Telephone Company, The Pacific Telephone and Telegraph Company, and Wisconsin Telephone Company.

Bellcore: The central service organization providing centralized technical and management services for the Regional Holding Companies. Formerly known as Bell Communications Research, Bellcore is in many ways the closest thing in the United States to a central standards organization for telecommunications equipment.

cable: A communications system which distributes broadcast programs and original programs and services by means of optic fiber, coaxial cables or other cable facilities. In some cable TV systems there is provision for interactive (both way) applications, including telephone service.

cellular: A mobile telephone service employing a network of low-power transmitters, each covering a specific geographic area or *cell*, that provides continuous interconnection for a mobile telephone user as he moves from one cell to another.

commercial mobile radio services (CMRS): Radio system using low-power transmitters providing coverage in a limited area but linked (usually by cable) with other similar transmitters operating at different frequencies. The whole system enables radio frequencies to be reused economically, and enables good telephone service to be provided in moving handsets by switching control from one transmitter cell to another as the mobile user moves across an area.

dialing parity: When telephone customers have the ability to automatically route their calls (without first dialing an access code) to the telecommunications service provider of their choice from among two or more telecommunications service providers.

direct broadcast satellite (DBS): Satellite service, usually via spot-beam antenna with a relatively small footprint on earth, so that the received signal is sufficiently strong to be picked up using small and inexpensive antennae at the viewer's own premises.

duopoly: A market situation in which two competing sellers hold the controlling power of determining the amount and price of a product or service offered to a large number of buyers.

exchange: A central office telephone switch.

exchange access: The offering of access to telephone exchange services or facilities for the purpose of the origination or termination of telephone toll services (long distance).

Federal Communications Commission (FCC): In the United States, a board of seven commissioners, appointed by the President, with the power to regulate all interstate and foreign electrical communications systems originating in the United States, including radio, television, facsimile, telegraph, telephone, and cable systems.

franchise: Contractual agreement between a cable television operator in the United States and the governing municipal authority. Under federal regulation a franchise, certificate, contract or any other agreement that amounts to a license to operate.

interconnection: The connection of telephone equipment to a network, also the connection of one carrier with another; *i.e.*, the interface between carriers.

interexchange: Any connection between exchanges. Generally used to refer to long distance services.

interLATA: Services which originate and terminate in different local access and transport areas.

intraLATA: Services which originate and terminate in the same local access and transport area.

Local Access and Transportation Area (LATA): An area served by a single local telephone company. Long distance calls are generally inter-LATA calls, and are handled by an interexchange carrier. Circuits with both end-points within the LATA (intra-LATA calls) are generally a local telephone company's responsibility.

local exchange: An exchange where subscribers' lines are terminated.

local exchange carrier: A provider of telephone exchange service or exchange access.

local loop: The circuit (usually a two-wire path) connecting a subscriber's station with the line terminating equipment in a central office. (Four-wire loops are sometimes provided for leased circuits used for data.)

microwave: A term loosely applied to those radio frequency wavelengths which are sufficiently short to exhibit some of the properties of light. Commonly used for frequencies from about 1 GHz to 30 GHz.

network element: A facility or equipment used in the provision of a telecommunications service. Such term also includes features, functions, and capabilities that are provided by means of such facility or equipment, including subscriber numbers, databases, signaling systems, and information sufficient for billing and collection or used in the transmission, routing, or other provision of a telecommunications service.

number portability: The ability of users of telecommunications services to retain, at the same location, existing telecommunications numbers without impairment of quality, reliability, or convenience when switching from one telecommunications carrier to another.

paging: To summon a person, exact whereabouts unknown, to the telephone or otherwise deliver him a message. Some paging systems use a selective radio signal to summon the called person to the nearest telephone. More sophisticated systems deliver voice messages, or text messages displayed on a strip of LCDs, to the person carrying the paging unit.

personal communications services (PCS): Radio services that free individuals from the constraints of the wireline public switched network. Similar in concept to cellular, but generally utilizing smaller cells.

Regional Holding Company (RHC): Any of the seven regional companies created by the AT&T divestiture to assume ownership of the Bell Operating Companies. These are: U S West, BellSouth, Pacific Telesis, SBC Communications, NYNEX, Bell Atlantic, and Ameritech.

resale: To hire circuits or services from a major carrier and resell them to individual users.

satellite master antenna system (SMATV): Distribution of television signals to users via a small dish receiver feeding cables to subscribers in the service area concerned.

Signaling System 7 (SS7): International common channel signaling system recommendations established by the International Consultative Committee for Telephone and Telegraph.

specialized mobile radio (SMR): Two-way mobile radio telephone systems used in the past for dispatch services.

spectrum: A range of frequencies of radiant phenomena; the electromagnetic spectrum, which includes the entire range of wavelengths or frequencies of electromagnetic radiation extending from gamma rays to the longest radio waves and including visible light.

tariff: 1. The schedule of rates and regulations governing the provision of telecommunications services. 2. A document filed with a regulatory body by a common carrier which: defines service offered, establishes rates customer will pay, and states general obligations of the common carrier and customer.

telecommunications: The transmission, between or among points specified by the user, of information of the user's choosing, without change in the form or content of the information as sent and received.

telecommunications carrier: Any provider of telecommunications services.

telecommunications service: The offering of telecommunications for a fee directly to the public, or to such classes of users as to be effectively available directly to the public, regardless of the facilities used.

telephony: The engineering science of converting voices and other sounds into electrical signals which can be transmitted by wire, fiber or radio and reconverted to audible sound upon receipt.

video dial-tone: Access to video services provided through a Bell Operating Company.

Bibliography

BOOKS AND PERIODICALS

John Brooks, *Telephone, the First Hundred Years*, Harper & Row, New York, New York, 1975.

Stuart N. Brotman and Morton I. Hamburg, *Communications Law and Practice*, Law Journal Seminars-Press, New York, New York, 1995.

George Calhoun, *Wireless Access and the Local Telephone Network*, Artech House, Boston, Massachusetts.

Dan Carney, "Congress Fires Its First Shot in Information Revolution," *Congressional Quarterly*, February 3, 1996, p. 289.

Steve Coll, *The Deal of the Century, The Break Up of AT&T*, Athenum, New York, New York, 1986.

"Cal. PUC Okays Rates for Resale of Local Telephone Service," *Communications Daily*, Volume 16, No. 5, March 14, 1996.

Robert F. Copple, "Cable Television and the Allocation of Regulatory Power: A Study of Demarcation and Roles," *Federal Communications Law Journal*, Volume 44, No. 1, December 1991.

John E. Cunningham, *Cable Television, Second Edition*, SAMS Publications, 1981.

Ralph B. Everett, "Special Report: Telecommunications," *Legal Times*, November 20, 1995, page S28.

Federal Communications Law Journal, Volume 48, No. 2, March 1996.

"Federal Regulatory Developments," *Inside Telecom*, July 17, 1995.

William E. Francois, *Mass Media Law and Regulation*, Grid Publishing, Inc., Columbus, Ohio, 1982.

David A. Garbin, Roger J. O'Connor and Joseph A. Pecar, *The McGraw-Hill Telecommunications Factbook*, McGraw-Hill, New York, New York, 1993.

Lawrence Gasman, *Telecompetition: The Free Market Road to the Information Highway*, Cato Institute, Washington, D.C., 1994.

James Harry Green, *The Dow Jones-Irwin Handbook of Telecommunications*, Dow Jones-Irwin, Homewood, Illinois, 1986.

Tim Greene and David Rohde, "Telecom In Transition," *Network World*, February 19, 1996, page 12.

Peter W. Huber, Michael K. Kellogg and John Thorne, *Federal Telecommunications Law*, Little, Brown and Company, Boston, Massachusetts, 1992.

Peter W. Huber, Michael K. Kellogg and John Thorne, *The Telecommunications Act of 1996, Special Report*, Little, Brown and Company, Boston, Massachusetts, 1996.

"Is Cable Telephony Here Yet?", *Cable World*, March 25, 1996, page 37.

Anne P. Jones and Harry W. Quillan, "Broadcasting Regulation: A Very Brief History," *Federal Communications Law Journal*, Volume 37, No. 1, January 1985, pages 107-112.

Graham Langley, *Telephony's Dictionary, Second Edition*, Telephony Publishing Corp., Chicago, Illinois, 1986.

William C. Y. Lee, *Mobile Cellular Telecommunications Systems*, McGraw-Hill, New York, New York, 1989.

William C. Y. Lee, *Mobile Communications Engineering*, McGraw-Hill, New York, New York, 1982.

Chris McConnell, "Ownership Spotlight Moves to FCC," *Broadcasting & Cable*, February 12, 1996, page 16.

Max D. Paglin, Editor, *A Legislative History of the Communications Act of 1934*, Oxford University Press, New York, New York, 1989.

C. Joseph Pusateri, *Enterprise in Radio: WWL and the Business of Broadcasting in America,*
University Press of America, Washington, D.C., 1980.

Christopher Stern, "New Law of the Land," *Broadcasting & Cable*, February 5, 1996, page 8.

Christopher Stern, "Coming Soon: TV Ratings," *Broadcasting & Cable*, February 19, 1996, page 6.

Alan Stone, *Wrong Number, The Breakup of AT&T*, Basic Books, Inc., New York, New York, 1989.

Telco Competition Report, Volume 5, No. 6, March 28, 1996.

Telco Competition Report, Volume 5, No. 7, April 11, 1996.

Telco Competition Report, Volume 5, No. 8, April 25, 1996.

"Telecom Q&A; How Telecom Legislation will Affect the Media," *Electronic Media*, February 12, 1996, page 30.

Peter Temin with Louis Galambos, *The Fall of the Bell System, A Study in Prices and Politics*, Cambridge University Press, Cambridge, United Kingdom, 1987.

Warren's Telecom Regulation Monitor, Volume 1, No. 1, February 12, 1996.

Warren's Telecom Regulation Monitor, Volume 1, No. 3, February 26, 1996.

Warren's Telecom Regulation Monitor, Volume 1, No. 4, March 4, 1996.

Warren's Telecom Regulation Monitor, Volume 1, No. 6, March 18, 1996.

Richard E. Wiley, "I Want My HDTV," *New York Times*, February 17, 1996, Section 1, Page 23, column 2.

FEDERAL COMMUNICATIONS COMMISSION PROCEEDINGS

Amendment of the Commission's Rules to Establish New Personal Communications Services, GN Docket No. 90-314, *Notice of Inquiry*, 5 F.C.C.R. 3995 (1990).

Amendment of the Commission's Rules to Establish New Personal Communications Services, GN Docket No. 90-314, *Notice of Proposed Rule Making and Tentative Decision*, 7 F.C.C.R. 5676 (1992).

Amendment of the Commission's Rules to Establish New Personal Communications Services, GN Docket No. 90-314, *Second Report and Order*, 8 F.C.C.R. 7700 (1993).

Implementation of Sections 3(n) and 332 of the Communications Act, GN Docket No. 93-252, *Notice of Proposed Rule Making*, 8 F.C.C.R. 7988 (1993).

Implementation of Sections 3(n) and 332 of the Communications Act, GN Docket No. 93-252, *Second Report and Order*, 9 F.C.C.R. 1411 (1994).

Implementation of Sections 3(n) and 332 of the Communications Act, GN Docket No. 93-252, *Third Report and Order*, 9 F.C.C.R. 7988 (1994).

Common Carrier Competition (Federal Communications Commission, Common Carrier Bureau Spring 1995).

Annual Report and Analysis of Competitive Market Conditions with respect to Commercial Mobile Services, FCC 95-317, August 18, 1995.

Second Annual Report (Assessment of the Status of Competition in the Market for the Delivery of Video Programming), CS Docket No. 95-61, FCC 95-491, released December 11, 1995.

Amendment to the Commission's Rules to Permit Flexible Service Offerings in the Commercial Mobile Radio Services, WT Docket No. 96-6, *Notice of Proposed Rule Making*, FCC 96-17, *summarized* 61 Fed. Reg. 6189 (Feb. 16, 1996).

Interconnection Between Local Exchange Carriers and Commercial Mobile Radio Service Providers, CC Docket Nos. 95-185, 94-54, *Notice of Proposed Rulemaking*, FCC 95-505, *summarized* 61 Fed. Reg. 3644 (Feb. 1, 1996), *Supplemental Notice*, FCC 96-61, 61 Fed. Reg. 6961 (Feb. 23, 1996).

Notice of Proposed Rulemaking, CS Docket No. 96-57, FCC 96-117, released March 20, 1996.

Common Carrier Competition (Federal Communications Commission, Common Carrier Bureau Spring 1996).

Implementation of the Local Competition Provisions in the Telecommunications Act of 1996, CC Docket No. 96-98, *Notice of Proposed Rulemaking*, FCC 96-182, *summarized* 61 Fed. Reg. 18311 (Apr. 25, 1996).

Report and Order, CS Docket No. 96-85, FCC 96-154, reprinted in 61 Fed. Reg. 18968, April 30, 1996.

Memorandum Opinion and Order on Reconsideration, CC Docket No. 88-2 Phase I, FCC 90-134, 5 FCC Rcd 3084; 5 FCC Rcd 3530 (1990).

Notice of Inquiry, CC Docket No. 91-346, FCC 91-383, 56 FR 65721 (1991).

Notice of Proposed Rulemaking and Order Establishing Joint Board, CC Docket No. 96-45, FCC 96-93, released March 8, 1996.

607

Notice of Proposed Rulemaking, CC Docket No. 96-98, FCC 96-182, released April 19, 1996.

CONGRESSIONAL MATERIALS

Conf. Rep. No. 102-862, 102d Cong., 2d Sess. (1992).
Conf. Rep. No. 104-458, 104th Cong., 2d Sess. (1996).

H.R. Rep. No. 98-934, 98th Cong., 2d Sess. (1984).
H.R. Rep. No. 102-628, 102d Cong., 2d Sess. (1992).
H.R. Rep. No. 103-111, 103rd Cong., 1st Sess. 259-60 (1993).
H.R. Rep. No. 103-213, 103rd Cong., 1st Sess. 494 (1993).
H.R. Rep. No. 104-204, 104th Cong., 1st Sess. (1995).

Omnibus Budget Reconciliation Act of 1993, Pub. L. No. 103-66, Title VI § 6002(b), 107 Stat. 312, 392 (1993).

Telecommunications Act of 1996, P.L. 104-104.

Antitrust Communications Reform Act, H.R. 3626.

Communications Competition and Infrastructure Reform Act, H.R. 3636.

Communications Reform Act of 1994, S. 1822.

Communications Act of 1995, H.R. 1555.

Congressional Quarterly, 1995 Weekly Report, pp. 503, 802, 862, 1411, 1496, 1628, 1727, 1994, 2175, 2347, 2787, 3298, 3734, 3796, 3881.

Index

GOVERNMENT INSTITUTES ORDER FORM

4 Research Place, Suite 200 • Rockville, MD 20850-3226 • Tel (301) 921-2323 • Fax (301) 921-0264
Internet: *http://www.govinst.com* • E-mail: *giinfo@govinst.com*

3 EASY WAYS TO ORDER

1. Phone: **(301) 921-2323**
Have your credit card ready when you call.

2. Fax: **(301) 921-0264**
Fax this completed order form with your company purchase order or credit card information.

3. Mail: **Government Institutes**
4 Research Place, Suite 200
Rockville, MD 20850-3226
USA
Mail this completed order form with a check, company purchase order, or credit card information.

PAYMENT OPTIONS

❏ **Check** (*payable to Government Institutes in US dollars*)

❏ **Purchase Order** (this order form must be attached to your company P.O. **Note:** All International orders must be pre-paid.)

❏ **Credit Card** ❏ VISA ❏ 🖤 ❏ ▓▓

Exp.____/____

Credit Card No. _____

Signature _____
Government Institutes' Federal I.D.# is 52-0994196

CUSTOMER INFORMATION

Ship To: (Please attach your Purchase Order)

Name: _____

GI Account# (*7 digits on mailing label*): _____

Company/Institution: _____

Address: _____
(please supply street address for UPS shipping)
_____

City: _____ State/Province: _____

Zip/Postal Code: _____ Country: _____

Tel: ( ) _____

Fax: ( ) _____

E-mail Address: _____

Bill To: (if different than ship to address)

Name: _____

Title/Position: _____

Company/Institution: _____

Address: _____
(please supply street address for UPS shipping)
_____

City: _____ State/Province: _____

Zip/Postal Code: _____ Country: _____

Tel: ( ) _____

Fax: ( ) _____

E-mail Address: _____

Qty.	Product Code	Title	Price

❏ **New Edition No Obligation Standing Order Program**
Please enroll me in this program for the products I have ordered. Government Institutes will notify me of new editions by sending me an invoice. I understand that there is no obligation to purchase the product. This invoice is simply my reminder that a new edition has been released.

15 DAY MONEY-BACK GUARANTEE
If you're not completely satisfied with any product, return it undamaged within 15 days for a full and immediate refund on the price of the product.

Subtotal_____
MD Residents add 5% Sales Tax_____
Shipping and Handling (see box below)_____
Total Payment Enclosed_____

Within U.S:	**Outside U.S:**
1-4 products: $6/product	Add $15 for each item (Airmail)
5 or more: $3/product	Add $10 for each item (Surface)

SOURCE CODE: BP01